THE PAPERS OF

Clarence Mitchell Jr.

THE PAPERS OF

Clarence Mitchell Jr.

Volume IV, 1951–1954

Denton L. Watson, *editor*

Edward Austin Bradley, *assistant editor*

Reginald H. Pitts, *assistant editor*

OHIO UNIVERSITY PRESS

ATHENS

Ohio University Press, Athens, Ohio 45701

www.ohioswallow.com
Printed in the United States of America

Ohio University Press books are printed on acid-free paper ∞ ™
The paper used in this publication meets the minimum requirements of the American National Standard for Information Sciences—Permanence of Paper for Printed Library Materials, ANSI Z39.48-1992.
18 17 16 15 14 13 12 11 10 5 4 3 2 1

Publication of *The Papers of Clarence Mitchell Jr.* has been made possible by by grants from the National Historical Publications and Records Commission of of the National Archives and Records Administration and the Harry Frank Guggenheim Foundation and by the sponsorship of the State University of New York College at Old Westbury.

Dust jacket: Photo of Clarence Mitchell Jr. by Surlock Studio, courtesy of Elmer Henderson papers.
Frontispiece: Photo of Clarence Mitchell Jr., Library of Congress.

Library of Congress Cataloging-in-Publication Data

Mitchell, Clarence M. (Clarence Maurice), 1911–1984.
[Papers. Selections]
The papers of Clarence Mitchell, Jr. / Denton L. Watson, editor, Edward A. Bradley, assistant editor, Reginald H. Pitts, assistant editor.
p. cm.
Includes bibliographical references and index.
ISBN 0-8214-1603-0 (cloth : v. 1 : alk. paper) - ISBN 0-8214-1604-9 (cloth : v. 2 : alk. paper)
1. Mitchell, Clarence M. (Clarence Maurice), 1911–1984-Archives. 2. African Americans-Archives. 3. Civil rights workers-United States-Archives. 4. African Americans-Civil rights-History-20th century-Sources. 5. African Americans-Legal status, laws, etc.-History-20th century-Sources. 6. Civil rights movements-United States-History-20th century-Sources. 7. United States-Race relations-History-20th century-Sources. I. Watson, Denton L. II. Bradley, Edward A., 1969– . III. Pitts, Reginald H., 1955– . IV. Title.
E185.97.M63A25 2005
323'.092-dc22

2005022302

To Juanita Jackson Mitchell

The Papers of Clarence Mitchell Jr.

CONTENTS

Volume III

Volume IV

DOCUMENTS

Reports of the Washington Bureau under Clarence Mitchell Jr.

1951

1954

APPENDIXES

THE PAPERS OF

Clarence Mitchell Jr.

Monthly Report, January 31, 1951

DRAFT

Monthly Report
Director of the Washington Bureau
NAACP
January 31, 1951

The primary concern of the Washington Bureau for the first month in the New Year has been the unceasing effort to get an FEPC Order issued by the President.[1]

The Director has met with M. Stuart Symington, Chairman National Resources Board, Dave Niles, Assistant to the President and Charles Wilson, Director of Defense Mobilization, to enlist their aid in getting the order issued immediately.[2]

A copy of the proposed Order has been submitted to Mr. Wilson. Mr. Wilson expressed agreement with the proposed order and promised to give it immediate support.[3]

A proposed executive order has been submitted to the Bureau of the Budget and is being considered there.

The newly proposed site for the Atomic Energy project is South Carolina and has raised the problem of the use of Negro manpower in the construction stage of this operation, along with other problems that will affect colored people living in that area.[4]

The Director arranged and attended a conference which was held in Augusta Georgia, on January 26, 27, and 28, with NAACP officials and representatives of labor and business in that area, and AEC and Dupont officials.

The Director listed the following points to be discussed in the Conference.

1. Protection to assure persons who own property in the construction site the full and fair compensation for the loss of their homes, lands, etc.
2. Assurance that qualified skilled colored persons will be used in employment, transportation, housing and use of facilities on the project.
4. Establishing liaison between A.E.C. Officials and local colored citizen in the area of the project.

The Director is also setting up a similar conference to be held in Paducah, Kentucky with local representatives and A.E.C. Officials to discuss the problems of colored people seeking employment in the atomic Energy project there.[5]

The increased inductions of men into the Armed services have raised additional problems of segregation in the Services. The Director has met with Mr. Eugene M. Zuckert, assistant Secretary of the Air Force and Assistant Secretary Earl D. Johnson of the Army and Colonel Campbell C. Johnson Assistant to Director of Selective Service and will seek an appointment with the Assistant Secretary of the Navy to make suggestions on handling draftees and volunteers.

The Washington Bureau has received several complaints concerning the treatment of colored draftees and inductees. We have been sent pictures of the crude and unsanitary accommodations for colored draftees in Houston Texas.[6]

We received a report from Sergeant Hebert Bradshaw who was brutally beaten by peace officers and a civilian in Brownsville, Tennessee, while enroute to a camp in Geneva, New York.[7]

From Minnesota came the report that colored members of the Minnesota National Guard training at Camp Rucker, Alabama were being segregated at the camp, and mistreated in the nearby towns. The Camp Rucker incident brought protests to Governor [Luther W. (Wallace)] Youngdahl and Senators [Hubert H.] Humphrey and [Edward J.] Thye.[8]

The Director testified before the Senate Armed Services Committee on January in opposition to the confirmation of the appointment of Millard E. Caldwell as Director of Civilian Defense. At the time of the testimony was given, the confirmation of Mr. Caldwell was not officially before the committee.[9] This was an irregularity in Committee procedure.

Later that afternoon, on the same day the committee reached the nomination and voted to confirm it. On Tuesday, January 16, with 15 Senators on the floor and Senator NcKellar of Tennessee presiding, the Senate confirmed the appointment in a rush-rush-move. As a result the liberal Senators who had pledged to vote against the confirmation were not there to give opposition.

The Director takes this opportunity to express his thanks to his secretarial staff, especially Mrs. Mae Hendricks for her cooperation and devotion to her job for working long hours on Saturday, January 13 to have the testimony ready on the short notice that was given by the Senate Committee.

On January 24, the director testified before the Preparedness Sub-committee of the Senate Armed Services committee conducting manpower hearings to urge safeguards against segregation and discrimination based on race legislation that might be proposed by that committee.[10]

MISCELLANEOUS:

The Washington Bureau received a complaint from Mr. Howard Pinn concerning his dismissal as deck steward on the S.S. America because he was thought to be a bad security risk. The Director has been informed that the Coast Guard has cleared Mr. Pinn as a bad security risk. The director has requested the National Maritime Union and the Coast Guard to reinstate Mr. Pinn.

The Director has urged Mr. Robert Goodwin, Executive Director of the Office of Defense Manpower, Department of Labor call a meeting with Capital Transit Officials and representatives of the Washington Community to discuss the continued refusal of that Company to hire colored street car and bus operators.[11]

The Director has been appointed to the Special Advisory Committee to the War Claims Commission.[12]

The Director has opposed the Bill proposed by the National Education Association because it does not contain safeguards against segregation.

The Director has been informed by Dr. J.E. Bowman of the National Dental Association that NAACP's position will be supported by that Association. The C.I.O. also supports the position of NAACP.

The Director has requested the Chairman of the National Mediation Board, Mr. John Thadd Scott for an interpretation of the new amendments to the Railway Labor Act. Our interpretation makes grounds for attacking segregation and jim-crow auxiliaries, and other discriminatory features in Railway Labor.[13]

The Director has registered a complaint to Mr. Roy E. Larsen, Chairman of the National Citizens Committee for the Public Schools against that committee's endorsing Arlington county, Virginia Schools.

The complaint outlines the waste involved in maintaining a dual school system and woeful state of public education where decent schools are denied because of racial segregation.[14]

The Director has registered a complaint with Mr. Paul M. Herzog Chairman of the National Labor Relations Board against its adoption of the decision in matter of Youngs Motor Freight Lines and the International Teamsters Union.

The Board refused to find that the Young Motor Company was guilty of unfair labor practices when it fired five colored truck drivers for joining the Teamsters Union.[15]

The Director submitted testimony to be included in the hearing record on the renewal of Reciprocal Trade Agreements.[16]

SPEAKING ENGAGEMENT

1. Graduation speaker at Banneker Junior High school, January 24, 1951.

MS: NAACP IX: 200, DLC.

1. This was EO 10308. See also, among others, 12/5 and 12/28/51; in appendix 1, this vol., 12/20/50; 6/25/51 for a parallel struggle by the National Council for a Permanent FEPC; and the headnote on the Struggle for a Permanent FEPC, 1942–54, vol. III.

2. Materials on this meeting and other activities related to the FEPC struggle are in NAACP II: A-257, DLC. In the newsletter of January 12, 1951, Mitchell reported that the NAACP, in the meeting on January 4, had won from Charles E. Wilson "potent new support" for its campaign to get President Truman to issue an executive order creating an FEP agency. In addition to the executive order with enforcement powers, he said, Wilson had "promised full cooperation" on the NAACP's struggle for:

> "Appointment of qualified colored persons on the non-salaried policy-making boards and committees established under Mr. Wilson's direction. (We are particularly interested in those boards and committees that will deal with problems of manpower and training.)

Effective liaison through a top staff member who will have direct access to Mr. Wilson. (NAACP WB newsletter, 1/12/51, MP)

Walter White, who also participated in the meeting, confirmed that Wilson was in "complete accord with the principle of full use of manpower on the basis of skill alone and [he and Symington] were deeply interested in the suggested methods of achieving this goal which were put forth by the representatives of the NAACP. The NAACP submitted a memorandum containing specific recommendations [outlined by Mitchell] for guaranteeing that manpower will be used to the fullest capacity without discrimination based on race." Report of the Secretary for the Month of January, 1951, EC.

3. The NAACP, at its annual meeting on January 2, 1951, adopted a resolution commending the president for appointing Charles E. Wilson director of defense mobilization and also congratulated Wilson upon his appointment. Wilson, president of General Electric Company, previously had been chair of the President's Committee on Civil Rights. Minutes, 1/2/51, EC.

4. At a meeting with four top AEC officials on December 28, 1950, in Washington, Mitchell, accompanied by Earle Fisher, discussed approaches to problems that would arise for blacks at the proposed site of the AEC plant for producing fissionable materials in South Carolina. The plant was to be built by the du Pont Company, which would have few restraints on its operation because the AEC wanted the facility to begin production as soon as possible. Memorandum by Fisher recapitulating the discussion at the meeting, 12/28/50, NAACP WB-8, DLC. See also, among others, 2/5 and 5/3/51.

5. See, most immediately, 2/2, 2/5, and 3/5/51; in appendix 1, this vol., 12/20/50, 2/21/51.

6. See, most immediately, 12/31/50 and 2/2/51.

7. Mitchell urged the air force to "work for swift and vigorous punishment of those responsible for the attack," and he sent Zuckert a copy of Bradshaw's statement. Mitchell letter to Zuckert, 1/18/51, NAACP WB-141, DLC. See subsequent developments at 2/5 and 3/5/51.

8. Mitchell said the Minnesota National Guard's experiences in the South was a "special phase of the problem" of segregation of military personnel and inductees, adding "we presented that formally on January 8" [1951], in a letter to Earl D. Johnson, assistant secretary of the Department of the Army. On January 13, 1951, Mitchell wrote Governor Youngdhal, commending him for his action on the Minnesota National Guard. Mitchell's letter to Jonas G. Schwartz, 1/31/51, NAACP WB-141, DLC. Another portion of this letter was cited at 12/4/50. See also 2/2, 3/5, and 12/28/51.

Walter White, also involved in this struggle, reported that on January 9, 1951, he telegraphed the secretaries of defense, army, navy, and air force regarding complaints about this problem at Camp Rucker. On January 17, 1951, he received a letter from James C. Evans, secretary of defense, saying that appropriate investigations had been ordered and that the NAACP's "apprehension over possible discrimination and related disturbance in the immediate future" [had been] "used to alert officers and commands having direct jurisdiction." Evans also said that although he was not in a position then to say through what channels the official response would be provided, attention was then being given to the NAACP's message, which would assist in correcting conditions leading to the complaints. Report of the Secretary to the Board for January 1951, EC.

9. See Mitchell's testimony and Caldwell's response, both on 1/15/51, *Hearings*, 1–14; see also note at 2/2/51 for extended background on this struggle.

10. See 1/24/51, *Hearings*, 861–73; see also 2/2, 3/5, 4/4, 5/3, 6/4, and 8/31/51.

11. For background, see the headnote on Street and Local Railways, vol. I.

12. This was the Committee on War Claims (1873–1946), which was abolished under the Legislative Reorganization Act of 1946, with its jurisdiction transferred to the Senate Judiciary Committee and the executive agencies. See http://www.archives.gov/legislative/guide/house/chapter-06-war-claims-.html.

13. Mitchell and Waddy, 5/18/50, *Hearings*, 242–309. In the 1/12/51 newsletter, Mitchell addressed this issue as follows:

> One of the last bills passed in the 81st Congress was S. 3295 which permits union shop and dues check-off contracts in the Railroad industry.
>
> The bill did not contain language suggested by the NAACP. However, friendly senators and congressmen did get some protective language in the committee report on the bill. This language will be of use in court when plaintiffs bring action against discriminatory agreements between management and labor in the railroad industry.
>
> We are immediately asking the National Mediation Board to assure us that the intent of Congress, as set forth in the report, will be followed in the administration of the law.
>
> The language in the report is as follows:

"During the course of the hearings before the sub-committee, evidence was introduced showing that the constitutions of some labor organizations established qualifications for membership which cannot be met by some railroad employees.

"The proposal was made by Senator Lehman that your committee's intention be made clear that such employees were not to be deprived of their employment as a result of the exercise of the right extended by this bill.

"Your committee desires to make it clear that the proviso clauses in paragraph eleventh (a) are designed to protect such employees; thus if an employee is denied membership or is eligible for membership only on terms and conditions not generally applicable to other members, he cannot be requested to give up the job because of failure to join a labor organization.

"Furthermore, if membership is denied or if an employee is expelled from membership for any reason other than his failure to tender uniformly required periodic dues, initiation fees and assessments, he cannot be required to relinquish his job because of failure to join or remain a member of a labor organization.

"Your committee also desires to make it clear that nothing in this bill is intended to modify in any way the requirement that the authorized bargaining representative shall represent all the employees in the craft or class, including non-union employees as well as members of the union, fairly, equitably and in good faith. (See *Steele v. Louisville and Nashville Railroad Co.*, 323 U.S. 192, and *Tunstall v. Brotherhood of Locomotive Firemen and Enginemen*, 323 U.S. 210.)" (Newsletter, 1/12/51, MP)

14. For background, see Caplan, "Virginia Schools: A Study in Frustration," *Crisis* 58 (January 1951): 5–11, 61–63; Robinson, "The Virginia School Fight—A Clarification," *Crisis* 58 (April 1951): 228–29.

15. In the 1/12/51 newsletter, Mitchell provided this additional information:

We have registered a vigorous protest against a recent decision of the National Labor Relations Board in the case of the Young's Motor Freight Company of Houston, Texas. This company employed colored truck drivers for years, but maintained an open shop. From statements given by the company, it was cheaper to use colored drivers. Colored drivers were also employed in the Company's Beaumont, Texas, shop.

During the summer of 1949, the colored drivers in Houston were approached by the Teamster's Union. They decided to attend a meeting called by the union. The company suddenly fired all of its colored drivers in Houston. The reason given was that customers were complaining about impertinence and other improper conduct on the part of the drivers. They were replaced with white men.

The union then organized the company's Beaumont establishment. The employees went on strike, but when the employer told them that the company could not afford to pay the union wage scale, they dropped out of the union and went back to work. They are still employed.

The Board's Trial Examiner, Lee J. Best, ruled that the company had violated the law by interfering with its Houston employees when they attempted to organize. However, he also held that the company did not violate the law when it dismissed the colored employees. He was upheld in this decision by Paul M. Herzog, Board Chairman, and members Abe Murdock and Paul L. Styles.

The net result of this is that the company is now free to keep the white employees who replaced the colored men. The union may organize these white individuals if they are not already members. The only losers are the colored men who got fired. (Newsletter, 1/12/51, MP)

Mitchell told Herzog that "the record in this case shows that the colored employees were being exploited under open shop conditions. As long as these employees were content to work at wages under the union scale, there was no possibility of being discharged because the company knew that the employment of white men would cost more in wages." Mitchell letter to Herzog, 1/15/51, in NAACP WB-141, DLC.

16. This was the Trade Agreement of 1934. *Congress and the Nation*, 193–96.

Monthly Report, February 2, 1951

February 2, 1951

MONTHLY REPORT OF WASHINGTON BUREAU

Civil Rights Legislation

At least seventeen civil rights bills have been introduced in the House and Senate. The Administration has again sent its omnibus civil rights bill and a proposed anti-lynching statute to Congress. These were introduced by Chairman Celler of the Judiciary Committee in the House. In the Senate, Chairman McCarran of the Judiciary Committee has turned them over to a subcommittee headed by Senator Eastland of Mississippi.[1]

A bill aimed at those who attempt to hold persons in involuntary servitude has also been sent to Congress by the Department of Justice.[2] Senator McCarran has also referred this to the Eastland subcommittee. Other members of the subcommittee are Senators Kefauver, Langer, O'Conor, and Hendrickson.

Senators Humphrey and Morse have introduced a resolution to limit debate in the Senate by a majority vote. Senator Lehman is planning to introduce the same resolution he introduced in the 81st Congress on this subject at the time this report is written. Senator Ives and eleven other Republicans introduced an FEPC Bill on January 18, 1951.[3]

Since the Senator made it clear that he also hoped the President would issue an executive order on the same subject, the Director sent him a letter of commendation for his action. A portion of Senator Ives' reply is included.

> "You may have noted that Senators Jenner and Capehart of Indiana, and Martin and Duff of Pennsylvania are co-sponsors of the FEPC Bill which I have introduced. It occurs to me in this connection that Indiana and Pennsylvania are two states where special concentrated effort on behalf of state FEPC legislation should be made this year."[4]

Executive Order FEPC

A few days ago, the Director was given a copy of the latest version of the proposed FEPC order. After studying it, the Director transmitted it to Mr. Charles E. Wilson, Director of the Office of Defense Mobilization, with suggested changes. Mr. Wilson has advised that he has forwarded the suggestions to the Bureau of the Budget.[5]

Armed Services

Following the direction of the National Board in its meeting on October 9, 1950, the Director has held meetings with the Army and Air Forces on suggestions offered by the NAACP to avoid segregation of volunteers and draftees in the South. Meetings were held with Earl D. Johnson, Assistant Secretary of the Army, Eugene M. Zuckert, Assistant Secretary of the Air Force, and Colonel Campbell Johnson, Assistant to the Director of Selective Service.[6]

At the time this report is written, a meeting is also scheduled with Secretary Matthews of the Navy Department. It appears that the Services may agree to our proposal on housing and feeding of draftees or volunteers on a non-segregated basis, although there is some contention that our proposal would be too expensive.

There seems to be considerable resistance to our proposal that racial designations be eliminated from records of service personnel. The Navy and the Air Force argue that such records are necessary to check on the progress of integration. Selective Service is rapidly eliminating all racial designations.[7]

Meanwhile, we have received reports of brutal treatment of colored men in uniform in the South.[8] The Bureau has referred to the Assistant Secretary of the Air Force a complaint from Sergeant Herbert Bradshaw, a member of the Air Force, who said that he was brutally beaten by white civilian police in Tennessee.[9]

With Senator Humphrey of Minnesota, the Bureau urged the Department of the Army to make certain that the integrated National Guard of Minnesota would not be reorganized into an all white unit when it was sent to Camp Rucker, Alabama.[10] The Department of the Army advised that the following would be the policy on integrated national guard units:

"With regard to the general question of integrated National Guard units ordered into active Federal service, it is the present policy of the Department of the Army to retain, insofar as practicable, individual members of all such units within the unit in which they have enlisted and trained.

"While certain individuals may be transferred because of special qualifications and in accord with military necessity, such transfers will be made only under procedures equally applicable to all enlisted personnel in any Army unit without regard to race."[11]

The Director appeared before the Senate Armed Services Committee on January 24, 1951, and asked for the following safeguards in the new legislation on compulsory military service[12]:

1. A provision giving protection to service personnel against wanton attacks by peace officers and civilians.
2. Organization of all new units without segregation.
3. A ban against housing or feeding personnel of the Armed Services in private establishments that require racial segregation.
4. Elimination of racial designations from all forms and records of military personnel.

Caldwell Appointment

The Director appeared in opposition to the confirmation of Ex-Governor Millard F. Caldwell of Florida as Chief of Civil Defense.

Caldwell was approved in the Senate by unanimous consent with about fifteen senators on the floor. His views on voting and whether colored people should be called "mister" making interesting reading in the senate record on the hearing. However, he pledged that he would be fair to all in performing his duties.[13]

Capital Transit Company

The Director has requested that the Federal Manpower authorities make the Capital Transit Company a number one item on the program for full utilization of labor. Manpower officials advise that they are working with management and the union to settle the question of whether colored people shall be employed as platform workers.[14] At the time this report is written, important meetings are under way, according to Edward Keenan, Assistant Executive Director of the Office of Defense Manpower.

Since there have been frequent reorganizations in Government's manpower set-up, it is hoped that this problem will be settled before any new shake-up takes place.

H-Bomb Plant in South Carolina

The Director arranged a meeting in Augusta, Georgia, with officials of the Atomic Energy Commission, the DuPont Company, and the Corps of Engineers to discuss plans for full use of the colored labor supply on the new H- Bomb site in South Carolina.

A full report on this is available and it is hoped that the report will be read.[15] A similar meeting has been arranged for the H-Bomb site near Paducah, Kentucky. This will be held in February.[16]

Railway Mediation Board and NLRB

The Bureau has asked Senator Lehman to join in obtaining important commitments from the National Mediation Board on the new amendment to the Railway Labor Act. We have asked for commitments which will insure that colored workers will not be required to join Jim-Crow auxiliaries under the new union shop provisions. The Board has declined to rule on this point for the NAACP in the absence of a specific case. We hope that Senator Lehman's request will be acted upon.[17]

In response to the Bureau's protest against its decision in the Young Motor Freight Company Case in Houston, Texas, the NLRB has promised to restudy its decision. In this case, the Board held that the firing of all colored drivers by the Company, after they attended a union meeting, was not a violation of the Labor Relations Act. The Company contended that it had planned to fire the men before they decided to join a union. They were replaced with white drivers.[18]

Immigration Problems

The Research Assistant has become rather expert on certain immigration problems.[19] Because of their human interest, the Director submits a brief statement on three of these cases handled by the Research Assistant.

1. Mr. John G. Jackson's case was referred from the New York Office in December 1950. His case involved his petition on behalf of his Japanese wife, a citizen of Great Britain, for admittance to the United States.

   Mr. Jackson encountered difficulties in London with the U.S. Consul. Public Law 717 governing his case was obtained and supplied. Mr. Jackson's petition was successfully approved January 16, 1951, according to information received from the Immigration Service.

2. Corporal Wilbert Wilson was confronted by a similar problem. His petition on behalf of his Oriental wife was refused. After inquiries at the Immigration Service, Corporal Wilson has been advised to seek the aid of the Red Cross to establish a home in the United States for his wife, and then petition again because he is covered by Public Law 717.

3. The third case involved a petition for naturalization of Mr. Arnold Gordon in Boston, Massachusetts. Our Boston Branch sent an urgent message stating that Mr. Gordon's petition was being delayed because of his membership in the NAACP.

Mr. Maurice A. Roberts, Assistant Chief of the Investigation Section of the Immigration and Naturalization Service informed the Research Assistant that the NAACP is not under investigation by the Immigration Service, and Mr. Gordon's petition should not be delayed because of his membership in the NAACP and that his field office in Boston would be notified immediately.

It is increasingly clear that the title Research Assistant is not an accurate term. He has given the Director valuable assistance in preparing for hearings on the Caldwell appointment, the Manpower legislation, and Defense Housing legislation. In addition, he is handling a great many matters involving specific complaints. A few of these are listed:

Mr. Norman T. Thomas, who charges that he was wrongfully dismissed by the T.V.A. because of activity with the Alabama NAACP; Miss Julia Cobb, who is charging the Naval Hospital at Bethesda with discrimination based on race[20]; Mr. J. K. Haynes, who charges that he is being denied an opportunity to operate a trade school for veterans in Louisiana; and others.

Speaking Engagements, Etc.

The Director was the commencement speaker at the Banneker Junior High School this month. He also spoke at the Friendship Baptist Church in Aiken, South Carolina, for the branches of that State. Other engagements in Washington, Virginia, and Maryland were also filled. The Director represented the NAACP at advisory meetings called by Federal agencies in the fields of housing and war claims.

The Research Assistant attended meetings for the Bureau on social legislation and migratory workers.

MS: NAACP II: A-670, DLC.

1. This report is complemented by 2/21/51 in appendix 1, this vol. See also, in appendix 1, this vol., 12/20/50. At its annual meeting on January 2, 1951, the board adopted the following program prepared by Mitchell for the 82nd Congress:

> In making plans for the legislative program in the 82nd Congress, two factors should be taken under consideration. The first is that President Truman will quite likely establish by executive order a fair employment practice agency affecting defense industries. The second factor is the probable strategy that the Republican minority will follow.
>
> It is unlikely that the Republicans will pass up an opportunity to precipitate a floor fight on some civil rights legislation. At the same time, they may withhold enough votes in the Senate to prevent final passage of such legislation.
>
> The following are suggestions for obtaining some constructive results from the 82nd Congress.
>
> 1. When the President issues an executive order setting up a fair employment practice Board, we must carefully follow the appropriations of this agency and turn the spotlight on any committee members in the House or Senate who fail to give it their full support.
>
>   On the floor of the House, we must be prepared for the raising of points of order and, of course, in the Senate, we must be prepared for some kind of filibuster. The Administration must take the responsibility of getting favorable rulings on points of order and we must be fully advised on when these rulings will take place in order that we may be prepared to rally supporting votes.
>
>   In the Senate, the administration must take the responsibility of tying the FEPC appropriations with vital defense legislation so that those who stage a filibuster against FEPC will have a difficult time justifying their position. We, in turn, must be prepared to rally supporting votes to prevent FEPC appropriations from being set aside for separate consideration.
> 2. The issuance of an executive order by the President will free civil rights organizations to make an all out fight for a rules change in the Senate. After the experience on Alaska and Hawaii Statehood, it may be possible to get support from organizations not necessarily friendly to FEPC if the issue is on change of rules.
> 3. If we fail in the rules effort, we should capitalize on past speeches made by Republican leaders on the effectiveness of the 64 vote cloture rule. Wherry and others have repeatedly said the 64 vote rule would work on an anti-lynching bill. Undoubtedly, they will say the same thing on any debate in changing the rule.
>
>   It is suggested that if the fight on the rules change fails, we should try to get the President to call a bi-partisan meeting of the Senate and House leaders. At that time, the White House could issue a press statement saying that the President had sought to implement the civil rights program as far as it was within his powers by setting up an executive order FEPC. The statement could then point out that the President had requested the leaders of both parties to attempt to get an anti-lynching bill through the 82nd Congress. I suggest the anti-lynching bill because if the anti-poll tax bill is called, undoubtedly, there will be an attempt to substitute a constitutional amendment for it.

These suggestions do not embrace the entire legislative program of the Association but they do affect our planning the basic civil rights bills. In my opinion, it will be very useful to talk over with the President whatever plan we finally agree upon. Thereafter, I think it would be most useful if the President could arrange a meeting between the Senate Majority Leader, the House Majority Leader, and a few leaders in the civil rights field. This meeting should be off the record and for the purpose of discussing the suggestions I have made. (Minutes, 1/2/51, 10–11, EC)

2. This was H.R. 2118, which proposed to amend various sections of the U.S. Code in order to prohibit attempts to commit proscribed offenses, namely, slavery and peonage. Mitchell told White that in his letter of transmittal to the Eastland Subcommittee of the Senate Judiciary Committee of January 17, 1951, Peyton Ford, deputy attorney general, said that during the fiscal year ending June 30, 1950, the Department of Justice had received eighty-five complaints concerning possible peonage and involuntary servitude. During the current fiscal year, he said, Peyton reported that thirty-three complaints had been received. Mitchell memorandum to White, 2/6/51, "Civil Rights Bills Proposed by the Department of Justice," NAACP WB-111, DLC.

3. In a letter of January 19, 1951, to Senator Ives, Mitchell thanked him and his "fellow sponsors" for introducing the FEPC bill. Among other things, Mitchell noted that the "unhappy fate of FEPC legislation in the 81st Congress" indicated that supporters had to expect "formidable opposition from a minority of senators." For that reason, he expected President Truman to issue an executive order creating a temporary FEPC "to fill the gap" until Congress passed such a bill. Mitchell's letter, 1/19/51, NAACP II: A-657, DLC. See also, in appendix 1, this vol., 9/21/51 for varying approaches.

4. For later activities involving Charles E. Wilson, director of the Office of Defense Mobilization, see 5/3/51, where Mitchell's report to Walter White on important points discussed with Wilson is also cited.

5. See also 1/31 and 12/5/51; in appendix 1, this vol., 6/25/51. On December 14, 1950, Walter White and A. Philip Randolph wired President Truman, urging him to include in his declaration of a national emergency an executive order establishing the Fair Employment Practices Commission. They sent copies to Secretaries Dean Acheson, George C. Marshall, Maurice Tobin, and Oscar Chapman and to Senators Irving Ives, Herbert Lehman, Wayne Morse, Hubert Humphrey, and James E. Murray, as well as to W. Stuart Symington, chair of the National Security Resources Board. The wire said:

> In view of your courageous and consistent stand in behalf of equality of opportunity for all Americans, we appeal to you to include in your declaration of national emergency an Executive Order establishing a Fair Employment Practices Commission with authority to assure the maximum employment of all workers regardless of race, color, religion, ancestry or national origin.
>
> Millions of members of minority groups, now working at lower than their best and most needed skills, are partially or wholly unemployed because of discriminatory practices, constitute the greatest available reservoir for meeting our critical manpower needs.
>
> Establishment of an effective FEPC will do more than increase our productive capacity. It will strengthen morale and national unity, and will demonstrate to the peoples of the world that in mobilizing for the defense of freedom we are applying those principles of human dignity and individual liberty which chiefly distinguish our Democracy from totalitarianism.
>
> At a time when all Americans are to be asked to make sacrifices, to accept controls on prices, wages and other facets of our economy, it is unthinkable that we shall permit the full utilization of our resources to be impaired by uncontrolled discriminatory employment practices. (Report of the Executive Secretary to the Forty-first Annual Meeting, 1/2/51, EC)

This request was reinforced by a letter from Sen. Hubert H. Humphrey to Eisenhower, proposing that he issue an executive order establishing such a commission to halt discrimination in defense industries. Minutes, 1/51, EC.

The board also adopted a resolution at its annual meeting commending Truman on Wilson's appointment. Following their meeting with Wilson, White and Mitchell met with him and Stuart Symington, chair of the NSRB, and found them "in complete accord with the principle of full use of manpower on the basis of skill alone" and without discrimination. They were "deeply interested" in the methods the NAACP suggested in a memorandum they submitted for achieving that goal. Minutes, 1/51, EC. See materials on this meeting in NAACP II: A-257, DLC.

6. For the board's suggestions, see Minutes, 10/9/50, EC. The meeting was held on November 10, 1950. Mitchell letter to Earl B. Johnson; that and other materials are in NAACP WB-141, DLC. See also, among others, 12/21/50, 1/31 and 3/5/51.

7. For the roots of this struggle, see the headnote on Race, Creed, Color, or National Origin on Employment Application Forms, vol. I. As NAACP labor secretary, Mitchell stepped up this struggle in May 1947 by challenging the navy's policy of designating race on forms for reporting injuries or occupational diseases. The navy responded that designating "race" had "been particularly advantageous to all employees concerned regardless of race," and it provided examples of such a need in its study of accidents and occupational diseases patterns, where the information was essential. See Mitchell's letter of 5/2/47 to Commander R. C. Williams of the navy and the response of 5/14/47 from Alan Turnbull Jr., head, Accident Analysis and Injury Compensation Section, Office of Industrial Relations, Navy Department, attached to Mitchell's memorandum of 5/21/47 to Madison Jones on the Communications for Health Committee, in NAACP II: A525, DLC. See also Mitchell's letter of 1/8/51 to Eugene M. Zukert, assistant secretary of the air force, and other materials in NAACP WB-141, DLC; among others, 12/4 and 12/21/50; in appendix 1, this vol., 12/31/50.

8. See 1/31, 3/5, 4/4, 5/3, 6/4, and 8/31/51.

9. For reports on Sergeant Bradshaw, see also 1/31, 3/5, and 8/31/51. In his testimony before the Senate Preparedness Subcommittee on S. 1, on January 24, 1951, Mitchell said that NAACP members were very concerned about the mistreatment of black servicemen and servicewomen. At the same time, they had expressed "praise for new non-segregation policies of the Air Force and the Navy" but "strongly condemned" continuing segregation in the army. "The overwhelming majority of our members believe that the Government" [does not] "give sufficient and necessary protection to colored members of the Armed Services when they are in the South," he said. 1/21/51, *Hearings*, 862. In reiterating those complaints before the House Committee on Armed Services on March 8, 1951, he said there was "hardly a home or family in the United States that" [was] "not affected in some way by pending" [UMT legislation (H.R. 1752)]." 3/8/51, *Hearings*, 845. See 3/5/51 for immediately following developments in this struggle.

10. See Mitchell letter, 1/8/51, to Earl D. Johnson, assistant secretary of the army, in which he explained that the Minnesota problem was part of a larger picture, together with other materials in NAACP WB-141, DLC. See also 1/31, 3/5, and 12/28/51.

11. Also working on this problem was Walter White, who sent a telegram on January 9, 1951, to the secretary of defense, secretary of the army, secretary of the navy, and secretary of the air force about complaints regarding the treatment of African American inductees and recruits from Minnesota who were on duty or scheduled to go on duty at Camp Rucker, Alabama. On January 17, 1951, James C. Evans, the civilian assistant to the secretary of defense, responded that the department had ordered investigations into the NAACP's expressions of concern. He said such "apprehension over possible discrimination and related disturbance in the immediate future have been used to alert officers and commands having direct jurisdiction." Evans assured the NAACP that the Defense Department was working to correct the alleged problems. Report of the Secretary, 1/51, EC.

For background on this struggle, see Dalfiume, *Desegregation of the U.S. Armed Forces*, 159–62.

12. 1/24/51, *Hearings*, 862.

13. See 1/31/51 for an earlier report. As part of a group of twelve persons meeting with Eisenhower on February 28, 1951, White presented the NAACP's program to the president and also informed him of the "bitterness" of African Americans over Caldwell's appointment. White reported that the "President seemed to be annoyed and said Caldwell was the only one of 15 persons he had called who was willing to accept the job." The board adopted a resolution urging NAACP members not to accept any position within the civil defense program, such as air raid warden or nurse's aide, as long as Caldwell remained as its head, and it urged those who were already involved 'in such operations to resign. In keeping with this resolution, which he had offered, Judge Hubert T. Delaney resigned from his civil defense position. Minutes, 3/12/51, EC. White said the NAACP's actions were "to serve notice on the president" that he" had to watch his appointments so that there would be no more Caldwells and to "put Caldwell on guard." Minutes, Committee to Implement Board Decision on the Caldwell Appointment, 3/12/51, EC. See also editorial, *Crisis* 58 (March1951): 183–84.

Actually, in opposing the appointment during the meeting with the president, White went against Mitchell's recommendations. For Mitchell, the lesson was that the appointment showed the administration was capable of avoiding delays in Congress with its program if it really tried. So he advised White that, because of his close personal relationship with Truman, "which we should preserve," he would not recommend "an all out attack" in an article White was evidently contemplating. Instead, Mitchell proposed "a cool analysis with suggestions on what" [could] "be done to repair the broken fence." Mitchell letter to White, 2/15/51, NAACP II: A-584, DLC.

Subsequently, Caldwell invited White and four other NAACP leaders to a civil defense conference in Washington on May 7 and 8, 1951, where Truman was scheduled to speak. White responded that it would be impossible to accept the invitation "unless and until" Caldwell repudiated his testimony before the Senate Armed Services Committee on January 15, 1951, in which he (1) reiterated his opposition to the Supreme Court's decision outlawing disfranchisement of blacks through the white Democratic primaries and admitted that he had urged the South to resist that decision; (2) admitted that he refused to follow common courtesy in addressing American citizens irrespective of race; and (3) espoused regional education as a means of evading the abolition of segregation in southern tax-supported schools as the Court had ordered. Report of the Secretary for March, 4/9/51, EC.

See also Ivey, "Facts about Regional Education," *Crisis* 57 (November 1950): 628–32, 674–75; "Press for Caldwell Revival," *Crisis* 58 (April 1951): 267, 269, where the NAACP reported that Mitchell had testified before the Senate Armed Services Committee on January 15, 1951 (*Hearings*, 1–10), in opposition to Caldwell's confirmation and that Walter White had written to Truman on February 21, 1951, expressing the board's "sense of shock" at the appointment. The *Crisis* report noted that White reiterated his charges against Caldwell in a meeting with the president on February 28, 1951. For subsequent developments, see note at 12/28/51.

14. Noting the long struggle to get the Capital Transit Company to hire black operators, Mitchell warned Robert Goodwin, executive director of the Office of Defense Manpower in DOL, that its segregation policy would "again be a cause for great concern and possibly serious trouble," meaning riots, unless it was resolved. Mitchell's letter to Goodwin, 1/5/51, NAACP WB-10, DLC. For background, see the headnote on Street and Local Railways, vol. I.

15. See also the 1/16/51 reply from Summer T. Pike, acting AEC chair, to Mitchell's 12/1/50 complaint about discrimination; detailed report of 2/5/5. Materials are in NAACP WB-8, DLC; see also 1/31 and 5/3/51.

16. See 3/5/51; in appendix 1, this vol., 12/20/50 and 2/21/51.

17. See Mitchell and Waddy, 5/18/50, *Hearings*, 242–309; among others, 1/31/51.

18. In response to Mitchell's protest of January 12, 1951, relative to PL 914, John Thad Scott Jr., chair of the National Mediation Board, reaffirmed for the lobbyist the functions of his agency, which were "primarily those of mediating labor disputes." Mitchell, of course, Scott said, appreciated "that any alleged violations of the law" were issues for the courts to resolve, and it was impossible for him "to forecast with any degree of accuracy the extent and character of labor disputes which may arise in connection with approaches which may be made by labor organizations to secure the union shop, etc." John Thad Scott Jr.'s letter to Mitchell, 1/26/51, NAACP WB-141, DLC. See also, in appendix 1, this vol., 10/31/48 for the broader implications of this struggle.

19. The NAACP was much more deeply involved in fighting discrimination in U.S. immigration policy than Mitchell indicated here. See, in appendix 1, this vol., 9/30/52 for White's testimony on immigration and naturalization.

20. Julia Cobb said she was certified to the Bethesda Naval Hospital by the Civil Service Commission as a clerk typist. The hospital called her in for an interview but upon seeing that she was black, said the job required knowledge about bookkeeping and machine operation, qualifications she did not possess. Ultimately, an "applicant with experience," a veteran who was a transferee from another department, was chosen. Memorandum from Earle Fisher to Mitchell, 10/30/50, NAACP IX: 67, DLC.

NAACP Report on "H" Bomb Project in South Carolina, February 5, 1951

NAACP REPORT
ON
"H" BOMB PROJECT IN SOUTH CAROLINA

[February 5, 1951]

The Government of the United States is acquiring 250,000 acres of land in the State of South Carolina for construction of facilities to make the Hydrogen Bomb.[1] The project will be built and operated by the DuPont Company. It will cost $600,000,000.00.

The location makes it impossible for the Federal Government to avoid facing squarely its responsibility to see that there is no segregation or discrimination based on race. The population figures make this mandatory, even if we forget for the moment that the contract with the DuPont Company contains a non-discrimination clause.

Colored people are over 42 percent of the total population in South Carolina. The project is located in Aiken and Barnwell Counties in South Carolina.[2] Census figures reveal that there are 20,921 colored people in Aiken County out of a total population of 49,916. In Barnwell County colored people number 12,618 or more than 50 percent of the total population of 20,138. In these two counties colored people own or operate more than 2,000 farms covering 180,000 acres of land. The buildings and land of these farms are worth nearly $5,000,000.00.

Residents of the area estimate that at least 2,500 colored people will be forced to vacate their property, homes and business to make way for the H-Bomb Project. Thousands will seek work on the construction gangs building the plants. Hundreds of others will seek work when the plant is completed. Maximum employment on construction is expected to reach 30,000. The plant may employ 6,000 persons when it is completed. It is anticipated that the first operating personnel will begin work in July 1951.

For the colored people there are three main problems to be resolved. These are:

1. Displacement, with the loss of property, homes and jobs
2. Employment as skilled workers in construction and operation of the plant

3. Avoiding extension of segregation, housing facilities, schools and transportation in the community.

The Director of the NAACP's Washington Bureau arranged a meeting with Government officials and South Carolina citizens in Augusta, Georgia, on January 26, 1951, to discuss these three points.

Conference with Atomic Energy Officials and Others

The chairman of the NAACP Committee is Dr. C. C. Johnson, a business man in Aiken. Other members of the committee are J. C. Artemus, a member of the South Carolina AF of L executive committee; H.J. Hardy, soil conservation expert; J. M. Hinton, business man and president of the South Carolina NAACP State Branches; R. A. Brooks, business man and President of the Aiken NAACP Branch; Eugene A. R. Montgomery, executive secretary of the South Carolina State Conference of branches; Mr. William Willburn of the Augusta, Georgia, NAACP; and the writer of this report.

We met with Mr. Arthur L. Tackman and Mr. G. O. Robinson representing AEC; Mr. J. W. Mercke and Mr. H. J. Feinen, representing the DuPont Company; and Mr. Gordon Britten, representing the Corps of Engineers.

Displaced Persons

Mr. Britten gave helpful information to the committee on rights of persons who will be displaced. He advised that property owners may accept payment for land, homes, or businesses in such amount as the Government deems the property is worth. However, if the owners are not satisfied, they can seek additional money by court action. Acceptance of the money paid by the Government, as its estimate of what the property is worth, does not prevent the individual from seeking the additional amount that he believes he is entitled to receive.

Since not everyone will leave the area at the same time, many farmers were undecided about whether they should plant crops in the spring,. Mr. Britten advised that the Government would pay the proper value of crops if the owners of the land were forced to vacate it before harvesting. Later, at a public meeting, it developed that a large number of individuals present were greatly concerned about this particular problem and were pleased to know that it would be taken care of.

Some effort is being made through the Department of Agriculture to relocate the displaced farm workers. However, this does not appear to be adequate. The Atomic Energy officials and the DuPont Company officials indicated that first preference will be given in employment to qualified displaced persons. Unfortunately, however, the sharecroppers in the area, and those who are wage earners on farms, face a problem with their employers and land owners. Some of the individuals affected allege they have been told they would be fired from their present employment or displaced from their holdings, if they filed applications for work on the site.

Employment

The Atomic Energy and Dupont officials both pledged their full cooperation in seeing to it that there is no discrimination in employment because of race.
They were very cooperative on all matters discussed.

However, this is the appropriate place to say that, in the eyes of the colored community, the project has gotten off to a bad start on employment. All of the persons who visited the AEC offices noted that the only visible colored employees, out of the large number of persons working there, were those who appeared to be janitors. In visiting the construction site, one could see a number of surveyors, truck drivers, watchmen, and other employees; but, here again, colored people were absent.

A plan of segregating colored people in the Federal building at Aiken has developed. Previously, persons visiting the building were not segregated. Now residents advise that those who go to the building, even on business not related to the H-Bomb project are met by an officious receptionist who enforces segregation among those waiting to see various officials. This information is not given to charge either the DuPont Company or AEC with conscious discrimination at this time. It is included to show that unless there are proper safeguards, the worst South Carolina patterns will prevail.

The DuPont officials stated that after all available and qualified displaced persons are hired, the local carpenters' union in Augusta, the employment service, and the newspapers will be notified of the hiring needs. It was agreed that information would be sent to the colored newspapers at the same time it is sent to the white papers. The committee left the addresses of the important colored papers in the area.

There is considerable danger in the present plan of using the employment service and the local unions in Augusta. The State Federation of Labor is seeking broader arrangements for handling the construction workers. Mr. R. C. Waites, Secretary of the Columbia, South Carolina, Building and Construction Trades Council has described this plan as follows:

> "Inasmuch as 'H' Bomb project of Aiken, Barnwell Counties, South Carolina come under jurisdiction of Columbia Council we propose the following: That a charter be granted South Carolina Building and Trades Council composed of Charleston, Columbia, Greenville and Spartanburg and this council service project accordingly. All cards be handled by state council."

If the plan proposed by Mr. Waites is accepted, Mr. Artemus, who is a member of the State Executive Council of the AFL, will be in a position to give useful services. If it is not accepted, Mr. Artemus believes it will be very difficult for skilled colored construction workers, particularly carpenters and painters, to get on the project.

The committee was able to locate one or two colored men who said that they were members of the white carpenters' local in Augusta. Mr. Myron Mason, a resident of Aiken, said that he had talked with the head of the carpenters' union in Augusta and had been promised referral when the work began. Mr. Mason is a member of the carpenters' union in Columbia, although he lives in Aiken.

Since there are very few colored people in construction labor unions in Augusta, any plan that uses Augusta as the channel for referral will undoubtedly result in serious discrimination. We urged that DuPont officials broaden their plan to include state representatives. We are advised that some representatives of international unions will be sent into the area to work with officials of the DuPont Company in obtaining the necessary labor supply. We also asked that Mr. Artemus have official information on hiring needs.

We discussed training and employment on the regular staff when operations actually begin. It will be necessary to discuss this further with other DuPont officials and also with the AEC at a later date. We were advised that training plans in the area probably would not be perfected for several months.

Housing and Project Facilities

The housing problems in the surrounding area will be acute unless there is rapid construction of new dwellings. Present plans indicate that there will be considerable reliance upon rooming houses. Presumably, this supply of living space will be exhausted almost immediately. The AEC plans to furnish estimates of its housing needs to appropriate government agencies. It was suggested by the Committee that the AEC should use its influence to see that housing is handled on the basis of first come, first served, with no discrimination because of race.

We also discussed the question of whether South Carolina laws on segregation would apply to the project. Mr. Tackman stated that he was unable to answer that question at this time but would indicate the answer at a later date. We advised him that, in the opinion of the NAACP, South Carolina laws on segregation did not apply to the project area and segregation on the site would only lead to waste of manpower and needless duplication of facilities.

It was agreed that Mr. Montgomery would maintain an informal liaison with the DuPont and AEC officials. We were advised that Mr. Hunter Kennedy, representing the AEC, had opened offices in the town hall at Ellenton, South Carolina, and would serve as a coordinator for AEC.

COMMUNITY PATTERNS

At a quick glance, this area of South Carolina is a fearful place. There are Jim-Crow waiting rooms in stations, hundreds of shacks and rundown houses in what are referred to as Negro areas, dilapidated schools staffed by poorly paid teachers, and active Ku Klux Klan groups which seek to intimidate colored and white people. These are the bad aspects of the area.

There are, however, a number of good factors which should be used in establishing the pattern of hiring, housing, and training on the AEC project. First, there is responsible colored leadership which can be relied upon for advice. These persons include the officials of the Pilgrim Life Insurance Company in Augusta. This is a million dollar business and it was suggested that the AEC and DuPont officials should visit it to see what is possible in the area.

The Johnson Brothers, who are colored, operate a drug store on a busy corner of Richland Street in Aiken. This is a large, well-stocked business which would be an asset to any community. The customers who come to the store include a heavy white trade. In the same block, there is a kind of super-market where colored men work as meat cutters and serve all customers. The colored doctor and dentist in Aiken have white patients.

In the city of Aiken, the writer of this report had a room on Edgefield Avenue. This has been a mixed neighborhood for a great many years. In fact, the house opposite the home in which the writer stayed is occupied by a white person.

When we visited the rural area of Barnwell and Aiken Counties, one of the first stops was a filling station and restaurant operated by Mr. William Bonner, who is colored. During a rather extended discussion of his problems, it was possible to observe that Mr. Bonner has a great many white customers. He occupies a neat, solidly constructed dwelling. It will be necessary for him to sell his place since it is on the H-Bomb site. Mrs. Bonner said that the white customers are sometimes cordial and a few are hostile. Recently, one customer ordered a coca cola and gave the clerk on duty a $10.00 bill. Suddenly the customer smashed the bottle and demanded his $10.00 back, saying, "I didn't know this was a nigger place." During our conversation, a number of white customers came in and accepted service. A few left on discovering the filling station was operated by colored people. All of those who came in had South Carolina tags on their cars.

We visited the farms of a number of persons and found that they adjoin property of white persons in almost every instance. Typical of the prosperous farmers were Mr. R. L. Myers and the family of Rouse Brothers. Mr. Myers also cuts lumber for pulp and paper industries. He mentioned that he had just offered an owner $10,000 for the right to cut timber on certain land. He did not mention how much profit could be made on this deal. The Rouse Brothers have 550 acres of land. Their farm is well stocked with cattle, pigs, turkeys, and chickens. They have modern farming equipment, including a combine and tractors. In the past, they have taken their own produce as far as Washington D. C., for sale.

These illustrations are given to show that the colored population of the area, whether rural or urban, must not be regarded as an ignorant, poverty stricken group. Some of them will suffer sever financial losses and great difficulties unless the Government aids them in rehabilitation. Most of them will be a valuable source of skilled labor in construction or permanent employment on the project after suitable training.

Although the Ku Klux Klan is active, the colored people are not intimidated. A few days before the writer was in Aiken, the Klan held a rally and one observer present reported that the NAACP was subject of a vicious and disgusting attack. As is well known, the Klan members have also beaten white people in South Carolina as well as colored. Mr. Hinton was recently kidnapped by members of the Klan. Nevertheless, the meeting called by the NAACP on January 26 was packed. One of the trustees of the Friendship Baptist Church, where the meeting was held, said that it was the first time in twenty years that the church gallery had been filled.

It is apparent that most of the colored people are not going to be intimidated by the Klan or any of the political groups that may seek to keep them from enjoying the full benefits of the project. However, the Government should make certain that there is no intimidation in the area.

CLARENCE MITCHELL
Director, NAACP Washington Bureau
100 Massachusetts Ave., N. W.
Telephone National 5794
February 5, 1951

MS: NAACP WB-8, DLC.

1. See 1/31, 2/2, and 3/5/51; in appendix 1, this vol., 12/20/50 and 2/21/51.
2. In addition to 12/20/50, in appendix 1, this vol., where Mitchell mentioned that the NAACP would hold a meeting with the AEC on December 5, 1950, the records show that he repeatedly met with AEC officials on discrimination problems. See materials in NAACP WB-8, DLC.

Monthly Report, March 5, 1951

March 5, 1951

MONTHLY REPORT OF WASHINGTON BUREAU

Armed Services

A move to end violence against members of the Armed Services came Wednesday, February 28, 1951, when ten senators, at the urging of the NAACP, introduced an amendment to S.1, the pending legislation on universal military training.[1]

Sponsors of the amendment are Senators Lehman, Humphrey, Douglas, Ives, Hendrickson, Benton, Murray, Kilgore, Green, and Pastore.[2] A plea to branches to make an all out effort to get the amendment passed was made by Walter White, Executive Secretary of the NAACP, after Senator Lehman, chief sponsor, called on his fellow senators to vote favorably on the recommendation.

The proposal is one of four suggested additions to the Manpower Bill offered by Clarence Mitchell, Director of the Association's Washington Bureau, in testimony before the Armed Services Committee of the Senate on Wednesday, January 24, 1951.[3]

The amendment is the same language offered several years ago by Secretary of War, Henry L. Stimson.

The other three points of the NAACP's proposal called for the ending of all segregation in the Armed Services, a ban against the use of Jim-Crow facilities for housing or feeding members of the Armed Services and the elimination of all racial designations in records.

Most of the senators who introduced the amendment against violence have pledged that they will also work to achieve the other three recommendations of the Association.

Six of the sponsors met with officials of the Department of Defense on Monday, March 5, to discuss the status of integration. A report on this conference is being prepared.[4]

The Executive Secretary and the Director of the Washington Bureau, also, joined Senator Hubert Humphrey and a delegation from Minnesota in a meeting with Secretary of the Army Frank Pace, General Lawton Collins, and General Miles Reber. The Minnesota delegation was concerned about discriminatory practices of the Armed Services.[5]

Manpower Utilization

Grim aspects of job discrimination were revealed when the Director of the Washington Bureau visited Paducah, Kentucky, this month. An example of what is happening was given when the local employment service admitted that out of 400 persons referred for work on the new AEC plant site not one was colored. Skilled colored electricians were offered jobs as window washers and colored clerical workers were "assured" that they would get maid jobs.[6]

The South Carolina State Conference reports that the DuPont Company has hired a colored man in its personnel department at the AEC site in Aiken.

It will be necessary for the Washington Bureau to do a great deal of follow-up work in Washington on both of these problems. The visits made to the sites will be helpful.[7]

As reported last month, the Bureau is actively working on the Capital Transit Company's hiring policies.[8] The latest report from the U. S. Employment Service is that the owner has agreed to hire colored platform workers, but the union (Amalgamated Association of Street and Electric Railway Employees of America, AFL) has intimated that its members oppose integration of colored workers.[9]

Housing Legislation

Amendments requiring non-segregation provisions in the pending Defense Housing Act were requested by the Director of the Bureau in a hearing before the Senate Committee on Banking and Currency.[10]

Testimony given for the Association pointed out that in a recent visit to South Carolina the Director of the Washington Bureau lived in a mixed neighborhood. Senator Maybank (D., S.C.) was a surprise corroborating witness. He interposed to say that in his home-town (Charleston) there was also integration in some residential areas.

The NAACP proposed that the legislation be amended to require that all defense housing and community facilities provided by the bill be available on a non-segregated basis.

Theodore M. Berry, member of the Cincinnati, Ohio, City Council, supported the NAACP's position. Mr. Berry, who was present to urge that Cincinnati be designated as a key defense area, said that Federal support of the NAACP's proposal would make it easier for local officials to take a similar position.[11]

Grain for India

The Director represented the Association before the House Foreign Affairs Committee in a plea for grain for India. The Committee seemed favorably disposed toward the idea and subsequently approved a plan for sending grain to India.[12]

Specific Cases

The Research Assistant met with the Personnel Director of TVA at the Washington Bureau to discuss plans for settling the complaint of Mr. Norman Thomas a former employee of TVA.

This matter is of great interest in Alabama because there is a belief among some people there that Mr. Thomas was dismissed for NAACP activity.

The Public Buildings Administration has designated Mr. Louis V. Melici, Acting Chief of the Protective Section, to work with the Research Assistant on several knotty problems involving guards, who charge that they were denied upgrading, and taxi drivers who allege that Virginia interests are trying to force them out of the state. The Director attended one of the meetings with government officials on the taxi cab problem.

Approximately twenty-five drivers were present. The Virginia interests were represented by a lawyer from that state. The Director wishes to report that the matter was handled very well by the Research Assistant.[13]

Additional problems affecting the Veterans Administration, the Public Health Service, the Bureau of Agricultural Economics, and the Treasury Department are also being handled by the Research Assistant.

One of the pressing problems in the Veterans Administration is a complaint that twenty veterans were ousted from a plumbing school because of an alleged altercation with an instructor. The men are being denied further training benefits because of the incident.

Meetings, Speeches, Etc.

The Director spoke at meetings in Paducah, Kentucky; Cleveland, Ohio; Calvert County, Maryland; Baltimore, Maryland; Washington, D.C., and other areas during the past month.

It was also necessary to attend the usual quota of government advisory committees on which the Director serves. Making plans for the amendment to S.1 has required a great many meetings at the Capitol but staff members of the senators working with us have been most cooperative.

MS: NAACP II: A-670, DLC.

1. The association's proposed amendment to S. 1 read as follows:

The National Association for the Advancement of Colored People recommend that the following provisions be added to S. 1:

It is further provided that wanton attacks by peace officers on civilians against service personnel shall be a Federal crime (enforced by appropriate sanctions).

All new units will be organized without segregation.

Inductees or draftees in the Armed Services will not be fed or housed in any establishments (private or public) that requires segregation.

Racial designations shall be eliminated from all forms and records of military personnel. (Mitchell's draft, NAACP WB-141, DLC)

Mabel D. Jackson, secretary to Walter White, related to him a message from Mitchell that the story on the S. 1 amendment in the *New York Times* on March 2, 1951, "was not presented in the proper perspective." Mitchell also asked White to ask the *Times* to correct the story in which he, Mitchell, was reported to have said there was no hope for the civil rights program in Congress. Jackson memorandum to White, 3/2/51, NAACP II: A-185, DLC. See Mitchell's detailed update on the "Status of Civil Rights Legislation in the 82nd Congress," NAACP II: A-185, DLC. See, most immediately, 1/31 and 2/2/51. For the continuation of the struggle for protections against violence, see 4/4, 5/3, 6/4, and 8/31/51.

2. See 8/31/51 for directly related development.

3. 1/24/51, *Hearings*, 861–73.

4. See 8/31/51.

5. The NAACP related the experiences of men from Minnesota who had suffered discrimination at Camp Rucker, Alabama; Camp Attebury, Indiana; and Camp Leonard Wood, Missouri. In response to demands for an end to those practices, General Collins, army chief of staff, agreed to eliminate racial designations from travel orders and to address other complaints. Senator Humphrey said he would not support a University Military Training program that continued segregation in the army. Report of the Secretary for March 1951, EC. See also 1/31, 2/2, and 12/28/51.

An inescapable problem, however, was the attitude within the military "that the question of the environment surrounding Camp Rucker is a civilian matter." Letter from James C. Evans, civilian assistant to the secretary of defense, 2/13/51, NAACP WB-141, DLC.

6. See, most immediately, 1/31, 2/2, 2/5, and 5/3/51; in appendix 1, this vol., 12/20/50 and 2/21/51.

7. See also 12/4 and 12/21/50, 5/3 and 8/31/51. At the same time, a "Summary and Recommendations" of February 1951, prepared by the NUL, documented similar discrimination in the tricity area of Pasco-Kennewick-Richland in Washington, where "tremendous change" had also occurred after the Federal government began to construct the Hanford Works in 1943. Benton and

Franklin counties, with a combined population of 13,000 in 1910, had 65,000 by 1950. The Negro population of these 2 counties, which was 25 in 1910, increased to the present estimate which is between 1,400 and 2,000. Pasco, with 27 Negroes in 1940, found itself with 2,000 or more during the height of activities in 1948. The North Richland barracks and trailer camp had a combined Negro population of several hundreds in 1948 in an area where few, if any, had resided a few years before that time. Even Kennewick, which has not had a Negro permanent resident for about 30 years, had Negro families occupying a trailer camp within its borders during the "boom" period. The population of the area is still small compared with that of many American metropolitan districts, but the great increase in the past decade and the importance of the product being processed here give the Tri-City area a national significance today.

There are only 2 Negroes on public payroll in the Tri-City area, not including those employed at Hanford Works. Both of these are women and both have janitorial jobs—one for a state agency (Employment Security Department), and the other for a Federal agency (United States Post Office). Negroes are employed neither by the City of Pasco nor Kennewick, nor by either of the 2 counties or the state. At Hanford Works, 2 Negroes, a clerical worker and a mail handler, have recently been employed by the AEC. General Electric Company, the prime contractor with a much larger total work force, has a few Negroes in clerical and janitorial jobs. GE stated that it was contrary to its policy to reveal the exact number in these. Negroes hold skilled and semi-skilled jobs with the construction contractor at Hanford Works, except in selected crafts using workers from unions which have no Negro members. There are several such unions. Negroes enjoy good relationship, however, in those unions in which they are members. (The "Summary and Recommendations" was from the "Review of the Economic and Cultural Problems of the Tri-city Area," prepared by the Department of Research and Community Projects, NUL, a copy of which is in MP)

8. See also, among others, 8/31 and 12/28/51.

9. See also, among others, 12/20/48, 12/21/49, 8/31/51.

10. Mitchell's testimony, 2/20/51, *Hearings*, 477–90; see 4/4, 8/31, 12/5, and 12/28/51.

11. See 4/4/51 for a later report.

12. Mitchell's testimony was supported by White in his report to the board. White recommended that the board request that branches, the press (particularly the Negro press), and cooperating organizations give their support to the government food gift to India. The board accepted his recommendation. Minutes, 3/51, 8, EC.

In his testimony on the India Emergency Act of 1951, Mitchell told the House Committee on Foreign Affairs that White's observations, based on the executive secretary's recent visit to India, were that "failure to obtain help in meeting the food shortages caused by drought, locusts, and earthquake may possibly result in Nehru's loosing his desperate fight against communism. . . . No informed person can deny that should Nehru's government be overthrown there is no hope whatever of preventing capture of all of Asia by Russia." 2/21/51, *Hearings*, 103–5. Ultimately, the Congress handed Truman a setback by voting to provide aid in the form of a straight loan. *Congressional Quarterly Weekly Report*, 1951, 996.

13. No designated report by Fisher on discrimination against taxi drivers at the Pentagon cabstand was found. However, he provided James C. Evans, civilian assistant to the secretary of defense, with a detailed outline of the problem and suggestions for resolving them. Earle W. Fisher's letter to Evans, 12/4/50. See also Fisher's letter to Louis V. Melici, acting chief, Protective Section, GSA, 3/1/51, in which he again recommended restoration of the previous system of operation and offered other suggestions for resolving the "present difficulties." NAACP WB-176, DLC.

Monthly Report, April 4, 1951

April 4, 1951

MONTHLY REPORT OF WASHINGTON BUREAU

Armed Services

As this report is written, there is a strong indication that as a matter of policy the Republican Party will vote to retain the Winstead amendment in the current Draft and Universal Military Training legislation. The Winstead amendment provides for segregation in the Armed Services.[1]

Congressman Melvin Price of Illinois has agreed to introduce an amendment striking out the Winstead proposal. Congressman Franck Havenner of California has agreed to introduce an amendment which would make assaults on members of the Armed Services a Federal offense. Congressman Jacob Javits of New York has a general amendment against segregation which he will propose from the floor.[2]

On the anti-violence amendment, we have the additional handicap of a letter from General G. C. Marshall which states that the Department of Defense believes that members of the Armed Services need legislative protection against violence but not in the pending legislation.[3]

Meanwhile, on the general question of integration in the Armed Services, the Director has had a meeting with [Brig. Gen.] General B. M. McFadyen [Fayden], Chief of Military Personnel Division. This meeting was arranged by Mrs. Anna Rosenberg, Assistant Secretary of Defense. A detailed report on this meeting is available.[4] So far as integration is concerned, there is very little of it in the ground forces. The following two paragraphs taken from our letter to Mrs. Rosenberg on results of the conference should be noted.

"The conference revealed that the Army has shown a few colored troops the promised land of integration in basic training units and some specialties. However, the vast majority of ground troops are still in the bondage of segregation.

"There is integration during basic training at Fort Dix, New Jersey; Riley, Kansas; Knox, Kentucky; Jackson, South Carolina; Breckenridge, Kentucky; Ord, California; Roberts, California; Wood, Missouri, and Chaffee, Arkansas. However, our discussion at the meeting revealed that most of the colored people entering the Army are sent to existing colored units as replacements. Even those who are integrated during the period of basic training are sent to segregated units when they have completed their training."[5]

Defense Housing Legislation

S. 349, the Senate Defense Housing Bill, has been reported out of committee. Senator Douglas and Senator Ives sought unsuccessfully to get NAACP proposals into the bill.[6] These proposals would have eliminated segregation in housing and community facilities provided under the bill.

The committee did agree to one brief statement on the subject of racial problems in housing. This appears on page 41 of the report from the Committee on Banking and Currency. The statement is as follows: "Your committee expects that in the provision of housing by the Federal Government under this title and in the provision, or operation and maintenance, of community facilities and services assisted by this title there shall be equality of treatment of persons of all races, religions, and national origins who are to be served by them."[7]

We shall continue our efforts to get an amendment on the floor.

Note: In view of the pressure of work in Washington at this time, this report is necessarily brief. An effort will be made to include what has been left out in the report submitted next month.

MS: NAACP II: A670, DLC.

1. On March 15, 1951, the House Armed Services Committee wrote in an amendment to the UMT bill giving draftees a choice of serving in racially segregated or nonsegregated units. *Congressional Quarterly Weekly Report*, 3/16/51, 411. See also, among others, 3/5/51; in appendix 1, this vol., 4/24/51. See also Report of the Secretary to the Board on "Washington Activities," 2/16–3/16/51, NAACP II: A-655, DLC; Mitchell, "Status of Racial Integration in the Armed Services," 205–7; and Watson, *Lion in the Lobby*, 206–7.

2. See 3/5 and 12/28/51 for related activities.

3. This was the NAACP amendment to S. 1, the pending UMT legislation. See 1/24/51, *Hearings*, 861–73; 1/31, 2/2, 3/5, 4/4, 5/3, 6/4, and 8/31/51; in appendix 1, this vol., 7/21/51.

4. The meeting with MacFayden (Mitchell's spelling here) was held on March 15, 1951. In a follow-up meeting on May 1, 1951, in the office of Peter Seitz, assistant to Anna Rosenberg, Maj. Steve Davis provided a detailed report on behalf of MacFayden on the following six topics: the question of increasing the number of African Americans from nonsegregated National Guard units that had been called to active duty; the continuing study of the use of military installations for housing and feeding draftees in order to avoid the use of segregated facilities; the continuing study of the question of racial designation; the number of African Amerians who were sent to all-black units instead of integrated basic training centers when they entered the army; problems of segregation in facilities and other aspects of camp life; and the role of DOD in seeking legislation to protect members of the armed services against assault and physical violence. James C. Evans also attended this meeting. Mitchell memorandum to Walter White, 5/17/51, NAACP II: A-655, DLC.

The May 1, 1951, conference produced "some changes" in the Department of the Army's racial policies, and Mitchell had learned that "further consideration" was being given to additional changes. Mitchell's letter to Seitz, 8/6/51, NAACP WB-133, DLC.

MacGregor explains that "Departmental interest in racial affairs quickened noticeably" when" Gen. George C. Marshall, who succeeded Louis A. Johnson as secretary of defense, "appointed the brilliant labor relations and manpower expert Anna M. Rosenberg as the first Assistant Secretary of Defense for Manpower and Personnel." MacGregor cites a letter from Rosenberg to him, 9/23/71; see also his interview with James C. Evans, 13/9/71, both of which are in CMH Files. MacGregor, *Integration of the Armed Forces*, 392n50. Borklund, *Men of the Pentagon*, 121–24.

5. Mitchell's letter to Rosenberg, 3/26/51. Helping Mitchell considerably in this struggle were Sen. Hubert Humphrey, who was on a first-name basis with Rosenberg, and Rep. Jacob Javits (R-N.Y.), who pressed the struggle to end segregation at Fort Dix, New Jersey. Mitchell's letter to Rosenberg and

related correspondence from Humphrey and Javits, as well as reports, such as "Summary of Advances in the Utilization of Negro Manpower in the Army," 3/7/51, are in Records of the Office of the Secretary of Defense, 291.2, Central Decimal File 1951, 190/25/34/7, RG 330, NARA, College Park, Md.

6. See 3/5, 8/31, 12/5, and 12/28/51.

7. On February 27, 1951, the House Committee on Banking and Currency approved the administration's $3 billion defense housing program. *Congressional Quarterly Weekly Report,* 3/2/51, 314.

On March 20, 1951, the Senate Banking Committee approved S. 349 to encourage housing construction in defense areas. A similar bill, H.R. 2988, calling for mortgage insurance up to $3 billion, remained pending on the House calendar after the House voted on March 14 not to take up the measure for the time being; *Congressional Quarterly Weekly Report,* 3/16/51, 406. Then, on April 5, the Senate opened debate on S. 349. *Congressional Quarterly Weekly Report,* 4/6/51, 518.

As debate in the Senate loomed, Senators Paul Douglas (D-Ill.) and Irving Ives (R-N.Y.), at the NAACP's request, sought to get antisegregation language into the bill. Mitchell feared that under the proposed defense housing program, vast sums would be spent or insured by the federal government for housing and community facilities where the population was increasing because of defense activities.

Without the protective language, he said, southern whites intended to use the federal largesse to extend segregation "on a handsome scale." As an example, he cited a statement by Sarah Busch of the Aiken, South Carolina, Chamber of Commerce that her community needed a "municipal building to incorporate . . . police chief's office, white and colored police cells, playgrounds, one each white and colored; swimming pools, one each white and colored." Mitchell noted that "Mrs. Busch even asked for two parks costing $20,000 each. One for white and the other for colored," and he said similar ideas were "lurking in the minds of many other planners in Dixie." He therefore urged NAACP branches and other supporters to let their representatives and senators know that they wanted safeguards against segregation in S. 349 and H.R. 2988; otherwise, they would wake up one day and find that their tax dollars were "being spent to fasten an incredible system of segregation on new industrial areas of the South." Newsletter, 3/21/51, NAACP II: A-655, DLC. Defense Housing and Community Facilities Development Act of 1951, S. 349, Report of the Committee on Banking and Currency, 3/21/51, 82nd Cong., 1st sess. v. 2, no. 187–403, CIS Serial Set, Fiche 1, p. 41.

But on August 15, 1951, the House approved S. 349, the Defense Housing Bill, to authorize government aid to home construction in defense areas. The measure authorized $1,635,000,000 for the program. The Senate approved the final compromise version on August 20, 1951, and the House followed suit on August 22. *Congressional Quarterly Weekly Report,* 8/17/51, 1231, and 8/24/51, 1268.

Monthly Report, May 3, 1951

May 3, 1951

MONTHLY REPORT OF WASHINGTON BUREAU

The Washington Bureau has commented extensively on the defeat of the Winstead segregation amendment in the April Newsletter and also in an article submitted to the Crisis for publication. Therefore, no lengthy comment is made on that issue at this time. It is important to note that 44 delegates from 11 key states came to Washington and spent 3 days working to defeat the Winstead Amendment. During their visit, they talked with nearly a hundred Congressmen. It is the opinion of the Director of the Washington Bureau that this ensured defeat of the Winstead proposal.[1]

An amendment to protect members of the Armed Services against assaults and physical violence was defeated.[2] It is the opinion of the Director of the Bureau that this amendment was defeated for two main reasons.

1. Secretary George C. Marshall of the Department of Defense opposed the amendment. He stated that he thought it should be considered as separate legislation.[3]
2. Some of our supporters in Congress thought that if the Havenner Amendment passed the southern Congressmen could successfully argue that the Winstead Amendment should be retained. Such reasoning had little merit, of course, but it was effectively used against the amendment.

We are asking that this be introduced as a separate bill since many people who opposed it as an amendment have pledged that they will support it as a separate bill.[4]

Segregated Hospitals

As noted in previous reports, H.R. 314, which is Congressman Rankin's Bill setting up a Jim Crow Veterans Hospital at the Booker T. Washington Birthplace in Virginia, was denied passage on the unanimous consent calendar twice. However, Congressman Rankin has succeeded in getting the Rules Committee to clear his bill and it is now on the union calendar of the House. This means that it can be brought up at a time when Mr. Rankin feels he can get it passed.[5]

We are working against this proposal and have numerous pledges of support. However, it will require a process of patient watching to catch it when it is brought up for a vote and also it will require considerable cooperation on the part of Congressmen in order that they will be available when needed to vote against it.[6]

Electoral College Resolution

H. J. Res. 19, which is Congressman Gossett's Resolution to change the electoral college system in a manner which would give greater advantage to southern states in national elections, is again troubling us. It will be recalled that this Resolution was defeated when brought to the House floor by Congressman Gossett in the 81st Congress.[7] A subcommittee of the House Judiciary Committee has the matter under consideration. We have been advised confidentially that the subcommittee intends to approve H. J. Res. 19, although the chairman of the subcommittee has indicated that no final action has been taken. We are working with members of the subcommittee and the full Judiciary Committee in the hope that we may halt this measure there.[8]

Apprentice Training Legislation

In the 81st Congress, several attempts were made to nullify a favorable decision of the Federal Fair Employment Board. This decision has enabled colored veterans to take apprentice training as plate printers in the Bureau of Engraving. The attempts in the 81st Congress on the part of those who sought to cancel out the Board's decision were unsuccessful.[9] However, these same interests have persuaded Congressman Robert Ramsay of West Virginia to introduce H.R. 1507 and H.R. 290. These bills have the same purpose as those introduced in the 81st Congress. We are urging West Virginia NAACP leaders to ask Congressman Ramsay to abandon these bills.[10]

Florida and North Carolina Elections

We have requested Chairman Guy Gillette of the Senate Subcommittee on Privileges and Elections for an opportunity to make a plea for an investigation of the 1950 senatorial elections in North Carolina and Florida. We have been advised by Senator Gillette that an effort will be made to grant our request.

Segregation in the Armed Services

The Washington Bureau has been holding a number of meetings with representatives of the Department of Defense on certain critical problems bearing on segregation and other difficulties in the Armed Services. The Department of Defense has been gathering data on NAACP suggestions that (1) racial designations be eliminated on forms and records,[11] (2) draftees and volunteers be housed and fed on Government installations in areas where local businesses refuse to accommodate them on a non-segregated basis,[12] and (3) that additional colored people be assigned to integrated national guard units as those units are called into active duty.[13] A report on how these proposals will be handled has been promised us.

The Bureau was advised in a meeting on May 1 that segregated swimming arrangements at Fort Custer in Michigan have been ordered discontinued following the Association's protest and similar complaints we filed about segregation in other forts or camps are being processed.

So many individuals and organizations protested about segregation at Fort Dix, New Jersey, that it is certain that many people will claim credit for ending the unfair practices there. The Washington Bureau notes for the record that Fort Dix was among the installations that the NAACP complained about in the meeting with Assistant Secretary of the Army Earl D. Johnson on November 10, 1950. He promised correction at that time.

The following is a quote from a memorandum dated November 29, 1950, from the Director of the Bureau to Mr. White.

> "On point 2, which dealt with segregation at Fort Dix, I suggested that the procedure followed in Camp Ord might be applied to Fort Dix. I am not familiar with the plan at Camp Ord, but it was mentioned favorably in your telegram. Mr. Johnson stated that he thought this could be arranged."

The Department of Defense advised us later that the practices of segregation had been corrected.[14]

Meeting with Charles E. Wilson

As the Secretary's alternate, the Director of the Washington Bureau, joined with representatives of other organizations in a meeting with Charles E. Wilson, Director of the Office of Defense Mobilization on April 13, 1951. A full report on this has been submitted.[15]

Meeting with Secretary Dean Acheson

Again representing Mr. White, the Director of the Washington Bureau, joined with representatives of other organizations in a meeting with Secretary Dean Acheson of the State Department. This meeting is also discussed in a separate report along with information on a follow-up meeting with the Director of Personnel in the State Department.[16]

Atomic Energy Commission

In previous reports, we have discussed the Atomic Energy projects at Paducah, Kentucky, and Aiken, South Carolina. As a result of information received from a reliable source the Washington Bureau has filed charges against the Atomic Energy Commission on behalf of Mrs. Barbara Banks and Miss Evelyn Mills of Paducah. We charged that AEC officials violated Executive Order 9980 by refusing to interview these applicants when they sought jobs as clerical workers. We are continuing a broad program affecting both of these areas. This requires action on specific complaints and the overall hiring practices.[17]

We recently received a letter of appreciation from South Carolina for work done by Mr. Fisher on a housing project in that area. We were advised that plans were under way to make this project available to whites only. Mr. Fisher's action in Washington with the AEC officials halted these plans. Meanwhile, we have received a new report from South Carolina stating that colored carpenters seeking work were told "no colored needed today."[18]

Investigation of Baltimore Employment Service

In line with action mentioned on the AEC, the Washington Bureau has had numerous requests for investigations of various types of employment discrimination. One such request from Baltimore has revealed a terrible pattern of discrimination in the local employment service. The investigation of this discrimination is still under way.[19] However, some of the preliminary results show that during the months of August, September, and October in 1950, 562 white people were placed in government jobs but only 46 colored people were placed. Under the clerical and professional placements, it is shown that during September 1950, 1009 white people were referred while only 15 non-white people were referred. During November 1950, 1335 white people were referred and only 42 non-white people were referred. These figures undoubtedly could be duplicated in a number of other offices of the employment service around the country. They serve to warn against optimistic statements about the large number of jobs colored people are getting and rosy presentations on the decline of discrimination in employment because of the abundance of defense contracts, etc.

Mob Action Against Florida Residents

Mr. James Gallon and his son, James, Jr., came to the Washington Bureau last month from Greensboro, Florida. They stated that they had been beaten with ax handles during an argument with a white store owner in their own home town of Greensboro. The store owner was assisted by a mob of white persons and the Gallons were forced to flee from the local community. They have stated that they are unwilling to return to Florida. Unfortunately, the Department of Justice advised that it had no grounds for acting in this case. Hence, we have assisted the men in getting employment in Washington. The facts on their case have been sent to the Florida State Conference of NAACP Branches for the present campaign to get an anti-lynching bill passed in Florida.[20]

Important Specific Cases

Special attention is directed to the following matters which are among the things being handled by Mr. Fisher.

1. Elmer N. Fassett, a veteran, sought assistance of the NAACP for himself and other men who were denied their right to continue any kind of training under the G. I. Bill. Mr. Fassett and other men were dropped from a plumbing course in Baltimore, Maryland, following an alleged disorder in class. Mr. Fisher worked with representatives of the Baltimore Branch and the Veterans Administration on this case. On April 4, the VA announced that Mr. Fassett and other veterans

similarly barred from training because of the incident would be reinstated to full benefits of the law.

2. Mr. Fisher represented William H. Howard, an employee dropped by the Federal Security Agency, at a hearing on April 12. This case is significant because it appears that Mr. Howard was released by a supervisor who objected to his efforts to eliminate racial discrimination in the section where he was employed.[21]

3. The Research Assistant met with Charles H. McGuire, Director of National Shipping Authority, to discuss the problem of employment of colored officers. Mr. McGuire stated that he would see what could be done on an informal basis to gain employment for these men. A letter has been sent to Mr. McGuire urging action on his part to see that the non-discrimination clauses are enforced in the General Agency Agreements in order that the colored officers might have an opportunity to work.[22]

MS: NAACP II: A-670, DLC.

1. The vote to defeat the amendment followed a plea by Representatives Adam Clayton Powell Jr. of Harlem and William Dawson of Chicago, two African Americans. Report of the Secretary for the Month of April, 5/14/51, 2, EC. See also, in appendix 1, this vol., 4/4/51, and 4/24/51; Mitchell, "People vs. Winstead of Mississippi"; and Watson, *Lion in the Lobby*, 205–7.

2. See 1/31, 2/2, 3/5, 4/4, 6/4, and 8/31/51, where an excerpt of the newsletter, 7/25/51, in the notes, summarizes the whole struggle.

3. Even though General Marshall opposed the amendment, he apparently still supported its purpose. Pressing the issue, Mitchell subsequently noted for the House Committee on Armed Services that Marshall was reported in the *New York Times* to have said, "We must develop some system that will permit us to reduce the standing force without weakening our military posture. We plan to put into the ranks of the National Guard basically trained men; that is, those who have had at least four months' military training. So the fundamental concept of our plan isn't just universal military training. Primarily it is to vitalize our military Reserve system."

Mitchell told the committee that since his last appearance before it (3/8/51, *Hearings*, 844–56), the former secretary of defense had issued a semiannual report for January 1 through June 30, 1951, in which he said, regarding the subject of integration in the armed services:

> Considerable progress was also made in carrying out the President's 1948 directive on equality of treatment and opportunity in the armed services.
>
> During the 12 months the policies developed by the Army, Navy, Air Force, and Marine Corps in previous years were being implemented without untoward incidents.
>
> Additional evidence was provided to support the conclusion that the effectiveness of Negro personnel increases in a marked degree as individual employment, based on proficiency and merit, is substituted for employment in large segregated units. Combat operations of all of the Armed Forces in Korea demonstrated the feasibility of the established policies as well as the advantages that can be derived from their implementation. (1/30/52, *Hearings*, 2983; see also 2/14/52, *Hearings*, 502–10)

4. Walter White reported to the NAACP board that NAACP branches in eleven key states sent forty-four representatives to Washington in an all-out lobbying effort to defeat the Winstead amendment to the draft UMT bill. The delegates also worked to gain support for the amendment sponsored by Franck Havenner (D-Calif.), which made it a federal offense to assault or murder a member of the armed services. He reported that Mitchell's and the delegates' work "contributed considerably to the elimination of the Winstead Amendment from the Barden Bill which the representative of North Carolina had offered as a substitute for the administration-sponsored draft bill. The vote was 176 to 126."

Subsequently, by a vote of 138 to 123, White reported, the House eliminated the segregation amendment to the draft bill. The vote to eliminate the Winstead amendment followed an effective plea by Representatives William Dawson (D-Ill.) and Adam Clayton Powell Jr. (D-N.Y.). The NAACP-sponsored amendment to protect servicepeople against assault by local police officers and civilians was defeated by a vote of 63 to 46. The administration opposed enactment of this amendment, and the vote was taken when most of the amendment's supporters were absent from the floor. Report of the Secretary for the Month of April, 5/14/51, 2, EC.

5. See, among others, 10/31/47, 12/4/50, 6/4/51; in appendix 1, this vol., 2/21, 5/29, and 6/21/51.

6. H.R. 314 proposed to spend $5 million to build a VA hospital at Booker T. Washington's birthplace in Franklin County, Virginia. Part of Mitchell's struggle to defeat Rankin's effort included sending allies a copy of his May 23, 1951, letter to members of Congress in which he insisted that, rather than reverting to the Jim Crow practice during World War I of squeezing all African American veterans into the hospital at Tuskegee Institute, Alabama, the present program of admitting them to nonsegregated hospitals throughout the country should be accelerated. In another letter, written June 5, 1951, to Adam Clayton Powell Jr., Mitchell said he hoped the Harlem representative would explain on the House floor to his fellow lawmakers that it "would be one of the worst possible ways of discriminating against colored veterans" if they bought the contention that the hospital was intended to honor Washington's memory. Copies of both letters are in NAACP WB-10, DLC.

The bill was soundly defeated after organizations attending a May 22–23, 1951, conference organized by the Washington bureau wrote to 315 House members opposing it. Watson, *Lion in the Lobby*, 207.

7. See 3/3/50, where Mitchell mentioned the memorandum by John A. Davis, "Proposed Lodge Gossett Amendment," which is in appendix 1, this vol., and 7/8/50, where he reported its defeat.

8. See 6/4, 8/31, 11/5, and 12/28/51; in appendix 1, this vol., 5/29/51; and Watson, *Lion in the Lobby*, 332–33.

9. The bill involved was S. 3050, which was defeated in the Senate on April 19, 1950. See 5/1 and 7/17/50 for earlier efforts and 12/7/53 for the continuing struggle.

10. See 12/4/50 for an earlier report on the effort to strengthen the national defense training program.

11. "An NAACP delegation from Minnesota, joined by Walter White and Sen. Hubert Humphrey of Minnesota, protested the Army's segregation policy in a meeting with Secretary of the Army Frank Pace; Maj. Gen. Miles Reber; Gen. Lawton Collins, chief of staff; and Earl Johnson, assistant to Secretary Pace. The NAACP delegation related the experiences of servicemen from Minnesota who had suffered discrimination at Camp Rucker, Alabama; Camp Atterbury, Indiana; and Camp Leonard Wood, Missouri, and urged the army leaders to correct the problem. General Collins agreed the army would eliminate racial designation from travel orders and take other steps to end the complaints. Humphrey said he would not support a UMT program that continued segregation in the army. Report of the Executive Secretary to the Board, March 1951, EC. Next, Walter White and Clarence Mitchell held a conference with Mrs. Anna Rosenberg, assistant secretary of defense in charge of national manpower, urging the elimination of racial designations on travel orders for servicemen and the issuance of an order banning segregation of Army personnel from induction through assignment to troop units. Report of the Secretary for the Month of March 1951, 4/9/51, EC." See also selections from Report of the Secretary to the Board, 2/16–3/16/51, NAACP II: A-655, DLC.

12. See 1/31/51.

13. Ibid.

14. See also 12/4/50.

15. Mitchell's 4/26/51 memorandum to Walter White on the 4/13/51 meeting as well as another on 4/19/51 noted in White's report are in NAACP II: A-257, DLC. White told the board that a subcommittee of the original White House group working on manpower problems met separately, first with Charles E. Wilson, director of defense mobilization, and subsequently with Acheson on April 13, 1951. At the first conference, Wilson agreed with the requests of the group and said he would appoint a black assistant to deal with the general policy relative to African Americans. He reported that Wilson said Dr. Arthur Fleming, assistant to the director for manpower, Office of Defense Mobilization, would be available to work with the subcommittee on specific problems raised regarding efforts to integrate African Americans into every phase of the nation's defense mobilization.

At the second meeting later that day, Acheson was similarly sympathetic and requested that the committee consult with Haywood T. Martin, director of personnel at the State Department, on policies related to integrating African Americans in the domestic and foreign services.

Mitchell, again representing the NAACP at the conference on April 19, 1951, reported that:

(1) Mr. Martin would welcome a list of recommendations from our full committee of a qualified Negro to work in his office and be responsible to him on general personnel problems of the State Department. Pending this appointment, he would accept recommendations from the full committee of a qualified Negro in an advisory or consultant capacity to aid him on the general personnel of his department, specifically related to the issue discussed at the meeting with the group.

(2) He would welcome recommendations from the full committee of a list of persons whom the committee believes are qualified for specialized service in the State Department, both in the administrative field and the foreign service. He would accept recommendations by the Committee of promising persons for the Internship Program of the State Department.

(3) He would welcome helpful suggestions from the full committee in the procedure presently being used by his department as it might affect the employment of Negro citizens. (Report of the Secretary to the Board, 5/14/51, EC)

16. See Report of the Secretary for April, 5/14/51, EC. Among other things, Mitchell reported that Acheson "said he was interested in correcting any racial discrimination that might exist in the Department." Mitchell memorandum to White, 4/26/51, NAACP II: A-257, DLC. For a follow-up report, see 6/4/51.

17. See 12/4 and 12/21/50, 1/31, 2/2, 2/5, and 3/5/51 for Mitchell's intensification of the AEC struggle and 12/28/51 for the results of his efforts.

18. Mitchell had discussed these problems in a meeting in December with AEC officials in Washington that Fisher had attended. See 1/31/51.

19. See, next, 8/31/51.

20. See 12/4/50, where a resolution deploring this type of violence is cited; Walter White got the NAACP annual meeting to adopt the resolution on January 1, 1951.

21. Mitchell reported that the Howard case concluded as follows: "A hearing was held under agency grievance procedure appealing the dismissal. This hearing board upheld the original Administrative action. The record was then sent to the head of the agency. The administrator upheld the action of the hearing board. On the record Mr. Howard was dismissed as of July 15, 1951." Project Report, NAACP WB, 1–7/53, NAACP WB-33, DLC.

22. Mitchell provided a fuller summary of this case:

> We were requested by representatives of sixty colored merchant marine officers to contact the National Shipping Authority in an effort to see why colored merchant marine officers were not able to find employment during this period of increased activity in the shipping industry.
>
> The National Shipping Authority has placed blame with the Masters, Mates and Pilots Union. We have made efforts to arrange a meeting to discuss this matter.
>
> Congressman Edward J. Hart, Chairman of the House Merchant Marine Committee has been sent copies of our correspondence with Mr. Charles H. McGuire, Director of N.S.A. No report of action by this office has been made." ("Project Report," NAACP WB, 1–7/51, NAACP WB- 33, DLC)

Monthly Report, June 4, 1951

June 4, 1951

MONTHLY REPORT OF WASHINGTON BUREAU

Protection of Members of the Armed Services Against Assaults and Violence

Congressman Franck Havenner (D., Calif.) has introduced H.R. 4301, a bill to provide protection for members of the Armed Services against assault and other forms of violence. A similar bill is being studied in Senator Lehman's office for introduction in the near future.[1]

Rankin Hospital Bill

As was expected, Congressman Rankin is trying to maneuver consideration of his H.R. 314, the Jim-Crow Veterans Hospital Bill at a time when he feels that he can get it through the House. At the time this report is written, consideration of the bill has been postponed twice. Fortunately, these postponements have occurred at a time when it was useful to opponents of the legislation.[2]

H. J. Res. 19

We are still trying to get enough votes in the Judiciary Committee to defeat H. J. Res. 19. This is Congressman Gossett's resolution on the electoral college reform. At present, we have five pledges against the proposal. They are Congressmen Kenneth P. Keating, Byron G. Rogers, Clifford P. Case, Angier L. Goodwin, and William T. Byrne. We are asking branches to get firm commitments against it from congressmen who have declined to give us final pledges in Washington.[3]

Follow-up on the Department of Defense

In prior reports, we have mentioned the follow-up action we are taking with members of Mrs. Rosenberg's staff concerning various aspects of discrimination against members of the Armed Services.[4] A report on the latest conference has been submitted to the Secretary.[5] Meanwhile, we have received from Kansas City, Missouri, a new instance of humiliating treatment given inductees. In this instance, the complainant was refused hotel accommodations.

Air Force Training

In response to a complaint submitted by the Washington Bureau on behalf of men stationed at Walker Air Force Base, Roswell, New Mexico, we have an interesting statement of policy.

The men complained because they were denied admission to courses offered at the New Mexico Military Institute at the expense of the Air Force. Following a conference between the Secretary and Mr. Thomas K. Finletter, Secretary of the Air Force, the Bureau sought action on this complaint. The Air Force through John A. McCone, Acting Secretary of the Air Force, has stated the following:

"The Air Force is urging all its personnel, without regard for race or color, to avail themselves of these educational opportunities; however, since the facilities in the local communities are used, Air Force personnel must necessarily meet the schools' established entrance requirements.

"The Air Force has no jurisdiction over these entrance requirements to the civilian institutions. Therefore, in areas in which segregation is practiced and school facilities are not available for Negro personnel it is necessary for the Air Force to make special arrangements for instructors to conduct classes on the base. The Commanding Officer of Walker Air Force Base has recently completed arrangements with the Eastern New Mexico University to conduct classes on the base starting June 11, 1951. These classes are open to all personnel and to date over two hundred officers and airmen have completed registration."[6]

Follow-up Action on State Department Meeting

At the request of the Department of State, we have suggested that several well-qualified individuals visit the Department's employment office for interviews. Although these people have not yet been employed, it appears that their applications are being considered favorably.

One individual who mentioned that he felt his application was not being considered by the Department has since been employed in a responsible position. In fairness, it should be pointed out that in this case we did not have an opportunity to formally discuss it with the State Department. It appears that the notice for him to report for duty came following our meeting with Secretary Acheson. Presumably, the sudden notice to report is due to Mr. Acheson's pledge of a general effort to assure all people of employment on the basis of merit.[7]

Meeting with General Electric

At the request of the Schenectady NAACP Branch, the Director of the Washington Bureau met with Mr. E. J. Riley, Manager of Employee Relations, to discuss problems of employment, upgrading, and training. The G. E. official pledged correction of specific complaints submitted by the branch and also agreed to work out a suggested policy change which should result in better use of qualified colored persons.

Other Matters

A number of important complaints and problems on a variety of matters are being handled by the Bureau. Mr. Fisher's assignments include complaints against the Department of Agriculture concerning employment; a charge that the Cice Steel Company in Houston, Texas, fired a colored employee because he joined the Ornamental Iron Workers Union; and an alleged Air Force failure to promote a captain to a position because of his race.

Mr. Fisher's prompt handling of a complaint that the Washington Police Department was not giving draft deferments to colored policemen has resulted in a satisfactory settlement with deferment for the officer who brought the original complaint. The Police Department has also assured us that all officers will be given proper deferment without regard to race.

The Bureau is pleased to report also that a complaint from Birmingham, Alabama, against the local employment service has resulted in the Veterans Administration refusing to use that agency as a source of recruiting workers for a new hospital being built in the area.

Complaints involving failure to enforce non-discrimination clauses in a wide variety of Government contracts are being handled in the Bureau. Some of these of particular interest include the Bendix Aviation Corporation in Kansas City, Missouri; the Naval Ordnance Plant in Indianapolis, Indiana; and the Chrysler Tank Arsenal Plant in Delaware.

The Director and Mr. Fisher work on these matters jointly, but Mr. Fisher has been doing an excellent job in handling the technical details which must be explored on these cases. Needless to say, almost anyone of the complaints is a full time job in itself.

Speaking Engagements, Etc.

During the past month, the Director spoke at a branch meeting in Grand Rapids, Michigan; at the Maryland State Conference of Branches; and the Schenectady Branch in New York. Mr. Fisher spoke for a meeting of the Staten Island NAACP Branch.

MS: NAACP II: A-670, DLC.

1. See 1/31, 2/2, 3/5, 4/4, 5/3, 6/4, and 8/31/51, note 13, where an excerpt from the 7/25/51 newsletter summarizes the struggle.

2. The Rankin proposal was defeated by a vote of 223 to 117. Mitchell memorandum to all NAACP branches, 4/1952, NAACP II: A-185, DLC. See also, among others, 5/3 and 12/28/51; in appendix 1, this vol., 2/21, 5/29, and 6/21/51.

3. See 5/3, 8/31, 11/5, and 12/28/51; in appendix 1, this vol., 5/29/51.

4. See 4/4/51.

5. See Mitchell's letter to Rosenberg, 3/26/51, Records of the Office of the Secretary of Defense, 291.2, Central Decimal File 1951, 190/25/34/7, RG 330, NARA, College Park, Md.

6. This compromise by the air force was in keeping with the agreement Walter White had obtained, which was as follows:

> On March 31, Thomas K. Finletter, Secretary of the Air Force, telephoned that the integration program of the Air Force had encountered a serious snag in a demand of 17 Southern states forced by Senators Allen J. Ellender of Louisiana that all training of air force personnel at Southern schools would be subject to the segregation laws of the Southern state.
>
> Mr. Finletter explained that certain subjects were not provided for in air force installations which necessitated sending of trainees for these particular courses to schools close to the air forces bases. Mr. Finletter informed the Secretary that a proposal had been made that each trainee thus sent to an outside school be given the option of refusing to go to a segregated school in which event he would be sent to one in a non-segregated state. In a letter dated April 6 the Secretary strongly opposed any surrender by the Air Force because yielding on any significant point might prove to be the opening wedge in stopping integration. Since these schools claim that their enrollment and income were dropping to such an extent as to put them in jeopardy and since they would be paid generously by the Government for such training it was urged that they be told they could not secure such contracts unless they were willing to train all on an equal basis. In the event of refusal by the schools, it was urged that trainees either be sent to schools outside the segregation field or that facilities be established on the air forces bases for such training.
>
> Mr. Finletter informed the Secretary on April 30 in Washington that the latter course had been decided upon and that training schools in all necessary subjects will be established by September 1st. (Report of the Secretary for April 1951, 5/14/51, EC)

7. See 5/3/51 for an earlier report and Mitchell's memorandum to White, 4/26/51, on the 4/19/51 meeting, NAACP II: A-657, DLC.

Monthly Report (for June, July, August) August 31, 1951

REPORT OF WASHINGTON BUREAU
FOR
MONTHS OF JUNE, JULY, AND AUGUST

[August 31, 1951]

Senate Rules Change[1]

Hearings have been set for the first two weeks in October on proposed changes in the Senate rules on limitation of debate.[2] List of possible witnesses have been agreed upon in meetings with interested organizations. Senator McFarland has announced that he hopes the Senate will be able to adjourn on October 1. However, this is a subject of some debate at this time and it is difficult to know whether the October 1 adjournment will actually take place. In any event, plans are going forward for the October hearings.[3]

The Housing Crisis

Housing problems of minority groups in the United States are at a critical stage.[4] The Federal Government is underwriting or supporting in various ways the building of public housing, private housing, and slum clearance programs. We have considerable evidence that in many instances the Federal Government is actually promoting the extension of racial segregation. We have prepared a statement on this which it is presumed the Secretary will bring up at the Board meeting.[5]

When S. 349, the Defense Housing Bill, was under consideration, Senators Douglas and Ives, after unsuccessfully seeking incorporation of non-segregation amendments in the Bill[6] itself, did obtain a statement in the Committee Report on the Bill concerning equality of treatment.[7] When the Bill was debated in the House, non-segregation amendments were kept off of the floor by the Administration with one exception. This exception was Congressman Javits' amendment dealing with community facilities. This amendment was defeated because it was opposed by Congressman

Multer of New York. Congressman Multer argued that he had been assured by the Housing Agencies that the problem raised by Congressman Javits was being taken care of by administrative regulations.[8] Following the passage of the Bill, Congressman Multer discussed his position at length, both in correspondence and personally, with the Director of the Bureau. He stated that he was going to take the problem to the President.[9]

The Bureau prepared a memorandum for the Congressman.[10] He sent a letter to the President urging action.[11] Other Congressmen have followed suit. The Bureau has also outlined the problem to Mr. Raymond Foley, Administrator of the Housing and Home Finance Agency, by letter and in conversation. It is clear, however, the NAACP must plan some dramatic action in this field. Also, it is clear that on the basis of our legislative experience, we are the only major organization in the country that has taken an all out position against segregation in housing. There are many other organizations that agree with the principle of no segregation, but either oppose or are indifferent to the possibility of having this principle included in legislation. Therefore, it seems important that, in any action planned on the housing front, the NAACP must take the leadership, although it would be well to welcome the support of other organizations.[12]

Armed Services

In the March Report of the Washington Bureau, we mentioned that Senators who sponsored an NAACP amendment to the Draft Bill had agreed to meet with the Department of Defense to discuss ways of speeding up integration. These Senators would not agree to place a non-segregation amendment on the floor for debate in the Draft and Universal Military Training Bill, but said that they would work for acceleration of the program of integration in the Armed Services. Six of them met at the Department of Defense on March 5, 1951. They obtained a pledge that the Universal Military Training Program would function on a non-segregated basis and they also obtained certain pledges on action to advance integration. Therefore, the recent announcement that the Army would abolish segregation in the Far Eastern Theater is one of the first concrete results of this conference.[13] The following statement from an official of the Department of Defense to one of the Senators is submitted for the Board's information:

> "I feel very strongly that whatever advances have been made in the elimination of discrimination and segregation in the Army, recently, should be credited not only to officials in the Department of Defense, but also to you and the Senators who are associated with you.
>
> "I feel, as you do, that things still remain which must be done to eliminate race and color segregation in the Army, and I am certain that every effort will be made to accomplish this desirable goal."

The Senator who received this communication felt that it would not be advisable to make it public, hence, the names of the Defense official and the Senator are not included in this written report. We have been assured that plans are under consideration for an announcement concerning integration of the Armed Services in the European Theater. Regrettably, full integration at home appears to be last on the list.[14]

Anti-Violence Legislation

We have been somewhat depressed by the difficulty we have encountered in getting legislation designed to protect members of the Armed Services against assaults and physical violence introduced in the Senate.[15] The delay has been caused by factors which are beyond the control of Senator Lehman, who is the chief sponsor of this bill. Mr. Julius Edelstein of his office has done a splendid job in assuring full support of Government agencies for this bill. So far, he has obtained clearance from the Department of Defense, the Treasury Department, and the Department of Justice. The Department of Defense has promised a statement on instances in which violence occurred and also has promised to define what is meant by the word "duty," since this appears to be a matter of considerable importance in the minds of members of the Senate.

Unfortunately, Senators Wiley, Ferguson, and O'Conor who are members of the Senate Judiciary Committee have not pledged that they will sponsor this legislation. Their sponsorship would do much to increase its chances of passage. We have not yet given up hope of getting them. The CIO has suggested that the bill be amended to exclude the possibility of having it apply to strike situations.

No Segregation on AEC Projects

The Atomic Energy Commission advised the Director of the Washington Bureau at a luncheon meeting that, pursuant to NAACP urging, it had instructed all contractors at Paducah and South Carolina that there would be no segregation in "cafeterias, eating facilities, wash-rooms, lavatories, etc." This action was taken by AEC after a careful study of practices of non-segregation on several southern Army posts. Senator Maybank, according to the Augusta Chronicle, has issued a statement implying that AEC appropriations may be cut because of this action.[16]

The AEC has also advised that it was assigning one of its top employees to make a special drive for eliminating the bottlenecks which in the past have prevented qualified colored people from getting skilled jobs with AEC or its various contractors. This official was also present at the luncheon. At the Bureau's request, the AEC confirmed its non-segregation policy in writing. It was also agreed that a meeting on problems of South Carolina employment and other matters would be held in that state with AEC officials on September 17. This meeting has been arranged.[17]

The Director of the Washington Bureau wishes to point out that the mere adoption of a policy does not assure that there will be absolutely no segregation on the project. However, with this policy in hand, the Association can police these projects effectively and stamp out segregation. The value of such a program cannot be over estimated. Also, such effective legal action as can be undertaken will help to make the AEC operations in the South a model of industrial activity.[18]

Cox Resolution

Congressman Cox of Georgia has introduced H. Res. 364 which provides for an investigation of foundations that to quote him have "disbursed funds irresponsibly to aid organizations which made a profession of stirring up class and race dissention throughout the South."[19] The list of persons cited by Cox as Communist fronters includes Dr. Ira D. Reid and Miss Lillian Smith. This resolution has been reported out by the Rules Committee. Apparently, Cox brought it up at a time when members pledged to oppose it were not present. Unfortunately, these members have been very noncommittal on whether they were actually at the meeting which, of course, was closed.

Both Congressman Dawson and Majority Leader, John McCormack, have pledged their opposition to this resolution. At the time this report is written, we have not yet obtained a commitment from Minority Leader, Joseph Martin, although we are still seeking it. We have placed the problem before him and hope that he will pledge opposition to the Resolution. The House will return for business on September 12. At that time, Cox may seek to bring up this Resolution and we are urging all liberal Congressmen to be on hand to defeat it.

Jim-Crow in VA Hospitals

In the May report, we pointed out that H.R. 314, Congressman Rankin's Jim-Crow Hospital Bill was on the calendar for action in the House. We are glad to report that this measure was defeated by a vote of 223 to 117.[20] Some indication of what conditions would be like if the bill had passed is given by a case we have received from Alabama. In this situation, a veteran who was in need of treatment in Montgomery, Alabama, was sent to Tuskegee for treatment because that was "the facility for colored veterans" although there was a hospital within four miles of his home. The hospital at Tuskegee is forty miles from his home.

We have taken this matter up with the Veterans Administration and, although we have received one report from Admiral J. T. Boone, Chief Medical Director of the Veterans Administration, we are not satisfied with it and we are taking further action.

Another illustration of the constant Jim-Crow tendencies in the Veterans hospitals has come from the institution located at Kecoughtan, Virginia. Here, the local officials of the hospital placed a sign over a door leading to the dining-room designating it as a colored entrance. We received an anonymous complaint on this and promptly took action. The hospital authorities demurred, but finally removed the sign.[21]

Maritime Employment

In a number of our reports, we have mentioned the consistent work which has been done by Mr. Fisher of the Washington Bureau staff on problems of colored officers in the Maritime industry. A small reward has come through his efforts in that the Merchant Vessel Booker T. Washington has been restored to active service and one of the colored officers who has been a complainant has been hired by the Luckenbach Steamship Company which operates the ship.

Mr. Fisher's plan of action, however, includes a much more extensive attack on this problem. He has advised the Maritime Administration of the Department of Commerce that "Articles 1, 2, and 12 of the General Agency Agreement between the Administration and the ship operators place sufficient power and authority in the National Shipping Authority to insist and demand that the agent shipping companies discontinue immediately their denial of employment to colored Merchant Marine officers solely because of race." Mr. Fisher indicates that there are 160 ships taken out of the "lay up" fleet because of Government demands. These vessels have openings for nearly one thousand officers.

Other Employment Facts

As we gear up for the defense program, there is continuing evidence for the need of national fair employment practice machinery.[22] In our report of May 1951, we mentioned that the employment service in the City of Baltimore has been guilty of extensive discrimination in making referrals to Government agencies. An investigation of these complaints has shown that the local employment service received over one hundred discriminatory requests from Government agencies. This report was promptly squelched by state officials who sent, instead, a statement to Washington that they had found no discrimination.[23]

The national office of the employment service, at our request, has been negotiating with officials of the Capital Transit Company to obtain agreement that colored people will be employed as platform operators. So far, no favorable results have been reported. We have also been granted time to oppose a fare increase requested by the Capital Transit Company before the Public Utilities Commission on September 24.[24]

We have received reports of discrimination from Ford plants in Norfolk, Virginia, and Chicago, Illinois. It appears that in these cases cooperation of the contracting agencies and the United Automobile Workers may produce some favorable results. On the other hand, the Caterpillar Tractor Company of Peoria, Illinois, engaged in extensive recruitment in Alabama, but, although it used the facilities of the employment service in Illinois and Alabama, refused to take any colored applicants. The Illinois Employment Service has said it is powerless to halt this kind of discrimination.

The Bendix Aviation Corporation Plant in Kansas City, Missouri, which is working on an Atomic Energy Commission contract, refused to employ colored girls who applied for jobs as clerk typists. The complainants left the establishment, and, on calling over the telephone, were told that there were plenty of openings. Apparently, the employer thought that the telephone callers were white. This matter has been placed before the Atomic Energy Commission and the Bendix Aviation Corporation Plant by the Washington Bureau.[25]

A great many other complaints of this kind are coming into our office and we are seeking to obtain some adjustment with the help of the contracting agencies. However, these complaints emphasize the fact that discrimination is still with us in spite of the high level of employment and numerous improvements in various parts of the country.

We have been advised that the legislative difficulties that the President has encountered on various parts of his program have effectively prevented issuance of an executive order on fair employment practice. However, it appears that the possibility of getting such an order is not entirely lost.[26]

Lodge-Gossett Resolution

Congressman Gossett of Texas has resigned from Congress, but his H. J. Res. 19, which eliminates the electoral college, has been reported out of the House Judiciary Committee and the Senate Judiciary Committee. In the Senate, this Resolution is sponsored by Senator Lodge of Massachusetts.[27] We have been advised that these actions were taken as a kind of farewell present to Congressman Gossett. However, we are making plans for conducting a floor fight, as we did successfully in the House last year, if it is necessary. Senator Lodge discussed his position on this with us.[28] It is as follows:

1. He did not seek action in the Senate Judiciary Committee and was out of town at the time the measure was reported out of the committee. He will not seek favorable action on it unless it is passed by the House.
2. If the House passes the Resolution, he will give us another opportunity to argue the merits of our opposition before he seeks action on the floor.

Chickland Cafe

During the Month of July, the proprietor of a night club known as the Chickland Cafe decided to open the establishment for colored patrons in an effort to boost his business. This cafe is located at Capitol Heights in Maryland, just across the District line. Although the proprietor expected to attract colored business mainly, he also admitted white patrons. This action resulted in mob violence and the destruction of his property by white residents in the town of Capitol Heights. Extensive reports have been written on this incident and recommendations for action have been made. It is clear that the hoodlums who caused the trouble had also caused trouble when the establishment was operated for white patrons only. Apparently, these elements had the full support of the local law enforcement officers in Capitol Heights.[29]

Birmingham Killings

The Director of the Washington Bureau accompanied Mr. Emory O. Jackson to a meeting in the Department of Justice for the purpose of seeking action on numerous police killings in Birmingham and Alabama. Mr. Jackson submitted information showing that since 1948 the Alabama police have murdered 52 colored people. Twenty-six of these killings occurred in the City of Birmingham. Peyton Ford, Deputy Attorney General, has advised that the Department of Justice is investigating these complaints. Mr. Ford has since resigned from the Department, but it appears that the investigation is continuing.[30]

The National Airport

Being mindful of the fact that, when the national airport was being constructed, plans to have a segregated arrangement for handling colored passengers were perfected with the acquiescence of the Department of Commerce, we have asked Secretary Charles Sawyer to give assurance that the new airport which will be built at Burke, Virginia, will not have segregated facilities. Secretary Sawyer stated that "it will be a long while before there will be any need to face the problem of segregation at the Burke airport. We will not have acquired the property for many months and after that many other things must be done before it will be in operation. I can assure you, however, that so far as it lies within my power there will be no segregation permitted."

Railroad Jim-Crow

We have received a complaint from a passenger on the Atlantic Coast Line who charges that the railroad forced her to sit in a Jim-Crow coach, although numerous seats were available in modern coaches set aside for white people. We have taken this matter up with the Atlantic Coast Line Railroad.[31]

Recreation Suits

Residents in the vicinity of the Rosedale playground in Washington have asked the Washington Bureau to act in their behalf because colored children are barred from play. Nearly one hundred parents signed a petition requesting action.[32] At a meeting with representatives of the parents, Mr. Frank Reeves, Chairman of the Washington Branch Legal Redress Committee and other citizens, plans were made for legal action. Mr. Reeves has filed one suit on behalf of another group of parents in another area and plans similar action on behalf of the parents in the Rosedale area.

Friends of the Association have prepared a very impressive letter for the signature of the Director of the Washington Bureau setting forth the legal arguments on why the Commissioners in the District of Columbia have ample authority to end segregation in all play areas. This document, which was four pages in length, has been submitted to the Commissioners of the District.[33] Mr. Fisher also appeared on behalf of the Association and made a presentation at a public hearing held by the District Commissioners. The action of the Bureau is designed to supplement the action of the Washington NAACP Branch.

MS: NAACP II: A-656, DLC.

The date 8/31/51 is assigned for editorial purposes.

1. In his February 2, 1951, report, Mitchell presented the legislative picture in the House and Senate. But until he could remove the filibuster roadblock, passage of civil rights legislation was nothing but a dream. His January 21, 1951, revised report to Walter White on the "Status of Civil Rights Legislation in the 82nd Congress" reinforced his concern about the comprehensive picture:

> To date, 40 bills and two resolutions on Civil Rights have been introduced in the House. These include three worthless compromise measures offered by Congressmen Hayes of Arkansas and Rogers of Florida.
>
> In the Senate, there are seven civil rights bills and three resolutions on this subject. Senator Lehman and others have introduced an anti-filibuster resolution which is, of course, the key to passing Civil Rights legislation in the Senate.
>
> The bills introduced in the House include four submitted to Congress by the Department of Justice. They are H.R. 28, the Anti-Lynching Bill; H.R. 29, the Omnibus Civil Rights Bill; H.R. 1320, which would eliminate the Poll Tax, and a new Bill, H.R. 2118. H.R. 2118 proposed to amend Sections 1581, 1583, and 1584 of Title 18, U.S. Code, so as to prohibit attempts to commit the offenses therein proscribed (slavery and peonage). All of these bills have been introduced in the House. On June 25, Senator Humphrey will introduce these in the Senate.
>
> It is important to note that five FEPC bills have been introduced in the House. However, their fate is sealed because they have been referred to the Labor Committee headed by Barden of North Carolina. The Senate Bill would be given friendly committee consideration, but there is the filibuster hurdle to be overcome.
>
> Other Civil Rights legislation proposed includes Abolition of Segregation on Common Carriers, no discrimination in the National Health Insurance Program, no discrimination in Educational Finance, Fair Housing Practices, and Equal Rights Act for the District of Columbia.
>
> Congressman Clifford Case of New Jersey and Franck Havenner of California have introduced bills to protect members of the Armed Services against assault and other violence at the hands of civilians or peace officers. A similar bill is being prepared for introduction in the Senate. (6/21/51 memorandum to Walter White, in NAACP WB-163, DLC)

See 10/4, 11/5, 11/30, and 12/28/51; "Still No FEPC," editorial, *Crisis* 58 (June-July 1951): 395; Report of the Secretary for September 1951, EC; Mitchell, "These Are the Issues," *Crisis* 59 (October 1952:): 483–86; and Watson, *Lion in the Lobby*, 166–70.

2. Pressing Mitchell to seek changes in the cloture rule was the fact that, as he reported to Walter White, forty civil rights bills and two resolutions had been introduced in the House. They included four submitted by the Department of Justice. They were H.R. 28, the Antilynching bill; H.R. 29, the Omnibus Civil Rights bill; H.R. 1320, to eliminate the poll tax; and a new bill, H.R. 2118, to amend Sections 1581, 1583, and 1584 of Title 18, U.S. Code, which barred slavery and peonage. He said Senator Humphrey would introduce these bills in the Senate. Mitchell memorandum, 6/21/51, to White, NAACP WB-163, DLC.

3. See 10/4, 11/5, 12/5, and 12/28/51 reports for his subsequent efforts in this struggle.

4. Drawing on a speech by Robert C. Weaver at the National Conference on Discrimination in Housing, on May 29, 1952, Walter White noted for the NAACP board that between 1935 and 1950, though approximately 2,761,000 dwelling units were built under the FHA insurance program, no more that 50,000 of them were available to nonwhites. White memorandum, 6/3/52, to NAACP board, 6/9/52, MP. See also statement of the Southern Regional Council on "Blighted Housing and Bomb Violence" in Report of the Secretary for May, 6/9/52, EC. See also 3/5, 4/4, 12/5, and 12/28/51; in appendix 1, this vol., 2/21/51; Crosby, "America's Segregated Cities," *Negro Digest* 9 (August 1951): 82–94.

5. See 3/5, 4/4, 12/5, and 12/28/51; amendments sought by Mitchell before the Senate Committee on Banking and Currency, 2/20/51, *Hearing*, 477–81; Minutes, 9/10/51, EC.

6. 2/20/51, *Hearings*, 477–81; and Berry, 2/20/51, *Hearings*, 481–505. S. 349 was enacted as the Defense Housing and Community Facility and Services Act of 1951, which Truman signed on September 1, 1951. The law authorized $50,000,000 for government-constructed defense housing, set aside $1.5 billion in FHA mortgage insurance for privately financed housing in defense areas, and extended the VA direct loan program to July 1, 1953. *Congress and the Nation*, 483–484.

7. Defense Housing and Community Facilities Development Act of 1951. Report of the Committee on Banking and Currency, S. 349, 3/21/51, 82nd Cong., 1st sess. S. Rpts. v. 2, 41. See 12/28/51 for expanded comments on the committee's report.

8. But, the NAACP would insist, the policy set forth by Raymond Foley, HHFA administrator, in a letter of 11/26/51 to Multer clearly permitted continued segregation. See also 2/6/51.

9. On August 15, 1951, the House passed S. 349 in substantially the same form as the Senate had approved it. *Congressional Quarterly Weekly Report*, 8/17/51, 1231–32; the House agreed to the conference report on August 21. *Congressional Quarterly Weekly Report*, 8/24/51, 1268.

10. Mitchell said the real reason for Multer's opposition was an off-the-record agreement among members of Congress that southern supporters of the bill should not be "embarrassed" by having to vote for it with favorable language on racial matters included. NAACP press release, 8/16/51, NAACP II: A-208, DLC. See also 12/28/51.

11. Mitchell recommended to Truman that he issue "to the responsible Federal agencies an Executive Order governing the administration of Titles II and III of the Defense Housing and Communities Facilities Act of 1951" that would be designed to end the glaring discrimination problems in the federal housing program. Minutes, 9/1/51, EC.

12. Mitchell was equally forceful in expressing the NAACP's concerns about the simple need for the federal government to provide an adequate supply of public housing. A resolution adopted by the NAACP board on May 14, 1951, asserted that "public housing holds out the greatest promise of changing the pattern of discrimination and segregation which means inequality and divisiveness and injustice." Copy of resolution in NAACP II: A-308, DLC. On June 11, 1951, he issued the following statement:

> The situation now is that the Senate has passed a housing bill which authorizes the construction of 35,000 public housing units a year for the next four years. However, when that measure was voted on in the Senate, Senator Lehman and a number of other liberal Senators voted against the provision requiring 35,000 units a year because the adoption of that provision had the effect of striking out another provision which would have authorized 130,000 units a year.
>
> In other words, incorporation of this amendment which was offered by Senator Knowland had the effect to reducing the number of units which were authorized in the bill. That situation is further complicated by the fact that the man who offered the original provision in the bill providing for 130,000 units was Senator Maybank of South Carolina. He, of course, has served notice that he will make a motion to strike out the 130,000 unit provision because the Supreme Court had ruled there must be no segregation. However, when he offered his proposed amendment, Senator Knowland objected to it and thereafter Knowland made his motion to ask for the 35,000 units and that is why it is so very complicated.

> There are no units of public housing authorized by the bill passed by the House. For that reason, the measure must go to a conference between the House and Senate. A few days ago, a motion was made for the appointment of a Conference Committee. There was an objection, so the House members were not appointed. However, inevitably there will be a Conference Committee appointed and inevitably some kind of bill will be passed. A fight will be on as to whether the House conferees will agree to the Senate authorization of 35,000 or whether they will insist on a House version of no units at all. Re: Clarence Mitchell's statement on housing (via long distance), June 11 [1951], NAACP II: A-316, DLC.

At its meeting in May, the NAACP board deplored the House's limiting the number of public housing units that would be constructed in the fiscal year beginning July 1, 1951, to 5,000. Subsequently, the number was increased to 50,000. Copy of Minutes, 5/14/51; NAACP press release, 8/16/51, both in NAACP II: A-308, DLC.

13. On July 1, 1951, General Ridgway received a message from the Department of the Army approving "deactivation of the 24th Infantry and your general plan of integration of Negroes into all units (with the temporary exception of the 40th and 45th Divisions)." MacGregor, *Integration of the Armed Forces*, 444.

See 3/5/51, where Mitchell reported on the introduction of an amendment to S. 1, the UMT bill, and on the conference of the sponsors with DOD officials.

14. See also, among others, 11/5 and 12/28/51; materials in NAACP II: A-656, DLC.

15. Mitchell reported:

> Protection for members of the Armed Services against assaults and other violence is provided in two bills, H.R. 4301 and H.R. 4442 in the House. Senator Lehman and others will introduce a similar bill in the Senate.
>
> H.R. 4301 was introduced by Congressman Franck Havenner (D., Cal.), May 31, 1951. H.R. 4442 was introduced by Congressman Clifford Case (R., N.J.), June 13, 1951.
>
> The proposed legislation extends to members of the Armed Services the protection given to members of the Coast Guard and other Federal officials under sections 1114 and 111 of title 18, U.S. Code. These sections of the U.S. Code impose heavy fines and other penalties on persons who commit stated offenses against Federal officers.
>
> In March, when the Universal Military Training Legislation was before the Senate, the NAACP sponsored an anti-violence amendment offered by Senator Herbert Lehman (D., N.Y.).
>
> In April, when this legislation reached the House for action, the amendment was sponsored by Congressman Franck Havenner. On both occasions, the anti-violence amendents were defeated. Many members said, however, that they would support it as separate legislation.
>
> Mrs. Anna M. Rosenberg, Assistant to the secretary of Defense, has assured the Director of the Washington Bureau that the Department of Defense will support the legislation. The Department of Defense stated in a letter to the Director, "There has been no change in our belief that such a bill is desirable to extend to Army, Navy, and Air Force officers and enlisted men the same type of protection that is afforded by law to other classes of Federal officers." (7/25/51, newsletter, MP)

16. It is not clear whether the luncheon was the July 5 meeting with AEC officials that Mitchell reported on in a July 16, 1951, memorandum.. However, he stated that at the July 5 meeting, discussion also involved protecting from dismissal any AEC employee who filed a lawsuit challenging segregation at Oak Ridge, Tennessee. Mitchell memorandum to Thurgood Marshall, 7/16/51, NAACP WB-8, DLC. See also 2/5/51 and other references cited there.

17. At the bottom of the "Suggested Agenda" for the September 17 meeting was the notation that the meeting was actually held December 14, 1951. NAACP WB-8, DLC. Mitchell noted on the agenda that he had included an excerpt from the 1951 Senate Hearings on the Defense Housing Act, S. 349, the full report of which can be found in 2/20/51, *Hearings*, 477–81. For Mitchell's earlier notes on his activities related to the hearings on the Defense Housing Act, see 3/5 and 4/4/51 reports. See also 2/2, 3/5, 5/3, 8/31, and 12/28/51.

Mitchell actually visited South Carolina on September 17, but according to the memorandum he submitted to Thurgood Marshall, he did so to collect evidence for proposed legal action challenging job discrimination at the AEC's Savannah River works. Based on the information Mitchell had provided, Constance Baker Motley, a member of Marshall's legal staff, said it appeared that the du Pont Company had a closed-shop agreement with the unions involved. Such agreements, she said, violated the Labor-Management Relations Act of 1947 (the Taft-Hartley Act) and therefore could only have been oral agreements. Mitchell's memorandum, 9/20/51, and Motley's analysis of 11/28/51 are in NAACP WB-8, DLC.

18. See Mitchell's 7/16/51 memorandum to Marshall informing him of his discussion with AEC officials about possible lawsuits; see also his 9/20/51 memorandum on "Proposed Legal Action at Savannah River Works of Atomic Energy Commission." Marshall evidently assigned the matter to Constance Baker Motley of his staff. See her memorandum of 11/28/51 to Mitchell analyzing data gathered by him on September 17 on AEC discrimination in South Carolina. These materials, as well as others from the NUL regarding similar problems in the tricity area of Pasco-Kennewick-Richland (in Washington State), are in NAACP WB-8, DLC. See 12/4 and 12/21/50, 2/2, 3/5, and 5/3/51 reports for earlier developments.

19. See 11/5 and 12/28/51, 5/8, 6/5, and 12/31/52; in appendix 1, this vol., newsletter, 5/28/52, and 7/52.

20. See *Congressional Quarterly*, 1951; Watson, *Lion in the Lobby*, 207; materials in NAACP WB-185, DLC.

21. See, among others, 5/3 and 12/28/51.

22. Both the NAACP and the National Council for a Permanent FEPC marked the tenth anniversary of Roosevelt's wartime FEPC by noting that June 25, the first anniversary of the start of the Korean War, was also a time to assess the impact of the continuing problem of racial discrimination in employment. See materials in NAACP II: A-257, DLC.

23. See also, among others, 5/3/51.

24. See 2/2 and 5/3/51.

25. See report on other AEC problems above.

26. See 12/28/51.

27. See also, among others, 3/3/50, 5/3, 6/4, and 12/28/51.

28. This battle was resumed formally on April 27, 1951, when Mitchell wrote fifteen members of Congress to express his disappointment that he had learned H.J. Res. 19, the revived Lodge-Gossett resolution, seemed to have the approval of a subcommittee of the House Judiciary Committee. He explained that the NAACP had consistently opposed the measure because it would increase the influence of southern states in national elections. The letter and other materials are in the "Lodge-Gossett" folder, NAACP WB-126, DLC.

A companion report by Mitchell stated:

> Congressman Ed Gossett of Texas is leaving the House of Representatives on July 31. As a going away present, the members of the House Judiciary Committee reported out (by voice vote [where votes were not recorded], of course) his anti-Negro and anti-Semitic H.J. Res. 19.
>
> This Resolution abolished the electoral college in national elections, but does not penalize southern states for denying the ballot to colored voters. The net effect would be to give the South greater power in national elections.
>
> The NAACP worked to defeat this measure in the 81st Congress and won by a vote of 210 to 134. As soon as the 82nd Congress got started, Gossett was right back with his proposal.
>
> He said himself that, if it becomes law, the major parties would not have to include FEPC in their platforms to win votes in Harlem. He also said that it would reduce the influence of New York Jews in national elections.
>
> It would be a good idea to ask the following members of the House Rules Committee to vote against H.J. Res. 19 when it comes before that group:
>
> Congressman Hugh B. Mitchell
> Congressman James J. Delaney
> Congressman Ray J. Madden
> Congressman Adolph J. Sabath
> Congressman Leo E. Allen
> Congressman Clarence J. Brown
> Congressman Henry J. Latham
> Congressman Harris Ellsworth
>
> Also, let your Congressman know that you want him to oppose it if it reaches the floor. (Newsletter, 7/25/51, MP; for a companion report, see 5/29/51 in appendix 1, this vol.)

For Mitchell's summary of the first phase of this struggle, see 12/21/50; in appendix 1, this vol., 2/50, 5/29/51.

29. The violence erupted on July 6, 1951, when the Chickland Club on Capitol Heights in Prince Georges County, Maryland, just over the border of the District of Columbia, opened on a nonsegregated basis. It involved two near-riots by a mob of five hundred angry whites, as well as three fires, apparently set by arsonists. The Washington, D.C., branch of the NAACP and the Maryland State Conference of NAACP Branches charged that the Capitol Heights and Prince Georges County police did nothing to end the violence until late into the night, after patrons had left the club. In a letter to the *Washington Post*, Mitchell charged that the club owner "was forced to bow to mob rule." "What is there to stop the same elements from closing a hardware store, a day nursery or even a church?" he asked. Clippings from the *Washington Post* (dated only "7/51"), clippings from other newspapers, and Mitchell's letter to the *Post* (undated) are in the folder Mob Violence, Brutality, NAACP IX: 42, DLC.

30. The report, dated July 3, 1951, and provided by the Birmingham NAACP branch, was as follows:

> Through 1948, peak of the Dixiecrat Revolt in the South and the Mid-Year of 1951, there were listed 52 Negro citizens in Alabama killed by law enforcement officers. This list may not be complete because there was no scientific way to keep a true listing of all the violence in this area. But those police-slayings listed in this report, taken from newspaper clippings and NAACP reports, is fairly accurate.
>
> Of this 52 police-slayings, 26 were in the City of Birmingham. In another view, 35 of these 52 police-caused deaths were in Jefferson County or the Birmingham area. All 14 of the police-killings listed for 1948 were in Jefferson County. This was the year the Dixiecrat Revolt was organized in July of 1948 at the City Auditorium one hot Saturday.
>
> Most of these slayings by Law Enforcement Officers were ruled "justifiable homicide." In Birmingham, a police officer was indicted, tried and freed by a jury in 1949. In 1948 a Negro slew a deputy sheriff and in turn was killed by sheriff deputies.
>
> Presumably, there has not been a careful study made of this area of violence over the past four years.
>
> This report is hardly more than [a] loose listing of those reported cases of violent deaths in which law enforcement officers have been involved. (NAACP II: A-656, DLC.)

Another report, "Mob Violence, Lawlessness and Law Enforcement," stated that "there was no decline during 1950 from the high level of racial violence noted in 1949. While there were no killings which fell within the technical definition of deaths by lynching as compared with three lynchings in 1949 and one in 1948, there were nine attempted lynchings and a large number of other forms of violence stemming from racial or religious bigotry." The organized effort to get legal action to end this violence was led by Ruby Hurley, NAACP southeast regional coordinator, whose office was then in Birmingham.

At the national level, the legal department, led by Thurgood Marshall as special counsel, handled these complaints. As Mitchell said to Marshall, "Where questions or problems to be referred to the Justice Department do not involve legal technical problems, I shall prepare correspondence for your signature and send it to New York." Mitchell's goal was to avoid duplication of action. Mitchell's letter to Marshall, 7/23/51, NAACP WB-189, DLC. See also "Minutes of May 15, 1952, Meeting at Birmingham to Discuss Ways of Reducing Violence in the South Arising from Racial and Religious Tension," and other materials in NAACP WB-189, DLC.

This violence was the newest form in the South, which caused the NAACP to continue pushing for antilynching legislation in Congress and other protections through the Department of Justice. See also, for example, 5/8/52.

31. See the headnote on the Struggle to End Jim Crow Travel, vol. III.

32. Mitchell came to the conclusion that a lawsuit was the only remaining alternative to getting the local D.C. government to end segregation at the playgrounds after Milo F. Christiansen wrote to inform him that the Recreation Board's policy was "to make every possible and realistic effort toward the removal of racial segregation in public recreation in such sequence and at such rate of progression as may be consistent with the public interest, public order and effective administration." Mitchell forwarded a copy of the letter to Robert Carter, NAACP assistant special counsel, with the recommendation that "it seems time that we entered a lawsuit against the Board." Next, he organized a meeting of interested D.C. residents at the Washington bureau to plan the lawsuit. Christiansensen's letter to Mitchell, 5/3/51, Mitchell's letter to Carter, 5/8/51, and other materials are in NAACP IX: 226, DLC.

33. A copy of the letter of 7/19/51 is in NAACP WB-59, DLC.

Monthly Report, October 4, 1951

Monthly Report
Director
Washington Bureau
NAACP
October 4, 1951

WASHINGTON BUREAU

In order that the hearings on the Senate Rules change (S. Res. 41, S. Res. 53, S. Res. 105 and S. Res. 203), may appear in proper focus, the Washington Bureau devotes its monthly report to this subject.[2] There are many other important matters to be presented but we shall include them in next month's report. A detailed statement on the Rules Change appears in the Washington Bureau Newsletter of September 21, 1951. Copies will be furnished upon request.[3]

In preparing for the hearings which began on October 2, we have been troubled by the uncertainties of the Senate's adjournment date. This date was scheduled to be October 1. We had reliable assurances that the Senate would not adjourn on that date but since many daily papers were carrying front page stories that the Senate would adjourn on October 1, the Director of the Washington Bureau has had a king size headache assuring witnesses and other interested persons that the hearings would actually take place.[4]

Senator Hayden, Chairman of the Committee, had originally talked in terms of seven days of testimony for proponents. This was cut down to two and extended to four. Some of our witnesses were unable to attend so the time was cut again to three days. These days were October 2 and 3 (The October 1 date had to be changed because it was a Jewish holiday) and October 9.

Into these three days we have crammed the testimony of twenty-five scheduled witnesses. It appears that a few more may come in if their schedules can be properly fitted to the Committee's requirements.

These witnesses did an excellent job. The entire hearing record would be very expensive, but the Washington Bureau recommends that the NAACP publish a small pamphlet for the education of the public on this subject. It is recommended that this pamphlet feature the testimony of Mr. White, all Senators who have appeared or will appear on the 9th and a few of the other witnesses—especially Walter Reuther. It is hoped that this pamphlet will also contain some expertly prepared but simply stated arguments that our branch people may use in discussing this technical subject with Senators when Congress adjourns.

The hearings were held during sessions of the Senate. For that reason Senator Hayden did not fill his post of committee chairman when testimony was being taken. The committee voted that the hearings would be before the full committee. Senator Benton was named chairman for the hearings and Senator Monroney of Oklahoma sat with him. However, it was agreed that any member of the committee who cared to do so could sit in on the hearings as he or she (Senator Margaret Chase Smith) found time to do so. It should be noted that Senator Douglas, although not a committee member, came to the hearings and sat in the audience during Mr. White's testimony to show his interest.

Because we must work with all Senators, the Director does not like to single out any particular Senator for praise in matters of this kind. However, the record should show that the warm and spirited statements made by Senators Lehman and Humphrey were worth recording for their frank presentations. At the time this report is written Senator Morse has not testified but has indicated that he will appear on the 9th.

Senator Monroney has shown a very commendable attitude in the hearings. Although he is not an advocate of the Civil Rights program of the President, he has expressed the desire to change the rules so that a filibuster may be broken. His attitude towards witnesses has been friendly. This gives hope that some other opponents of Civil Rights may be won over to support the rules change. It is regretted that this hope is slim but it must not be abandoned.

Senator Benton has been the ideal chairman for the hearings. In spite of a heavy schedule of his own, he has given ample time to witnesses and maintained a congenial spirit throughout the hearings. Mr. Darrell St. Claire, Chief Clerk of the Committee, has been extremely helpful to the Director.

Throughout the hearings there has been the unanswered question "can we succeed in changing the rule?" The Director believes that the rule can be changed. *It is urged that no one in the NAACP join with the defeatist who see this as a hopeless fight.* These hearings are only the beginning. We must use them to make the country aware of the issue and to show how the present rule came about. We have a chance to alter the course of American history by making it possible for the Senate to vote when the majority of its members are ready to do so.

The Director wishes to go on record as thanking the New York Staff for the fine coordination that was worked out on this project. It has been necessary to call on the Executive Secretary at odd hours and in a somewhat too frequent manner, considering his other duties. However, he did not at anytime turn down a request for action.[5]

The Washington Office Staff has also been faithful in performing the numerous odd jobs and regular assignments that are needed in such hearings. This, too, is submitted for the record.

Mr. Paul Sifton of UAW, Mr. Julius Edelstein of Senator Lehman's office, Mrs. Violet M. Gunther and Mr. John Gunther of ADA, Mr. Herman Edelsberg of B'nai B'rith, and Mrs. Mary Alice Baldinger on behalf of ACLU have constituted a small informal sub-committee with the Director to work on details in connection with the hearing.

MS: NAACP II: A-666, DLC.

1. This date is based on that of the Secretary's Report, September, 1951, a copy of which is in NAACP II: A-666, DLC.

2. At a meeting on September 13, 1951, of organizations interested in changing the Senate rules, the following persons participated: Julius Edelstein, administrative assistant to Senator Lehman; Will Maslow of the AJCong.; Theodore Brown of the BSCP; Paul Sifton of the UAW; Violet Gunther of the ADA; Theodore Laskes of the AJCong.; Sol Rabkin of the ADL; George Silver of the JLC; Arnold Aronson of the NCRAC; Eunice H. Carter of the NCNW; Sam Tappis of the AVC; and Herbert Monte Levy of the ACLU. Walter White, Roy Wilkins, Henry Lee Moon, and Mitchell represented the NAACP.

The group's primary concern was setting a date, as Mitchell reported, for the Senate committee hearing on changing the rules and the subjects. The group agreed that all the organizations would support the principles of the Lehman resolution (S. Res. 105) and the Morse-Hymphrey (S. 41) resolution. The group did not agree to suppport the Ives or Wherry proposals. The group accepted Aronson's suggestion to develop arguments under the following five major headings: the impairment of governmental efficiency by filibusters; the constitutional and parliamentary arguments against the filibuster; the foreign implications of the filibuster; the historical record of the effects of filibustering; and a solid summary of all arguments. Participants were assigned to get others to testify. NAACP, WB-33, DLC.

3. See 8/31, 11/5, and 12/28/51.

4. Minutes, 9/10/51, EC. For the initial announcement, see 8/31/51.

5. See White, 10/2/51, *Hearings*, 34–63.

Monthly Report, November 5, 1951

November 5, 1951

MONTHLY REPORT OF THE WASHINGTON BUREAU

Closing of Cloture Hearings

On October 23, 1951, the Senate Committee on Rules and Administration formally closed hearings on resolutions to limit debate. The last witnesses were Senator Carl Hayden of Arizona, whose testimony supported in general the principle of a vote by two-thirds of the members of the Senate present in limiting debate, and Senator Richard Russell of Georgia, who expressed vigorous opposition to the proposals to change the rules. It is interesting to note that Senator Russell tried to avoid the civil rights issue in his prepared statement. During the exchange of questions between Senator Russell and Senator William Benton, Chairman, the former stated that he would do everything in his power to defeat any proposal to change the rules, but did not make a flat statement that he was entirely certain of winning.[1]

Baltimore Branch Railway Suit

Beginning on page 13 of the NAACP Annual Report for 1950, there is discussion of the action of the Washington Bureau when the Railway Labor Act was being amended in the 81st Congress.[2] The first test of the effectiveness of the legislative action taken by the Bureau is now being made.

Employees of the Baltimore and Ohio Railroad in Baltimore have sought to join Local 511 of the Brotherhood of Railway and Steamship Clerks. This union has a union shop agreement with the B & O Railroad. When the men sought to join Local 511, they were told that they must join 6067 which is a segregated local. We discussed this problem with President George Harrison of the union. He promised to correct it and see that the men were admitted to Local 511. However, the notice posted by the union required that applications for membership be submitted by November 1, 1951. When this date passed and neither Mr. Harrison nor any representatives of the union gave written assurances that the men would be admitted to Local 511, suit was filed in the Federal Court in the District of Columbia on behalf of James P. Taylor, Howard Taylor, and Charles Blake.[3]

January Legislative Problems

Congress adjourned on October 20, 1951. It will reconvene on January 8, 1952. We have prepared a statement for branches on important legislative problems, in addition to the senate rules change and civil rights, which we must face when the lawmakers return to their desks. Among them are the following:

1. In the closing days of the first session, Congress passed H.R. 5411, which provided for aid to schools in defense impacted areas. This school aid program was originally a part of the Defense Housing and Community Facilities Act. The NAACP sought to have non-segregation amendments in the entire legislation. The fate of our efforts is set forth in other reports.

   The net effect of the language of H.R. 5411 would be to halt, and, in some cases, eliminate entirely existing non-segregated schools on military posts located in states where separate schools are maintained by law. Fortunately, the President has vetoed this bill, but it will undoubtedly face us when Congress reconvenes.

   There is also under consideration in the Senate S. 1631 which provides Federal funds for land grant colleges for agricultural extension work and S. 337 which is designed to aid students seeking a medical school education. In all of these bills, we are confronted with an unwillingness on the part of liberal Congressmen and Senators to introduce non-segregation amendments. Many of those who could make an effective fight and provide good leadership feel that the need is so great that, even if Federal funds go to support segregation, in the long run the schools will be improved.

One of the jobs confronting our branches during the recess period is to get across to Congressmen and Senators the importance of supporting non-segregation amendments.

2. The District of Columbia Fire Department has a policy of segregating colored and white firemen. When the Commissioners of the District announced that segregation would be ended during the Month of October, the white firemen immediately objected. It appears that, if the action of the Commissioners had been carried out according to schedule, this problem would be of no importance. Unfortunately, however, when Congressman James Davis of Georgia introduced H.R. 5696, the action of integration was delayed until January when Congress reconvenes.[4]

   As soon as the announcement of integration was made, the Washington Bureau asked various members of the Senate and House District of Columbia Committee to assure the Commissioners that their action had the support of Congress. Prompt response came from Senators Matthew Neely of Virginia and James Duff of Pennsylvania. House members were not as prompt, although Congressmen Edward Sittler of Pennsylvania and Arthur Klein of New York reported that they had verbally assured the District Commissioners of their support. There is very little chance that this bill would get through Congress, but it is important that our branches register their opposition to it.

3. H. Res. 364 which was introduced by Congressman Cox of Georgia to harass foundations is another measure which must be defeated. Apparently, the foundations themselves are under the wrong impression that such an investigation under the direction of Congressman Cox would do no harm since they "have nothing to hide." It would appear that the foundations have not realized the type of inquiry Congressman Cox is capable of staging.[5]

4. The Electoral College Resolution, H. J. Res. 19, is on the calendar and probably will be brought up at a time which best serves the interest of those who want to see it passed.[6]

5. H.R. 5307, introduced by Congressman John Rankin of Mississippi, would invalidate the laws of 1872 and 1873 on civil rights in the District of Columbia. This legislation is also in the category of token opposition from the South, but, nevertheless, keep an eye on it.

Loyalty Developments

The Director spent a few days running down alleged investigations of a Board Member of the NAACP. This member is a candidate for public office. The party opposing him inserted an ad in one of the daily papers which contained this question addressed to him, "Why would a witness say that there was a rumor that you were being investigated by the Un-American Activities Committee?" One daily newspaper also advised the NAACP Board Member that a person representing himself as an investigator for the State Department had mentioned that he was checking on the candidate's loyalty. All of the reports of investigation by Congress and Executive Agencies proved to be false.[7]

The Director was asked to give information on a college sorority. The request came from a lawyer representing an individual who was charged with being a bad security risk. Among other things, the charges stated that his wife was a member of the sorority.[8]

Defense Program

Mr. Charles E. Wilson, Director of the Office of Defense Mobilization, through one of his assistants, advised interested organizations that he wished to have a qualified person appointed as an Assistant General Counsel in the Office of Defense Mobilization. The General Counsel of ODM discussed this appointment with Mr. Oliver Hill of Richmond, Virginia, but Mr. Hill declined. However, we are advised that a second individual is being considered and may be appointed by the time this report is read.[9]

Following an unproductive conference with Mr. J. R. B. Crigler, Vice President of the Chesapeake and Potomac Telephone Company in Washington, the Director requested Mr. Wilson to set in motion plans for enforcing non-discrimination provisions in Government contracts with the local Telephone Company. It will be recalled that during meetings with Mr. Wilson the Association and other organizations were advised that ODM would study ways of enforcing the non-discrimination clauses in the defense contracts. We have been advised by Mr. Arthur S. Flemming, Assistant to the Director, that action on our request is being considered. Such action, of course, would be an important precedent for other areas.[10]

Speaking Engagements

The Director spoke at meetings in Aiken, South Carolina; Snow Hill and Baltimore, Maryland; Baton Rouge, Louisiana; Norfolk, Virginia; Washington, D.C.; and New York City.

MS: NAACP II: A656, DLC.

1. See White, 10/2/51, *Hearings*, 34–63; also, most immediately, 8/31, 10/4, and 12/28/51.

2. See 12/21/50 for this discussion; for the published version to which he referred, see NAACP *Annual Report*, 1950, 13–15.

3. The case was filed in the U.S. District Court for the District of Columbia against the Brotherhood of Railway and Steamship Clerks, Freight Handlers, Express and Station Employees, and the Baltimore and Ohio Railroad Company. This was a Baltimore NAACP branch lawsuit. The attorneys of record for the plaintiffs were Joseph C. Waddy, Howard Jenkins (both of Washington), Juanita Jackson Mitchell, and John R. Hargrove (both of Baltimore).

Under the Railway Labor Act, employees were not to be forced to leave their jobs if they refused to join a union that denied them membership under the same terms and conditions that were generally applicable to other employees. In the B & O case and a similar matter involving employees of the Washington Terminal, the NAACP contended that it was illegal to require that African Americans join Jim Crow unions as a condition of keeping their jobs. Although no court decision would be rendered in either of these cases, the NAACP would win because the unions involved agreed to admit African American employees on a nonsegregated basis. Mitchell's letter to Elias G. Burnett, 4/7/53. Mitchell's letter, the text of the lawsuit, and related materials are in NAACP IX: 197, DLC. See also, among others, 12/21/50, 12/28/51, 10/6, 12/3, and 12/31/52.

4. See also, among others, 11/30 and 12/28/51; "Brief History of Integration in D.C. Fire Department [1919–1957]," by M. H. Sutton, fire chief, in NAACP WB-59, DLC.

5. See, among others, 8/31 and 12/28/51.

6. See, most immediately, 8/31 and 12/28/51.

7. This board member apparently was Channing H. Tobias, who was investigated extensively by the House Un-American Activities Committee and was listed in 1940 as a member of the American League for Peace and Democracy and the National Federation for Constitutional Liberties, an important communist front organization. In 1941, Tobias had also signed a statement defending the Communist Party during the time of the Stalin-Hitler Pact when the communist front American Peace Mobilization was at the height of its activities. Mitchell memorandum to Walter White, 10/17/51, NAACP WB-126, DLC.

8. See the headnote on National Origin, Alienage, and Loyalty, vol. I.

9. See 5/3 and 5/31/51.

10. Mitchell's undated report on these efforts stated:

> In 1951 the Washington Bureau of the NAACP submitted complaints to the Committee on Government Contracts charging that the Chesapeake and Potomac Telephone Company of Washington and Baltimore refused to hire colored girls as operators. The charge was supported by specific cases. We also submitted to the committee a brief summary of our experiences with the management of the company. In all meetings, the management freely admitted that it would not hire colored operators despite the fact that there was a non-discrimination clause in its contracts with the Federal Government.
>
> We have been advised that a sub-committee has obtained agreement from the Telephone Company that colored operators will be hired eventually in Washington. The company has taken what the sub-committee says is a first step. This is the transfer of colored clerical workers from a segregated office to the main downtown office where they work on a non-segregated basis. In response to inquire on when the company will take the next step and place operators on the job we have been told that this will be done in "the company's own time and its own way." We have not had any information on what is being done about the Baltimore complaint. (NAACP WB-5, DLC.)

See also 12/28/51, as well as the headnote on the Telephone Industry, vol. I.

Communication to Branches on Important Legislation in the New Congress, November 30, 1951

DRAFT

November 30, 1951

COMMUNICATION TO BRANCHES ON IMPORTANT LEGISLATION IN THE NEW CONGRESS[1]

While members of the Congress and the Senate are at home, it is important to ask them the following questions. When you have obtained the answers, please send them to the Washington Bureau at 100 Massachusetts Avenue, N.W., Washington D.C.

Question 1. Will you support the Lehman or Morse proposal to limit debate in the U.S. Senate, and, thereby, eliminate filibusters which at present are blocking civil rights legislation?[2]

Background Information

At present, Senate rules require 64 votes of Senators before debate can be limited. Two attempts to limit debate under this rule have failed. One was May 19, 1950. The vote was 52 to 32. The other was July 12, 1950. The vote was 55 to 33. Senator Lehman and others have introduced S. res. 105. The Lehman Resolution limits debate by a majority of the members of the Senate present and voting after 15 days of debate. The Lehman Resolution also provides that debate may be limited by a vote of two-thirds of the Senators present 48 hours after a cloture petition is filed.

Senator Morse and Senator Humphrey have introduced S. res. 41. This resolution seeks to change Rule XXII by permitting application of cloture by majority vote. A Senator ay yield a part or all of the period of time he is entitled to speak to any other Senator. The senator to whom the time has been yielded is then entitled to speak for the time yielded plus the period of the time he is allowed. This Resolution repeals subsection 3 of Rule XXII which prohibits the application of the cloture rule to proposals to change any standing rule of the Senate.

Either of these Resolutions would be effective in controlling filibusters. The Senate Committee on Rules has completed hearings on these and other proposals. This question applies to Senators only.

You should seek to obtain a definite commitment from your Senators that will support either S. Res. 105 or s. Res. 41. Don't let Senators evade the issue by saying that the rules change fight is so difficult that it should be avoided because this is an election year.

Question 2. Will you support Fair Employment Practice Legislation with enforcement powers, and, if President Truman issues an executive order setting up an FEPC, for defense industries, will you vote to give it appropriations?[3]

Background Information

Experience has shown that Fair Employment Practice Legislation must have clear enforcement provision if it is to be effective. At present, some Senators and Congressmen are wavering between strong legislation with enforcement powers and a weak type of legislation which would not require enforcement.

Senator Taft represents the school of thought which favors a weak bill. Senator Humphrey is one of the leaders of the forces seeking a strong bill. A copy of Senator Humphrey's statement on civil rights legislation is enclosed.

While we are trying to get an FEPC by legislation, we are also urging President Truman to sep an FEPC by executive order. Senator Richard Russell and others will, undoubtedly, seek to cut off appropriations for such an agency, if the president establishes it. Therefore, it will be necessary to have commitments that Senators and Congressmen will support appropriations for an agency of this kind.

Question 3. Will you support non-segregation clauses in important legislation?[4]

Background Information

The pattern of segregating the South is breaking under repeated attacks made by the NAACP through the courts. The South cannot possibly continue to finance segregation in public schools, housing, recreation, and other services unless it has outside help. Southern Congressman and Senators are seeking such help through various bills which provided for Federal aid to schools, Federal Assistance in medical education, and federal aid to defense areas where expanded Federal operations have placed a serious burden on public facilities.

Typical of the southern action is Senator Lister Hill's move which included in H.R. 5411 a proviso that state laws would be followed in school programs assisted under this legislation. This bill was vetoed by the President, but it will be up for consideration again when Congress returns.

You should urge your Senators and congressmen to vote against it unless the discriminatory language is removed. You should also urge them to incorporate positive language forbidding the expenditure of the funds provided by this bill for segregation.

Further information on this phase of our legislative activity may be found in the NAACP Annual Report for 1950 on pages 13, 14, and 15.

This school aid program was originally a part of the Defense Housing and Community Facilities Act. The NAACP sought to have non-segregation amendments in the entire legislation.

There is also under consideration in the Senate S. 1631 which provides Federal funds for land grant colleges for agricultural extension work and S. 337 which is designed to aid students seeking a medical school education. In all of these bills, we are confronted with an unwillingness on the part of liberal Congressmen and Senators to introduce non-segregation amendments. Many of those who could make a effective fight and provide good leadership feel that the need is so great that, even if Federal funds go to support segregation, in the long run the schools will be improved.

Question 4. Will you oppose H.R. 5696 which aims to maintain segregation in the District of Columbia's Fire Department?[5]

Background information

The District of Columbia Fire Department has a policy of segregating colored and white firemen. When the Commissioners of the District announced that segregation would be ended during the month of October, 1951, the white firemen immediately objected. It appears that, if the action of the Commissioners had been carried out according to schedule, this problem would be of no importance. Unfortunate, however, when Congressman James Davis of Georgia introduced H.R. 5696, the action of integration was delayed until January when Congress reconvenes.

As soon as the announcement of integration was made, the Washington Bureau asked various members of the Senate and House District of Columbia Committee to assure the Commissioners that their action had the support of Congress. Prompt response came fro Senators Matthew Neely of Virginia and James Duff of Pennsylvania. House members were not as prompt, although Congressmen Edward Sittler of Pennsylvania and Arthur Klein of New York reported that they had verbally assured the District Commissioners of their support. There is very little chance that this bill would get though Congress, but it is important that our branches register their opposition to it.

Question 5. Will you oppose H. Res. 364? This Resolution proposes to create a Congressional committee to investigate tax exempt educational and philanthropic funds and foundations.[6]

Background Information

On August 1, Congressman Cox of Georgia introduced H.Res. 364. Although the sponsor of this resolution says he plans to investigate whether foundations are using their resources for un-American activities, it appears that a major objective of this resolution is to embarrass organizations seeking to overcome race prejudice in the South.

On page A 5046 of the Congressional Record of August 1, Congressman Cox attacks the Rosenwald Foundation for "stirring up class and race distinction throughout the South."

The Rosenwald Fund is no longer in business, but most of its money was spent to overcome the frightful inequities of the segregated school system of the South. The shotgun nature of the Congressman's approach is demonstrated by his listing of Dr. Ira DeA. Reid among "leading Communists and Communist fronters" who received fellowships from the fund. Dr. Reid is colored. He is also one of the most distinguished sociologists in the Untied States. At present, he is teaching at Haverford College in Pennsylvania. There are many outstanding southern white people who also received fellowships from this fund.

Since one of the chief purposes of this resolution seems to make some kind of attack on colored and white people who wish to eliminate race prejudice in the United States, we urge that it be defeated.

Question 6. Will you oppose H.J. Res. 19? This Resolution changes the national system of elections by abolishing the electoral college.[7]

Background Information

This Resolution was defeated in the 81st Congress by a vote of 210 to 134 because of a strong fight against it led by the NAACP.

During the debate in the house, Congressman Clifford Case (R., N.J.), who led the fight against the proposal, pointed out that if it had been in effect during the last national election the State of Georgia alone would have had greater influence in determining the outcome of the election than the most populous states outside the Solid South.

Joining Mr. Case in opposing the legislation, Congressman Chet Holifield (D., Cal.) said, "One electoral vote in California represents 168,862 voters. In South Carolina, it represents 17,821 or about a 10 to 1 difference. This is not changed by the bill."

Both Mr. Case and Mr. Holifield pointed out that because it would mean greater strength for conservative factions, passage of the resolution at this time would kill the chances of keeping civil rights legislation as a part of the platforms of major parties. This was the avowed purpose of Representative Ed Gossett (D., Texas), one of the sponsors of the Resolution.

Question 7. Will you oppose H.R. 5307? This bill seeks to promote segregation in Washington.[8]

Background Information

H.R. 5307, introduced by Congressman John Rankin of Mississippi, would invalidate the laws of 1872 and 1873 on civil rights in the District of Columbia. This legislation is also in the category of token opposition form the South, but, nevertheless, keep an eye on it.

MS: NAACP WB-111, DLC.

1. This "communication" was prepared at the suggestion of Roy Wilkins, who felt the branches would benefit from an outline of items the national office would like to have them discuss with their representatives and senators. Wilkins's memorandum, 10/24/51, to Walter White. It does not appear, however, that this document was sent out. Mitchell prepared a brief, itemized list of "Important Questions to Be Asked of All Congressional Candidates" that apparently was distributed instead. Contrasted with a detailed compilation of civil rights bills and their authors that Mitchell also prepared, the draft "communication" emphasized the bills Mitchell thought were most important at that time and provided helpful background for understanding their significance. These and other related materials are in NAACP WB-111, DLC.

2. See, most immediately, 10/4 and 12/28/51, as well as the headnote on the NAACP and the Filibuster, vol. III.

3. See, most immediately, 12/28/51; in appendix 1, this vol., 6/25/51; and the headnote on the Struggle for a Permanent FEPC, 1942–54, vol. III.

4. The enforcement of nondiscrimination clauses in federal contracts was the key feature of EO 10308, issued on December 3, 1951. See 12/5/51.

As a measure of the importance the NAACP placed on the nondiscrimination provisions, Walter White on December 3, 1951, wrote to the governors of New York, New Jersey, Connecticut, Pennsylvania, Indiana, Ohio, Illinois, and Massachusetts, urging them to use their influence with their congressional delegations to prevent southerners from sharing in the use of federal grants to support racial segregation. He noted that their eight states paid more than 50 percent of the federal tax revenue during the fiscal year ending June 30, 1951. By contrast, ten southern states carried only 9 percent of the federal burden. White said that the citizens of the eight northern states were bearing the added tax burden because of segregation in the South, and so he asked them to "take official notice of the federal programs for housing, schools and other benefits."

Athough southern states needed financial help, he said, "such help should be given on the condition of not wasting money on segregation." So he asked the eight governors to urge members of Congress from other states to "give full support to language forbidding expenditure of federal money for segregated facilities. Such language should be included in all bills for housing, schools, hospitals and other proposals for giving assistance to the states." Report of the Secretary for 12/51 and 1/52, EC.

5. See, most immediately, 11/5 and 12/28/51; "Brief History of Integration in D.C. Fire Department [1919–1957]," by M. H. Sutton, fire chief, in NAACP WB-59, DLC.

6. See, most immediately, 11/5 and 12/28/51.

7. See, most immediately, 8/31 and 12/28/51.

8. The thrust of this attack was on the "lost laws," which the Supreme Court resoundingly held valid in *John R. Thompson Co., Inc. v. District of Columbia* in 1953. See, most directly, 6/15/53.

Monthly Report, December 5, 1951

December 5, 1951

MONTHLY REPORT OF THE WASHINGTON BUREAU

EXECUTIVE ORDER

The Executive Order establishing a committee to police non-discrimination clauses in defense contracts was a disappointment because of its lack of enforcement powers and limited scope.

However, this order can be converted into a useful instrument for combatting discrimination in defense industries. A great part of its effectiveness will depend on how vigorously it is administered and how closely we watch its operations. At present over four million persons work in defense industries and by the fall of 1952 it is estimated that this number will rise to eight and one half million.

A brief review of the NAACP efforts to get the President to act shows that since the start of the Korean War the Association led the effort to get an order issued. We joined in the preparation of a much stronger and broader order. Although it was not accepted by the President, this stronger order may yet be obtained and some of its enforcement provisions may be accomplished under the present order.[1]

It will be remembered that an executive order on employment was one of the factors included in the director's legislative program submitted at the beginning of the year.[2]

With all of its apparent weaknesses, this order can have the effect of speeding up legislative action on FEPC. One fight must be made to prevent Congressional action to cut off funds for the new committee created by the order. Such action will take the form of riders to appropriations for the various contracting agencies. Senator Humphrey has announced that he plans to tie in hearings on the need for FEPC legislation with the overall study of the Defense effort. The new agency should help to produce up to date facts on what is happening to minority groups.[3]

Housing Threat

The issuance of the executive order on employment reminds us that the President has not yet acted to correct flagrant policies of segregation that now exist under the Federal Housing program.[4]

At present the housing agencies have taken the position that even when colored people are displaced from areas because of Federally aided housing programs, nothing can be done by the Federal government to require that the new housing be open to all persons without regard to race.

Regulations governing the administration of the Defense Housing Act were issued in November by the Housing and Home Finance Agency. These regulations clearly permit segregation in defense housing.

The director recommends that the Association continue to work for remedies to the present problem. However, it is also suggested that as an organization we should explore the question of whether present Federal Housing policies of segregation so seriously impede our overall drive for civil rights that we should withdraw our support from the agencies and the programs they administer.

School Segregation at Fort Bragg

Elementary Schools at Fort Bragg, North Carolina are operated on a non-segregated basis. Children of high school age who live on the post are sent to segregated schools in Fayetteville, North Carolina. The director has requested Mr. Oscar Ewing, Administrator of the Federal Security Agency, to take the necessary steps to provide non-segregated high schools at the Fort.[5]

Segregation in National Park Areas

The Washington Bureau has requested the Department of Agriculture to end regulations which permit segregation in the Pisgah National Forest. Lyle F. Watts, chief of the Forest Service of the Department of Agriculture, states that these regulations were set up at the request of colored people from Atlanta.

November Travel

During November the director made trips to Oklahoma, Virginia, Alabama and Kentucky for speeches and other official business.

The C.I.O. publication "Economic Outlook" cited employment discrimination as seen by the NAACP Washington Bureau in an important article on FEPC.

MS: NAACP II: A-656, DLC.

1. Statement by the president, "On Establishing the Committee on Government Contract Compliance," 12/3/51, Truman, *Public Papers of the Presidents*, 1951, 640. See also 1/31, 2/2, and 12/28/51; in appendix 1, this vol., 12/20/50, 6/9/52.

In a note to "Newsletter Readers," dated December 19, 1951, Mitchell explained that because of the importance of EO 10308 that Truman issued on the enforcement of nondiscrimination clauses in government contracts, he was instead sending them a copy of the order. Upon the president's announcement of the order, he stated, the Washington bureau had issued the following statement: "Since the start of the Korean War we have been urging action by the President. We are disappointed because of the weaknesses and lack of enforcement powers in this executive order. However, we must work to make the most of it and at the same time seek ways of strengthening it." Mitchell to Newsletter Readers, 12/19/51, MP.

The members of the committee were: Dwight G. Palmer, president, General Cable Corporation (chair); James Carey, secretary-treasurer, CIO, and president of IEU-CIO; Irving Engel, AJCom.; Oliver W. Hill, former member of the Richmond, Virginia, city council and a member of the national NAACP Legal Committee; Dowdal Davis, editor of the *Kansas City Call*; George Meany, secretary-treasurer, AFL; Russell Forbes, deputy administrator, GSA; Michael J. Galvin, undersecretary of labor; Everett L. Hollis, general counsel, AEC; and John D. Small, chair, Munitions Board, DOD. Report of the Secretary for 12/51, also 1/52, EC.

2. See 1/31/51.

3. Upon further reflection, Mitchell said, "We must remember that no matter how well the Committee does its job, it will not be a substitute for a legislative FEPC." Mitchell, "President Truman's FEPC," *Crisis* 59 (January 1952): 5–8.

4. See 3/5, 4/4, 8/31, and 12/28/51 for Mitchell's activities on discrimination in housing during the year.

5. This demand was part of Mitchell's broader struggle to protect African American soldiers and their families stationed in the South against segregation. See 1/24/51, *Hearings*, 861–73. In also addressing similar segregation problems at Fort Bliss and Fort Sam Houston in Texas, Fort Sill in Oklahoma, and Fort Belvoir in Virginia, Mitchell noted that their continuing existence was a "shocking departure from the stand taken by President Truman in 1951 when he vetoed H.R. 5411, a school aid bill, because it contained language designed to introduce segregation in schools on military posts." Mitchell's letter to Robert A. Lovett, secretary of defense, 10/2/52, and NAACP WB press release, 10/4/52, both in NAACP WB-171, DLC. See also, among others, 12/28/51.

Annual Report, December 28, 1951

December 28, 1951

ANNUAL REPORT OF THE WASHINGTON BUREAU

Located at the seat of our National Government, the Washington Bureau must handle a wide variety of NAACP business with the legislative and executive branches of Government. The Executive Secretary, the Director of the Bureau, and one assistant handle the kinds of problems set forth in this report. The Director has omitted a number of items which have been mentioned in monthly reports during the year. Almost any subject we have listed, could be discussed at length, but we have tried to compress each with the hope that the report would be read in full. Some items are necessarily shorter than others. They also are far down in the body of the report. Neither their brevity nor their position means that we consider them unimportant.

Action Against the Filibuster

Hearings on Changing the Senate Rules on Debate opened on October 2, 1951, before the Senate Committee on Rules and Administration.[1]

Walter White, Executive Secretary of the NAACP, headed a delegation in May which conferred with Senators Ernest W. McFarland, Majority Leader and Kenneth Wherry, Minority Leader (now deceased), on the need for changing the present Senate Rules on debate in order to permit passage of Civil Rights Legislation.

Senator Wherry, who was a member of the Rules Committee, obtained a unanimous vote from the committee to hold open hearings. The hearings were held on S. Res. 41, S. Res. 52, S. Res. 105, and S. Res. 203.

At present, Senate rules require 64 votes of Senators before debate can be limited. Two attempts to limit debate under this rule have failed. One was May 19, 1950. The vote was 52 to 32. The other was July 12, 1950. The vote was 55 to 33. Senator Lehman and others introduced S. Res. 105. The Lehman Resolution limits debate by a majority of the members of the Senate present and voting after 14 days of debate. The Lehman Resolution also provided that debate may be limited by a vote of two-thirds of the Senators present 48 hours after a cloture petition is filed.

Senator Morse and Senator Humphrey introduced S. Res. 41. This Resolution seeks to change Rule XXII by permitting application of cloture by majority vote. A Senator may yield a part or all of the period of time he is entitled to speak to any other Senator. The Senator to whom the time has been yielded is then entitled to speak for the time yielded plus the period of the time he is allowed. This Resolution repeals subsection 3 of Rule XXII which prohibits the application of the cloture rule to proposal to change any standing rule of the Senate.

The NAACP and other organizations interested in Civil Rights Legislation testified in favor of S. Res. 41 and S. Res. 105.

S. Res. 52, introduced by Senator Ives and Senator Lodge, proposes that 49 votes be required to invoke cloture. It does not suggest that subsection 3 of Rule XXII be changed.

S. Res. 203 was introduced by Senator Wherry. It requires that two-thirds of the Senators vote for cloture before debate can be limited. It also does not suggest a change in subsection 3 of Rule XXII.

Thirty-four witnesses, including fifteen Senators, testified at the hearings or submitted statements for the record. Nine of the Senators supported the rules change. Two were undecided or at least did not commit themselves for the record. Four were opposed to any change in the rules.

Senator Morse dramatically charged, during the hearings, that the present rule requiring 64 votes for cloture was the result of a deal between Southern Senators and those outside of the South on the issue of public power. A direct quote from Senator Morse's testimony is as follows:

> "It was very interesting that a little over a year after—to show in part the way this rule came on the books—we had before the Senate three great transmission line issues, one involving the Southeast, one the Southwest, and one the Pacific Northwest.
>
> "The Pacific Northwest transmission line issue came later, it was the third one. The Southeast one passed by a substantial vote. The southwestern was closer. The third one was to be the northwestern, and one of my very good friends from the South called me into the cloakroom and said, 'Wayne, I don't think you should go to a vote on this one this afternoon.' I said, 'I had better take the majority we obtained on the last vote and run.' He said, 'I can't vote with you.' In the past he had never failed to vote in favor of the principle of the government building what we called the gridback transmission lines to load centers, and then entering into contracts with private utilities over those transmission lines for the service of their customers.
>
> " . . . my Southern friend went on to say that while he and some of his associates had always stood shoulder to shoulder with the rest of us in having the Government build the gridback transmission lines, they could not do so in this instance. Any other principle would result in the private utilities getting control of these dams, at dam site.
>
> " . . . after the southeastern and southwestern had passed, I was advised that we would not win in the Northwest. Why? Because at the time the Wherry compromise cloture rule was adopted in the Senate, what I had warned on the floor of the Senate that very night was a reality. Some deals had been entered into in exchange for votes on the cloture resolution for votes on a certain transmission power line issue."

The hearings were held during sessions of the Senate. For that reason Senator Hayden did not fill his post of committee chairman when testimony was being taken. The Committee voted that the hearing would be before the full committee. Senator Benton was named chairman. Senator Monroney of Oklahoma sat with him. However, it was agreed that any member of the committee who cared to do so could sit in on the hearings as he or she (Senator Margaret Chase Smith) found time to do so. It should be noted that Senator Douglas, although not a committee member, came to the hearings and sat in the audience during Mr. White's testimony to show his interest.

Senator Benton was the ideal chairman for the hearings. In spite of a heavy schedule of his own, he gave ample time to witnesses and maintained a congenial spirit throughout the hearings. Mr. Darrell St. Claire, Chief Clerk of the Committee, was extremely helpful to the Director.

Throughout the hearings there was the unanswered question "can we succeed in changing the rule?" The Director believes that the rule can be changed. It is urged that no one in the NAACP join with the defeatist who see this as a hopeless fight. These hearings are only the beginning. We must use them to make the country aware of the issue to show how the present rule came about. We have a chance to alter the course of American history by making it possible for the Senate to vote when the majority of its members are ready to do so.[2]

Civil Rights Bills

We have no doubt about the votes to pass civil rights bills, if we can overcome the filibuster.[3] The two test votes previously mentioned in this report (May 19 and July 12) showed this.

The Southern Senators understand Arithmetic. They know that, while we would lose some votes because certain Senators do not agree with specific features of proposed civil rights laws, we do have enough to win by a comfortable majority. Hence, they fight desperately to protect the one weapon that they have. That is endless talk.

During 1951, various Congressmen and Senators introduced Anti-Lynching, Anti-Poll Tax, FEPC, Anti-Jim Crow Travel Bills, and other civil rights proposals.

In the opening days of the first session of Congress, the Administration sent its omnibus civil rights bill and a proposed anti-lynching statute to Congress. These were introduced by Chairman Celler of the Judiciary Committee in the House. In the Senate, Chairman McCarran of the Judiciary Committee turned them over to a subcommittee headed by Senator Eastland of Mississippi.

A bill aimed at those who attempt to hold persons in involuntary servitude was also sent to Congress by the Department of Justice. Senator McCarran referred this to the Eastland subcommittee, also. Other members of the subcommittee are Senators Kefauver, Langer, O'Conor, and Hendrickson.

Senator Ives and eleven other Republicans introduced an FEPC Bill on January 18, 1951.

On June 25, 1951, Senator Hubert Humphrey introduced bills on all major civil rights subjects including those referred to the Eastland subcommittee by Senator McCarran.

Other Important Legislation

Armed Services

The integration of the Air Force and Navy is a major triumph of democracy, but this advance was threatened by Congressman Winstead of Mississippi who, with the help of some Northern Republicans, wrote an amendment into the UMT Bill which would have reestablished segregation in the Navy and the Air Force.[4]

This amendment was defeated by the combined efforts of Congressmen William Dawson, Melvin Price, and Adam Powell, and delegates from NAACP Branches in key states who came to Washington and helped to gather the votes that were needed to defeat it.[5]

A move to curb violence against members of the Armed Services came on February 28, 1951, when ten Senators, at the urging of the NAACP introduced an amendment to S. 1, the legislation on Universal Military Training. This amendment was defeated in the House and Senate.[6]

Sponsors of the amendment are Senators Lehman, Humphrey, Douglas, Ives, Hendrickson, Benton, Murray, Kilgore, Green, and Pastore.

The proposal is one of four suggested additions to the UMT Bill offered by the Director of the Association's Washington Bureau, in testimony before the Armed Services Committee of the Senate on January 24, 1951.[7]

The amendment is the same language offered several years ago by Secretary of War, Henry L. Stimson.

The other three points of the NAACP's proposal called for the ending of all segregation in the Armed Services, a ban against the use of Jim-Crow facilities for housing or feeding members of the Armed Services and the elimination of all racial designations in records.[8]

Six of the sponsors met with officials of the Department of Defense on March 5 to discuss ways of speeding up integration. These Senators would not agree to place a non-segregation amendment on the floor for debate in the Draft and Universal Military Training Bill, but said that they would work for acceleration of the program of integration in the Armed Services. They obtained a pledge that the Universal Military Training Program would function on a non-segregated basis and they also obtained certain pledges on action to advance integration.

The Executive Secretary and the Director of the Washington Bureau, also, joined Senator Hubert Humphrey and a delegation from Minnesota in a meeting with Secretary of the Army Frank Pace, General Lawton Collins and General Miles Reber. The Minnesota delegation was concerned about discriminatory practices of the Armed Services.[9]

Following the direction of the national Board in its meeting on October 9, 1950, the Director held meetings with the Army and Air Forces on suggestions offered by the NAACP to avoid segregation of volunteers and draftees in the South. Meetings were held with Earl D. Johnson, Assistant Secretary of the Army, Eugene M. Zuckert, Assistant Secretary of the Air Force, and Colonel Campbell Johnson, Assistant to the Director of Selective Service.

With Senator Humphrey of Minnesota, the Bureau urged the Department of the Army to make certain that the integrated National Guard of Minnesota would not be reorganized into an all-white unit when it was sent to Camp Rucker, Alabama. The Department of the Army advised that the following would be the policy on integrated national guard units:

> "With regard to the general question of integrated National Guard units ordered into active Federal Service, it is the present policy of the Department of the Army to retain, insofar as practicable, individual members of all such units within the unit in which they have enlisted and trained.
>
> "While certain individuals may be transferred because of special qualifications and in accord with military necessity, such transfers will be made only under procedures equally applicable to all enlisted personnel in any Army unit without regard to race."[10]

On the general question of integration of the Armed Services, the Director had a meeting with General B.M. McFadyen, Chief of Military Personnel Division in April.

This meeting was arranged by Mrs. Anna Rosenberg, Assistant Secretary of Defense. The following two paragraphs taken from our letter to Mrs. Rosenberg on results of the conference should be noted.

> "The conference revealed that the Army has shown a few colored troops the promised land of integration in basic training units and some specialties. However, the vast majority of ground troops are still in the bondage of segregation.
>
> "There is integration during basic training at Fort Dix, New Jersey; Riley, Kansas; Knox, Kentucky; Jackson, South Carolina; Breckenridge, Kentucky; Ord, California; Roberts, California; Wood, Missouri, and Chaffee, Arkansas. However, our discussion at the meeting revealed that most of the colored people entering the Army are sent to existing colored units as replacements. Even those who are integrated during the period of basic training are sent to segregated units when they have completed their training."[11]

When the Army announced that it would integrate troops in the Far East, it became clear that the Association's consistent attack on segregation was bearing fruit.[12] One of six Senators who met with Defense officials in March received the following statement in a letter from a high Defense official:

> "I feel very strongly that whatever advances have been made in the elimination of discrimination and segregation in the Army, recently, should be credited not only to officials in the Department of Defense, but also to you and the Senators who are associated with you.
>
> "I feel, as you do, that things still remain which must be done to eliminate race and color segregation in the Army, and I am certain that every effort will be made to accomplish this desirable goal."[13]

The Senator who received this communication felt that it would not be advisable to make it public hence, the names of the Defense official and the Senator are not included in this written report. We have been assured that plans are under consideration for an announcement concerning integration of the Armed Services in the European Theater. Regrettably, full integration at home appears to be last on the list.

After the defeat of the anti-violence amendment, Congressman Franck Havenner, who sponsored it in the House, introduced it as a separate bill (H.R. 4301). Senator Lehman has promised to introduce a similar bill in the Senate.

Other Important Legislation (continued)

Veterans Hospitals

During the year, we received from Alabama a complaint that a colored veteran had been denied admission to a Veterans Administration Hospital in Montgomery and sent instead to Tuskegee which is forty miles away. Admiral J. T. Boone, the Chief Medical Director of the Veterans Administration, has informed us that:

> "If a colored veteran applies at the Montgomery Hospital, a bed for him is secured at Tuskegee, and if a white veteran applies at Tuskegee, that hospital makes arrangements for his admission to Montgomery."

This disgraceful condition would have been expanded under the terms of a bill that Congressman Rankin introduced in the 82nd Congress. He said that a "group of niggers" had asked him to introduce it and added that they wanted to "be to themselves." It would have established a segregated hospital in the name of Booker T. Washington. The NAACP rallied the support of friendly Congressmen in defeating this bill. It was knocked out by a vote on a parliamentary maneuver executed by Congressman Powell. There is no doubt that if this bill had passed the practices of segregation in the Veterans Administration would be increased everywhere. It is a common experience to find that many hospitals operated by the VA try to send critically ill veterans to Tuskegee, even though there are facilities more immediately available. Fortunately, in most cases, we can halt such practices when they come to our attention, but the job would have been harder if we had not defeated the Rankin proposal.[14]

Housing

Housing problems of minority groups in the United States are at a critical stage.[15] The Federal Government is underwriting or supporting in various ways the building of public housing, private housing, and slum clearance programs. We have considerable evidence that in many instances the Federal Government is actually promoting the extension of racial segregation. We have prepared a statement on this which will be furnished upon request.[16]

When S. 349, the Defense Housing Bill, was under consideration, Senators Douglas and Ives, after unsuccessfully seeking incorporation of non-segregation amendments in the Bill itself, did obtain a statement in the Committee Report on the Bill concerning equality of treatment.[17] This appears on page 41 of the report from the Committee on Banking and Currency. The statement is as follows:

> "Your committee expects that in the provision of housing by the Federal Government under this title and in the provision, or operation and maintenance, of community facilities and services assisted by this title there shall be equality of treatment of persons of all races, religions, and national origins who are to be served by them."[18]

When the Bill was debated in the House, non-segregation amendments were kept off of the floor by the Administration with one exception. This exception was Congressman Javits' amendment dealing with community facilities. This amendment was defeated because it was opposed by Congressman Multer of New York. Congressman Multer argued that he had been assured by the Housing Agencies that the problem raised by Congressman Javits was being taken care of by administrative regulations. Following the passage of the Bill, Congressman Multer discussed his position at length, both in correspondence and personally, with the Director of the Bureau. He stated that he was going to take the problem to the President.

The Bureau prepared a memorandum for the Congressman. He sent a letter to the President urging action. Other Congressmen have followed suit. The Bureau has also outlined the problem to Mr. Raymond Foley, Administrator of the Housing and Home Finance Agency, by letter and in conversation.[19]

At the time we asked Congress to act, there were no regulations which would meet this problem. There are none now.

The Housing Agencies, on the advice of their lawyers and after counseling with White House advisers, have taken the position that the Federal Government cannot require those who build housing with Federal assistance to refrain from segregating or excluding tenants or buyers solely because of race.

In Aiken, South Carolina, an extensive program of housing on vacant land will be made possible by the Federal Government. This housing is being built for persons who will be employed on the H-Bomb project of the Atomic Energy Commission.[20]

At present, in Aiken, the colored and white citizens have a varied housing pattern. There are some neighborhoods which are entirely colored, but there are others where colored and white citizens live side by side or on the same streets.[21]

Instead of the following the better of these two patterns, the Housing agencies have elected to follow the worst and will support a program of separate housing developments for colored people.

In Savannah, Georgia, there is a neighborhood known as the Old Fort Area where colored persons are concentrated and have lived for years. The Public Housing Program will eliminate the slums, remove the colored people, and build a project for whites only. Once this land is cleared and the housing developed, it will be a highly desirable neighborhood.

In Baltimore, Maryland, plans are under way to engage in an extensive redevelopment program for the clearing of two neighborhoods which are almost entirely colored. Under this program, the Federal Government will pay two-thirds of any loss the City may suffer in the land assembly.

One of these programs is known as the Waverly Project and colored people will be excluded entirely from it. The other is in the vicinity of the famous Johns Hopkins Hospital and only a very small number of colored people, if any, will be permitted to live in it once the present housing has been demolished.

In short, these areas which are being cleared could be occupied by colored people as long as they were slums, but, once they become a place of decent dwellings, even those who have the money to buy or rent the housing made possible with the assistance of the Federal Government will be excluded.

In Nashville, Tennessee, there is a neighborhood in the vicinity of the Capital where a program of improvement is being undertaken. In the present slum area, there are some white people who live in the neighborhood, but the majority of the occupants are colored.

Under the program of development now planned, the colored people will be dispersed to other areas and none but white individuals will be permitted to return to the neighborhood.

The Housing Program of the Federal Government as currently administered in the entire South, all of the border states, and in a few northern communities, is one of the greatest single factors underwriting segregation with tax money.

The colored people of the United States who have lived for so long in slum areas have been the chief supporters of the programs of Federal Housing. It is ironic that their loyalty to these programs is now being rewarded by a master plan of segregation which would please even Herman Talmadge of Georgia.

The NAACP has brought this problem to the attention of the President. The latest statement to Mr. Truman is from the Executive Secretary and states the following:

> "The present policy of the Housing Agency is the exact opposite of the Government stand taken by the Department of Justice in the restrictive covenant cases.[22] It places the Government of the United States in the anomalous position of opposing restrictive agreements by private owners but giving support for such unwritten agreements through its housing program.
>
> "We strongly urge that this question receive immediate attention and that the housing agencies be instructed to halt any assistance unless there is assurance that the dwellings made available will be open to all qualified persons without regard to race."[23]

Other Important Legislation (continued)

Miscellaneous Bills

1. In the closing days of the first session, Congress passed H.R. 5411, which provided for aid to schools in defense impacted areas. This school aid program was originally a part of the Defense Housing and Community Facilities Act. The NAACP sought to have non-segregation amendments in the entire legislation. The fate of our efforts is set forth in the Section of this report dealing with Housing.

   The net effect of the language of H.R. 5411 would be to halt, and in some cases, eliminate entirely existing non-segregated schools on military posts located in states where separated schools are maintained by law. Congressman Javits of New York and McCarthy of Minnesota opposed it but without success. Fortunately, the President has vetoed this bill, but it will undoubtedly face us when Congress reconvenes.[24]

   There is also under consideration in the Senate S. 1631 which provides Federal funds for land grant colleges for agricultural extension work and S. 337 which is designed to aid students seeking a medical school education. In all of these bills, we are confronted with an unwillingness on the part of liberal Congressmen and Senators to introduce non-segregation amendments. Many of those who could make an effective fight and provide good leadership feel that the need is so great that, even if Federal funds go to support segregation, in the long run the schools will be improved.

2. The District of Columbia Fire Department has a policy of segregating colored and white firemen. When the Commissioners of the District announced that segregation would be ended during the Month of October, the white firemen immediately objected. It appears that, if the action of the Commissioners had been carried out according to schedule, this problem would be of no importance. Unfortunately, however, when Congressman James Davis of Georgia introduced H.R. 5696, the action of integration was delayed until January when Congress reconvenes.[25]

   As soon as the announcement of integration was made, the Washington Bureau asked various members of the Senate and House District of Columbia Committee to assure the Commissioners that their action had the support of Congress. Prompt response came from Senators Matthew Neely of Virginia and James Duff of Pennsylvania. House members were not as prompt, although Congressmen Edward Sittler of Pennsylvania and Arthur Klein of New York reported that they had verbally assured the District Commissioners of their support.

3. H. Res. 364 which was introduced by Congressman Cox of Georgia to harass foundations is another measure which must be defeated. Apparently, the foundations themselves are under the wrong impression that such an investigation under the direction of Congressman Cox would do no harm since they "have nothing to hide." It would appear that the foundations have not realized the type of inquiry Congressman Cox is capable of staging.[26]

4. Congressman Gossett of Texas has resigned from Congress, but his H. J. Res. 19, which eliminates the electoral college, has been reported out of the House Judiciary Committee and the Senate Judiciary Committee. In the Senate, this Resolution is sponsored by Senator Lodge of Massachusetts. We have been advised that these actions were taken as a kind of farewell present to Congressman Gossett. However, we are making plans for conducting a floor fight, as we did successfully in the House last year, if it is necessary. Senator Lodge discussed his position on this with us.[27] It is as follows:

   a. He did not seek action in the Senate Judiciary Committee and was out of town at the time the measure was reported out of the committee. He will not seek favorable action on it unless it is passed by the House.

   b. If the House passes the Resolution, he will give us another opportunity to argue the merits of our opposition before he seeks action on the floor.

5. H.R. 5307, introduced by Congressman John Rankin of Mississippi, would invalidate the laws of 1872 and 1873 on civil rights in the District of Columbia.[28]

Executive Agencies

Government Contracts

High on the list of important items on the Washington Bureau's 1951 agenda was the need for an FEPC established by executive order of the President.[29]

During the year, the Executive Secretary and the Director joined in meetings with various government officials on this matter. Several of the conferences were with Mr. Charles F. Wilson, Director of the Office of Defense Mobilization. In these meetings, Mr. Wilson promised that he would try to set up machinery for enforcing the non-discrimination clauses in Government contracts.[30]

When President Truman issued Executive Order No. 10,308 which seeks to obtain compliance with the non-discrimination clause, the Director of the Bureau issued the following statement:

> "Since the start of the Korean War, we have been urging action by the President. We are disappointed because of the weaknesses and lack of enforcement power in this executive order. However, we must work to make the most of it and at the same time seek ways of strengthening it."

A.E.C. Segregation Ban

The Atomic Energy Commission advised the Director of the Washington Bureau that, pursuant to NAACP urging, it had instructed all contractors at Paducah and South Carolina that there would be no segregation in "cafeterias, eating facilities, wash-rooms, lavatories, etc." This action was taken by AEC after a study of practices of non-segregation on several southern Army posts.

The AEC also advised that it was assigning one of its top employees to make a special drive for eliminating the bottlenecks which in the past have prevented qualified colored people from getting skilled jobs with AEC or its various contractors. At the Bureau's request, the AEC confirmed its non-segregation policy in writing.

The Director and representatives of the South Carolina NAACP Branches met with AEC officials at the H-Bomb plant site in Aiken on December 14. This was the Director's third visit of the year to Aiken. The policy of no segregation at the plant site appears to be working satisfactorily.[31]

The AEC is processing the applications of colored stenographers and scientists. The chief problems are the failure of the DuPont Company (which will operate the plant and is now handling construction) to hire colored white collar workers and acute discrimination against colored skilled construction workers. Also, a vast program of wasting Federal money to build separate schools, parks, and other facilities is being pushed by surrounding local communities.[32]

The Paducah, Kentucky, site of AEC production has also received a great deal of attention from the Washington Bureau this year. Latest reports indicate that some small progress is being made in clerical and skilled employment. However, there is not clear evidence that the Carbon and Carbide Company which will operate this plant has kept its promise to the NAACP that it would employ colored people as trainees. We have received reports that the company intends to do so, but we are still awaiting final confirmation in the form of action.[33]

Executive Agencies (continued)

State Department

On April 13, the Director joined representatives of other national organizations in a meeting with Secretary Dean Acheson. The purpose of the meeting was to place before the Secretary problems of employment discrimination in his Department. We have had a number of follow-up meetings with various State Department officials. However, what has been achieved is not yet extensive enough to report.[34]

Defense Agencies

Representatives of the same organizations that met with the Secretary of State also met with other Agency heads, especially those carrying out the Defense Program, to urge fair employment of minorities within the agencies. These meetings are still being held from time to time.

Manpower Problems

Baltimore Branch Railway Suit

Beginning on page 13 of the NAACP Annual Report for 1950, there is discussion of the action of the Washington Bureau when the Railway Labor Act was being amended in the 81st Congress. The first test of the effectiveness of the legislative action taken by the Bureau is now being made.[35]

Employees of the Baltimore and Ohio Railroad in Baltimore have sought to join Local 511 of the Brotherhood of Railway and Steamship clerks. This union has a union shop agreement with the B and O Railroad. When the men sought to join Local 511, they were told that they must join 6067 which is a segregated local. We discussed this problem with President George Harrison of the union. He promised to correct it and see that the men were admitted to Local 511. However, the notice posted by the union required that applications for membership be submitted by November 1, 1951. When this date passed and neither Mr. Harrison nor any representatives of the union gave written assurances that the men would be admitted to Local 511, suit was filed in the Federal Court in the District of Columbia on behalf of James P. Taylor, Howard Taylor and Charles Blake.[36]

Meeting with General Electric

At the request of the Schenectady NAACP Branch in May, the Director of the Washington Bureau met with Mr. E. J. Riley, Manager of Employee Relations, to discuss problems of employment, upgrading, and training. The G.E. official pledged correction of specific complaints submitted by the branch and also agreed to work out a suggested policy change which should result in better use of qualified colored persons.

The Schenectady Branch has informally advised the Director that a number of promises made at the meeting have been carried out.

Capital Transit Company

The Director has requested that the Federal Manpower authorities make the Capital Transit Company a number one item on the program for full utilization of labor. Manpower officials advise that they are working with management and the union to settle the question of whether colored people shall be employed as platform workers.[37]

Washington Telephone Company

Following an unproductive conference with Mr. J. R. B. Crigler, Vice President of the Chesapeake and Potomac Telephone Company in Washington the Director requested Mr. Wilson to set in motion plans of enforcing non-discrimination provisions in Government contracts with the local Telephone Company. We have been advised by Mr. Arthur S. Flemming, Assistant to the Director, that action on our request is being considered.[38]

Other Important Happenings

Birmingham Killings

The Director of the Washington Bureau accompanied Mr. Emory O. Jackson to a meeting in the Department of Justice for the purpose of seeking action on numerous police killings in Birmingham and Alabama. Mr. Jackson submitted information showing that since 1948 the Alabama police have murdered 52 colored people. Twenty-six of these killings occurred in the City of Birmingham. Peyton Ford, who was then Deputy Attorney General, advised that the Department of Justice would investigate these complaints. Mr. Ford has since resigned from the Department.[39]

Chickland Cafe

During the Month of July, the proprietor of a night club known as the Chickland Cafe decided to open the establishment for colored patrons in an effort to boost his business. This cafe is located at Capitol Heights in Maryland, just across the District line. Although the proprietor expected to attract colored business mainly, he also admitted white patrons. This action resulted in mob violence and the destruction of his property by white residents in the town of Capitol Heights. It is clear that the hoodlums who caused the trouble had also caused trouble when the establishment was operated for white patrons only. Apparently, these elements had the full support of the local law enforcement officers in Capitol Heights.[40]

Other Important Happenings (continued)

The National Airport

Being mindful of the fact that, when the national airport was being constructed, plans to have a segregated arrangement for handling colored passengers were perfected with the acquiescence of the Department of Commerce, we have asked Secretary Charles Sawyer to give assurance that the new airport which will be built at Burke, Virginia, will not have segregated facilities.[41] Secretary Sawyer stated that,

> "It will be a long while before there will be any need to face that problem of segregation at the Burke airport. We will not have acquired the property for many months and after that many other things must be done before it will be in operation. I can assure you, however, that so far as it lies within my power there will be no segregation permitted."

Florida and North Carolina Elections

We have requested Chairman Guy Gillette of the Senate Subcommittee on Privileges and Elections for an opportunity to make a plea for an investigation of the 1950 senatorial elections in North Carolina and Florida. We have been advised by Senator Gillette that an effort will be made to grant our request.

Caldwell Appointment

The Director appeared in opposition to the confirmation of Ex-Governor Millard F. Caldwell of Florida as Chief of Civil Defense.

Caldwell was approved in the Senate by unanimous consent with about fifteen senators on the floor. His views on voting and whether colored people should be called "mister" make interesting reading in the Senate record on the hearing. However, he pledged that he would be fair to all in performing his duties.[42]

Recreation Suits

Residents in the vicinity of the Rosedale playground in Washington have asked the Washington Bureau to act in their behalf because colored children are barred from play. Nearly one hundred parents signed a petition requesting action. At a meeting with representatives of the parents, Mr. Frank Reeves, Chairman of the Washington Branch Legal Redress Committee, and other citizens, plans were made for legal action. Mr. Reeves has filed one suit on behalf of another group of parents in another area and plans similar action on behalf of the parents in the Rosedale area.[43]

Friends of the Association prepared a very impressive letter for the signature of the Director of the Washington Bureau setting forth the legal arguments on why the Commissioners in the District of Columbia have ample authority to end segregation in all play areas. This document, which was four pages in length, was submitted to the Commissioners of the District. The action of the Bureau is designed to supplement the action of the Washington NAACP Branch.[44]

Speaking Engagements, Etc.

During the year, the Director spoke in Alabama, Georgia, Kentucky, Louisiana, Maryland, Michigan, New Jersey, New York, Ohio, Oklahoma, Pennsylvania, South Carolina, Virginia and Washington, D.C.

MS: MP.

1. 10/2/51, *Hearings*, 34–63. See also 10/4 and 11/5/51 reports; in appendix 1, this vol., 9/21/51.
2. See the headnote on the NAACP and the Filibuster, vol. III.
3. Mitchell reported:

On June 25, 1951, Senator Hubert Humphrey (D., Minn.) introduced eight Civil Rights Bills. The bills are co-sponsored by Senators Benton, Douglas, Lehman, Morse, Murray, Neely, and Pastore. The bills are as follows:

S. 1732, a bill to prohibit discrimination in employment because of race, color, religion, or national origin.

S. 1733, a bill to protect persons within the United States from lynching.

S. 1734, a bill outlawing the poll tax as a condition of voting in any primary or other election for national officers.

S. 1735, a bill to strengthen the Federal Government machinery for the protection of civil rights by establishing a Commission on Civil Rights in the Executive Branch of Government, creating a joint Congressional Committee on Civil Rights, and by reorganizing the Civil Rights activities of the Department of Justice through establishing a Civil Rights Division in the Department under an Assistant Attorney General.

S. 1736, a bill to provide relief against segregation and other forms of discrimination in interstate transportation.

S. 1737, a bill to strengthen existing civil rights statutes.

S. 1738, a bill to protect the right to political participation by effectively protecting individuals against intimidation, coercion, and other interferences with the right to vote.

S. 1739, a bill to strengthen the criminal laws relating to peonage, slavery, and involuntary servitude.

Similar bills were submitted to the Senate earlier this year, but Chairman McCarran of the Senate Judiciary Committee referred them to Senator Eastland of Mississippi for "study." (Newsletter, 7/25, 1951, MP)

4. See, among others, 3/5 and 4/4/51.
5. See 4/4 and 5/3/51; Mitchell, "The People v. Winstead of Mississippi," *Crisis* 58 (May 1951): 307–11.
6. For the amendment, see 3/5/51.
7. 1/24/51, *Hearings*, 861–73.
8. Ibid.
9. See 3/5/51.
10. See also 1/31, 2/2, and 3/5/51.
11. See 4/4/51. MacGregor, *Integration of the Armed Forces*, 392.
12. See 5/28/52 in appendix 1, this vol., which also comments on the NAACP's struggle to win political support for its legislative battle; MacGregor, *Integration of the Armed Forces*, 442–45.
13. See 8/31/51.

14. See also White, 2/3/48, *Hearings*, 100–121; among others, 6/4/51; in appendix 1, this vol., 5/29/51; statements by Dr. W. Montague Cobb, representing the National Medical Committee of the NAACP, on S. 1414, and Robert L. Carter of the American Veterans Committee. White, Cobb, and Carter testified before the Subcommittee on Veterans Affairs of the Senate Committee on Labor and Public Welfare on S. 1414 and H.R. 3814 (Booker T. Washington Hospital Bills). Drafts of their statements and other materials are in NAACP WB-185, DLC.

15. See, most immediately, 3/5, 4/4, 8/31, and 12/5/51 for Mitchell's earlier activities on discrimination in federally funded housing.

16. NAACP Memorandum, 1/11/52, on "The Authority and Power of the Administrator of the Housing and Home Finance Agency, the Federal Housing Administration, the Public Housing Administration, and the Division of Slum Clearance and Urban Redevelopment, Constituent Units of the Housing and Home Finance Agency, to Prohibit Discrimination in Federal and Federally-Aided Housing Programs Administered by Them," MP.

17. S. 349 became the Defense Housing and Community Facilities and Services Act of 1951. See 8/31/51.

18. Defense Housing and Community Facilities and Services Act of 1951. Report of the Committee on Banking and Currency, to accompany S. 349, 3/21/51, p. 41.

19. See 8/31/51.

20. The report noted that the large atomic energy installation to be constructed by the AEC on the acquired 250,000 acres in Aiken and Barnwell counties would require the direct employment of 6,000 persons. With the inclusion of employees and service personnel, there thus would be a permanent increase of upwards of 30,000 people in the area. So the number of construction workers used to build the plant and the permanent population would be about 35,000 at its peak.

To avoid creating "government-owned towns," private developers individually or in groups would be encouraged to develop the land for housing and commercial enterprises, and they would be given opportunities to buy the land for those purposes. Financing for housing construction would be made available through the FHA and other government agencies and private sources. Report of the Committee on Banking and Currency, to accompany S. 349, 3/21/51, p. 403.

21. See 2/2, 5/3, and 8/31/51.

22. The official position of the Truman administration on racial restrictive covenants was as follows:

> The Government is of the view that judicial enforcement of racial restrictive covenants on real property is incompatible with the spirit and letter of the Constitution. . . . It is fundamental that no agency of the government should participate in any action which will result in depriving any person of essential rights because of color or creed. Kurland and Casper, *Landmark Briefs of the Supreme Court of the United States*, 46:233–34.

See also Vose, *Caucasians Only*, 160.

The AEC's housing practices also had a direct impact on its employment practices. Consequently, in a meeting on December 14, 1951, discussions were centered on the agenda Mitchell had prepared. The first item was: "Formulation of plans to guarantee that no agreements with labor unions, policies of the contractors or subcontractors, local customs, or any other factor will be allowed to prevent the employment of qualified colored persons who seek available jobs on the AEC staff as construction workers or in the plant when it is completed." Mitchell requested that this policy also apply to existing or future training programs.

In addition to seeking to have specific job discrimination cases adjusted, he sought assurance that there would be no segregation on the plant site and that this policy would be extended to transportation facilities. He also requested that the company tolerate "no subtle attempts to enforce segregation by occupational discrimination or in other ways."

Finally, he asked that the company adopt a policy barring discrimination in housing on the AEC site. To emphasize that demand, he gave AEC officials an excerpt from the 1951 Senate Hearings on the Defense Housing Act, S. 349 (2/20/51, *Hearings*, 477–81). "Suggested Agenda for Meeting with AEC Officials in South Carolina on September 17, 1951," held 12/14/51, NAACP WB-8, DLC. See also 1/31/49.

23. The NAACP board authorized White to issue the statement following discussion of his report on the policy adopted by Raymond Foley, HHFA administrator, under the Defense Housing and Community Facilities Act of 1951. White was guided by the opinion of the NAACP special counsel, which was outlined in the following list:

"1. There is nothing in this statement which prohibits segregation in defense housing provided directly by the Federal Government (HHFA). Mr. Foley, at an off-the-record conference on

October 4, 1951, stated that this policy would, in certain areas, permit of segregation where a non-segregation policy could not be enforced. However, he stated that if the only available housing for a Negro family for example was in a white project, the Negro family would be entitled to such a facility.

"2. With respect to community facilities and services, the statement clearly permits of a separate but equal policy.

"3. With respect to privately financed defense housing, the Administrator's statement of policy calls for a determination of defense housing needs in terms of race and color, i.e., the need for minority group in-migrant workers will be determined separately and such information made available to private developers as a separate item. In other words, a proposal made to Foley at the off-the-record meeting on October 4, 1951, to the effect that the housing needs be determined without reference to race and color has not been accepted.

"Therefore, this statement by Foley represents, in our opinion, absolutely no progress over the policy which existed during World War II." (Minutes, 12/10/51, EC)

24. Truman killed by pocket veto H.R. 5411, which authorized federal construction, maintenance, and operation of elementary and secondary schools in areas where federal defense activities had put an unsupportable burden on the local taxpayers. He said the "basic purpose" of the bill was good, but he noted in a memorandum disapproving it ""that it represented "a backward step in the efforts of the federal government to extend equal rights and opportunities to all our people." Southern members inserted a segregation rider in the closing days of the 82nd Congress. *New York Times*, 11/3/51, 10. See http://www.google.com/search?as_q=Truman+veto_HR+5411+1951. See also12/3/52.

25. See 11/5 and 11/30/51.

26. See also 11/5/51, 5/8, 6/5 and 12/31/52; Newsletter, 5/28/52 and 10/3/52, both of which are in appendix 1, this vol.

27. See also, among others, 6/4 and 8/31/51. Alfred Baker Lewis, a member of the board, in a letter of September 17, 1951, to Mitchell, said of the prospects of defeating the amendment: "We are a little worse off in the House this year than we were last year, which makes me really worried. In the first place, the liberal Democrats are distinctly fewer since the 1950 election, and in the second place, the House Rules Committee held it up last year and reported it out this year." See "Lodge-Gossett" folder in NAACP WB-126, DLC. Among the materials in the folder is Mitchell's letter of December 18, 1952, to Arthur Krock, a *New York Times* reporter, responding to his column of the same date on the Electoral College:

> On February 1, 1950, the Senate defeated a proposal by Senator Langer that Presidents be elected by popular vote. I am glad to say that Senator Lodge supported the Langer plan.
>
> However, most of the other advocates of changing the electoral system seem to be afraid of election by direct vote of the people. Their opposition to choice by popular vote inevitably leads to the conclusion that they are not really interested in reform but a possible transfer of influence from big states to less enlightened areas of the country.

28. Watson, *Lion in the Lobby*, 224.

29. See, among others, 12/5/51.

30. One topic of discussion was the continuing refusal of the Chesapeake and Potomac Telephone Company to hire African American women as operators. See 11/5/51.

31. See Mitchell's memorandum of 12/27/51 to Constance Baker Motley on the H-bomb plant at Aiken, South Carolina, in NAACP WB-8, DLC; also see 8/51.

32. See, most immediately, 8/31/51; also see 12/20/50 and 2/21/51, both of which are in appendix 1, this vol.

33. See 8/31/51.

34. Meeting with Secretary of State Dean Acheson.

35. See 12/21/50 for this discussion.

36. See 11/5/51 for the filing of the first test case and, subsequently, among others, 10/6 and 11/5/52.

37. See, among others, 8/31/51.

38. See 11/5/51.

39. The NAACP used incidents of racial violence like these to support its struggle for an anti-lynching law in Congress and to obtain other protections from the executive branch. See, for example, the NAACP's reaction to the killing of Harry T. Moore, state coordinator of NAACP branches in

Florida, and his wife, Harriet, by a dynamite bomb on Christmas night 1951, Report of the Secretary for December 1951 and January 1952, EC; also see 5/2/52, where Mitchell reported on his continuing struggle for an antilynching law, and "That Is a Shameful Record," editorial, *Atlanta World*, 7/13/51, 6, denouncing the killing of ten blacks in less than two years (copy in NAACP IX 42, DLC); *New York Times*, 12/27/51, i.

40. See 8/31/51.

41. See headnote on the Struggle to End Jim Crow Travel, vol. III.

42. See note at 2/2/51 for extended sources cited earlier. According to Earl Dickerson, NAACP board member, the Caldwell appointment was "but another indication of the low esteem in which the present administration holds the Negro citizenry." "Press for Caldwell Removal," *Crisis* 58 (April 1951): 267, 269. See also "Civil Rights Conference," *Crisis* 58 (May 1951): 328, 330.

43. This action was initiated through a petition with ninety-seven signatures protesting the exclusion of African American children from the Rosedale Playground in the Northeast section of Washington and requesting the NAACP to take legal action to abolish this discrimination. Earlier, Mitchell had forwarded to Robert Carter, NAACP assistant special counsel, a letter from the District Board of Recreation on the playground, expressing his conclusion that it was time that the NAACP entered a suit against the board because of its segregation practices. Mitchell's letter, 5/8/51, to Carter; and letter of 6/25/51 from Earl W. Fisher, WB research assistant, to Carter, both in NAACP IX: 226, DLC.

A WB "Statement on Rosedale Playground," 1/16/52, announced that the lawsuit was suspended:

> The NAACP attorney is holding the filing of the Rosedale Playground case in abeyance until disposition by the court of two motions which are pending in the District Court and upon which a hearing is scheduled for February 4, 1952. The reason why this is being done is in order that we might profit by any ruling that this court may make for the pending case of the Trinidad Playground and the Wheatley School Playground which was filed in August 1951. This case involves the same questions which are involved in the Rosedale Playground case and there will be some advantage to be gained by holding your file on Rosedale. (NAACP IX: 226, DLC)

See 12/7/53.

44. This actually was a five-page letter of July 19, 1951, to Bernard L. Robinson, the engineer commissioner for the District of Columbia, in which he said that "*the Recreation Board's promise* to 'make every possible and realistic effort toward the removal of racial segregation in public recreation' has become 'a promise to the ear, to be broken to the hope'" (emphasis Mitchell's). Mitchell's letter to Robinson, 7/19/51, NAACP WB-59, DLC. See also 8/31/51.

Monthly Report, February 6, 1952

February 6, 1952

MONTHLY REPORT OF THE WASHINGTON BUREAU

SENATE RULES COMMITTEE

On January 29, 1952, the Senate Rules Committee reported out S. Res. 203 which is the least effective of all of the anti-filibuster resolutions that the group considered.[1] It will be recalled that S. Res. 203 was introduced by Senator Wherry of Nebraska (now deceased). It provides that two-thirds of the senators present and voting shall be required to invoke cloture. It also changes the voting date on a cloture petition from the "following calendar day but one" to the "fifth calendar day but one."

Apparently this resolution had the support of the so-called small state senators. Also, members of the Committee who favored other resolutions decided to vote out the Wherry Resolution in order that the Committee might send something to the Majority Leader for consideration on the floor.

Senator Benton deserves the highest commendation for his determined effort to bring this matter to a vote in the Committee. He also announced that he would pursue the fight on the floor.

For the sake of the record, the senators who were present have been requested to give a statement on how they voted. So far, we have statements from Senators Dirksen, Gillette, Benton, and Lodge.[2]

Senator Lodge did not attend the Committee meeting. We have expressed our disappointment to him about his failure to be present. The senator has recorded his position as follows:

> "It was physically impossible for me to get to the meeting in time, but I have instructed the Clerk of the Committee to record my position on this issue. I have, in the meantime, received a report of the voting, and I can assert positively that my presence would not have changed the result in any way.
>
> "If the majority leader decides to bring this Resolution up for action in the Senate, it will, of course, be possible to amend it on the floor. The action of the Committee, therefore, should not be taken as being final in any sense of the word. The mere fact that a cloture resolution is going onto the Senate Calendar is, in itself, a big step forward, even if we both happen to agree on the substantive inadequacy of the particular form in which it was reported."

Senator Gillette recorded his position as follows:

"The Rules Committee of the Senate reported out the Wherry Resolution relative to cloture rules. I shall support the resolution though I have very hope that we can bring it to a vote in the Senate at an early date."

The Director has also talked with Senator Gillette. It is difficult to know what he means in the words we have underlined.

Senator Dirksen's position is recorded as follows:

"I shall certainly be guided by a desire to work out a practical rule which among other things will be entirely fair, will prevent hasty and ill-considered proposals but at the same time make possible a consideration of measures and motions."

TESTIMONY BEFORE HOUSE COMMITTEE ON ARMED SERVICES

The Director appeared before the House Committee on Armed Services on January 30, 1952, to ask for the inclusion of safeguards against segregation and violence in H.R. 5904.[3]

At the Director's request, the Department of Defense answered an inquiry on whether colored persons who would receive Universal Military Training could thereafter be admitted to reserve components in the various states. The Department of Defense lists the following states as places where colored persons may be admitted to the National Guard on a non-segregated basis:

California, Connecticut, Illinois, Massachusetts, Minnesota, New Jersey, New York, and Wisconsin.

The Department of Defense also listed the following as places in which training could be obtained on a segregated basis:

The District of Columbia, Maryland, the State of Washington, Indiana, Michigan, West Virginia, Kentucky, and Ohio.[4]

Since the National Guard units will serve as the reserve components, the conclusion is inescapable that under a UMT program, colored people could get their full training on a non-segregated basis in only eight states.

During the hearing, some of the members of the Committee wanted to know whether Pennsylvania and Maine should be on the list of the states in which colored persons would be admitted to National Guard units on a non-segregated basis. The Department of Defense has advised that these states were intentionally omitted.

SEGREGATION IN CEMETERIES

During the January Board meeting, there was discussion about Private Thomas Reed being denied burial in a privately owned cemetery at Phoenix, Arizona. We were in touch with our Arizona representatives on this matter and were advised that the parents of Private Reed preferred to resolve the issue and have their son buried in Phoenix. Fortunately, they won and the cemetery agreed to burial in a non-segregated veterans section.[5]

Following the Board's instructions, the Director queried the Department of Defense on its policies on national cemeteries. The following is the Department's reply:

> "You may recall the history of this development when The Honorable Kenneth Royall was Secretary of War. There was no change in regulations but it was directed that no new sections providing for segregation by rank, race, or creed would be developed in any national cemeteries.
>
> "It was understood that those unfilled sections already developed on a segregated basis might be filled in accordance with the earlier policies. Even so, wherever the next-of-kin of any deceased veteran raised objection, burial would be made without further question in a non-segregated section, provided same has already been developed in the particular cemetery."[6]

In simple language, the Defense Department admits that it still has segregated sections in national cemeteries (including Arlington), but does not insist that colored soldiers be buried in such sections if relatives object.

THE HOUSING CRISIS

The Executive Secretary, Board Member Dr. Robert C. Weaver, and the Director, met with Mr. Raymond Foley, Administrator of the Housing and Home Finance Agency, on January 11, 1952, to discuss policies of Government agencies.[7] The heart of our presentation was as follows:

> "The chief threat to progress in eliminating Negro ghettos comes from the Federal Government itself through the operations of the Housing and Home Finance Agency and its constituent agencies.
>
> "Under the Slum Clearance and Urban Redevelopment Program, colored residents of some areas that will be cleared are being forced to move out while white persons will be the only racial group admitted to the new rental or sales housing to be erected on the cleared site.
>
> "In several cities, public housing projects will be built in areas where colored people have lived for many years but when the new projects are completed they will be designated for white occupancy.
>
> "The Defense Housing Program will, undoubtedly, follow the same pattern of segregation now in effect under the other housing operations. The policy set forth in the Administrator's letter to Congressman Abraham J. Multer, dated November 26, 1951, clearly permits continued segregation.[8]
>
> "This is the time for the Housing Agencies to deny any assistance or finances unless there is a guarantee that the housing made available will be open to all qualified applicants without regard to race.

"Because the present course of the Housing Agencies is a serious threat to the gains made by the NAACP and other organizations through court action against restrictive covenants, we are confronted with this question: 'Is it better to oppose the Housing Program, as such, and, thereby, halt Federal action in this field than to let the present program continue and within the next five years face a new and more terrible kind of restriction on the use and occupancy of Housing imposed with the help of the U.S. Government itself?'"

The Legal Department prepared an excellent brief which was submitted to Mr. Foley and is now under study.[9] We are awaiting Mr. Foley's reply.

SEGREGATION AT AIRPORTS

On behalf of the Birmingham, Alabama, and Baltimore, Maryland, NAACP Branches, the Washington Bureau has requested the Civil Aeronautics Administration to use its power to halt segregation in the airport facilities in those two states. The Baltimore request grows out of a change in policy in that city. The old airport served colored people while the new airport which has the title of "Friendship" denies them service in the dining-room.

In Birmingham, we acted at the request of Mr. Emory O. Jackson who advised us that city officials were seeking Federal funds with which to expand airport facilities.[10]

COMPLAINTS OF JANITORS IN SAN ANTONIO, TEXAS

Back in May of 1950, we received from Mr. Harry V. Burns, President of our San Antonio, Texas, NAACP, a statement about a complaint of colored janitors at the Kelly Air Force Base. These men were reclassified from janitors to laborers. The result was a substantial loss is pay because of this reclassification.

The 14th Regional Office of the U.S. Civil Service Commission ruled that the action at Kelly Field was improper and ordered the men restored to their former rank and pay.

The Air Force appealed the case to the Civil Service Commission and the Washington Bureau entered the picture by supporting the action of the Civil Service Regional Office.

On February 1, 1952, the Civil Service Commission advised that "these cases and others similar to them were held in abeyance for a considerable period of time pending a complete study of the problems [in] relation to the position coverage of the Classification Act of 1949 under Section 202(7). The Commission has completed its study of these cases and is pleased to advise you that the decision of the Fourteenth Region has been sustained and the agency and individuals concerned have been so advised."[11]

PUBLICATIONS

The Director invites members of the Board to read an article on the President's FEPC published in the January *Crisis.* The purpose of this article was to appraise the potential value of this agency if it is properly administered. At the time the article was written, the President had not made the appointments of committee members. These appointments have been made and several of the members are conscientious persons.[12]

The Director has passed on to some of the members suggestions for operating in a manner which should produce some results in spite of the weakness of the order.[13]

MS: NAACP II: A-656, DLC.

1. Despite these efforts, Senator McFarland had informed Mitchell in a very confidential meeting that the present situation in the Senate was such that no progress could be made on the rules change in this session of Congress. Mitchell memorandum to Walter White on "Conferences with Senator McFarland and Senator Douglas," 1/17/52, NAACP II: A-185, DLC.

2. See 3/5, 5/8, and 7/52, as well as the headnote on the NAACP and the Filibuster, vol. III.

3. The typescript of Mitchell's statement for the House Committee on Armed Services urging support for an amendment to the UMT bill to bar segregation training and service in reserve units is dated January 29, 1952, but he testified on January 30. He recalled that in his testimony before the committee on March 8, 1951, he recommended the inclusion of four safeguards in H.R. 1752, a similar bill that was then being considered. The NAACP in 1951 asked for the elimination of racial segregation in all units of the armed services, a prohibition against the use of segregated facilities for housing and feeding servicepeople, protection of servicemen and servicewomen against violence in "our own country," and the elimination of all racial designations in forms and records of service personnel. Mitchell cited a statement by Gen. George C. Marshall on the success of nonsegregated fighting units in the Far East. So, he said, if the UMT plan "cannot have full value unless the persons trained become a part of reserved components, then, automatically, the colored citizens of the United States will be placed at a disadvantage in the 40 states which either exclude them from the National Guard altogether or require that they belong to segregated units." Mitchell typescript statement, 1/29/52, NAACP WB-150, DLC; 1/30/52, *Hearings,* 2982–99. Related materials are in NAACP II: A-656, DLC. See also 2/14/52, *Hearings,* 502–10. For references to Mitchell's previous testimony before the Senate Armed Services Committee on 1/26/51 and the House Armed Services Committee on 3/8/51, see 2/2 and 12/28/51. See, furthermore, 3/5/52.

4. This information came from Civilian Assistant to the Secretary of Defense James C. Evans, in his letter to Mitchell of 1/28/52, a copy of which was included with Mitchell's testimony of 1/30/52, at page 2992, cited above.

5. The concern was aroused by a *New York Times* story on January 7, 1952, reporting that the body of an African American killed in Korea remained unburied until the trustees of the private Greenwood Memorial Park Cemetery in Phoenix, Arizona, could clarify its policy on whether he could be buried in the veterans' section. *New York Times,* 1/7/52, 3. The board adopted a resolution to ask the president to authorize the burial of the GI at Arlington National Cemetery. Minutes, 1/7/52, EC.

6. This was a long, ongoing struggle. On April 16, 1947, Walter White wrote to Gen. George Horkan regarding an order of the War Department (Bulletin 11) that American soldiers killed in World War II were to be segregated in national cemeteries. White asked Horkan to "do his utmost to 'get the War Department to change this unnecessary and gratuitous action.'"

On April 26, 1947, after apparently reading a public announcement that the War Department had issued a subsequent statement barring discrimination due to race or rank in the burial of war dead, White wrote the secretary of war expressing his appreciation for the reversal on behalf of himself and the NAACP. Report of the Secretary to the Board for May [1947], EC; Report of the Secretary of Veterans' Affairs, 5/47, 6/47, EC.

7. See Weaver, "Habitation with Segregation," *Crisis* 59 (June-July 1952): 347–53, 402–3.

8. For Multer's position on S. 349, the Defense Housing Bill, see 8/31/51.

9. See NAACP Memorandum, 1/11/52, on "The Authority and Power of the Administrator of the Housing and Home Finance Agency, the Federal Housing Administration, the Public Housing Administration, and the Division of Slum Clearance and Urban Redevelopment, Constituent Units of the Housing and Home Finance Agency, to Prohibit Discrimination in Federal and Federally-Aided Housing Programs Administered by Them," MP.

10. See also 12/28/52.

11. See 11/3/50 for initiation of this case and 12/3/52 for affirmation of the Civil Service Commission's ruling.

12. See Mitchell, "President Truman's 'FEPC,'" *Crisis* 59 (January 1952): 5–8. The persons Truman appointed to his Committee on Government Contract Compliance were Dwight Palmer (chair), James B. Carey, Dowdal H. Davis, Irving Engel, Oliver W. Hill, and George Meany. Palmer was then chair of the board of General Cable Corporation; Carey was secretary-treasurer of the CIO; Davis was general manager of the *Kansas City Call*; Engel was chair of the executive committee of the American Jewish Committee; Hill was a prominent African American attorney in Richmond, Virginia, involved in major civil rights cases; and Meany was secretary-treasurer of the AFL. Representing government agencies on the committee were Russell Forbes, deputy administrator of the GSA, who also represented the Defense Materials Procurement Agency; Michael J. Galvin, undersecretary of labor; Everett L. Hollis, general counsel for the AEC; and John D. Small, chair of the Munitions Board, Department of Defense. See Transcript, "The President's News Conference of January 10, 1952," The American Presidency Project, Harry S. Truman: 1945–1953, available online at www.presidency.scsb.edu/site/docs/pppus.php?admin=033&year+1952&id=7; see also press release, 1/10/52, with this same information, in NAACP II: A-200, DLC.

13. Mitchell unsuccessfully attempted to win the NAACP board's support for an earlier plan under which the Department of Justice would secure enforcement of nondiscrimination clauses in government contracts by getting an injunction. Copy of the related discussion, Minutes, 12/10/51, NAACP II: A-200, DLC. See also 6/5/52, in appendix 1, this vol., Mitchell's 6/9/52 statement before the committee.

Monthly Report, March 5, 1952

March 5, 1952

MONTHLY REPORT OF THE WASHINGTON BUREAU

STATUS OF RULES CHANGE

Senator William Benton has prepared a minority report on S. Res. 203 reported out by the Senate Committee on Rules. We are advised that Senator Theodore Green will also sign this minority report. Senator Green's absence from his office apparently has delayed his signing of the report. When his signature is obtained, the committee report will be filed and placed on the Senate calendar.[1]

As stated in last month's report, we have asked committee members to give us a written statement on how they voted in committee. The line up of replies will be given in next month's report when it is hoped that we will have them all in.[2] So far, we have heard from Senators Everett M. Dirksen, Guy M. Gillette, Robert C. Hendrickson, Henry Cabot Lodge, Jr., A. S. Mike Monroney, and Margaret Chase Smith.

HEARINGS ON CIVIL RIGHTS LEGISLATION

Senator Hubert Humphrey has advised that in April he will hold hearings on FEPC legislation in connection with an overall inquiry that he will be making on the use of manpower in the present emergency.[3] We are asking the House Judiciary Committee to hold hearings on Anti-Lynching legislation. Similar requests for hearings are being made to the Interstate Commerce Committees of the House and Senate on Anti-Jim Crow Travel legislation.[4]

UNIVERSAL MILITARY TRAINING LEGISLATION

In the hearings on UMT Legislation before the Senate Armed Services Committee, Senator Kefauver officially stated that his vote for the Russell segregation amendment in the 81st Congress could not be interpreted to mean that he now favors segregation in the Armed Services. This statement by the Senator was made in response to testimony by the NAACP.[5]

In the House, Congressmen Powell, Javits, and Havenner agreed to introduce anti-segregation and anti-violence amendments to the UMT legislation. These amendments were suggested by the NAACP and Congressmen were urged to vote against the legislation if they were not included. As a result of parliamentary maneuvering, the UMT Bill was shelved before these issues could come to a vote.

It is interesting to note that the Department of Defense officially stated that there would be no segregation in the basic training of UMT. However, the Department did not make a clear cut commitment on training in Reserve Components. The Reserve Component training covers a longer period than the basic training. In this connection, it is suggested that pledges made by the Department of Defense last year be noted. These are mentioned on page 5 of the mimeographed annual report of the Washington Bureau.[6]

ALASKA STATEHOOD BILL

Although the admission of Alaska to statehood is technically not a civil rights issue, some work was done on specific Senators in an effort to get their support for a vote against a motion to recommit the bill. The Senators who pledged to vote against recommitment were Senators Ives and O'Conor. They had been listed as doubtful and did vote against recommitment. Senator Saltonstall who was also asked to vote against recommitment did not comply with the request. He voted for recommittal.

Senator Lodge was out of the city at the time of the vote but he, too, was listed as opposing statehood for Alaska. The bill was recommitted by one vote (45 to 44). Among the southerners voting against recommitment were Senators Holland, Kefauver, and Sparkman.[7]

LEGISLATION ON PROBLEMS OF THE BLIND

We have had a number of requests to support a bill setting up a temporary national committee on the problems of the blind. We have requested that the House Committee on Education and Labor begin hearings on this proposed legislation.

COMMITTEE ON GOVERNMENT CONTRACT COMPLIANCE

The Committee on Government Contract Compliance has held its first meeting and is now selecting an executive director. We have explored the possibilities of getting Mr. Robert Ming to have his name submitted for consideration. Needless to say, he would be an outstanding choice. Meanwhile, Mr. Wilfred Leland, who is at present the executive director of the Minneapolis Fair Employment Committee, has been interviewed by a number of the committee members. Mr. Leland has had extensive experience in Government and on FEPC matters. If either is selected, it is anticipated that we will have a very cooperative relationship.[8]

We have presented to the committee the problem of discrimination in the Washington Telephone Company. In the most recent case, the local company agreed to accept an operator who was transferred to Washington from New York. The company withdrew its offer of a job when it interviewed the operator and found that she was colored. Since the policies of the company had been placed before the Office of Defense Mobilization prior to the issuance of Executive Order 10, 308, it has been suggested that the committee and ODM work jointly on it. We have submitted to the chairman of the committee and some of the members certain suggestions for strengthening this operation. These suggestions are now under consideration.[9]

ALONG THE D.C. SEGREGATION FRONT

Sergeant Jesse Teverbaugh, who holds the Silver Star, is a member of the Marine Corps. He was denied admission to the Warner Theater in Washington when he presented a pass that had been given by an officer on the Post at Quantico, Virginia. The picture was about the exploits of Sergeant Teverbaugh's outfit in Korea.

We joined him in a meeting with the manager of the theater. The manager apologized for the incident and invited the Sergeant to stay to see the picture. Sgt. Teverbaugh remained and no further incident occurred. We are suggesting that the

Department of Defense should follow up on this since the pass was distributed through official channels.[10]

The Sadler Wells Ballet was presented in Washington in February and there was no segregation in the audience at the Capital Theater. Sometime ago, we asked the Metropolitan Opera Company to assure us there would be no segregation when it comes to the Capital Theater in Washington. The Metropolitan Opera Company referred the matter to S. Hurok. We have asked Mr. Hurok to assure us that there will be no segregation.[11]

MS: NAACP II: A-670, DLC.

1. See 2/6, 5/8, and 7/52; Benton, "Need for a Suitable Cloture Rule," *Crisis* 59 (February 1952): 83–88. In a cover letter to Walter White, Mitchell said that, subsequent to dictating this report, he had a call from Benton's office indicating that the report on S. Res. 203 would be filed in the Senate on Thursday, March 6. Benson would file his minority report immediately after Jenner filed the majority report, according to the present plans, he said. Mitchell to White, 3/5/52, NAACP II: A-670, DLC.

2. The report for March seems to be missing; the May 8, 1952, report had nothing on the rules change effort. However, Mitchell, in a report on the Senate's action on March 11, 1949, said that a ruling by Vice President Alben Barkley, president of the Senate, that cloture applied to a motion to take up S. Res. 15 (which was to change the Senate rules) could have been sustained by a shift of three votes in favor of the civil rights forces. Mitchell memorandum to NAACP branches in Iowa, Kansas, Missouri, Nebraska, and Wisconsin on "The Role of Your States in Civil Rights," 3/23/52, NAACP II: A-185, DLC. See also 7/52.

3. Humphrey held the hearings. See 5/8/52.

4. For background, see Alexander, "Recent Trends in the Law of Racial Segregation."

5. 1/30/52, *Hearings*, 2982–99.

6. See 12/28/51.

7. The bill was killed on February 27, 1952. Mitchell memorandum to all NAACP branches, 4/19/52, NAACP II: 185, DLC. Southern senators opposed statehood for Alaska because some of them feared that adding the territory to the Union would add two more pro—civil rights senators who would help beat filibusters. Mitchell memorandum to NAACP Branches in Missouri, Kansas, Iowa, Nebraska, and Wisconsin on "Role of Your States in Civil Rights."

8. Dwight Palmer of General Cable Corporation was appointed chair of the Committee on Government Contract Compliance. See 2/6/52.

9. See, in appendix 1, this vol., 6/9/52; Mitchell, "President Truman's FEPC."

10. Mitchell said that experience showed the importance of not distributing any theater passes or other entertainment tickets unless the armed services were assured that those who attempted to use them would be free to do so regardless of race. Furthermore, he said, if a civilian organization such as the NAACP could have corrected the injustice at the Warner Theater, "a great deal more could be accomplished if the Department of Defense itself showed such interest on behalf of members of the Armed Services." Mitchell's letter to Robert A. Lovett, secretary of defense, 3/12/52, NAACP WB-133, DLC.

11. See, most immediately, 2/4/53.

Monthly Report, May 8, 1952

May 8, 1952

MONTHLY REPORT OF THE WASHINGTON BUREAU

FEPC HEARINGS

The Humphrey Subcommittee of the Labor Committee in the Senate conducted hearings on fair employment practice legislation. In preparing for these hearings, the Senate Labor Committee consulted with the Washington Bureau for the purpose of determining employer witnesses and others who would give a picture of discrimination in the United States at present. Among the employers recommended by the Bureau were RCA and International Harvester. Both of these companies appeared and made statements that are useful.

The Executive Secretary testified for the Association and he was accompanied by the Director of the Bureau.[1]

Charges against specific companies made by the NAACP are now being investigated by the staff members of the Senate Labor Committee. Also, for the first time, it appears that the Executive Agencies of Government, in compliance with a request from Senator Humphrey, will make a determination on the extent of under-utilization of minority groups.

THE COX RESOLUTION

By a vote of 194 to 158 on April 4, 1952, the House passed the Cox Resolution which provides for investigation of foundations and other organizations.[2]

Organizations interested in keeping the Cox Committee from becoming a real witch-hunt urged that liberal elements in Congress be represented on the committee. The members of the committee are Cox of Georgia, Chairman; the Democrats are Hays of Arkansas, O'Toole of New York, and Forand of Rhode Island; the Republicans are Goodwin of Massachusetts, Simpson of Pennsylvania, and Reece of Tennessee.

The NAACP has urged the members of Congress to vote against any appropriation for this committee, since the House Ways and Means Committee is already conducting an investigation of organizations that may be abusing their tax exempt status. Hence, the Cox Committee would be a duplication of the work of the Ways and Means Committee, if Cox intended to conduct a fair investigation.

VOTING RECORDS

The Washington Bureau has prepared and distributed voting records for a number of states. These records contain narrative accounts that have been arousing a considerable amount of interest in the places where they have been used. As rapidly as the Washington workload will permit, we are assembling other records and hope shortly to have them completed for all states.[3]

ANTI-LYNCHING BILL

For months, extensive discussions have been going on over at the Senate about the possibility of action on an Anti-Lynching Bill in this session of Congress. At the time report is written, these discussions are still in progress. Needless to say, there are those who are seeking to water-down any Anti-Lynching Bill that might be considered. On the other hand, there is a strong move to get a worthwhile bill.[4]

SPEAKING ENGAGEMENTS

The Director of the Washington Bureau has made visits to Michigan, Georgia, Pennsylvania, Massachusetts, Delaware, Maryland, and North Carolina.

Because of the necessity to prepare for these visits and numerous other matters that are before the Bureau at this time, this report is brief and emphasizes only some important highlights of the Washington scene.

MS: NAACP II: A-656, DLC.

1. 4/17/52, *Hearings*, 141–63; see also 3/5 and 7/31/52; related materials in NAACP II: A-257, DLC. Mitchell reported to the board that Humphrey had set a deadline to get the bill reported out early in May. The previous year, he said, Humphrey had stated that he was going to have hearings on manpower legislation and that he would include the FEPC question. Mitchell said he worked with him, and he finally decided to place the emphasis on FEPC. Inasmuch as the bureau had tried to be selective in getting people to testify, such as representatives of International Harvester, RAC, and state and local FEPC groups, White and Walter Reuther, president of the UAW, could testify in a capsule hearing with the objective of getting the bill out early in May. Minutes, 4/14/52, EC.

2. See, among others, 12/28/51, 6/5 and 12/31/52.

3. These reports reinforced the NAACP's voter registration campaign. Commenting on one being conducted by the North Carolina State Conference of NAACP Branches, Mitchell told the board that he had prepared a summary of important issues for the organization as well as the voting records of representatives and senators from North Carolina. Initially, he said, delegates were unable to see how bad the records of their representatives and senators were. "But when the district representatives were permitted to stand up and speak about the voting records of their representatives, it became clear to the people how bad the situation was." Minutes, 4/14/53, EC. Mitchell's memorandum to North Carolina branches on the voting records of their representatives and senators, 3/22/52, is in NAACP II: A-188, DLC.

4. Getting action on a federal antilynching bill was one of the issues Mitchell discussed earlier with Senators McFarland, majority leader, and Paul Douglas. Mitchell's memorandum to Walter White, 1/17/52, NAACP II: A-185, DLC. See also 6/5/52.

The struggle for an antilynching bill was influenced dramatically by the dynamite bomb, the new form of racial violence that was symbolized by the blast on Christmas night 1951 that killed Harry T. Moore, Florida state coordinator of NAACP branches, and his wife, Harriet. In addition to seeking protections in Washington, the NAACP, at a meeting in Jacksonville, Florida, on January 19 and 20, 1952, adopted plans to increase the voter registration of African Americans throughout the South, and it created a committee composed of state conference presidents from fifteen southern states to increase the association's political action campaign in the region. See detailed report of related NAACP activities, Report of the Secretary for December 1951 and January 1951, EC.

Monthly Report, June 5, 1952

June 5, 1952

MONTHLY REPORT OF THE WASHINGTON BUREAU

SENATE JUDICIARY COMMITTEE

The Director of the Washington Bureau has reminded Senator McFarland, the Majority Leader, that the Senate Judiciary Committee, while refusing to act on Anti-Lynching Legislation, reported out a proposed Constitutional Amendment to prevent seizure of private property in less than a week. The Majority Leader insists that he is trying to get the Committee to act on an Anti-Lynching Bill in this session.[1]

COX COMMITTEE

The House Administration Committee is scheduled to vote on whether the Cox Committee (which is set up to investigate foundations and charitable organizations) shall have money with which to operate. At the time this is written word of a possible postponement of the vote has reached us. The vote was scheduled for Thursday June 5. Although some Congressmen who opposed the creation of the committee say that they favor giving it an appropriation, we have urged friendly committee members to vote against funds for Cox.[2]

MUTUAL SECURITY ACT

The Executive Secretary and the Director sought the inclusion of language in the Mutual Security Bill which would assure Dependent Over-Seas Territories of Point IV assistance in public health, industrial production, economic development, and agriculture. We proposed an amendment covering Western Hemisphere Countries that was adopted by the House Committee. The specific language we suggested for Africa and Asia was not accepted, but Point IV officials believe that other language inserted by Congressman John Vorys of Ohio will accomplish the desired objectives for Africa and Asia. The Executive Secretary and the Director discussed the entire matter with Mr. Vorys at some length.[3]

IMMIGRATION BILL

After a gallant fight by a small band of liberals in the Senate, the McCarran Immigration Bill passed. However, those who opposed the legislation are rallying the country with the hope of getting and sustaining a Presidential veto.[4] A large part of the work on this Bill was done by Mr. William Pryor of the Washington Bureau.

KELLY FIELD WAGE DISPUTE

The Director of the Bureau represented colored employees of the Kelly Field Air Base in Texas at a hearing before the Civil Service Commission this month. The employees were formerly under classified Civil Service ratings but have been transferred to ungraded area ratings. Under the area ratings, classified janitors and charwomen become laborers.

The pay rate is then based on what local non-government laborers are paid. The loss in pay ranges from sixteen to thirty cents an hour. Other benefits of the classified Civil Service are also lost. Approximately fifty areas of the South are affected.

Mrs. Susie Henderson, a charwoman from Atlanta, Georgia, was present at the hearing. She told the NAACP that her loss because of reclassification might amount to as much as $500 a year. Mrs. Henderson was employed at Fort McPherson. The Department of the Army changed her job classification, then transferred her to other duties, and, subsequently, dismissed her.

The Kelly Field employees have been fighting the problem since 1949 with the help of Mr. Harry Burns, President of the San Antonio NAACP, and Mr. Harold S. Nelson, a lawyer.

NAVY SEGREGATION

The Executive Secretary of the NAACP has written a strong letter to the Secretary of the Navy urging that segregation in the Navy Yards at Charleston, South Carolina, and Norfolk, Virginia, be ended.[5] An excerpt from the Secretary's letter spells out the present problem.

> "It is a real cause for alarm that Rear Admiral W. McL. Hague, Chief of the Office of Industrial Relations, has announced that the Navy's policy is as follows on segregation. 'Segregated facilities are provided at Naval Stations—

a. Where the Station is subject to the laws of the community in which located, and the laws of the community require segregated facilities, or
b. Where, although the Station is not subject to local laws, segregated facilities are the norm in the community because of law, mores, or customs, and the conversion to common facilities would, in the judgment of the Commanding Officer, result in definite impediment to productive effort.'

"We ask that you order the end of all racial segregation in the Yards at Charleston and Norfolk. We also ask that Admiral Hague's statement of policy be completely eliminated and that there be substituted for it a policy of no racial segregation in facilities and services at any Naval establishments."

SCHOOL CONSTRUCTION

The Director has urged the Bailey Subcommittee of the House Labor Committee to deny funds for school construction unless there are appropriate safeguards against segregation in the schools that will be built.

INTEGRATION IN EUROPE

The Director, in reporting that integration in the Armed Services in Europe is under way, calls attention to the annual report of the Bureau, dated December 28, 1951. The report gave details on the action of the Association to speed up integration in the Armed Services and pointed out that integration got under way in the Far East following conferences at the Pentagon between friendly Senators and Defense Department officials. A quote from the report states -

> "We have been assured that plans are under consideration for an announcement concerning integration of the Armed Services in the European Theater. Regrettably, full integration at home appears to be last on the list."

During a recent visit to Washington, the Executive Secretary was assured by the Department of Defense that integration in Europe would be accomplished. We have urged the Department of the Army to make public the order which called a halt to segregation in the European Theater. Secretary Pace has promised to do this but so far we have not received the written order.

PRESIDENT'S COMMITTEE ON GOVERNMENT CONTRACT COMPLIANCE

The Bureau has again urged the President's Committee on Government Contract Compliance to take prompt action on a pending complaint against the Telephone Company in Washington. We believe that a satisfactory settlement of this case would get the Committee off to a good start. The issue involved is the Company's failure to hire colored operators.[6]

MS: MP.

1. See 10/6/52; in appendix 1, this vol., 5/28/52, where Mitchell commented on the national political scene. This newsletter, which also reported on the struggle to integrate the armed services, is cited at 12/28/51.

2. See 5/8 and 12/31/52.

3. This struggle involved the Mutual Security Program, for which the Truman administration won from Congress a grudging increase over 1951 in economic aid for Europe. *Congress and the Nation,* 169, 171. This struggle also involved attempts to revise the country's immigration policy that were led by Sen. Patrick A. McCarran (D-Nev.). *Congress and the Nation,* 222; Minutes, 3/10/52, EC.

4. The NAACP opposed the McCarran bill because it would restrict immigration to the United States from the British West Indies. It therefore urged the authors of the bill to include the British West Indies in the British quota rather than in a separate island quota, which, Mitchell told the board, would restrict the immigration of people of African descent to one hundred from each colony. As a result, the board voted to "call upon the authors of the bill to include the Britist West Indies in the British quota rather than in a separate island quota." Minutes, 3/10/52, EC. See also, among others, 12/31/52; in appendix 1, this vol., 5/28, 6/3, and 9/30/52; *Congress and the Nation,* 222–23.

5. See text of letter, 5/26/52, to Dan A. Kimball, secretary of the navy, and related materials in NAACP WB-142, DLC. See also, most immediately, 5/1/50, 10/6/52, 4/3/53; in appendix 1, this vol., 10/3/52; and Watson, *Lion in the Lobby,* 236–38.

6. See Mitchell's statement before the committee, 6/9/52, in appendix 1, this vol., and 10/6/52.

Special Report on Congress, July 1952

[July 31, 1952]

[SPECIAL REPORT ON CONGRESS]

This is the year when the people of the United States have their opportunity to reward those who have been good public servants in Congress and the White House. It is also the year for penalizing and throwing out of office those who have been poor custodians of the public welfare. This is an election year.[1]

For the members of the N.A.A.C.P. and all who cherish human freedom the most important yardstick for measuring candidates is civil rights.

All over the country our branches have been active in pressing the drive to increase the number of registered voters. In the Baltimore, Maryland branch, for example, the drive for increased registration resulted in an increase of colored voters that was almost three times as great as the increase of white voters. You will hear, today, the reports of Alabama, Georgia and North Carolina. But let me say this first, there are 2,800,000 colored people twenty-one and over in the South. We must not rest until every single one of them who is sound of mind is a registered voter.

Presented in stark reality, the goals of increased registration this year are two. They are:

1. The election of and keeping in office those candidates who believe in and work for civil rights legislation, and
2. The defeat of the enemies of civil rights whether they be in the South, the North or wherever they may be.

The Congressman and Senators who really fight for civil rights are frequently the targets of special interests that seek to defeat them and in doing so, use the civil rights issue to appeal to voters who may have racial or religious prejudices. We must stand behind those Representatives and Senators who support our cause in Congress—whether they be Democrats or Republicans. The only way to give them effective support is to register and vote.

During this session we hope to impress upon you the fact that the enemies of civil rights are not necessarily confined to the South. Now is the time to identify those foes of human freedom so that you may know them by name. We offer you the facts on their records, it is up to you to decide whether you want to have them remain in office or whether, as their employers, you want to hand them a dismissal notice.

The May 28 Newsletter of the Washington Bureau gave you a thumbnail sketch on the records of the candidates who are running for President.[2] Therefore, I shall not take time to go into those records here unless I am asked to do so during the question period. But I shall discuss the records of Senators and Congressmen in Key Northern and Western States whose fate may well rest in your hands and the hands of all friends of civil rights.

On March 11, 1949, Vice President Barkley, presiding in the United States Senate, called for a vote on Senator Richard Russell's appeal from a ruling by the chair that cloture applied to a motion to take up a measure. In non-technical terms, the Vice President's ruling was a powerful blow against the foes of civil rights. If it had been sustained, it would have spelled the doom of the filibuster. The Vice-President's ruling was overturned by a vote of 46 to 41. If there had been a shift of three votes the result would have been 44 to 43 and it is certain that today much of the civil rights legislation would be now law.[3] Among those who voted with the South against the ruling of the Vice-President are the following Senators who are up for re-election this year.

1. Williams of Delaware (paired)
2. Jenner of Indiana
3. Thye of Minnesota
4. Kem of Missouri

5. Butler of Nebraska
6. Bricker of Ohio
7. Martin of Pennsylvania (paired)
8. Watkins of Utah
9. Cain of Washington

I wish to direct your attention to significance of those voted paired on this issue. These votes are not counted in the total. However, they show that when a Senator takes the trouble to be paired against a measure in which you are interested he is taking extra pains to let you know that he is so much opposed to what you want that he wishes to make a record of his views even though it does not change the result.

All of these Senators can show you how they voted favorably on other issues when they knew it was not possible for us to win. But on this crucial vote, the most important vote affecting civil rights in the 81st Congress, they were on the wrong side.

On February 22, 1950, the House voted 222 to 178 to substitute a weak and toothless FEPC bill for the Powell Bill.[4] The Powell Bill contained the enforcement powers that are so necessary for the success of legislation in this important field. Here a shift of only twenty-three votes would have given us victory. At that time over 100 Northern Border State and Western Congressman joined with Rankin of Mississippi in the vote to destroy FEPC.

TABLE 1

	P+4	Lucas	Lehman	Alaska	Humph.	Hst Veto
Williams (Del) (R)	W	R	W	R	W	W
Jenner (IND) (R)	W	R	R	W	R	W
Thye (Minn) (R)	W	R	W	R	R	W
Kem (MO) (R)	W	R	R	W	W	W
Butler (NEB) (R)	W	R	W	W	W	W
Bricker (Ohio) (R)	W	R	W	W	W	W
Martin (PA.) (R)	W	R	R	R	W	W
Watkins (Utah) (R)	W*	W	R	R	W	W
Cain (Wash.) (R)	W	R	W	R	W*	W
	Point 4	Lucas Amend	Lehman Amend	Alaska Statehood	Humphrey motion to recommit McCarran Immigration Bill	Vote on Truman Veto of above

These same Congressmen had another chance to show their views on racial matters on April 4, 1952, in the 82nd Congress when by a vote of 194 to 158 the House gave Cox of Georgia the authority to investigate charitable organizations that he said were stirring up class and racial strife in the South.[5] His prize example of this was the Rosenwald Fund. This Fund, as you know, is not out of business. However, between 1917 and 1948 it spent 22 million dollars to build 5,000 schools for colored children, for grants to four major colored universities, for health facilities and for the training of many colored and white people who are now leaders in the United States. A shift of 19 votes would have defeated the Cox proposal. But here 55 [65][6] allies of the Dixiecrats joined Cox in this move against those who are working for better race relations in the South. These sixty-five, supporters of Rankin and Cox, are the hard core of the alliance between the Dixiecrats and those [who] come from other areas of the country. Here are their names:

California (7)
Anderson
Bramblett
Jackson
McDonough
Phillips
Poulson
Werdel

Colorado (1)
Hill

Illinois (4)
Allen
Chiperfield
Chauncey Reed
Velde

Iowa (3)
Dolliver
Jensen
Talle

Kansas (4)
Cole
Rees
Scrivener
Wint Smith

Maryland (1)
Edward T. Miller

Massachussets (3)
Goodwin
Martin
Nicholson

Michigan (4)
Blackney
Crawford
Hoffman
Shafer

Minnesota (4)
Anderson
Andresen
O'Hara

Missouri (2)
Jones
Dewey Short

Montana (4)
D'Ewart

Nebraska (1)
A.L. Miller

New York (4)
Cole
Gwinn
Kilburn
Taber

Ohio (5)
Clarence Brown
Clevenger
Elston
McCulloh
Weichel

Pennsylvania (8)
Dague
Fenton
Gavin
Graham
Benjamin F. James
Kearns
McConnell
Van Zandt

S. Dakota (1)
Lovre

Kentucky (4)
Chelf
Golden
Gregory
Morton

Wyoming (1)
Barrett

Washington (1)
Horan

Wisconsin (1)
Davis

TABLE 2

	Point 4	Rankin	Cox $	Rules	Exception
Calif.					
Anderson (R)	W	W	W	W	No vote on first Cox
Bramblet T. (R)	W	W	W	W	No vote on first Cox
Jackson (R)	R	R	W	W	
McDonough (R)	R	R	W	R	No vote on first Cox
Phillips (R)	W	R	W	W	
Poulson (R)	R	O	W	R	No vote on first Cox
Wedel (R)	W	W	W	W	
Colo.					
Hill (R)	W	R	W	R	
Ill.					
Allen (R)	W	R	W	W	
Chiperfeld (R)	W	R	W	W	No vote on first Cox
C. Reed (R)	W	O	W	W	No vote on first Cox
Velde (R)	W	W	W	R	No vote on first Cox
Iowa					
Dolliver (R)	W	R	W	W	No vote on first Cox
Jensen (R)	W	W	W	W	
Talle (R)	W	R	W	W	
Kan.					
A. M.Cole (R)	W	R	W	W	
E. H. Rees (R)	W	R	W	W	
Scriuner (R)	W	R	W	W	
Wint Smith (R)	W	O	W	W	
MD.					
Miller (R)	W	W	W	W	
Mass.					
Goodwin (R)	W	R	W	W	
Martin (R)	W	R	W	W	
Nicholson (R)	W	W	W	W	
Mich.					
Blackney (R)	W	W	W	W	No vote on first Cox
Crawford (R)	W*	O	W	W	
C.E. Hoffman (R)	W	O	W	W	No vote on first Cox
Shafer (R)	W	W	W	W	

TABLE 2 *(cont.)*

	Point 4	Rankin	Cox $	Rules	Exception
Minn.					
Andersen (R)	W	R	W	R	
Andresen (R)	W	R	W	W	
Ohara (R)	W	W	W	R	
Mo.					
Jones (D)	R	O	W	R	
Short (R)	W	W	W	W	
Mont.					
D'Ewart (R)	W	R	W	W	
N.Y.					
Wis. Cole (R)	W	R	W	W	
Gwinn (R)	W	R*	W	W	
Kilburn (R)	R	O	W	W	
Taber (R)	W	R	W	W	
Ohio					
C. Brown (R)	W	W	W	W	
Clevenger (R)	W	W	W	W	
Elston (R)	W	R	W	W	
McCulloch (R)	W	R	W	W	
Weichel (R)	W	R	W	W	No vote on first Cox
Penna.					
Dague (R)	W	R	W	R	
Fenton (R)	W	R	W*	W	
Gavin (R)	W	R	W	R	
Graham (R)	W	R	W	W	
James (R)	W*	R	W	R	
Kearns (R)	W	R*	W	W	
McConnell (R)	W	R	W	R	
Von Zandt (R)	W	R	W	R	
S.Dak.					
Louvre (R)	W*	R	W	R	
K.Y.					
Chelf (D)	R	W	W	R	
Golden (R)	W	W	W	R	
Gregory (D)	R	W	W	W	
Morton (R)	R	W	R*	R	No vote on first Cox
	Point	**Rankin**	**Cox $**	**Rules**	**Remarks**
Wash.					
Horan (R)	W	R	W	R	
Wisc.					
Davis (R)	W	R	W	R	
Wyo.					
Harrison (R)	Not seated	O	X	Not seated	Not seated when FEPC cameup
Barrett	W	Replaced		W	(No longer in)

With one or two exceptions, these Congressmen come from states where colored people enjoy the right to vote without a single restriction of any kind. In these states there are also numerous, labor, church and civil organizations that would help to get these Congressmen to vote right or defeat them.

Almost always in Northern states it is possible to select candidates on a basis of fitness for office. Often in the South it is not possible to make a choice between men on the basis of which is better. Usually it is a choice of the lesser of two evils. This was the case in the 1950 election race between Dixiecrat Strom Thurmond and Senator Olin Johnston in South Carolina. It will be the case in Mississippi this year when John Rankin must compete for his seat with another Dixiecrat names Abernethy. Defeat of Rankin would not only rid Congress of a very objectionable character, but it would also release the House Veterans Committee from his ruthless control as chairman.

In many cases it would be wise to vote against some southern incumbents, because this would free an important committee from their domination and make it possible for a more liberal person to be chairman. This would be true in North Carolina whose Graham Barden heads the House Labor Committee. Defeat of Barden would mean that Congressman Kelley of Pennsylvania or Congressman Powell of New York would be chairman under a democratic administration. This committee, under Barden's rule, has bottled up FEPC, Education bills and other useful legislation. His defeat would break the log jam.

The importance of getting the vote registered in the South cannot be overemphasized. As an illustration of the important potential in this region we offer Alabama's first Congressional District. In four of the seven counties of this district colored people outnumber the white population. In one of the four, Wilcox County, colored people outnumber whites nine to one.

The rewards of registration are demonstrated in North [the remainder of the text is missing]

MS: MP.

This incomplete original carries a notation at the top in Mitchell's handwriting that seems to read "July 1952 83rd." Nevertheless, although Mitchell provided the affirmation that "this is an election year," which 1952 was, he wrote "83rd" next to what in all likelihood is a partially punched-out "2," as done to place the document in an office binder. Thus, the only conclusion that can be reached about the "83rd" is that he made the notation to remind himself of something about the approaching 83rd Congress in 1953 that he did not want to forget.

1. The Forty-third Annual Convention of the NAACP at Oklahoma City, Oklahoma, on June 28, 1952, affirmed this militant tone by urging the two major political parties to include in their platforms the nine-point civil rights plank that had been endorsed by fifty-three national organizations at the LCCR sponsored by the NAACP and by a meeting of national African American organizations. "Political Action," *Crisis* 59 (August-September 1952): 446–47. See also "Party Platform Pledges on Civil Rights," *Crisis* 59 (October 1952): 480–81; Mitchell, "These Are the Issues," *Crisis* 59 (October 1952): 483–86; in appendix 1, this vol., 10/3/52.

2. See 11/5 and 12/28/51, 5/8, 6/5, and 12/31/52; in appendix 1, this vol., 5/28/52.

3. *Congressional Record Daily Digest,* 3/10/49, D111 of *Congressional Record* 2125–59, 2166–75; *Congressional Record Daily Digest,* 3/11/49, D114 of *Congressional Record* 2214, 2227–76; *Congressional Record Daily Digest,* 3/12/49, D117 of *Congressional Record* 2312–55. See also, in appendix 1, this vol., 3/10/49 and 10/3/52. For the more detailed report of Leslie Perry on this struggle, which he was leading, see 2/49 in NAACP II: A-656, DLC.

4. See 3/3/50; *Congress and the Nation*, 1618; White with Mitchell, 4/17/52, *Hearings*, 141–63.

5. See also 8/31, 11/5, and 12/28/51, 2/6, 3/5, 5/8, 6/5, and 12/31/52; in appendix 1, this vol., 5/28/51 and 10/3/52.

6. Mitchell's correction.

Monthly Report, October 6, 1952

October 6, 1952

MONTHLY REPORT OF THE WASHINGTON BUREAU

UNION SHOP IN THE RAILWAY INDUSTRY

The Washington Railroad Terminal has signed a union shop agreement with several unions, including the Brotherhood of Railway Carmen.[1] This union still has a provision in its constitution requiring that colored employees join Jim-Crow locals which are under the supervision of white locals. Approximately 400 colored employees at the Terminal are within the jurisdiction of the Carmen.

On their behalf, we have asked the Terminal whether it will dismiss them if they refuse to join the Jim-Crow local. The terminal has replied that,

> "I call your attention to Section 4 of the agreement which provides that nothing in the agreement 'shall require an employee to become or to remain a member of the organization if such membership is not available to such employee under the same terms and conditions as are generally applicable to any other member, or if the membership of such employee is denied or terminated for any reason other than the failure of the employee to tender the periodic dues, the initiation fees, and assessment (not including fines and penalties) uniformly required as a condition of acquiring or retaining membership.' You will note that this provision of the agreement conforms with the provision of the Railway Labor Act as amended to which you refer in the fourth paragraph of your September 24 letter."

It will be recalled what when the Railway Labor Act was amended to permit union shop agreements in this industry, the NAACP sought the inclusion of language that would provide adequate safeguards against discrimination by unions that deny membership to colored people on the basis of race or shunt them into Jim-Crow locals.[2]

The first test of the effectiveness of language that Congress did include came in Baltimore, Maryland, in 1950, when some employees of the Baltimore and Ohio Railroad refused to join a Jim Crow local set up by the Railway Clerks. When this matter was taken into court by the Baltimore branch, the union promptly stated, under oath, that it would not require colored people to join a separate local as a condition of remaining on the job. The employer also said, under oath, that none of the colored employees faced dismissal because they refused to join a separate local.[3]

The three plaintiffs in the case are still on the job although they were denied membership in the white local when they applied for it. Meanwhile, two colored men have been admitted to the white local and employees who voluntarily joined the Jim-Crow local are considering the possibility of abolishing their lodge and joining the white local.[4]

SCHOOL SEGREGATION ON ARMY POSTS

On behalf of complainants from Fort Bliss and Fort Sam Houston in Texas, Fort Sill in Oklahoma, and Fort Belvoir, Virginia, we have asked Secretary Robert M. Lovett of the Department of Defense to abolish the practice of requiring children of colored service personnel to attend schools off the military posts while white children are given schools on the posts usually with transportation, new buildings and hot lunches.[5]

This practice, which Army officials pretend is done to conform with state laws, is another illustration of how the policy of integration in the Army is being delayed and sometimes even set back by persons in policy making positions who are determined to thwart the President's program of ending segregation.

U.S. COAST GUARD

The U.S. Coast Guard Station at Curtis Bay, Maryland, has denied proper work experience and promotion opportunities to colored technicians who are skilled in work on Sonar, Loran and Radar. On behalf of these employees, the NAACP is seeking a hearing under the provisions of the Fair Employment Order 9980. Some of the employees report that, in an effort to stall off the investigation, some supervisors are offering chances for promotion to certain workers if they will agree to testify against the complainants who made the first charges. Needless to say, these offers have been rejected.

TELEPHONE COMPANY

Although we have had frequent assurance that it is at work on the problem, the President's Committee on Government Contract Compliance has not yet broken down the hiring practices of the Chesapeake and Potomac Telephone Company, operating in Washington and Baltimore, which result in the exclusion of colored operators. Dwight R. G. Palmer, Chairman of the Committee, advises that he is personally working on this problem. Meanwhile, at least twenty new cases have come in against the Company.[6]

NAVY YARD SEGREGATION

While it is not a problem strictly within the jurisdiction of the Government Contract Compliance Committee, we have placed the matter of segregation in the Norfolk, Virginia, and Charleston, South Carolina, Navy Yards before the Contract Compliance group. We have done so on the ground that these establishments, as large employers, have an important effect on the policies of private industry. The Navy Yards in question have separate lavoratories, restaurants, and drinking fountains. These practices have been approved by the Secretary of the Navy despite our protests.[7]

CIVIL SERVICE COMPLAINTS

Approximately twenty-five colored persons who passed a written examination for the job of investigator in the Fourth Region of the Civil Service Commission were disqualified because they "failed" to pass oral examinations.

One question asked on the oral examination was:

> "If you were investigating a postmaster in North Carolina, would you accept an invitation from him to go to lunch at the Rotary Club?"

When we filed charges of discrimination on behalf of most of those who were disqualified, the Civil Service Commission and the Fair Employment Board offered to see that the complainants were given a new oral examination. We are awaiting the outcome of this development, but have not withdrawn the complaint.

MS: MP.

1. See 2/4/53, where Mitchell reported that blacks were finally admitted to the brotherhood.

2. "Full compliance with the Railway Labor Act as amended in 1950 requires that neither colored people nor white people may be parties to the exclusion of any applicant from membership under the union shop agreement at the Washington Terminal on the basis of race and, thereafter, seek the dismissal of such applicant for failure to join a segregated local [716]." Mitchell's letter to James Langsen, general chairman, Brotherhood of Railway Carmen, 2/12/53, NAACP IX: 196, DLC.

3. The plaintiffs were James P. Taylor, Howard Taylor, and Charles Blake, all of Baltimore. The lawsuit was filed against the Brotherhood of Railway and Steamship Clerks, Freight Handlers, Express and Station Employees as well as the Baltimore and Ohio Railroad Company in the U.S. district court in Washington, D.C. NAACP IX: 197, DLC. See also, among others, 11/5/51.

4. See also 11/5 and 12/31/52.

5. See press release, 10/4/52, with letter to Lovett attached, in appendix 1, this vol.; "Negroes Protest Segregation at Ft. Bliss Schools," *El Paso Herald*, 10/4/52, 1, and collection in NAACP WB-171, DLC; 11/5, 12/3, and 12/31/52; 2/4/53; Watson, *Lion in the Lobby*, 241–42.

6. See 6/5/52; in appendix 1, this vol., Mitchell's 6/9/52 statement before the committee; 12/31/52; related materials in NAACP II: A-200, DLC.

7. See, also, most immediately, 6/5/52, 4/3/53. Mitchell's letter, 9/18/52, to Robert R. Granville, executive director of the President's Committee on Government Contract Compliance, further noted that because the Norfolk yard was headquarters for various European companies cooperating with the United States in defending democracy against communism, segregation there posed the danger that "an extremely ugly international incident" could occur if "one of the colored citizens of these European countries" were humiliated while he performed his official duties there. Mitchell's letter to Granville, 9/18/52, and related materials are in NAACP WB-142, DLC.

Monthly Report, November 5, 1952

November 5, 1952

MONTHLY REPORT OF THE WASHINGTON BUREAU

SEGREGATION IN SCHOOL LOCATED ON ARMY POSTS

Last month, we reported that we have a number of complaints charging that colored school children are either segregated on Army posts or sent to separate schools in nearby communities in Virginia, Texas, and Oklahoma.[1]

The Department of Defense previously has contended that it was legally required to follow these practices of racial segregation. Senator Hubert Humphrey joined us in presenting vigorous arguments against the practices and pointing out that there is no legal requirement that segregation be followed.[2]

Now the Federal Security Agency, which administers the law that the Department of Defense says requires segregation, denies that the schools in question come under this particular law. The FSA has stated that the policy of segregation or non-segregation is entirely up to the Department of Defense. We have recently been advised officially by the Department of the Army that Secretary Lovett has referred our arguments to the Secretary of the Army for study.[3]

FHA POLICIES

On October 10, 1952, the Director of the Washington Bureau joined with Dr. Robert C. Weaver and other individuals in a meeting with Mr. Walter Greene, FHA Commissioner.

At a recent public meeting, Mr. Greene had stated that FHA would work for the building of additional open occupancy housing which would be available for qualified persons without regard to race. We discussed this FHA policy and found that, while the Commissioner had made a public statement about it, actually no practical steps had been taken to implement it. We also found that FHA had no plans to change its policy of giving insurance on housing which it knows will be for whites only. This means that, in spite of recent favorable publicity which FHA was able to obtain, actually the agency continues to be an important factor in willfully extending housing segregation.[4]

UNION SHOP IN THE WASHINGTON TERMINAL

We have continued to hold meetings with colored employees of the Washington Terminal who, under the Railway Labor Act, are now covered by a union shop agreement.

We are contending that the Brotherhood of Railway Carmen, which has jurisdiction over several hundred of these employees, cannot force them to take out memberships because it will not admit them to parent locals but, instead, requires that they join subordinate Jim-Crow locals. The deadline for submitting applications to join the union is November 15.

A few of the men have filed applications to the white local. However, in one case, the applicant was told verbally that he would not be admitted. We have advised the men to make all applications in writing and send them by registered mail.[5]

ATOMIC ENERGY COMMISSION

The Atomic Energy Commission is again on our active list with complaints from Chicago and South Carolina.[6]

In the Chicago case, a colored scientist charges that he was wrongfully dismissed by the Argonne Laboratory which is a University of Chicago project for AEC.

In the South Carolina complaint, a colored electrician alleges that he has been denied employment, although he has made frequent trips to the AEC plant site and also to the electrical unions of the AFL which have the bargaining rights.

UNITED STATES COAST GUARD

In response to NAACP requests, the United States Coast Guard has undertaken an extensive investigation of discriminatory employment practices involving several hundred individuals at Curtis Bay, Maryland.

VA JIM CROW HOSPITAL IN ST. LOUIS

Following the Washington Bureau's protest about a plan to operate a new Veterans Administration hospital in St. Louis on a segregated basis, the VA has advised us that it has not yet decided what the racial policies of the hospital will be. We assume that additional protests will cause the VA to operate this hospital on a non-segregated basis and have advised the St. Louis branch accordingly.

CIVIL SERVICE APPEALS

During the Month of October, a considerable amount of time was required for the handling of Civil Service appeals coming from Colorado and North Carolina.

In the Colorado complaint, a colored electrician charged that he was wrongfully disciplined while working in Pueblo.

In the North Carolina case, colored applicants, who were denied jobs because of race and subsequently won in their effort to prove that the Postmaster of Durham had discriminated against them, have not been hired although a year has elapsed since their victory.

We have placed this matter before the Post Office Department and have been promised corrective action.[7]

REQUESTS FOR INFORMATION

The Washington Bureau has received an unusually large number of requests for information on fair employment practice legislation. Most of these requests come from school and college students who are debating the issue.

We also received during the campaign numerous requests for copies of the mimeographed voting records prepared by the Washington Bureau on individual states.

SPEAKING ENGAGEMENTS

During the Month of October, the Director spoke at meetings in Maryland, Massachusetts, North Carolina, Rhode Island, and Virginia.

MS: MP.

1. See, most directly, 2/4, 10/6, 12/3, and 12/31/53.

2. See materials in NAACP WB-171, DLC.

3. Mitchell told the board that the FSA in effect acknowledged that the policy of segregation or nonsegregation was entirely up to DOD. The Department of the Army, as a result, told Mitchell that Secretary Lovett had referred the NAACP's arguments to the secretary of the army for study. Minutes, 11/10/52, EC. See 10/6/52 for a previous report.

4.The meeting, no doubt, was covered by Weaver in his article "Habitation with Segregation," *Crisis* 59 (June-July 1952), 347–53, 402–3. This article was an address that Weaver originally gave at the National Conference on Discrimination in Housing on May 20, 1952.

5. See, most immediately, 10/6/52 and 2/4/53, where Mitchell reported that blacks were finally admitted to the Brotherhood of Railroad Carmen. See also 5/10/50 for his initial attempts to amend the Railway Labor Act; in appendix 1, this vol., 6/7/50.

6. See, among others, 12/28/51.

7. For historical background on the problem, see the section on the Post Office Department in the headnote on Relationships with Federal Agencies, vol. I.

Monthly Report, December 3, 1952

December 3, 1952

MONTHLY REPORT OF THE WASHINGTON BUREAU

ANTI-FILIBUSTER MEETINGS

During the month, the Director has participated in two meetings in Washington on anti-filibuster strategy in the 83rd Congress. Several Senators who must give leadership in this effort have promised to discuss plans for action on or about December 15 when they return to Washington.[1]

CONGRESS COMMITTEE CHAIRMEN

We have asked each prospective chairman of committees, handling civil rights bills, in the 83rd Congress to meet with the Director to discuss plans for hearings, etc. Absence from the city by Senators and Representatives is a handicap. However, it appears that these discussions will be given top place on their agenda's when they return.

THE SECRETARY OF INTERIOR

Because of the extensive progress against segregation in Washington made by the Department of the Interior under Secretary Oscar Chapman and others, we are urging the West Coast Branches to talk with the Secretary-designate, Governor Douglas McKay of Oregon. We have asked them to seek a firm commitment that present integration in swimming pools, golf courses, and other activities under Interior's control be continued and expanded.[2]

U.S. STEEL MEETING

The Director joined with the Secretary, Dr. Robert C. Weaver, and Mrs. Constance Motley in a meeting with Mr. E. E. Moore and other U.S. Steel executives on November 17. We discussed employment and housing in the area of the new steel plant that the company is building in Bucks County, Pennsylvania. The Steel Company apparently will follow a good course of no discrimination in employment. The company officials were more cautious on housing, but they appeared very receptive to suggestions. Mr. Moore will replace Ben Fairless as President of U.S. Steel in January.[3]

STATUS OF WASHINGTON TERMINAL DISPUTE

We have requested Secretary of Labor, Maurice Tobin, to aid in working out an "honorable way to avoid trouble" at the Washington Terminal where the Brotherhood of Railway Carmen is trying to force hundreds of colored car cleaners, repairmen, crew workers, and others into a Jim-Crow union under a union shop agreement. The Labor Department is at present studying the legal aspects of our request. Meanwhile, it appears that the union has stepped up a kind of war of nerves to force colored employees to join the separate local. So far, most are standing firm and refusing to join.[4]

APPEAL VICTORIES

Two significant decisions on administrative appeals handled by the Washington Bureau were made this month. Both involve substantial financial questions.

1. After two years of hearings and correspondence, the Civil Service Commission has ruled favorably for colored employees at Kelly Air Base, Texas, who contended that their pay was unlawfully reduced by an Air Force personnel action changing them from classified employees to workers subject to local wage rate patterns.[5]

   The Washington Bureau handled the matter on behalf of the San Antonio Branch and others in Texas. At the hearings, it developed that the problem was almost south-wide in scope and involved a number of military establishments. The legal representatives of the Army and Air Force opposed our claim. The Navy Department, also, sent an observer. The favorable ruling of the Civil Service Commission means that hundreds of employees affected by the action may now seek the pay they lost because of reclassification.

2. We joined with the Red Cross in appealing a decision of the Veterans Administration in Maryland which held that a veteran who was seeking training as a bricklayer could not receive payments under the G.I. Bill of Rights because his formal application for training was not received prior to the applicable delimiting date, which in his case was August 28, 1951.

   Evidence obtained in the appeal showed that on August 2, 1951, the veteran had clearly, although informally, told the VA that he intended to enter the training course. The Board of Veterans Appeals made the training benefits retroactive to August 2, 1951.

SEGREGATION IN SCHOOLS ON MILITARY POSTS

Mrs. Anna Rosenberg, Assistant Secretary of Defense, has agreed to meet with the NAACP on the question of ending segregation of school children on military posts. Senator Hubert Humphrey is joining us at this meeting. Two scheduled dates were changed because of conflicts in the Rosenberg and Humphrey commitments. However, it is expected the meeting will take place within two weeks.[6]

ATLANTA BUFFER HOUSING PROJECT

Mr. C. L. Harper, President of our Atlanta Branch, has advised that the City of Atlanta is planning to build a public housing project which will be for white persons. The project is to be placed in a strategic location for the purpose of halting the expansion of colored home owners into certain white neighborhoods, according to Mr. Harper.

We have registered a protest against the project and have asked Mr. Harper for additional information. Atlanta daily papers report that some colored people have approved the idea of building the project.[7]

STATE DEPARTMENT MEETING

This month, the Director met with Deputy Under-Secretary of State, Carlisle Humelsine. He gave assurance of a progress report on integration in the State Department. He also promised that the present project aimed at increasing the number of qualified colored persons in the Department will not be terminated by the present administration.[8]

TRI-STATE FEPC MEETING

The Director joined with Mr. Gloster Current, Director of Branches, in a tri-state meeting for FEPC legislation in Detroit on November 30. The meeting was for the purpose of making plans for State FEPC legislation in Michigan, Ohio, and Illinois.[9]

MS: NAACP II: A-656, DLC.

1. The meeting was held December 12, 1952, in the office of the Washington bureau and, subsequently, in Senator Lehman's office. Mitchell told Walter White that Bill Welch in Lehman's office said the senator "had definitely decided that he would make a motion to change the rules on the opening day" of the Senate. He said Lehman would also contend that the Senate "is a new rather than a continuing body, and, therefore, privileged to adopt a new set of rules." It was expected, Mitchell said, that Senators Irving Ives, Paul Douglas, and Hubert Humphrey would support him. Another meeting, scheduled for December 30, 1952, was to be a strategy session, Mitchell said. Mitchell's letter to White, 12/22/52, NAACP WB-111, DLC.

2. Douglas McKay was appointed secretary of the interior on January 21, 1953. See www.nndb.com/people/040/000116689/. See, among others, 12/28/51; "Progress Highlights in Race Relations in the Decade—1942–1952," by E. B. Henderson, president, the Washington Fellowship, in NAACP II: A-363, DLC; Indritz, "Racism in the Nation's Capital," *Crisis* 59 (October 18, 1952): 355–57.

3. See follow-up at 10/6/53.

4. Mitchell's letter to Maurice Tobin, 11/25/52. Tobin responded that it would appear the matter was one that came before the National Mediation Board, which was primarily responsible for administering the Railway Labor Act. Mitchell's letter to Tobin, 11/25/52, and Tobin's response, 12/5/52. So Mitchell appealed to Leverett Edwards, chair of the National Mediation Board, for help in resolving the dispute. Approximately three hundred African American employees within the jurisdiction of the Brotherhood of Railway Carmen flatly refused to join the segregated Local 716, he said. When some of them sought loans from a credit union at the Washington Terminal, they were required to show receipts for joining fees or dues from the Brotherhood of Railway Carmen, which, of course, they did not have. They also charged that a top union official was advising them that they were required to join the Brotherhood of Railway Carmen.

Mitchell recalled that:

> during the hearings on the Railway Labor Act amendment providing for union shop in the industry, Mr. George M. Harrison, Grand President of the Brotherhood of Railway Clerks, appeared as a representative of all Railway Unions and stated that "it would be indefensible for the union to come in here and ask Congress to permit the union to negotiate an agreement to compel everybody to join the union that holds the contract and then for the union to say, 'No, we won't take you in because you are a colored fellow,' and so forth, and he would therefore lose his job. We are not here asking for that. To the contrary, we say that kind of union-shop agreement cannot be made. . . ." This statement appears on page 23 of the Hearings before the Subcommittee of the Committee on Labor and Public Welfare, 81st Congress, Second Session, May 1 to May 23, 1950.

But the National Mediation Board said it had no "jurisdiction to oversee or otherwise control the operation of collective bargaining contracts negotiated in accordance with the Railway Labor Act." Mitchell's letter to Leverett Edwards, 12/12/52; response of E. C. Thompson, secretary, National Mediation Board, to Mitchell, 12/18/52, NAACP IX: 192, DLC. See also, among others, 10/6/52, 2/4 and 10/6/53.

5. See 11/3/50 for initiation of this case and 2/6/52 for the original, favorable ruling of the Civil Service Commission.

6. This meeting was the result of Hubert Humphrey's letter of October 16, 1952, to Rosenberg that Mitchell had drafted and sent to Max M. Kampelman, legislative counsel to Humphrey, with the request that the senator send it to the assistant secretary of defense. Humphrey's letter, as edited and sent, referred to Rosenberg's of June 16, 1952, to the senator, in which she said that regulations at Fort Bliss, Texas, that required black children to attend segregated schools off the post while white children attended schools on the post were based on PL 874, 81st Congress. The NAACP Washington bureau, Humphrey said, had advised him that "the practices of segregation now include Fort Sam Houston, Texas, Fort Sill, Oklahoma, and Fort Belvoir, Virginia, among others."

Rosenberg's letter to him, Humphrey stated, cited "specifically, Section 7(a) of this Law, which provides that there shall be no interference by Federal department, agencies, officers, or employees with the direction, supervision, control of personnel, curriculum, or program of instruction of any school or school system of any local or state educational agency." That provision, Humphrey said, "was included for the purpose of safeguarding standards of curriculum and personnel, but not for the purpose of requiring that any military establishment enforce racial segregation in schools located on Federal property." He continued:

> Had segregation been the intent of this language, I would have objected vigorously at the time this legislation was before the Labor and Public Welfare Committee of the Senate, of which I am a member. Those who favor segregation incorporated wording subject to interpretation as favoring segregation language in a later bill passed in the first session of the 82nd Congress, but that bill, H.R. 5411, was vetoed by the President. [See 12/28/51.]
>
> You will recall that the President's memorandum of November 2, 1951, disapproving H.R. 5411, contains these specific words:
>
> "Unfortunately, the Congress has included one provision in this bill which I cannot approve. This provision would require a group of schools on Federal property which are now

operating successfully on an integrated basis to be segregated. It would do so by requiring Federal schools on military bases and other Federal property to conform to laws of the States in which such installations are located. This is a departure from the provisions of Public Laws 815 and 874, which required only that the education provided under these circumstances should be comparable to that available to other children in the State."

Thus the President has clearly stated that there is no requirement in Public Law 874 that schools on Federal property be segregated on the basis of race. In addition, I was a member of the Senate sub-committee that handled H.R. 7940, now Public Law 874, when it was before the 81st Congress. At no time did the House or the Senate include any language that would require the segregation of children by race on military posts.

Because there was "no justification in the legislative history of Public Law 874 for the policies of segregation at Fort Bliss," Humphrey therefore urged the Department of Defense to change these policies so as to permit all children without regard to race to attend schools on military posts. He stressed that this was the first time that the practices of local communities were "being extended to Federal property under the guise of compliance with Federal law." Mitchell's letter of October 9, 1952, to Kampelman and a copy of Mitchell's draft and Humphrey's edited version of October 16, 1952, along with other materials, are in NAACP II: WB-171, DLC. See also 10/6, 11/5, and 12/31/52 and, most immediately, 2/4/53.

7. See, for related activities, 2/6/52, where the NAACP charged that the chief threat to progress in eliminating ghettos came from the FHA, and 9/9/53 for a similar struggle in Birmingham, Alabama.

8. The department was also preparing a report for the NAACP to show what favorable changes in its employment policies had taken place since their discussions began. Minutes, 11/10/52, EC. See 4/5/53.

9. See the headnote on the Struggle for a Permanent FEPC, 1942–54, vol. III.

Spotlight on the Nation's Capital, December 31, 1952

[December 31, 1952]

SPOTLIGHT ON THE NATION'S CAPITAL

The Washington Bureau, under the direction of Clarence Mitchell, acts as the eyes and ears of the NAACP in the executive chambers and legislative halls of our federal government. Alert to all legislative and proposed legislation, it constantly advances the position of the Association that civil rights of minority groups must be safeguarded in any and all bills. Testimony on behalf of the NAACP is presented at countless hearings before committees and subcommittees and the Bureau works closely with executive agencies handling the administration of the laws. In this time of intense defense activity, the Bureau is increasingly active in combating discrimination in areas of activity involving defense production, the armed forces, the Veterans Administration, Atomic Energy Commission, and all other federal agencies.

THE FILIBUSTER REMAINS

As the year drew to a close, the chief weapon in the battle of the diehard obstructionists against passage of civil rights bills—the filibuster—had still not been conquered.[1]

On January 29, 1952, after hearings held at the urging of the NAACP and other organizations, the Senate Rules Committee reported out S. Res. 203, least effective of all the anti-filibuster resolutions that the group considered.[2] Introduced by Senator Wherry of Nebraska (now deceased), S. Res. 203 provides that two-thirds of the senators present and voting shall be required to invoke cloture. It also changes the voting date on the cloture petition from the "following calendar day but one" to the "fifth calendar day but one."

Senator Lehman and others offered a plan that would permit a majority of senators present and voting to limit debate after fourteen days of filibustering. Even thereafter, senators could still talk one hour each or a total of an additional 96 hours. Senators not wishing to use their time could give it to others. The Lehman proposal, S. Res. 105, also permits limitation of debate after forty-eight hours of filibustering, but only if two thirds of the Senators present and voting agree. Moreover, it would halt filibusters against rules changes.

Senator Ives also had a resolution before the rules committee. The Ives resolution requires 49 votes to halt a filibuster. As submitted to the committee the Ives proposal did not require a change in that part of the present senate rule limiting debate (Rule 22,) which permits unlimited filibuster against any proposals to change the rules. In the majority report, submitted by Senator Jenner of Indiana, the hearings were described as the most extensive of any on this subject. Senator William Benton, who served as chairman of the committee during the hearings, prepared a minority report. Senator Francis Green joined him in saying: "We favor Senate Resolution 105. This would give the Senate a means by which it could operate effectively in an emergency, where time is of the essence, and also permit it to follow a procedure to handle needed legislation other then that of urgent character where time need not be calculated in terms of hours." Other objections to S. Res. 203 were noted by Senators William C. Hendrickson and Henry Cabot Lodge. The committee report was placed on the Senate calendar but Congress adjourned without taking action on it. The Senate is therefore still operating on the rule adopted by the 81st Congress, requiring the votes of two-thirds of the Senate membership, or 64 Senators, to break a filibuster.[3]

FEPC HEARINGS

The only committee of Congress that held a hearing on civil rights bills in 1952 was the Senate Labor Committee. The NAACP worked very closely with Senator Humphrey, chairman of the subcommittee that conducted the hearings. The Executive Secretary testified for the Association.[4] During these hearings Senator Humphrey and Senator Ives developed a bill (S. 3368) which would establish an FEPC with enforcement powers. The agency carrying out the program would be called the "Equality of Opportunity in Employment Commission." This bill was reported favorably by the Senate Labor Committee and placed on the calendar.[5]

It would establish a Committee to handle fair employment problems and would cover firms engaged in interstate commerce and employing fifty or more persons. The commission could issue directives, enforceable by federal courts to halt discrimination in employment. There is also a new provision which permits, but does not require, the commission to cede jurisdiction to FEPC bodies in states with laws that the commission considers adequate.

The Congress adjourned without taking action on the bill; however, two very valuable reports were issued as a result of the hearing, one on State and Municipal Fair Employment Legislation and the other on Employment and Economic Status of Negroes in the United States.[6]

NO SPECIFIC CIVIL RIGHTS BILLS

During the 82nd Congress there were many discussions on possible civil rights action, but in each case opponents of civil rights refused to permit bills to come to the floor unless they were emasculated. Thus there was no action on specific bills on FEPC,[7] anti-lynching, anti-poll tax,[8] or anti-Jim Crow travel.[9] Bills to give Alaska and Hawaii statehood and to establish home rule in the District of Columbia were killed. Fortunately, there also died a resolution which would abolish the electoral college in presidential elections and give greater power to the South in the naming of presidential candidates.[10]

The McCarran-Walter Immigration bill passed Congress over the President's veto. This legislation is extremely complicated and contains numerous passages which discriminate against immigrants on the basis of race and nationality. However, some of those who supported this bill felt that it contained benefits for certain groups in which they were interested.[11]

COX COMMITTEE

Using his power on the Rules Committee, the late Congressman Cox of Georgia succeeded in getting a resolution passed on April 4th, providing for an investigation of foundations and organizations to determine whether they are "stirring up class and race distinction throughout the South." The vote was 194 to 158.[12] This committee got $75,000 with which to operate and held hearings which produced nothing particularly new on foundations and charitable organizations. Representative Brooks Hays of Arkansas succeeded to the chairmanship of the committee upon the death of Mr. Cox.[13]

The Executive Secretary and the Director of the Washington Bureau sought inclusion of language in the Mutual Security Bill which would assure dependent overseas territories of Point IV assistance in public health, industrial production, economic development and agriculture. The NAACP supported an amendment covering Western Hemisphere countries that was adopted. The net effect of these changes in the law is more direct assistance to colonies in becoming self-sufficient. The Director and the Executive Secretary discussed the problem at considerable length with Congressman Vorys of Ohio before he inserted these changes.[14]

UNION SHOP AGREEMENTS IN THE RAILWAY INDUSTRY

When the Railway Labor Act was amended to permit union shop agreements in the industry, the Washington Bureau asked that adequate safeguards be included against discrimination by unions that deny membership to Negroes on the basis of race or shunt them into Jim Crow unions.

Congress included some language to this effect, although it was not as strong as that recommended by the NAACP. The first test of the effectiveness of this language came in Baltimore, Md., when employees of the Baltimore and Ohio Railroad refused to join a Jim Crow local of the Brotherhood of Railway Clerks. When the matter was taken into court by the Baltimore Branch, union officials promised under oath that Negroes would not be required to join a separate local as a condition of remaining on the job. The employer also said that none of the Negro employees would be dismissed because they refused to join a Jim Crow local. The plaintiffs in the case were denied membership in the white local, but no effort has been made to dismiss them. Two other Negroes were admitted to the white local but "old guard" employees have continued to maintain the Jim Crow local.

At the end of the year a similar case involving Negro employees of the Washington Terminal and the Brotherhood of Railway Carmen, the recognized union, was pending. Negro employees refused to join the union's Jim Crow auxiliary and sought the aid of the Washington Bureau in resisting discharge by the Terminal.[15]

VOTING RECORDS

To justify its position as the Association's eyes and ears in Washington, the Bureau carefully checks the records of all representative and senators. Sometimes in an election year the cry of partisanship is raised by those who have bad records or by their selfish supporters. However, the favorable comments outnumber the unfavorable.

This year the Bureau prepared narrative records for each state, including each man's record sine 1948. Also included was information on sponsorship of good or bad legislation. Compilation of these records was done largely by William Pryor, assistant to the director. In some instances the record cause senators and representatives to make pledges clarifying previously vague positions on civil rights questions.

The Director found these records useful in visits to various states during the election campaign. The records also played an important part in the register and vote campaign.[16]

THE TRANSITION PERIOD

When a new President moves into the White House many valuable programs get lost or delayed because of uncertainties surrounding their future. The Executive Secretary and board members met with General Eisenhower in November for top level commitments on civil rights. As a follow-up the Director of the Washington Bureau submitted a memorandum to Senator Lodge for consideration by President-elect Eisenhower.[17] Senator Lodge at that time was serving in a liaison capacity between General Eisenhower and the executive agencies of government.

The memorandum asked:

1. That the new administration give early assurance that the functions of the Fair Employment Board established in the U. S. Civil Service Commission by Executive Order No. 9980 will be continued and fully implemented to prevent discrimination in federal employment.
2. That the Committee on Government Contract Compliance be continued and strengthened. This committee, set up by Executive Order No. 10,308, was established to obtain compliance with the non-discrimination clause in all government contracts. Until a Federal FEPC is established by law, this group will fill an important place in assuring minority groups of fair treatment by employers holding government contracts.[18]

   The NAACP gave the leadership to the movement which resulted in the setting up of the Fair Employment Board[19] and the Contract Compliance Committee.[20] An NAACP complaint resulted in a board decision establishing the principles that appointing officers must be able to prove that all appointments made in accordance with the Civil Service "rule of three" are made solely on the basis of merit and fitness and that the appointment of members of minority groups on a quota or percentage basis is not in accordance with selection on the basis of merit and fitness.
3. That segregation in schools maintained on military posts for the children of military personnel be halted and that the Navy policy of allowing local commanders to establish segregation facilities for civilian workers in shore establishments be rescinded.[21]
4. That the policy of the Housing and Home Finance Agency of giving federal assistance to segregated private and public housing be stopped by executive action, to bring federal policies in line with decisions of the U. S. Supreme Court.
5. That the U. S. Department of State continue the employment of a consultant to help identify and eliminate the factors that have prevented the employment and upgrading of qualified Negroes and members of other minority groups.[22]

OTHER ACTIVITIES

Other activities of the Washington Bureau included the handling of problems with the Atomic Energy Commission,[23] the Veterans Administration,[24] discrimination in certain private companies,[25] and segregation in airports.[26]

The Director visited approximately twenty states during the year for speaking engagements or other Association business. He continued a weekly newspaper column for the Washington edition of the Afro-American and contributed articles to The *Crisis* and the *Nation* magazines.

MS: NAACP "Annual Report," 1952, 15–20.

1. See the headnote on the NAACP and the Filibuster, vol. III.

2. 10/2/51, *Hearings*, 34–63.

3. In preparation for another attempt to change the filibuster rule on the opening day of Congress in January 1953, Mitchell and Walter White held three meetings with a number of senators during the previous month to develop strategy, but those attempts, too, failed. Mitchell letter on the meetings to White, 12/22/52, and NAACP Washington bureau telegram to a group of NAACP leaders, 12/31/52, stating that Senators Ives and Lehman would make a bipartisan effort to end filibusters when Congress opened on January 2, 1953, and urging them to organize support, both of which are in NAACP WB-111, DLC. See also 6/15/53 for Mitchell's report on the failure of the attempts in January.

4. White, with Mitchell, 4/17/52, *Hearings*, 141–61. See also 2/4/53.

5. "The only Congressional action on civil rights in 1952 was approval by Senate committees of FEPC legislation and of a proposal to relax the Senate cloture rule. Neither was debated on the floor." *Congress and the Nation*, 1619. *Congressional Quarterly Weekly Report*, 4/11/52, 351; 4/18/52, 371; 4/25/52, 394; 5/9/52, 455; 7/5/52, 710.

6. The introductory note to the employment and economic status report explained that the material was culled from a wide variety of sources to highlight the major facts. Two general facts seemed to emerge, it noted. The first was that in almost every significant economic and social characteristic that could be measured—including length of life, education, employment, and income—African Americans, as a whole, were less well off than white citizens. The second was that in regard to almost every characteristic, the differences between the two groups had narrowed in recent years. Employment and Economic Status of Negroes in the United States, Staff Report to the Subcommittee on Labor and Labor-Management Relations of the Committee on Labor and Public Welfare, U.S. Senate, 82nd Congress, 2nd sess., 2/18/53.

For the second report, the introductory note explained that this and others that would be issued were designed to contribute to the understanding of the problems that impelled the subcommittee and the Committee on Labor and Public Welfare to recommend for favorable action the federal equal opportunity for employment bill and to promote reasoned and informed attitudes toward that measure. State and Municipal Fair Employment Legislation, Staff Report to the the Subcommittee on Labor and Labor-Management Relations of the Committee on Labor and Public Welfare, U.S. Senate, 82nd Congress, 2nd sess., 2/20/53. The chair of the Subcommittee on Labor and Labor-Management Relations was Hubert H. Humphrey.

Mitchell's optimism that prospects for an early consideration of FEPC legislation in the 83rd Congress appeared "very bright" was based on his conversations with senators and representatives and a pledge from Sen. Robert A. Taft that he was contemplating holding hearings on the Taft-Hartley law as soon as the Senate was organized; after that, he knew of nothing that would take priority over FEPC. NAACP WB press release, 12/10/52, NAACP WB-111, DLC. See also the headnote on the Struggle for a Permanent FEPC, 1942–54, vol. III.

7. See the headnote on the Struggle for a Permanent FEPC, 1942–54, vol. III.

8. See the headnote on the Struggle to Abolish the Poll Tax, vol. III.

9. See the headnote on the Struggle to End Jim Crow Travel, vol. III.

10. See, among others, 12/28/51; in appendix 1, this vol., 2/28/50.

11. See, most immediately, 6/5/52; in appendix 1, this vol., 5/28, 6/3, and 9/30/52; *New York Times*, 1/11/53, 4E.

12. See 5/8 and 6/5/52 for earlier developments.

13. See, among others, 6/5/52; in appendix 1, this vol., 7/31/52.

14. Congress passed the Mutual Security Act of 1952 on May 28, 1952. *Congressional Quarterly Weekly Report*, 5/30/52, 546. Making a strong argument for the adoption of the Point IV program, White said:

> With the exception of the amendment that benefits Western Hemisphere colonial countries, most areas under the rule of the major powers can receive assistance from the United States only in connection with plans for defense of the North Atlantic Area.
>
> This means that the colonial people in Africa and Asia come in solely as fifth wheels to the European war machine.
>
> The colonial people of the world are determined to have freedom and they may become the enemies of anyone who even appears to stand between them and liberty. The Association's amendments would help to show clearly that the United States does not intend to have its foreign aid program used to support the colonial system. (Report of the Secretary for May 1952, 6/9/52, EC)

15. See, among others, 10/6, 11/5, and 12/3/52, 2/4/53; in appendix 1, this vol., 6/7/50; 5/18/50, *Hearings*, 242–309; 6/7/50, *Hearings*, 242–309.

16. Mitchell explained the importance of the summary of the voting records on representatives and senators to the board. He said when he presented it at a one-day statewide conference in North Carolina, most delegates at first did not realize how bad the records of their congresspeople were. "But when the district representatives were permitted to stand up and speak about the voting records of their representatives, it became clear to the people how bad the situation was." Minutes, 4/14/52, EC. See also 5/8/52.

17. Mitchell letter to Henry Cabot Lodge Jr., 12/4/52, listing the matters they discussed during their meeting that day, NAACP II: A-200, DLC. For details of the items Mitchell discussed with Lodge and related developments, see Watson, *Lion in the Lobby*, 215.

18. In another letter to Dwight Palmer, chair of the President's Committee on Government Contract Compliance, on December 4, 1952, Mitchell informed him of his meeting with Lodge that day, specifically noting their discussion of "Item 2," which urged strengthening of the committee and stressed the need to see that it did "not go out of business by default." Mitchell told Palmer that Lodge assured him of General Eisenhower's interest in the committee and that his administration wished to give "considerable attention" to the problems it was considering. Mitchell letter to Palmer, 12/4/52, NAACP II: A-208, DLC.

19. See 8/31/48 and, subsequently, related documents.

20. See 12/5/51 for report on EO 10308 creating the President's Committee on Government Contract Compliance, related texts throughout, and Mitchell's statement, 6/9/52 in appendix 1, this vol.

21. See 10/6, 11/5, and 12/3/52 and, most immediately, 2/4/53.

22. See 4/3, 5/4, 6/1, and 9/9/53.

23. One problem involved discrimination in employment by the du Pont Company at Savannah River and segregation in the schools of Oak Ridge, about which he complained to the AEC. Gordon Dean, AEC chair, told Mitchell that regarding the reported assertion by a representative of the du Pont Company that it was not bound by the nondiscrimination clause, he had instructed the company's Savannah River office to make an investigation of the matter and to provide an early report.

Regarding the employment of African American scientists by the company, it was the AEC's understanding the du Pont had offered technical positions to four blacks and that one of them had accepted a position and was scheduled to report for work in the summer.

Regarding segregated schools at Oak Ridge, the AEC had "had this matter under study for some time in view of the cases before the Supreme Court." Dean's letter to Mitchell, 4/10/53, NAACP WB-171, DLC.

24. See, among others, 8/31 and 12/28/51.

25. Among the private companies in which Mitchell was consistently seeking to end employment discrimination were telephone and railroad companies.

26. See 2/6/52.

Monthly Report, February 4, 1953

February 4, 1953

MONTHLY REPORT OF THE WASHINGTON BUREAU

CIVIL RIGHTS LEGISLATION INTRODUCED

In the Senate, the Ives-Humphrey FEPC Bill, S. 692, has been introduced and contains enforcement powers. In keeping with previous discussions between themselves and other persons, Senators Ives and Humphrey have not called this bill an FEPC proposal. Instead, it is titled "Federal Equality of Opportunity in Employment Act."[1]

Senator Dirksen has introduced a bill, S. 1, which would provide for investigation of discrimination in employment and other civil rights problems. It contains no enforcement powers, although it sets up a commission to make inquiries on discrimination. The commission would have subpoena powers.[2]

Other civil rights and related measures include three proposals to change Rule 22, an Anti-Lynching Bill, Anti-Poll Tax Bill, Anti-Jim Crow Travel Bill, a bill strengthening and expanding civil rights functions for the Department of Justice, a proposal to approve and strengthen Federal civil rights statutes, an anti-peonage bill, a bill to protect servicemen from mistreatment by civilians in the United States, a proposal to establish a human rights commission, a bill to outlaw segregation in the District of Columbia, and the Alaska and Hawaii Statehood Bills.[3]

As has been reported in the press, southern Senators have introduced a Constitutional Amendment to outlaw the Poll Tax.[4]

In the House, the civil rights proposals are very numerous. There are five proposed FEPC Bills with enforcement powers, five Anti-Lynching Bills, six Anti-Poll Tax Bills, three anti-discrimination proposals, three bills outlawing segregation in the Armed Services, two designed to strengthen the Federal civil rights statutes, two Anti-Jim Crow Travel Bills, two proposals to establish a Federal human rights commission, one bill to outlaw segregation in the District of Columbia, one anti-peonage bill, one proposal to strengthen the civil rights functions of the Department of Justice, a bill forbidding Federal aid to national guards which discriminate on the basis of race, a bill forbidding discrimination in administration of Federal funds, a bill for fair education practices and a bill for fair housing practices.[5]

LABOR LEGISLATION

We have had a number of discussions with Senators and Congressmen about proposed amendments to the Taft-Hartley Law. Chairman McConnell of the House Committee has discussed the problem at length and has agreed that the Association's testimony will be heard in March.[6] We have requested the advice of the legal staff on language which would outlaw segregation in unions. In this connection, it is interesting to note that the language used in the Railway Labor Act, together with supplemental statements in the Committee Reports on this legislation, has brought about the admission of colored persons to Local 364 of the Brotherhood of Railway Carmen at the Washington Terminal.[7]

We have mentioned this problem in previous reports.[8] However, in a formal hearing on January 28, where William T. Scott, an employee of the Washington Terminal, was threatened with dismissal for failure to join the Brotherhood under the union shop contract at the Terminal, Mr. Edward Hickey, Jr., lawyer for the Carmen, stated that on Monday, January 26, the union had decided to admit colored people into their white local. The request for dismissal of Mr. Scott was withdrawn by the union when he offered his membership and it was accepted for the formerly all white local.[9] The men admitted on January 26 had applied for membership in the white local after talking with the NAACP.

Since the constitution of the Carmen provides that colored people must be members of the separate locals except where such separation is in violation of the law, Mr. Hickey stated that he was authorized by the organization to say that the international officers of the union did not desire to interpret or apply the constitution in any way which would be incompatible with any civil law.

Mr. Joseph Waddy, Washington, D. C., attorney, and the Director of the Washington Bureau had appeared on Mr. Scott's behalf to contend that the action of dismissing Mr. Scott for failure to join the Jim Crow union was a violation of the Railway Labor Act as amended in 1950 following NAACP testimony and efforts of others, including Mr. Waddy, to have safeguards included in the law.[10] We have never been satisfied with the language but it does appear that it can be used effectively against segregation.[11]

ANTI-JIM CROW TRAVEL

The Interstate and Foreign Commerce Committee headed by Representative Charles A. Wolverton invited sponsors of Anti-Jim Crow Travel legislation to testify at brief hearings on January 28.[12] Later, the committee will schedule hearings on these bills and witnesses other than Congressmen will be permitted to testify. The committee heard Congressman Adam C. Powell, Jr., on January 28.[13] Congressman William L. Dawson was also invited to testify but postponed his appearance temporarily. It will be recalled that following the November elections, we urged Congressman Wolverton and Senator Charles Tobey, Chairman of the Senate Committee, to make an early start on bills to end segregation in interstate travel.

SEGREGATION IN SCHOOLS ON FEDERAL PROPERTY

Senators Duff, Henrickson, Ives, Morse, Humphrey, and Lehman have joined us in urging that the Department of Defense conclude action designed to outlaw segregation in schools on military posts. We had discussed this matter extensively with top Defense officials of the past Administration.

After considerable discussion, the Department of Defense and the U. S. Office of Education finally admitted in writing that there were no legal barriers preventing them from admitting children of all service personnel to schools on military posts, even though such schools were run by local authorities.[14]

We made an unsuccessful effort to have an order to implement these findings sent out just before Assistant Secretary Anna Rosenberg left her post in the Department of Defense. Unfortunately, she did not do this and we have placed the matter before Dr. John Hannah who will succeed Mrs. Rosenberg.[15]

Also unresolved in the Department of Defense is the question of segregation in certain Naval establishments. It is interesting to note that Mrs. Rosenberg sought to clear up this problem but Under-Secretary Whitehair of the Navy Department did not answer her inquiries on it until January 22, two days after she had left the Pentagon. In his memorandum to Mrs. Rosenberg, Under-Secretary Whitehair said, "Although our concern over this problem is mutual, the approach of a military establishment will naturally differ from that of the officials of the NAACP. . . . A direct order from the Secretary of the Navy, no matter how forceful, would not only fail to eliminate the basic social causes of the problem but would only antagonize the opposing forces involved."

At the time Mr. Whitehair signed this communication, he was Acting Secretary of the Navy replacing Dan Kimball.[16]

MS: MP.

1. See also 6/1, 6/15, and 12/31/53, 2/28, 3/9, and 12/31/54, as well as the headnote on the Struggle for a Permanent FEPC, 1942–54, vol. III.

2. Mitchell informed the board that although Sen. Everett Dirksen had introduced a weak FEPC bill without enforcement powers, Irving Ives and Hubert Humphrey had introduced strong bills. He said he had concluded that there would be "a strong disposition to get out Sen. Dirksen's bill or some variation of it as an administration sponsored plan of action in this field." Minutes, 2/9/53, EC. A year later, at the beginning of the second session of the 83rd Congress, Dirksen offered some very important insights into his philosophy on civil rights, which presaged a dramatic confrontation with Mitchell in 1964 during the struggle over the scope of Title VII of the civil rights bill. See 2/54, where Dirksen's philosophy is noted.

3. In the recommendations on a legislative program that he prepared and gave to Walter White, Mitchell said that, in addition to seeking hearings on the various proposals to amend Senate Rule XXII, the NAACP should seek hearings on FEPC legislation. Mitchell memorandum, 2/6/53, to White, MP. See also 3/3 and 5/4/53.

4. For more detail on some of these bills, see a summary of them in NAACP WB-111, DLC.

5. In a comprehensive letter to senators that covered the proposals in this paragraph, Mitchell urged them to take action on civil rights legislation. The "positive and effective civil rights program" the NAACP was advocating, he explained, was provided in the statement he authored entitled "These Are the Issues," which was published in the *Crisis* in October 1952. Furthermore, the Senate Labor Committee's report, "Employment and Economic Status of the Negro in the United States," presented a "compelling argument on the need for action." The committee reported that although the annual income of African Americans had risen from $364 in 1939 to $1,295 in 1950, the income of whites had risen from $956 to $2,481 over the same period. He explained further that whenever the federal government considered social legislation, such as laws regarding federal aid to education, housing, or affecting the armed services, the civil rights question arose because those programs were frequently marred by segregation. Further, segregation affected not only blacks living in the South but also blacks and whites from the North who, as civilians, were often sent below the Mason-Dixon Line to perform "duties vital to the national defense." Mitchell's letter, 1/9/53, NAACP II: A-183, DLC.

At the same time, Mitchell called Walter White's attention to a page-one *Washington Post* story that said southerners were backing a compromise civil rights bill (S. 535) that their friend Sen. Hubert Humphrey had introduced as a "starter" measure in the desperate hope of getting some action on such legislation in Congress. Mitchell explained that Humphrey had said he did not mean to imply in any way that his bill would "take the place of FEPC legislation." Mitchell acknowledged that he himself had not taken a position on such legislation, and he asked White for his opinion. Mitchell's letter, 1/26/53, to White, and *Washington Post* article, 1/26/53, in NAACP II: A-185, DLC.

6. More specifically, the NAACP amendment sought to prevent any employees from being excluded from membership or placed in a separate union or denied adequate representation solely because of race, religion, or national origin. 3/31/53, *Hearings*, 2055–78. See also 3/3, 4/3, 4/30, 5/4, and 6/1/53, as well as the headnote on the NAACP, the Taft-Hartley Act, and the National Labor Relations Board, vol. III.

7. No court decisions were rendered in either the B & O or the Washington Terminal cases because the unions themselves ended segregation. Mitchell's letter to Elias G. Burnett, 4/7/53, NAACP IX: 197, DLC.

8. See 11/5, 12/3, and 12/31/52.

9. See 5/31/50, where Mitchell reported that a strong effort had been made to amend the act to permit establishment of the union shop and the dues checkoff system in the industry.

10. See 11/5/51; 10/6/52; in appendix 1, this vol., 6/7/50.

11. See also 5/31, 7/17, 8/31, and 12/21/50; 6/7/50, *Hearings*, 285–302. The testimony of Mitchell's former FEPC colleague, Theodore E. Brown, representing the International Brotherhood of Sleeping Car Porters, precedes the statement (pp. 273–85). See also 5/18/50, *Hearings*, 242–309.

12. See, most recently, 12/31/52, Mitchell's "Recommendations on Legislative Program"; Alexander, "Recent Trends in the Law of Racial Segregation"; and the headnote on the Struggle to End Jim Crow Travel, vol. III.

13. No published record of Powell's closed-session testimony of 1/28/53 on Jim Crow travel was found, but see his public testimony at 5/13/54, *Hearings*, 55; see also Mitchell, 5/13/54, *Hearings*, 39.

14. This was a direct continuation of the efforts Mitchell reported at 12/4/52. In a letter of January 10, 1953, Rosenberg advised Earl J. McGrath, commissioner of education, that

> the fact that segregation has been practiced in schools which are on military installations has been a matter of concern to the Department of Defense.... I know that, in exercising your discretion under this Act, you may wish to take this important matter into your consideration and I would appreciate your letting me know whether you consider it proper that children be required to attend a segregated school on a Federal installation under a program financed to a considerable degree by Federal money. It is our feeling that this practice is unsatisfactory and is violative not only of the policy of the Department of Defense but also contravenes the policy set forth by the President.

On January 15, 1953, McGrath replied:

> If it is the policy of the Department of Defense not to permit segregated education on any property within its control, whether that education be local school agencies under Section 3 (Public Law 874) or by the Commissioner of Education operating under Section 6 (Public Law 874), this agency would, of course, be guided by such a policy.... In any case in which the local

educational agency is not able to provide education on an integrated basis, the Commissioner would then be under the necessity of making other arrangements for education of such children.

From these exchanges, Mitchell told John A. Hannah, it was clear that there remained "only the necessity of taking the mechanical action needed to end racial segregation in all schools on military posts." Mitchell's letter to Hannah, 1/21/53, and other materials are in NAACP WB-171, DLC, and in OF 142 A 4 (1), DDEL. See also 12/31/52, 2/4, 4/3, 5/4, 6/15, 10/6, and 12/7/53, 2/17/54.

15. Roger W. Jones, assistant director for legislative reference, however, showed another possible reason why Rosenberg did not act. Unlike McGrath with his obfuscatory reasoning, he flatly concluded that under PL 874, "schools located on non-Federal property and operated by State and local authorities are segregated or non-segregated as the State law prescribes. No authority exists to require such schools to be non-segregated." Regarding schools located on federal property and operated by federal agencies, he said, existing law provided for administrative discretion as to whether they should be segregated. Moreover, the law, contained discretion as to whether locally operated schools on federal property should be segregated. The policy then was that they were segregated or nonsegregated depending on state laws for regular state and local schools. Roger W. Jones memorandum for Mr. Shanley, on "Segregation Issues Involved in Temporary Extension of Public Law 874," 81st Congress, OF 142 A 4 (1), DDEL. See, next, 4/3 and 11/4/53.

16. Mitchell pressed this concern by telling Robert B. Anderson, secretary of the Department of the Navy, that the segregation at the yards in Norfolk, Virginia, and Charleston, South Carolina, was approved by Secretary Francis P. Whitehair in a memorandum of January 22, 1953, to Rosenberg. Since Rosenberg retired on January 20, Mitchell said, there had been no response to the memorandum, so the segregation had become official navy policy. As Anderson knew, Mitchell stated, President Eisenhower had strongly repudiated "this kind of injustice in his press conference on March 19." He therefore asked that all racial segregation be ended at the navy yards and that "a general policy statement be issued by the Navy Department ending racial segregation wherever it existed in naval establishments."

Mitchell next reminded Hannah that although the president had said "forthrightly that he was opposed to racial segregation where federal funds [were spent]," the secretary of the navy had revealed that the chief executive's wishes were not being implemented at the Norfolk and Charleston navy yards. Mitchell followed up this complaint with a letter to Maxwell Rabb, assistant to Governor Adams at the White House, in which he said he had learned that Marvin J. Ottllie, in the Office of Industrial Relations in the Navy Department, was the "real author of the various Navy communications endorsing segregation at these yards." He therefore urged Rabb to "act to see that the answer to this letter clearly supports a policy of no segregation in all Navy establishments, including the yards at Charleston and Norfolk." Mitchell's letters to Anderson, 3/30/53, Hannah, 5/4/53, and Rabb, 5/28/53, and other related materials are in NAACP WB-142, DLC. See 11/2/53 for the successful results of this struggle.

Monthly Report, March 3, 1953

March 3, 1953

MONTHLY REPORT OF THE WASHINGTON BUREAU

TAFT-HARTLEY AMENDMENTS

In preparation for committee consideration of NAACP amendments to the Taft-Hartley Act we have had conferences with committee members in the House and Senate. Senator Alexander Smith (R-N.J.) who is chairman of the Senate Labor Committee arranged a meeting with the committee counsel to discuss NAACP proposals.

The proposals we have discussed would have the effect of ending segregation in labor unions that make use of the National Labor-Management Relations Act in collective bargaining. This, of course, would include every major union outside of the jurisdiction of the Railway Labor Act.

George Weaver and Roy Reuther of the CIO have been furnished copies of the NAACP amendments. They have agreed to study them and we hope that they will get full CIO backing for them.[1]

The Taft-Hartley legislation is the first major field in which there will be a chance to establish the principle of non-segregation in the 83rd Congress. Hence, it is important that the amendments be given strong support.[2]

JIM CROW TRAVEL

Mr. William Pryor of the Washington Bureau has made an excellent compilation of segregation laws for use in the anti-jim crow travel hearings.

The extent and vicious implications of these laws challenge any belief that segregation in inter-state travel is a thing of the past. It is still possible for a railroad conductor in South Carolina to put a colored man off the train for refusing to obey the jim crow law, pursue him if he runs and take him to jail.[3]

A very excellent study has been released by Fisk University. This study shows what happens to passengers traveling on certain crack trains as well as on ordinary accommodations. In one or two instances the study contains information that has been changed by circumstances (e.g. it apparently assumes that the Maryland Intra-State jim crow travel law is still in effect) but it is a very useful document.[4]

HOUSING APPOINTMENT

The appointment of ex-Congressman Albert M. Cole as administrator of the Housing and Home Finance Agency apparently is a signal that the Administration intends to make an important shift in National Housing Policies. The director of the Washington Bureau testified on the Cole appointment. We stressed the importance of finding out whether Mr. Cole intended to junk the public housing program and also whether he would, as administrator, oppose present practices and policies of segregation in HHFA.[5]

Senator Ives (R-N.Y.) gave valuable support on these matters, but Mr. Cole did not make a firm commitment that the public housing program would not be altered considerably.[6] It is not extravagant to say that his testimony could even be interpreted to mean that the program may be abandoned. On segregation he stated that he was personally opposed to it, but he surrounded his personal views with enough qualifications to leave the door wide open for continued segregation.[7]

JUSTICE APPOINTMENT

At the request of the Texas branches we have asked that the Justice Department hold up the appointment of John Lee Smith as a U.S. attorney in that state. We are awaiting information from Texas on the evidence that warrants opposition to this appointment.

CIVIL DEFENSE APPOINTMENT

Appointment and confirmation of ex-Governor Val Peterson as head of Civil Defense settles a question raised by the Columbus Branch of the NAACP. The branch feared that this post would go to an individual from Columbus who had a distinct anti-minority group bias. We discussed this with members of the Ohio delegation in Congress who seemed to know that the post would go to Peterson.

MICHIGAN STATE FEPC LAW

The director of the Washington Bureau had the good fortune to be in Lansing, Michigan at the time of the NAACP led mobilization for a state FEPC law. Bishop George W. Baber of the A.M.E. Church and Mr. Edward Turner, president of the Michigan State Conference of NAACP Branches, deserve great credit for their work in this matter. Eight hundred persons came to Lansing to lobby for FEPC. They made a wonderful impression and showed the effectiveness of the Association in Michigan. The groups co-operating on this made an impressive list. There seems to be a good chance that a law will pass

DR. A. POWELL DAVIES

The pastor of All Souls Unitarian Church, Dr. A. Powell Davies, created a stir of conscience in Washington by announcing that he would not knowingly eat in a Washington Restaurant that refused service to colored people. We sent him a note of commendation and received a cordial reply.[8]

MS: NAACP II: A-537, DLC.

1. Both the AFL and the CIO approved the amendments. Minutes, 5/11/53, EC.

2. For the amendments, see 3/31/53, *Hearings,* 2055–78. See also the headnote on the NAACP, the Taft-Hartley Act, and the National Labor Relations Board, vol. III; for other efforts on this issue during the second session of the 83rd Congress, 2/4, 4/3, 4/30, 5/4, 6/15, 11/4, 12/31/53, and, in appendix 1, this vol., 8/10/53.

3. See the headnote on the Struggle to End Jim Crow Travel, vol. III.

4. Herman H. Long, "Segregation in Interstate Railway Coach Travel," Race Relations Department, American Missionary Association, Board of Home Missions, Congregational Christian Churches, Fisk University, a copy of which is in NAACP IX: 12, DLC.

5. 3/2/53, *Hearings,* 27–34. See also the headnote on Segregation in Federal Housing Programs, vol. III.

6. Testifying for himself, Cole said that although he was personally opposed to public housing, he would, as head of HHFA, administer the law as written. He also said he was "unqualifiedly opposed" to segregation in public housing. 3/2/53, *Hearings,* 1–26. (In addition to Mitchell, the only other person who testified against Cole's nomination was Elmer W. Henderson, director of the American Council on Human Rights. See 3/2/53, *Hearings,* 28–34.) Still, as a member of Congress, Cole voted against the Housing Act of 1949 and voted to cut PHA funds, causing the CIO to brand him "an outspoken enemy of the housing program." Another reason critics were wary of Cole's appointment was that in 1952, he voted to authorize the Cox Committee, which subsequently investigated charitable organizations and civil rights groups in the South, allegedly because they were subversive. *Congressional Quarterly Weekly Report,* 3/6/53, 289–97.

7. In conjunction with this March 3, 1953, report, the board discussed Mitchell's "Recommendations on Legislative Program," of February 6, 1953, which was attached to the agenda for its March 9 meeting. The board then voted to create the National Legislative Committee to study the memorandum in order to provide a subsequent report to the board. Minutes, 3/9/53, EC. Mitchell's 2/6/53 memorandum is also cited at 2/4 and 5/4/53.

8. See 6/15, 11/4, 12/7, and 12/31/53, 9/29, 12/6, and 12/31/54.

Monthly Report, April 3, 1953

April 3, 1953

MONTHLY REPORT OF THE WASHINGTON BUREAU

TAFT-HARTLEY TESTIMONY

The Executive Secretary and the Director of the Washington Bureau made a joint appearance before the House Labor Committee to seek anti-segregation amendments to the Taft-Hartley Act.[1]

Chairman Samuel McConnell displayed a friendly interest in the Association proposals. Congressman Powell, who is a member of the Committee, said he intended to introduce the amendments.

KEATING SUB-COMMITTEE

We have furnished the Keating Sub-committee with information on police brutality in Alabama, Maryland, and North Carolina. This Sub-committee of Congress was established to investigate whether the Department of Justice had agreements with various cities and states that prevented Federal investigation of civil rights violations. Congressman Keating, chairman, and Congressman Rogers, a ranking minority member, pledged that they would make a thorough inquiry on whether the Department had failed to act in these cases because of agreements with local police officials.[2]

PRESIDENTIAL ACTION AGAINST SCHOOL SEGREGATION

In a rapid fire development, President Eisenhower took action on the question of segregation in schools on military posts. The past action of the Bureau on this problem is so extensive that we shall not review it here.[3]

Mrs. Alice Dunnigan of the Associated Negro Press asked the President on March 19 what would be done about the matter. He said he would investigate it. At the time of the President's answer to Mrs. Dunnigan we suggested that this matter could be settled before the next White House conference.[4] We reminded White House contacts that we had given full details on how this matter could be taken care of shortly after the President took office. We had also prepared a memorandum which was sent over to the White House by Congressman Powell on March 19. Acknowledgement of receipt of the memorandum was made by Mr. Wilton B. Persons, Special Assistant to the President, on March 28, 1953.[5]

A day before his next press conference, the President announced through his press officer that all segregation in schools on military posts would be abolished. Schools operated by the military are to end segregation in September.[6] No time schedule was announced for schools on Military posts but operated by local school officials. Needless to say we must take a considerable amount of follow-up action on this, but we expect to settle the problem.[7]

The Director wishes to say a special word of commendation for Mrs. Dunnigan because she raised the question at the press conference.

MEETING WITH NEW HOUSING AND HOME FINANCE CHIEF

The Director had a meeting with Albert Cole, new head of the Housing and Home Finance Agency, concerning policies of that agency. Mr. Cole insisted that he will follow the President's announced policy of no segregation in matters supported with Federal funds. The conference was informal and Mr. Cole agreed to a more extensive meeting with NAACP officials when we will discuss policies needed to halt Federal support of segregation in housing. The NAACP views on this were set forth during hearings on Mr. Cole's nomination.[8]

GOVERNMENT CONTRACTS COMPLIANCE COMMITTEE AND FAIR EMPLOYMENT BOARD

The Executive Secretary sent to the President a request that the Government Contracts Compliance Committee and the Federal Fair Employment Board be revitalized.[9] In his press conference of April 2, the President said that he would check on the appointment of a chairman for the Government Contracts Compliance Committee. We have prepared a memorandum for the White House urging that action on the Committee be linked with action on the Fair Employment Board.[10]

NAVY SEGREGATION

We have asked the Secretary of Navy to implement the President's non-segregation policy by ending Jim-Crow facilities at the Norfolk and Charleston Navy Yards as well as in all other Naval establishments.[11]

ATOMIC ENERGY SEGREGATION

We have asked the chairman of the Atomic Energy Commission to implement the President's non-segregation policy by abolishing Jim-Crow in schools and other facilities in the government owned town of Oak Ridge, Tennessee.[12]

STATE DEPARTMENT

Donold B. Lourie, Under Secretary for Administration in the Department of State, has authorized the release of a long promised State Department report on personnel matters. This report is a significant document prepared by Dr. John A. Davis, consultant in the Department. The Director expects to follow up action on it after it has been read and discussed with our Executive Secretary.[13]

FEDERAL SECURITY ADMINISTRATION

This month, we had a constructive meeting with Mrs. Oveta Culp Hobby, the new head of the Federal Security Agency. We discussed policy matters on funds administered by FSA. Now that the agency has been given Cabinet status, we expect she will be able to give attention to questions we raised.[14]

MS: NAACP II: A-537, DLC.

1. See 3/31/53, *Hearings,* 2055–78. See also the headnote on the NAACP, the Taft-Hartley Act, and the National Labor Relations Board, vol. III, as well as 2/4, 3/3, 4/30, 5/4, and 6/1/53 for other efforts on this issue during the second session of the 83rd Congress.

2. The principal sanctions against official brutality and private racial violence were laws enacted during Reconstruction, but these were limited. *Congress and the Nation,* 1603. The NAACP was also deeply involved in police brutality problems in New York. Report of the Secretary, 3/9/53, EC.

3. On March 25, 1953, Eisenhower once more showed the power of the presidency in resolving the internal impasse over the integration of schools on army posts. He announced that, at his request, the secretary of the army had provided him with a memorandum addressing a question he had received the previous week during his news conference. The secretary of the army informed him, Eisenhower said, that "by the opening of the school term next Fall all schools operated by the Army under provisions of Section 6 of Public Law 874 will be on a completely integraged basis."

Eisenhower said further that the secretary had indicated that army commanders were surveying the question "designed to bring about agreement with local authorities for integrating the schools. If such integration is not achieved, other arrangements in these instances will be considered." Eisenhower memorandum for the secretary of defense, 3/25/53, OF 142 A 4 (1), DDEL.

See also 2/4, 5/4, 6/15, 10/6, 11/4, and 12/7/53, 2/17/54; collection in NAACP WB-171, DLC; "Ike Orders Probe of Segregated Schools at Fort Belvoir and Other Posts in South," *Washington Post,* 3/20/53; Watson, *Lion in the Lobby,* 241–45.

4. President's news conference, 3/19/53; Eisenhower, *Public Papers of the Presidents,* 108; MacGregor, *Integration of the Armed Forces,* 487–90; Watson, *Lion in the Lobby,* 236–38; excerpts of president's news conference, 3/19/53, NAACP WB-171, DLC.

5. Among this collection is a speech by Harlem representative Adam Clayton Powell Jr., in which he explained to the House that Mitchell had told him

> about a conference with some local school officials in a defense impacted area of Maryland. The conference was necessary because four colored boys had been refused admission to a trade

school which was the only institution in the city offering the particular type of training the children were seeking. The head of the school board said that separate training would be offered for the children and that a whole staff of teachers would be hired, expensive equipment would be purchased, and even a new building would be built if necessary. I am sure that I do not need to tell you who is expected to pay for that kind of waste. It is the people of Rhode Island, Massachusetts, and other states where there is no segregation in public schools who will pay for it in Federal taxes. (General File, White House Central Files, Box 910, "Segregation, 1952–53," DDEL)

6. *Washington Post*, 3/20/53.

7. See, among others, 2/4/53. Mitchell told Robert Carter, NAACP assistant special counsel, that the president's statement had "not solved the whole problem." As an example, he sent Carter a copy of his April 21, 1953, letter to John A. Hannah, assistant secretary of defense, in which he explained that despite the president's "very forthright statement on this matter," the Department of the Army had not as yet given any indication that it "actually was taking steps to end segregation in schools located on military posts, but assisted in various ways by local school authorities."

Furthermore, Mitchell told Carter, "we are running into a number of interesting problems with the Atomic Energy Commission concerning Oak Ridge. Oak Ridge is owned entirely by the Federal Government but operates a strict pattern of segregation in schools, theaters, restaurants, and other activities of the community." Mitchell's letter to Carter and related materials are in NAACP WB-171, DLC.

8. 3/2/53, *Hearings*, 27–34. See also 3/3/53.

9. White wired the president, expressing his grave concern over the inactivity of the Fair Employment Board of the Civil Service Commission and the Committee on Contract Compliance. He noted that these agencies had been dormant since the administration assumed office, "and he urged that vacancies on them be filled and that they be instructed to make the maximum effort to end discrimination in their areas of responsibility." Report of the Secretary for March 1953, 4/14/53, EC.

10. See 4/3, 5/4, and 8/21/53 for Mitchell's background on this eventually successful effort; Watson, *Lion in the Lobby*, 226–27.

11. See also, most immediately, 10/6/52 and 5/4/53; Mitchell's letter of 3/30/53 to Robert B. Anderson, secretary of the navy, and other materials on navy segregation of civilians in NAACP WB-142, DLC.

12. See 5/4/53 and materials in NAACP WB-9, DLC.

13. This report was sent to Mitchell by E. N. Montague, director of office personnel, Department of State. Letter from Montague, 3/31/53, NAACP II: 617, DLC. Regarding the appointment of Davis as a consultant on minority employment, Walter White told Montague that the work was "important not only to the progress of fair treatment at home, but also to our good name abroad." White said his observation was the result of "considerable travel to other nations of the world." White to Dean Acheson, secretary of state, 6/17/52, NAACP II: A-617, DLC. See also Minutes, 11/10/52, EC; among others, 12/31/52, 5/4, 6/1, and 9/9/53.

14. In a get-acquainted meeting with Hobby on March 12, Mitchell mentioned the NAACP's concerns over the continuing use of federal funds to support separate schools in some states and thus extend segregation there. He subsequently affirmed for her in a letter the role of the U.S. Office of Education in distributing approximately $300 million under Public Laws 815 and 874 without having any information on how this money was divided in states with racially separate schools. He stressed that even more serious was that some of this money was spent to promote and extend racial segregation on military posts. The Office of Education, he added, also had "no safeguards against racial discrimination in the use of federal funds for vocational education." Mitchell to Hobby, 3/16/53, NAACP IX: 98, DLC. But in a letter of May 18, 1953, Hobby reiterated the standard position that "schools located physically on military bases but operated by State and local authorities, are subject to the Constitution and laws of the States in which they operate." A year later, Hobby still held to this position. Hobby to Senator Hubert Humphrey, 5/18/53, NAACP WB-171, DLC. See also 4/28/54; Watson, *Lion in the Lobby*, 245.

On April 11, 1953, Hobby was sworn in as the first secretary of the new Department of Health, Education and Welfare. She became the second woman ever to hold a cabinet post. *Congressional Quarterly Weekly Report*, 4/17/53, 493.

Report on Washington, April 30, 1953

[April 30, 1953]

WASHINGTON IN 1953

The Republican Party has been in power for nearly three months. The following is a brief summary of the Washington scene as of this date:

FEPC

President Eisenhower is opposed to FEPC with enforcement powers. Also opposed are Senator Robert A. Taft, Majority Leader, and Speaker Joseph Martin of the House of Representatives.

In the Senate, FEPC Bills must be passed upon by the Labor and Public Welfare Committee. Senator Irving Ives is chairman of a subcommittee which will consider his own bill (S. 692).[1] This is a wholly acceptable proposal and hearings on it are expected to follow consideration of amendments to the Taft-Hartley Act.[2]

The FEPC Bill in the House must be considered by the Committee on Education and Labor. The chairman of this committee is Congressman Samuel K. McConnell, Jr. Like Senator Taft and Speaker Martin, Mr. McConnell opposes FEPC with enforcement powers, but is willing to have hearings on the legislation after his committee disposes of amendments to the Taft-Hartley Act.

ANTI-FILIBUSTER RESOLUTIONS

On January 2, 1953, a bi-partisan group of Senators agreed on the following strategy with regard to a rules change in the Senate, and, thereby, elimination of the filibuster as a weapon in stalling civil rights bills.[3]

Senator Clinton Anderson (D., N.M.) was to introduce a motion to consider the adoption of rules for the Senate of the 83rd Congress. If this motion had prevailed, Senator Ives was to introduce a motion to revise Rule XXII. This rule at present requires 64 votes to halt a filibuster.

The Anderson motion was defeated when Senator Taft made a motion to table it on January 7. The tabling motion won by a vote of 70 to 21. Taft was supported by 41 Republicans and 29 Democrats. Voting against Taft were 5 Republicans and 15 Democrats.

Senator Taft says that he favors a rules change, but has not yet indicated when he thinks it should be considered by the Senate.

There are 48 G.O.P. votes in the Senate and there are 25 Democrats in that body from outside the Solid South. With the vote of Senator Wayne Morse, Independent, there are 74 votes which should be for civil rights, and, therefore, capable of breaking a filibuster under the present rule. Unfortunately, experience shows that, unless the Republican leadership can use persuasive powers that have not been revealed in the past and unless the Democrats can convince certain Western and Border State members to change previous voting habits, we can count on only a total of 59 votes. This is more than enough to pass legislation but not enough to halt a filibuster under the present rule. Nevertheless, Senator Taft insists that a filibuster can be broken under the existing rule.[4]

HOUSE RULES

In the House, the chief bottleneck on constructive legislation is the Rules Committee. On January 3, by a voice vote, the House adopted its old rules, thus, continuing the power of the Rules Committee, which is now headed by Congressman Leo Allen of Illinois.

Congressman Herman Eberharter of Pennsylvania was unsuccessful in getting consideration of a resolution which would allow committee chairmen to force House consideration of legislation which their committees approve but which the Rules Committee does not clear within twenty-one days after receiving it.[5]

OTHER CIVIL RIGHTS MEASURES

In other types of legislation in the civil rights field, there are some hazards because of "working agreements" in Congress, but there is no strong opposition to them from the leaders of the Republican Party. Hence, it is entirely possible that, if the Republican leadership is convinced that it must act in the field of civil rights, it may move to pass a weak Anti-Lynching Bill, a good Anti-Jim Crow Travel Bill, an acceptable plan to reorganize and strengthen the functions of the Department of Justice in the field of civil rights, or possibly worthwhile legislation to protect members of the Armed Services against assault and violence at the hands of civilians.[6]

There is, however, a serious possibility that the leadership of the Republican Party in the House and Senate may accept a Constitutional Amendment to repeal the Poll Tax (Alabama, Arkansas, Mississippi, Texas, and Virginia still require payment of Poll Taxes) in lieu of a bona fide law ending this brake on voting in the South. It is well known, of course, that Senator Holland of Florida and other southern members of Congress consider this as a practical step in meeting civil rights demands.[7] Needless to say, it is not an acceptable step nor even a reasonable compromise on the issue of civil rights.

HAWAII STATEHOOD

The House has passed a bill to make Hawaii a state. Smothered in committee is a bill to give similar status to Alaska. The Senate may face a filibuster when the Hawaii Bill comes up, but southern members of Congress are divided on this measure. In the House, it was supported by Congressmen from Texas, Georgia, Louisiana, and other anti-civil rights areas. The vote favored statehood by 274 to 178.[8]

NON-SEGREGATION AMENDMENTS

The 83rd Congress will have ample opportunity to implement the pledge of President Eisenhower that he would do all in his power to see that the Federal Government itself does not promote racial segregation and discrimination.[9]

Our first opportunity to evaluate the Administration's plans in this field will come when the Taft-Hartley legislation, now under consideration in the House and shortly scheduled for hearings in the Senate, is reported out of the Senate and House Committees.[10]

On March 31, NAACP testimony urging inclusion of non-segregation provisions in this law to protect colored working people against forced membership in Jim Crow Unions or complete exclusion from unions that wish to remain lily-white will be presented to the House Labor Committee. We have already advised the Party leadership of our desire to have these amendments in the law.[11]

We are, also, urging that all legislation providing for Federal grants to the states include non-segregation provisions.

This month, the U.S. Office of Education announced that it had spent 315,000,000 dollars for aid to schools in Defense impacted areas of the country. In response to a request by Congressman Adam Clayton Powell, the U.S. Office of Education has advised that it has no means of determining whether this money is spent equitably in the states which require separate schools.

We already know that, under present laws, the colored people of the separate schools are cheated out of approximately 7,000,000 dollars a year in funds administered by the U.S. Department of Agriculture for use in the land grant colleges. These funds are apportioned among the states on the basis of population. The colored people are counted in the total population and, therefore, help to determine the size of the grant. After that, no check is made by any Federal Agency to determine whether colored citizens receive any part of these benefits.[12]

POSSIBLE ACTION BY EXECUTIVE BRANCH

In the field of action which may be taken by the President without approval of Congress, there are many things which may be done immediately. We have already presented suggestions to the White House and the appropriate Executive Agencies.[13] These include:

1. Abolition of the remaining segregation in the Armed Services and ending such segregation as presently exists in schools on military posts or in the various Federal establishments.
2. Ending practices of segregation in all aspects of Federal Aid to Housing whether this be through direct grants or insurance.
3. Strengthening the machinery for eliminating segregation and discrimination in the Federal Service with special emphasis on certain specific departments of government that have had notorious records of discriminating against colored applicants.
4. Appointing only those individuals to the Federal Service who will faithfully administer the laws in a non-discriminatory manner and who will act vigorously to eliminate segregation from all matters or activities under their jurisdiction. This, of course, includes the various Commissions and Boards of the District of Columbia.[14]

Special tribute is due the District of Columbia Branch, under its President Eugene Davidson, because it has pressed vigorously and persistently for action to eliminate segregation in the Nation's Capital.[15]

MS: NAACP II: H-8, DLC.

1. See 6/1/53 for report on Ives's comments about this proposed hearing. In a memorandum to White, Henry Lee Moon, director of public relations, said Mitchell had talked to the counsel of the committee and to Ives, and they both had agreed to introduce the long amendment that the WB director had submitted in his testimony at the hearings in April. Moon said Mitchell believed that although the senators on the committee were favorable, they needed some indication of support. Mitchell reported that Ives feared introduction of his amendment would precipitate a filibuster and that he had previously indicated this issue should be included in and settled by FEPC legislation. See Moon's complete memorandum and other materials in NAACP II: A-257, DLC; 4/29/53, *Hearings*, 488–97.

2. 4/29/53, *Hearings*, 2186–96. For other efforts on this issue during the first session of the 83rd Congress, see 2/4, 3/3, 4/3, 5/4, and 6/1/53. See also the headnote on the NAACP, the Taft-Hartley Act, and the National Labor Relations Board, vol. III.

3. *Congressional Quarterly Weekly Report*, 1/2/53, 11–12. See also the headnote on the NAACP and the Filibuster, vol. III.

4. The defeat in the perennial struggle to modify the Senate filibuster rule occurred despite the all-out fight waged by Walter White and Mitchell. Speaking for the fifty-three national organizations in the LCCR, White said this was "a negation of the democratic process." Taft bluntly told the delegation led by White that in his view, the Senate was a continuing body and as such was not required to adopt rules at the beginning of a new Congress, as was the House. Statement by White, 1/2/53, and NAACP press release, 1/3/53, NAACP WB-111, DLC.

Mitchell, in a "My dear Senator" letter, stressed the need to pass the NAACP's program he had advocated in his article "These Are the Issues," which appeared in the October 1952 *Crisis*. He also stressed the "compelling argument on the need for action" that was contained in the report of the Senate Labor Committee, "Employment and Economic Status of the Negro in the United States," which showed that, although the annual income of African Americans had risen from $364 in 1939 to $1,295 in 1950, the income of whites had risen from $956 to $2,481 in 1950. Mitchell's letter, 1/9/53, WB-111, DLC.

5. *Congressional Quarterly Weekly Report,* 1/2/53, 11–12, 13. For the evolution of the power of the Rules Committee, see Engel, "The Seven Conservatives Who Bottleneck Our Laws," *Reporter,* 8/5/53, a copy of which is in NAACP II: 188, DLC. See also 6/15/53.

6. See 2/4/53.

7. See the headnote on the Struggle to Abolish the Poll Tax, vol. III.

8. On March 10, 1953, the House passed a bill, H.R. 3575, to grant eventual statehood to Hawaii (*Congressional Quarterly* gives the vote as 274 to 138). *Congressional Quarterly Weekly Report,* 3/13/53, 333. See also 6/15 and 11/4/53; 7/9/53, *Hearings,* 429–30.

9. In his State of the Union message, Eisenhower said he would "use whatever authority exists in the office of the President to end segregation in the District of Columbia, including the Federal government and any segregation in the armed forces." Eisenhower, *Public Papers of the Presidents,* 1:30–31.

The NAACP responded that it was "encouraged" by Eisenhower's "affirmation," and it applauded his recommendation for revision of the discriminatory McCarran-Walter immigration act and his repudiation of "that unreasoned suspicion that accepts rumor and gossip as substitutes for evidence" in the loyalty and security program.

> However, the Association regrets that the President places such great reliance upon "persuasion" as a means of achieving "equality of rights of all citizens of every race and color and creed." Our oft-stated conviction is that legislation is required to achieve this objective just as it is required to maintain the rights of labor, of industry and of individuals. Of the notable gains made in race relations in recent years, very little has been the result of persuasion. Court decisions, executive orders, economic factors and legislation have been the prime movers in attaining these results.
>
> In a democracy it should be unnecessary to persuade citizens to live up to the basic principles of their government. The very idea of persuasion carries with it the assumption that one group of citizens has the right to confer upon other citizens the rights which are inherent in our concept of democracy and explicit in our constitution. (Report of the Secretary to the Board of Directors for the Month of February 1953, EC)

10. 4/29/53, *Hearings,* 2186–96.

11. 3/31/53, *Hearings,* 2055–78. See also, among others, 5/31 and 7/17/50, 11/5/51,10/6/52, 2/5/53.

12. In a February 6, 1953, memorandum to Walter White, which the board considered at its March 9, 1953, meeting, Mitchell said that on federal aid to education, it was more important than ever for the NAACP to insist that nonsegregation provisions be a condition of federal aid. Mitchell memorandum to Walter White, 2/6/53, MP; Minutes, 3/9/53, EC. See also, among others, 11/30/46, 12/21/50; in appendix 1, this vol., 3/16/48.

13. For the first positive response, see 8/21/53.

14. Mitchell presented these suggestions on what the executive branch could do to end segregation to Attorney General Herbert Brownell. See 5/4/53.

15. Eugene Davidson served as assistant director with Mitchell at the FEPC from 1943 to 1945.

Monthly Report, May 4, 1953

May 4, 1953

MONTHLY REPORT OF THE WASHINGTON BUREAU

VISIT TO ATTORNEY GENERAL BROWNELL

The Secretary and Director met twice with the Attorney General, Mr. Herbert Brownell, this month to discuss certain policy matters in the Civil Rights field.[1]

At the first meeting, the Attorney General stated that he had assigned members of his staff to explore the question of how far the President could go in eliminating segregation in the District of Columbia.[2]

In the second meeting, which was held on May 1 and attended by representatives of 50 national organizations of the Leadership Conference on Civil Rights, the following points were discussed:

1: Strengthening the Civil Rights Section of the Department of Justice by giving it morepersonnel and assigning an assistant attorney general to handle this special function.

2: Strengthening and reviving the President's Committee on Government Contract Compliance.

In discussing these points, Mr. Brownell said that he would take action to strengthen the Civil Rights Section of the Department, although he did not commit himself to the specific plan offered by the organizations.

Mr. Maxwell Rabb of the White House staff and Mr. J. Lee Rankin, Executive Adjudications Division of the Department of Justice, were present at the meeting and both stated that they are working on plans to revive and strengthen the Government Contract Compliance Committee's function in the Federal Service.[3] Also present were Mr. William P. Rogers, Deputy Attorney General of the Justice Department, Mr. J. Walter Yeagley, First Assistant, Criminal Division, Justice Department, and Mr. Arthur B. Caldwell, Chief of the Civil Rights Section, Department of Justice.

The Attorney General promised that he would try to arrange a meeting of representatives of the organizations with President Eisenhower, but said that he would like to have another session with us before doing so.

The Executive Secretary, who served as spokesman for the group, and the Director of the Washington Bureau suggested that the conference with the President might well include consideration of certain possibilities for legislative action in the 83rd Congress.[4]

INTEGRATION IN SCHOOLS ON MILITARY COSTS

The Executive Secretary and the Director met with Dr. John Hannah, Assistant Secretary of Defense, to follow up on President Eisenhower's commitment that segregation would be abolished in schools on military posts.[5] We also checked on whether the Navy Department is eliminating segregation in the yards at Charleston, South Carolina, and Norfolk, Virginia, as requested by the NAACP.

Dr. Hannah was cordial and emphatic in pledging that the President's promise to end segregation in schools on military posts would be carried out. However, Dr. Hannah stated that plans for integration have been delayed in schools on 21 military posts because Mrs. Oveta Culp Hobby, Secretary of the Department of Health, Education, and Welfare, has asked for more time to study the problem. We expressed displeasure at Mrs. Hobby's request and pointed out that the problem has been studied so long that any fair arrangement would require integration in all schools on military posts in the Fall term.[6]

In discussing the question of segregation in the Navy Yards, Dr. Hannah requested that we submit an official statement on the problem. We had already officially sent it to the Secretary of the Navy, but we had reason to believe that a negative answer was in the making. We have sent Dr. Hannah a similar letter on this matter.[7]

SCHOOLS AT OAK RIDGE, TENNESSEE

As stated in last month's report, we have taken up with the Atomic Energy Commission the question of eliminating segregation, particularly, in the schools in Oak Ridge, Tennessee, which is a Government owned community. We have had an extensive meeting with officials of the Atomic Energy Commission on this subject and have received a list of hazards which the AEC believes it will encounter if it abolishes segregation. We are preparing an answer to these problems with the help of Mr. Robert Carter of the legal staff. This matter is now actively before the top officials of AEC.[8]

STATE DEPARTMENT MEETING

As a follow up on employment practices of the State Department, the Director met with Mr. Edwin N. Montague, Director of Office Personnel; Mr. Robert F. Woodward, Chief of Division of Foreign Service Personnel; Mr. Edward T. Wailes, Assistant Secretary for Administration-Designate, and Dr. John A. Davis, Personnel Consultant.

Unfortunately, the meeting came on the same day that the House Appropriations Committee heavily cut State Department's funds. However, we discussed specific plans to improve employment opportunities in the State Department. A separate memorandum on this has been submitted to the Secretary.[9]

It is apparent that we must also have a meeting on this with the Secretary of State in the near future.

TAFT-HARTLEY AMENDMENTS

Senator Irving M. Ives, has advised, at the time this report is being written, that he will introduce the NAACP's amendments to the Taft-Hartley legislation.[10] He is supported by all of the Republicans on the Senate Labor Committee, with the exception of Senator Taft. He advised that Senator Taft is not opposed to the NAACP's amendment but wishes to study it. Senator Taft also stated a similar view to the Director of the Washington Bureau.[11]

Senators Kennedy, Neely, and Lehman have agreed to join Senator Ives in sponsoring the amendment at the time of this writing. We expect, also, Senators Douglas and Murray will support it but we have not gotten a definite commitment from them.[12]

Senator Lehman also has an amendment of his own which he may introduce. His amendment was framed to meet the problem raised by the NAACP in our testimony before the Committee on April 29.[13] However, it does not use the specific language offered by the Association and is not as extensive in scope. Needless to say, however, either the Ives proposal or the Lehman proposal would substantially improve our lot in this field.

APPROPRIATIONS IN HOUSING CUT

The Director appeared before the Senate Appropriations Subcommittee headed by Senator Saltonstall of Massachusetts to urge restoration of cuts in the Housing appropriation which eliminate all new public housing contracts and also cut in half the staff of the Racial Relations Service in the Housing and Home Finance Agency.

The Executive Secretary, who was enroute to Richmond and Norfolk for NAACP meetings, remained in Washington to join the Director in expressing the Association's desire to have the cuts restored.[14]

ANTI-JIM CROW TRAVEL

Mr. Robert Carter has forwarded to the Washington Bureau a serious problem in which a young Lieutenant of the Air Force was disciplined for failing to obey Jim Crow Laws in Alabama. It appears that he was in interstate travel at the time.[15]

We have offered this to Senator Charles Tobey, Chairman of the Interstate and Foreign Commerce Committee, and Congressman Charles Wolverton, Chairman of the House Committee on Interstate and Foreign Commerce. We have also given this story to key Senators and Congressmen by way of urging that action be taken on the Jim Crow Travel Bill.

FEPC HEARINGS.

Senator Ives has advised that hearings will begin on FEPC legislation May 19. They will last for the balance of the week. The Senator is anxious to have top officials of organizations that are on record in support of FEPC.

We have previously indicated that Senator Ives had pledged to hold FEPC hearings at the close of the Taft-Hartley hearings in the Senate Labor Committee.[16]

VISITS TO NORTH CAROLINA

The Director of the Washington Bureau visited North Carolina twice this month to aid in stimulating register and vote campaigns in Charleston and Gastonia.

The Director also made visits to New Jersey and Virginia.

MS: NAACP II: A-537, DLC.

1. These efforts involved implementing the recommendations of *To Secure These Rights* as well as the agenda of the Washington bureau and the Leadership Conference on Civil Rights. Among the several recommendations Mitchell offered Walter White were, for example: a strategy for getting the Senate Rules Committee to report out promptly a workable rules change based on a new proposal by Senator Ives, S. Res. 31, for controlling filibusters; getting hearings on FEPC legislation; and getting quick action on "certain civil rights proposals which have less opposition than FEPC." Mitchell memorandum to White, 2/6/53, MP. See also 2/4 and 3/3/53.

2. This meeting was on April 24, 1953. In preparation for the meeting, a subcommittee of the LCCR met on April 17 to discuss possible action on segregation in the capital. Several lawyers were then preparing a legal document outlining powers the president could use to end segregation in the District of Columbia. Mitchell memorandum to Roy Wilkins, 4/20/53, NAACP II: A-350, DLC.

3. See 4/3 and 8/21/53 for Mitchell's eventually successful efforts.

4. The topics at the May 1, 1953, meeting with Brownell were determined by an LCCR steering committee at a meeting on April 21. For a detailed report on the May meeting, see memorandum from Arnold Aronson, LCCR secretary, to "All Cooperating Organizations," 5/12/53, NAACP II: A-350, DLC. Attached are a "Memorandum to the Attorney General on Implementation of the Nondiscrimination Provisions in Government Contracts" and a "Memorandum to the Attorney General on Administrative Action to Improve the Civil Rights Machinery of the Department of Justice."

5. See, most immediately, 2/4, 4/3, 6/15, 10/6, 11/4, 12/7, and 12/31/53; Watson, *Lion in the Lobby*, 244–45.

6. See related materials in NAACP WB-171, DLC; for subsequent developments, see 6/15, 10/6, and 12/7/53, 2/17/54.

7. See also, most immediately, 4/3 and 10/6/53; in appendix 1, this vol., 8/21/53.

8. See 4/3/53 and materials in NAACP WB-9, DLC.

9. See also, most recently, 12/3 and 12/31/52, 6/1 and 9/9/53.

10. The amendments were drafted by NAACP attorneys and approved by the AFL and CIO. Minutes, 5/11/53, EC. Summarized, the four parts stated:

> It shall be an unfair labor practice for an employer or labor organization to discriminate against or segregate any member of the labor organization or any member of the craft or class of employees represented by the labor organization with respect to any of the purposes of this Act or with respect to referrals for hiring, upgrading, promotions, lay-offs, retrenchment, membership in the labor organization or any other term or condition of employment or membership. (Typescript of statement, 4/29/53, MP, which appears in 3/31/53, *Hearings*, 2055–78; 4/29/53, *Hearings*, 2186–96)

Mitchell effusively thanked Ives for introducing the amendments. He noted that although the "enactment of national labor legislation in 1933 made possible the growth of great economic morality in the field of labor relations," Congress regrettably had "never included in this legislation any adequate safeguards against some of the cruelest types of discrimination solely because of race." The amendments Ives offered, he said, were intended to fill that gap. Mitchell letter to Irving M. Ives, 5/5/53, NAACP II: A-337, DLC. See also *New York Times*, 5/6/53.

11. See 2/4, 3/3, 4/3, 4/30, and 6/1/53, and the headnote on the NAACP, the Taft-Hartley Act, and the National Labor Relations Board, vol. III.

12. Also joining as sponsors were Senators Barry Goldwater (R-Ariz.), John F. Kennedy (D-Mass.), and William A. Purtell (R-Conn.). The only members of the Senate Labor Committee who did not support the amendment were Robert A. Taft (R-Ohio) himself and Lister Hill (D-Ga.).

13. 4/29/53, *Hearings*, 2186–96.

14. 4/25/53, *Hearings*, 488–97.

15. This was Lt. Thomas Williams of Camden, New Jersey, who was a member of the air force taking instructor pilot training at Craig Air Force Base in Selma, Alabama. Williams, 5/13/54, *Hearings*, 40–55. See also the headnote on the Struggle to End Jim Crow Travel, vol. III.

16. Those hearings on FEPC were not held. Mitchell prepared a "Summary on FEPC Hearings," stamped 5/25/53, with Ives's verbatim promise to hold the hearings on May 19–22, 1953, in the *Congressional Record*, 5/1/53, 4427. But he subsequently announced (*Congressional Record*, 5/15/53, 5137) that the hearings had been postponed, to begin on the second week of January, the week of January 10, 1954. But those hearings, too, were postponed. See 2/28/54. They were eventually held in February 1954. White, 2/25/54, *Hearings*, 141–58. See also 3/9/54.

Monthly Report, June 1, 1953

June 1, 1953

MONTHLY REPORT OF THE WASHINGTON BUREAU

DEVELOPMENTS ON AMENDMENTS TO TAFT-HARTLEY ACT

The status of amendments to the Taft-Hartley Act is very cloudy at the time this report is written. One draft prepared by the Senate Labor Committee staff omits any reference to the problem of racial discrimination. However, all of the sponsors of the Ives amendment are standing firm in their commitments to us. Meanwhile, the staff draft has been denounced by labor leaders as worse than the Taft-Hartley Act itself.

Support of the Ives proposal, with suggestions for changes, has been voiced by the CIO.

At the time this report is written (May 28), we cannot make a prediction on what the schedule will be on Congressional action on the whole Taft-Hartley Act. Hence, we are unable to state when the Ives proposal will reach the floor. Meanwhile, Senator Lehman has introduced S. 1897. This bill would achieve considerable correction of present problems, but it is not as inclusive as the Ives Bill which Senator Lehman, also, sponsors.[1]

FEPC POSTPONEMENT

For the use of anyone who may wish to answer inquiries, the following sequence on FEPC is included in this report.

1. At the beginning of the 83rd Congress, the NAACP urged that early hearings be held on FEPC Bills. Republican leaders agreed that such hearings would follow hearings on the Taft-Hartley Act in the Senate.
2. When Taft-Hartley hearings ended in the Senate, Senator Ives made the following statement which appears on page 4427 of the Congressional Record for May 1, 1953:

   Mr. Ives: "Mr. President, I wish to announce that beginning on Tuesday, May 19, and continuing through May 19, 20, 21, and 22, and presumably the first 3 days of the following week, the Subcommittee on Civil Rights of the Committee on Labor and Public Welfare will hold hearings in the old Supreme Court Chamber, on Senate Bill 692, a bill to prohibit discrimination in employment because of race, color, religion, national origin, or ancestry.

   "In this connection, I urge all civic groups of national importance who are interested in this subject to be represented at the hearings. Most of all, I would urge those who are represented to have the heads of their organizations present to testify. I happen to know that many outstanding organizations in the United States favor this type of legislation, but, unfortunately, too many times the heads of the organizations themselves do not see fit to appear. I believe the time has come when they themselves should be present at the hearings."
3. Senator Ives advised the NAACP and others that he was unable to get some witnesses he wanted because they could not appear at the May hearings. He announced that hearings would be postponed until the week of January 10, 1954.[2]

HOUSING APPROPRIATIONS

The Senate restored cuts in housing appropriations which would have knocked out public housing and cut the Racial Relations staff of the housing agencies severely.[3] The measure now goes to conference between the House and Senate.

On May 7, the director met with Mr. Albert M. Cole, Administrator of the Housing and Home Finance Agency. We submitted to him a memorandum on how the housing agencies could and should abolish segregation in matters under their jurisdiction.[4] Mr. Cole's response is set forth in the following points:

1. Mr. Cole stated that he personally feels that he should follow the suggestions made in our memorandum, but that it will be necessary to talk it over with his associates in the Housing field such as the head of FHA, the head of PHA, and others. He said, also, that he felt because of the great significance of what we suggest it should, also, be cleared with the highest level in the Administration.

2. We requested a statement on when we could get a specific answer from him. He said that he wanted to assure us that the answer given would be definite and not evasive. He said, also, that he could not give a specific time limit but would like for us to check with him again in 30 days for a progress report.

HOWARD UNIVERSITY AND FREEDMEN'S HOSPITAL APPROPRIATIONS

Cuts given by the Appropriation Committee of the House to Howard University and Freedmen's Hospital were restored in part on the House floor because of a vigorous effort made by Congressman Adam Clayton Powell, Jr., and Mrs. Margaret Sitt Church of Illinois.

We, also, reminded the House leadership that the practice of making cuts which would curtail programs, under which colored persons were being treated fairly, was serious indictment of the Republican Party. As a further safeguard, we asked seventeen key Republicans in the House to make certain that the Powell and Church amendments were kept in on final passage of the bill. The amendments were kept in.[5]

JIM CROW TRAVEL

Congressman Wolverton, Chairman of the House Committee on Interstate and Foreign Commerce, has asked that we submit a list of persons who should be called to testify on the Jim Crow Travel Bills. He pledged that he would hold hearings but has not yet set a date.

Executive agencies are sending replies to a Senate request that they give their opinions on the Anti-Jim Crow Travel Bill before the Senate Committee. We have protested a statement from the Department of Defense which showed very little interest in the bill. We pointed out that, because of the effect of Jim Crow Travel regulations on service personnel the Defense Department should be among the leaders seeking enactment of this law.[6]

STATE DEPARTMENT

As elsewhere in Washington, there is great confusion in the Department of State because of budget cuts and investigations. In last month's report, we stated that we had held a conference on personnel matters in the Department. One of the top officials with whom we met has resigned, another has been dropped on budgetary technicality, and a third may leave any day. Only one of those present at the meeting, Mr. Edward T. Wailes, Assistant Secretary for Administration, seems firmly placed. He has just been confirmed by the Senate. However, we are trying to pick up the pieces.

MS: NAACP II: A-537, DLC.

1. See also 2/4, 3/3, 4/3, 4/30, and 5/4/53, as well as the headnote on the NAACP, the Taft-Hartley Act, and the National Labor Relations Board, vol. III.

2. See, most immediately, 2/4 and 6/15/53.

3. 4/25/53, *Hearings*, 488–97.

4. See also 4/3/53.

5. Mitchell listed these points in his report to Walter White on the meeting with Cole. On March 19, 1953, he had "met informally" with Cole, the new head of the HHFA. At that time, they discussed housing policies that led to segregation. They agreed to have this subsequent meeting, and Mitchell left with Cole his January 11, 1952, memorandum on the problem.

On July 27, 1953, Mitchell led a meeting with Cole that included: George Weaver and William Oliver, CIO; Dr. Dorothy Ferebee and Jeanette Brown, NCNW; Elmer Henderson and James Scott, ACHR; Archibald Carey and Robert E. Merriam, City Council of Chicago; Reginald Johnson, NUL; and Fern Colborn and Irving Kriegefield, National Federation of Settlements and Neighborhood Centers. Mitchell reported that the most important result of the meeting was the unanimity of support the participants expressed for the NAACP's strategy for eliminating segregation in housing. Mitchell memoranda to White, 3/20, 5/7, and 7/2/53, NAACP II: A-309, DLC.

6. See the headnote on the Struggle to End Jim Crow Travel, vol. III.

A Report from Washington, June 15, 1953

A REPORT FROM WASHINGTON

[June 15, 1953]

Republicans have had six months of power in Washington. This is a brief appraisal of what has happened up to Monday, June 15, which is the time this report is written. Obviously, in this statement, we are omitting many things in an effort to give only the highlights.[1]

THE WHITE HOUSE

On the credit side of the ledger, President Eisenhower merits praise for following through on NAACP urging that segregation in schools on military posts be abolished.[2] The Chief Executive has promised to end it and, in September, all such schools run by the Federal authorities will be integrated. However, there are twenty-one schools which are jointly run by local authorities and the U. S. Government, although most of the cost is paid by Uncle Sam. Here, we are encountering stubborn resistance by local officials and sabotage by some Federal officials. A detailed statement on this problem has been prepared by the Washington Bureau and is available at the Convention.[3]

On the credit side, also, is the splendid way in which the White House and the Department of Justice supported the U. S. Supreme Court in declaring segregation in Washington restaurants unlawful. With the blessing of the White House and the Justice Department, enforcement of the non-segregation law began at 8:00 A.M. on June 10.[4]

Among the major matters which can be resolved by the President without the help of Congress are:

Ending segregation in all housing programs assisted by the Federal Government;

Strengthening the Fair Employment Board in the Federal Service and the Government Contact Compliance committee which polices the non-discrimination clause in Federal contracts;

Ending segregation in all Federal establishments, especially those in Norfolk and Charleston (S.C.) where segregation is rampant under present Navy policy; and

Appointment to Federal office of only those persons who will faithfully administer the laws in a non-discriminatory manner.

Apropos of this last mentioned action, we urged the U.S. Attorney General not to appoint John Lee Smith of Lubbock Texas, as U.S. Attorney for the northern district of that state. On June 2, the Dallas News reported that Mr. Smith had withdrawn his name because, "I do not think Attorney General Brownell would approve my appointment. He is strongly opposed to racial segregation and my position favoring it is well-known."[5]

THE CONGRESS

To date, the members of Congress have concentrated on investigations, budget cutting and Tidelands Oil. The House Appropriations Committee gave deep and unfair cuts to Howard University, Freedmen's Hospital and the Housing Program. At the time this report is written, the final appropriations have not been acted upon.[6]

The following is a summary, as of June 15, on matters of interest to the NAACP:

Discrimination in Employment

A major chance for action in the field of employment discrimination came when Senator Irving Ives (R., N.Y.) and Congressman Adam Powell (D.,N.Y.) introduced NAACP amendments providing non-segregation safeguards to the National Labor Management Relations Act.

In the Senate, where rules permit joint sponsorship of bills, the following Senators are supporting the Ives proposal (S. 1831):

Republicans Smith (N.J.), Aiken (Vt.), Griswold (Nebr.), Purtell (Conn.), and Goldwater (Ariz.)

Democrats Murray (Mont.), Neely (W. Va.), Douglas (Ill.), Lehman (N.Y.), and Kennedy (Mass.)

S. 1831 is no substitute for FEPC, but it is a major part of the NAACP's long standing policy of seeking such safeguards in legislation.[7]

S. 692, the Ives-Humphrey FEPC Bill was originally scheduled for hearing on May 19, but the date was changed to January 10, 1954, because some witnesses invited by Senator Ives could not be available in May. In the House, no hearings have been set on FEPC, although they have been requested by the NAACP.[8]

Anti-Filibuster Resolution

On January 2, 1953, a bi-partisan group of Senators agreed on the following strategy with regard to a rules change in the Senate, and, thereby, elimination of the filibuster as a weapon in stalling civil rights bills.[9]

Senator Clinton Anderson (D., N.M.) was to introduce a motion to consider the adoption of rules for the Senate of the 83rd Congress. If this motion had prevailed, Senator Ives was to introduce a motion to revise Rule XXII. This rule, at present, requires 64 votes to halt a filibuster.

The Anderson motion was defeated when Senator Taft made a motion to table it on January 7. The tabling motion won by a vote of 70 to 21. Taft was supported by 41 Republicans and 29 Democrats. Voting against Taft were 5 Republicans and 15 Democrats.[10]

On May 12, the Senate Rules Committee suddenly reported out S. Res. 20. This was during the Tidelands Oil Debate. However, no move has been made to schedule debate on this or any other anti-filibuster resolution. S. Res. 20 was introduced by Senator Jenner and is the least desirable. S. Res. 63 introduced by Senator Lehman, S. Res. 41 by Senator Morse, and S. Res. 31 by Senator Ives offer workable plans for ending filibuster.

Senator Taft says that he favors a rules change, but has not yet indicated when he thinks it should be considered by the Senate.[11]

There are 48 G.O.P. votes in the Senate and there are 25 Democrats in that body from outside the Solid South. With the vote of Senator Wayne Morse, Independent, there are 74 votes which should be for civil rights, and, therefore, capable of breaking a filibuster under the present rule.

Unfortunately, experience shows that, unless the Republican leadership can use persuasive powers that have not been revealed in the past and unless the Democrats can convince certain Western and Border State members to change previous voting habits, we can count on only a total of 59 votes. This is more than enough to pass legislation but not enough to halt a filibuster under the present rule. Nevertheless, Senator Taft insists that a filibuster can be broken under the existing rule.[12]

House Rules

In the House, the chief bottleneck on constructive legislation is the Rules Committee. On January 3, by a voice vote, the House adopted its old rules, thus, continuing the power of the Rules Committee, which is now headed by Congressman Leo Allen of Illinois.

Congressman Herman Eberharter of Pennsylvania was unsuccessful in getting consideration of a resolution which would allow committee chairmen to force House consideration of legislation which their committees approve but which the Rules Committee does not clear within twenty-one days after receiving it.[13]

Other Civil Rights Measures

In other types of legislation in the Civil Rights field, there are some hazards because of "working agreements" in Congress, but there is no strong opposition to them from the leaders of the Republican Party. Hence, it is entirely possible that, if the Republican leadership is convinced that it must act in the field of Civil Rights, it may move to pass a weak Anti-Lynching Bill, a good Anti-Jim Crow Travel Bill, an acceptable plan to reorganize and strengthen the functions of the Department of Justice in the field of Civil Rights, or possibly worthwhile legislation to protect members of the Armed Services against assault and violence at the hands of civilians.

There is, however, a serious possibility that the leadership of the Republican Party in the House and Senate may accept a Constitutional Amendment to repeal the Poll Tax (Alabama, Arkansas, Mississippi, Texas, and Virginia still require payment of Poll Taxes) in lieu of a bona fide law ending this brake on voting in the South. It is well-known, of course, that Senator Holland of Florida and other southern members of Congress consider this as a practical step in meeting Civil Rights demands. Needless to say, it is not an acceptable step nor even a reasonable compromise on the issue of Civil Rights.[14]

Hawaii Statehood

The House has passed a bill to make Hawaii a state. Smothered in Committee is a bill to give similar status to Alaska. The Senate may face a filibuster when the Hawaii Bill comes up, but southern members of Congress are divided on this measure. In the House, it was supported by Congressmen from Texas, Georgia, Louisiana, and other anti-Civil Rights areas. The vote favored Statehood by 274 to 178.[15]

Non-Segregation Amendments

We already know that under present education laws, the colored people of the separate schools are cheated out of approximately 7,000,000 dollars a year in funds administered by the U. S. Department of Agricultures for use in the land-grant colleges.

These funds are apportioned among the states on the basis of population. The colored people are counted in the total population, and, therefore, help to determine the size of the grant. After that, no check is made by any Federal Agency to determine whether colored citizens receive any part of these benefits.

The U. S. Office of Education has announced that it had spent 315,000,000 dollars for aid to schools in Defense impacted areas of the country. In response to a request by Congressman Adam Clayton Powell, the U. S. Office of Education has advised that it has no means of determining whether this money is spent equitably in the states which require separate schools. Congress is now considering legislation extending these laws. Here is an excellent opportunity for legislators to back up the President by inserting a non-segregation clause in this legislation.[16]

A similar chance is offered in Housing Bills (S. 2103 and H.R. 5667) now pending.[17]

Treaties.

The Senate Judiciary Committee on June 15, by a vote of 9 to 5, reported out a Constitutional Amendment which would limit the Treaty making power of the President.[18] Some of its supporters said it was necessary to halt Civil Rights advances in the United States. This is a false and thoroughly dishonest argument. The NAACP is on record against the amendment.[19]

MS: NAACP II A-298, DLC.

1. See, in appendix 1, this vol., newsletter, 8/10/53, for an extension of this report.

2. See materials in NAACP WB-171, DLC; 4/3 and 10/6/53; MacGregor, *Integration of the Armed Forces,* 489–92.

3. See 2/17/54 for combined highlights of the campaign; Watson, *Lion in the Lobby,* 244–45.

4. See 3/30/50 for earlier development in the famous "lost laws" case of *District of Columbia v. the John R. Thompson Company, Inc.,* in which the Justice Department joined the district in asking the Supreme Court to uphold two statutes forbidding restaurants to refuse to serve blacks. The Supreme Court on June 8, 1953, upheld one of the laws, that of 1873, in a very limited opinion that for the time being left intact the *Plessy v. Ferguson* separate but equal doctrine. *New York Times,* 6/9/53, 1; Arthur Krock, "A Very Limited Decision against Segregation," *New York Times,* 6/9/53, 26. See also 3/3, 11/4, 12/7, and 12/31/53, 9/29, 12/6, and 12/31/54; Watson, *Lion in the Lobby,* 224.

5. See also 11/4/53.

6. *Congressional Quarterly Weekly Report,* 5/29/53, 703. See also 6/1/53.

7. See, most immediately, 5/4/53.

8. Mitchell, nevertheless, was able to testify on S. 692 before the House Committee on Banking and Currency. See 6/23/53, *Hearings,* 203–5. See also 2/4, 6/1, and 12/31/53, 2/28, 3/9, and 12/31/54, as well as the headnote on the Struggle for a Permanent FEPC, 1942–54, vol. III.

9. This activity was in keeping with plans that had been made in a meeting on December 18, 1952, and another held subsequently at which Sen. Herbert Lehman was reported to have agreed to make a motion on the opening day of Congress in January to change the rules. Another meeting of senators

had also been scheduled for December 30, 1952, to test the firmness of support. Mitchell letter to Walter White, 12/22/52, NAACP WB-III, DLC; *Congressional Quarterly Weekly Report*, 1/2/53, 11–12. See also 4/30/53; Watson, *Lion in the Lobby*, 323.

10. *Congressional Quarterly Weekly Report*, 1/9/53, 43. See also the headnote on the NAACP and the Filibuster, vol. III.

11. *Congressional Quarterly Weekly Report*, 5/15/53, 638.

12. See White, *Man Called White*, 170–71.

13. *Congressional Quarterly Weekly Report*, 19/9/53, 44. For a historical review of the almost total power of the Rules Committee, see *Congressional Quarterly Weekly Report*, 1953, 288. See also Engel, "The Seven Conservatives Who Bottleneck Our Laws," *Reporter*, 8/5/52, a copy of which is in NAACP II: A-188, DLC; 4/30/53, 9/29/54.

14. See the headnote on the Struggle to Abolish the Poll Tax, vol. III.

15. 7/9/53, *Hearings*, 429–30. *Congressional Quarterly* gives the vote as 274 to 138. See *Congressional Quarterly Weekly Report*, 3/13/53, 333.

16. For Eisenhower's declaration that he could see no justification for discrimination in the spending of federal funds, see president's news conference, 4/19/53, Eisenhower, *Public Papers of the Presidents*, 108. See also, among others, 12/21/50, 4/3, 4/30, and 11/4/53.

17. Mitchell pressed for a provison to the Housing Act amendments of 1953 barring discrimination in mortgage insurance and loans on the basis of race, color, religion, or national origin. 6/18/53, *Hearings*, 264–67; 6/23/53, *Hearings*, 203–5. S. 2103 became law on June 30, 1953. It extended defense and military housing programs for one year, but it did not include a nonsegregation provision. *Congress and the Nation*, 484.

18. This was the famous Bricker amendment. On January 7, 1953, John Bricker (R-Ohio) and sixty-three cosponsors introduced in the Senate S.J. Res. 1, a proposed constitutional amendment to restrict the treaty-making power of the president. *Congress and the Nation*, 110–11.

Mitchell began attacking the amendment in a letter to senators dated January 9, 1953, in which he pressed them to take "urgent action on a broad range of civil rights legislation." Some supporters of the Bricker proposal, he explained, argued that unless the treaty-making power was included as an amendment, the government could find itself "committed to anti-lynching or other civil action" legislation "because of some treaty agreed upon with foreign Governments." Mitchell's letter, 1/9/53, NAACP II: A-185, DLC.

19. The importance that the NAACP placed on the Bricker amendment was demonstrated by Walter White's forgoing having a guest on his April 9, 1953, broadcast radio program on WLIB and its affiliated stations, instead devoting the period to his statement on the Ohio Republican senator's initiative. See 4/9/53 in appendix 1, this vol.

The board, furthermore, adopted a resolution opposing the amendment because it would "gravely restrict presidential treaty-making power and seriously impair the flexibility of our foreign relations." Minutes, 4/13/53, EC. See also *Congressional Quarterly Weekly Report*, 4/10/53, 466–67; among others, 11/4/53.

Background on NAACP's Successful Drive for Action against Discrimination by Government Contractors, August 21, 1953

August 21, 1953

BACKGROUND ON NAACP'S SUCCESSFUL DRIVE FOR ACTION AGAINST DISCRIMINATION BY GOVERNMENT CONTRACTORS

The *New York Times*, on August 14, carried a page one story with a headline stating that, on August 13 at Denver, Colorado, President Eisenhower had set up a panel to end bias in U. S. Contracts.[1] The story also said that the committee would be composed of fourteen members who would "seek compliance by all plants working for the Government."

The President appointed vice President 'Nixon to head' the committee. In another page one story in the *Times*, on August 20, Mr. Nixon said:

> "Where taxpayers' funds are involved, all segments of the population should have equal opportunity. From 39 billion to 40 billion is spent annually on Government contracts. This is about one-fourth of all money spent in a year on production in the United States."

Obviously, the action of the President and the work of the committee he appointed is big news. Behind the news is the story of the work of the NAACP in getting the President to act. The following are some of the highlights:

1. The original order establishing a Government Contract Compliance Committee was issued by President Truman after a long series of efforts by the NAACP.

   Following the November election, it became apparent that some members of the committee were planning to wind up the agency's affairs and submit a final report.

   If the committee had voluntarily ended its existence, it would have been difficult and perhaps impossible to get the function re-established in the new administration. Therefore, the Director of the NAACP's Washington Bureau moved quickly to avoid a close-out of the committee by meeting with Senator Henry Cabot Lodge, Jr., who was then serving as liaison man for the new administration.

   The date of this meeting was December 4, 1952, and the following excerpt from a Bureau letter sent to Mr. Dwight Palmer,[2] Chairman of the President's Committee on Government Contract Compliance, is of importance:

"Today, I met with Senator Henry C. Lodge, Jr., who, as you know, was designated by General Eisenhower to maintain a liaison with executive agencies in Washington. Item 2. on the agenda discussed with Senator Lodge was as follows:

> "Executive Order No. 10,308 established a Committee on Government Contract Compliance. This Committee is at present working out programs from obtaining compliance with the non-discrimination clause in all government contracts. Until a Federal FECP is established by law, this group will fill an importance place in assuring minority groups of fair treatment by employers holding government contracts. Strengthening of the functions of this group is needed. Also, every effort should be made to see that it does not go out of business by default."

"I told the Senator that I understood the Committee would meet on Monday, December 8. Senator Lodge assured me that General Eisenhower is definitely interested in the function of the Committee on Contract Compliance and that the new administration will wish to give considerable attention to the problems that your Committee is handling. I asked and received Senator Lodge's permission to give you this information."

"I hope the Committee will continue to function and do everything possible to avoid a break in its work."

Mr. Palmer replied on January 19, 1953, as follows:

> "Last Friday, January 16th, we submitted our report to the President and as of the same day I tendered my resignation as chairman and member of the committee. Such members as remain, I assume, will submit their resignation subject to the convenience of the President. The staff, as presently constituted, will continue substantially as is or until a newly completed Committee makes new assignments."

Since executive orders continue in effect until rescinded or canceled by the President, the way was open to get the new administration to strengthen and revive the committee.

As one of his last official acts, President Truman sent a copy of the committee's report to President-elect Eisenhower by special messenger.

2. In February, the Director of the Washington Bureau discussed the status of the Contract Compliance Committee with a member of the President's staff.

   In March, Mr. Walter White sent the following telegram to the President:

   "We are gravely concerned about the lack of action in recent weeks on the part of the Fair Employment Board of the Civil Service Commission and the Committee on Contract Compliance. We urge that the vacancies on these committees be filled and that they be instructed to make the maximum effort to end discrimination in their areas of responsibility."

   Mrs. Alice Dunnigan of the Associated Negro Press, also discussed the status of the Contract Compliance Committee with the Director of the Washington Bureau, and, thereafter, raised a question in the President's Press Conference which was as follows:

"I understand before leaving office President Truman sent you a report of the Contract Compliance Committee, which was set up to eliminate discrimination in plants with Government contracts. That committee doesn't have a chairman now and many of the members are resigning. What steps have been taken or are being taken to appoint a chairman to that committee and to revitalize the committee?"[3]

The President promised to look into the matter and give a report at a later press conference.

In April, additional information on the need for an executive order to revitalize the committee was submitted to the White House by the Director of the Washington Bureau. By this time, of course, the whole matter was being considered by the Bureau of the Budget and several other agencies of Government. The Executive Secretary and the Washington Bureau Director also discussed the need for action in this field with Attorney General Herbert Brownell.

The Executive Secretary and the Washington Bureau Director arranged a meeting for the Leadership Conference on Civil Rights with the Attorney General in May. Mr. Maxwell Rabb of the White House staff was also present at the meeting. Several matters were discussed at this meeting, including the Government Contract Compliance Committee. Mr. Brownell and Mr. Rabb gave assurances that the order would be issued.[4]

To emphasize the importance of action, the Executive Secretary of the NAACP called on branches in key communities throughout the country to give a first hand picture of discrimination in their cities. This information was submitted to the Government by the Executive Secretary.[5]

The Washington Bureau remained in constant contact with the White House on the executive order and enjoyed excellent cooperation from Mr. Rabb.[6]

Now that we have the new committee, we must help to make it effective by submitting bona fide complaints against plants that have Government contracts to the Contracts Compliance Committee, U. S. Department of Labor, Washington, D. C.

Please send copies of all complaints to the Washington Bureau. Meanwhile, we will also vigorously continue our efforts to get Congress to pass an FEPC bill with enforcement powers.

Walter White
Executive Secretary, NAACP

Clarence Mitchell
Director
Washington Bureau, NAACP

MS: NAACP II: A-200, DLC.

1. This action by Eisenhower was intended to enforce EO 10479, which he issued on August 13, 1953. Mitchell also provided Walter White with a copy of the *Washington Star* editorial on August 17, 1953, that said the creation of the committee was "further evidence of the President's determination to use his legitimate powers to combat racial discrimination." The president's action, the *Star* said, was con-

sistent with his "stated views that his committee will emphasize education as an anti-discrimination tool, and that it will not seek to expand its work beyond the realm of Federal authority. The committee will not be limited to mere preachment, however, for Federal contracts can be denied to any bidder who practices discrimination in hiring or firing. Thus, an effective sanction is available, and the committee presumably will invoke it should need arise." Watson, *Lion in the Lobby*, 227–28.

2. Mitchell's letter to Palmer, 12/4/52, and his letter to Lodge, also of 12/4/52, listing the matters they had discussed during their meeting that day, are in NAACP II: A-200, DLC. See also 12/31/52.

3. White told Palmer "confidentially" that the reporter who asked Eisenhower about the Government Contract Compliance Committee at the president's news conference on April 2, 1953, had done so at Mitchell's request. White said: "I am sharing your letter with Mr. Mitchell, and we will work assiduously, I assure you, on your suggestion that the new chairman be, if not a Dwight Palmer, one as close to that model as possible, namely one who not only believes but has himself practice[d] fair employment practices." White asked Palmer whether he had anyone in mind whom he could suggest to the president as Palmer's replacement. White's letter to Palmer, 4/15/53, NAACP II: A-200, DLC.

4. See 5/4/53.

5. White asked eighteen NAACP branch leaders to make a "spot check of the present employment situation in certain key areas." He explained, confidentially, that he had shown Attornney General Herbert Brownell, when he and Mitchell met with him the previous week, a telegram he had received from Willard L. Brown, president of the Charleston, West Virginia, NAACP branch. Brownell, he said, expressed deep interest and asked him "if the same employment pattern existed in other cities." Although Brownell made no specific promises, White explained, he "gathered that he might use this information with the President, especially with respect to the President's Committee on Government Contract Compliance." White also said Brown provided him with the following information:

> Approximate employment status is following DuPont 5000 with 67 Negroes. Carbide and Carbon 9,600 with 83 Negroes. B. F. Goodrich Chemical 600 with 9 Negroes. Goodrich is a government FRC operation. All the other plants in valley employ Negroes in an even smaller degree. Most employment is janitorial and with little if any upgrading. The situation is grave with coal mining employment becoming less. Definite pattern of exclusion exists in most plants who do not adopt policy of employing one percent or less Negroes.
>
> Out of 4 plants employing more than 25,000 only 206 Negroes were employed. (White's memorandum, 4/27/53, NAACP II: A-200, DLC)

See, also, in appendix 1, this vol., 11/30/53.

6. Rabb initially was secretary of the cabinet and later associate counsel to the president in charge of civil rights. Parmet, *Eisenhower and the American Crusades*, 254–56; Watson, *Lion in the Lobby*, 226–27, 229.

Monthly Report, September 9, 1953

September 9, 1953

REPORT OF THE WASHINGTON BUREAU*

PRESIDENT'S COMMITTEE ON GOVERNMENT CONTRACT COMPLIANCE

The highlight of the summer was President Eisenhower's action establishing a new committee on government contract compliance headed by the Vice President. Even before the President took his oath of office, we had this important matter before him.[1] Getting action required months of work and conferences with government officials. We have set up a summary of the highlights on our effort to get action and copies have been sent to interested persons.[2] A few days after the order was issued, the Bureau Director received a small package from the White House. It contained a pen used by the President to sign Executive Order No. 10,479 creating the new committee.[3]

As is usually the case, the opposition to civil rights immediately got busy on a plan to challenge the new committee. However, the Bureau has urged the Vice President and the White House to tackle two major problems left on the agenda of the previous group. One of these is the Washington Telephone Company[4] and the other is the training programs of contractors operating Atomic Energy plants. It is well-known, of course, that the Washington Telephone Company refuses to employ colored operators. Solution of the Washington Telephone Company problem will be in line with the President's pledge to eliminate segregation from the Nation's Capital. We have made considerable progress in some aspects of AEC employment, but many new workers are being trained by the Dupont Company and the Carbide and Carbon Company which operate the installations in Aiken, South Carolina,[5] and Paducah, Kentucky.[6] Complainants allege that colored persons are barred from such training. A victory on this front in South Carolina will be significant because it is on the doorstep of Governor Byrnes.[7]

The Director of the Bureau believes that we can and must make considerable headway against employment discrimination through the new committee. We must also use its inevitable failures to emphasize the need for a fair employment practice law with enforcement powers.

NAVY SEGREGATION

The Navy Department announced on August 20 that Secretary Anderson had requested local commanders to end all segregation of races in their establishments.

Progress reports are to be given to the Secretary of the Navy at sixty day intervals. We can see no reason why the first report should not indicate the end of all segregation. Thus, victory in this long NAACP campaign seems certain.[8]

A. J. Clement, Jr., President of the Charleston, South Carolina, Branch recently sent a letter to the Washington Bureau enclosing an announcement issued by Captain T. T. Dantzler, Commander of the Charleston Navy Yard, that on and after September 14 drinking fountains in the Yard will no longer have signs restricting their use by races. The announcement said:

> "The Commander has received instructions from the Secretary of the Navy and the Commandant of the Sixth Naval District that he is to effect a progressive elimination of all barriers to the free use of facilities in the Shipyard which are now segregated according to race."

The Director has also reviewed a Navy report from Commanders in the South which shows many have already acted to end all segregation in their installations. The report has a space in which Commanders are requested to state how much trouble they have encountered in ending segregation. All say, "None."

We regret that the Navy did not order an immediate end to segregation everywhere, but, instead, required that it be done "progressively." Nevertheless, this is a far cry from the parting shot of Acting Secretary of the Navy, Francis Whitehair, who said in an official report on January 22, 1953:

> "The approach of a military establishment will naturally differ from that of officials of the NAACP . . . A direct order form the Secretary of the Navy, no matter how forceful, would not only fail to eliminate the basic cause of the (segregation) problem but would only antagonize opposing forces involved."[9]

VETERANS ADMINISTRATION

Among the Federal establishments which stubbornly cling to segregation, few are more important than the hospitals and facilities of the Veterans Administration. The new Administrator, Mr. Harvey V. Higley, and members of the President's staff now have this problem before them. It appears that in the near future we shall be able to win a complete change of policy so that each veteran may be served without segregation.

The new Administrator advises that his staff believes segregation is necessary for the medical well-being of certain mentally disturbed patients.[10] Dr. Montague Cobb, Chairman of the NAACP's National Health Committee, has agreed to answer the VA on this point.[11]

HOUSING PROBLEMS

The Administrator of Housing and Home Finance Agency, Mr. Albert M. Cole, held a series of what he called shirt-sleeve conferences in Washington for the purpose of determining the Administration's new policy on housing. The Director represented the Association at one of these Washington conferences and presented our view that any Federally assisted housing should be operated on a completely nonsegregated basis.[12]

The Administrator, thereafter, held conferences of a similar nature in various parts of the country. The Bureau arranged for representatives of the NAACP to be present at these conferences. As far as we can determine from reports these Association representatives vigorously supported the argument that all segregation should be abandoned.

We note with particular interest and pleasure a newspaper headline from the West Coast indicating that Franklin Williams made a very forceful presentation at the San Francisco hearing. This is especially gratifying because some of the local forces attempted to prevent Mr. Williams from appearing, but after we advised the Administrator that he was being frozen out the appearance was arranged.

Additional conferences of this kind are scheduled in October. We are alerting the branches to request an opportunity to be heard.[13]

The question of Federal funds being used to support segregation in matters under the jurisdiction of Mr. Cole was brought forcefully to his attention by citizens of Alabama who joined Mrs. Ruby Hurley, Southeast Regional Secretary, at a meeting in Washington, which the Bureau arranged on August 1.

The members of the group from Alabama were Mr. Oscar Adams, attorney; Mr. Orzelle Billingsley, attorney; Reverend H. W. Scruggs, Pastor of Thankful Baptist Church and Chairman of the Home Owners Protective League; Reverend John W. Goodgame, Pastor of the Sixth Avenue Church; and Reverend J. L. Ware, Pastor of the Trinity Baptist Church, President of the Birmingham Baptist Ministers Conference, President of the Greater Birmingham Emancipation Association, and Corresponding Secretary of the Alabama Baptist State Convention.

The delegation pointed out that, under present plans in Birmingham, approximately 2,000 colored people are to be displaced to make way for a multi-million dollar health center which will be studded with Jim-Crow arrangements. The Birmingham citizens told Mr. Cole that they did not object to any plan for improving the city and eliminating slums, but they strongly objected to spending Federal money for any program that would result in segregation.

Mr. Cole, after hearing the group, promised that at a later date he would give a final decision on whether the Federal Government would support the City of Birmingham in this venture.[14]

STATE DEPARTMENT

The NAACP's program to increase the employment of qualified colored persons in the Department of State has been thrown into severe jeopardy by two factors; one, the Congress has slashed the appropriations of the Department so much that there is more of an atmosphere of firing than hiring in the Department at this time; and, two, some political individuals and Department officials who are opposed to integration of colored people have combined forces in halting a program under the direction of Dr. John A. Davis. This program which Dr. Davis carried on as a consultant was designed to show the basic problems in the State Department that result in exclusion of qualified colored persons.[15]

MS: NAACP II: A-537, DLC.

1. A copy of EO 10479, issued 7/9/53, and other materials are in NAACP II: A-208, DLC. In conjunction with a meeting he held with Henry Cabot Lodge Jr., Mitchell provided a detailed and substantive list of issues that the NAACP wanted to have addressed. For instance, Mitchell urged that the Eisenhower administration strengthen and continue the Committee on Government Contract Compliance. Mitchell letter to Lodge, 12/4/52, NAACP WB-111, DLC.

2. See 8/21/53, as well as the headnote on the Struggle for a Permanent FEPC, 1942–54, vol. III.

3. See also 6/29/54; Watson, *Lion in the Lobby*, 227, 229.

4. See 3/5 and 6/5/52; in appendix 1, this vol., 6/9/52 and 11/30/53; and the headnote on the Telephone Industry, vol. I.

5. See 2/5/51 for a special report on the atomic energy plant in South Carolina.

6. See 5/3/51.

7. In a September 10, 1953, press release, the NAACP announced that Mitchell had asked the President's Committee on Government Contract Compliance to consider pending complaints the Washington bureau had submitted against the Chesapeake and Potomac Telephone Company in Washington, as well as the companies in charge of atomic energy facilities in Aiken, South Carolina, and Paducah, Kentucky. The NAACP explained that the cases had been pending since the previous Truman administration committee. The press release said Mitchell believed that if the committee resolved these complaints at the outset of its work, that "would pave the way for highly effective action in other industries." NAACP press release, 9/10/53, NAACP II: A-208, DLC. The NAACP followed up on this request by submitting to the Committee on Government Contracts recommendations for improving its work. Memorandum from Walter White and Mitchell, 11/30/53, MP.

8. The announcement by Robert B. Anderson, secretary of the navy, called for "complete elimination" of racial segregation among civilian employees at forty-one naval shore stations in the South. The navy, however, had forty-three shore installations from Virginia to Texas. It said that a recent survey showed segregation existed in about half of them, with discriminatory practices ranging from "minor in most instances to substantial in a few cases." The order was aimed primarily at a naval base at Norfolk, Virginia, and the big naval shipyard at Charleston, South Carolina. The navy was the only branch of the services with a civilian segregation problem. It was forced to end the segregation because the problem of following "local custom" on racial matters had become a "source of embarrassment" to President Eisenhower. Mitchell said, "We hope that at the end of the first sixty-day interval the commanders will report that all Jim Crow facilities have been eliminated." *New York Times*, 8/21/53, 9.

Mitchell reported on the initiation of the campaign at 2/5/51 and on its intensification at 6/5/53. See, next, 10/6, 11/2, 11/4, and 12/31/53, 6/29/54; MacGregor, *Integration of the Armed Forces*, 474.

9. This action resulted from a strong push by the board, which sent the following telegram to the president:

> The Board of Directors of the National Association for the Advancement of Colored People is shocked to learn that the Navy Secretary is continuing racial segregation in the yards at Charleston, S.C., and Norfolk, Va. We strongly urge that this outright defiance of the national policy which you have so clearly reaffirmed be corrected and that the Secretary of the Navy be instructed to end racial segregation in all activities and establishments under its jurisdiction. We are gravely concerned that the Department of the Army is actually making new arrangements with local communities to continue segregation in schools on military posts, despite your statement that such practices cannot be legally or morally justified. We respectfully urge that you order the ending of segregation in all schools on federal property beginning in the fall term and that all contracts with local authorities that permit segregation in schools on federal property be abrogated. (Minutes, 6/8/53, EC)

See also 10/6/53, as well as additional materials in NAACP II: A-341, DLC. For a narrative account of this victory, see Watson, *Lion in the Lobby*, 236–38.

10. September 1953, nevertheless, was when the official program for ending segregation in all VA hospitals began. Mitchell, 6/29/54; J. Francis Pohlhaus, Report on Negro Veterans, 2/25/56, NAACP WB-151, DLC, used in vol. V appendix. See also, among others, 3/9/54.

11. Evidently, Cobb helped influence Higley's changed position. See also Watson, *Lion in the Lobby*, 258.

12. Mitchell's position was that the NAACP should continue to insist that the federal government "cease being a party to programs of housing segregation, whether such programs be extensive or, as alleged in this case [of Birmingham], for limited use only." Mitchell's letter to Atty. Oscar W. Adams of Birmingham, 7/20/53, NAACP WB-92, DLC.

At the meeting with Cole on August 14, 1953, the NAACP delegation expressed the concern that Birmingham planned to clear an area where two thousand African Americans were living to build a medical center on the land. The plan originally also provided for housing units. Tax experts recommended that if blacks were permitted to live in the new housing, the city would receive a much-needed boost in income. City officials, however, first announced that the housing would be for whites only. Later, the plan was revised to provide only limited dormitories for white employees of the medical center.

The plans included setting aside one part of the African American area for small businesses, such as retail stores and shops. The city refused to agree that those shops would be open to all business-people without regard to race. Additionally, the delegation said that the city had not provided a workable plan for rehousing the families that would be displaced by the project. The Birmingham delegation pointed out that even though housing and business facilities in the area would be limited, they should be open to everyone. The delegation also charged that "an incredible pattern would prevail in the new set-ups." That pattern apparently would have followed that of a hospital, which required black patients to use a freight entrance. The delegation charged, "Often patients find themselves riding on the same elevator with garbage cans."

Plans for the medical center included a park that, under Birmingham city ordinances, would be off limits to blacks. Regarding another aspect of the plans, the delegation said it was ironic that space that could be used for badly needed housing would be "converted into badminton courts—for whites only."

The delegation said that slum clearance was a good idea, but in Birmingham, the federal government was being asked to participate in a program of "Negro clearance." The delegation urged Cole not to approve the program unless guarantees were given that all housing, businesses, or facilities made possible by the clearance would be available to everyone on a nonsegregated basis. Report on meeting of Birmingham Delegation with Housing Officials at 1626 "K" Street, N.W., Washington, D.C., 8/14/53, NAACP WB-92, DLC. Mitchell accompanied the delegation and apparently prepared this report on the meeting. See also the much more detailed "Appraisal of the Birmingham Redevelopment Plan, Medical Center Site A," by the Birmingham NAACP branch, on which the report of the meeting was based, in NAACP WB-92, DLC. See also 12/7/53.

13. See also, among others, 3/3, 4/3, and 6/1/53; in appendix 1, this vol., 8/10/53.

14. See also the headnote on Segregation in Federal Housing Programs, vol. III; 3/2/53, *Hearings*, 27–34; Watson, *Lion in the Lobby*, 252–57.

15. Integration of professional personnel at the State Department was one of the problems the NAACP Washington Conference considered in 1941. See 2/7/42 in appendix 1, this vol.. Mitchell continued to pursue this issue, at times with the help of such supporters as John A. Davis. See, for example, 5/4 and 6/1/53.

Monthly Report, October 6, 1953

October 6, 1953

REPORT OF THE WASHINGTON BUREAU

FAITH AND CUSTER IN GEORGIA

Early in September a group of little colored children left home for school in Georgia. They arrived at the school building where white children were also present. Classes started. An observer would not have been able to tell the difference between this school and one like it in New York or Boston. By a quirk of good fortune the school was named Faith. The incident referred to took place at Fort Benning, Ga., where because of the NAACP's long campaign jim crow was ended this fall. The last stand of segregation in the Custer School, also on the post, is now in the past, too. Both schools are integrated.

Elsewhere in the U.S. the picture is not as cheerful. Segregation still persists in twenty-one schools located on posts but operated by local authorities.[1] This month at a press conference Assistant Secretary of Defense John M. Hannah, was quoted as saying that segregation would be abolished in the fall of 1955. In response to a protest from the Washington Bureau, Mr. Hannah said he was not quoted correctly and that: "we have insisted that the military services eliminate segregated schools 'not later than' September 1, 1955.

"My attitude on racial integration is firmly fixed and well known and I do not expect to vary from it. However, it is a little discouraging to be criticized by your organization when we are trying to accomplish the objectives that you seek, and to which I subscribe."[2]

In Temple, Texas, Brigadier General Edward G. Farrand of Fort Hood denied that the Bureau was right in saying that he was ignoring the President's program for ending segregation. He has leased land to local school authorities to operate a jim crow school. His explanation was: "Negotiations to (lease the land) were started long before the President's policy was announced." The unanswered question is: Who gave the authority to continue the negotiations after the President spoke?[3]

THE WALLS ARE TUMBLING DOWN

"The walls are really tumbling down, signs are being taken down all over the Navy Yard and the Naval Base. It seems that the base is a little ahead of the yard, however, I receive messages almost daily of the signs being taken down in the various shops.

"The signs are removed for the most part on Saturday while most of the personnel are not at work and then again they will not just paint out the signs but rather they will paint the whole side of a building or of a room and, of course, forget to paint the words "White" and "Colored" on the side of the room or building.

"The whole matter is very pleasing to the men and women working in the installations."

This was a report sent to the Bureau by Jerry or [O.] Gilliam, president of the Norfolk, Va., branch on progress of non-segregation program inaugurated by the Navy in facilities for civilian employees in shore establishments.[4]

U.S. POST OFFICE (COLORED SECTION)

The NAACP's campaign to end discrimination in the sprawling establishments of the Post Office Department has been going on for a long time. John LeFlore of the Mobile Branch asked the Bureau to support his request that segregation in locker rooms, work assignments and other facilities be ended in all post offices. We did so and reminded the Postmaster General that jim crow in the post office extends as far north as Baltimore, Md.

An Associated Press story on the NAACP's protest broke at the time the Postmaster General was in Maine making a speech about the post office being "clogged with antiquated methods, expensive fussiness and just plain bad habits." In an editorial the Springfield (Mass.) Daily News said:

"While the Postmaster General is seeking ways of providing better service at lower costs, in justice to the career employees and public, maybe he should also give some attention to (the) complaint that justice is being denied some postal workers because of color. . . . If we are to have improved service, let's have it for all."[5]

WE CALLED THE DOCTOR

When the Veterans Administration said that in certain hospital cases racial segregation had medical value we promptly called the doctor—in this case Dr. Montague Cobb, chairman of the Association's National Health Committee.[6] He agreed to answer the VA on this point. A part of his letter said: "Mr. Clarence Mitchell, Director of the Washington Bureau of the NAACP has asked me to comment on your letter to him of August 20 in which you state that there are certain areas in which some degree of segregation has been found necessary for the well being of patients, with particular reference to the field of neuropsychiatry, and, that the safety of patients must always be the first consideration.

"The number of mental conditions which might predispose to emotional explosions of the type you suggest, is, in the first place, limited, and secondly, not every individual suffering from such conditions is a uniform, potential ignition fuse for a racial outbreak.

"The careful grading of patients by psychiatrists both as to overt and covert behavior is the proper and scientific way to determine the degrees of social liberty which may be permited individual patients. Outbursts between individuals of the same racial group are certainly common enough to render it obvious that to presume a common denominator of racial hostility in large or small groups of the mentally ill from various causes and on this presumption to erect a segregative barrier within them is unsound and unscientific.

"The states of New York and Massachusetts have long been leaders in provisions for the care of mental patients. The facilities in these states are not segregated and the patients consist not only of the customary so-called racial groups but many other groups, cultural, national, etc., yet these states have not found it necessary to segregate cultural or ethnic groups to provide safe and proper care.

"In well known institutions in a southern locality such as St. Elizabeth's Hospital here in Washington and John Hopkins Hospital in Baltimore, integrated group therapy classes for mental patients have been and are being successfully operated.

"A final consideration is that segregated facilities generally result in the minority group patients receiving the inferior part of whatever care is provided, however good or bad this may be. This is inescapable from the very nature of the differential and would apply to brand new Veterans Administration Hospitals as well as to other institutions."

We have forwarded the letter to the White House. At the time this report is written the VA has not found a suitable answer to the Cobb letter.[7]

U.S. STEEL CONFERENCE

This month the bureau director joined the executive secretary, Dr. Robert C. Weaver and Charles Shorter, Secretary of the Philadelphia Branch in a conference with officials of U. S. Steel and others on problems of employment and housing in Bucks County, Pennsylvania, where the company has a giant new plant.[8]

MARINE CORPS SEGREGATION

Piloted by William Pryor of the Washington Bureau, an NAACP inquiry is under way on segregation of some colored marines into a stewards category where they serve as personal maids and lackeys for top officers.[9] Mr. Pryor quotes one Marine as saying:

"Sometimes when I'm off duty, I go out to the 'boondocks' and pitch a tent just to see how it feels to be a marine."

WINGS CLIPPED BY JIM CROW?

On behalf of Lt. Thomas E. Williams of the Air Force we are making an inquiry to determine whether he is being ousted from the service because he protested against segregation on an interstate bus.[10]

MS: NAACP II: A-537, DLC.

1. See 2/4, 4/3, 5/4, 6/15, 9/9, and 12/7/53; MacGregor, *Integration of the Armed Forces,* 494.

2. In a statement of October 12, 1953, nevertheless, Hannah said that within eight months from that date, segregation would end in all army units. Mitchell, "Status of Racial Integration in the Armed Services," 203–13. The air force and the navy were already "completely integrated," he told *U.S. News & World Report,* and the army was about 95 percent integrated. That meant, he said, there were no black men in the navy or air force who were serving in "colored" units. In the army, there were a few such units, but they were being disbanded rapidly. *U.S. News & World Report* 35 (October 16, 1953): 100. See collection in NAACP WB-171, DLC.

3. See, especially, 2/17/54.

4. See, most immediately, 9/9 and 11/2/53.

5. See the headnote on Relationships with Federal Agencies, vol. I.

6. See 10/47 for Mitchell's early involvement in this struggle; 5/3/51, among others, for subsequent developments; and, for the later phases, 11/4 and 12/7/53, among others.

7. The VA had no suitable response to Cobbs's challenge other than to end its policy of segregation. Actually, the VA had told the NAACP in April 1949 that its policy was to avoid segregation of patients in its hospitals, except when integration would create a "situation, or mental condition [that] might presumably retard the recovery of patients." See 6/29/54; Watson, *Lion in the Lobby,* 258, 411, 414.

8. E. E. Moore, president of U.S. Steel, at the meeting on September 24, 1953, reported that there were approximately 32,252 blacks employed in the company's plants around the country. A year earlier, there had been 18,000. In the Bucks County plant, however, there were only 70 blacks out of 3,000 employees, and they were unskilled.

On housing, Walter White and Weaver pressed the steel officials on whether they had used their influence to correct the discriminatory practices of the owners of a Levittown housing project in Bucks County from which blacks had been totally excluded. The steel officials were also asked whether they were using their leadership to prevent the repeat of patterns of racial exclusion in new housing for workers in Bucks County. White reminded them that Fairless Village, a new housing project in the area, apparently had the support and blessing of the company, since it was named for the chairman of the board of U.S. Steel. There were no blacks living in that development, and it was suggested that it, too, should be open to everyone without regard to race.

Because there was considerable confusion about whether U.S. Steel was discriminating against black applicants at the Fairless Works, members of the group suggested that the company issue a public statement in writing on its employment policies and circulate it widely. They also urged the company to adopt a positive position and provide some leadership in correcting existing discrimination in housing in Bucks County. The steel officials said they would cooperate on the request, but they "did not make a specific promise on what they would do." The group agreed that the NAACP should hold another meeting to discuss approaches to the Bucks County problem. At that point, White's report said: "It was suggested that Bucks County Council should issue the call for the meeting and it would be held in that area." Report of the Secretary for September, 10/12/53, EC.

At a subsequent meeting on November 5, 1953, the NAACP, along with the NUL, the American Friends Service Committee, and the Bucks County Human Relations Council, pressed to get blacks into Levittown and Fairless Village. Because "all other avenues had been exhausted," they decided to prepare a memorandum for President Eisenhower on the use of FHA funds to build segregated housing. Minutes, 11/9/53, and Report of the Secretary for November, 12/14/53, EC. See also 12/3/52, as well as the headnote on Segregation in Federal Housing Programs, vol. III.

9. Responding to Mitchell's letter of October 1953 about the Marine Corps practice of assigning blacks to the Stewards Branch, Brig. Gen. R. H. Ridgley Jr. said a very "small number" of men "enlist for *Steward Duty Only* [emphasis Ridgley's]. They enlist for that duty of their own volition, after the type of duties they must perform are explained to them by the recruiter. As a matter of fact, during the

month of September 1953, only fourteen (14) enlisted for Steward Duty Only." Mitchell responded, "We know that official policy is as you have stated; we also know there are occasional deviations." He continued, "For instance, despite policy, the fact remains that our observer of some years in the Corps has known of only one white steward. It is flatly incredible that only one white man chose steward duty and that all others having an affinity for that type of job should be Negroes." Ridgley letter to Mitchell, 10/9/53, and Mitchell's letter, 10/9/52, responding to Ridgley, NAACP IX: 67, DLC. See also 5/5/54; in appendix 1, this vol., 12/31/50. For the history of this practice, see MacGregor, *Integration of the Armed Forces*, 107–8.

10. See 12/7 and 12/31/53 for fuller accounts of this case.

Monthly Report, November 2, 1953

November 2, 1953

REPORT OF THE WASHINGTON BUREAU

Ending of segregation in the Charleston, S.C. Navy Yard cafeteria was page one news in Charleston. A newsreel of the event was shown in South Carolina theaters and possibly other southern cities.[1]

The Washington Bureau this month devotes its entire written report to a discussion of the elimination of racial segregation at the Charleston, S.C., Navy Yard. We are doing this because the Charleston situation may be an indication of what will happen in the south when segregation is eliminated in other more extensive aspects of community life. As of Monday October 19 the Charleston Yard ended segregation in its cafeteria. Previously, segregation in the use of drinking fountains had been abandoned by the Navy on September 14. The Yard has not yet eliminated segregation in restroom facilities, although, it is anticipated that this will be done in the near future.

On the first day of integration a crowd of whites blocked the entrance to the cafeteria. Colored employees were formerly confined to the first floor to the building and whites used the second floor. Also, industrial employees of the Yard eat at 12:00 noon and clerical employees eat at 12:30. Most of those in the crowd were industrial workers and they prevented other whites from entering the cafeteria by shouting and insulting them. However, newspaper reports said that the crowd was in a joking mood. At 12:30 the industrials went back to work and the white clerical employees used the cafeteria in numbers approximating the normal crowd. Fifteen colored employees used the upper floor formerly reserved for whites. They sat at separate tables.

Mr. Thaddeus G. Fraser, an employee at the Yard, initiated action against segregation and he was supported in his effort by the Washington Bureau. He has provided us with a chronological report on what happened when segregation ended in the cafeteria. It is as follows:

"Tuesday (20th), about 600 to 700 spectators gathered immediately after the whistle blew for dinner, all white. Since, I understand, that the Captain of the Yard returned and called a meeting of the masters, and must have informed them that people entering the cafeteria must not be interfered with. This message had been passed along to the White workers, and on this day, though a greater number assembled they were orderly, and did in no way interfere with anyone.

"There were many Naval officers and many police officers in evidence this day, and all through the rest of the week. Approximately 40 Negroes ate this day upstairs. The white industrial workers fell off to about 20 and about 30 white clerical workers. About 100 colored workers also congregated after they ate their dinner.

"Wednesday (21st), the crowd of spectators fell off to about 400. The spectators are always industrial workers. The white industrials still boycott the cafeteria only about 20 industrials, and about 60 clericals using the facilities this day. An official picture was taken of the crowd today. A few white women appeared in the crowd of spectators today. Everyone is peaceful, but everyone is also very tense. There's no fault to be found with cafeteria service at anytime.

"Thursday (22nd), only about 300 spectators today. No disorder whatever. Lots of officers still in evidence. Approximately 60 Negroes ate upstairs approximately 75 whites mostly clericals ate. Boycott still on. Tenseness slightly relaxed today.

"Friday (23rd), about 100 Negroes ate upstairs. The colored people seem to be taking the situation in stride. Not overdoing nor shy. About 20 white industrials, and about 80 white clericals. This being pay day, and everyone going to cash their checks only about 150 congregated today."

The Charleston News and Courier interpreted the action of the 15 colored employees who ate on the first day as a move to force white people to eat with colored at the same tables. In an editorial on October 21 the News and Courier said "Although in the past equal dining facilities had been provided for whites and Negroes, there had been no integration of the races at mealtime—which apparently is one of the goals of the National Association for the Advancement of Colored People."

The Washington Bureau answered this editorial in a letter which was prominently published promptly in the Courier on October 27. The text of the Bureau's letter is as follows:

"It is interesting to note that although your editorial took the colored people to task for eating at different tables you did not say anything about the large number of whites who imposed their will on fellow workers by congregating at the building's only entrance. Your own news story of October 20 states "*the second shift, apparently unaware of the earlier disturbance, ate as usual.*" Thus it would appear that the drop in use of the cafeteria could in a large part be attributed to the presence of a derisive crowd using the deadly weapon of ridicule.

"The State of South Carolina does not exist in a vacuum. As you well know, the Governor of South Carolina, is representing this country at the U.N. and Congressman James P. Richards of your state is the ranking member of the House Foreign Affairs Committee. You also invited General Mark Clark to come to the Charleston to head The Citadel. I am sure General Clark could tell you that in Korea the Communists constantly used racial discrimination in the United States as a weapon of war. I am sure that Governor Brynes and Mr. Richards are aware of this also, although they might not admit that they are.

"Hence, South Carolina cannot afford to have patterns of segregation which make any person from your state appear ridiculous in a world discussion on human rights. Even if there are people in the state who think they can afford the dubious luxury of racial segregation it is unfair for them to make the rest of the country suffer for their myopia."

A letter from Mr. Charles H. Monson, a white employee at the Yard appeared in the Courier on October 24. The text is as follows:

"When I first came to Charleston last February, it was with the preadvised knowledge of the racial situation in the South . . . and with much additional advice on how to get along in relation to it. Being a native Californian and unfamiliar with the issue as it now stands, I came with a firm of determination not to involve myself or argue my views in the matter. After all, I hadn't been out of the state 20 years . . . so I made the trip with an open mind, deciding to keep my mouth shut and my eyes and ears open so that I might gain a firsthand impression of this so-called "problem."

"So far I've withheld comment and put off writing this, but the article on page one October 20 headed "Non-Segregated Dining Cuts Navy Yard Cafeteria Trade" made it impossible to keep my views to myself any longer.

"I was brought up in a neighborhood which was composed of a fair number of Negro families; I went to school and church with their children—all with the child's unconcerned outlook. I grew up with that same attitude, remembering my father's advice to "judge a person for what he is, and not for the color of his skin or shape of his eyes."

"So you have a problem out here. I doubt it, but let's examine the issue squarely. You shove your Negro population to the rear of your buses, segregate them in your theaters, ball parks, and by social pressure, generally force them into the slum districts (and some I've seen here can't be any worse than those of Los Angeles or San Francisco; which is comparable to some of the best pigsties I've seen) . . . and to what end? I fail to see what you think you're solving by all this, and haven't had anyone yet explain it to me to any degree of satisfaction.

"As for this asinine demonstration put on by some of the "superior" whites at the Navy Yard, nothing would please me more than to learn at a future date that some of them fainted at their work-benches from acute and prolonged malnutrition."

A few other South Carolina publishers commented on this incident and one editorial appeared in the Anderson Independent on October 23.

This provoked a reply from the Charleston News and Courier in an editorial on October 26. It was as follows:

"The News and Courier, like the Anderson Independent, opposed the forced mixture of races in eating places. But the record should be set straight.

"President Roosevelt, by his Executive Order No. 8802, prohibited "discrimination" in the employment of workers in defense industries or by the Government. This set the whole pattern for what has followed.

"President Truman ended separation of the races in the armed forces. Long before President Eisenhower took office, whites and Negroes were eating in the same mess halls and sleeping in the same barracks.

"Under President Truman, the government successfully backed legal action which required many white graduate schools to admit Negroes. The Truman administration also backed action to force ALL public schools to mix the races and to force EVERY SINGLE EMPLOYER in the country to mix the races.

"While Fair Dealers in the South accuse Mr. Eisenhower of being pro-Negro, Fair Dealers in the North accuse Mr. Eisenhower of being anti-Negro—since he would not support the FEPC. The Fair Dealers can't have it both ways at once."

The record should also include a letter from a colored woman which was published in the News and Courier on the same day that the Washington Bureau's letter appeared. One of the disturbing quotes in this letter is as follows:

"I have read about the non-segregated cafeteria at the Navy Yard and the thing that aroused my interest most is the fact that those 14 or 15 Negroes dispersed themselves about the room occupying some 14 of the eight-place tables in the dining hall.

"What those white employees did was no more than what I, personally, would have done if the situation were vice versa. Even if there were no segregation in the beginning, it would still be wrong to act in the manner in which those Negroes did. I do believe that everyone, regardless of race, is entitled to some privace of their own. If I were sitting in that cafeteria, with or without a relative or friend of mine, I would not appreciate a white person or even a Negro with whom I did not associate to be so rude as to intrude at the table at which I am dining, for if I am in the position to leave that place I would do so.

"The National Association for the Advancement of Colored People is, and has been for a long time, fighting for that they call "equal rights." Well, what do you consider as being equal rights? No one is holding the Negroes back from doing anything that they want to among themselves. There are Negroes who have just as much or more than some white people. If they were fighting for this non-segregation business, well, it was granted at the Navy Yard, but what happened? A pitiful few acted like hoodlums.

"What difference does it make what color you are? I am a Negro and I'm proud to be one. Does anyone know what color soul he has? God doesn't look for color. He looks to see whether or not your soul is clean." Mrs. Emma Ophelia Smalls, Station A, Box 6.

In Washington the Director of the Bureau maintained contact with the Navy Department and the White House on the Charleston situation to make certain that every possible precaution was taken to avoid any physical violence. It appears that the Federal authorities were alert, although, we do not believe that the Navy Department should have permitted the crowd to congregate in front of the cafeteria. The Navy said that an attempt to disperse the crowd would probably have "bad reactions" it was the significance in the News and Courier editorial which we quote. In speaking of the Navy's move to end segregation the Courier said "The Federal order, which we deplore, appears to be here to stay."

The Bureau believes that the following conclusions can be drawn from this incident.

1. The Navy Department made a serious error in gradually eliminating segregation. If all segregation had been ended when bans on the use of drinking fountains were moved the opposition would not have had an opportunity to build up the kind of following which caused the demonstration at the cafeteria entrance. It is still possible that the ending of segregation in the restrooms may provoke further demonstrations.
2. The prominence given to the Bureau's letter seems to indicate that this channel to favorable public opinion would be very useful when other intergration occurs. Perhaps we should study a plan of stimulating correspondence in such situations to make certain that both sides of the questions are properly aired.
3. The editorial reply of the News and Courier to the Anderson Independent charge that the ending of segregation was an Eisenhower venture rather than a continuation of existing policies of the Roosevelt and Truman administration is a healthy sign. It is another reminder that those who wish to promote race prejudice in National elections may find that their schemes backfire after the election is over.

MS: NAACP II: A-200, DLC.

1. Published as Mitchell, "Negroes Now Eat Upstairs," 585–88, 638–39. See, most immediately, 10/6 and 11/4/54; in appendix 1, this vol., 8/21/53. In a press statement, the president noted that of sixty installations in the South on federally owned property, only one reported partial segregation. White House press release, 11/11/53, and other related materials are in NAACP WB-142, DLC.

Important Civil Rights Legislation in the 83rd Congress, November 2, 1953

November 2, 1953

IMPORTANT CIVIL RIGHTS LEGISLATION IN THE 83RD CONGRESS[1]

In the Senate, the Ives-Humphrey FEPC Bill, S. 692, has been introduced and contains enforcement powers. In keeping with previous discussions between themselves and other persons, Senators Ives and Humphrey have not called this bill an FEPC proposal. Instead, it is titled "Federal Equality of Opportunity in Employment Act."[2]

Senator Dirksen has introduced a bill, S. 1, which would provide for investigation of discrimination in employment and other civil rights problems. It contains no enforcement powers, although it sets up a commission to make inquiries on discrimination. The commission would have subpoena powers.

Other civil rights and related measures include four proposals to change Rule 22 (of the several proposals introduced, S. Res. 63 introduced by Senator Lehman, S. Res. 41 by Senator Morse, and S. Res. 31 by Senator Ives offer workable plans for ending filibuster. S. Res. 20 introduced by Senator Jenner is the least desirable), an Anti-Lynching Bill, Anti-Poll Tax Bill, Anti-Jim crow Travel Bill, a bill strengthening and expanding civil rights functions for the Department of Justice, a proposal to approve and strengthen Federal civil rights statutes, an anti-peonage bill, a bill to protect servicemen from mistreatment by civilians in the Untied States, a proposal to establish a human rights commission, a bill to outlaw segregation in the District of Columbia, and the Alaska and Hawaii statehood Bills.

Southern Senators have introduced a Constitutional Amendment to outlaw the Poll Tax, S.J. Res. 25.

In the House, the civil rights proposals are very numerous. There are five proposed FEPC Bills with enforcement powers, five Anti-Lynching Bills, six Anti-Poll Tax Bills, three anti-discrimination proposals, three bills outlawing segregation in the Armed Services, two designed to strengthen the Federal civil rights statutes, two Anti-Jim Crow Travel Bills, two proposals to establish a Federal human rights commission, one bill to outlaw segregation in the District of Columbia, one anti-peonage bill, one proposal to strengthen the civil rights functions of the Department of Justice, a bill forbidding Federal Aid to national guards which discriminate on the basis of race, a bill forbidding discrimination in administration of federal funds, a bill for fair education practices, and a bill for fair housing practices.[3]

MS: NAACP II: A-185, DLC.

1. Mitchell prepared this report at Walter White's request for discussion at the November 9, 1953, NAACP board meeting on what Congress had done on civil rights after the elections and what the association thought it should do. The report is complemented by 11/4/53.

At the October board meeting, White recommended:

(1) That the Association invite heads of Negro organizations to sit down together and appraise the legislative situation and issue a statement, non-partisan in character, for the guidance of the thinking of colored people, and impressing again upon the political parties that the Negro is an independent voter.

(2) That we activate registration among Negro voters, in the North as well as the South.

(3) That a second meeting be held in December or early January of the top leadership of organizations—labor, church and others working on civil rights legislation, for unified action.

(4) In January when Congress begins, we again sit down with the top leadership of selected members of the larger organizations of the group comprising the Leadership Conference, and then see the majority and minority leaders of both houses of Congress to let them know something must be done about civil rights legislation in the next session of Congress.

In their discussion of the recommendations during the board meeting, William H. Hastie, Henry Lee Moon, Mitchell, Joel Spingarn, Robert Weaver, and Franklin H. Weaver agreed that the staff should do an analytical appraisal of what constructive action the national administration had taken on civil rights, where it had failed, and what the NAACP ought to do in the next session of Congress. Mitchell was assigned to do the appraisal. Minutes, 10/13/53, EC.

2. See White, 2/5/54, *Hearings*, 176–91, as well as, previously, 4/17/52, *Hearings*, 141–58.

3. See the congressional statements of Mitchell, Leslie Perry, Walter White, Roy Wilkins, and other NAACP representatives in the bibliography for the organization's official positions on these bills.

A Report from Washington, November 4, 1953

[November 4, 1953]

A REPORT FROM WASHINGTON

Republicans have had eleven months of power in Washington. This is a brief appraisal of what has happened up to Wednesday, November 4, which is the time this report is written.[1]

THE WHITE HOUSE AND THE EXECUTIVE AGENCIES

On the credit side of the ledger, President Eisenhower merits praise for following through on NAACP urging that segregation in schools on military posts be abolished. The Chief Executive has promised to end it, and, in September, all such schools run by the Federal authorities were integrated.[2]

There was only one major post on which Federally operated schools were still segregated. This was at Fort Benning, Georgia. It is significant that the integration in these schools was accomplished peacefully and successfully despite opposition from Governor Talmadge. However, there are twenty-one schools which are jointly run by local authorities and the U.S. Government, although most of the cost is paid by Uncle Sam. Here, we are encountering stubborn resistance by local officials and sabotage by some Federal officials.

On the credit side, also, is the splendid way in which the White House and the Department of Justice supported the U.S. Supreme Court in declaring segregation in Washington restaurants unlawful. With the blessing of the White House and the Justice Department, enforcement of the non-segregation law began at 8:00 A.M. on June 10.[3]

In response to urgings of the NAACP, the President continued and strengthened the Committee on Government Contract Compliance. This group is actively working on several important complaints of discrimination in employment by government contracts. It is too early to say how effective it will be but the outlook is good.[4]

A program of ending segregation of civilian employees in approximately 20 shore establishments was undertaken by the Navy Department following long and insistent prodding by the NAACP. One of the significant developments of this program was the ending of segregation in the cafeteria at the Charleston, South Carolina, Navy Yard. This action received extensive coverage in the Southern press and radio. There was also a newsreel on it.[5]

The Veterans Administration is committed to end all segregation in its hospitals and domiciliary establishments. This action is also being taken because of NAACP efforts and the President's interest.[6]

The Department of Defense has announced that, by June 1954, it is expected that all segregation will be ended in the Armed Services. We still have active complaints alleging segregation by other Federal establishments, but it seems clear, however, that the Administration intends to eliminate such problems.[7] Regrettably, sometimes the length of time taken to achieve the result leaves much to be desired.

Among the major matters which can be resolved by the President without the help of Congress are:

1. Ending segregation in all matters under Federal or local government control in Washington
2. Ending segregation in all housing programs assisted by the Federal Government.
3. Strengthening the Fair Employment Board in the Federal Service. (This Board handles problems of discrimination in government employment as distinguished from the function of the committee handling discrimination by government contractors.)
4. Appointment to Federal office of only those persons who will faithfully administer the laws in a non-discriminatory manner.

The NAACP urged the U. S. Attorney General not to appoint John Lee Smith of Lubbock, Texas, as U. S. Attorney for the northern district of that state. On June 2, the *Dallas News* reported that Mr. Smith had withdrawn his name because, "I do not think Attorney General Brownell would approve my appointment. He is strongly opposed to racial segregation and my position favoring it is well-known."[8]

The Attorney General again declined to appoint a foe of civil rights as U. S. Attorney on October 30. State Senator Warren Gill of Oregon, who had strong party backing in his state, was refused post of U. S. Attorney in Oregon. Senator Gill had opposed the Oregon civil rights bill on the grounds that owners of establishments serving the public had a right to discriminate.

THE CONGRESS

The first session of the 83rd Congress concentrated on investigations, budget-cutting, and Tidelands Oil. The House Appropriations Committee gave deep and unfair cuts to Howard University, Freedmen's Hospital, and the Public Housing Program.

Discrimination in Employment

Senator Irving Ives (R., N.Y.) and Congressman Adam Powell (D., N.Y.) have introduced NAACP amendments providing non-segregation safeguards to the National Labor Management Relations Act.

In the Senate, where rules permit joint sponsorship of bills, the following Senators are supporting the Ives Proposal (S. 1831):

Republicans	Smith (N.J.), Aiken (Vt.), Griswold (Nebr.), Purtell (Conn.), and Goldwater (Ariz.)
Democrats	Murray (Mont.), Neely (W. Va.), Douglas (Ill.), Lehman (N.Y.), and Kennedy (Mass.)

S. 1831 is no substitute for FEPC, but it is a major part of the NAACP's long standing policy of seeking such safeguards in legislation.

The chance for passage of S. 1831 increased when Senator Ives replaced the late Senator Taft as Chairman of the Subcommittee which will consider action on amendments to the Taft-Hartley Act. It is very important that the President support the principle of the Ives Amendment in any message he sends to Congress on amending the Taft-Hartley Act.[9]

S. 692, the Ives-Humphrey FEPC Bill was originally scheduled for hearing on May 19, but the date was changed to January 10, 1954, because some witnesses invited by Senator Ives could not be available in May.

In the House, no hearings have been set on FEPC, although they have been requested by the NAACP. Congressman Samuel McConnell, Chairman of the House Committee, is personally opposed to a workable FEPC.[10]

Anti-Filibuster Resolution

On January 2, 1953, a bi-partisan group of Senators agreed on the following strategy with regard to a rules change in the Senate, and thereby, elimination of the filibuster as a weapon in stalling civil rights bills.

Senator Clinton Anderson (D., N.M.) was to introduce a motion to consider the adoption of rules for the Senate of the 83rd Congress. If this motion had prevailed, Senator Ives was to introduce a motion to revise Rule XXII. This rule, at present, requires 64 votes to halt a filibuster.

The Anderson motion was defeated when the late Senator Taft made a motion to table it on January 7. The tabling motion won by a vote of 70 to 21. Taft was supported by 41 Republicans and 29 Democrats. Voting against Taft were 5 Republicans and 15 Democrats.

On May 12, the Senate Rules Committee suddenly reported out S. Res. 20. This was during the Tidelands Oil Debate. However, no move has been made to schedule debate on this or any other anti-filibuster resolution. S. Res. 20 was introduced by Senator Jenner and is the least desirable. S. Res. 63 introduced by Senator Lehman, S. Res. 41 by Senator Morse, and S. Res. 31 by Senator Ives offer workable plans for ending filibuster

There are 47 G.O.P. votes in the Senate and there are 26 Democrats in that body from outside the Solid South. With the vote of Senator Wayne Morse, Independent, there are 74 votes which should be for civil rights, and, therefore, capable of breaking a filibuster under the present rule.

Unfortunately, experience shows that, unless the Republican leadership can use persuasive powers that have not been revealed in the past and unless the Democrats can convince certain Western and Border State members to change previous voting habits, we can count on only a total of 59 votes. This is more than enough to pass legislation but not enough to halt a filibuster under the present rule.[11]

House Rules

In the House, the chief bottleneck on constructive legislation is the Rules Committee. On January 3, by a voice vote, the House adopted its old rules, thus, continuing the power of the Rules Committee, which is now headed by Congressman Leo Allen of Illinois.

Congressman Herman Eberharter of Pennsylvania was unsuccessful in getting consideration of a resolution which would allow committee chairmen to force House consideration of legislation which their committees approve but which the Rules Committee does not clear within twenty-one days after receiving it.[12]

Other Civil Rights Measures

In other types of legislation in the Civil Rights field, there are some hazards because of "working agreements" in Congress, but there is no strong opposition to them from the leaders of the Republican Party.

It is entirely possible, therefore, if the Republican leadership is convinced that it must act in the field of Civil Rights, it may move to pass a weak Anti-Lynching Bill, a good Anti-Jim-Crow Travel Bill, an acceptable plan to reorganize and strengthen the functions of the Department of Justice in the field of Civil Rights, or possibly worthwhile legislation to protect members of the Armed Services against assault and violence at the hands of civilians.

There is, however, a serious possibility that the leadership of the Republican Party in the House and Senate may accept a Constitutional Amendment to repeal the Poll Tax (Alabama, Arkansas, Mississippi, Texas, and Virginia still require payment of Poll Taxes) in lieu of a bona fide law ending this brake on voting in the South.[13]

It is well known, of course, that Senator Holland of Florida and other southern members of Congress consider this as a practical step in meeting Civil Rights demands. Needless to say, it is not an acceptable step nor even a reasonable compromise on the issue of Civil Rights.

Hawaii Statehood

The House has passed a bill to make Hawaii a state. Smothered in committee is a bill to give similar status to Alaska. The Senate may face a filibuster when the Hawaii Bill comes up, but southern members of Congress are divided on this measure. In the House, it was supported by Congressmen from Texas, Georgia, Louisiana, and other anti-civil rights areas. The vote favored Statehood by 274 to 178.[14]

Non-Segregation Amendments

We already know that, under present education laws, the colored people of the separate schools are cheated out of approximately 7,000,000 dollars a year in funds administered by the U.S. Department of Agriculture for use in the land grant-colleges.

These funds are apportioned among the states on the basis of population. The colored people are counted in the total population, and, therefore, help to determine the size of the grant. After that, no check is made by any Federal agency to determine whether colored citizens receive any part of these benefits.

The U. S. Office of Education has announced that it had spent 315,000,000 dollars for aid to schools in Defense impacted areas of the country. In response to a request by Congressman Adam Clayton Powell, the U. S. Office of Education has advised that it has no means of determining whether this money is spent equitably in the states which require separate schools.

Here is an excellent opportunity for legislators to back up the President by inserting a non-segregation clause in this type of legislation and other Federal grants to states.[15]

Treaties

The Senate Judiciary Committee on June 15, by vote of 9 to 5, reported out a Constitutional Amendment which would limit the Treaty making power of the President. Some of its supporters said it was necessary to halt Civil Rights advances in the United States. This is a false and thoroughly dishonest argument.[16]

The NAACP is on record against the amendment. It appears that this will be an important issue in the next session of Congress.

MS: NAACP II: H-8, DLC.

1. This report is complemented by that of 11/2/53, "Important Civil Rights Legislation in the 83rd Congress," which was prepared at Walter White's request. It was discussed at the November 9, 1953, board meeting by Earl Dickerson, Mitchell, Robert Weaver, and White. Minutes, 11/9/53, EC.

2. See, especially, 10/6/53.

3. See 3/3, 6/15, 12/7, and 12/31/53, 9/29, 12/6, and 12/31/54.

4. See 12/31/53.

5. See, most immediately, 11/2 and 12/31/53, 6/29/54.

6. See, among others, 10/6 and 12/7/53.

7. See 2/2/53, where the first step by Eisenhower to end segregation in schools on army posts is cited. Eisenhower's memorandum of March 25, 1953, also said that the secretary of the army had indicated that army commanders were conducting a survey in preparation for implementing "the question designed to bring about agreement with local authorities for integrating the schools." Eisenhower memorandum for the secretary of defense, 3/25/53, OF 142 A 4 (1), DDEL.

8. See also 6/15/53.

9. See, most immediately, 5/4/53.

10. See the headnote on the Struggle for a Permanent FEPC, 1942–52, vol. III.

11. See the headnote on the NAACP and the Filibuster, vol. III.

12. For the significance of Mitchell's concern about changing the power of the House Rules Committee, see Watson, *Lion in the Lobby*, 185–86. See 4/30/53; *Congressional Quarterly Weekly Report*, 1/9/53, 43–44.

13. See the headnote on the Struggle to Abolish the Poll Tax, vol. III.

14. *Congressional Quarterly Weekly Report*, 3/13/53, 333. See also 6/15/53.

15. See also, among others, 12/21/50, 4/30 and 6/15/53.

16. See also, among others, 6/15 and 12/31/53; in appendix 1, this vol., 4/9/53; *Congress and the Nation*, 110–11.

Monthly Report, December 7, 1953

December 7, 1953

MONTHLY REPORT OF THE WASHINGTON BUREAU

CIVIL RIGHTS LEGISLATION

This month, Senator Irving Ives discussed with the Director of the Washington Bureau responses to his invitation to witnesses to appear at FEPC hearings scheduled January 10, 1954. The Senator has asked outstanding clergymen, labor leaders, business men, and educators to testify. His first replies have been disappointing. A publisher, three business men, and a Bishop have answered but expressed doubt about whether they can be present. In one case, a person making the response stated that he could possibly be present but would not be able to support the idea of an FEPC with enforcement powers.[1]

The Bureau has also requested that the Republican leaders include Civil Rights on the agenda when they meet with President Eisenhower on December 17–19 to discuss the legislative program of the second session of Congress.[2] Senator Ives promised to urge that Civil Rights legislation be included in the discussions. The persons receiving the NAACP's request were the Honorable Joseph Martin, Speaker of the House, Senator William Knowland, Majority Leader, Senator Leverett Saltonstall. Majority Whip, and Senator Homer Ferguson, Chairman of the Policy Committee. Of these, only Senator Ferguson has given a favorable reaction. He has stated the following:

"As you know, I have introduced both anti-lynch and anti-poll tax measures and am deeply interested in this field of legislation. I anticipate that the field of civil rights will be covered during the White House discussions."

AIR FORCE OUSTER

We have been making representations on behalf of Lt. Thomas Williams, who was ousted from the U.S. Air Force allegedly because of an economy move to reduce personnel, but, in reality, because he refused to accept segregation while a passenger on an inter-state bus in Florida. We have had three meetings with Air Force officials on this case, and, also, on the question of reprimanding officers who refuse to accept segregation.[3]

H. Lee White, Assistant Secretary of the Air Force, now has the Williams' case before him. The Assistant Secretary has also promised to issue a statement on the question of reprimanding officers who refuse to obey segregation laws that the U.S. Supreme Court has declared unconstitutional. Unfortunately, Lt. Williams has been shifted to reserve status by the Air Force after he was given an extension of approximately thirty days following NAACP protest.

We have also placed before the Air Force charges presented by Lt. K. M. Richmond. Lt. Richmond states that the Commanding General at Chanute Field in Illinois called him a Communist during a discussion about segregation in the barber shop on the post. Lt. Richmond's report states that the General later withdrew the charge of Communism in the conversation. However, this incident would not have arisen had the Air Force established a policy of non-discrimination in barber shops on the posts. We believe that correction of the basic policy on a nation–wide basis is required and have requested the Air Force to do this.

It is recommended that if pending conferences with Assistant Secretary White do not result in the reinstatement of Lt. Williams, a protest be sent to the President by the Board and/or the Executive Secretary.

BUREAU OF PRINTING AND ENGRAVING

A serious crisis has arisen in the Bureau of Printing and Engraving. As a result of application of the principle of Executive Order 9980, colored employees were permitted to take apprentice training as plate printers beginning in 1951. This was the first time in the history of the Bureau of Engraving that colored persons held such jobs.[4]

This year, the Treasury suddenly removed the apprentices from their jobs on the grounds of economy. Although the source of information cannot be disclosed at this time, the Director of the Bureau is convinced that the Fair Employment Board has recommended that the men be put back on their jobs. The matter is now under consideration at the White House.

The Director is absolutely certain that the so-called economy move is only another attempt of the Treasury to keep the printing force entirely white. Hence, it is recommended that, since this matter is currently before the White House, a strong message be sent to the President on behalf of the men who have been displaced. It is also recommended that the message be released to the press from New York.[5]

SEGREGATION IN SCHOOLS ON MILITARY COSTS

The Bureau has again directed the attention of the Department of Defense to delays in integration of schools on military posts. The new admonition to the Department was prompted by the newspaper story in the *Sherman Democrat* of Sherman, Texas, stating that a new school would be built on the Perrin Air Force Base for whites only. This school was to be ready for occupancy in 1955 which is the same year that the Defense Department says segregation in schools on military posts will be finally ended.

We have not had an official statement from the Department on this matter, but Assistant Secretary of Defense, John Hannah, stated in a press conference that the 1955 deadline would still be followed and he was undertaking an investigation of the Perrin Air Force Base school. He stated that this school would probably not be built if local authorities insisted upon having it segregated. We also are advised, unofficially, that Dr. Hannah is meeting with officials of the U.S. Office of Education on this question.[6]

STATUS OF HOUSING PROBLEMS

The Bureau notes three important developments in the Housing field:

1. At the invitation of the Housing Agencies, we have submitted suggestions on program and structure of the Federal Housing set-up.[7] This information has been sent to the President's Advisory Committee on Housing.[8] Our recommendations may be basically summed up by the following:
   - a. A first requirement is the establishment of a national housing policy that will result in a supply of dwellings at reasonable sale and rental rates which will be open to all persons without regard to race, religion, or national origin. The government has no business supporting any other kind of policy.
   - b. Agencies set up to implement this policy should be under the direction of one government organization with final authority to resolve differences that may arise among them and to coordinate their activities.
   - c. Establishment of more central direction of the housing activities of government would not be successful if the person heading the program was partial

to any particular phase of it. Therefore, we believe that the type of coordinated administration we suggest can be successful if it is directed by an impartial person who will be able to consider the total housing program.

2. The Washington Bureau has been representing citizens of Birmingham in their opposition to a redevelopment project which would clear out colored families from an area of that city to make way for a hospital development. The Association's protest, of course, has been based on the lack of positive assurance that the displaced families would be re-housed adequately, and, also, because there was no assurance that the redeveloped site would be used for the benefit of colored and white persons alike.[9]

   This month, the Housing and Home Finance Agency approved a loan for redevelopment subject to conditions which the City of Birmingham must meet.[10] As soon as the local and regional representatives of the NAACP advise us on the outcome of conversations they are having with Birmingham officials, we shall take further steps in this matter.[11]

3. The City of Baltimore is again in the Housing arena following an announcement that 950 colored families will be displaced from a site which will be used for state office buildings.

   In directing the attention of the Housing officials to this new problem, the Washington Bureau reminded them that in a previous redevelopment program, also protested by the NAACP, colored displaced persons were paid an average of $3,726 for their homes by the Redevelopment Commission while white people received an average of $4,108 for theirs. On the other hand, colored families paid an average of $7,836.84 for dwellings in other areas after they were displaced while white families similarly displaced paid only $6,126.25. Thus, the cost of the redevelopment program for colored families was $2,000 more than for whites. In addition, of course, colored families have been denied access to the housing in the redeveloped area.[12]

ORDER OF D.C. COMMISSIONERS ON SEGREGATION

The Commissioners of the District of Columbia issued an order abolishing segregation in agencies of the District with certain notable exceptions. The exceptions include the D.C. Fire Department, the Recreation Board, and certain other Public Welfare institutions. According to the order, segregation will be abolished later in all of these.[13]

In the case of the Recreation Board, the Commissioners contended that they do not have the authority to order the end of segregation. However, in this agency, too, it is expected that segregation will be eliminated.[14]

The Bureau Director and the President of the D.C. Branch both urged Administration officials to have the order cover all agencies. The Director expressed the strong belief that if the Commissioners were unwilling to give a blanket order a piece-meal approach might be worse than none at all. Nevertheless, the Commissioners issued the order and it was severely criticized by residents of Washington. The editorial comment of the *Washington Post* seems appropriate here.

> "We doubt very much that this kind of compromise contributes any more to expediency than it does to principle. Piece-meal abandonment of discrimination entails a repetition and prolongation of the wrench away from outmoded patterns of behavior. The only way to abandon discrimination is to abandon it."

VETERANS HOSPITALS

We have received some very encouraging reports on abolition of segregation in Veterans hospitals, but, because of the length of the Bureau's report, we will not include them at this time.[15] However, it should be noted that apparently the Veterans Administration has abandoned the concept that segregation is necessary for medical reasons in hospitals handling neuro-psychiatric cases.[16]

HOTEL SEGREGATION

A teacher in Dayton, Ohio, requested the help of the Bureau in obtaining hotel accommodations for an all colored class which will visit Washington in May or June. Mr. William Pryor of the Bureau staff checked hotels and discovered that most of the moderate price hotels would accept the group only if colored children were a small part of the total number.

A news story on the incident appeared in *Jet* magazine and the teacher advised us, on the instruction of her superiors, she did not wish to make an issue out of the matter. She stated that, if necessary, the students would stay at an uptown colored hotel. However, we have offered the Burlington Hotel which is in the downtown section. This hotel has advised that it follows the policy of accommodating whatever group a reliable transportation company brings to it and this would include an all colored group.

LIFE MEMBERSHIP

Mr. Presly Holliday is a resident of the U.S. Soldiers Home. The Director has only a rough idea of Mr. Holliday's age but he appears to be at least 70. Mr. Holliday has paid a total of $250.00 on a life membership but refuses to let his name be published. He has suggested, instead, the story of his gift be told without use of his name as a means of encouraging other soldiers to give to the NAACP.

ADMISSION OF ABDULLAHI ISSA TO THE UNITED STATES

After many weeks of negotiations, numerous telephone calls, and meetings by the Director of the Bureau, Mr. Abdullahi Issa, a representative of the Somali Youth League of the Territory of Somaliland, was readmitted to the United States to present a plea on behalf of his people at the United Nations. After handling this case, the Director's sympathies for persons caught in the meshes of red tape are greatly increased.[17]

DENIAL OF APPOINTMENT TO OREGON SENATOR BILL

The Director of the Washington Bureau handled some aspects of the Oregon protest against the appointment of State Senator Warren Gill as U.S. Attorney. It is pleasing to note that Mr. Gill was not appointed because he opposed civil rights legislation in his home state.

SPEAKING ENGAGEMENTS

The Director of the Washington Bureau had speaking engagements during the Month of November in Petersburgh, Virginia, and Philadelphia and Pittsburgh, Pennsylvania.

MS: NAACP II: A-537, DLC.

This report is a direct follow-up to those of November 2 and 4, 1953, which Mitchell prepared at Walter White's direction for the development of strategy in the next session of Congress.

1. See 12/31/53 for new schedule of hearings.

2. The board approved the sending of the following wire to the president:

> We have been advised by Senator Homer Ferguson, chairman of the Senate Policy Committee, that civil rights will be on the agenda at the forthcoming series of conferences that you will hold with leaders of Congress to plan the legislative program for the new congress. Despite the steady and continuing march of progress in the courts and the executive branch of government on civil rights, the Congress has been guilty of woeful neglect by failing to pass much-needed laws to safeguard the rights of all of the people in the United States.
>
> We approach a possible business setback in our economy with no national law to prevent wholesale racial discrimination in employment. In all the many pronouncements on revising the Taft-Hartley law, there is no sign that the vital Ives Amendment against discrimination in matters under the jurisdiction of NLRB will be approved by the White House. It is significant that each member of the Senate Labor Committee except one is a sponsor of this amendment. In today's Board meeting we heard the shocking details of the arrest of a colored officer of the Air Force [Lt. Williams, 10/6, 12/7, and 12/31/53] because he refused to accept segregation while he was a passenger on an inter-state bus. Yet no hearings have been held on pending bills to put an end to segregation in inter-state travel. We strongly ask you to urge the leaders of Congress that they have a duty to consider and pass legislation which protects and strengthens the American heritage of civil rights for all. We ask that your message to Congress offer a ringing challenge and a call for action in this vital field. (Minutes, 12/14/53, EC; see also 12/31/53)

3. See 10/6/53 for initial mention of this case and 12/31/53.

4. Subsequent to his May 3, 1951, report, Mitchell continued to monitor developments at the Bureau of Printing and Engraving, as shown in his memorandum of August 3, 1953, which provides a history of this struggle dating back to 1938, and other documents in the collection. Mitchell memorandum, 8/3/51, NAACP WB-18, DLC. See 12/31/53 for the continuing effort.

5. Mitchell targeted all three branches of government for protests. As an example, in 1952, he complained to John W. Snyder, secretary of the treasury, that the Bureau of Printing and Engraving, as in the past, was seeking to ignore the list of eligible hires "because a fair system of naming individuals to vacancies would have inevitably resulted in the appointment of colored persons." Mitchell's letter to Snyder, 2/13/52, NAACP WB-18, DLC. See also 2/28 and 3/9/54.

6. See 2/4, 4/3, 5/4, 6/15, and 10/6/53, 2/17/54; materials in NAACP WB-171, DLC.

7. Albert Cole, whose appointment as HHFA administrator Mitchell had vigorously opposed, regarded the Eisenhower administration's deliberations over the future of pubic housing as "our Number One policy issue." Hunt, "How Did Public Housing Survive the 1950s?" 200. For the NAACP's related activities, see also, among others, 12/31/53, 2/28 and 3/9/54, as well as the headnote on Segregation in Federal Housing Programs, vol. III.

8. The deliberations of Eisenhower's decisive 1953 Presidential Advisory Committee on Government Housing Policies and Programs showed the program's fragility and the relationships between public housing, urban redevelopment, and the FHA. Hunt, "How Did Public Housing Survive the 1950s?" 194.

9. This battle was central to the NAACP's broader struggle to stop the federal government from displacing thousands of black inner-city families from their communities. Subsequent to the NAACP delegation's meeting with Albert Cole in Washington (see 9/9/53), the administrator "and members of the shirtsleeves conferences" began holding hearings on the federal housing program with local groups around the country. Ruby Hurley, secretary of the Southeast Regional NAACP Office, led one such meeting in Birmingham in October and repeated the NAACP's complaints that had been made to Cole in Washington. Letter from Mabel W. Spencer, secretary to Hurley, 10/6/53, with Birmingham NAACP Branch Statement, NAACP WB-92, DLC.

Mitchell next recommended that Walter White obtain the NAACP board's approval to write Eisenhower requesting that his administration not approve the Birmingham redevelopment project until the city "gives positive assurance that there will not be any racial segregation in [the related] housing or medical facilities." Mitchell memorandum to White, 10/7/53, NAACP WB-92, DLC. No record was found regarding White bringing this recommendation to the board.

Instead, early in December, representatives of the NAACP and of community and church organizations held a meeting with the mayor of Birmingham and the director of Slum Clearance and Redevelopment of the Housing Authority, Birmingham District; they reiterated the concerns that had been expressed to Cole at the August 14, 1953, meeting in Washington. Ruby Hurley informed the board that although NAACP representatives had made no commitments at the meeting, the mayor issued a statement to the press afterward that caused some to accuse the NAACP of having "sold out." Consequently, the NAACP would seek another meeting to clarify (1) press accounts that "a hotel and motel" were to be built in the area of the planned medical center; (2) when blacks would be appointed to the city's planning, zoning, relocation, and other boards; and (3) who was "going to build the proposed Negro hospital, etc." Report of the Secretary for November, 12/14/53, EC.

Earlier, White had stated that developments had shown housing and city officials in Birmingham had "finally come to the realization that the NAACP [was] a force to be reckoned with," since Washington had granted money to other cities but not Birmingham. The regional NAACP office, he said, felt that "the Medical Center Redevelopment program was as strategically important for us as the Civil War was for the institution of slavery." Report of the Secretary for October, 11/9/53, EC.

10. On November 25, 1953, HHFA announced that it had allocated on that day $4,058,000 in loans for the medical center and $858,780 in a capital grant. In reaffirming that step, J. W. Follin, HHFA director, told Ruby Hurley that "this allocation was made only after a most careful and sympathetic consideration of the racial aspects mentioned" in her telegram of February 9, 1954, to Albert Cole again deploring HHFA's "apparent disregard of the colored people of Birmingham and the pronouncements of the Chief Executive" in his housing message of January 25, 1954. Follin's letter to Hurley, 2/12/54; Hurley's telegram, 2/9/54 to Cole and related materials are in NAACP IX 3, DLC; "Special Message to the Congress on Housing," 1/25/54, Eisenhower, *Public Papers of the Presidents, 1954*, 197–201. See also 4/21/54, *Hearings*, 686–92.

11. See 9/9/53, 3/9/54.

12. See, among others, 3/9 and 5/5/54.

13. Samuel Spencer, president of the District of Columbia Board of Commissioners, notified Eisenhower of the board's desegregation order in an attempt to bring the district into "accord with that of the Federal Government." He recalled Eisenhower's State of the Union message on February 2, 1953, in which the president promised to use all available powers to end segregation in the nation's capital. The commissioners ordered all the city's agencies to hire and discharge employees without regard to race, creed, or color. In addition to the Fire Department, the order exempted the schools and recreation facilities that were operated independently, even though they were under the district government budget control. *New York Times*, 11/26/53, 28. See also, among others, 11/5/51, 9/29/54.

14. See 12/28/51 for developments leading to the Washington bureau's involvement in attacking segregation in recreation facilities. See also 3/3, 6/15, 11/4, and 12/31/53, 12/6 and 12/31/54 for other aspects and later developments in this struggle, as well as Burkart, "Yonder Sits the Rocking-Chair," *Crisis* 59 (December 1952): 619–24, for an overview of segregation and discrimination in the capital.

15. Mitchell provided a full report on the NAACP's victory in this struggle at 6/29/54. See also, most immediately, 11/4 and 12/31/53.

16. The VA's abandoning of the concept that segregation in its hospitals was necessary for medical reasons resulted from the NAACP's strong protests, which Dr. Montague Cobb lodged with the agency. See 10/6/53; materials in NAACP, WB-185, DLC; Watson, *Lion in the Lobby*, 258.

17. Italy, administrator of the Somaliland trust territory, had outlawed the Somali Youth League (SYL). Between 1940 and 1950, the NAACP assisted the SYL in its efforts at the United Nation to prevent the return of the territory to Italy. "Somali Youth League," *Crisis* (October 1952): 516.

Annual Report, December 31, 1953

[December 31, 1953]

NAACP'S WASHINGTON BUREAU—SUMMARY OF 1953 HIGHLIGHTS

THE RIGHT TO WORK

President Eisenhower reestablished by Executive Order No. 10,479 the Government Contract Committee which has the duty to enforce the non-discrimination clause in government contracts on August 13, 1953.[1]

Among the historical items in the Washington Bureau is the pen used by the President to sign the Executive Order. It was sent to the Bureau Director from the White House.

— — —

A serious crisis has arisen in the Bureau of Printing and Engraving. As a result of a favorable decision before the Federal Fair Employment Board, colored employees for the first time were permitted to take apprentice training as plate printers beginning in 1951. This year, the men were suddenly removed from their jobs for "economic reasons." Since this action has the effect of reversing the Fair Employment Board's decision, the question now, is will the President uphold the Bureau or the Fair Employment Board?[2]

— — —

Senator Irving Ives introduced S. 1831 which is an amendment to the National Labor Management Relations Act. It would bar segregation and discrimination in matters under the jurisdiction of NLRB.[3]

Others joining Mr. Ives on this amendment are Senators Smith of New Jersey, Aiken of Vermont, Griswold of Nebraska, Purtell of Connecticut, Goldwater of Arizona, Murray of Montana, Neely of West Virginia, Douglas of Illinois, Lehman of New York, and Kennedy of Massachusetts.[4]

A similar amendment was introduced in the House by Representative Adam Clayton Powell (D.,N.Y.), and Representative Jacob Javits (R., N.Y.).[5]

— — —

Hearings on the Ives-Humphrey FEPC Bill, S. 692, will begin in the U.S. Senate on January 12 through 15 and January 19 through 21, 1954.[6]

OUSTING JIM-CROW FROM THE CLASSROOM

President Eisenhower merits praise for following through on NAACP urging that segregation in schools on military posts be abolished. The Chief Executive has promised to end it, and, in September, all such schools run by the Federal authorities were integrated.

There was only one major post on which Federally operated schools were still segregated. This was at Fort Benning, Georgia. It is significant that the integration in these schools was accomplished peacefully and successfully despite opposition from Governor Talmadge. However, there are twenty-one schools which are jointly run by local authorities and the U.S. Government, although most of the cost is paid by Uncle Sam. Here, we are encountering stubborn resistance by local officials and sabotage by some Federal officials.

Recent information we have received from Assistant Secretary of Defense, John A. Hannah, and the new U.S. Commissioner of Education, Dr. Samuel Brownell, gives us reason to hope that this problem will be resolved in 1954.[7]

— — — — —

We are also seeking the end of segregation in schools run by the Atomic Energy Commission. On April 2, we urged Mr. Gordon Dean, who was then Chairman of AEC, to end segregation in the schools at Oak Ridge, Tennessee. In subsequent conferences with AEC officials, we learned that a segregated system resulted in considerable financial loss to the Federal Government. It is interesting to note that on

December 23 the Oak Ridge Town Council voted to ask the President to end segregation on the schools there. We have reminded the new AEC Chief, Mr. Lewis L. Strauss, that segregation in Oak Ridge Schools is not only immoral, but it is also economically unsound.[8]

TAKING THE CHUCKLE OUT OF THE KREMLIN

No doubt the halls of the Kremlin vibrate with chuckles when U. S. soldiers are the victims of segregation and police brutality here at home. When we have successfully concluded the following, there will be more smiles over here and less joy in hostile propaganda mills abroad. A Navy move on this front helped civilian employees.

1: Lieutenant Thomas Williams was dropped from the U. S. Air Force after he was arrested in Florida for failing to accept segregation on an inter-state bus.[9]

2: Corporal Lee Roy Cail was arrested in Richmond, Virginia, because he attempted to give medical assistance to a soldier who was shot. The victim of the arrest wears numerous decorations for similar action on battlefields in Africa, Italy, the Philippines, and Korea. In Richmond, his reward was 107 days in jail and demotion to private because the army considered him AWOL when he was in prison.

3: U. S. soldiers en route from Columbia to Fort Jackson, South Carolina, were jailed and fined, just prior to going on overseas duty, because they did not obey the driver's interpretation of the Jim-Crow laws of that state while on a bus.

4: Private James E. Wade of Camp Polk, Louisiana, was severely beaten by Leesville, Louisiana, policemen because he "was just a smart nigger who needed the— beat out of him."

H. Lee White, Assistant Secretary of the Air Force, now has Lieutenant Williams' case before him. The Assistant Secretary has also promised to issue a statement on the question of whether service persons who refuse to obey segregation laws that the U. S. Supreme Court has declared unconstitutional should be disciplined by superior officers.

Congress has before it bills which will end segregation in inter-state travel and give protection to members of the Armed Services who are the victims of local police brutality. If these bills pass in 1954, democracy will win another round in the battle for world leadership.[10]

The Navy Department has issued official instructions to end all segregation in shore establishments in the South. This climaxes a long campaign waged by the NAACP to end segregated drinking fountains, Jim-Crow restaurants, and other forms of humiliation of civilian employees working in southern Naval establishments. Latest reports show that order is being carried out successfully even in Georgia, Mississippi, and South Carolina.

Action in this field was initiated by the Washington Bureau at the request of Jerry O. Gilliam of Norfolk, Virginia, and Thaddeus Fraser of Charleston, South Carolina.[11]

A GOOD PRESCRIPTION FOR WILLING PATIENT

Government officials usually hand out a lot of advice, but seldom do they accept any. Veterans Administrator Harvey Higley is not in this class. He has tackled the long standing problem of segregation in veterans hospitals. At one point, he regarded hospitals for mental patients as areas in which progress would be most difficult. At the Bureau's request, Dr. Montague Cobb, Chairman of the Association's National Health Committee, and Dr. Jerome D. Frank of Johns Hopkins Hospital advised Mr. Higley that there was no medical necessity for segregation in mental hospitals.

George L. Holland, Assistant to the Administrator of the Veterans Administration, who has persistently worked against segregation in VA hospitals estimates that all will be integrated by March of 1954.[12]

Important hospitals in many southern states have already changed. Some of these are at Little Rock, Arkansas; Jackson, Mississippi; Nashville, Tennessee, and Oklahoma City, Oklahoma.[13]

YOU STILL SUPPORT JIM-CROW HOUSING

The Federal Housing Program, which is supported by your tax money, is still the greatest single force in promoting housing segregation in the United States.[14] The Bureau has told the Housing officials that:

> "The national housing policy should result in a supply of dwellings at reasonable sale and rental rates which will be open to all persons without regard to race, religion or national origin. The government has no business supporting any other kind of policy."

A policy of no segregation in any Federally-assisted housing program can be established immediately without the help of Congress. This is a major challenge to the new Administration.[15]

DISTRICT OF COLUMBIA SEGREGATION

Although notable strides have been made in ending segregation in Washington theaters and restaurants, a number of areas are still troublesome. Most of the Washington hotels have established quotas for colored guests. The public recreation program under the Government of the District of Columbia is still segregated.[16]

LEGISLATIVE OUTLOOK

The Congress is still handicapped by rules that permit filibusters and other delaying tactics.[17]

In the Senate, there is a friendly Labor Committee that is handling FEPC legislation. However, the House Committee is not favorable for a FEPC with enforcement powers.

Anti Jim-Crow Travel, Anti-Lynching, and Anti-Poll Tax Bills are being mentioned as possible items for consideration by G.O.P. leaders.[18]

The House has passed a bill to make Hawaii a state.[19] Smothered in committee is a bill to give similar status to Alaska.[20] The Senate may face a filibuster when the Hawaii Bill comes up, but southern members of Congress are divided on this measure. In the House, it is supported by Congressmen from Texas, Georgia, Louisiana, and other anti-civil rights areas. The vote favored Statehood by 274 to 178.

The Senate Judiciary Committee on June 15, by a vote of 9 to 5, reported out a Constitutional Amendment which would limit the Treaty making power of the President. Some of its supporters said it was necessary to halt civil rights advances in the United States.[21] This is a false and thoroughly dishonest argument.

The NAACP is on record against the amendment. It appears that this will be an important issue in the next session of Congress.[22]

MS: NAACP II: A-537, DLC.

1. At a conference on November 30, 1953, with Maxwell Rabb, counsel to the president, James P. Mitchell, secretary of labor, and J. Ernest Wilkins, vice chair of the President's Committee, Walter White and Mitchell urged the committee to take "speedy action" on cases involving the telephone company and Capital Transit Company in Washington; the atomic energy installations in Paducah, Kentucky, and Aiken, South Carolina; and defense industries in West Virginia, where serious discrimination problems had been documented. NAACP press release, 12/3/53, and other materials pertaining to the conference are in NAACP II: A-200, DLC. See also 8/21 and 9/9/53 and the headnote on the Struggle for a Permanent FEPC, 1942–54, vol. III.

2. See, among others, 12/7/53, 3/9/54.

3. See also 12/7/53.

4. See also, most immediately, 5/5/53, 8/21/54; 1/29/54, *Hearings*, 3177–84.

5. See 6/23/53, *Hearings*, 203–5.

6. See also 2/4, 6/1, 6/15, and 12/31/53, 2/28, 3/9, and 12/31/54.

7. Information the NAACP had received showed that the states were paying very little of the costs for operating schools on military posts, giving the federal government considerable leverage in pushing for full cooperation with integration orders. So Mitchell recommended that "all leases for school property on military posts be voided if local authorities seek to use this as a pretext for failing to comply with the Defense Department directive." In sum, the information showed the need for an overall declaration by the federal government that would end segregation in all federally operated schools or schools on federal territory that were "operated jointly by contributions from local governments and any type of Federal funds." Memorandum on "Recent Developments in the Matter of Segregation in Schools on Military Posts and Other Federal Areas," 2/19/54. See also 10/6/53; Watson, *Lion in the Lobby*, 241–46.

8. See also 4/3 and 5/4/53.

9. See also 10/6 and 12/7/53.

10. In addition to Mitchell's efforts in Congress, Robert Carter reported to the board that the NAACP had filed a complaint against eleven companies with the Interstate Commerce Commission, asking it to issue an order banning the segregation of interstate passengers by railroads, stations, and

restaurants in states where such practices occurred. The complaint was filed on behalf of the NAACP as an organization and seventeen individuals, including one white person. Minutes, 12/14/53, EC.

11. See also, most immediately, 11/4/53, 6/29/54.

12. See materials on George L. Holland in NAACP WB-185, DLC. Mitchell's relationship with Holland began when the lobbyist was executive secretary of the St. Paul Urban League in Minnesota from 1937 to 1941. See Watson, *Lion in the Lobby*, 107, 411.

13. See also, most immediately, 12/7/53, 3/9/54; Watson, *Lion in the Lobby*, 258; materials in NAACP WB-185, DLC.

14. At the December 14, 1953, board meeting, Robert C. Weaver, a member, urged his associates to get a copy of the report of the President's Advisory Committee on Housing. "The new administration's approach will emphasize conservation. There will be no more housing for low income groups. The Association will have to direct its thoughts as to what can be done to prevent new segregated communities." Minutes, 12/14/53, EC.

15. Mitchell's anxiety was further increased by his knowledge that Eisenhower, leading the Republican Legislative Conference on December 17, 1953, noted then that Cole had presented for consideration his department's program "with special emphasis on assisting low income families in obtaining good housing accommodations." "Statement by the President on the First Day of the Republican Legislative Conference in the Cabinet Room," 12/17/53, Eisenhower, *Public Papers of the Presidents*, 1953, 848. See also "Notes on the Legislative Leadership Conference," 12/17–19/53, DDE, Papers of the President, Legislative Meeting Series, DDEL; handwritten notes on presentation by Albert Cole, 12/17/53, WHO, Office of Staff Secretary, Legislative Meeting Series, L-6 (2), DDEL; 9/9 and 12/7/53, 2/28 and 3/9/54; and the headnote on Segregation in Federal Housing Programs, vol. III.

16. See also 3/3, 6/15, 11/4, and 12/7/53, 9/29, 12/6, and 12/31/54.

17. See also the headnote on the NAACP and the Filibuster, vol. III.

18. Mitchell provided Walter White with an overall direction in a memorandum on "Recommendations on Legislative Program," 2/6/53, MP, which has been used at 2/4, 3/3, and 5/4/53. See also 12/7/53; Mitchell, "These Are the Issues," *Crisis* 59 (October 1952): 483–86, which he prepared for the Democratic and Republican parties in the 1952 national elections.

19. The House passed the bill on March 10, 1953. See also, among others, 4/30/53.

20. Attempts to grant Alaska statehood got bogged down in procedural maneuvers, regarding whether to consider this effort separately from that involving the struggle over Hawaii statehood. *Congressional Quarterly Weekly Report*, 5/15/53. See also, among others, 6/15 and 11/4/53.

21. *New York Times*, 6/16/53, 1, 13.

22. This effort was initiated by Sen. John W. Bricker (R-Ohio), who, on January 7, 1953, along with sixty-three cosponsors, introduced S.J. Res. 1, a proposed constitutional amendment to limit the treaty-making power of the president. *Congress and the Nation*, 110–11. See also 9/29/54.

Recent Highlights in the NAACP Campaign against Segregation in Schools on Military Posts, and Additional Steps in Integration of Schools on Military Posts, February 17, 1954

[February 17, 1954]

On March 25, 1953, the White House announced that President Eisenhower had sent a memorandum to the Department of Defense on racial segregation in schools on military posts. If properly carried out, the President's memorandum dooms Jim-Crow in all schools on military posts. Already, it has been announced that beginning in the Fall term segregation will end in the Federally operated schools on military posts.

The NAACP is working to make certain that the memorandum will also end segregation in schools located on military posts but operated by local school officials. We shall accomplish this objective, but let no one believe that it does not require a considerable amount of additional effort.

A volume could be written on what we did to reach our present position on this matter. However, we have compressed happenings of the last six months into this short statement. We pay tribute to Mrs. E. N. Williams of El Paso, Texas, and the many Army wives both white and colored, who cannot be named but who, with Mrs. Williams, have worked in local communities to support the effort being made in Washington.

Deserving praise, also, are Mrs. Alice Dunnigan of the Associated Negro Press, who raised this question at a White House Press Conference, and Mrs. Sarah McClendon, a white native Texan, who faithfully and fairly reported developments through the chain of newspapers she serves as Washington correspondent.[1]

January 10, 1953: As a result of a conference between Mrs. Anna Rosenberg, Assistant Secretary of Defense, Senator Hubert Humphrey, the NAACP, and other Defense officials, Mrs. Rosenberg informed the U. S. Office of Education that it was her Department's desire to end segregation in all schools on military posts, if such action did not conflict with legal requirements (Public Law 874) of funds administered by the Office of Education.

January 15, 1953: Commissioner Earl J. McGrath advised the Department of Defense that nothing in existing Federal Laws prevented the ending of racial segregation in schools on military posts. He said,

"If it is the policy of the Department of Defense not to permit segregated education on any property within its control, whether that education be by local school agencies under Section 3 (of P.L. 874) or by the Commissioner of Education operating under Section 6 (schools operated solely by Federal Government) this agency would, of course, be guided by such a policy. It would be necessary in that event to determine in each case whether any local educational agency which now providing education on a segregated basis is able to provide such education on an integrated basis. *In any case in which the local educational agency is not able to provide education on an integrated basis, the Commissioner would then be under the necessity of making other arrangements for education of such children.*"

January 27, 1953: Senators Duff, Hendrickson, Morse, Ives, Lehman and Humphrey joined the NAACP in urging that the Department of Defense conclude the work started by Mrs. Rosenberg and order integration in all schools on military posts. The communications were addressed to Dr. John A. Hannah, Assistant Secretary of Defense, who replaced Mrs. Rosenberg.

February 4, 1953: The Director of the NAACP's Washington Bureau, in a White House meeting, submitted a memorandum on a number of problems including the school question. We had previously outlined the same matters in a conference with

Senator Henry Cabot Lodge, Jr., when he was serving as liaison man for President-elect Eisenhower. Senator Lodge promised to discuss the questions with the new Chief Executive. He also pledged that the new President would follow through and end racial segregation in schools on military posts.

February 20, 1953: Colonel Frank C. Norvell, Executive Assistant in the Office of the Secretary of Defense, wrote that the Army was taking steps which would "result in education of dependents on Army posts without racial considerations." However, he declined to give a date on which full integration would be achieved.

March 19, 1953: Mrs. Alice Dunnigan, White House reporter for ANP after discussing the matter with the NAACP, asked the President at his press conference whether segregation in schools on military posts would be ended.

On this same date, Congressman Adam Clayton Powell, Jr. submitted an NAACP memorandum on this subject to the President. Acknowledgment on behalf of the President was made by General Wilton B. Persons, Special Assistant to the President.

March 25, 1953: The President announced that segregation in all Federally operated schools on military posts would be ended by the Fall term. He also pledged that military Commanders would negotiate with local authorities to achieve similar results in schools located on military posts but operated by local or state authorities.

May 1, 1953: Dr. John Hannah, Assistant Secretary of Defense, informed the Executive Secretary and the Director of the Washington Bureau that the Department of Health, Education, and Welfare had suggested that integration in schools on 21 military posts should be delayed.

June 3, 1953: Congressman Adam Powell placed an NAACP statement in the *Congressional Record* charging that integration was being held up by the Department of Health, Education, and Welfare. He also urged the President to end segregation.

June 11, 1953: An NAACP wire to the President urged action to end segregation in the 21 schools.

ADDITIONAL STEPS IN INTEGRATION OF SCHOOLS ON MILITARY POSTS FEBRUARY 17, 1954

June 11, 1953: Congressman Powell at a hearing before the House Committee on Education and Labor obtained admission from U.S. Office of Education officials that money could be transferred from the States to Defense installations to operate schools on a non-segregated basis. He also obtained a listing of locations of segregated schools.

September 16, 1953: Dr. Hannah announced at a press conference that segregation in schools on military posts would be ended by the fall of 1955. The NAACP said it could see no reason for delay. The Association also charged that "military officials entered into new contracts to keep schools on posts segregated even after the President had clearly stated such policies should end."

September 17, 1953: The NAACP received report that the end of segregation at Fort Benning, Ga., schools (operated entirely by Federal Government) had been accomplished.

September 23, 1953: Senator Humphrey protested to the President about continued segregation in schools on military posts that are operated by the states.

September 23, 1953: Dr. Hannah advised the NAACP "we have insisted that military services eliminate segregated schools not later than September 1, 1955." He also said: "my attitude on racial integration is firmly fixed and well known and I do not expect to vary from it.["]

November 6, 1953: Sherman, Texas, Democrat in page one story announced new school would be built at Perrin Air Force Base. The story also stated that the school would be ready for occupancy about 1955 and would be for whites only. The NAACP protest caused Defense officials to halt plans for segregated school.

November 23, 1953: The NAACP protested to Major General William S. Biddle's dedication of segregated school at Fort Hood. The school is operated by officials of Killeen, Texas, (Mrs. Hobby's hometown.)

December 18, 1953: Commissioner Samuel Brownell of the U.S. Office of Education advised the director of the Washington Bureau that details for ending segregation in schools of 21 posts that are operated under state supervision had been agreed upon in meeting with Dr. Hannah.

January 12, 1954: The Wilson order was sent to the Navy, Air Force and Army.

MS: MP.

The date of this document is based on the second part of Mitchell's report, beginning at June 11, 1953.

1. See, most immediately, 12/7/53, 2/28, 3/9, 5/5, 6/29, 9/29, 11/4, and 12/31/54. The struggle to desegregate schools on military posts was subsumed by the broader struggle related to the NAACP's victory in the *Brown v. Board of Education* case. See also materials on this struggle in NAACP WB-171, DLC; MacGregor, *Integration of the Armed Forces*, 488–98; Watson, *Lion in the Lobby*, 241–46; Mitchell, "Status of Racial Integration in the Armed Services."

Monthly Report, February 28, 1954

[February 28, 1954]

DEPARTMENT OF HEALTH, EDUCATION AND WELFARE

Mrs. Jane M. Spaulding is the first casualty of the jim-crow attitude of Mrs. Oveta Culp Hobby, Secretary of Health Education and Welfare. Although Mrs. Spaulding signed a resignation, she was actually forced out of the Department with the acquiescence of the White House. A full memorandum on this has been prepared by the bureau.[1]

It appears that Howard University is the next target. Several faculty members of the University have been called on the carpet by the FBI because of membership in the Washington Chapter of the Lawyers Guild.[2] A study is being made under the supervision of Nelson Rockefeller, Under Secretary of HEW, to determine whether Federal funds should be withdrawn from Howard.

SEGREGATION OF SCHOOLS ON MILITARY POSTS

An order dated January 12 and signed by Secretary of Defense Charles E. Wilson requires the end of all segregation in schools on military posts not later than September 1955. A summary of the NAACP's work in this matter has been prepared.[3]

SEGREGATION AT THE U.S. SOLDIERS HOME

Segregation at the U.S. Soldiers home in Washington has long been a trouble spot. This month the Department of the Army advised that it would end segregation following a persistent association campaign.[4] Unfortunately, this is not a closed case because the Army said segregation would be ended "gradually." We are still at work on this.

JIM CROW TRAVEL BILL

Chances are better than even that an anti-jim crow travel bill may pass in this session of Congress. Extensive work has been done on this.[5]

FEPC HEARINGS

It is well known now that January FEPC hearings were postponed. In a counter move a sub-committee of the Senate Judiciary Committee started hearings on bills which would establish a Civil Rights Commissions without enforcement powers.[6] We appeared in opposition to these bills as substitutes for FEPC with enforcement powers.[7]

TAFT-HARTLEY HEARINGS

Following a vigorous protest by the Bureau to our friends on the Senate Labor Committee, the director was heard in the current Taft-Hartley hearings on the President's recommendations.[8] Staff members of the committee and Senator Smith had tried to bar an NAACP appearance. One member of the committee received a note from Senator Smith (prior to the director's appearance) saying that he (Smith) had "worked out an arrangement with his colored friends about testifying." Apparently Senator Smith had hoped to use this to give the impression that we did not wish to be heard. At the hearing Senator Smith asked whether we wanted our proposed amendments or hearings on FEPC. We said we wanted both.

AIR FORCE AND ARMY POLICY

The assistant secretary of the Air Force advised this month that superior officers will not be permitted to discipline colored troops for violating jim crow laws when in interstate travel.[9]

The army also advised that in response to our protest none of soldiers arrested at Fort Jackson on Thanksgiving night during a dispute about jim crow seating on a bus would be disciplined.[10] It also advised that the matter had been referred to the Department of Justice for whatever action may be warranted. This has since been confirmed by the Department of Justice.

HOUSING POLICY

Following our meeting with the President the director met with Albert Cole, administrator of the Housing and Home Finance Agency to ask that the following be included in the President's message to Congress on housing include clear language announcing that no more Federal Aid would be given for segregated housing. The language we suggested was not included in the message.[11] It should be added that we made a similar effort to have a statement included in the President's labor message.[12] We talked with Secretary James Mitchell of the Labor Department on this without success.

LIFE MEMBERSHIP

This month Mr. Presly Holliday, a retired soldier who is nearly blind made his last payment on a life membership. His check is for $250.

NATIONAL ASSOCIATION FOR THE ADVANCEMENT OF WHITE PEOPLE

William Pryor has prepared an interesting report on the National Association for the Advancement of White People that has opened a chapter in Washington.

MEETING WITH THE SECRETARY OF THE TREASURY

The director had an interesting meeting with the Secretary of the Treasury on behalf of Bureau of Engraving Employees. If the mission is successful it will be a major victory for fair employment. The Secretary was cordial and promised co-operation. We shall see what comes of it.[13]

MS: NAACP II: A-670, DLC.
This roughly typed, unfinished text was preceded by the following note: "Dear Mabel: The following is a brief report I have typed myself at 7:00 pm. The past three weeks have been very, very rugged. Please get it in if you can. Clarence."

The editor has incorporated Mitchell's corrections in the text, thus providing the clean text he had intended.

1. Spaulding, in her letter of resignation, said she was leaving to take another position in the War Claims Commission because it offered opportunities for advancement. Apparently, she was under the impression she would be receiving a higher salary. But, Mitchell said, "a move was under way to cut" sharply her salary at Health, Education and Welfare (HEW) and limit her job functions. HEW's announcement said Spaulding had been with the department since April 14, 1953. In the absence of Hobby, Nelson A. Rockefeller, acting secretary, accepted her resignation. Mitchell said HEW was an important agency, but he did not believe much could be accomplished in improving racial conditions there under Hobby. Spaulding's letter, 1/21/54, to Hobby; Rockefeller's letter, 2/22/54, and HEW's news release, 2/2/54; letter from Floyd Howard Skinner, 2/20/54, to Mitchell regarding the developments involving Spaulding; Mitchell's response to Spaulding, 2/21/54, all of which are in NAACP IX: 98, DLC.

Hobby had confirmed Mitchell's worst fears when, testifying before the House Interstate and Foreign Commerce Committee in a series of such appearances, she presented her plans to change all grant-in-aid programs from an "earmarked" to a "state-plan" basis. She began allocating each state its share of grant funds earmarked by Congress for specific purposes, such as for control of cancer or for education in home economics. Under her plan, each state was allowed to set up its own plans for these federally funded programs. *New York Times*, 3/5/54, 12. See also 4/3/53.

Hobby's policy for funding federal grant-in-aid programs was anathema to Mitchell's struggle to get the government to adopt nondiscrimination protections for such programs, especially for hospital construction and the operation of schools in defense-impacted areas. See note 3 below.

2. The National Lawyers Guild, controversial because of its aggressive espousal of liberal causes, was then battling the attempts by the attorney general to list the organization as communist. Within the NAACP itself, membership in or association with the guild was causing divisions. At its March 9, 1954, meeting, the board voted 19 to 3 not to approve or recommend any participation amicus curiae in the ongoing proceedings in which the National Lawyers Guild was seeking an injunction against

the attorney general to prohibit him from proceeding further in listing it as a communist organization. Minutes, 3/9/54, EC.

3. Memorandum for the Secretary of the Army, Secretary of the Navy, Secretary of the Air Force, from the Secretary of Defense, 1/12/54. Seeking to squelch fears that Hobby would not support the integration of schools on military posts, Wilson announced:

> There is absolutely no truth to stories attributed to authoritative sources that the Department of Health, Eduction and Welfare has opposed integrated schools on military bases. Quite to the contrary, Mrs. Hobby and the Department of Health, Education, and Welfare have actively assisted the Defense Department in working out a program to end segregation in schools at the earliest possible moment in line with President Eisenhower's statement issued last Spring. . . .
>
> Since the schools are located on military property the basic responsibility for making the determination as to when the abolition of segregation should occur is that [of] the Department of Defense.
>
> Both the Department of Health, Education and Welfare and the Defense Department are working actively on the solution of this problem, and we have mutually set September 1, 1955, as the time for its complete solution. (DOD press release, 2/1/54, MP. See also Wilson memorandum, 1/12/54; Hobby's response to Wilson, by way of a detailed memorandum to the president, 4/13/54, on her understanding of the three conditions involving schools operated on federal posts, and other related materials are in NAACP IX: 98, DLC)

See also, most immediately, 2/17, 3/9, 5/5, 6/29, 9/29, 11/14, and 12/31/54.

4. Mitchell had been complaining about segregation at the Soldiers' Home in Washington at least since 1952, when Thomas J. Simmons, first lieutenant in the Office of the Assistant Secretary of Defense, sent him a copy of the War Department's letter of July 8, 1944, to commanding generals of the army air forces, all service commands, and the military district in Washington. The letter informed them that effective compliance with War Department policies providing equal opportunity to enjoy recreational facilities on each post, camp, and station would be obtained through inspection by responsible commanders and inspectors general. Simmons told Mitchell that even though the directive might not have included the U.S. Soldiers' Home, it was hoped that Mitchell would be successful in his approaches. Simmons memorandum to Mitchell, 9/30/52, attached to the War Department's letter, 7/8/44, NAACP IX: 60, DLC.

The Soldiers' Home in Washington was established in 1851 as an "asylum for disabled veterans." A brief history is available at http://www.afrh.gov/afrh/wash/whistory.htm.

5. See also, among others, 12/31/53, 5/5 and 6/4/54, as well as the headnote on the Struggle to End Jim Crow Travel, vol. III.

6. This is a continuation of the struggle reported on at 2/4/53. In a proposed statement of January 17, 1954, Mitchell said: "For the second time, Senator [H. Alexander] Smith has dealt FEPC a deadly blow. In 1947, although he was a sponsor of the bill, he made a drastic proposal to weaken it. This year, he has over-ridden the wishes of the sponsors and postponed the hearings. This action on his part will effectively destroy chances for passing the bill in this session of Congress." The statement accompanied a memorandum that was used in a press release by the NAACP national office on January 7, 1954. NAACP II: A-256, DLC. See also 2/4, 6/1, 6/15, and 12/31/53, 3/9 and 12/31/54.

7. In his testimony on Dirksen's bill, S. 1, and on another, S. 535, to establish a commission on civil rights, Mitchell said that neither measure "would effectively remedy basic problems in the field of civil rights" because they "emphasize the study aspect of problems in human relations rather than an action program." Dirksen, though, was emphatic in his opposition to any bill like the one Mitchell was seeking because, in his view, it required "an education not a compulsive approach to the problem" of civil rights. 1/26/54, *Hearings*, 43, 44.

On March 3, 1954, the Civil Rights Subcommittee of the Senate Labor and Public Welfare Committee concluded hearings on S. 692, to prohibit employment discrimination because of race, color, creed, or national origin. *Congressional Quarterly Weekly Report*, 3/5/54, 293. See also 12/31/54.

8. 1/29/54, *Hearings*, 3177–84. See also materials on Taft-Hartley in NAACP IX: 12, DLC.

9. See, in appendix 1, this vol., NAACP Washington Bureau press release, 1/25/54, announcing the change of policy.

10. The Reverend J. M. Hinton, president of the South Carolina State Conference of NAACP Branches, requested the national office's help following the mass jailing of forty-seven African American

soldiers in Columbia, South Carolina, when another soldier with whom they were traveling refused an order to move from a seat beside a white girl on a public bus. The men, stationed at Fort Jackson, were fined, but the city recorder refused to permit appeals from the soldiers on grounds that the twenty-four-hour period allowed for notices of appeals had expired. The NAACP also insisted that although the charges were against only one soldier, forty-seven others were jailed, whereas the three white passengers on the same bus who had been taken to the city jail were freed without being booked.

As a result of the branch department's widespread protests and Mitchell's involvement, Fort Jackson announced a new policy on civil arrests that provided for the release of military personnel arrested by Columbia police to military police at the base. Except in regard to traffic or major offenses, civilian authorities would take no action against soldiers stationed on the base. Report of the Secretary to the Board for January, 2/8/54, EC. For other problems involving African American soldiers at Fort Jackson, see 3/9/54.

For combined reports on both developments, see 12/7/53.

11. Mitchell recalled this January 13, 1954, meeting with Eisenhower in his May 7, 1954, memorandum to Walter White and related there his disappointment with how the NAACP's suggestions had been handled in the president's January 25 message to Congress on housing. NAACP WB-91, DLC. See 12/28/53 for a summary of the NAACP's suggestions on the program and structure of the federal housing programs. Mitchell also wrote Cole expressing his concern over a press conference the HHFA chair had given, in which he said some HHFA policies would be guided by local views on race. Mitchell to Cole, 2/5/54, NAACP WB-91, DLC. See also 3/9 and 5/5/54, as well as the headnote on Segregation in Federal Housing Programs, vol. III.

12. "Special Message to the Congress on Labor-Management Relations," 1/11/54, Eisenhower, *Public Papers of the Presidents*, 1954, 40–44.

13. See Mitchell's memorandum, "Summary of Apprentice Plate Printers' Problems," 2/3/54, to George M. Humphrey, secretary of the treasury, NAACP WB-18, DLC; see also 12/7/53, 3/9/54.

Monthly Report, March 9, 1954

March 9, 1954

MEETING WITH U.S. COMMISSIONER OF EDUCATION: On Friday, February 19, Dr. Buell Gallagher, Dean Charles Thompson, the Executive Secretary, and the Director of the Washington Bureau met with Dr. Samuel M. Brownell, U.S. Commissioner of Education.

We discussed the role of the U.S. Office of Education in the light of a possible Supreme Court decision ending segregation in public schools.[1] We, also, submitted a memorandum on developments following Secretary of Defense Wilson's order requiring the end of segregation in schools on military posts.[2]

Dr. Brownell stated that a report on suggested actions by the U.S. Office of Education is being prepared. The report will be designed to offer plans for action no matter what type of decision the U.S. Supreme Court gives. He also promised to handle promptly various questions raised in a memorandum which we submitted concerning developments in schools on military posts and other related matters.[3]

HEARINGS ON FAIR EMPLOYMENT PRACTICE LEGISLATION: The Executive Secretary and the Bureau Director testified at hearings on S. 692, which is a bill to prevent discrimination in employment. We stressed the importance of enacting a bill with enforcement power.

Regrettably, several persons seemed to believe that S.1, which is a bill introduced by Senator Dirksen of Illinois, would be an acceptable substitute for S. 692. The Dirksen Bill does not have any enforcement powers. Also, while S. 692 is before the Senate Labor Committee, the S.1 is in the hands of the Senate Judiciary Committee.[4]

SCUTTLING THE PRESIDENT'S HOUSING MESSAGE: In our January report, we mentioned the President's reference to minority group housing problems in his message to Congress on January 25.[5] Despite the President's statements, the Housing, and Home Finance Agency continues to support the Birmingham Slum Clearance program which has the effect of ousting colored residents from the area where they are now living and replacing their living space with hospital and health facilities that will operate on a Jim-Crow basis.[6]

Similar plans are still underway in Baltimore, Maryland, and Paducah, Kentucky. In these cases, however, housing will be built in the cleared area but strict rules of exclusion or segregation will be followed in the new dwellings.[7]

The Bureau Director had an opportunity to witness the dramatic impact of current housing policies when he visited Savannah, Georgia. A white public housing project has been built on land formerly occupied by colored persons. The new buildings and clean streets of this project are completely surrounded by shacks and unpaved streets. The slum area that remains is still occupied by colored people.[8]

GRANTS TO HOSPITALS: Mrs. Oveta Culp Hobby, Secretary of the Department of Health, Education, and Welfare states that she is powerless to prevent a Federal grant of $1,500,000.00 to the city hospital at Houston, Texas, even though that institute refuses to permit colored doctors to use its facilities.

We have asked Mrs. Hobby to restudy this question and to submit the matter to the Attorney General for a ruling. We contend that the Health, Education, and Welfare Department does have the authority and the duty to prevent the use of Federal money in such obviously discriminatory situations.[9]

U.S. SOLDIERS HOME: In last month's report, we mentioned an Army pledge that segregation would be ended at the U.S. Soldiers Home. We had reservations about this promise because it was based on a principle of gradualism. Meanwhile, those who favor segregation apparently succeeded in obtaining a legal opinion in the Department of the Army that the Secretary of the Army did not have authority to order Home officials to end segregation.

The Director of the Bureau has been advised confidentially that at one point the Judge Advocate General's Office was prepared to rule that the Secretary of the Army could order the end of segregation, but this ruling was halted because of pressures. We have appealed to Secretary of Defense Wilson on this matter, because it again reveals how prejudiced subordinates are able to thwart the President's program of ending racial segregation in all Government operations.

During the consideration of this matter, the chief complainant, Mr. John R. Bates, was assaulted by another resident of the Home. The other resident was colored, but Mr. Bates has advised us that this man opposed efforts to end segregation.

TORTURE OF TRAINEE AT FORT JACKSON: The Bureau received an anonymous letter stating that a Private Jeff McGriff had been forced to stand in front of a hot stove at Fort Jackson, South Carolina, by two white soldiers. As a result of this ordeal, Pvt. McGriff, who is colored, fainted and was later treated for serious burns.

We placed the matter before Assistant Secretary of the Army, Mr. Hugh Milton, for investigation and action. The report is authentic. The Army sentenced the two offenders to a year in prison and gave them bad conduct discharges.

From all indications, the Army had started action against the offenders before the Bureau complaint was filed. If this is true, it is a healthy sign.[10]

FAIR EMPLOYMENT CONTEST: Behind the scene in official Washington, there is a serious struggle between the Bureau of Printing and Engraving and the Fair Employment Board. At stake is the question of whether the Board's decision permitting colored veterans to be trained as plate printers will be junked by the Bureau of Engraving under another guise of economy.

Last month, we mentioned that the Bureau Director had a conference with the Secretary of the Treasury on this matter. The Secretary has ruled that, after current lay-offs are completed, the veterans will be returned to the training that the Board stipulated they should receive as vacancies develop in the plate printer's staff.[11]

We are not satisfied with this ruling by the Secretary because it is not clear how long the men must wait before there will be any vacancies. Meanwhile, the legislative representative of the plate printers union has threatened the Civil Service Commission and the Treasury with reprisals through Congress if the men are permitted to continue their training.[12]

VETERANS ADMINISTRATION SEGREGATION: In connection with our efforts to spur the ending of segregation in Veterans hospitals and domiciliary facilities, we have had a number of conversations with officials who are interested in this matter.

At one point, we were advised that the VA hospital at Tuskegee, Alabama, was resisting the program of no segregation. After investigation of this matter, the Director was able to advise the Veterans Administration that the officials at the hospital at Tuskegee do not oppose integration and would welcome it. These officials have quite properly pointed out that integration in the VA hospitals must include staff as well as patients.[13]

MS: NAACP II: A-656, DLC.

1. See 2/17/54.

2. This was a follow-up to a meeting Mitchell had with Brownell on December 21, 1953, when they discussed (1) the integration of schools on military posts where local authorities were responsible for those schools, (2) the role of the Office of Education in administering federal funds that were spent in states with segregated schools, and (3) the role of the U.S. Office of Education should the Supreme Court outlaw segregation.

White also reported that the "Commissioner agreed to call fairly soon an off-the-record conference of key educators and representatives of key organizations interested in the whole question of public acceptance of the Supreme Court decisions when handed down." Mitchell memorandum on his meeting with Brownell, 12/21/53, NAACP IX: 98, DLC; Report of the Secretary for the Month of February, 3/9/54, EC.

The gist of Mitchell's February 19, 1954, memorandum was that several local school districts had indicated the states were spending very little money for the operation of schools on military bases. Mitchell therefore believed that those schools could be integrated by September 1954 at no greater cost to the federal government than at present. He recommended that all leases for school property on military posts should be voided if local authorities sought to use the ostensibly higher costs of operation as a result of desegregation "as a pretext for failing to comply with the Defense Department Directive." Mitchell said that delays in carrying out the nonsegregation order could only cause unnecessary confusion. Mitchell memorandum, 2/19/54, NAACP WB-171, DLC. See also, most immediately, 2/17, 2/28, 5/5, 6/29, 9/29, 11/4, and 12/31/54.

3. On May 11, 1954, with her testimony before the Subcommittee on Education of the Senate Labor and Public Welfare Committee on S. 359, S. 2601, and S. 2779, all of which involved federal aid to school construction, Oveta Culp Hobby, secretary of HEW, submitted a letter objecting to passage of the measure under the subcommittee's consideration. In that letter, she argued that no general federal aid to schools should be recommended until state and White House conferences were held to determine what resources localities had for meeting school construction needs. *Congressional Quarterly Weekly Report*, 5/14/54, 621.

4. See 2/4, 6/1, 6/15, and 12/31/53, 2/28 and 12/31/54; 1/26/54, *Hearings*, 75–77; White, 2/25/54, *Hearings*, 176–91.

5. In his message, Eisenhower said that "the administrative policies governing the operations of the several Housing Agencies must be, and they will be, materially strengthened in order to assure equal opportunity for all of our citizens to acquire, within their means, good and well-located homes. We shall take steps to insure that families of minority groups displaced by urban redevelopment operations have a fair opportunity to acquire adequate housing; we shall prevent the dislocation of such families through the misuse of slum clearance programs; and we shall encourage adequate mortgage financing for the construction of new housing for such families on good, well-located sites." "Special Message to Congress on Housing," 1/25/54, Eisenhower, *Public Papers of the Presidents, 1954*, 193–200. See also 2/28/54.

6. See 2/28 and 5/5/54; Mitchell's "Recommendations on Present Housing Problems," memorandum to White, 5/7/54, cited at 6/4/54; in appendix 1, this vol., 12/9/54.

7. Reiterating this widespread problem, Mitchell reminded Cole that Eisenhower had "clearly stated that slum clearance must not result in Negro clearance, but [that is] exactly what would happen under present redevelopment plans in Baltimore and Birmingham. In the case of Baltimore, I understand that one of your representatives visited the city but obtained most of his information from the same people who are responsible for undemocratic housing policies." Mitchell letter, 2/5/54, to Cole, NAACP WB-91, DLC.

8. See the headnote on Segregation in Federal Housing Programs, vol. III.

9. The $1.5 million was for improving the City-County Hospital at Houston even though it refused to permit African American doctors to use its facilities to treat patients and denied them other courtesies commonly extended to white professionals. Hobby maintained that there was no provision in the Hospital Survey and Construction Act that would permit the Public Health Service to refuse federal aid to a hospital solely on the basis that the hospital would not allow black doctors to use its facilities for treatment of their patients. She acknowledged that the act contained specific provisions pertaining to nondiscrimination; however, they applied to the admission of patients, not to the staffing practices of the hospital. Congress, she said, had considered an amendment to the act that would have authorized the surgeon general "to prescribe regulations to assure that hospitals receiving aid could be used by all licensed practitioners in the community," but it was defeated. To date, she said, the Public Health Service had not received a formal application for federal aid for construction of the City-County Hospital at Houston. However, if an application was submitted that met the statutory requirements for approval, the surgeon general was required by the act to approve it. Hobby's letter to Rep. Adam Clayton Powell, Jr., 2/4/54, NAACP IX: 98, DLC.

10. Initially, Maj. Gen. William. E. Bergin, adjutant general, had replied to Mitchell's complaint of February 25, 1954, that the Department of the Army was not aware of the incident involving McGriff. Mitchell responded that it was "extremely puzzling" to have received his letter. He said that after lodging his initial complaint, he had received information that the men who had mistreated McGriff had been court-martialed and given dishonorable discharges. Subsequently, Maj. Gen. John A. Kikin, acting

adjutant general, confirmed for Mitchell that the men had been punished as he had heard. Mitchell's letter to Bergin, 2/25/54; Bergin's letter to Mitchell, 3/16/54; Mitchell's letter to Bergin, 3/31/54; Kikin's letter to Mitchell, 4/30/54, all of which are in NAACP IX: 59, DLC. For other problems involving African American soldiers at Fort Jackson, see 2/28/54.

11. The text of the letter from George Humphrey, secretary of the treasury, that bothered Mitchell said: "With the dismissals of plate printers that must be made between now and July 1, we will have no plate printers left in service, who were hired after the time the apprentice program began, who are not veterans. It is impossible to substitute apprentices for any of them. But we will, when vacancies occur in the future, reinstate apprentices in the order of their seniority before any plate printers are hired from the outside." Humphrey to Mitchell, 2/11/54, NAACP WB-18, DLC. At the end of the year, this matter would still be unresolved. See 12/31/54.

12. See, among others, 12/31/53, 6/29 and 9/29/54.

13. See also, among others, 9/9 and 12/7/53, 6/29/54; materials in NAACP WB-185, DLC.

Monthly Report, April 12, 1954

[MONTHLY REPORT]

WASHINGTON BUREAU

[April 12, 1954]

TAFT-HARTLEY AMENDMENT: The Senate Labor Committee has reported out revisions of the Taft-Hartley Act, but Senator H. Alexander Smith (R-N.J.) arbitrarily refused to permit Senator Herbert H. Lehman (D-N.Y. to offer a non-discrimination amendment in the committee. Senator Smith had the full support of his Republican colleagues when he acted.[1] This means that refusal to permit consideration of the amendment was a party policy decision and not simply the individual stand of Senator Smith. Senator Lehman and Senator Ives are expected to offer amendments from the floor.

In the House, where the committee has had a much more turbulent series of sessions than the Senate, an all inclusive amendment proposed by the NAACP and Congressman Powell was not accepted. However, the committee did vote approval of two amendments which were offered by Mr. Powell and which will be very useful in situations where employers and unions join in seeking to require that colored people become members of jim crow locals as a conditions of being hired or keeping their jobs. The Powell amendments make this unlawful.[2]

TRAVEL BILL: Senator John W. Bricker (R-Ohio), who is chairman of the Senate Committee on Interstate and Foreign Commerce has formally notified Andrew Schoeppel, sub-committee chairman, that hearings are to be held on S. 2672, which is the Ives-Butler Anti-jim crow Travel bill. Senator Butler (R-Md.) has promised the director of the bureau that he will ask permission to conduct the hearings himself. He expects to limit them to one day in order that the bill may be reported out.

In the House Congressman Wolverton (R-N.J.), who is chairman of the Committee on Interstate and Foreign Commerce seems very indefinite about his plans, but we have called upon the White House for support in getting action.

By a fortunate coincidence, Miss Ethel Payne of the Chicago Defender asked President Eisenhower at his press conference on March 24 whether he favored the bill. The President promised to check with the Department of Justice and make a later report. The director met with the Deputy Attorney General to discuss the bill on March 29, 1954.

HOUSING: The fate of public housing is somewhat muddled, but at this point it appears certain that the housing agencies do have authority to start construction of 33,000 units.[3] The director attended a meeting with the housing administrator, Albert Cole, on March 29. The discussion in this meeting indicated that the administration is expecting the Senate to rescue and clarify the President's proposal. Under the administration's plan the house Appropriations Committee would have authorized 33, 000 units a year for the next four years in public housing. The appropriations committee included language to terminate the public housing program after completion of 33,000 units. This was struck out on a point of order on the floor of the house. The administration contends that the housing agencies may still build units authorized by Congress last year. However, it is expected that the Senate will straighten out the present tangle through action by the Appropriations Committee and also the senate Banking and Currency Committee.

When the House considered the Administration's housing bill (H.R. 7839) amendments offered to include public housing were defeated. Non segregation amendments offered by Congressman Powell and Javits were also defeated on April 2 by votes of 110 to 87 and 113 to 74. This bill has not been reported out as yet by the Senate Banking and Currency Committee. It does not at present contain any authorization for public housing.[4]

FREEDOM FULFILLMENT CONFERENCE: The success of the Freedom Fulfillment Conference on March 10 is apparent. However, the director wishes to include a word of appreciation to members of the staff of the Washington Bureau who worked long and consistently to take care of many, many details connected with the Conference. In addition, Mrs. Hendricks and Miss Swanson obtained the services of four volunteer clerical workers, three receptionists and one housewife who kept the office open while the staff was at the Departmental Auditorium on March 10. Most of these persons have regular jobs. Not only did they work at night in the bureau after their regular hours when we were preparing for the Conference, but they also took time off from their jobs on the day of the Conference.[5]

MS: Report of the Secretary to the Board of Directors, 4/12/54, EC.

1. Congressional Quarterly Weekly Report, 4/2/54, 425. See also, most immediately, 2/28 and 5/5/54.

2. For Eisenhower's labor recommendations, which did not include civil rights provisions, see *Congressional Quarterly Weekly Report,* 2/19/54, 204. The House Education and Labor Committee, on

March 9, 1954, voted 25 to 2 to approve an amendment by Powell making it an unfair labor practice for a union to deny memberships to workers beause of race, religion, or national origin. *Congressional Quarterly Weekly Report,* 3/13/54, 323; 4/2/54, 425.

3. See *New York Times,* 6/4/54, 1; note at 5/5/54 for an explanation of the "muddled situation" to which Mitchell refers.

4. The bills (S. 2938 and H.R. 7839), sponsored by Sen. Homer E. Capehart (R-Ind.) and Rep. Jesse P. Wolcott (R-Mich.), were designed to reduce direct federal participation in housing and to encourage private industry to play a greater role in providing housing for all income groups. "Blueprint for Better Homes," *Congressional Quarterly Weekly Report,* 2/26/54, 237. For related action, see *Congressional Quarterly Weekly Report,* 3/2/6/54, 390; 4/2/54, 419.

5. The Fighting Fund for Freedom campaign was planned in conjunction with the association's birthday on February 12. It was an all-day conference that was held in the Inter-departmental Auditorium of the Labor Building.

Addressing the conference were President Eisenhower; Ralph J. Bunche, member of the NAACP board; Daisy E. Lampkin, member of the NAACP board; Sen. Herbert H. Lehman, member of the NAACP board; Arthur B. Spingarn, president, NAACP; Channing H. Tobias, chair, NAACP board; Carl Johnson, representing the Midwest NAACP; Kelly Alexander, representing the southern NAACP; and Walter White. White said thirteen hundred persons from thirty-six states attended. Alexander, Johnson, and Franklin H. Williams, representing the West Coast, gave regional reports. Minutes, 1/4/54, 2/8/54, Report of the Secretary to the Board of Directors, April 12, 1954, EC. "Remarks at Conference of the National Association for the Advancement of Colored People," 3/10/54, Eisenhower, *Public Papers of the Presidents,* 310–11.

Monthly Report, May 5, 1954

May 5, 1954

TAFT-HARTLEY AMENDMENTS

The most pressing problem in Washington at the time this report is written is the fate of non-discrimination amendments to the Taft-Hartley Act. During the first session of Congress, all members of the Senate Labor Committee, except the late Senator Taft and Senator Hill of Alabama, were sponsors of an NAACP non-discrimination amendment offered by Senator Ives.[1]

When the second session got underway, the Republican members, following the leadership of Senator H. Alexander Smith, began to cool off on the proposal. When a vote was taken to report out the present bill (S. 2650) before the Senate, all Republicans voted solidly against any amendments.[2]

Now that the issue has been brought to the floor, Senator Lehman and Senator Ives have introduced non-discrimination amendments. However, the Democrats are committed to a strategy of first trying to vote to recommit the bill to committee. Thereafter, if recommital fails, amendments will be considered. Apparently, the Republicans plan to get agreement from southern Democrats to support a motion to table the Ives and Lehman amendments.[3]

We have urged State Conference Presidents and key branches to ask their Senators to support the Ives and Lehman amendments since either of them would be worthwhile.

HEARINGS ON ANTI-JIM CROW TRAVEL

Hearings on bills to end segregation in interstate travel will begin in the House on May 12 and run through May 14.[4] Chances for House action appear very good.

We have had several agreements with Senators on how the matter would be handled in the Senate, but, as yet, hearings have not been scheduled. At present, it is planned that there will be a one day hearing in the Senate. This hearing should be held before a subcommittee headed by Senator Schoeppel of Kansas. However, Senator Butler of Maryland, who is a member of the subcommittee and a sponsor of the bill, has requested Senator Schoeppel to let him conduct the hearings. At this time, it appears that Senator Schoeppel will agree to this procedure.[5]

SENATE APPROPRIATION HEARINGS

The Bureau Director appeared before a Senate Appropriations subcommittee headed by Senator Saltonstall of Massachusetts. The original purpose of the appearance was to support public housings. However, the Administration through Housing Administrator Albert Cole, told the subcommittee that it would seek to salvage the full public housing program through the Senate Banking and Currency Committee. The NAACP statement was made, but we presume that the Administration believes it can get some public housing built this year despite the muddled situation created by the House Appropriations Committee.[6]

During the NAACP appearance, there was considerable discussion about the problem faced by minority groups in redevelopments programs.[7] The National Director of the Redevelopment Program and a representative of the Baltimore Planning Commission were also at the hearing. Baltimore is an example of how major cities discriminate against minorities in the redevelopment program. The Redevelopment Director and the Baltimore representative challenged statements made by the NAACP.

In the ensuing discussion, Senator Saltonstall insisted that the Bureau Director and the Baltimore representatives arrange a meeting in Baltimore to compose their differences.[8] The Senator also asked the NAACP for specific language which would be useful in meeting the problem. The language was submitted. Also, meetings were held with Redevelopment officials in Washington and Baltimore. Both of these sessions lasted many hours. The director can only report that these sessions revealed information that supports our contention that the Redevelopment Program, as presently operating, works an unnecessary hardship on colored people and very little is done about it.[9]

HEALTH HEARINGS

The Director appeared before the Senate Subcommittee on Health to urge adoption of safeguards against discrimination in hospital grants.[10]

SEGREGATION IN SCHOOLS ON MILITARY POSTS

Former Secretary of the Navy Anderson (who succeeds Mr. Roger Kyes as Deputy Secretary of Defense) has submitted an interesting report to the Bureau in connection with the matter of segregation in schools on military posts. It is the instruction sent out to all shore stations of the Navy and Marine Corps.[11] The Director has not had time to analyze and appraise it.

RESIGNATION OF WILLIAM PRYOR, JR.

William Pryor, Assistant to the Director, resigned from the Bureau this month to accept a government post in Indo-China. Mr. Pryor's resignation comes at a bad time in that his work load must be carried by the Director as best he can. Needless to say, this will creates some unfortunate gaps in matters to be handled.

MS: NAACP II: A-656, DLC.

1. On January 29, 1954, the Senate Labor and Public Welfare Committee concluded hearings on on the president's fourteen-point program to revise the Taft-Hartley law, and the House Education and Labor Committee began its hearings on proposed changes to the law on February 24, 1954. *Congressional Quarterly Weekly Report,* 2/12/54, 188; 2/26/54, 254. Senate debate on S. 2650 proposing twelve changes in the Taft-Hartley law began May 3, 1954. On May 5, the Senate agreed unanimously to limit debate on the bill and amendments to it, starting on May 7. For a background on developments in the Senate following Eisenhower's labor message to Congress of January 11, 1954, see *Congressional Quarterly Weekly Report,* 5/7/54, 582. See also 2/28/54, 4/12/54; 1/29/54, *Hearings,* 3174–84.

2. See 4/12/54.

3. *New York Times,* 5/5/54, 27. On May 7, the Senate killed the amendments to the Taft-Hartley law. *New York Times,* 5/8/54, 1. On May 5, Walter White wired Senators William S. Knowland, Homer Ferguson, Leverett Saltonstall, and H. Alexander Smith and asked them to rally the support of their party behind the identical Lehman and Ives amendments. These measures would make it illegal for either employers or unions to discriminate in hiring or granting union membership against anyone because of race, creed, color, national origin, or ancestry. Report of the Secretary for April, 5/10/54, EC.

4. Powell, 5/13/54, *Hearings,* 55–65; Mitchell, 5/13/54, *Hearings,* 39; Lieutenant Johnson, 5/13/54, *Hearings,* 40–55; Carter and Mitchell, *Hearings,* 96–118.

5. Hearings before the House Interstate and Foreign Commerce Committee began on May 12, 1954; *Congressional Quarterly Weekly Report,* 5/14/54, 621. See also, among others, in appendix 1, this vol., 8/10/53, as well as the headnote on the Struggle to End Jim Crow Travel, vol. III.

In his statement to the committee, Rep. John W. Heselton explained that H.R. 7304 was designed to end the existing "patchwork pattern of handling the seating or accommodations for passengers traveling in interstate commerce." The various court decisions, he said, had established the principle that racial segregation was an unnecessary burden on interstate commerce. Some carriers complied with the decisions, and others did not. Consequently, both black and white passengers entered "a kind of 'no-man's land'" when they passed through certain states. One of the earliest cases was *Hall v. DeCuir*, in which the U.S. Supreme Court held that enforcement of the Louisiana civil rights statute requiring equal treatment of black passengers was an unconstitutional burdon on commerce and could not validly be applied to a carrier. In *Mitchell v. United States*, the Court held that railroads were required to make available to blacks the same type of services and accommodations as were available to whites. In *Morgan v. Virginia*, the Court overturned the conviction of the black passenger, Irene Morgan, who had refused to move to the rear of the vehicle, and held that the application of the Virginia segregation laws to interstate commerce constituted a burden on commerce in violation of the commerce clause. And in *Henderson v. United States*, the Court held that segregation in a dining car practiced pursuant to the rules and regulations of the Southern Railway Company, whereby one table was reserved exclusively for black passengers, was a violation of the Interstate Commerce Act.

Heselton presented to the committee for its record a copy of a memorandum of June 9, 1953, issued by the River Division of the Frisco Railroad Company, which dealt with segregation of passengers riding between St. Louis and southern points in Tennessee and Alabama. He said it was interesting to note that curtains separating black and white passengers were put up when the train was southbound out of Arkansas and taken down when it reached the border of Arkansas on its northbound trip. "On reading this memorandum, one must ask the question, 'What is so different about the people of Arkansas that a curtain would not be necessary within their borders while it would be required in Tennessee and Alabama?'" Heselton's statement, 5/12/54, NAACP IX: 12, DLC.

6. See 4/12/54 for the earlier mention of the "muddled situation," which resulted from scandals exposed on April 2, 1954, after the House had acted over widespread discrepancies that had to be resolved in the Senate-House conference. The scandals involved irregularities in government insurance programs covering loans for home improvements as well as mortages for multifamily rentals. The major difference between the measures going to conference, as Mitchell noted, was that the House bill contained no provision at all for public housing. *New York Times*, 6/4/54, 1.

Mitchell urged the committee to "clarify the present confusion in the field of public housing [by] authorizing the construction of 140,000 new public housing units for the next four years, as proposed by President Eisenhower." The present need was as critical as it had been in 1953, when he had expressed concerns, he said. (6/18/53, *Hearings*, 264–67; 6/23/54, *Hearings*, 203–5.) "It is still impossible to see how we can have a productive slum clearance and redevelopment program without public housing." See 4/21/54, *Hearings*, 689–92. See also the headnote on Segregation in Federal Housing Programs, vol. III. For Congress's attempt to deal with the "muddled situation," see "Federal Housing under Fire," *Congressional Quarterly Weekly Report*, 6/11/54, 721–24.

7. Challenging Mitchell's assertion to the Senate Appropriations Subcommittee that people in Birmingham were adversely affected by the proposed redevelopment program, James W. Follin, director of the Slum Clearance and Redevelopment Section in the HHFA, said that Mitchell did not have any specific facts to support his statement. Mitchell therefore asked Ruby Hurley, secretary of the Southeast Region NAACP, to send a telegram to Sen. Leverett Saltonstall, chair of the subcommittee, with information Mitchell provided to support the NAACP's contentions. Mitchell's letter to Hurley, 4/21/54, and related materials are in NAACP WB-91, DLC.

8. The problem in Baltimore centered on the Waverly project. Richard L. Steiner explained to the subcommittee of the Committee on Appropriations headed by Saltonstall that he had been director of the Baltimore Redevelopment Commission for eight years but had never met Mitchell. The lobbyist responded that he was certain Steiner had met his wife, Juanita, who was a lawyer in Baltimore representing the NAACP branch there. 4/21/54, *Hearings*, 691–92.

9. During the discussions, Saltonstall mentioned the role of the Banking and Currency Committee in these matters. For Mitchell's testimony there, see 3/25/54, *Hearings*, 893–900; see also 12/7 and 12/31/54, 2/28 and 3/9/54, and subsequent reports.

10. See 4/21/54, *Hearings*, 847–56.

11. See also, most immediately, 2/17, 2/28, 3/9, 6/29, 9/29, 11/4, and 12/31/54; Mitchell, "Status of Racial Integration in the Armed Services."

Monthly Report, June 4, 1954

June 4, 1954

STATUS OF ANTI-JIM CROW TRAVEL BILL

The House Committee on Interstate and Foreign Commerce has completed hearings on various bills which would end segregation in interstate travel.[1] Unfortunately, the White House now appears to be blocking action on this legislation.

At the time this report is being written, executive agency comments on the bills are being bottled up in the White House. Committee members are holding up a vote on the legislation because the agency comments have not been received.

On Friday, May 28, Congressman Adam Clayton Powell, Jr., discussed this delay with Deputy Attorney General William Rogers. Mr. Rogers promised that the Justice Department reports would be sent forward, according to Mr. Powell.

In the Senate, Senator Andrew Schoeppel, chairman of the subcommittee in charge of the proposed legislation, has not scheduled hearings. This subcommittee is supposed to be awaiting the lower House action. Here again the delay seems traceable to the White House. Curiously enough, one of the reported reasons for the White House's slow-down is the Supreme Court's decisions outlawing racial segregation.[2] Prior to the time the Court handed down the decisions some of the members of the House Committee said action on the Travel Bill should be held up until the Supreme Court handed down its decisions.

PUBLIC HOUSING

Repercussions from the Supreme Court's decisions are being felt in the housing field.[3] Senator Burnet Maybank proposed that an amendment which he had offered to restore public housing to the Administration's housing program (H.R. 7839) be stricken out. Senator Maybank, who has long been a sponsor of public housing, says he now opposes it because it must be non-segregated. He, therefore, proposed that no new public housing starts will be made after 1954.[4]

The Bureau warned Senators (particularly, Republicans) that the Maybank action has created a situation in which the followers of public housing from the North, who voted for his plan to kill public housing, would also be voting in favor of racial segregation.[5] Their action, it was pointed out might determine the outcome of some closely contested elections in northern states, and, thereby, decide which of the major Parties will be in control of the Congress in 1955.

The Maybank pro-segregation move was defeated by a voice vote on June 3. The Senate then approved a Republican sponsored move to provide for construction of 140,000 public housing units at the rate of 35,000 a year. Some liberal Senators, including Lehman, Ives, and Morse, opposed this because the public housing program was not adequate. The measure now goes to a conference between the House and Senate. The bill passed by the House does not provide for any public housing. Hence, there is a dangerous possibility that the program approved by the Senate may be whittled down further in conference or knocked out completely.[6]

PRO-SEGREGATION BILLS

Senator James Eastland and Congressman John Bell Williams, both of Mississippi, have introduced Constitutional amendments to nullify the Supreme Court's decisions outlawing segregation. These proposed amendments have been referred to the Judiciary Committee in the House and Senate.[7] We have notified members that we oppose these proposals. Of course, no one anticipates approval of the resolutions.

CONSTITUTIONAL AMENDMENT ON POLL TAX

Senator Holland's proposal to eliminate the Poll Tax by Constitutional amendment was given quick approval by Senator Langer's Judiciary subcommittee following a brief hearing. Senator Langer declined to hear testimony by the NAACP against the amendment. We have notified members of the full committee that we were denied a hearing and asked that they vote against Holland's proposal.

WASHINGTON SCHOOL BOARD

It now appears that there will be integration in some schools in Washington in September. The major problem centers on a plan offered by the Superintendent of Schools to undertake integration in a manner that will permit continued concentration of colored children in certain schools. The plan has not been adopted, but the Board will give further consideration to the method of accomplishing integration on June 23.

This item is included for information purposes only, since the NAACP leadership in handling this problem is in the hands of the D. C. Branch of the NAACP, rather than the Bureau.[8]

FEDERAL GRANTS TO STATES

The Director has had conversations with a number of southern and border states members of Congress about the future of government grants-in-aid now that the Supreme Court has outlawed racial segregation.[9] We have consistently urged the inclusion of safeguards against segregation in the expenditure of monies made available though these grants. This includes such diverse fields as health, agriculture, schools, and recreation. One southern member has said it might be fruitful for an off-the-record discussion of this situation with the so-called liberal bloc of southern members of Congress.

OTHER MATTERS

Because of the length of this report, other matters receiving attention by the Bureau at this time are omitted. However, it should be noted that on April 8 we asked for an opportunity to appear before the Air Force Academy Site Selection Commission which is studying a site for the Air Force Academy. We wished to express opposition to any site in a southern state where facilities surrounding the Academy would be segregated. Apparently, an appearance will be unnecessary because the Air Force has announced that consideration has been narrowed to three sites, all outside the South.

SPEAKING ENGAGEMENTS

In the past two months, the Director has had speaking engagements in Pennsylvania, Maryland, South Carolina, and Washington, D. C.

MS: NAACP II: A-670, DLC.

1. On May 12, 1954, the House Interstate and Foreign Commerce Committee began hearings on the bills. *Congressional Quarterly Weekly Report*, 5/14/54, 621. See 5/5/54; 5/13/54, *Hearings*, 39. The House Rules Committee refused to let the measure come to a vote, thus killing it. See also 8/21 and 12/31/54.

2. *Brown v. Board of Education.*

3. The ripple effects of *Brown*, which were historical both constitutionally and socially, were felt especially in this instance in *Housing Authority of San Francisco et al. v. Banks et lal.* In its ruling on May 24, 1954, in *Banks*, the Court refused to overrule a California court decision that African Americans had to be admitted to a San Francisco housing project. Responding, Maybank, who had been the Senate leader in the fight for public housing, said: "Now that the Supreme Court has seen fit to reverse an acceptable and working pattern . . . I must oppose my own amendment. . . . The Supreme Court has brought about the denial of much needed benefits to the people for whom they are primarily intended." *Congress and the Nation*, 485. See also *New York Times*, 5/25/54, 1; 6/4/54, 1.

Just before the Supreme Court's decision in *Brown*, Mitchell suggested to Walter White that the NAACP board should request a joint meeting with the president, the attorney general, and the administrator of HHFA to obtain a definite agreement that, in the future, the government would provide no aid in housing unless there was an assurance that the facilities would be open to qualified persons without regard to race. Mitchell memorandum to White, 5/7/54, NAACP WB-91, DLC. See also, most immediately, 3/9, 5/5, 6/29, 8/21, 9/29, 11/4, and 12/31/54; in appendix 1, this vol., 12/9/54; 4/21/54, *Hearings*, 686–92; and the headnote on Segregation in Federal Housing Programs, vol. III.

4. Maybank further said that when a housing bill (H.R. 7839) reached the House floor, he would move in the Senate to strike from President Eisenhower's housing program any continuance of public housing. *Congressional Quarterly Weekly Report*, 5/28/54, 671. The Senate, which granted Eisenhower's request for thirty-five thousand new public housing starts a year over a four-year period, rejected Maybank's amendment. *Congressional Quarterly Weekly Report*, 6/4/54, 709. See 6/29/54 for follow-up discussion; 8/21/54 for discussion following passage of the Housing Act of 1954.

5. Mitchell reminded the Senate Subcommittee on Appropriations that in his appearance before it a year earlier, he had stressed the number of people, particularly African Americans, who were being displaced by slum clearance and community redevelopment projects. About one-half of those people, he said, were eligible for public housing. The picture in 1954 had not changed very much, he stated. 4/21/54, *Hearings*, 686–92.

6. *New York Times*, 6/4/54, 1. Because of unresolved differences between the House and Senate over public housing, both bodies approved resolutions extending existing housing laws for thirty days. *Congressional Quarterly Weekly Report*, 6/5/54, 804. In addition to the Supreme Court's decision in *Brown*, its refusal to hear the San Francisco Housing Authority's appeal of a decision that struck down its discriminatory practices alarmed Maybank. Hunt, "How Did Public Housing Survive the 1950s?" 207.

7. Eastland's initial reaction to the Supreme Court's decision was, "The South will not abide by nor obey this legislative decision by a political court." Reactions from other lawmakers, from the North and South, were also provided. On May 24, 1954, Eastland introduced a proposed amendment to the Constitution, S.J. Res. 159, to prevent interference with state powers "to regulate health, morals, education, marriage and good order." *Congressional Quarterly Weekly Report*, 6/4/54, 696, 704.

8. Racial integration of the schools in the District of Columbia began uneventfully on September 13, 1954. *New York Times*, 9/15/54, 17.

9. Consequently, Oveta Culp Hobby, secretary of HEW, on May 11, 1954, submitted a letter to the Subcommittee on Education of the Senate Labor and Public Welfare Committee, objecting to passage of the measures being considered on the grounds that no general federal aid to schools should be recommended until state and White House conferences to determine the resources of localities for meeting school construction needs were held. *Congressional Quarterly Weekly Report*, 5/14/54, 621. The Chamber of Commerce of the United States also announced on May 28, 1954, that it had asked Congress to defer action on proposed federal aid for school construction "until the need for such legislation has been fully demonstrated." *Congressional Quarterly Weekly Report*, 6/4/54, 701. For the NAACP's position, see, for example, 3/25/54, *Hearings*, 893–900; 4/21/54, *Hearings*, 686–92; 4/21/54, *Hearings*, 847–56; 5/20/54, *Hearings*, 248–52.

Desegregation by Presidential Order and Legislative Record of 1954 Candidates, June 29, 1954

DESEGREGATION BY PRESIDENTIAL ORDER
AND
LEGISLATIVE RECORDS OF 1954 CANDIDATES

[ca. June 29, 1954]

The executive branch of government has played a vital role in desegregation of various government facilities. This program was started under the Roosevelt and Truman Administrations, but it has been accelerated considerably under the Eisenhower Administration. For their accomplishments in this field, the three Presidents deserve the warmest praise.

There is no doubt that some of the important road-blocks to integration have been removed solely because the Chief Executive, in response to the continued protest of the NAACP and other allied forces, has instructed that a change be made.

It is not possible to list all of these charges, but, for this discussion, we have selected typical cases in order that the role of the executive branch in this field may be illustrated by practical examples.

This presentation also deals with the incredibly shabby record of the legislative branch of the government. The record demonstrates the complete failure of President Eisenhower to urge that the Congress take any positive action in the field of civil rights.

There is strong evidence that this Administrative has deliberately blocked possible action by the legislative branch in the field of civil rights.

It should be added that dismal record of the Republican Party in legislation seems to have the full cooperation of the Democrats. There is no reason for believing that the result would have been any different if the Democrats had been in control of the 83rd Congress. There is no reason to believe that the present leaders among the Democrats will do a better job in the civil rights field, if they control the 84th Congress.

SEGREGATION OF CIVILIANS IN NAVY YARDS

The NAACP campaign to end segregation in the shore establishments of the Navy was started by branches in Norfolk, Virginia, and Charleston, South Carolina. The Washington Bureau initiated action on complaints by these branches in 1951.[1]

These complaints charged that civilian employees were required to use segregated rest-rooms, drinking foundations, and restaurants. We asked for the ending of segregation in the two establishments where we had specific complaints. We also asked that the Navy adopt a policy that would forbid racial segregation in any of its operations.

The Navy Secretary, under President Truman, refused to abolish segregation because "local customs must be followed in situations of this kind."

One of the strongest telegrams of protest coming from our Convention in Oklahoma City in 1952 urged President Truman to correct this discrimination. No corrective action was taken and the matter remained unsettled until the Secretary of the Navy, following President Eisenhower's policy, ordered the end of segregation in all Naval establishments.

On November 11, 1953, the President reported that "of sixty (Navy) installations on Federally-owned property" in the South only one had not completed the program of eliminating segregation. The one exception was the Charleston Navy Yard which had ended segregation everywhere except in the wash-room facilities. This was ended later. On May 18, 1954, the Director of the Washington Bureau and representatives of the Charleston, South Carolina, branch made a tour of the Navy Yard in that city. We found no segregation in facilities.

In his official statement, the President said this is an "accomplishment of which we all can be proud and I congratulate the Secretary of the Navy and his Department on a job very well done indeed." The Director of the Washington Bureau wishes to be on record as sharing the President's view on this matter.

It should also be noted that these Naval establishments are located in the states of Alabama, Georgia, Florida, Maryland, North Carolina, South Carolina, and Virginia.

The President's November announcement showed that facilities in Kentucky, Tennessee, and Texas were listed as integrated when first reports were made in August 1953.[2]

SEGREGATION IN SCHOOLS ON MILITARY POSTS

The Washington Bureau has prepared a statement on the ending of segregation in the Armed Services which will appear in the *Journal of Negro Education*, published by the Bureau of Educational Research, Howard University, on July 15, 1954.[3]

One of the important aspects of discrimination in the Armed Services is racial segregation in elementary and high schools on military posts. These schools are divided into two groups. One group is operated by the Military under Section 6 of Public Law 874 and the other group is operated by local boards of education under Section 3 of the same law.

The President formally requested elimination of the segregation practice in 1953.[4] At that time, sixty-three military posts offered school facilities to children of parents either living on or working on Federal property.

Under previous Administrations, segregation had been banned in all of the Section 6 schools, except the school at Fort Benning, Georgia. In 1953, there were twenty-one posts where Section 3 schools were segregated. In addition, colored children, were barred from certain schools in the Canal Zone. The Canal Zone school system includes 17 elementary schools, 5 junior high schools, and 2 high schools.

The Department of Defense has announced that all segregation will be ended in schools on military posts by September 1955.

Segregation was abolished in the school at Fort Benning, Georgia, in September 1953. Of the twenty-one posts, only Fort Belvoir, Virginia has publicly announced that it will end segregation in September 1954. However, we are awaiting an official report which may show that others in this group are planning to end segregation this year.

New schools at Fort Myer, Virginia, and the Craig Air Force Base in Alabama will open on a non-segregated basis in September 1954. However, these schools and the schools at Fort Belvoir will be operated by the Federal Government because the local authorities have declined to run them if colored children are admitted. All schools in the Canal Zone will be open to colored children in September 1954.

There was no evidence that any Cabinet officer sought to block the program of integration in schools on military posts under the Truman Administration. However, there is ample evidence to demonstrate that Mrs. Oveta Culp Hobby, Secretary of the Department of Health, Education, and Welfare, did request a delay in the school integration program under the Eisenhower Administration.[5]

VETERANS ADMINISTRATION

The Veterans Administration has officially declared that segregation must end in its hospitals and domiciliary facilities. The NAACP has long pressed for realization of this objective.[6]

Within the Veterans Administration, Mr. George Holland, Assistant to the Administration, has consistently urged and worked for the abolition of all racial segregation in the facilities of this agency.[7]

Mr. Harvey Higley, the Eisenhower appointed Administrator, is the first chief of the Veterans Administration to give full personal backing to the policy of no segregation.[8]

Scrutiny of the cost of operating Veterans Hospitals shows that, aside from the moral liability of racial segregation in these hospitals, the financial waste caused by separation of the races is enormous. For example, we list the cost of building similar VA hospitals in six cities. All hospitals listed below are General Medical.

Location	*Beds*	*Cost*
New Orleans	496	$8,140,000
Chicago	"	$8,032,000
Ann Arbor	"	$7,951,000
St. Louis	"	$7,686,000
Cincinnati	"	$7,810,000
Oklahoma City	"	$7,487,000

It will be noted that the hospital in New Orleans which was built on a plan to maintain racial segregation is more expensive than any of the other five which were not built on a plan to keep racial separation. Fortunately, even the New Orleans hospital has now been instructed to end racial segregation.

On the basis of the above figures, it would be fair to say that the saving would run anywhere from $100,000 to over a half million dollars in each hospital of this kind. Factors taken into consideration in computing the cost difference are plumbing, recreation rooms, dining-rooms, and other wasteful dual facilities.

A survey in 1946 revealed that approximately 65 hospitals practiced some form of segregation or total exclusion by race. Forty-seven of the 65 were in the South. Of the 47 in the South, 14 excluded colored people completely. Northern hospitals having colored wards in 1946 were Wood, Wisconsin, Coatesville, Pennsylvania, and Hines, Illinois.

In April 1949, the V.A. said:

> "It is our policy to avoid segregation of patients wherever this can be done without creating a situation, or a mental condition, which might presumably retard the recovery of the patients.
>
> "In providing hospitalization under the laws administered by V.A. our first and all important consideration is for the welfare of the hospitalized veterans. The V.A. is not, and will not become, an agency for social change.
>
> "In those instances where it has been determined that the integration of white and colored patients would work a hardship upon the patients or interfere with their recovery, exception has been made to the general policy and local custom has been followed.
>
> "We shall continue our efforts to provide equally and impartially for every veteran, regardless of his race, creed or color, the finest service available."

The official program of ending racial segregation in all VA hospitals and domiciliary facilities began in September 1953.

It is important to remember that the specific instances of departures from the top policy must be constantly exposed if we are to obtain complete adherence to the national policy. Branches are urged to investigate conditions at any Government facilities in their areas and to report to the Washington Bureau on whether racial segregation is practiced in these facilities.

FAIR EMPLOYMENT BOARD AND COMMITTEE ON GOVERNMENT CONTRACTS

The Bureau reminds the branches that, because of the Association's efforts, we have two Federal agencies which are charged with the responsibility of eliminating discrimination in employment. These are the Federal Fair Employment Board, located in the U.S. Civil Service Commission, Washington, D.C., which operates under Executive Order No. 9980 and the Committee on Government Contracts, located in the

U.S. Department of Labor, Washington, D.C. which is established to police the non-discrimination clause which is in all Government contracts under Executive Order No. 10,479.[9]

Neither of these committees can be considered as a substitute for a Federal Fair Employment Practice Law under any circumstances. However, they can perform valuable functions if we insist that they act on specific problems and complaints which we present.

As frequently happens in the executive branch, these committees are sometimes blocked by powerful Government officials who for one reason or another wish to prevent fair employment.[10]

We now have a specific case on this point involving the Treasury Department and the Bureau of Engraving and Printing. The Treasury Department apparently with the sanction of the White House permits continued discrimination against apprentice-trainees by denying them opportunity to continue their instruction in this field of employment. *A Federal Fair Employment recommendation that this discrimination be corrected has been suppressed.*[11]

HOUSING POLICIES

In recent years, Federal executive policies in housing have been the greatest single factor in promoting residential racial segregation. This is still true.[12] The record of Federal practices is so bad and so extensive that it cannot be compressed into a few paragraphs.[13]

It should be noted that on January 25, 1954, the President made the following statement in his Housing Message to Congress:

"It must be frankly and honestly acknowledged that many members of minority groups, regardless of their income or their economic status, have had the least opportunity of all of our citizens to acquire good homes. Some progress, although far too little, has been made by the Housing Agency in encouraging the production and financing of adequate housing available to members of minority groups. However, the administrative policies governing the operations of the several housing agencies must be, and they will be, materially strengthened and augmented in order to assure equal opportunity for all of our citizens to acquire, within their means, good and well-located homes. We shall take steps to insure that families of minority groups displaced by urban redevelopment operations have a fair opportunity to acquire adequate housing; we shall prevent the dislocation of such families through the misuse of slum clearance programs; and we shall encourage adequate mortgage financing for the construction of new housing for such families on good, well-located sites."[14]

Nothing has been done by the Housing Agencies to implement the promise made in this message.[15]

THE LEGISLATIVE RECORD

The only record to date of the Republican controlled Congress' views on civil rights is that of January 7, 1953, when, as a matter of Party policy, the Republicans voted solidly with the southern Democrats to continue Senate rules which permit filibusters.[16]

The only Republicans who voted in favor of changing the rules were Senators Duff (Pa.), Hendrickson (N.J.), Ives (N.Y.), Kuchel (Calif.), and the late Senator Tobey of New Hampshire.

Since that time, the President and the leaders in the House and Senate have systematically ignored all pleas for action on civil rights legislation.

The nearest we have come to getting officially endorsed action has been in a bill to penalize segregation in interstate travel.[17] Hearings on this bill have been held in the House, but the House Committee has not reported out the bill at the time this statement is written because the executive agencies of Government, which must obtain clearance from the Bureau of the Budget before submitting reports on pending legislation, have not sent in their reports.

The conclusion is inescapable that these reports are being held up by the White House. In addition, the Senate Committee has refused to act on the bills because the House Committee has not acted.

The Senate Labor and Public Welfare Committee has reported out S. 692, a Federal Fair Employment Practice Bill with enforcement powers. However, the House has no plan for considering this bill in committee and it is obvious that under the present rule S. 692 would face a filibuster in the Senate.[18]

Perhaps one of the worse sins of the 83rd Congress is the passage of a hospital construction act which permits segregation in public hospitals that receive Federal aid. Northern Senators and representatives have flatly refused to support the principle that safeguards against segregation in such hospitals should be incorporated in this bill. The fact that this legislation was passed after the Supreme Court decisions outlawing segregation shows the grim problem facing us in the future as we continue the battle against Government endorsed segregation.[19]

Generally speaking, the grants to states for social welfare and other programs that benefit large numbers of people have the support of a coalition of liberal northern and "less conservative" southern members of Congress. The members of this group believe that inclusion of non-segregation provisions in such legislation will force the southern group to vote against the entire bill—no matter how beneficial it may be. Hence, the northern liberals (both Republicans and Democrats) usually oppose including non-segregation clauses in such measures.

The one bright spot so far in the record of the 83rd Congress is the defeat of an amendment by Senator Maybank of South Carolina which would have struck out public housing from the Housing Act of 1954 because of the Supreme Court decision outlawing segregation in California public housing. The Maybank amendment was defeated by a voice vote on June 4.

The only Senators who made statements for the record on the date this vote was taken were Senator Maybank, who spoke in favor of his own amendment, Senator Knowland, the Majority Leader, who urged the Maybank amendment be defeated, and Senator Lehman, who expressed his opposition to the Maybank amendment. However, the overwhelming nature of the vote shows that it was heavily supported by many Senators, and, in this instance, the Congress was prevented from going on record in favor of defying the Supreme Court.[20]

We must publicize and stress the records of members of the Senate and House if we are to overcome the present stalemate in Congress on civil rights. We are now at the place where our steadily increasing voting strength will effectively persuade members of the House and Senate to support civil rights, if they believe that the voters at home are carefully following what happens in Washington.

One of the finest illustrations of an effective use of voting records comes from the State of Oklahoma where Mr. Roscoe Dunjee, editor of the *Black Dispatch*, has published the record of Senator Kerr, who is up for reelection this year. We have asked Mr. Dunjee for a folio of his printed statements on Senator Kerr, and now have that available for distribution at the Convention.

The NAACP does not endorse candidates for election, but it is under a mandate from its constituents to supply the record of office-holders. We have these records in the Washington Bureau, but they will serve no useful purpose unless they are given the kind of publicity and attention that Mr. Dunjee has provided. It is strongly urged that his example be followed throughout the country.

We have at the Convention the individual records of the Congressmen and Senators. We also have samples of mimeographed records which we prepare in the Washington Bureau. Many of these have been distributed in state and regional conferences. We have not prepared a new supply for this Convention because it is anticipated that Congress will adjourn July or early in August. At that time, a record on each state will be prepared embracing the entire 83rd Congress and it will be available upon request.

The foregoing statement was presented at the NAACP National Convention in Dallas, Texas, June 29 to July 4, 1954

MS: MP.

Although this report contains some of the information that is in other reports, it is published because it is the most concise.

1. For initial mention of and report on this problem involving civilians at navy yards, see, respectively, 5/1/50 and 6/5/52.

2. See 9/9, 10/6, 11/2, 11/4, and 12/31/53.

3. Mitchell, "Status of Racial Integration in the Armed Services."

4. See 4/3/53; president's news conference, 3/19/53; Eisenhower, *Public Papers of the Presidents*, 108.

5. See, among others, 2/17/54; materials in NAACP WB-171, DLC.

6. See also, among others, 3/9 and 9/29/54.

7. See 12/31/53; materials in NAAACP WB-185, DLC; Watson, *Lion in the Lobby*, 107, 411.

8. See 9/9/53.

9. For reports on Truman's issuance of EO 9980, see 12/1/48 and, in appendix 1, this vol., 11/7/47, and 8/20/48; on Eisenhower's issuance of EO 10479, see 9/9/53.

10. See the headnote on Struggle for a Permanent FEPC, 1942–54, vol. III.

11. For Mitchell's initial reaction to the Federal Fair Employment Board's recommendation, see

3/3/50. For detailed backgrounders on the ending of the apprentice program, see letter, 7/9/53, from A. W. Hall, director of the Bureau of Engraving and Printers, to a Mr. Longhorn, and another from Hall to Raymond F. Cooke, 4/23/54, in NAACP WB-18, DLC. See also, among others, 3/9 and 9/29/54.

12. See, in appendix 1, this vol., 2/1/49, as well as the headnote on Segregation in Federal Housing Programs, vol. III. See also, most immediately, 6/4 and 5/5/54.

13. Mitchell recommended to Walter White that the board should request a joint meeting with the president, the attorney general, and the housing administrator to obtain a "definite agreement that in the future the Government will give no aid of any kind in the Housing program unless there is an assurance that housing and/or facilities will be open to qualified persons without regard to race." Mitchell memorandum to White, 5/7/54, NAACP WB-91, DLC.

14. *New York Times*, 1/26/54, 1, 12; "Special Message to the Congress on Housing," 1/25/54, Eisenhower, *Public Papers of the Presidents, 1954*, 193–200.

15. At Eisenhower's news conference on May 5, 1954, Ethel Payne of the Defender Publications repeated her April 7, 1954, question to the president "as to whether the several housing agencies had issued any regulations to implement the statement in your Housing Message to Congress, that everything should be done to assure good and well located homes for all citizens." As far as she had learned, she told Eisenhower, "no such specific regulations have been forthcoming." She cited Levittown in Pennsylvania as an example of communities where members of minority groups had been barred. The president responded that the "only hope of getting a detailed report" was to go to the FHA itself. *New York Times*, 5/6/54, 18. See also Walter White's assertion that Eisenhower had "assured him personally that no Federal moneys would be used for segregation." *New York Times*, 5/18/54, 16.

16. *Congressional Quarterly Weekly Report*, 1/9/53, 43–44. On January 18, 1954, Sen. Clinton P. Anderson (D-N.Mex.) proposed in a Senate speech that the cloture rule (Rule XXII) should be changed so that debate could be terminated by a vote of two-thirds of all senators voting, rather than two-thirds of all elected senators, as was then required. Sen. William F. Knowland (R-Calif.), Republican floor leader, said he respectfully declined the invitation "for a double filibuster," instead of a single filibuster, "prior to a vote on Hawaiian statehood." Knowland said the Republican Policy Committee might consider the matter at some future date, but in the interest of expediting the president's program, he would not do so before February. *Congressional Quarterly Weekly Report*, 1/22/54, 97. See also 4/30/53 and materials in NAACP WB-111, DLC.

17. 5/13/54, *Hearings*, 39, 96–118.

18. White, 2/25/54, *Hearings*, 176–91.

19. 4/21/54, *Hearings*, 847–56; *Shelley v. Kramer*; See also Watson, *Lion in the Lobby*, 158, 251.

20. "During consideration of the Omnibus Housing Act of 1954, the House by non-recorded votes rejected anti-discrimination and anti-segregation amendments. No such amendments were offered in the Senate, but a move to delete the public housing features of the bill in view of the Supreme Court's anti-segregation decisions never reached the floor." *Congress and the Nation*, 1616.

A Summary of the Civil Rights Record of the 83rd Congress, August 21, 1954

August 21, 1954

A SUMMARY OF THE CIVIL RIGHTS RECORD OF THE 83RD CONGRESS

The 83rd Congress closed, as it began, with a record of failure on civil rights proposals.

Until the final day, Congressman John Heselton (R., Mass.) made a gallant fight to obtain approval of H.R. 7304, a bill which would have ended all segregation in interstate travel by imposing a fine of $1,000 on carriers if they separated passengers on the basis of race.[1]

The fate of H.R. 7304 was similar to treatment given proposals to eliminate filibusters and other delaying tactics when the Congress met in 1953. At that time, the Senate by a vote of 70 to 21 tabled a motion by Senator Clinton Anderson (D., N.M.) which would have paved the way for adoption of an anti-filibuster rule in the Senate. The Anderson motion, which was tabled on January 7, 1953, was opposed by 41 Republicans and 29 Democrats. By a voice vote on January 3, 1953, the House killed a proposal to eliminate the power of its Rules Committee to block legislation.[2]

H.R. 7304 was a combination of bills introduced by Congressmen Adam Clayton Powell (D.,N.Y.), William L. Dawson (D., Ill.), Heselton and others. Its counterpart in the Senate was S. 2672, introduced by Senators Irving Ives (R., N.Y.) and John M. Butler (R., Md.). The Senate refused to act on the bill until it was passed by the House.

After long delays, the House Interstate and Foreign Commerce Committee held hearings on the travel bills in May of 1954. Some of the committee members said that they wanted to see "what the Supreme Court would do in the school cases." After the Court handed down its decision, some of the same persons suggested that "it would be a good idea to let the dust settle before bringing up any other civil rights proposal."[3]

Finally, on July 21, 1954, the House Committee reported out the bill by a vote of 19 to 7. It was then referred to the House Rules Committee which has the power to kill legislation or send it to the floor for a vote. Congressman Leo Allen (R., Ill.), chairman of the Rules Committee, told his constituents that he could not act on the bill because the leadership of the House thought it was too late in the session.

On Tuesday, August 3, Mr. Heselton sought to move to have the rules of the House suspended in order that the bill might be passed. In order to make this move, it was necessary for him to have the consent of Majority Leader Charles Halleck (R., Ind.)

and Minority Leader Sam Rayburn (D., Tex.). Mr. Halleck agreed but Mr. Rayburn refused.

Numerous unsuccessful attempts were made to get Representative Rayburn to change his mind and permit the bill to come to the floor under suspension of the rules. Republican leaders and the White House were urged to ask Chairman Allen to reconsider and give the bill a favorable rule in his committee. These efforts continued until the Congress adjourned.

Throughout the session, there was some reason to believe that the Administration might get behind H.R. 7304 and get it passed.[4] In the case of FEPC and other civil rights measures, at no time did it appear that the Administration would give even mild support to them.

Senator Everett Dirksen (R., Ill.) introduced S. 1, which would establish a commission to investigate discrimination. This legislation was generally regarded as an attempt to set up an FEPC without enforcement powers. The bona fide FEPC Bill, S. 692, was introduced by Senators Ives, Hubert Humphrey (D., Minn.) and others.

The Dirksen Bill was referred to the Senate Judiciary Committee and the Ives-Humphrey Bill was referred to the Senate Labor Committee.[5]

The NAACP opposed the Dirksen Bill when hearings were held on it in the Senate Judiciary Committee. It was not reported out. The Ives-Humphrey Bill was reported out by the Senate Labor Committee with only Senator Lister Hill (D., Ala.) opposing it.

Democratic Senators James Murray (Mont.), Mathew Neely (W.Va.), Paul Douglas (Ill.), Herbert Lehman (N.Y.), and John F. Kennedy (Mass.) all supported an FEPC with enforcement powers. All of the Republicans on the committee, except Senator Ives, expressed reservations about enforcement powers. The other Republicans are H. Alexander Smith (N.J.), William A. Purtell (Conn.), Barry Goldwater (Ariz.), John Sherman Cooper (Ky.), and Robert W. Upton (N.H.).

Chairman Sam McConnell (R.,Penn.) did not at any time schedule hearings on FEPC legislation. He is opposed to a bill with enforcement powers.

All member of the Senate Labor Committee, except Senator Hill, joined in sponsoring S. 1831, which was a non-discrimination amendment to the Taft-Hartley Act. A similar amendment was sponsored in the House by Congressman Powell. The House Committee approved part of the Powell Amendment but did not report out a bill.[6] The Senate Committee reported out a bill without amendment S. 1831. When the Senate Bill was sent back to committee after it reached the floor, all consideration on amendments to the Taft-Hartley was dropped.[7]

The Senate and House Committees on Banking and Currency ducked the issue of segregation when they considered (H.R. 7839) the Housing Act of 1954.[8] However, Senator Burnett Maybank brought the issue to the floor in reverse when he proposed an amendment which would strike all public housing from the bill because the U.S. Supreme Court upheld the banning of segregation in public housing in California.[9] The Maybank proposal was defeated by an overwhelming voice vote in the Senate on June 4, 1954.

The only Senators who made statements for the record at that time were Majority Leader William Knowland (Cal.) and Lehman, who both opposed the Maybank Amendment, and Senator Maybank.[10]

Outside the strictly civil rights aspects of housing, it should be noted that the 83rd Congress so curtailed the public housing program that many believe it has been consigned to a lingering but certain death.[11]

Congress ignored requests for protection against practices of segregation when it passed the Medical Facilities Survey and Construction Act. This legislation makes grants to the states for hospitals and other health needs. Under its terms, states may maintain "separate but equal" facilities and still receive Federal funds.[12]

S. 2601, a bill to give emergency aid for school construction, also, contained language recognizing the state program of "separate but equal school systems." This language was struck out following NAACP protests and the bill passed the Senate. However, it died in the House. Senator Cooper of Kentucky, chairman of the subcommittee which considered the bill, pledged that the objectionable language would be omitted.

Senator James Eastland (D., Miss.) and Representative John Bell Williams (D., Miss) introduced S. J. Res. 159 and H. J. Res. 532 which proposed amendments to the U.S. Constitution for the purpose of setting aside the Supreme Court decisions in the school cases. Both of these proposals died in committee.

The Congress passed S. 3378 which revises the Organic Act of the Virgin Islands. A number of the residents of the Islands opposed the feature of this bill which gives the Governor sweeping power to reorganize the executive branch of government. Congressman Powell obtained approval of an amendment which required that the Governor obtain the approval of the Islands' legislature before putting reorganization plans into effort. In a conference between the House and Senate, this was modified to provide that the Governor may reorganize the present executive branch in the Islands without the consent of the legislature, but all future reorganization must be done with the consent of the legislature.[13]

Bills to give Statehood to Hawaii and Alaska were killed in the House and Senate.[14] Legislation to give Home Rule to the District of Columbia was also killed.[15]

Anti-Lynching, Anti-Poll Tax, and other civil rights bills had no consideration, except a proposal of Southern Senators to outlaw the Poll Tax by Constitutional Amendment which was taken up but died in the Senate Judiciary Committee.[16]

Perhaps it is significant that in giving the record of the 83rd Congress, beginning on page A-6263 of the Congressional Record for August 20, Majority Leader Knowland mentioned the Supreme Court decision against segregation in public schools, ending segregation in the Armed Services, action against segregation in the Nation's Capital, appointment of colored persons to government jobs and other actions of the executive branch. His report does not mention FEPC, Anti-Jim Crow Travel, and other civil rights bills which the Congress failed to act on.

From this, it would appear that the members of the 83rd Congress will run on civil rights records made by the Supreme Court and the Executive Branch. It remains to be seen what the voters will think of this.

MS: NAACP II: A-185, DLC.

This report was sent to Walter White on August 27, 1954, with the following comment: "This is the legislative record of the Administration on civil rights. A record also including the executive actions will be prepared later." For the later report, see 9/29/54.

1. *Congressional Quarterly Weekly Report,* 5/14/54, 621.

2. *Congressional Quarterly Weekly Report,* 1/2/53, 11; 1/9/54, 43.

3. 5/13/54, *Hearings,* 96–118. See also, among others, 5/5 and 6/4/54; materials in NAACP IX: 12, DLC.

4. In the report to accompany H.R. 7304 from the Committee on Interstate and Foreign Commerce, Representative Wolverton noted that the bill did not establish a new policy but simply reaffirmed and clarified the general policy already adopted by Congress in several statutes (which implicitly existed in common law) against discrimination with respect to travel on common carriers operating in interstate transportation. Wolverton's report, NAACP IX 12: DLC. See also 5/5, 6/4, 9/29, and 12/31/54.

5. See, among others, 3/9 and 9/29/54; 1/26/54, *Hearings,* 75–77; White, 2/25/54, *Hearings,* 176–91.

6. *Congressional Quarterly Weekly Report,* 3/12/54, 323.

7. See 4/12/54.

8. See 6/4/54 for earlier activity related to H.R. 7839. Signed by Eisenhower on August 2, 1954, the Housing Act of 1954 amended the 1949 act. In addition to authorizing thirty-five thousand public housing units for one year, it provided, under the new term *urban renewal,* $500 million for rehabilitation of existing residences and construction of new housing in blighted urban areas. *Congress and the Nation,* 485–86. The Senate never considered the amendments Mitchell had proposed (3/25/54, *Hearings,* 893–900), which the House had rejected. See also *New York Times,* 8/8/54, IV-5.

Adding to this August 21, 1954, report, Mitchell told the board that he was seeking to have Attorney General Herbert Brownell

> take drastic action in Chicago to bring an end to the rioting in connection with the *Trumbull Park Homes.* A constructive meeting was had with Mr. Brownell on the matter at which time he said he would explore the possibility of invoking a statute which provides fines for persons destroying government property. Later he said he had been advised by his people in Chicago that the damage to property was so small that they might lose the case in court, which would make the situation worse. Another part of the conference is still current. Our position is that situations like Trumbull Park would not exist if the government gave no assistance to public housing which discriminated on the basis of race. Attorney General Brownell agreed to set up a conference when Mr. Cole, HHFA Administrator, would be present, after which the matter would go to the President. Mr. Brownell is arranging that meeting at which time it is hoped that the government will come out with an over-all policy of no assistance to housing if there is to be discrimination. (Minutes, 9/13/54, EC)

9. *Congressional Quarterly Weekly Report,* 5/28/54, 671. See 6/4/54 for the earlier report.

10. *Congressional Quarterly Weekly Report,* 6/4/54, 709.

11. For a review of the Omnibus Housing Act of 1954, see *Congress and the Nation,* 485–87. See also, most recently, 5/5 and 9/29/54, as well as the headnote on Segregation in Federal Housing Programs, vol. III.

12. Signed into law on July 12, 1954, the Medical Facilities Survey and Construction Act (H.R. 8149) embodied the president's requests of January 18, 1954, for expansion of the Hill-Burton hospital construction program. *Congress and the Nation,* 1136. See also 9/29/54; 8/21/54, *Hearings,* 847–56.

13. At the June meeting of the board, Mitchell reported on the NAACP's efforts to get Congress to revise the Organic Act of the Virgin Islands and recommended that the board support passage of a different bill, S. 2475, which was backed by the Farmers Union. The resolution noted the NAACP's dissatisfaction with S. 3378 and another bill, H.R. 5181, which, it said, actually represented "a backward step through denying to the local legislature the power to approve or disapprove executive department reorganization." The resolution, which the board adopted, called on Congress "to correct these defects." Minutes, 6/14/54, EC. See also, most recently, 9/28 and 12/31/54.

14. On July 26, 1954, the House Rules Committee tabled a request for a rule to send to conference H.R. 3575, the Hawaiian statehood bill, as amended by the Senate to include Alaskan statehood. Afterward, when asked if this action killed statehood for this session, Allen told a reporter, "I would presume so." *Congressional Quarterly Weekly Report,* 7/30/54, 993. See also, most immediately, 12/31/53; 9/29/54.

15. Home rule for the District of Columbia was killed despite Eisenhower's strong support. State of the Union message, *New York Times,* 1/8/54, 10; *New York Times,* 12/14/54, 1. *Congressional Quarterly*

Weekly Report, 3/12/54, 314. See also 9/29 and 12/31/54; "Should District of Columbia Citizens Have Right to Vote?" Serial Scholastic, 10–11.

16. See headnote on Struggle to Abolish the Poll Tax.

Civil Rights under the Eisenhower Administration, 1953–54, September 29, 1954

CIVIL RIGHTS UNDER THE EISENHOWER ADMINISTRATION 1953–1954[1]

[September 29, 1954]

We have had two years or Republican control of the National Government. The question arises, what has the new leadership done in the field of Civil Rights? A short answer to this question is, the Executive Branch of Government under President Eisenhower has taken substantial steps in the direction of full democracy for all.

The Legislative Branch, also under the leadership of President Eisenhower, has done nothing.

Under the Eisenhower Administration, the Truman program of integration in the Armed Services has been carried forward until it is now an accepted policy.

The Navy Department has ended all racial segregation of civilian employees in its shore establishments in the South. In May 1954, inspection by the Director of the Washington Bureau of the Charleston, South Carolina, establishment, which was the last holdout, showed no segregation in facilities. Many of these Naval establishments are in Alabama, Georgia, Florida, Maryland, North Carolina, South Carolina, and Virginia. Establishments in Kentucky, Tennessee, and Texas had been reported integrated at the time of a prior report in November 1953. The Truman Administration had followed a policy of accepting local custom in these matters.[2]

The President formally requested elimination of segregation in all schools on military posts. As a result, the Department of Defense has announced that all segregation will be ended in such schools by September 1955. The Truman Administration had ended segregation in all military post schools completely under the control of the Department of Defense, except at Fort Benning, Georgia. This was integrated in September 1953. Twenty-one other schools were conducted by the Department of Defense in conjunction with local authorities. Of these, the schools at Fort Belvoir, Virginia, were integrated in September 1954. Local educational officials who formerly operated the Fort Belvoir schools refused to do so and the supervision is now directly in the hands of the Federal Government. We have no report on the status of integration in the other twenty locations.

All schools in the Canal Zone, which were previously segregated, opened in September 1954 on a non-segregated basis. Two new schools, at Fort Myer, Virginia, and Craig Air Force Base, Alabama, opened in the Fall of 1954 on a non-segregated basis.

Naval authorities at the Bainbridge, Maryland, base defied the Department of Defense policy of non-segregation in schools on military posts. At this location, the Naval officials signed an agreement with the Cecil County (Md.) school officials to provide a school for white children only on Navy property. When colored children sought admission to the school, they were denied entrance on the basis of race. At the time of this report, top Naval authorities in Washington are still supporting the Bainbridge policy.

In connection with the integration of military post schools, it should be noted that the Secretary of Health, Education, and Welfare, Mrs. Oveta C. Hobby, sought to delay the school integration program.[3]

POLICY OF NONSEGREGATION

The Administration-appointed Veterans Administrator, Mr. Harvey Higley, is the first chief of that agency to give full support to a policy of non-segregation. Under his direction, the official program of ending segregation in all VA hospitals and domiciliary facilities began in September 1953. In July of 1954, the Veterans Administration officially announced that the program was completed.[4]

The President has continued and strengthened the Truman Administration's Committee on Government Contracts, which is charged with eliminating discrimination in employment by private employers working under governmental contracts. On September 2, 1954, he signed an Executive Order strengthening the non-discrimination clause which must be included in all contracts entered into by the Federal Government. Vice President Nixon is now Chairman of the Committee.[5]

This Committee is now actively working to eliminate employment discrimination in the Telephone Company and Street Car Company in Washington, D.C.[6]

The Eisenhower Administration has continued the Federal Fair Employment Board which was established by President Truman's Executive Order 9980. This Board is charged with responsibility of the eliminating of discrimination in Federal employment. In a very important case, it appears that the White House has failed to back this Board in its finding of discrimination against the Treasury Department. The Board ruled that elimination of Apprentice Training in the Bureau of Printing and Engraving, under the guise of economy, was in reality a continuation of the Bureau's practice of keeping this particular occupation for whites only. At the time of this report, the Board's decision is still being suppressed by the White House.[7]

The most prominent field in which a responsible Executive agency has resisted change relating to discrimination has been that of housing. The Housing Program of the Government has been the greatest single force in the Nation promoting housing segregation. Despite the President's plea for adequate housing for minority groups, no action has been taken by the Housing Agencies to implement the President's statement on this subject which was made in his January Housing message to Congress.[8]

The Attorney General of the United States, Mr. Herbert Brownell, took part in cases before the Supreme Court and lower courts advancing the cause of civil rights. Chief of these were the school segregation cases and the Thompson Restaurant Case, in which his office filed briefs and argued as *amicus curiae.*[9] In the Thompson Case, which established the validity of the law prohibiting segregation in restaurants in the District of Columbia, the argument of the Department of Justice was particularly effective and greatly contributed to a favorable decision.

On June 8, 1953, the U.S. Supreme Court declared that segregation in Washington restaurants was illegal. The Commissioners of the District of Columbia, who are appointed by the President, began enforcement of the Supreme Court decision on June 10, 1953.[10]

The Attorney General also assisted the cause of civil rights by screening out applicants for positions who were known opponents of civil rights. In Oregon, Senator Warren Gill, who had opposed the Oregon Civil Rights Bill, was refused appointment as United States Attorney because of his views. In Texas, a pro-segregation candidate, John Lee Smith, withdrew as applicant for the office of United States Attorney. He announced that his views on civil rights were unacceptable to Attorney General Brownell.

PRESIDENT FAVORS COMPLIANCE

The District of Columbia Government has made progress in eliminating discrimination and segregation in its operations. On September 18, 1954, the long-planned integration of the local Fire Department, which had been blocked during the Truman Administration, was put into effect.[11]

The District Government now requires contractors to sign a non-discrimination clause similar to that contained in Federal contracts.[12] Steps have been taken to eliminate discrimination in hiring by District agencies. Public recreation facilities have been integrated.[13]

Integration in the public schools of Washington, D.C., began in September 1954 as a result of the U.S. Supreme Court decisions.[14] The program of integration was in the hands of the local Board of Education which is appointed by the Courts in the District of Columbia, and, therefore, not directly subject to the control of the President. However, it is generally understood that the President himself favored complete compliance with the Supreme Court decision in Washington, D.C.

The new Administration has stated that it would give opportunity for employment in Government Service without regard to race.

Senator William Knowland, Majority Leader, listed the following appointments of colored persons in his report on the 83rd Congress:

"Delegate to United Nations; legal counsel, Post Office Department; minority groups consultant, Labor Department; member, Caribbean Commission; Ambassador to Liberia; adviser and consultant, War Claims Commission; member, Federal Parole Board[15]; Register, Treasury Department; adviser on business affairs, Commerce Department; Special Assistant to Commissioner of Public Housing on Racial Affairs; Advisory Committee on Government Housing Policies and Programs; member, International Development Advisory Board; assistant counsel, Foreign Operations Administration; Governor of Virgin Islands; Assistant Secretary, Labor Department; head of United States Educational Mission to Afghanistan; National Board of Field Advisers to Small Business Administration, and member of Board of Foreign Scholarships."

Inclusion of the Knowland list in this report is not intended to indicate that the appointments made are all significant or important. It is offered as an example of what the Republican Party itself believe to be a good record.

NO SENATE RULES CHANGE

The President did not publicly request Congress to pass any civil rights legislation. When the Secretary of Labor endorsed an FEPC with enforcement powers, the President stated in a press conference that the Secretary of Labor was not speaking for him.[16]

The Congress opened with an attempt to change Senate rules to make it easier to break a filibuster, which device has been used to kill all civil rights legislation. Senator Clinton P. Anderson (D., N.M.) introduced a motion to consider adoption of rules for the 83rd Session. Had this motion prevailed, Senator Irving Ives (R.,N.Y.) was to introduce a motion to revise the Senate rule relating to filibusters. The late Senator Robert Taft (R., Ohio), however, moved to table Senator Anderson's motion. Senator Taft's motion was adopted by a vote of 70 - 21, thereby killing any chance to change the rules. Taft was supported by 41 Republicans and 29 Democrats. His motion was opposed by 5 Republicans and 15 Democrats.[17]

In the House, too, an attempt to modify the rules so as to prevent legislative bottlenecks was defeated. By a voice vote, the House adopted its old rules, continuing the power of its Rules Committee, which has used its power to block civil rights and other progressive legislation. Congressman Herman Eberharter (D., Pa.) attempted unsuccessfully to have a resolution passed which would allow committee chairmen to force House consideration of bills approved by their committees but blocked by the Rules Committee.[18]

In the Senate, two bills providing fair employment practices were introduced. The first, sponsored by Senator Everett Dirksen (R., Ill.), lacked enforcement powers and was opposed by civil rights organizations. It was referred to the Senate Judiciary Committee, which did not report it out. The second, co-sponsored by Senators Ives (R., N.Y.) and Humphrey (D., Minn.) was reported favorably by the Senate Labor Committee. All other members of the Committee, except Senator Lister Hill (D., Ala.)

joined Senator Ives and Humphrey in supporting this legislation. Senators Murray (D., Mont.), Neely (D., W.Va.), and Douglas (D., Ill.), Lehman (D., N.Y.), Kennedy (D., Mass.), Humphrey, and Ives favored an FEPC with enforcement powers. The other favorable committee members, Senators Smith (R., N.J.), Purtell (R., Conn.), Goldwater (R., Ariz.), Cooper (R., Ky.), and Upton (R.,N.H.) expressed reservations on enforcement powers. Faced with a certain filibuster if this bill was acted on, the Senate did not take it up for debate.[19]

In the House, despite requests for hearings on FEPC legislation by the NAACP and other interested organizations, Representative Samuel McConnell (R., Pa.), Chairman of the House Labor Committee, refused to conduct such hearings or take any action on the proposed legislation. Representative McConnell has opposed a workable FEPC.[20]

Senator Ives and Representative Adam Clayton Powell (D., N.Y.) sponsored a bill to add non-segregation safeguards to the National Labor Relations Act. In the Senate, the following members joined in co-sponsoring this legislation: Republicans Smith (N.J.), Aiken (Vt.), the late Senator Griswold (Nebr.), Purtell (Conn.), and Goldwater (Ariz.), and Democrats Murray (Mont.), Neely (W.Va.), Douglas (Ill.), Lehman (N.Y.), and Kennedy (Mass.).[21] The House Committee approved part of the Powell Amendment but did not report out a bill. The Powell Amendment died when the Senate referred the bill amending the Taft-Hartley Act back to committee. Led by Senator Smith of New Jersey, all Republican sponsors of the amendment withdrew their support in committee when a proposed revision of the Taft-Hartley Act was reported out.[22]

HOUSING SEGREGATION

In the field of Housing, both the Senate and House Committees on Banking and Currency ducked the issue of segregation when they considered the Housing Act of 1954.[23] The issue was raised in reverse, however, when the late Senator Burnet Maybank (D., S.C.) proposed an amendment which would strike all public housing from the bill because of a Supreme Court ruling upholding a decision in the California Court ending segregation in public housing. This proposal was defeated by an overwhelming voice vote in the Senate. The only Senators who made statements for the record on this bill, other than Senator Maybank, were Majority Leader Knowland (R., Cal.) and Lehman (D., N.Y.), both of whom opposed the proposal. Final action by Congress on the Housing Act so curtailed public housing as to foreshadow its early death.[24]

In other welfare and public works building programs, the 83rd Congress failed to take action which would prevent segregation in the use of Federally-built and supported facilities. The Hospital Construction Act, even though passed after the Supreme Court decision outlawing segregation, did not contain any safeguards against segregation. Under the terms of this appropriation bill, the states may provide so-called "separate but equal" facilities and still receive Federal funds.[25]

A Senate Bill to provide emergency aid for school construction contained language recognizing the "separate but equal" doctrine. At the urging of the NAACP, Senator John Sherman Cooper had this language struck out in committee and the bill passed the Senate. The bill died in the House.[26]

These grants to states for social welfare programs generally have the support of liberal northern and less conservative southern Congressmen. The liberals (both Republicans and Democrats) feel that inclusion of non-segregation clauses in this type of legislation will lead to southern opposition to the entire bill. For this reason, in fear that the legislation will be rejected entirely, they refuse to take a strong stand for non-segregation.

FAILURE TO PASS LEGISLATION

The strongest bid made to pass civil rights legislation in the 83rd Congress was the attempt to end Jim-Crow travel restrictions in interstate commerce. Until the final day of the Congressional session, Congressman John Heselton (R., Mass) made a gallant effort to obtain approval of H.R. 7304, which would provide penalties for carriers separating persons in interstate commerce on the basis of race. H.R. 7304 was a combination of bills introduced in the House by Representatives Heselton, Powell, Dawson (D., Ill.), and others. Its counterpart in the Senate was S. 2672, introduced by Senators Ives and Butler (R., Md.). The Senate refused to take action until the House passed the bill.

In the House, after long delays, the Interstate and Foreign Commerce Committee held hearings on the travel bills in May 1954. Finally, on July 21, the Committee reported out the bill by a vote of 19–7. Congressmen who voted for the bill in Committee were: Republicans Wolverton (N.J.), Hinshaw (Calif.), Hale (Maine), Hoffman (Ill.), Beamer (Ind.), Springer (Ill.), Schenck (Ohio), Carrings (Pa.), Warburton (Del.), Derounian (N.Y.), Pelly (Wash.), and Younger (Calif.)—Democrats Crosser (Ohio), Klein (N.Y.), Granahan (Pa.), Mack (Ill.), Moulder (Mo.), and Staggers (W.Va.)

It was then referred to the House Rules Committee. Congressman Leo Allen (R., Ill.), Chairman of that Committee, said he could not act on the bill because it was too late in the session.

In the closing days of the session, Congressman Heselton sought to have the rules of the House suspended so the bill might be brought before the House. To do this, it required the consent of the leadership of both Parties. Speaker Martin (R., Mass.) and Majority Leader Halleck (R., Ind.) were agreeable to this proposal, but Minority Leader Rayburn (D., Tex.) refused his consent. Despite constant urging, Representative Rayburn refused to relent. Likewise, Representative Allen was adamant in his refusal to release the bill from his committee.

Representative Heselton stated his belief that Congress would have passed this legislation had it been given an opportunity to vote. He announced his intention to reintroduce it at the next session of Congress.

Representative William Granahan (D., Pa.), who sponsored a bill similar to that of Congressman Heselton, also announced his intention of pressing for the passage of his bill in the next Congressional session.[27]

Statehood for Hawaii and Alaska, favored by the NAACP, failed of passage this session. The House passed a bill approving Hawaiian Statehood. This was amended in the Senate to include Alaska and sent back to the House, where no further action was taken.[28]

Home Rule for the District of Columbia was also considered by Congress, but, likewise, failed of passage.[29]

A proposal by southern Senators to outlaw the Poll Tax by Constitutional Amendment was taken up by the Judiciary Committee, but died there.

Other proposed Constitutional Amendments, sponsored by Senator James Eastland (R., Miss.) and Representative John Bell Williams (D., Miss.) designed to set aside the Supreme Court decisions in the school cases, died in committees.

A bill revising the Organic Act of the Virgin Islands was amended to give residents a voice in future reorganization of the Islands' Government. This amendment was one of several suggested by the NAACP and offered on the floor by Congressman Powell. A number of the Islands' residents opposed the original bill which gave the Governor power to reorganize the Executive Branch of Government without the consent of the Islands' Legislature. As finally passed, the bill provides that the Governor may carry out reorganization of the present Executive structure in the Islands without the consent of the Legislature. However, all future reorganization must be with the consent of the Legislature.[30]

Some supporters of the Bricker Amendment, limiting the President's treaty-making power, urged its adoption as necessary to halt the civil rights progress in the United States. This is a false argument, used to exploit the prejudices of some persons for political advantage. The NAACP was one of the many organizations which opposed the Bricker Amendment. This Amendment was defeated in the Senate.[31]

The failure to pass any civil rights legislation during this session of Congress must be shared by the Administration, its Congressional leaders, and the leadership of the minority Party. Any action taken on such legislation was by individual Congressmen, unsupported by their Party leaders.

REPORT RELEASED

This report was released September 29, 1954

MS: NAACP II: A-182, DLC.

1. This report is complemented by that of 8/21/54.
2. See, among others, 6/29/54.
3. See, most immediately, 2/17, 2/28, 3/9, 5/5, 6/29, 11/4, and 12/31/54.
4. See also, among others, 6/29 and 12/31/54; correspondence between Mitchell and Higley and other materials in NAACP WB-185, DLC.

5. On September 2, 1954, Eisenhower signed EO 10557, Approving the Revised Provision in Government Contracts Relating to Nondiscrimination in Employment. Deputy Attorney General William P. Rogers earlier had announced the text of the revision. It strengthened the Committee on Government Contracts by defining the prohibited discriminatory employment practices based on race, color, religion, or national origin, and it provided for the posting of a notice in conspicuous places of employment by the contractor in order to acquaint employees and applicants for employment with the provisions of the nondiscrimination clause. Press release, 4/22/54, President's Committee on Government Contracts, NAACP II: A-208, DLC. See also materials in NAACP II: A-200, DLC; Donnelly Collection of Presidential Executive Orders, available at http://www.conservativeusa.org/eo/eisenhower.htm.

6. A hearing in January held by the Senate District Committee on the Capital Transit Company (CTC) impasse, though long-winded and inconclusive, showed that the attitude within the company of accepting black platform workers was less rigid than in the past. William Pryor reported to Mitchell that CTC attorney Edmund L. Jones said the company had no objections to hiring black platform workers but that the white operators would "wildcat"; the union would not order them back to work, and neither would it arbitrate the matter. Anyway, Pryor reported Jones as saying, arbitration probably would not do much good because if the wildcatters were forced back to work under such a ruling, "that would be involuntary servitude."

Sen. Wayne Morse, however, noted that the union had said it had no objection to the hiring of black platform workers; therefore, if the whites wildcatted, they would be doing so in violation of union policy, as each man entering the union had sworn not to discriminate. Morse noted further that the union had insisted on arbitrating the pension plan, and thus, the company could insist on arbitrating the ending of segregation. Furthermore, Morse said, there was no doubt that an arbitration board would find the wildcatters in violation of their contract if they did that. He said the men could appeal the arbitration ruling in court, as had been established in connection with the discussion on pension plans. Memorandum from Bill (William) Pryor to Mitchell, 1/19/54, NAACP WB-18, DLC.

After a struggle that was begun by the wartime FEPC, the CTC would employ its first blacks as operators of streetcars and buses in 1955. See volume V.

7. See, among others, 3/9, 6/29, and 12/31/54.

8. See, most immediately, 3/9, 5/5, 6/4, 6/29, 8/21, and 12/31/54; in appendix 1, this vol., 12/9/54; Mitchell memorandum to Walter White, 5/7/54, "Recommendations on Present Housing Problems," NAACP WB-91, DLC.

At the board meeting in September, Mitchell again recalled Eisenhower's news conference on August 4, 1954, when he asserted that "where Federal funds and Federal authority are involved, there should be no discrimination based upon any reason that is not recognized by our Constitution." Mitchell urged the president to "give his position practical effect by establishing a clear policy that all rental or sale housing built with any form of government assistance . . . be open to all qualified persons without regard to race." He reiterated that the NAACP did "not approve of any program of special treatment as announced by Administrator Albert M. Cole" of the HHFA in Pittsburgh, Pennsylvania, on 9/8/54. He then said he would set up an advisory committee on minority housing." Minutes, 9/13/54, EC; 8/4/54, Eisenhower, *Public Papers of the Presidents*, 1954, 182.

9. *Brown v. Board of Education; John R. Thompson Company, Inc. v. District of Columbia.* On Brownell's action in *John R. Thompson Company, Inc.*, see Watson, *Lion in the Lobby*, 224. In that case, the Court ruled that restaurants in the District of Columbia could not legally refuse to serve meals to blacks who were well behaved. It held valid a statute enacted in 1873 that made it a criminal act for owners of eating places to refuse to serve any person solely because of race or color. *New York Times*, 6/9/53, 1.

10. See, most immediately, 3/2, 6/15, 11/4, 12/31/53, 12/6 and 12/31/54; *District of Columbia v. John R. Thompson Company, Inc.*; White, "How Washington's Color Line Looks to Me," NAACP reprint, NAACP II: K-1, DLC.

11. See also, most immediately, 12/7/53, 12/31/54.

12. Unlike the federal government, the District of Columbia had not required nondiscrimination clauses in contracts with firms with which it did business. Due to the NAACP's persistence, an announcement was made that beginning on November 16, 1953, all contracts amounting to $30,000 or more let by the district would include nondiscrimination clauses. Minutes, 10/53. Copy in NAACP II: A-200, DLC.

13. See, most immediately, 3/3, 6/15, 11/4, and 12/31/53, 12/6 and 12/31/54.

14. Watson, *Lion in the Lobby,* 225.

15. On September 29, it was announced that this appointee was made chair of the Federal Parole Board.

16. At the president's news conference on March 3, 1953, Alice Dunnigan of the Associated Negro Press asked Eisenhower to clarify a story circulating on Capitol Hill, which said that a letter sent by his labor secretary to the chair of the Senate Committee on Labor and Public Welfare endorsing the Ives equal employment opportunity bill, with enforcement powers, expressed the administration's position on the FEPC issue. Eisenhower replied that he had made his position clear "many dozens of times": he believed there were certain things that were "not best handled by punitive or compulsory Federal law." Secretary Mitchell, he said, was "allowed in his own person to have views different from me on certain particular details of governmental activity." Any other cabinet officer was "so allowed and so authorized," he added, and he did not "consider it any matter of disloyalty to me." Eisenhower, *Public Papers of the Presidents,* 1954, 293.

See also the text of Eisenhower's letter to Richard Nixon, September 4, 1953, in which the president said: "I have never agreed with the wisdom of enacting a so-called Federal FEPC law on the grounds that [among others] it would be ineffective and would undoubtedly by creating antagonisms, set back the course of progress by a good many years." Available at http://www.eisenhowermemorial.org/presidential-papers/first-term/documents/401.cfm.

17. For a detailed account of the battle, which led to the defeat on January 7, 1953, of the effort to change the rules at the beginning of the 83rd Congress, see *Congressional Quarterly Weekly Report,* 1/9/53, 43.

18. See *Congressional Quarterly Weekly Report,* 1/9/53, 44; also 4/30 and 6/15/53 for Mitchell's reactions to attempts to adopt a twenty-one-day rule for the House Rules Committee.

19. *Congressional Quarterly Weekly Report,* 3/5/54, 293. See also 2/28, 8/21, and 12/31/54.

20. See 8/21/54.

21. See, most directly, 5/4 and 12/31/53, 8/31/54.

22. See 4/12 and 8/21/54; progress report on "Labor Law Revision, *Congressional Quarterly Weekly Report,* 4/16/54, 481.

23. See 6/18/53, *Hearings,* 264–67; 6/23/53, *Hearings,* 203–5; 3/25/54, *Hearings,* 893–900. See also statement of Albert M. Cole, 6/16/53, *Hearings,* 4–15.

24. See *Congress and the Nation,* 485–87; 8/21/54.

25. Mitchell protested bitterly to Sen. H. Alexander Smith, of the Senate Labor and Public Welfare Committee, that the Senate passed H.R. 8149, a bill to amend the Hospital Survey and Construction Act provisions of the Public Health Service Act, even though it permitted continued federal aid to hospitals that denied admission to African Americans solely because of race. Mitchell's letter to Smith, 6/30/54, NAACP WB-111, DLC. See also 8/21/54; 4/21/54, *Hearings,* 847–56.

26. Hearings began on May 11, 1954, on S. 359, S. 2601, and S. 2779, all pertaining to federal aid to school construction. *Congressional Quarterly Weekly Report,* 5/14/54, 621. See 5/20/54, *Hearings,* 248–52; also 3/9 and 6/4/54.

27. See, among others, 6/29 and 8/21/54, as well as the headnote on the Struggle to End Jim Crow Travel, vol. III.

28. *Congressional Quarterly Weekly Report,* 2/5/54, 162; 3/5/54, 284; 3/12/54, 314.

29. See 8/21/54; *New York Times,* 12/14/54, 1, where Eisenhower urged the right to vote, locally and nationally, in the District of Columbia.

30. See, most recently, 8/21 and 12/31/54.

31. After a month-long debate that tied up action on President Eisenhower's legislation, the Senate on February 26, 1954, rejected the Bricker amendment by a lack on one vote, 60 to 31. The tide of support for the amendment ebbed after 1954. *Congress and the Nation,* 111–13. See also, among others, 12/31/53. For examples of news reports on the widely covered struggle, see *New York Times,* 1/21/54, 1, 1/23/54, 1, 1/24/54, 1. and 1/26/54, 1, 26; *Newsweek* (January 10, 1955), 20; "The Bricker Amendment," *Congressional Quarterly Weekly Report,* 1/15/54, 47–48.

Monthly Report, October 7, 1954

October 7, 1954

MONTHLY REPORT OF THE WASHINGTON BUREAU

Because of the importance of developments in school integration in Baltimore, Maryland, and Washington, D. C., the following is submitted as the Washington Bureau's Monthly Report. Originally, the emphasis of this report was to be on the executive and legislative record of the new Administration. Instead, a separate statement on that matter has been prepared and is available for distribution. In reading this report on the schools, it is important to keep in mind that integration began peacefully in Baltimore on September 7 and in Washington on September 13.

On Thursday, September 30, a small group of white women began picketing the Charles Carroll School in Baltimore. There are only twelve colored children at this school and all of them are in the kindergarten. The total school enrollment is 558. The school is located in a part of South Baltimore that is called "Pigtown." In this section of the city, there is a heavy concentration of unemployment, petty crimes, and other social problems.

Student Assaulted

During the lunch hour at the Gwynn's Falls Junior High School, which is located in a middle income residential area of Northwest Baltimore, a colored student was struck in the face by two white men who came on the school property. The student reported that one of the men asked him what time it was. When the student replied that he did not have a watch, the man struck him in the face. Both men then ran from the school property.

The Police Department staged a line-up which included the operator of a car that drove away from the school at the time the incident occurred. The child, who was the victim of the assault, was unable to identify the assailant in the line-up. The driver of the car said that he had come to the school to pick up his sister because he had heard there would be a race riot at the school.[1]

The Baltimore Sun, a daily newspaper which was giving extensive coverage to the Milford, Delaware, school disorders, carried a triple column picture of the pickets in a prominent place.

On October 1, the picketing spread to four other schools. These schools were No. 72, No. 22, No. 48, and Southern High School. All of these are in South Baltimore. The Gwynn's Falls Junior High School was not picketed on October 1.

Students at Southern High School, which not only had accomplished integration quickly and peacefully, but had also accepted the services of colored teachers, began a demonstration. The students carried crude signs advising, "Niggers Go Back to Africa," "Give Us Our School Back," and other slogans. The demonstrations soon approached riot proportions in that whites began threatening physical attacks on colored persons and colored persons began counter threats.

Throughout the days of Friday, Saturday, and Sunday, numerous people reported that inflammatory telephone calls were being made to parents of children in integrated schools. The calls falsely reported that a white girl had been stabbed to death by a colored boy, that schools had been burned down, that colored people were assembling to attack white people, and that white gangs were accepting invitations to have pitched battles with colored people.

Representatives of the Baltimore Branch and the Washington Bureau of the NAACP discussed with the Baltimore City Solicitor the possibility of seeking an injunction against the pickets. The City Solicitor said that he was unwilling to do this because it was necessary for him to prepare for an argument in a case set for Tuesday, October 5th. In this case, the National Association for the Advancement of White People, purporting to be acting on behalf of white parents, was seeking to obtain a court ruling that the Baltimore City School Board had acted illegally by integrating the schools prior to a final decree from the U.S. Supreme Court.[2]

The Baltimore Branch with help of the National Legal Staff then engaged in planning a program of its own to seek an injunction on behalf of parents whose children were being intimidated by the picketing of the integrated schools. Meanwhile, the Baltimore Chapter of the American Veterans Committee pointed out that the Baltimore City Code prohibited the interference with the attendance of school children, and, the picketing was, therefore, unlawful.

Picketing Spreads

On Monday, October 4, picketing was extended to include the Gwynn's Falls Junior High School and disruptive activity was started in the immediate vicinity of twenty other schools that had not experienced any trouble during the previous week. A parent of the student, who was assaulted on September 30, surveyed the Gwynn's Falls neighborhood at the time school was to begin. The parent found that, at strategic points several blocks away from the school, adults were directing children to return home.

A number of parents later verified that such interference with children had occurred in various parts of the city for several days. For example, the Baltimore Sun of October 6, 1954, carried a letter signed by a parent, B. L. Buckner, who said the following:

> "I am a white parent of five children attending Public School No. 22, Hamburg and Scott Streets. My children went to school Friday morning. Four of them were sent home.

"As long as pickets are causing trouble my children are forced to stay home. No parent wants their children mixed up in any racial mess such as is happening.

"The law must be enforced to the extent that all must be quiet and peaceful around our schools."

At the Gwynn's Falls Junior High School, adults and teen-agers not connected with the school created most of the disturbance. The children seemed bewildered and usually entered the school building when urged to do so. The pickets carried crude signs, but the slogans were carefully worded. The general run of signs stated, "Wake Up, Mr. Politician," "We Want Our Rights," and "Let the People Decide."

On the other hand, various persons were distributing highly inflammatory signs to the children. These signs, written on pieces of cardboard, read, "Niggers Go Back To Africa," "Kick Them Out," and other slogans. It was obvious from first-hand observation that the signs were being prepared and distributed systematically among the children. Some of the children who did not know what to do with the signs stuck them in shrubbery near the school, and went into the building.

The picket lines were obviously organized by experts and were serviced by several cars. The license numbers of these cars were obtained and a check revealed their ownership. One man, who appeared to be the supervisor of the picket line was using a car, Maryland tags HC-5493. The car is listed in the name of Preston Thomas Donaldson, 6332 Rollins Avenue, Washington, D. C. (The Maryland Commissioner of Motor Vehicles listed the address as Washington, but this street also runs across the Maryland line.)

Another important person on the picket line was a man who did not carry a sign, but held frequent conversations with pickets and serviced them with soft drinks. He was using a car, Maryland license, No. CE-9097. This car is listed in the name of Owen Bernard Hayes, 311 South Norris Street, Baltimore 23, Maryland.

A third car was at the Gwynn's Falls Junior high school during several hours of the picketing. There was no evidence that the occupants had a direct contact with the pickets. However, since it remained on the scene for such an extended period, the license was checked. This car is registered in the name of Emil Albert Teller, 3506 West Lexington Street, Baltimore, Maryland.

Another car was observed by Baltimore City Police in the vicinity of a school building. The occupant of this car had a map of the city on which various spots had been pin-pointed. The license number of this car was AG-9743. It is owned by Richard Dann, 3803 Park View Avenue, Baltimore.

The occupants of another car carried placards, soft drinks, and apples-on-the-stick and distributed the cards and refreshments to various school children. This car's license number is BE-1560 and is registered in the name of Margaret Wheeler, 4212 Morrison Street, Baltimore, Maryland.

A car with the license number BE-7185 had four occupants, all of whom had placards. This car is registered in the name of Robert Davidson, 2200 Greenmount Avenue, Baltimore, Maryland.

Other cars operating in conjunction with disorders in other parts of the city were: License number AE-9214, registered in the name of Elsworth Fendley, 3716 Flowerton

Road, Baltimore, and License number BJ-4359, registered in the name of Nick Puss Loskie, Jr., 1212 James Street, Baltimore.[3]

During the day of October 4, students, mainly from Southern High School in Baltimore, began seeking recruits for a march on the City Hall. Several hundred students participated in this march, but the majority of students at the integrated schools of Merganthaler, Polytechnic, and City College refused to join in the demonstration. At one point, police broke up a near fight between the white demonstrators and white students at one of the schools at which recruits were being sought. The demonstrating students marched through the downtown area in the face of on-coming traffic, but the police did not stop them until they reached a point near the Court House.

The "parade" route also passed Western High School, which is an all girls' school that has been integrated. None of the students from Western High School joined the line of march.

At one point in the parade, a mother dressed in a house coat rushed from her home and seized her son who was carrying a sign. She ordered him to get back to school or go to work.

Patrolman Sartorius, a traffic officer, said that he ordered some of the demonstrators to get out of the line of traffic, and, also asked them why they were staging the parade. Those interviewed were not certain why they were demonstrating, he said.

At another point, an observer was asked by a student how to spell the word segregation because he wanted to write it on a sign.

Baltimore Turning Point

The turning point in the Baltimore disorder came the evening of October 4, when the Commissioner of the Police announced that the picketing was interfering with the schooling of the children, and, therefore, was a violation of the law. He announced that pickets would be arrested.

On October 5th, pickets showed up at one or two points but were dispersed by the police. They then went to the court of Judge Cullen, who was hearing the anti-integration case of the NAAWP. In the court-room, they insisted on sitting by whites only and when seats were available by colored people they ostentatiously refused to accept the suggestions of bailiffs that they might be seated instead of standing. One member of the group made a considerable point of angrily arising from his seat and walking out of the court-room when a colored man sat beside him.

During the argument on the case, the lawyers for the NAAWP seemed much more interested in talking to their clients than they were in talking to the Judge. Most of the time, the counsel would turn from addressing the Judge and addressed remarks in the general direction of the assembled pickets and NAAWP members.

Arguments were concluded at noon and the Judge advised the spectators that he would announce his opinion at 3:00p.m. At 3:00 p.m., the pickets and others, who apparently were their sympathizers, assembled and filled the three rows of seats directly in front of the Judge. They sat in such a manner as to prevent any colored person getting into the seats.

When the Judge gave his opinion declaring that the Baltimore City School Board had acted legally in abolishing segregation, one of the group was heard to ask another, "What does that mean?" The other replied, "He just cut our throats."

Criminal Record of Bryant William Bowles, Jr.

The following is a partial criminal record of Bryant William Bowles, Jr., in the City of Baltimore, Maryland. These charges arose primarily when Bowles was operating an organization known as the Bryant's Home Improvement Company on Greenmount Avenue. The information on the Bowles criminal record was obtained by Mr. J. Francis Pohlhaus of the NAACP's Washington Bureau. Mr. Pohlhaus made his investigation after the Baltimore Branch of the NAACP received a suggestion from a confidential source that an inquiry about Bowles would show that he had a criminal record.

> Indictment #501/53 (January term, 1953) charged Bowles with larceny after trust of $5,000. The complaining witness was Edward W. Ericksen of New York. On August 18, 1953, he entered a guilty plea. On August 19, 1953, he withdrew this plea and Judge Moser struck out the verdict of guilty and postponed trial. On June 18, 1954, he was found not guilty by Judge Manley.
>
> Indictment #1952/53 charged Bowles with false pretenses. This was filed on May 4, 1953. On August 18, 1953, he entered a plea of guilty, then withdrew the plea on August 19, 1953. On June 18, 1954, he was found guilty before Judge Manley and on July 27, 1954, he was sentenced to one year in the Maryland House of Correction. Sentence was suspended generally on good behavior and on condition he make restitution. The complaining witness in this case was Charles F. Posqua.
>
> Five indictments were filed against Bowles on June 4, 1953, three charging him with failure to pay wages and two with false pretenses. After withdrawing guilty pleas, as in the other cases, he was found guilty by Judge Manley on all five counts on June 18, 1954. He was fined $25.00 and costs on each count.
>
> The false pretenses counts apparently were the result of passing bad checks. Complaining witnesses were John Grey and Louis A. Plummer. Complaining witnesses in the wage cases were John P. Gantt, John Kamler, and Timothy Mitchell.
>
> Mr. Bowles was represented in all cases by William J. O'Donnell, who was defeated when he sought the 1954 Democratic nomination for States Attorney in Baltimore.
>
> The Washington Star of October 7, 1954, carried this comment on the Ericksen case:
>
> > "Larceny after trust—October, 1952. 'Feloniously and fraudulently converted to this own uses' $5,000 entrusted to him by Capt. Edward W. Ericksen, a New York tugboat operator, to be applied in building of a six-unit motel at La Plata, Md. Contract between Ericksen and Bryant Roofing and Home Improvement Corp. March 10, 1953, Bowles signed agreement following civil action, handled by Sherbow & Sherbow, 1316 Munsey Building, Baltimore, to

pay Ericksen $1,000 on each of five successive Mondays starting March 16, 1953. With deduction for surveys, etc., the total due Ericksen, Sherbow & Sherbow says, is $ 4,700.

"On April 30, 1954, Edward F. Shea, jr., of Sherbow & Sherbow wrote to N. Peter Moser, assistant State's attorney, as follows:

'Our file further shows that on March 16, 1953, Mr. Bowles telephoned our office several times during the day and assured us he would appear with the payment that day. Mr. Bowles never appeared and never made any payments under the agreement."

In addition to the foregoing specific charges, Bowles' wife has advised the Baltimore City authorities that her husband is the victim of suicidal tendencies. On receiving this information, the Baltimore officials requested Dr. Guttmacher, a court psychiatrist, to examine Bowles. The result of this examination is in a sealed envelope in the Baltimore Probation Department.

Bowles, also, has a record of passing worthless checks while he was in the Marine Corps in Florida and later in Bel Air, Maryland. Most of these charges were dropped when he agreed to make restitution.

There has been considerable discussion about why city officials in Baltimore have not arrested Bowles again in order that he might be required to serve out the suspended sentence given by Judge Manley. Apparently, this arrest could be made if Bowles committed some new crime in Baltimore City. However, most of his personal activity in Maryland, since the Milford, Delaware, incident, has been carried on in Anne Arundel County, which is outside Baltimore jurisdiction. Nevertheless, it is clear that the NAAWP followers were the nucleus of the picketing groups.

It is quite likely that careful investigation of the license numbers included in this report would shed light on what appears to be a conspiracy to create friction in Washington and Baltimore, after the success in Milford, Delaware.

Trouble Spreads to Washington

On Monday, October 4, students at Anacostia and McKinley High Schools demonstrated against integration. These students carried the same type of crudely worded signs displayed by children in Baltimore. Threatened trouble at Eastern High School was averted when the principal called an assembly of students and urged them not to follow trouble-makers. All three schools reported a high rate of absenteeism on October 5. The Washington, D. C., Branch of the NAACP promptly moved on October 4 to get full police protection for all children. President Eugene Davidson also made a tour of the affected areas.

It should be noted that the Washington Star on October 7 carried an editorial stating that the total number of schools involved in the demonstration was "eight or nine out of 169" in the Capital. The Star also said that, out of the 103,334 school population in the District of Colombia, only about two per cent was involved in the absenteeism during the demonstration.

J. Francis Pohlhaus of the Washington Bureau reported as follows on October 5:

"I left the office of the Washington Bureau with Miss Dagney Johnson to make a tour of the trouble spots in the school strikes.

"We first visited Anacostia High School. As we approached the bridge, we saw some students coming across and more crossing the field below the bridge-a total of perhaps 200. Some of these said they were heading for Eastern or McKinley High Schools.

"We proceeded on to the Anacostia School. There were by this time no children on the outside. The only adults in evidence were residents who were standing on their lawns, apparently observing. I saw a teacher in the school yard and talked to him. He said that inside things were normal and a majority of students were in school.

"When we returned to the bridge, we found that the police had taken a stand about midway and refused to allow any students to cross the bridge in either direction. The students were trying to 'bum' rides across the bridge, but I saw no one picking any of them up. The police officers seemed to have the situation in hand. They kept the strikers off the road and on the sidewalks. About this time, I heard one of the police officials place a call for a dozen more men.

"We moved on to Eastern High School. Along the way, we saw about fifty students straggling along in the direction of that school. When we arrived, there was a small group assembled on the lawn of an apartment building at the southeast corner of 17th and East Capitol Streets. There were a number of adults here, who appeared to be residents. They were in conversation with the students, these were the only adults we saw in direct contact at any time with students.

"We circled the block several times. The school was well-guarded by police officers from all approaches. I tried to secure information from one of the officers, but he was non-commital. When we returned to the assembling point, about fifty strikers were there, but were being dispersed by the police. We saw two young colored boys who were acting as safety patrolmen, and decided to follow them. We lost them in the traffic jam, but it did not appear that they were having any trouble or were apprehensive.

"Returning to Anacostia, we found the crowd on the bridge completely dispersed, and the students going in different directions in small groups. The only sizable group left was being addressed by a minister, who was urging them to return to school. We followed some of these and found they went by the school, but did not go in. A few called names at children inside the school yard, but no incidents took place. One group crossed the path of a group returning to the school from a gym classes, but nothing occurred. Normal activity, including several outside gym classes, was going on at the school.

"We proceeded to McKinley (it was then about 11:30 a.m.). There was no outside activity there at all. Police were stationed around the school and several streets leading to the school were closed to traffic.

"In the course of our observation, we did not notice any adult leadership of the strikers. In fact, there appeared little leadership at all. The groups seemed to be milling about in a rather disorganized fashion.

"We noticed about five cars transporting students from school to school. There was only one that aroused suspicion. That was occupied by a group of youths who may have been above school age. It was a gray sedan, license number believed to be DC-V-5934. The driver was a youth with a Spanish-sounding name."

Action by Public Officials

In both Baltimore and Washington, School Officials moved promptly to reaffirm the principle of integration. They did so by issuing public statements and making radio and television appeals for students and parents to cooperate in ending the disorders. After a somewhat slow start, Baltimore Police began a stern program of maintaining order. The Washington Police Department appeared on the alert from the beginning of the trouble. On October 7, Bryant Bowles of the NAAWP visited Anacostia School to "counsel with the striking students." Police ordered him to leave. Several arrests were made in Baltimore and Washington in connection with the disorders.

The Mayor of Baltimore and the President of the D.C. Board of Commissioners called upon those responsible for the trouble to halt their activity.

Action by Private Groups

Numerous private groups, particularly, church organizations, held meeting to consider the problem. Out of these meetings came many useful statements and some direct appeals to persons who could be effective in preventing trouble.

On October 7, the Baltimore Evening Sun said it had received so many letters on the school disturbance (most of which supported the ending of segregation) that it would not publish them since the situation appeared to be returning to normal and such comment "would have little interest."

Conclusion

The events in Baltimore and Washington show that inflammatory newspaper stories and organized agitation can temporarily disrupt integrated schools. This experience also shows that prompt and firm law enforcement at the first sign of trouble can prevent its spread. At no time has their been any evidence that those responsible for the trouble had any substantial support from the majority of the people of Baltimore or Washington.

It is believed that a full investigation of the pickets in Baltimore, the officers of the NAAWP, and some of the so-called student leaders of the strike at Anacostia High School will reveal enough information to help prevent future occurrences of this kind.

MS: copy, NAACP WB-164, DLC.

1. The child in question was Mitchell's second son, Keiffer Mitchell, age nine. See Watson, *Lion in the Lobby*, 269–71.

2. The National Association for the Advancement of White People was the first and most widely publicized prosegregation group formed after the *Brown* decision. Founded by Floridian Bryant Bowles, the group organized a successful campaign of demonstrations and boycotts to overturn school integration efforts of the Milford, Delaware, school district in 1954. Bowles's attempts to apply the same techniques in Baltimore were thwarted by the efforts of the NAACP and other civic groups, and after the details of his criminal background came to light, he was indicted on a charge of violating state school laws. His blatant anti-Semitic activities also undermined his support at that time. However, the organization continued to exist until at least the mid-1960s. See Mitchell's report of 2/28/54; Fleming, "Resistance Movements and Racial Desegregation," 44–45; clippings file on the NAAWP (1963–64) in the Wilbur and Mary Alice Baldinger Papers, Walter P. Reuther Library, Wayne State University. In 1980, former Ku Klux Klansman David Duke of Louisiana formed another organization by the same name, which still exists.

3. None of these individuals has been further identified.

Monthly Report, November 4, 1954

November 4, 1954

MONTHLY REPORT OF THE WASHINGTON BUREAU

The 84th Congress

At the time this report is written, the issue of whether the Senate will be controlled by the Democrats is still in doubt.[1] The House is in the hands of the Democrats.

Under the control of the Democrats, the House presents many problems for civil rights bills. The Labor Committee which will handle FEPC Bills will have Graham Barden of North Carolina as chairman. He is anti-FEPC. The Judiciary Committee which will handle anti-lynching and other civil rights bills will be chaired by Emanuel Celler of New York, who is a sponsor of this type of legislation.

Under a gentleman's agreement reached in the House, just before adjournment Percy Priest of Tennessee is pledged to give early consideration to a bill to end segregation in inter-state travel which will come before his committee on Interstate and Foreign Commerce.

The most gloomy prospect of all, however, is the fact that Howard Smith of Virginia will control the Rules Committee of the House. This committee has the power to kill legislation even when it is favorably reported by committee that give it original consideration.

In the Senate, if the Democrats control, FEPC will receive most friendly consideration in the Labor and Welfare Committee headed by Senator James E. Murray of Montana.

Prospects are also bright in the Judiciary Committee which will be headed by Senator Harley Kilgore of West Virginia. The presence of Senator James Eastland of Mississippi, as the next ranking member of this committee, is most unpleasant.

The chairmanship of Senator Warren Magnuson on the Senate Committee on Interstate and Foreign Commerce will improve chances for prompt consideration of the anti-Jim Crow Travel Bill.[2]

Civil rights matters affecting the District of Columbia will be placed in some jeopardy in the House because John L. Millan of South Carolina will be chairman of the District Committee. However, pro-civil rights Senator Matthew Neely of West Virginia will be chairman of the Senate Committee.[3]

The prospect of a change in Senate Rules is about the same under Democrats as it would be under Republicans. Senator William Jenner of Indiana is chairman under the G.O.P and Senator Carl Hayden of Arizona, a supporter of the filibuster, will be chairman if the Democrats control.

There is also little to choose from in the leadership of both Houses. It is not apparent that there is any great difference between the views of Representative Sam Rayburn, the new speaker, and Representative Joseph Martin, the outgoing speaker so far as civil rights bills are concerned. Neither has shown any enthusiasm for this kind of legislation. A similar observation applies to Republican leader, Senator William Knowland of California, and Senator Lyndon Johnson, the Texas leader of Senate Democrats.

About Face on Schools

The Under-Secretary of the Navy has reversed President Eisenhower's policy of ending segregation in schools on military posts in one instance.[4]

The Under-Secretary admitted in a conference with Washington Bureau representatives that he had personally approved the opening of a segregated school at the Bainbridge Naval Station in Maryland. The Under-Secretary defended his action by saying this was an emergency arrangement. We have appealed to the Secretary of Defense to over-rule the Navy in this matter.

Housing Developments

Housing Administrator Albert Cole has been the center of considerable activity in Washington on what policy the Federal Government will follow in the field of housing.[5] Recently, Mr. Cole made a speech at Hampton Institute and newspaper reports seemed to show that the Government was moving into a firmer position against segregation in housing. A careful reading of the speech made by Mr. Cole does not show that the Administration has adopted the position that there will be no Federal aid to any kind of rental or sale housing unless there is a guarantee that all eligible persons may be admitted without regard to race.[6]

There seems to be a conscious effort on the part of the Housing Agencies to give the impression that they plan to attack segregation. However, the policy of permitting Government aid for all types of housing segregation continues.

There is no doubt that the Housing Agencies will seek to use the forthcoming White House conference on housing to get endorsement for policies that fall short of the position taken by the NAACP.[7]

Speaking Engagements

During the past month, the Director has visited branches in North Carolina, Wisconsin, Oregon, and the State of Washington.

The Bureau Counsel has filled engagements in Washington, D.C., and Virginia.

MS: copy, NAACP II: A-656, DLC.

1. The Democrats won control of the Senate by one seat, making Eisenhower the third president in the twentieth century (after Wilson and Truman) to face opposition majorities in both houses at midterm. *New York Times*, 11/7/54, E1. Another significant development was that Democratic control of the Senate made Lyndon B. Johnson majority leader.

2. See, most immediately, 8/21 and 9/29/54.

3. For the continuing effort to obtain home rule for the District of Columbia, see 9/29 and 12/31/54.

4. See, among others, 9/29 and 12/31/54.

5. See, among others, 9/29 and 12/31/54, as well as the headnote on Segregation in Federal Housing Programs, vol. III.

6. The occasion for Cole's address at Hampton University on October 29, 1954, was the dedication of the new Harkness Hall dormitory. There, Cole said that "the Federal government does not have the total responsibility [for providing] leadership in the affirmative use of authorities to correct" housing inequality. "The *basic responsibility lies inescapably with the citizen, the community leadership, and the private industry*" (emphasis Cole's). A copy of the address is in NAACP II: A-309, DLC. Against Cole's assertion, it is also essential to see the NAACP's memorandum of January 11, 1952, on "The Authority and Power of the Administrator of the Housing and Home Finance Agency, the Federal Housing Administration, the Public Housing Administration, and the Division of Slum Clearance and Urban Development, Constituent Units of the Housing and Home Finance Agency, to Prohibit Discrimination in Federal and Federally-Aided Housing Programs Administrated by Them." NAACP II: A-309, DLC.

7. See, in appendix 1, this vol., 12/9/54 for NAACP recommendations. Following the conference, Cole said it had offered "a very good start" on the problem of providing more and better housing for African Americans and other minority groups. *New York Times*, 12/11/54, 8. See also, among others, 6/29/54, as well as the headnote on Segregation in Federal Housing Programs, vol. III.

Report on Atomic Energy, Aiken, South Carolina, November 30, 1954

ATOMIC ENERGY

Aiken, South Carolina[1]

[ca. November 30 1954]

In 1950, the Washington Bureau received from individuals and the Aiken, South Carolina, branch complaints of discriminatory hiring by building trades unions and by DuPont, contracted by AEC to build and operate the plant. For construction work, union closed shops combined with jim crow locals to keep Negro carpenters, operating engineers, etc., off the job. Starting at the same time and ever increasing was Du Pont's discrimination in plant staffing.

Conferences with AEC at the national level and with AEC, the unions and Dupont at the local level were held to try to correct hiring pattern.[2]

As a result of these conferences and negotiations the AEC agreed that there would be a policy of no segregation on the plant site. This is an excellent gain. Four colored scientists have been employed in the area. This is also worthwhile. On the other hand, patterns of discrimination in employment continued throughout the construction work. Also, now that the plant is in production, colored people are denied opportunities to obtain on the job training which is available for whites. The DuPont company can truthfully say it is making mechanics out of white farmers, but it is also making janitors out of colored farmers who are just as qualified as the whites. This matter has been before the Committee on Government Contracts. Additional complaints were submitted to the Committee in 1953. So far, the committee has not resolved the problem.[3]

PADUCAH, KENTUCKY

Word of Paducah's situation first came to the Washington Bureau in 1951 via complaints from our branch there and some of the job bias victims. An NAACP official on the scene who had reported the fact to me faithfully, had also sought help in vain from the AEC locally. A full dress conference on employment was set for February, 1951.

Construction on the Paducah plant was contracted to one large firm, McGraw Co.; the plant was to be operated by the Union Carbide and Carbon Co. The unions, too much like Aiken, combined the closed shop with jimcrow locals to keep colored out.

The February, 1951 conference was attended by representatives of McGraw AEC, larger unions, and the NAACP. Though seemingly promising the meeting resulted only in slightly improved hiring policies. At one time, 63 colored carpenters were working at Paducah. But, 1. there were hundreds of white carpenters; 2. the colored were dropped first when there was work-contraction or cost cutting. Ostensibly to cut costs, the business agent of Negro carpenters was dismissed; however this followed closely his efforts for fairer policies.[4]

Hiring of electricians and brikclayers was never democratic. Token hiring existed. Clerical positions in plant staff were a little more open to colored than professional posts in which one Negro was placed. No non-whites were hired as trainees for production work.

Complaints were submitted to the Committee in 1952, but no settlement has been resolved as yet.

MS: copy, NAACP WB-9, DLC.

1. This report evidently was prepared as part of Mitchell's response to a complaint of November 21, 1954, from Robert A. Brooks, president of the Aiken NAACP branch, to Ruby Hurley, NAACP regional director, stating "that colored people [were] disappointed with the NAACP" because it had not accomplished much with the AEC discrimination problems. For the record, on November 24, 1954, Mitchell updated Brooks on what the NAACP had been doing, which included developing the nonsegregation agreement for the facility, hiring colored scientists and stenographers, and helping a farmer to get "several thousands of dollars due him from the Farmers Home Administration." The money had been approved in Washington but was being held up by local officials. Mitchell explained that "for a long time the NAACP's voice was the only force that insisted on fair play in the AEC's operations. I, too, wish that we could now report that we have solved the problem and there is no employment discrimination." Because that was not so, he said he was continuing to prod the AEC. Indeed, this issue would be revived in 1966 and 1967.

Copies of this report may have been sent to Ruby Hurley, Walter White, J. M. Hinton, and A. C. Redd, the NAACP officials to whom Mitchell sent copies of his reply to Brooks. A copy of Mitchell's letter of 11/24/54 and related materials are in NAACP WB-9, DLC. See 2/5/51 for an earlier report on Aiken and related references.

2. On the initial complaints regarding the Aiken facility, known as the Savannah River Plant, and the responses to them, see 12/21/50, 2/2, 2/5, 3/5, 5/3, and 8/31/51.

3. On the complaints to the Committee on Government Contract Compliance and its successor, the Committee on Government Contracts, see 9/9/53; in appendix 1, this vol., 11/30/53.

4. On the Paducah complaints and initial responses, see 3/5, 5/3, and 8/31/51.

Monthly Report, December 6, 1954

December 6, 1954

Legislative Outlook

During the past month, we have been having informal discussions with senators, representatives and members of their staffs on the outlook for civil rights legislation in the 84th Congress. At this time there are so many cross currents to be taken into consideration that it is somewhat risky to make any kind of suggestion on broad strategy to be followed when Congress convenes.

Generally speaking, it seems important to have two action meetings in Washington. One of these would be a small group of organization representatives who would meet with leaders of majority and minority in both houses to obtain commitments on legislative action. Thereafter a larger meeting should be made up of persons who come from specific Congressional districts and, if possible, who also know their Congressmen personally. It is unlikely that a meeting that brings a large number of people from a few states will have any significance.

Visits to Mississippi and Tennessee

In November the Director of the Bureau had the good fortune to meet with NAACP representatives in Tennessee and Mississippi. Oral and written reports have been made on the Mississippi visit. There was need for follow-up action on the visit to Mississippi.

The Director has sent letters to several persons who could give advice on how some of the economic pressures now being exerted to retard civil rights advances in Mississippi could be met. As yet no solutions have been obtained.

Richmond, Virginia

The Director was a speaker for the Richmond, Virginia, branch on the eve of the hearing before the State Commission set up to make inquiry on de-segregation.[1] The hearings held by the Commission were correctly thought of as a sounding board for anti-integration elements. However, it was apparent very early in the hearings that the pro-integration spokesmen presented their arguments much more effectively than their opponents.[2]

It is a tribute to the work of the Virginia NAACP that the meeting, which was held in the Mosque, was not segregated. The Mosque, of course, has been the subject of many controversies on the question of whether meetings held there would be non-segregated.

Inquiry from Jugoslavia

We have received an inquiry on race relations form the Government of Jugoslavia. We took this matter up with the State Department and the following statement from the Department should be of interest.

> "By virtue of their Marxist background, Yugoslav officials and the institutions which they operate are particularly interested in questions concerning the status of Negroes in the United Stares. During the period of close Yugoslav ties with Moscow, which ended in 1948, the Yugoslavs, of course, were subjected to all of the tendentious propaganda which the USSR publishes on the life of American Negroes. Since that time, Yugoslav articles on the subject have tended to become progressively more factual although residues of the earlier indoctrination persist.
>
> "In view of this background, and after further reflection, I think that it would be useful if you could furnish Mrs. Josimovic any or all of the information which she requests, or at least provide her with references to other books of publications where the data is available. Such information, the product of scholarly research in this country or elsewhere in Western Europe, can help to bring the question into a reasonable perspective for the Yugoslavs. Moreover, since it will give a true picture of developments and progress in this country, there is no cause for any concern that the information can do us any harm."

It should be noted that during the past month we have further discussions with the State Department on its own employment policies. These policies have not improved very much.[3]

Christmas Seals

During the month, it has been necessary to spend considerable time in meeting and correspondence in connection with the Christmas seal campaign. Since all other staff members could tell about their experiences in this field, the following is submitted with apologies to them.

One white donor returned the seals sent her (because she made a purchase last year) with the comment that "I have a number of friends among your people, but I must work on these matters in my own way." In the same mail was another letter from a white family saying, "Thanks for the seals." It contained a check for $100.00.

Hotels and Places of Amusement

The District of Columbia Branch and other groups, notably the AVC, have been working to get the Commissioners of the City to issue a proclamation declaring that existing laws forbidding segregation in hotels and places of amusements are valid and will be enforced. President Eugene Davidson of the branch has advised that the commissioners have now pledged that they will issue the proclamation but have asked that no comment be made until they act. If the promised schedule is followed, the proclamation will be published by the time this report is available to the board.[4]

MS: NAACP II: A-656, DLC.

1. Virginia State Commission on Interracial Cooperation. See Kluger, *Simple Justice*, 159.

2. In contrast to hearings of this nature, the NAACP held an Emergency Conference on School Integration in Philadelphia on November 26–27, 1954, to discuss how to handle problems arising from school integration in wake of the Supreme Court's May 17, 1954, *Brown v. Board of Education* school desegregation decision. Report of the Secretary to the Board, 12/13/54, EC.

3. See, most immediately, 4/3, 5/4/53.

4. See also 3/3, 6/15, 11/4, 12/31/53, 9/29, 12/7, 12/31/54 (emphasis Mitchell's).

Annual Report, December 31, 1954

1954 ANNUAL REPORT OF THE WASHINGTON BUREAU OF THE NATIONAL ASSOCIATION FOR THE ADVANCEMENT OF COLORED PEOPLE

[December 31, 1954]

The past year reveals that President Eisenhower remains committed to a policy of attacking racial segregation by Executive action. In several instances, subordinates have defied the Chief Executive's policy of refusing to permit Federal dollars to be used to promote discrimination. Others seek to slow down progress in this field.[1]

Examples of reluctance to promote the President's policies by the Executive Branch are as follows:

1. The Housing and Home Finance Agency and its constituents still give full Federal backing to programs that result in entire new communities for whites only. Federal sanction is still given to programs that force colored residents from areas that are to be redeveloped without adequate assurance that those displaced will be properly rehoused. There is a continuing program of approving all white housing projects and segregated public facilities on redeveloped land.[2]

2. On January 12, acting to implement previous statements by the President, Defense Secretary Charles E. Wilson issued a memorandum to the Secretaries of Army, Navy, and Air Force requiring that effective on that date no new schools would be opened on a segregated basis on military posts. The Department of the Army carried out this instruction when it opened a new school on the post at Fort Myer, Virginia. The Air Force reports that it took similar action when it opened a school at the Craig Base in Alabama. The Navy Department, with the approval of one of its highest officers, defied the order and opened a new segregated school on its base at Bainbridge, Maryland, in September 1954.[3]
3. The Department of Health, Education, and Welfare, in February 1954, reaffirmed its policy of giving Federal grants to hospitals even though they segregate colored patients and refuse to admit persons because they are being treated by colored doctors.[4]

While the President has given strong and constructive civil rights leadership to sometimes reluctant aides in the Executive Branch, he has consistently misjudged or been poorly advised on the possibilities of legislative action by Congress in the field.

Examples of the failure to challenge Congress to act on civil rights issues are:

1. The President omitted any reference to the need for civil rights safeguards in his proposed revision of the Taft-Hartley Act.[5] Nevertheless, even the conservative Labor Committee by a vote of 25 to 2 did agree to one amendment on this subject. A more comprehensive amendment was not acted upon because it did not have White House support.

   In the Senate, where a clear majority of members of the Labor Committee supported strong civil rights safeguards in the Taft-Hartley Act, Administration policy forced all Republicans on the committee to withdraw their support from the corrective suggestions. In this case, Senator Alexander Smith of New Jersey was the standard bearer of the anti-civil rights forces.[6]
2. After long delay because the Administration had not endorsed civil rights bills of any kind, the House Committee on Interstate and Foreign Commerce approved a bill to end segregation in interstate travel by the heavy majority of 19 to 7. Nevertheless, the Administration controlled House Rules Committee refused to let this measure come to the floor for a vote.[7]
3. An FEPC Bill with enforcement powers was reported favorably by the Senate Labor Committee, but was not supported by the Administration.[8]

CIVIL RIGHTS AND THE 1954 VOTE

The year 1954 sharply emphasized the sophistication of voters who favor civil rights legislation. The Washington Bureau had a heavy demand for the individual voting records of the Senators and Representatives. Republicans, such as Charles R. Jonas of

North Carolina and Edward T. Miller of Maryland, were able to win reelection in spite of the fact that their Democratic opponents tried to defeat them by citing civil rights advances under the Eisenhower Administration. On the other hand, liberal Democrats, such as Senators Paul Douglas of Illinois and Hubert Humphrey of Minnesota won overwhelming support of pro-civil rights voters because of their personal records. In the close Oregon race, which was won by Senator-elect Richard Neuberger, the outcome could easily have been different if Senator Guy Cordon had been able to point to a personal record of giving full backing to civil rights.

The reaction of pro-civil rights voters in the 1954 elections is a warning to both major parties that they will never get a comfortable margin of control in Congress until they show that civil rights pledges made at campaign times are adopted as party policy in the legislative caucuses when Congress is in session. When neither party has a good legislative record on civil rights, the Washington Bureau's experience shows that voters in key states give increasingly close scrutiny to the records of individual candidates. If this trend continues through the election in 1956, President Eisenhower will have the edge on the present leaders of the Democrats because the most influential members of that group have shown a fatal tendency to sacrifice civil rights in the interest of party harmony. Yet it is unlikely that even the President will be able to sweep anti-civil rights Republicans into office, if he runs in 1956.

THE 1954 LEGISLATIVE STORY

In the Senate, two bills on fair employment were introduced. The first, sponsored by Senator Everett Dirksen (R., Ill.), lacked enforcement powers and was opposed by civil rights organizations. It was referred to the Senate Judiciary Committee, which did not report it out. The second, co-sponsored by Senators Ives (R., N.Y.) and Humphrey (D., Minn.), and others was reported favorably by the Senate Labor Committee. All other members of the Committee, except Senator Lister Hill (D., Ala.) joined Senator Ives and Humphrey in supporting this legislation. Senators Murray (D., Mont.), Neely (D., W. Va.), and Douglas (D., Ill.), Lehman (D., N.Y.), Kennedy (D., Mass.), Humphrey, and Ives favored an FEPC with enforcement powers. The other favorable committee members, Senators Smith (R., N.J.), Purtell (R., Conn.), Goldwater (R., Ariz.), Cooper (R., Ky.), and Upton (R., N.H.) expressed reservations on enforcement powers. The Senate did not take up the bill for debate.[9]

In the House, despite requests for hearings on FEPC legislation by the NAACP and other interested organization, Representatives Samuel McConnell (R., Pa.), Chairman of the House Labor Committee, did not conduct such hearings or take any action on the proposed legislation. Representative McConnell is opposed to an FEPC with enforcement powers.[10]

In the field of Housing, both the Senate and House Committees on Banking and Currency ducked the issue of segregation by ignoring non-segregation amendments when they considered the Housing Act of 1954. The issue was raised in reverse, however, when the late Senator Burnet Maybank (D., S.C.) proposed an amendment which would strike all public housing from the bill because of a Supreme Court ruling upholding a decision in the California Court ending segregation in public housing.

The Bureau warned Senators that the Maybank action had created a situation in which the foes of public housing from the North, who voted for his plan to kill public housing, would also be voting in favor of racial segregation. Their action, it was pointed out, might determine the outcome of some closely contested elections in northern states.

The Maybank proposal was defeated by an overwhelming voice vote in the Senate. The only Senators who made statements for the record on this bill, other than Senator Maybank, were Majority Leader Knowland (R., Cal.) and Lehman (D., N.Y.), both of whom opposed the proposal. It should be noted that the Maybank proposal was made a few minutes after the Senate had formally recognized the presence in the Chamber of Representatives of the Turkish Government. American racial policies are of great interest in Turkey and the Middle East. Final action by Congress on the Housing Act so curtailed public housing as to foreshadow its early death.[11]

In other welfare and public works building programs, the 83rd Congress failed to take action which would end segregation in the use of Federally-built and supported facilities. The Hospital Construction Act, even though passed after the Supreme Court decision outlawed segregation, did not contain any safeguards against segregation.[12]

A Senate Bill to provide emergency aid for school construction contained language recognizing the "separate but equal" doctrine. At the urging of the NAACP, this language was struck out in committee and the bill passed the Senate. The bill died in the House.[13]

These grants to states for social welfare programs generally have the support of liberal northern and less conservative southern Congressmen. The liberals (both Republicans and Democrats) feel the inclusion of the non-segregation clauses in this type of legislation will lead to southern opposition to the entire bill. In all such grants, the Executive Branch could accomplish the desired result by administrative action. For that reason, the Bureau has continued to press for action by both Congress and the President with the hope that one or the other would act.

The strongest bid made to pass civil rights legislation in the 83rd Congress was the attempt to end Jim-Crow travel restrictions in interstate commerce, which has been mentioned before in this report. Until the final day of the Congressional session, Congressman John Heselton (R., Mass.) made a gallant effort to obtain approval of H.R. 7304, which would provide penalties for carriers separating persons in interstate commerce on the basis of race. H.R. 7304, as reported by the committee, was a combination of bills introduced in the House by Representatives Heselton, Powell, Dawson (D., Ill.), and others. Its counterpart in the Senate was S. 2672, introduced by Senators Ives and Butler (R., Md.), and S. 465 introduced by Senators Humphrey and others. The Senate refused to take action until the House passed the bill.

The committee held hearings on the travel bills in May 1954.[14] On July 21, the committee reported out the bill. Congressmen who voted for the bill in committee were: Republicans Wolverton (N.J.), Hinshaw (Cal.), Hale (Maine), Hoffman (Ill.), Beamer (Ind.), Springer (Ill.), Schenck (Ohio), Carrigg (Pa.), Warburton (Del.), Derounian (N.Y.), Pelly (Wash.), and Younger (Cal.)—Democrats Crosser (Ohio), Klein (N.Y.), Granahan (Pa.), Mack (Ill.), Moulder (Mo.), and Staggers (W.Va.).

It was then referred to the House Rules Committee. Congressman Leo Allen (R., Ill.), Chairman of that Committee, said he could not act on the bill because it was too late in the session.

In the closing days of the session, Congressman Heselton sought to have the rules of the House suspended so the bill might be brought before the House. The consent of the leadership of both Parties was required to do this. Speaker Martin (R., Mass.) and Majority Leader Halleck (R., Ind.) said they were agreeable to this proposal, but Minority Leader Rayburn (D., Tex.) refused his consent. Despite consent urging, Representatives Allen was adamant in his refusal to release the bill from his committee.

Representative Heselton stated his belief that Congress would have passed this legislation had it been given an opportunity to vote. He announced his intention to reintroduce it at the next session of Congress.

Representative William Granahan (D., Pa), who sponsored a bill similar to that of Congressman Heselton, also announced his intention of pressing for the passage of his bill in the next Congressional session.[15]

Statehood for Hawaii and Alaska, favored by the NAACP, failed of passage this session. The House passed a bill approving Hawaiian Statehood. This was amended in the Senate to include Alaska and sent back to the House where no further action was taken.[16]

Home Rule for the District of Columbia was also considered by Congress, but, likewise, failed of passage.[17]

A dubious proposal by southern Senators to outlaw the Poll Tax by Constitutional Amendment was taken up by the Judiciary Committee and died there.[18]

Other proposed Constitutional Amendments, sponsored by Senator James Eastland (R., Miss.) and Representative John Bell Williams (D., Miss.) designed to set aside the Supreme Court decisions in the school cases, died in committees. The Bureau had notified committee members of our opposition to these proposals.

A bill revising the Organic Act of the Virgin Islands was amended to give residents a voice in future reorganization of the Islands' Government. This amendment was one of several suggested by the NAACP and offered on the floor by Congressman Powell. A number of the Islands' residents opposed the original bill which gave the Governor power to reorganize the Executive Branch of Government without the consent of the Islands' legislature. As finally passed, the bill provides that the Governor may carry out reorganization of the present Executive structure in the Islands *without the consent* of the legislature. However, all future reorganization must be with the consent of the legislature.[19]

Some supporters of the Bricker Amendment, limiting the President's treaty-making power, urged its adoption as necessary to halt the civil rights progress in the United States. This is a false argument, used to exploit the prejudices of some persons for political advantages. The NAACP was one of the many organizations which opposed the Bricker Amendment. This Amendment was defeated in the Senate.[20]

The failure to pass any civil rights legislation during this session of Congress must be shared by the Administration, its Congressional leaders, and the leadership of the minority Party.

1954 ADVANCES BY EXECUTIVE BRANCH

Armed Services

The Armed Services of the United States continued to be one of the greatest forces for good or ill in racial relations in the United States. In 1954, the policy of racial segregation in the Armed Services was officially ended.[21] The Director of the Bureau has written an article for the *Journal of Negro Education* appraising the present situation.[22] In general, it is fair to say that there is a real desire to implement the new policy of integration. Nevertheless, there must be constant scrutiny of the Armed Services to prevent the growth of practices that will chip away and finally destroy the progress that has been made.

One of the major unresolved problems in the Armed Services is continued segregation in some schools on the military posts. The President formally ordered elimination of segregation in all schools on military posts. As a result, the Department of the Defense has announced, in January 1954, that all segregation will be ended in such schools by September 1955. The Truman Administration had ended segregation in all military post schools completely under the control of the Department of Defense, except at Fort Benning, Georgia. This was integrated in September 1953. Twenty-one other schools were conducted by the Department of Defense in conjunction with local authorities. Of these, the schools at Fort Belvoir, Virginia, were integrated in September 1954. Local educational officials who formerly operated the Fort Belvoir schools refused to do so and the supervision is now directly in the hands of the Federal Government.

All schools in the Canal Zone, which were previously segregated, opened in September 1954 on a non-segregated basis. Two new schools, at Fort Myer, Virginia, and Craig Air Force Base, Alabama, opened in the Fall of 1954 on a non-segregated basis.

Naval authorities at the Bainbridge, Maryland, base (as was said earlier in this report) defied the Department of Defense policy of non-segregation in schools on military posts. At this location, the Naval officials actually signed the agreement with the Cecil County (Md.) school officials to provide a school for white children only on Navy property. When colored children sought admission to the school, they were denied entrance on the basis of race. At the time of this report, top Naval authorities in Washington are still supporting the Bainbridge policy.

The Navy action of approving the segregated school in Maryland deserves the strongest condemnation because those who accepted the program were fully aware that they were violating established policy. When questioned, they sought to confuse the issue by pretending this was not a new school.

The Bureau is aware of forces within the Services that are seeking to delay integration in the remaining segregated schools on military posts beyond the target date of September 1955.

The far-reaching implications of integration were evident when word reached the Washington Bureau that the Navy was distributing 13,000 Jim Crow tickets for the Sugar Bowl Classic in New Orleans. These tickets actually carried a printed statement warning that any users other than members of the Caucasian race would be ejected from the game. As in the case of the Bainbridge school, top Navy officials knew about the embarrassment that this language on the tickets could cause the Government, but apparently they hoped to get away with it. The Secretary of the Navy repudiated the requirement and stated that all holders of the tickets distributed by the Navy would be admitted regardless of what was printed on the tickets.

Government Promotion of Jim Crow Housing

On par with the influence of the Armed Services in American life is the activity of the Federal Housing Agencies. Some of the largest all new cities in the United States are for whites only. They have been created and brought into being with the help of the Federal Housing Administration.

The housing program of the Government continues to be the greatest single force in the Nation promoting residential segregation. As late as December 1954, the Housing Agencies were still toying with the notion that progress in correction of this problem can be made without strong policy directives against it.

There must be continuing and unrelenting effort to obtain adoption of the following NAACP objectives which were submitted to the Housing Agencies at a conference in December. These recommendations have been made before by us.

1. All public housing must be open to tenants without regard to race. There will be no more "white" and "colored" projects. Tenant selection will be made on the basis of need for housing rather than on the basis of race.
2. There will be a contractual requirement that all housing and other facilities such as parks, playgrounds or hospitals erected or developed on land assembled through loans or grants under the Slum Clearance and Urban Redevelopment Program and the Urban Renewal Program would be open to all renters, buyers, and users without regard to race
3. On all housing on which there is FHA insurance or VA guarantee or a commitment for such insurance or guarantee, there shall be a contractual agreement binding on those who own the property or control the sale or rental of such property that there shall be no discrimination against persons seeking to lease, rent or purchase such property on account of race, creed, color or national origin.[23]

Government and Employment

The President has continued the Truman Administration's Committee on Government Contracts, which is charged with eliminating discrimination in employment by private employers working under governmental contracts. On September 2, 1954, he signed an Executive Order strengthening the non-discrimination clause which must be included in all contracts entered into by the Federal Government. Vice President Nixon is now Chairman of the Committee.

Unfortunately, this committee has lagged in performing its duties. Two of the major complaints sent to it by the Washington Bureau charging that the Capital Transit Company and the Chesapeake and Potomac Telephone Company refuse to hire colored operators are still unresolved.[24] In addition, there is a growing unrest throughout the country about the committee's failure to tackle flagrant cases of job discrimination.

The Eisenhower Administration had continued the Federal Fair Employment Board which was established by President Truman's Executive Order 9980 to eliminate employment discrimination within the Government itself.

A definite advance in Federal policy has been the recognition that physical segregation is discriminatory. The outstanding example of correction in this field is the Navy's halting of civilian segregation in its shore establishments. Many of these are located in Alabama, Georgia, Florida, Maryland, North Carolina, South Carolina, and Virginia. Most of them had segregated drinking fountains, segregated washrooms, and restaurants for whites only. The Truman Administration, which had been forthright on many other civil rights matters, had refused to act on this problem.[25]

In May of 1954, the Director of the NAACP's Washington Bureau visited the Charleston (S.C.) Navy Yard which was the last holdout. It, too, was completely integrated. As a fitting climax, the chief complainant who first brought the matter of segregation to the Bureau's attention was promoted to a supervisory job at the yard in 1954.[26]

That much needs to be done in the field of Government employment is evidenced by incredible cases that come to the Bureau's attention. One which is being handled at this time concerns a young woman who discovered a note in which her supervisor called her a darky and joked about how she got the "run-around" when she complained about unfair employment practices. When she brought the note to the attention of her superiors, she was fired for having the personal property (i.e. the note) of another employee in her possession.

A matter of continuing concern is an unresolved case at the Bureau of Printing and Engraving. The Fair Employment Board has ruled that elimination of plate printer apprentice training at the Bureau, under the guise of economy, is in reality a continuation of a previous practice of keeping this occupation for whites only. The Board's decision has been suppressed. However, Secretary of the Treasury George Humphrey has informed the NAACP that when new employees are needed in this occupation apprentices who were removed from training in the "economy" action will be given first choice of returning to their former training. As yet, no new persons are being hired.[27]

In the employment field, it is important to credit the Eisenhower Administration with integration in the District of Columbia Fire Department. Previous Administration officials always ran for cover on this problem. Pro-segregation elements in the Fire Department could always depend on southern Democrats to attack any official who sought integration. On September 18, 1954, the Eisenhower Administration accomplished integration in this department.[28]

It has been the Bureau's experience that obstructionist tactics on matters affecting civil rights in the Nation's Capital have been most vicious under the Democrats. Integration in swimming pools, golf courses, government cafeterias, as many other public places was accomplished by courageous officials in the Executive Branch during the Roosevelt and Truman Administrations. Always, these moves were under constant attack by important committee chairman in Congress.[29] Republican chairman of committees have usually cooperated with such moves under the Eisenhower Administration or at least they have kept quiet. The Fire Department matter is a good illustration of this point.

The Veterans Administration

The Administration-appointed Veterans Administrator, Mr. Harvey Higley, is the first chief of that agency to give full support to a policy of non-segregation. Under his direction, the official program of ending segregation in all VA hospitals and domiciliary facilities began in September 1953. In July of 1954, the Veterans Administration officially announced that the program was completed.

The Bureau believes that the Higley action is a definite policy that local installations are required to follow. However, experience has shown that such matters must be subjected to close follow-up action.[30] Accordingly, we have requested NAACP branches to visit these establishments and report to us whether segregation has been abolished. The states and the number of VA hospitals in each are as follows:

Arkansas	3	Louisiana	3	Oklahoma	-2
Florida	3	Maryland	3	S.C.	-1
Kansas	3	Mississippi	3	Tennessee	-4
Kentucky	4	North Carolina	4	Texas	-10
Virginia	-3	West Virginia	-4		

Returns from three states show that, as usual, the VA top office must follow up on its policy statement to see that it is carried out.

Kentucky reports complete integration at Louisville and Lexington, with two more facilities to be checked.

Louisiana reports segregation continuing in separate wards and in separate dining halls in New Orleans. Also, discrimination by nurses and doctors in addressing colored patients by their first names and whites by "Mr."

Virginia reports complete integration at Hampton, the continuation of segregation in recreational facilities and use of technical personnel at Roanoke. Richmond is yet to be reported.

Speaking Engagements

During the past year, the Director of the Bureau has spoken in fifteen states and covered approximately 25,000 miles in travel.

. . . This report was released December 1954.

MS: MP.

1. For government responses to this report, see *New York Times*, 12/30/54, 10.

2. See also, most recently, 12/31/53, 2/28, 3/9, 6/4, 5/5, 6/29, 9/29, 11/4, and 12/31/54; in appendix 1, this vol., 2/1/49 and 12/9/54; and the headnote on Segregation in Federal Housing Programs, vol. III.

3. See, most immediately, 2/17, 2/28, 3/9, 5/5, 6/29, and 9/29/54.

4. See 3/9, 6/29, 8/21, and 9/29/54.

5. During the 1952 presidential campaign, Eisenhower called for a repeal of the Taft-Hartley Act, and in his first State of the Union message, he promised revisions. But, as he explained in December 1953, he was advised that under no circumstances was he to recommend datailed amendments to the Taft-Hartley Act, "except only in the particular areas in which I promised Amendments during the campaign." Eisenhower, *Public Papers of the Presidents, 1953*, 28–29; Memorandum of Conversation with Roy Allison Roberts, 11/12/53, Series EM, AWF, Ann Whitman Diary Series, available at http://www.eisenhowermemorial.org/presidential-papers/first-term/documents/604.cfm.

Mitchell's frustrations went well beyond Eisenhower's refusal to seek reforms for the benefits of labor. In his special message on labor-management relations, Eisenhower made fourteen recommendations, but none was on civil rights. Special Message to Congress on Labor Management Relations, 1/11/54, Eisenhower, *Public Papers of the Presidents, 1954*, 40–44.

6. Smith, nevertheless, supported Mitchell on fair employment practice measures. See, for example, 9/39/54.

7. *Congressional Quarterly Weekly Report*, 5/14/54, 621. See also 5/5 and 6/4/54.

8. *Congressional Quarterly Weekly Report*, 3/5/54, 293, 254. See also 2/4, 6/1, 6/15, and 12/31/53, 2/28 and 3/9/54.

9. *Congressional Quarterly Weekly Report*, 3/5/54, 293, 254.

10. See the headnote on the Struggle for a Permanent FEPC, 1942–54, vol. III.

11. See, among others, 6/4 and 8/21/54.

12. See 3/9, 6/29, 8/21, and 9/29/54.

13. See 6/29, 8/21, and 9/29/54.

14. 5/13/54, *Hearings*, 39.

15. See, most immediately, 6/29, 8/21, 9/29, and 11/4/54, together with the headnote on the Struggle to End Jim Crow Travel, vol. III.

16. *Congressional Quarterly Weekly Report*, 3/12/54, 314. See also 9/29/54.

17. See also 8/21, 9/29, and 11/4/54.

18. The poll tax amendment was defeated.

19. See, most recently, 8/21 and 9/29/54.

20. See also, among others, 9/29/54.

21. For a summary, see MacGregor, *Integration of the Armed Forces*, 614–23.

22. Mitchell, "Status of Racial Integration in the Armed Services." See also the headnote on Ending Segregation in the Armed Services, vol. III.

23. These three points were the NAACP's recommendations to the Conference on Minority Housing Problems in Washington on December 9–10, 1954. Mitchell concluded the recommendations by stating: "We believe that the above position is the only honorable and legal position that the Federal

Government can take in this matter. It is also in line with President Eisenhower's policy of not permitting Federal funds to be used to promote racial discrimination." NAACP II: A-309, DLC. See also note 2 of this report for references.

24. For the CTC, see 9/29/54. Regarding the CTC, on September 28, 1952, Mitchell submitted another list of complainants that had been provided by the Baltimore NAACP branch to Robert R. Granville, executive director of the President's Committee on Government Contract Compliance. He explained that although the telephone company desperately needed operators, it refused to hire qualified African American applicants. He therefore urged prompt action to settle "this flagrant instance of racial discrimination by a Government Contractor." Mitchell letter to Robert R. Granville, 9/26/52, NAACP WB-5, DLC.

25. See, most immediately, 9/29/54.

26. See, especially, 11/2/53.

27. George Humphrey, secretary of the treasury, made this promise to Mitchell in a letter of 2/11/54, NAACP WB-18, DLC. See, among others, 3/9, 6/29, and 9/29/54.

28. For desegregation of the D.C. Fire Department, see 12/7/53, 9/29/54.

29. See 3/3, 6/15, 11/4, and 12/31/53, 9/29 and 12/6/54.

30. See also, among others, 9/29/54; materials in NAACP WB-185, DLC.

APPENDIX 1

Related Documents

Memorandum, Robert A. Ming, Jr., "A Labor Secretary," June 5, 1941

Memo to Walter White
Thurgood Marshall

[June 5, 1941]

The increasingly complex character of the problems which beset Negro workers make it imperative that the Association take immediate steps with respect to this situation. Since the staff of the National Office is already over-burdened in carrying out present assignments additional personnel is necessary to deal with the problems of Negro labor.[1]

At least one person together with necessary stenographer should be added to the National Office staff in the capacity of "Industrial Secretary" or "Labor Problems Secretary." Generally speaking the function of this staff member would be to deal with the problems of Negro workers as such and to coordinate the activities of the various branches in connection with such problems.

The work of such a Secretary in the labor field is peculiarly valuable at this critical time because of the NAACP's freedom form political financial or other control. If such a Secretary were employed by an organization suspected of Communist, Republican, Democratic or other political faith, his work might be almost completely nullified because of such political affiliation. Similarly, such an individual could not work as effectively if employed by an organization which received the bulk of its support from conservative foundations and individuals and from community chests. Between 65 and 70 per cent of the NAACP's income is contributed by Negroes themselves, which gives it a freedom from dictatorship as to policy and procedures which is unique. Thus, an NAACP Secretary of Industrial Relations would be able to do more effective work on behalf of the Negro and of labor relations generally than one employed by almost any other organization.

One of the important functions which could be performed by this individual would be that of coordinating the efforts of other organizations working in the field, such as the National Urban League, the American Civil Liberties Union, the Committee on Participation of Negroes in the National Defense Program, the Workers

Defense League, the Council for Democracy, and other organizations which are now interested or which may be interested through the effort of such an individual.

The peculiar position of Negro workers beset as they are with problems arising from their relationship not only which employers and government but also from their relationship with white workers and the Negro middle class requires that careful attention be paid to the selection of a person to fill this highly important place.

The person selected should be one having no binding political affiliations or obligations nor any commitments to any particular social or political philosophy other than that of the rights of workers to improve their working conditions by collective or other action and the right of Negro workers not to be discriminated against solely on account of race.

The urgent need of the Negro community for such service as this "Secretary" could render requires than the person selected should be one with a considerable knowledge of the field of labor relations and the problems of industrial and agricultural workers. Obviously, training of some individual in this field by the Association would be impossible in the light of the present emergency. In addition, such a "Secretary" must have the ability to win, not command, the respect of Negro workers in order that the fullest cooperation of such workers may be secured in the solution of their problems.

Among the specific things which this "Secretary" should do would be to:

1. *Contact employers and their personnel officers for the purpose of ascertaining the extent of discriminatory policy in the hiring and training of workers*. Where such practices are found this "Secretary" would aim at eliminating racial barriers by use of persuasion, education, coercion, or political and legal action if such are available. Special attention should be devoted to the admission of Negro youths to both public and private training classes in order that Negroes might avail themselves of the present shortage of skilled workmen as a means of acquiring industrial skills.

This employment-opportunity effort should include state and federal governments as employers, as well as private industry.

2. *Improve the relationships between organized labor unions and Negro workers in the jurisdiction of such unions*. This "Secretary" would deal with the problem of exclusion of Negroes from labor unions whether the ban depends upon constitutional or by-law provision, ritual or custom. In addition this "Secretary" would deal with the problem of the treatment of Negro workers already in unions or in the field of union activities where no prescription against their admission to membership exists. Under this head the "Secretary" would deal with the whole problem of the raising of Negro workers form their present status of "unskilled workers", promotions, seniority rights, union benefits, Negroes as strike breakers and the like. Such a "Secretary" should be available to advise Negro union members with respect to the best means available for the protection of t heir rights as union members and in the securing of the support of their unions for their efforts at more, better and more lucrative employment.

A large part of such "Secretary's" efforts should be directed at the education of Negro workers to the benefits of collective action in concert with their white fellow-workers, and as a corollary, education of white workers as to the necessity of joint solution of common problems, and the need for their assistance to Negro workers in the solution of problems which confront the latter.

3. *Organized community support for workers efforts through local branches*. Working closely with the "Coordinator of Branches" and other officers, this "Secretary" should aim at a cohesion of all the forces in any given community. In support of the efforts of the workers to improve their conditions, specifically there should be a campaign of education in the whole community with respect to the problems and needs of the workers and the solution available for such problems. Public assistance of the workers by support of strikes and strikers and of boycotts, establishment of worker's schools, and the exercise of political power at the polls to further the efforts of workers, can be secured by this means.

4. *To educate Negro workers with respect to benefits available under existing legislation*. A large number of Negro workers are totally ignorant of the rights which they have under such protective measure as "The Social Security Act," both state and federal, "Workmen's compensation Acts," "Minimum Wage and Maximum Hour Acts," etc.

Discriminatory practices in the enforcement of such legislation is all too common, and it can not be stopped unless the workers themselves know what their rights are and are trained to expect and demand them.

5. *To improve working and living conditions among Negro workers*. Even a casual glance at mortality [and] disease tables for Negroes shows clearly the great need that exists in this field. Many states have adopted socially beneficial legislation setting up safety regulations for industry, minimum housing standards, pure food minimums and the like. Discriminatory practices with respect to the enforcement of such measures in many situations denies to Negro workers the benefits available under such laws. This "Secretary" should deal with such situations. In addition he should actively further the low-cost housing movement, particularly for Negro workers, and should serve as a source of information for such workers of the availability of such low-cost housing as well as the availability of low-cost medical service in the various communities. In the same connection he should cooperate with, and stimulate the activity of, other groups such as the various associations of doctors, dentists, and nurses who are interested in this problem.

6. *To secure legal services for Negro workers for the protection OF THEIR RIGHTS*. In connection with all of the problems of Negro workers this "Secretary" should serve as a liaison officer between Negro workers and lawyers available for defense of worker's rights particularly the National Legal Committee of the Association and the lawyers with whom it has contact, to provide assistance wherever there might be legal remedies available. Particularly is this true where Negro workers are being deprived of their civil and political rights as a means of prevention of direct action by such workers aimed at improvement of their working and living conditions.

A minimum budget of $10,000 per year would be necessary for this activity. A salary of from three to four thousand dollars per year should be paid to the "Secretary," although a larger amount may be necessary in order to attract to this work a person of the type necessary to do this job. Secretarial services must be provided at a cost of about two thousand dollars per year. From the scope o activity outlined above it is obvious that a large amount of traveling expense would be incurred by such a "Secretary." In addition, the cost of printing and duplicating literatures which efficient and effective functioning of this office would require would necessitate an increase in the budget of the Association for such purposes. The work of the office of the special counsel would be increased as would the traveling expenses of such special counsel and other Association lawyers for which budget provision must be made.

It seems that a minimum estimate to cover all of these items would be $10,000 per year.

Justification for this extension of Association activity can be easily found in the increasing percentage of Negro unemployment as white, but not Negro workers, are absorbed in the defense effort. Increasing resentment on the part of government officers at demands for assimilation of Negro workers which such officers too frequently regard as an interference with emergency activity demands that private organizations shoulder the responsibility for improvement of conditions among Negro workers. The support which the Association has received in the past form the Negro community for its efforts on behalf of Negro Americans indicates that the Association offers a potent means of furthering the efforts of Negro workers. The problems are tremendous, the need is urgent. With means made available the Association can furnish a real service not only to Negro workers but to the American community as a whole.

June 5, 1941 W. R. Ming, Jr.

MS: NAACP II: A-337, DLC.

The date and format are based on Ming's original proposal.

1. For implementation of the proposal, see 7/25/46; in appendix, 3/7/47.

May 20, 1942.

MEMORANDUM

RE: MEETING OF WASHINGTON BUREAU STEERING COMMITTEE

(Messrs. Hastie, Ransom and Ming) AND MESSRS. WHITE AND REEVES—At residence of Judge Hastie.

The following matters were taken up and disposed of:

Formal Opening

It was the opinion of the committee that a formal opening of the office as contemplated by the National Office staff was inadvisable and with the concurrence of Mr. White it was decided that there would be no formal opening on May 31, but that an effort would be made to get the leading newspapers (Negro) to carry a mat announcing the opening of the office without charge to the Association. This mat would include a picture of the building. It was also agreed that an announcement card would be prepared and sent to a selected list of individuals and organizations, including each member of the Executive Committee of the District of Columbia Branch.

Telephone:

Mr. Reeves reported that in a conference at the telephone company today he was informed that because of an order by WPB, the only way we would be able to obtain telephone service is to obtain a letter from some responsible government official to the effect that the services which the Washington Bureau of the NAACP will offer are vital to the war effect, etc. Mr. White reported that when he received this information this afternoon he had requested Mr. Ulric Bell of the OFF to write such letter, and Mr. Bell had agreed promising to have the letter in our hands tomorrow.

Sign:

It was agreed that Mr. Reeves shall secure as soon as possible the erection of a sign, approximately 6' X 18," in the front yard of the premises, bearing the full name of the Association in gold letters on a blue background.[1]

Advisory Committee:

There was considerable discussion as to the purpose and function of the Advisory Committee and various names were considered. It was generally agreed that the purpose of the Advisory Committee was to advise and consult with the Director and Administration Assistant on strategy and to serve as a source of information to the Bureau on what was going on behind the scenes in government. That committee will consist of Messrs. Hastie, Ransom, Ming, Geo. Johnson, Chas. H. Houston and others to be named after further consideration. The Committee will meet regularly at the offices of Bureau from 12:30 to 1:30 P.M and luncheon will be served.

Conference of Negro Newspaper Editors:

Messrs. White and Reeves reported on the plans for this conference which is to be held at the Bureau on Saturday, May 30, at 10 A.M. Suggestions were made with regards to the extending of additional invitations which are to be sent out by Mr. White. These include Carter Wesley, Roscoe Dunjee, Donald Jones, Charlotta Bass, and the editors of the Washington Tribune, New Orleans Weekly, Philadelphia Independent, Atlanta World, etc. It was agreed that Mr. White, and if possible Mr. Wilkins, would come to Washington on Friday, May 29 for a meeting with the Committee to devise plans for the conduct of Saturday's meeting.

Clerk-Stenographer for Washington Bureau:

With knowledge that Mrs. Gertrude Stone had refused the job because of the long hours, it was agreed that Mr. White in acknowledging her letter of rejection would make reference to the fact that if need should develop for additional clerical personnel on a part-time basis she would be first considered. Mr. White reported that an effort would be made to obtain Miss Evelyn <Ellen> Terry of Philadelphia, if she meets the job qualifications and is interested.

OPA—Rationing—Consumer Education:

It was agreed that Messrs. Ming and Reeves would confer with Miss Frances Williams for the purpose of preparing a detailed memorandum on the subject which would be presented to Leon Henderson by Messrs. White and Reeves.

Office Hours:

It was agreed that the Bureau will open from 8:30 A.M. to 6:00 P.M., Monday through Friday, and from 8:30 A.M. to 1:00 P.M. on Saturdays. In order to maintain this schedule it is proposed that a staggered schedule of hours be worked out for the Washington Bureau and District of Columbia Bureau clerk- stenographers so that each shall work a maximum of 44 hours per week.

Conference of Organization and Group Representatives:

It was agreed that a conference of fraternal, church, labor and other organization and group representatives, similar to the aforementioned editors' conference, would be held at the earliest possible date. To aid in the preparation of the list to which invitations will be extended Mr. White is to send Mr. Reeves and the members of the Committee a copy of the list of organizations and groups which cooperated with the Association in the anti-lynching fight together with such additional suggestions as he may have.

MS: NAACP II: A-667, DLC.
1. These were the NAACP colors.

Findings and Recommendations, Washington Conference, N.A.A.C.P., July 4, 1942

REPORT OF FINDINGS AND RECOMMENDATIONS WASHINGTON CONFERENCE, N.A.A.C.P., JULY 4, 1942 BY CHARLES H. HOUSTON

The Fact Findings Committee of the Washington Conference, N.A.A.C.P., held July 4, 1942 at the office of the Washington Bureau, N.A.A.C.P. makes the following findings and recommendations:[1]

The Washington Bureau is distinctly an adjunct of the national office in New York and as such should concern itself with matters of general concern, as distinguished from matters local to the city of Washington. Such local matters should be left in the first instance to the District of Columbia Branch.[2]

As an adjunct of the national office The Washington Bureau will carry out the programs and policies of the national office, and no attempt is made here to designate or rate the national office policy and program.

The location of the Washington Bureau at the capital of the nation gives it a unique opportunity to serve as a focusing agency for coordinating the efforts of all organizations seeking governmental action in the field of civil rights. The Washington Bureau should keep a record on the formal pronouncements and vote of every member of Congress on matters affecting civil rights and democratic practices; and a record on the activities of all government officials in Washington in policy making positions in the same fields.

The Washington Bureau should build a file of organizations interested in civil rights and democratic practices. The file should cover the constitution and by-laws, and up-to-date list of national officers, and a notation of the special fields of interest of each organization. This file would be the reservoir from which the N.A.A.C.P. would draw wherever cooperative effort of several organizations is needed.

The Washington Bureau should serve, as far as personnel and funds will permit, as a clearing house for information and action strategy to cooperating organizations.

Within its own sphere the most important function of the Washington Bureau is to establish itself as that agency in Washington which stands unequivocably for complete fulfillment of the democratic ideal and the integration of the Negro into all phases of American life. To that end the following action program is now of prime importance:

A. Establishment of interracial units in the armed forces on the basis of horizontal integration: rank with rank where available. This includes female as well as male contingents.

B. Opening all categories and services of the armed forces to Negro men and women under identical conditions as those which other citizens have to meet. In this connection a percentage quota should not be accepted except negatively, to establish that prima facie when Negroes were not represented up their percentage of the population such fact should create an inference of discrimination.

C. Elimination of segregation in all leisure and recreational facilities for the armed forces.

D. Elimination of segregation in all facilities covering transportation, subsistence and public entertainment to any person in uniform.

E. Elimination of segregation in all facilities covering transportation and subsistence as applied to any person traveling on government orders.

F. Elimination of segregation in all government buildings, reservations and territories over which the Federal Government has exclusive jurisdiction.

G. Integration of Negroes in government service, including full and unrestricted opportunity to share without segregation or discrimination all government provisions for housing and sustenance of government employees.

H. Representation of Negroes on all local boards and agencies and integration of Negroes on all local staffs of boards and agencies participating in the war effort or post-war reconstruction.

I. Integration of Negro professional personnel in the State Department, particularly in those offices, bureaus and missions affecting non-Caucasian peoples.[3]

J. Closer affiliation and support of the War Manpower Commission and the President's Committee on Fair Employment Practice; and support of a program of civil and penal sanctions to be given the President's Committee on Fair Employment Practice for enforcement or its orders against discriminations.

K. Lobby activities in support of a Federal anti-poll tax law, and anti-lynching law, and a law for Federal Aid to Education.

It is recommended that a budget be worked out for the Washington Bureau in which a definite share should be allocated to cooperating organizations for the support; but it should be made clear exactly what services the Washington Bureau is to render these organizations for such support in order that organization lines may not be crossed. It is recommended that such services be a regular report on Congressional and government activities in Washington on a monthly basis; postal mailing Washington address; and a semi-annual one-day planning and program conference at the office in Washington.

December 15, 1942

MS: NAACP II: A-670, DLC.

1. In sending participants of the founding conference a copy of the Report of Findings, Walter White said that after operating slightly less than six months, the Washington bureau was already outgrowing its quarters. He continued:

> It is our hope soon to be able to add an expert to examine every bill and resolution introduced in both houses of Congress. As I believe I pointed at the July 4th conference, the enemies of democracy are shrewd and resourceful and often mask their attempts to deny rights and privileges to minorities like the Negro through ambiguous and hidden clauses, which only an expert can fathom. The preponderance of arch conservatives in the new Congress makes it all the more necessary that we be on our guard. The machinery of our Washington Bureau will be amplified to meet the growing needs and as our resources will permit.

The participants receiving White's letter were: Earl Adams, United Transport Service Employees; Herbert Agar, Freedom House; Willard W. Allen, National Negro Business League; William J. Arnold of Washington, D.C., NAPE; Roger Baldwin, American Civil Liberties Union; George Gordon Battle, Council against Intolerance; Mary McLeod Bethune, National Council of Negro Women; R. A. Billings, Phi Beta Sigma fraternity; Ivan A. Booker, National Education Association; G. Norman Branche, National Negro Insurance Association; Bishop R. A. Carter, CME Church, Chicago; Rachael V. Corrothers, Union for Democratic Action; Frank R. Crosswaith, Negro Labor Committee; Dorothy Detzer, Women's International League for Peace and Freedom; Lester B. Granger, National Urban League; Albert Hamilton, Workers Defense League; William H. Hastie; George E. Haynes, Federal Council of Churches; Dorothy I. Height, YWCA; Carl R. Johnson, Kansas City, Missouri (Kappa); George M. Johnson, deputy chair, Fair Employment Practice Committee; Harry W. Laidler, League for Industrial Democracy; Belford V. Lawson, Alpha Phi Alpha fraternity; Geraldine Lensh, Union for Democratic Action; Z. Alexander Looby, Omega Psi fraternity; Beatrice Mayor, Zeta Phi Beta sorority, Morgan State College; Louise McDonald, Alpha Kappa Alpha sorority; H. L. Medford, Washington, D.C. AMEZ, (African Methodist Episcopal Zion); W. Robert Ming Jr., Kappa Alpha Psi fraternity; T. W. Moore, New York City; Alberta Morris, Committee on Race Relations; Marjorie Penney, Young People's Interracial Fellowship; A. Philip Randolph, Brotherhood of Sleeping Car Porters; Leon A. Ranson, NAACP National Legal Committee; Leon A. Reid, National Dental Association; Jerome J. Rothschild, Philadelphia Anti-defamation Council; James E. Scott, Kappa Alpha Psi fraternity; Lillian A. Speight, March on Washington; Maurice Sugar, National Lawyers Guild; Channing H. Tobias, National Council, YMCA; Robert C. Weaver, War Manpower Commission; and J. Finley Wilson, IBPOE. W. White's letter, 12/17/42, to participants, NAACP II: A-670, DLC.

2. See also the founding purpose of the bureau of 7/4/42 that follows in appendix; for a broader explanation of its creation, see the introduction to volume III; Watson, *Lion in the Lobby*, 146.

3. Mitchell pursued this problem relentlessly. See, for example, 5/4, 6/1, and 9/9/53.

The Washington Bureau of the NAACP—Purpose, July 4, 1942

THE WASHINGTON BUREAU OF THE NAACP

[ca. July 4, 1942]

PURPOSE

That the National Association for the Advancement of Colored People, which for 34 years has sought diligently to foster and protect the civil and political rights of the Negro in the United States, may continue to perform this function in the most efficient manner possible, and since, particularly during the present national crisis, everything vital to the present and future welfare of all Americans in centered in and emanating from the Nation's Capital, it is deemed necessary and expedient to establish in Washington an office, adequately staffed, to serve as a "watch-dog" of the interests of Negroes in this county.[1] Specifically the function of the Washington Bureau will be to:

(1) Seek out an act upon all policies affecting directly or indirectly the welfare of the Negro in the armed services, employment, citizenship, etc.

(2) Secure and examine immediately upon introduction in Congress all bills and resolutions which may affect the welfare of Negroes.

(3) Prepare carefully documented and logically written memorandum briefs to support legislation which will improve the lot of the Negro, and also to oppose legislation which will injure the Negro, and present these, when necessary, to House and Senate Committees in public hearings.

(4) See that branches and the people of the country are informed of this legislation so as to bring pressure on Congressmen and Senators to vote against harmful bills and to support helpful ones.

(5) Prepare and send out at such periods as may be deemed most effective a mimeographed or printed "Behind the Scene" picture of matters of interest to Negroes. This service might be extended to all persons contributing a specified sum or over that sum to the support of the Bureau.

(6) Make personal contacts with Senators and Congressmen, client officers, department heads, members of the press and others, presenting the Negroes' side of the story.

(7) Cooperate as far as possible with other agencies or organizations interested in the same or similar objectives.

In addition to the above-described functions, the Washington Bureau will serve the general public:

(1) As a center of information on national issues affecting the Negro.

(2) As a source of information with respect to the governmental activities and records of public officials affecting directly or indirectly the interest of Negroes.

(3) For the purpose f receiving data on the denial of citizenship rights in local areas which can be remedied by federal action.

(4) As a meeting place for everyone who wants to see democracy function as it should.

MS: NAACP II: A-670, DLC.

The date is assigned based on the Reports of Findings and Recommendations by Charles H. Houston of instant date, also in appendix.

1. See the introduction to volume III for an explanation of the founding of the bureau.

[December 8, 1942]

COLORED FIREMEN KILLED OR WOUNDED

MISS. LA., & TENN.—LOWER MISS. VALLEY.

Negro brakemen wounded in vicinity of Wilson, La., in 1917 &1918, and a number murdered 1921–1922 (about five (5) killed—brakemen and firemen).[1]

Shootings & murders from 1931

9/7/31—Jack Taylor (brakeman) W. Durant, Miss.

9/7/31—Clove Sims (fireman)

11/7/31—Fred Harman (B) W. Aberdeen Junction, Miss.

11/10/31—Frank Kimcaird (F) killed at Canton, Miss.

Previously wounded 8/8/31, but recovered.

1/31—Pete Lewis (F.) W. McComb, Miss.

1/23/32—Gus Emory (F.) W. Canton, Miss.

2/4/32—Ed Cold (B.) K. Water Valley, Miss.

2/29/32—Sam Barnes (F.) W. McComb, Miss.

3/11/32—Turner Sims, (F.) W. McCombs, Miss.

3/19/32—Aaron Williams (F.) K. Vicksburg, Miss.

3/29/32—Wilbur Anderson (F.) K.

MS: NAACP II: A-208, DLC.

1. Winifred Raushenbush, secretary of the Citizen's Committee to Save Colored Locomotive Firemen's Jobs, sent Walter White this list with a letter dated December 8, 1942,in preparation for the FEPC's railroad hearings on January 25, 26, and 27. She told White that any information he or Charles Hamilton Houston, special counsel to the FEPC for the railroad hearings, could provide would be appreciated. The material, she said, was needed for general press releases and for a specific story that was to be ready that week. See the headnote on Struggle for a Permanent FEPC: 1942–54. Mitchell recalled this violence in explaining the need for affirmative action programs. Watson, *Lion in the Lobby,* 132–33.

December 31, 1942

REPORT OF ACTIVITIES, WASHINGTON BUREAU NAACP

1. Conference of Newspapermen, May 30, 1942:

On May 30th the Washington Bureau invited a selected number of leading Negro newspapermen to meet at its office for the purpose of determining how the Bureau could be of maximum service to Negroes and to the Negro press and also to charter the best plan of action to be followed in dealing with the growing tendency of certain government agencies to oppose the efforts of Negro newspapers and organizations which are too outspoken in their criticism of discrimination in the war program.

Among the newspapers represented were the *Afro-American* newspapers, the Associated Negro Press, Chicago *Defender,* Louisiana *Weekly,* New York *Age,* New York *Amsterdam Star-News,* Norfolk *Journal and Guide,* Philadelphia *Tribune,* and the Washington *Tribune.*

2. Conference, July 4th:[1]

Representatives of twenty-nine Negro and White national organizations met at the Washington Bureau on July 4th to support a program by which the cooperation of the organizations could be focused and unified through the Washington Bureau on problems affecting the Negro.

Discussion touched upon the Odell Waller case,[2] the fight for the Anti-Poll Tax bill, the color problem throughout the world, the question of Negroes in stenographic pools in government agencies, the elimination of discrimination and segregation in the armed forces, integration of Negroes into the air force, the place of Negro doctors in the army, relations between Negro workers and organized labor, vocational training for war industries, and the southern bloc in Congress.

All delegates pledged support to the Washington Bureau. A Findings Committee was appointed which later rendered a report. In this was stated the belief that within its own sphere the most important function of the Washington Bureau was to establish itself as that agency in Washington which stands unequivocably for complete fulfillment of the democratic ideal and the integration of the Negro into all phases of American life. In accordance with this profession, a definite program was detailed. It was recommended that a budget be worked out in which a definite share should be allocated to cooperating organizations, for the support of the proposed program. It was recommended that in return, the Washington Bureau perform certain services:

1. Regular monthly reports on Congressional and government activities in Washington
2. Use of the Washington Bureau as mailing address
3. Semi-annual and program conference at the Washington office.

3. Office of Defense Transportation:

On May 21st, the Executive Secretary, together with members of the legal staff of the N.A.A.C.P. held a conference with Joseph Eastman and requested that appropriate steps be taken to suspend application of Jim-Crow accommodations to Negro soldiers. Mr. Eastman indicated Willingness to cooperate. As with the exception of the director of O.D.T., the conferees later became members of the Advisory Committee to the Washington Bureau, the Bureau assumed responsibility for the memorandum of August 3rd which directed to Mr. Eastman's attention. The memorandum pointed out:

1. Segregation of races on public vehicles is undemocratic un-American.
2. Negro accommodations are generally inferior and insufficient.
3. Eight specific cases of segregation against colored soldiers, six of which dealt with interstate travel.
4. Morale of Negroes in support of war effort dangerously impaired by such factors.
5. National economy in use of transportation equipment seriously impaired.
6. O.D.T. by authority invested through Executive order 8989 requested to issue order to vehicles engaged in interstate transportation that they cease segregation of soldiers and defense workers and/or recommend necessary emergency legislation.

Mr. Eastman replied to the effect that he did not feel empowered to act in direct accordance with the request but reported that from time to time he might be able to improve certain conditions.

Unsatisfied with this reply, the Advisory Council met with a representative of the Department of Justice on December 8th who stated:

1. Eastman, under war powers, can require statements of policy from railroads, but there are no sanctions that he can exercise.
2. O.D.T.'s influence would be limited to buses which it could penalize through rationing devices.
3. Discrimination best attacked through the Interstate Commerce Commission.
4. Formal documented memorandum brief be filed with the Department of Justice regarding discrimination and including therein complaints which have previously been made to O.D.T.

4. Memorandum to Mrs. Roosevelt:

A memorandum regarding the policies and practices of the United States Employment service and the U.S. office of Education as those policies and practices operate upon the efforts of qualified Negroes to obtain employment in war industry, was directed by the Washing Bureau in a letter to Mrs. Roosevelt September 2nd. The memorandum pointed out that:

1. The USES was obligated to effectuate the purposes of Executive Order 8802 within the area of employment subject to its jurisdiction.
2. The USES aids and abets discrimination against workers in cases where it fills an order containing discriminatory specifications.
3. The USES issued Bulletin No. C-45, effective July 1, 1942, instructing state and local directors to ignore the provisions of Exec. Order 8802, and requiring them to accept and service orders for workers containing discriminatory specifications unless prohibited from so doing by state law.
4. The USOE is charged by statute with the responsibility of administrating federal funds provided for to finance war industry training programs throughout the country. In connection with this administration the congressional act provides that no trainee shall be discriminated against because of sex, race or color. . . .
5. There has been little change in the situation inspite of the fact that complaints were so numerous that the committee on Fair Employment Practices summoned Commissioner Studebaker before it to give account.
6. Both USES and USOE are subagents of the War Manpower Commission. It is inconsistent with reason to believe that the FEPC can become of increased importance as a part of an agency, two of whose constituents have notoriously bad records and whose policies and practices the FEPC has been seeking to correct.[3]

5. Use of special Buses for Negro Orchestras:

The N.A.A.C.P., with the direct assistance of the Washington Bureau, first began to work to lift restrictions on the use of buses for Negro orchestras when in June the Executive Secretary and his Administrative Assistant held a conference with certain O.D.T. officials and pointed out that transportation restrictions worked special hardship on Negro bands because discrimination against Negroes in the South and other parts of the country presented an obstacle to groups traveling. These bands, it was submitted, which had been whole hearted in making appearances at Army camps, would not be able to continue this contribution if their bus transportation were no longer available. The O.D.T consented to allot five busses to replace the approximately fifty used in such service prior to the date of restriction. It agreed to respect the recommendations of a responsible committee in considering applications for this service. As a result of this announcement, a conference was held at the National Office on September 12th, where representatives of O.D.T., Negro orchestras, booking agencies, and the N.A.A.C.P. formulated plans whereby the use of buses by Negro orchestras in the South could be permitted for a trial period. Having brought its efforts to a successful termination, the N.A.A.C.P. referred all further work to newly formed committee, the Transportation Coordinating Committee Under the Jurisdiction of the O.D.T.

6. Soldier Vote Bill:

It was largely through the efforts of the Washington Bureau in its ability to check on, and keep in direct contact with members of the House and Senate, that the N.A.A.C.P. was able to contribute its share in bringing pressure to bear on Congress for passage of the amendment permitting members of armed forces to cast absentee ballots in wartime primaries, irrespective of poll tax, for senators and representatives.[4]

7. Fair Employment Practice Committee:

Anticipating the difficulties which would arise as a result of the transferal of the F.E.P.C. from an agency with independent status to an agency under the supervision of W.M.C., the Washington Bureau directed a letter to President Roosevelt renewing the objection of the Association to the transfer on the grounds that the powers of the committee were submerged since the creation of area officers and the limiting of public hearings by will of the Commissioner of War Manpower.[5]

In October a second protest was registered by the bureau upon receipt of detailed information disclosing the serious budgetary and administrative handicaps under which the F.E.P.C. was laboring as well as advance intelligence of attempts at further emasculation.

8. Office of Price Administration:

At the insistence of N.A.A.C. P. branches in various parts of the country that discriminatory action on the part of O.P.A. officials is all too prevalent, the National Office, ably assisted by the Washington Brea, has brought to the immediate attention of the O.P.A. the fact that its failure to establish a forthright policy of non-discrimination has produce serious problems.

Factors involved in the issue include:

1. Failure to regulate rents, thereby permitting continued violation and exploitation of Negro tenants.
2. Failure to insure against racial discrimination in distribution of rationed materials by providing adequate safeguards in selection of members to rationing boards.
3. Failure to regulate price differential in comparable Negro and white neighborhoods.
4. Failure to insure against racial discrimination in hiring at regional, state, and area levels. (Instead of permitting Negroes on boards, O.P.A. has adopted a policy of complete segregation exemplified by the Richmond and Louisville cases which are violations in spirit of Executive Order 8802 and inconsistent with stated O.P.A. policy).

The fact that O.P.A. to date has not succeeded in presenting any satisfactory adjustments to the created situation above stated, has caused the Washington Bureau to assume leadership in combating these evils. It has collaborated with the National Office in obtaining data to sustain the contentions made. It has paved the way for aggressive protest on the part of the Richmond Branch with reference to the Richmond case. It is at present bringing increased pressure on an unwilling O.P.A. Industry Council, in spite of obstacles encountered by the resignation of Leon Henderson.

9. Closed Shop Agreement, Railway Employees:

In the latter part of September Mr. White called the attention of the Washington Bureau to the announcement that fifteen non-operating unions of the Railway Employees Department of the American Federation of Labor had served notice on Class I railroads that they sought modification of existing contracts to create a closed shop. The Washington Bureau immediately formulated plans for organized protest. Letters were subsequently drafted and sent to William Green and to Malcolm S. McLean pointing out:

1. Many if these same unions have color bars in their constitutions, by-laws, or rituals.
2. Many refuse to admit Negro railway workers into their general locals but organize Negro workers into Jim-Crow locals under definite policy of never letting a Negro worker rise higher in a craft than the position of helper, apprentice or assistant.
3. The proposed close shop agreement is illegal under Sect. 2-Fifth of the 1934 amendment of the Railway Labor Act.

4. Other closed shop agreements have worked to the decided disadvantage of the Negro worker.
5. Railroads are public utilities and should not cater to lily- whitism

The whole question is at present being studied by the F.E.P.C.

10. Negroes and Public Housing:

Incidents such as that at Hamtramck, Michigan, where tenants of a federal housing project voted a resolution restricting occupancy solely to whites prompted the N.A.A.C.P. to take on action on the problem of housing.[6] For its part, the Washington Bureau called representatives from the F.P.H.A. [Federal Public Housing Authority] and the N.H.A. [National Housing Authority] in for consultation on July 3rd. It was determined at this meeting that in light of recent developments in racial policy, it would be necessary to bring outside pressure to bear on certain housing officials in order to obtain a favorable reconsideration of basic policies as they affect Negroes. A conference with heads of the F. P.H. A. and the N. H. A. was proposed at which time a favorable statement pf policy would be requested. N.A.A.C.P. branches were to be informed concerning proper steps to take when local authorities violate the tenets of the anticipated authorized statement. Negro defense workers were to be urged to make early applications to all new housing developments.

At a conference held in November by the Advisory Council with representatives of F. P. H. A. and N.H.A., the defense housing program of Akron, Ohio, from which Negroes allegedly were banned, was discussed. Upon learning that Negroes in Ohio, through either apathy or general ignorance were not making application for defense hosing, the Akron branch was asked to provide Negroes with information on public housing and to request the cooperation of church and local groups in publicizing the existence of defense housing and its availability under law to eligible person regardless of race or color.

11. Anti-Poll Tax Bill:

During the month of November, a great deal of time was devoted by the Bureau to the Anti-Poll Tax bill. The Bureau polled seventy-five senators to secure their commitment to support the bill. Confronted by the filibuster ot reqiested [it requested] senators to vote for cloture, held conferences with congressional leaders to influence the breaking of the filibuster, and sought to crystallize public opinion against this type of legislative obstruction.

Since the defeat of cloture it has collaborated with the National Committee to Abolish the Poll Tax and other interested groups in formulating plans for further work on the bill, and for its reintroduction immediately after the convening of the 78th Congress on January 4. 1943.[7]

12. Wage Differentials:

During the early part of June the Washington Bureau discussed with the Anglo-American Caribbean Commission the matter of the abolition of wage differentials between Negro and white workers engaged in naval and army bases in the Caribbean district. It was reported that this differential was upheld by employers to prevent the out break of labor trouble between native Negro workers who are paid on a lower scale than those set by U.S. labor, and their employers.

In November the Washington Bureau formulated plans for protest to the War Labor Board against the recommendation of the Mediation Panel ordering wages 13c [cents] per hour below the union recommendation in classifications composed predominately of Negro workers, over against 4c [cents] below in groups of white at the Ingalls Birmingham Plant.

13. War Department:

James Harold vs. John McShain, Inc. and Theodore Lee: One of the first official acts of the Washington Bureau was the filling of a complaint for assault and battery on behalf of James Harold, government worker in the War Department Building at Arlington, Va., against John McShain, Inc., and Theodore Lee, agent of McShain. The latter maliciously and willfully attacked Harold as he was leaving the entrance of the cafeteria of the War Department in which he had been refused service.

Family Allowance and Allotment: Soon after governmental decision to transfer the Family Allowance and Allotment Branch of the War Department from Washington to Newark, N.J. was made in October, Negro employees complained that they had been uniformly discouraged from making the transfer. The ostensible reason given by the Department was lack of housing facilities in Newark for Negroes. Negroes who insisted on going, it was charged, were given low efficiency ratings which automatically precluded transfer. The Bureau made a careful investigation of the charges and found some evidence to sustain the allegations of discrimination. The Newark branch was requested to make an investigation of the housing facilities in Newark for Negroes and assist the Washington Bureau in overcoming the obstacle which might interfere with the transfer. The Bureau was assured by a representative of the War Department that an investigation of the unsavory situation had been ordered.

14. Civil Liberties:

Powell-Randolph: When it was reported that Rev. Adam Clayton Powell and A. Philip Randolph, together with a group of New York ministers, were insulted, denied their rights as citizens to enter the public galleries in the Senate, and later threatened by Capital police, the Washington Bureau immediately asked the members of the party to make personal affidavits as to the facts. This incident was brought to the attention of Senator Robert Wagner whose office has requested Col. Chesley W. Jurney to make a full investigation and strong disciplinary action against the policemen if the charges are found to be true.[8]

Miscellaneous: The Washington Bureau has lent valuable assistance to the National Office in the prosecution of civil liberties cases filed on behalf of Reverends Jackson and Young, and in the instances of Anna Russell and Roland Hayes.[9]

15. Vocational Training for Defense in the South:

Atlanta, Ga.: Complaints were ordered registered with the U.S. Office of Education by the Advisory Council of the Washington Bureau concerning discrimination against Negroes in defense training in Georgia. It was reliably estimated that over forty-two percent of the available labor supply in the Atlanta area, where the Bell Aircraft Corporation has set up a plant estimated to need from 25,000 to 40,000 workers, is of the Negro race. Despite the fact that federally financed defense training in skills needed by this plant has been provided white persons for months, it has thus far been denied, solely because of race, the more than 5000 Negroes who applied.

Alabama: Conflicting reports were registered with the Washington Bureau concerning the origin of an order that war training for Negroes had been stopped in Alabama. Protest from the Bureau led to the investigation of the Chief of Training for Manpower, who has asked for a complete investigation.

The Washington Bureau has also requested an independent investigation by Dr. E.W. Taggart to determine:

1. Courses stopped.
2. Number of Negroes deprived of training through stoppage.
3. Courses provided whites, denied colored.

16. War Manpower Commission:

The Washington Bureau, early in the fall of the year, sensed in the proposed legislation to control the nation's manpower, the dangerous possibility that Negroes would be forced into domestic, menial or other work. In the interest of safeguarding Negroes' rights, it began to study the legislation and to draft limitations to be placed in the measure to insure such protection.

When, by congressional authority, a sub-committee was appointed to study Senate Resolution 291, permission was obtained by the Washington Bureau to submit a statement which it had prepared on behalf of the Association. The statement covered certain areas and patterns of discrimination against Negroes in the war effort:

1. Defense training.
2. Non-employment and under-employment of Negro men.
3. Non-employment of Negro women in defense industries.
4. Specific limitations on the full use of Negro skill and ability by the armed forces.

In conclusion it urged that manpower shortage can be solved only by using to the fullest extent all available or potential albor without regard for segregation and discrimination.

17. Segregation in Government Agencies:

During the months of December a memorandum was drafted and directed to the F. E. P. C. requesting elimination of the undemocratic practice of segregation in government agencies. The memorandum pointed out:

1. Executive Order #8802 issued June 25, 1941.
2. Pres. Roosevelt's letter demanding abolition of segregation in government offices, written Sept.3, 1941.
3. Custom policy and usage of segregating Negroes in Federal Civil Service solely on account of race has no statutory authority and is therefore void.
4. Denounced segregation in public schools.
5. Denounced segregation in public vehicles.

18. Recommendations from the Washington Bureau Advisory Committee to the National Board of Directors, December 14, 1942.

I. That the Anti-poll be reintroduced in both houses of the Congress immediately after the convening of the 78th Congress.

II. That the N.A.A.C.P. sponsor the introduction of a bill in the Senate to provide for he reduction of southern representation of southern representation, as is explicitly provided in Section 2 of the Fourteenth Amendment of the constitution of the United States.

III. That the Board of Directors authorize an active campaign for an anti-lynching bill in the 78th Congress.

IV. That the N.A.A.C.P. in cooperation with the National Education Association and other agencies renew in the 78th Congress the campaign for Federal Aid to Education.

[Signed]
Julia E. Baxter.[10]

MS: NAACP II: A-667, DLC.

1. See, in appendix, 7/4/42.

2. For the story of Odell Waller, see Pauly Muray, "All of M. Davis," NYC Workers Defense League, 1942, available at http://catnyp.nypl.org/search/a?searchtype =X&searcharg=odell+waller&SORT=D&search.

3. See volumes I and II.

4. The Senate completed congressional action on the service members' absentee voting bill on September 10, 1942, providing for wartime suspension of poll tax laws in eight southern states, and sent it to the president. *New York Times*, 9/11/42, 9. See also Coleman, "The Uniformed and Overseas Citizens Absentee Voting Act," available at http://www.thememoraryhole.org/crs/more-report/RS20764.

5. Memorandum, "The Future of FEPC," NAACP II: A-208, DLC. Walter White protested that with the FEPC being placed in the WMC along with the U.S. Employment Service and the U.S. Office of Education, these agencies were in an anomalous situation in that the FEPC was charged with opposing the discrimination that they practiced. "A contribution of this sort can only lead to further skepticism and despair," he said. Walter White's letter to President Roosevelt, 9/15/42, NAACP II: A-208, DLC.

6. This was political, in addition to legal, action. See the headnote on Segregation in Federal Housing Programs.

7. See the headnote on Struggle to Abolish the Poll Tax.

8. Chesley Jurney was sergeant at arms of the Senate. See http://www.time.com/time/magazine/article/0,9171,754033-1,00.html.

9. Cases filed on behalf of Rev. Jackson, Rev. Young, Anna Russell, and Roland Hayes.

10. See the headnote on Struggle to Abolish the Poll Tax.

Will Maslow, Director of Field Operations **January 25, 1944**
Emanuel H. Bloch, Senior Fair Practice Examiner

Federal Policy against Discrimination by Reason of Race, Color, Creed, or National Origin.[1]

The concept of equality with respect to religion, race, or creed is rooted in the Constitution of the United States. The free exercise of religion and the prohibition against any law abridging the right thereof, is found in Article 1. With the abolition of slavery under Article 13 thereof, equal protection of the laws by virtue of race or color was given by Article 14 under the 'equal protection of the laws' clause and Article 15 which provides that

> "the right to citizens of the United States to vote shall not be denied or abridged by the United States or by any state on account of race, color, creed, or previous condition of servitude."

Implementation of these rights is found in what is commonly known as the 'Civil rights Law.' *1/*

Section 31 of this law *2/* provides

1/ U.S. Code–Title 8, Sec. 31, et seq.

2/ R. S. 2004.

> "*Race, color or previous condition not to affect right to vote.* All citizens of the United States who are otherwise qualified to vote at any election by the people of any state, territory, district, county, city, parish, township, school district, municipal, or other territorial subdivision, shall be entitled and allowed to vote at all such elections without distinction of race, color, or previous condition of servitude, any constitution, law, custom, usage, or resolution of any state or territory , or by or under its authority to the contrary notwithstanding."

Section 41 *3/* entitled 'Equal Rights under the Law,' gives "all persons within the jurisdiction of the Untied States . . . the same right in every state and territory to make and enforce contracts to sue or be sued, give evidence, and to the full and equal benefit of all laws and proceedings for the security of persons and property as is enjoyed by white citizens and shall be subject to like punishment, pains, penalties, licenses, and exactions of every kind and to no other." Equal rights to the enjoyment of property, the right to inheritance, purchase, etc., accorded by Section 42. 4/.

Section 43 provides for a civil action for deprivation of these rights. Section 44 prohibits "exclusion of jurors on account of race or color" to citizens. 5/

3/ R. S. 1977

4/ R. S. 1978

5/ Section 44 "*Exclusion of Jurors on Account of Race, or Color.*

"No citizen possessing all other qualifications which may be proscribed by law shall be disqualified for service as grand or petit juror in any court of the United States, or of any state, on account of race, color, or previous condition of servitude . . ."

In 1890 Congress passed "An Act to enable New Mexico and Arizona to form constitutions and state governments and be admitted into the Union on an equal footing with the original states." 6/ This act contained the following provisions, applicable to both Arizona and New Mexico:

"and said convention shall provide by an ordinance irrevocable without the consent of the United States and the people of said state . . .

First, that perfect toleration of religious sentiment shall be secured and that no inhabitant of said *state* shall be molested in person or property on account of his and her mode of religious worship.

Fifth, that said state shall never enact any law restricting or abridging the right of suffrage on account of race, color, or previous condition of servitude."

An Act to apply a portion of the public land to more complete endowment in support of the colleges for the benefit of the agricultural and mechanical arts. 7/ This Act contains the following provision: "provided that no money shall be paid out under this___

6/ U.S. Stat. Vol. 36, page 569, 570, Vol. 36, page 558, 559, June 20, 1910–Ch. 310, H.R. 18166, Pub. No 219.

7/ U.S. Stat. Vol. 26, page 418–October 30, 1890.

Act to any state or territory for the support and maintenance of a college where a distinction of race or color is made in the admission of students, but the establishment and maintenance of such colleges separate for white and colored students shall be held to be a compliance with the provisions of this act as the fund received in such state or territory be equitably divided as hereinafter set forth . . ."

Language disapproving, disallowing, or outlawing discrimination by reason of race, color, creed, or national origin is embodied in many of the Appropriations Acts enumerated below:

1. An Act for the relief of employment though the performance of useful public work and other purposes. March 31, 1933. 8/

"That in employing citizens for the purposes of this act no discrimination shall be made on account of race, color, or creed."

2. An Act to establish a Civilian Conservation Corps and for other purposes *9/* –June 28, 1937. Section 8 . . .

"provided that the Director may exclude from enrollment such classes of persons____________

8/ U.S. Stat Vol. 48, page 23, paragraph 1, Ch 17 S598, Pub. No. 5.

9/ U.S. Stat. Vol. 50, page 320, Sec. 8, Ch. 383–H.R. 6551 Pub. No 163.

as he may consider detrimental to the well-being or welfare of the Corps, except that no person shall be excluded on account of race, color, or creed . . ."

3. Emergency Relief Appropriations Act of 1937. *10/* Section 12 provides "any persons who knowingly and with intent to defraud the United States by means of fraud, force, threat, intimidation, or boycott, or discrimination on account of race, religion, political affiliation, or membership in a labor organization, deprives, or attempts to deprive or assists in depriving any person of any benefits to which he may be entitled under such appropriation shall be guilty of felony and be fined not more then $2000 and imprisoned not more than two years, or both. The provision of this paragraph shall be in addition to and not in substitution for, any other provision of existing laws."

4. Appropriations Act for relief purpose of June 21, 1938. *11/* Section 12 of this act contain similar language to that quoted in "3" above and provides for similar penalties.

10/ U.S. Stat. Vol. 50, page 357, Joint resolution making an appropriation for relief purposes–H.J. Res. 361 Pub. Res. No. 47.

11/ Joint resolution for work relief or otherwise to increase employment by providing loans and grants for public work projects. U.S. Stat. Vol. 52, page 814, Section 19, Ch. 554, H.J. Res. 679, Pub. Res. No. 122.

5. Joint resolution making an additional appropriation for work relief and relief for the fiscal year ending June 30, 1939. February 4, 1939 *12/* Section 3(b) "it shall be unlawful for any person to deprive, attempt to deprive or threaten to deprive by any means any person of any employment, purchase, work, compensation, or other benefit provided for or made possible by the Emergency Relief Act of 1938 or this joint resolution on account of race, creed, color . . ." Section 4 provides penalty of a maximum fine of $1000 or imprisonment for one year or both for a violation.

6. Relief Appropriations Act of June 30, 1939. *13/* Joint appropriations and work relief and relief for the fiscal year ending June 30, 1940, known as "Emergency Relief Appropriations Act of 1939." Similar language as above is found in this Appropriations Act. The penalty provided in Section 301 fixes a maximum fine of $1000 or imprisonment for one year, or both.

7. Joint resolutions for work relief and relief for the fiscal year ending June 30, 1940, "Emergency Relief Appropriations Act of 1939" for Work Projects

12/ U.S. Stat. Vol. 53, page 508.

13/ U.S. Stat. Vol. 53, page 939, Sections 28 and 30–H.J. Res. 24, Pub. Res. No. 24.

Administration and National Youth Administration. *14/* Section 30 (b) of this act contains language similar to the language employed in the joint resolution of February 4, 1939.

8. Joint resolution for work relief and relief for the fiscal year ending June 30, 1941–June 26, 1940—known as "Emergency Relief Appropriations Act–Fiscal year 1941." *15/* Section 27 of this Act contains the same prohibitive language as is contained in the Appropriations Acts listed above. The penalty for violation is increased to a maximum $2000 fine or two years imprisonment, or both.
9. Emergency Relief Appropriations Act, fiscal year 1942–July 11, 1941. *16/* Section 22 and section 24 of this Act contains similar language and provides similar penalties as above.
10. Emergency Relief Appropriations Act, fiscal year 1943. *17/* Sections 21 and 23 of this Act contains similar language and provides similar penalties as above.

14/ U.S. Stat. Vol. 53, page 937.

15/ U.S. Stat. Vol. 54, page 624–Ch. 432–H.J. Res. 544, Pub. Res. No. 88.

16/ Stat. Joint resolution for work relief and relief for the fiscal year ending June 30, 1942–U.S. Stat. Vol. 55, pages 405, 406, Ch. 266, H.J. Res. 193, Pub. No. 143.

17/ U.S. Stat. Vol. 56, page 643–July 2, 1942–Ch. 479, H.J. Res. 423, Pub. No. 651.

11. An Act to prevent pernicious political activities in appropriation funds for work relief or relief purposes– August 2, 1939. *18/* This Act contains similar language to 1 above. The penalty provided for violation is a maximum fine of $1000, imprisonment for one year, or both. (Section 4 and 8).
12. An Act to provide for the training of civil aircraft pilots and other purposes, June 27, 1939.*19/* The following language appears in section 2 of this Act:

"... provided, that in the administration of this Act, none of the benefits of training or programs shall be denied on account of race, creed, or color."

13. Act extending the classified Civil Service of the United States, November 26, 1940. *20/* Under Title 2 entitled "Extension of Classification Act," Section 3 (e) provides

"in carrying out the provisions of this title and the provisions of this title and the provisions of the Classification Act of 1923 as amended , there shall be no discrimination against any person, or with respect to the position held by any person, on account of race, creed, or color."

18/ U.S. Stat. Vol. 53, pages 1147, 1148.

19/ U.S. Stat. Vol. 53, pp. 856, Ch. 244, H.R. 5619, Pub. No. 153

20/ U.S. Stat. Vol. 54, pp. 1214, H.R. 960, Pub. No. 880.

14. The Appropriations Acts for the National Youth Administration of June 26, 1940. *21/* July 1, 1941. *22/* and July 2, 1942 *23/* contain language prohibiting and outlawing discrimination by reason of race, color or creed.

15. Appropriations Act for the Civilian Conservation Corps of June 26, 1940. *24/* This Appropriation is found in the Emergency Relief Appropriations Act for the fiscal year 1941. Section 38 states

"... provided further that no person shall be excluded from the training program authorized by this section on account of race, color or creed."

16. The Selective Service Training Act of 1940. *25/* Section 3(a) provides

"... provided that within the limits of the quota determined ..., any person, regardless of race or color, between the ages of 18 and 36, shall be_

21/ U.S. Stat. Vol. 54, page 593, para. 20, H.R. 9007, Pub. No. 665.

22/ U.S. Stat. Vol. 55, page 491, para. 21, 23, Pub. No. 146, H.R. 4426, Ch. 2629.

23/ U.S. Stat. Vol. 56, page 575, Ch. 475, H.R. 7181, Pub. No. 647.

24/ U.S. Stat. Vol. 54, page 626, Ch. 432, Pub. Res. 888, H.J. Res. 544.

25/ An Act to provide for the common defense by increasing the personnel of the armed forces of the United States and providing for its training. U.S. Stat. Vol. 54, page 885, Ch. 720, S4164, Pub. No. 783.

afforded an opportunity to volunteer for induction into the land or naval forces of the United States for the training and service prescribed ..."

Paragraph 4 (a)–Impartiality of Selection—

"provided that in the selection and training of men under this act and in the interpretation and execution of the provision of the act, there shall be no discrimination against any person on account of race or color."

Reference to religion was probably omitted in the above clauses because of the deferment of ministers of religion and conscientious objectors. *26/* This Act was amended December 20, 1941, by providing for the extension of liability of the military service and for the registration of the manpower of the nation to men between the ages of 20 and 45. *27/*

17. Appropriation Acts for the education and training of defense workers of October________________

26/ The Act states "nothing contained in this Act shall be construed to require any person to be subject to combatant service and training in the land or naval forces of the United States, who, by reason of religious training and belief is conscientiously opposed to participation in war in any form." If such persons are inducted, they are assigned to non-combatant service. There is an express provision deferring ministers of religion, etc.

27/ U.S. Stat. Vol. 55, page 246, Ch 602, H.R. 621, Pub. No. 360, Dec. 20, 1941.

9, 1949. *28/* The Act of July 1, 1941, *29/* The Act of July 2, 1942, 30/ and the Act of July 2, 1943, 31/ have the following provisions:

"No trainee under the foregoing appropriations has ll be discriminated against because of sex, race or color and where separate schools are required by law for separate population groups for the extent needed for trainees for each such group, equitable provisions shall be made for faculties and training of like quality."

18. Appropriations Act for the Acquisition and Equipment of public works made necessary by the defense program– June 28, 1941. *32/* Section 203 (a) (4) provides

"Public works shall be provided on the basis of need and in determining need, no discrimination shall be made on account of race, creed, or color." ______________

*28/*U.S. Stat. Vol. 56, page 10??, Ch. 780, H.R. 10589, Pub. No. 812

*29/*U.S. Stat. Vol. 56, page ???, H.R. 9936, Pub. No 548.

*30/*U.S. Stat. Vol. 56, page 580. H.R. 7181, Pub. No. 647.

31/ U.S. Stat. Vol. 57, page 504, 505, Ch. 221, H.R. 2935, Pub. No 135.

*32/*U.S. Stat. Vol. 56, page 363, Ch. 260, H.R. 4545, Pub. No. 137

19. The Appropriations Act providing for the training of nurses. *33/* (to provide for the training of nurses for the armed forces, government, and civilian hospitals, health agencies, and war industries through grants to institutions providing such training and for other purposes–June 15, 1943) In the section dealing with the appropriations of moneys, the following language is used:

" . . . provided that there shall be no discrimination in the administration in the benefits and appropriations made under the respective provisions of this act on account of race, creed, or color."______________

33/ U.S. Stat. Vol. 57, page 153, Ch. 126, H.R. 2664, Pub. No. 74.

MS: HqR5, Office Files of George M. Johnson, Director, Dec. 1941–Nov. 1945, Legal Division.

1. See volumes I and II for the beginning of the modern efforts under the FEPC to establish a national nondiscrimination policy.

Memorandum, Will Maslow, "Status of State FEPC Bills," March 27, 1945

March 27, 1945

MEMORANDUM

To: Mr. Malcolm Ross, Chairman
Mr. George M. Johnson, Deputy Chairman

From: Will Maslow, Director of Field Operations
RE: Status of State FEPC Bills[1]

Bills forbidding discrimination in employment have been introduced in nineteen states. These bills fall into two general categories: those creating a State FEPC and those conferring additional powers upon an existing state agency. With few exceptions, the bills forbid discrimination in employment because of race, color, creed, or national origin and are applicable to employers and trade unions. Some bills in addition cover state agencies and employment agencies. Many of the bills also direct the preparation of comprehensive educational programs.[1]

The procedure for the enforcement of these bills is substantially the same in most of the bills. They provide for an administrative hearing, the issuance of quasi-judicial cease and desist orders, and the enforcement of such orders in the courts. Some bills provide for an alternative criminal penalty.

The chief national groups pushing these bills are the CIO, the [...]

No bill has been introduced in any Southern state except Texas, and there the bill was applicable only to persons of Mexican or Latin America origin. In the North, however, a bill has been introduced in every industrial state.

A summary of the situation in each state follows:

[1]This is a preliminary non-technical survey. Mr. [Simon] Stickgold and I plan a detailed analysis of the text of the various bills, when legislative action on these bills is further advanced.
NAACP and the American Jewish Congress, each of which is circulating "model" bills throughout the country.

In many states the bills have been endorsed by the State Governors. In many, the State A. F. of L. is supporting these bills. Industry is either campaigning actively against the bills or has not taken any stand.

Two states have already passed laws: New York and Indiana, while in Kansas, Washington, and West Virginia bills have already been killed. Legislative hearings have been held or are being held in the following states: Massachusetts, Connecticut, Rhode Island, New Jersey, Pennsylvania, Wisconsin, Michigan, and California, and chances for some kind of bill are good in Massachusetts, New Jersey and Pennsylvania.

1. New York

Ives-Quinn Law becomes effective July 1, 1945, a comprehensive measure applicable to employers, trade unions, and employment agencies. The Commission Against Discrimination, an independent five-man salaried agency, is empowered to issue cease and desist orders, enforceable in the courts. Violation of its orders is also a misdemeanor. The Commission is empowered to create non-salaried auxiliary agencies (1) to study discrimination outside of employment, (2) to further goodwill through community effort, and (3) to prepare educational programs.

2. Indiana

Fleming-Brokenburr law, approved March 9, 1945, empowers Commission of labor to make comprehensive investigations of discrimination in employment based upon race, color, or creed (but not national origin), and to formulate programs for the elimination of such discrimination. Only $30,000 for next two years appropriated for this purpose.

3. Washington

House Bill 228 passed the House but died in the Senate. The legislature has since adjourned. The Bill (in the form in which it was approved by the House) made discrimination in employment because of race, creed, color, or national origin "unlawful." The bill was applicable to state agencies, employers of ten or more, trade unions, and any other "person". A commission of five members was to be created, consisting of the State Director of Labor and Industries or his nominee and four other members. These four other members were to receive $10 for each day of service. The Commission was to issue cease and desist orders enforcible in the courts, and violation of a court enforcement order was made a contempt of court. No appropriation was provided, a section in the bill providing for $75,000 being stricken. The bill also required non-discrimination clauses in each government contract, lease, or franchise.

4. Massachusetts

Seven different bills forbidding discrimination in employment have been introduced in the legislature, sponsored by the CIO, the American Jewish Congress, and a Special Recess Commission created by the Legislature. Hearings on these bills are now being conducted before a joint legislative committee. On March 20, Governor Tobin (Dem.) publicly endorsed these bills, declaring that "Massachusetts is opposed to anti-racism and bigotry, and will not countenance discrimination in employment. . . ." The bills have also been endorsed by Catholic and Protestant bishops and by Boston A.F. of L. spokesmen. Industry, however, is expected to oppose the bills.

In an effort to unify support, the CIO, the AJC, and the NAACP have withdrawn their prior proposals and have agreed upon a new bill drafted by a prominent Boston attorney.

Although the text of the new bill is not yet available, according to newspaper reports it is modeled upon the New York law. It creates a five-man salaried Commission, forbids discriminatory employment practices by employer (of 6 or more), labor unions, and employment agencies. Wilful violation of the Commission's orders in punishable by fine and imprisonment.

5. New Jersey

Two bills are being considered. The measure introduced by Assemblyman Hill, a Republican Negro, is endorsed by Governor Edge (Rep.). The other proposal, the Morrissey-Howell bill, is being pushed by Frank Kingdon, state chairman of the New Jersey Independent Citizens League.

The Hill bill (Ass. No. 321) creates a "Division Against Discrimination" in the State Department of Education consisting of the Commission of Education and a non-salaried "council" of seven members to be appointed by the Governor. The Commissioner is authorized to issue complaints, to conduct hearings, and to issue orders enforceable in the courts. Violation of the orders of the Commissioner is likewise a misdemeanor which under New Jersey practice requires an indictment before trial. The other provisions of the bill are similar to the Ives-Quinn law. $50,000 is to be appropriated to enforce the Act.

The Morrissey-Howell bill creates a new office, that of State Commission Against Discrimination, at an annual salary of $8,000. He is given power to issue orders after hearing. Violators of his orders would be punished as "disorderly persons" without the necessity of a criminal indictment. His orders can likewise be enforced in the courts which would have no power to review the Commission's findings of facts in the absence of fraud.

At the recent legislative hearings, AF of L and CIO state leaders endorsed the need for legislation. Governor Edge has, however, come to against the creation "of a costly new separate agency." The Newark Chamber of Commerce has urged a state-wide referendum before any bill is enacted.

6. Connecticut

Public hearings have been held by a joint legislative committee on three different bills. The one most likely to be reported in the Aaron bill (Senate 236) introduced by chairman of the joint committee and endorsed by Governor Baldwin (Rep.).

The Aaron bill is modeled upon the Ives-Quinn law in New York. It creates a five-man salaried full-time Commission with power to issue cease and desist orders, These orders are enforceable in the courts, which (unlike the procedure in the New York law) have the power to review the findings of facts of the Commission.

The Aaron bill is broader than the New York model. It is applicable to all employers of one or more persons (except that farmers employing four or less persons are excluded). It is explicitly applicable to state agencies. It declares that "Segregation" shall be deemed discrimination. Finally the Aaron bill makes it a criminal offense to resist or "interfere with" any Commission order.

7. Rhode Island

A House Committee has already reported out the Wrenn bill (H. 603) which has the support of Negro and Jewish groups. The House Committee made certain changes in the bill which are not yet available but which are reported in the press as strengthening amendments. The bill originally created a three-man Commission, each member receiving the $5,000, and allowed a total appropriation of $25,000. Otherwise, the bill is a comprehensive measure, applicable to employers of four or more, State agencies, labor unions, and employment agencies. An interesting feature is a provision making the orders of the Commission final unless the respondent appeals.

8. Pennsylvania

Two bills are being seriously considered and a public hearing is scheduled for March 27. The Brown bill (H. 354) introduced by a veteran Negro legislator, has support of CIO, Jewish , and Negro groups. The Brown bill creates a five-man commission with salaries of $10,000 each. The bill is applicable to all employers, state agencies, and labor unions. The orders of the Commission are enforcible in the courts. The Commission is also directed to prepare a comprehensive educational program with the cooperation of state educational authorities and is authorized to accept contributions from private sources for this purpose. Violation of the Act is punishable as a misdemeanor.

The Kephart-Bowers bill (S. 444) amends the Pennsylvania State Labor Relations Act to make discriminatory employment or membership practices by employers or trade unions unlawful. The Pennsylvania Labor Relations Board will, therefore, enforce the amendment in the same manner as it prevents unfair labor practices by employers and unions, i.e., by the issuance of orders enforcible in the courts.

Republican Governor Martin has expressed opposition to the creation of a separate commission because of the expense involved and has suggested that an existing state agency enforce the law. Thereafter, he stated that the Kephart-Bowers bill was not an administration measure and urged the sponsors of the various bills to work out a satisfactory compromise.

9. Wisconsin

Public Hearings have already been held by a joint legislative committee on the Tehan-Simmons bill (S. 131) which is endorsed by the State AF of L, the State CIO, and church, Negro, and Jewish groups. The bill was opposed however, by the State and Milwaukee Chambers of Commerce. Assemblyman Simmons is the only Negro legislator in Wisconsin, while Senator Tehan is the State Chairman of the Democratic Party.

The Tehan-Simmons bill forbids discriminatory employment practices by employers or trade unions and confers upon the Industrial Commission the power of forbidding such practices by the issuance of cease and desist orders, enforcible in the courts.

Only $10,000 is to be appropriated annually for the news duties conferred upon the Industrial Commission.

10. Michigan

A public hearing was held March 15 on the Carpenter bill (S. 134) which was endorsed by the State CIO, the Detroit district of the American Legion, and various churches, Negro, and Jewish groups. The Carpenter bill creates a four-man Commission with annual salaries of $7,500. It forbids discrimination by employers (of 8 or more), trade unions, and employment agencies.

A similar bill introduced by Rep. Ellstein, an officer of the Amalgamated Clothing Workers of America, is pending in the House.

Governor Kelly (Rep.) announced that he supports the Republican Party plank calling for a permanent FEPC but has not yet taken a stand on the state bills.

11. California

Governor Warren (Rep.) in his annual message to the State Legislature urged the creation of a "Commission on Political and Economic Equality" to report upon the necessity of new laws against discrimination. But without awaiting such a report, a group of fourr assemblyman, led by Negro Assemblyman Hawkins, has introduced a bill (Assembly No. 3) declaring discrimination in employment unlawful. The bill creates a five-man commission at annual salaries of $7,500 and provides for the issuance of enforcible cease and desist orders. Probably as a result of the FEPC's case against the Boilermakers Union, the bill specifically outlaws "second class or segregated membership" in trade unions. Violation of the Act is made a misdemeanor.[3]

Hearings on the bill were held before a legislative committee which reported adversely on the bill by a vote of 10 to 8. The bill was supported by the State CIO and Negro, Jewish, and civic groups.

12. Illinois

The Illinois bill (S. 156) is based upon a model bill circulated by the American Jewish Congress. It creates a five-man salaried commission with orders enforcible in the civil and criminal courts. "Auxiliary" unions based solely upon race or color are specifically forbidden. An appropriation of $100,000 is authorized. The president of the State AF of L has announced that he would support the Mills bill if it conforms to the "Federal Fair Employment Practice Act."(?)

13. Ohio

Several bills are pending in Ohio, none of which appears to have a chance of passage. Only the Metzenbaum bill (H.B. 88) is available, but according to press reports all are similar in principle to the Ives-Quinn law. The Metzenbaum bill applies to state agencies as well as employers and unions, requires government contracts to contain a non-discrimination clause, provides for the adoption of a comprehensive educational program, and appropriates $100,000. Governor Lausche, in his message to the legislature, asked it to consider creating a non-salaried Race Relations Committee without coercive powers to develop a program to eliminate discrimination.

14. West Virginia

Although a public hearing was held on the West Virginia bill, the legislature adjourned without taking any action on it. According to press reports, the State CIO opposed the bill because it might give the courts power over the internal affairs of unions. The state AF of L stated it had taken no stand on the bill but its representatives indicated that it was quite possible that existing law was adequate.

No copies of the bill sponsored by Democratic Representative Fleming Jones, the legislature's only Negro member, are available. Press clippings state that it created a State Commission whose orders were enforcible in the courts, with power to proceed against employers and trade unions.

15. Maryland

A bill has been introduced by Leon Rubenstein, Democratic delegate from Baltimore, but it has no chance of passage. No copies of the bill are yet available, but according to the press, it creates a State quasi-judicial agency with powers to issue orders against employers or trade unions, enforcible in the courts.

16. Colorado

A bill has been introduced by State Senator Brooks (Republican of Denver) which creates a three-man salaried commission with power to issue orders enforcible in the courts against employers or trade unions. Senator Brooks announced that his bill seeks to protect the 100,000 Spanish Americans the 12,000 Negroes, and 8,000 Japanese-Americans in the State. The bill is expected to die in Committee.

17. Texas

A bill forbidding discrimination in employment and in places of public accommodation based upon national origin, language, or ancestry was introduced by state senators Spears of San Antonio. The bill allowed persons discriminated against to sue in the civil courts for damage and was explicitly designed to protect persons of Mexican or Latin-American origin.

According to press reports, it was amended in Committee to apply only to discrimination in places of public accommodation, the employment features being stricken.

It is noteworthy that even the bill as first drawn excluded Negroes, Jews, Catholics, and Orientals.

18. Kansas

A bill introduced by Representative Towers, veteran Negro Legislator, has been killed by the Judiciary Committee. The Towers bill created a five-man commission with orders enforcible in the courts. An interesting provision made it unlawful to restrict union membership to an "auxiliary" local, because of race, creed, etc.

19. New Mexico

A bill has been introduced in the House by Representative Garcia (H. 193) but the text is unavailable. The Division of Labor Standards of the U.S. Department of Labor reports that it prohibits discrimination in the employment because of race, color, creed, national origin or ancestry by employers or trade unions and provides penalties for its violation. According to PM [magazine], the chances of passage are good because of the influence of Mexican-Americans in the State.

MS: HqR3, Office Files of Malcolm Ross, Will Maslow.

1. See the headnote on the Struggle for a Permanent FEPC, 1942–54.

2. See the headnotes in vol. I on the Shipbuilding Industry and the Boilermakers Union and on the FEPC and Unions.

Operating Manual for the Labor Committees of Branches, March 7, 1947

WASHINGTON BUREAU NAACP
100 MASSACHUSETTS AVE ., N.W.
WASHINGTON 1, D. C.

March 7, 1947

To the Branches:

Attached is an operating manual for the labor committees of branches.[1]

It will be appreciated if you will send to me the name and address of the Chairman of your Labor Committee. The National Committee is made up of the following persons:

Mr. Charles H. Houston
Mr. Alfred Baker Lewis
Mr. Palmer Weber
Mrs. Eleanor Roosevelt
Mr. A. Philip Randolph
Father Francis J. Gilligan
Mr. Walter P. Reuther
Mr. George L. P. Weaver
Mr. Willard S. Townsend
Mr. Boris Shishkin
Mr. Frank Fenton
Mr. Nelson Cruikshank

As soon as possible, I would like to have the names of those persons on your Labor Committee, and an indication of their labor union connections.

Any suggestions for revision of the manual in line with your experiences in your own community will always be welcomed.

Cordially yours,
Clarence Mitchell
Labor Secretary

Attachment

NAACP LABOR DEPARTMENT OBJECTIVES

1. Elimination of: discriminatory employment practices in industry and government which result in refusal to hire colored workers, wage differentials based on race, unequal opportunities for training and promotion, unfair dismissals, and segregation in employment because of race.
2. Greater participation of colored persons in the trade union movement.
3. Ending of segregated locals, auxiliaries, and any other discriminatory practices in labor unions.
4. Passage of state and federal FEPC legislation.
5. Inclusion of non-discrimination clauses in state and federal laws pertaining to the employment of persons in the execution of government contracts.
6. Joining with labor unions for the enactment of legislation favored by labor and for the repealing of unfavorable labor legislation.
7. Expanding and improving opportunities for vocational training on the basis of non-segregation.

STRUCTURE

The Secretary of the Labor Department is responsible to the Executive Secretary of the Association. The work of this department shall be coordinated with the activities of the Legal Department and the Branch Department by regular meetings with the Secretary and these department heads.

There shall be formed a labor committee of Board Members and such other persons as may be needed to further the objectives of this program. Labor committee shall also be formed in local branches as provided in Article III, Section 2 of the branch constitution. A special effort should be made to have C.I.O. and A.F.L. members on such committees.

DUTIES

The National Committee shall work with the Secretary in achieving the objectives of this program. This committee shall also make recommendations to the Board of Directors on the labor policy to be followed by the NAACP. This shall include recommendations on the endorsement or rejection of proposed labor legislation.

Branch labor committees shall initiate, within the framework of a specified operating procedure, positive action to achieve the objectives of this program.

Branch labor committees shall also receive and investigate complaints alleging discrimination because of race in hiring, upgrading, wage payments, training, or dismissals from employment. The committees shall take appropriate steps to adjust such complaints.

RELATIONSHIPS WITH UNIONS

It shall be the duty of branches to keep informed on the local practices of labor unions. This includes giving assistance in building the membership of those unions organizing on a non-segregated basis.

Some unions such as the United Automobile Workers have extensive machinery against discrimination. Branch labor committee should become familiar with this machinery and urge local union officials to make it work. In other cases, locals of international unions with discriminatory policies are working to eliminate such policies. This is true in the case of the International Association of Machinists. Although the union has a prohibition against Negroes in its ritual many locals have actually included colored persons and in recent conventions of the machinists, the vote to eliminate the color bar has gained new support. The branch committee can speed up this type of progress by informing the National Office of liberal persons in such unions who may be counted on to give support to a plan of ending discriminatory features.

LABOR LEGISLATION

The labor committee of the branch shall have the responsibility of reporting to the National Office any proposed city ordinances or state laws which are against the best interest of labor. Also, favorable legislation proposed shall be submitted to the National Office in order that the Association may have a uniform policy on such matters throughout the country. Such legislation shall be studied jointly by the labor and legal departments of the National Office. In submitting matters of this kind the recommendations of the branch shall be included. It is important that this phase of the program be given careful attention. Numerous state bills and proposed city Fair Employment Practice ordinances are being submitted in various parts of the country. The NAACP should endorse only the strongest and best of such legislative proposals. In addition, various state legislatures undertake the passage of hostile labor laws which should be defeated because of the adverse effect they have on the progress of organized labor with the resultant ill effect on colored persons.

By showing its recognition of the common objectives for both colored persons and labor, the NAACP will promote increased harmony between these groups.

VOCATIONAL TRAINING

The branch labor committee shall work with the education committee (where the latter exists) in evaluating local tax-supported vocational programs. Where such programs fail to offer equal opportunity for colored and white students, the labor committee shall take action to eliminate such inequality. The National Office Labor Department shall be kept informed on such matters in order that it may give advice and assistance in handling them.

ACTION ON COMPLAINTS

The National Office shall give advice on all cases submitted to it by branch committees, but obviously it cannot take action on each individual complaint *unless that complaint involves a policy question.* Thus, in cases where the hiring policies of an employer are generally satisfactory, individual charges of discrimination shall be handled by the local branches without reference to the National Office.

Individual complaints which do not involve policy matters received directly by the National Office shall be referred to the Labor Committee in the local branch nearest the source of the complaint. Branches will be informed of complaints involving policy received by the National Office.

The National Office shall be kept informed of all action taken by local branches on complaints involving policies of employers, labor unions, employment service officers, and training institutions. These types of complaints include charges that employers refuse to hire colored persons in skilled jobs, labor unions refuse to admit them to membership, adequate training facilities are not provided by local school authorities, and discrimination on the part of state or federal government officials in Civil service employment.

Copies of all correspondence sent to parties charged in policy cases shall be sent to the National Office as well as copies of reports on all conferences with such parties charged. The National Office will be able to offer advice in the handling of such cases and aid in the settlement. It will also make available a body of experience which will be useful to other branches in the handling of such cases.

Information Needed on Complaints:

Valid complaint shall contain the following information:

1. Name of party charged.
2. Date or period of the discriminatory action.
3. Persons or persons responsible for action complained of and their titles.
4. Brief description of what happened.
5. Brief description of the party charged, i.e., type of business, type of union, etc.

Refusal to Hire:

1. Check with the USES (Civil Service Commission in government cases) or other agencies working in the employment field in order to determine whether the party charged has submitted a request for workers and whether such request made any specification as to race of applicants.
2. Visit plant or agency to interview policymaking officer, such as manager of industrial relations, director of personnel, agency head, or other executive officials.
3. Determine what openings existed at the time of the alleged discrimination, what qualifications were required, who was hired for the opening and what qualifications did the individual have who was employed.
4. Determine whether the company has a union contract, and if so, get the names of officials who represent the union in bargaining with the employer and a copy of the contract.
5. Determine whether the firm is part of a national corporation, and if so, who is president and where are the headquarters. It is sometimes helpful to call in national management early in a case. This action can be taken by the National Office of the NAACP or the labor committee nearest the company headquarters.

Refusal to Upgrade:

1. *Determine whether the complainant made use of grievance procedure if the workers employed are represented by a union.*
2. If such procedure was not utilized by the complainant, refer him to the proper union official and request that the union give the NAACP a report on the outcome of the case. In such matters it will be necessary for the committees to become familiar with the union procedure, and the responsibility for explaining this shall rest with the A.F.L. or C.I.O. representatives on the committee.

3. In general, unions should be allowed a period of grace in which to take action on behalf of complainants. Although the length of this period is best left to the discretion of the local labor committee, it is suggested that a ten day period should be sufficient to show some progress in handling of the complaint. At the end of that period it would be advisable to check with the union to determine the status of the complaints if no report has been submitted.
4. If there is no union representing the workers at the plant, visit the establishment to determine the plan of promotion and ascertain qualifications required for a vacancy complained of. Also, determine whether the vacancy was filled and qualifications of the individual who got the job.

Refusal to Train:

1. Determine from complainant what qualifications were required for admission to the course.
2. Determine whether the complainant has the required qualifications.
3. Interview the party charged to check for verification of qualifications as outlined by the complainant. Any official written statement of such qualifications will, of course, be useful in making a determination.
4. As a further check, ascertain whether the persons admitted to the training have qualifications similar to or less than those of the complainant.
5. Determine whether the training program is supported in any way by federal, state, or city funds.

Wage Discrimination:

1. Obtain from the complainant description of duties performed on the job and rate of pay.
2. Get from complainant names of white employees doing similar work at higher rates of pay.
3. Obtain copies of statements in contracts or other written form showing differentials.
4. Remember that wage discrimination is not always obvious. In some cases employers use a few whites of lower qualifications with large numbers of colored persons simply to be able to say whites are doing the same work.

Discriminatory Dismissals;

1. *Did the complainant use his union grievance machinery, and, if so, what were the results?*
2. Ascertain whether the complainant alleges that his seniority warranted his retention, and, if so, obtain the names of persons with less seniority who were retained.
3. Obtain from the complainant the employer's version as he understands it of why he was dismissed.
4. Check complainant's story with any witnesses he may have and obtain their opinion of his ability as a worker.
5. If there is no union grievance machinery which may be used to handle this case, visit the plant directly and attempt to adjust the matter with a policy-making officer.
6. In Government cases, special Civil Service procedures are set up which govern the release of employees. The individual dismissed should be in the position to indicate whether he believes these regulations or procedures were violated in his case. If he does not know, a check should be made with the Civil Service Commission to determine what regulations covered his case and also whether they were followed by the agency dismissing him.

Discrimination by Unions:

1. Does the union have a closed shop contract with the employer or any other type of agreement which makes it necessary for employees to be or become members in order to remain on the job?
2. Are there constitutional or other barriers on which the union bases its action complained of. If so, be certain to obtain an exact statement on these.
3. Who is the international president of the union and what is his address?
4. Do the members and officers of the local wish to change any discriminatory policy they may be following, but are prevented from doing so by the international officers?
5. Make a personal visit to the union office to attempt a settlement. If you are unsuccessful forward all details to the Labor Secretary.

Address Communication to:
Clarence Mitchell
Labor Secretary
100 Massachusetts Avenue, N.W.
Washington 1, D.C.

MS: NAACP II: A-656, DLC.

1. See 6/5/41 in appendix for the original idea of an NAACP labor secretary, 7/25/46 for the labor department's objectives, and 8/1/46 for the proposed program.

NAACP Washington Bureau Press Release, Resolutions Urging Favorable Action of FEP Legislation, April 7, 1947

PRESS RELEASE

Labor Department, NAACP
100 Massachusetts Avenue, N.W.
Washington, D.C., April 7, 1947: Resolutions urging favorable action on Fair Employment Practice legislation and opposition to pending anti-labor bills were forwarded to each member of the House and Senate Labor Committees from the NAACP's Labor Department this week.[1]

These resolutions, passed at regional conferences of the Association in San Francisco, California and Charleston, South Carolina, represented the views of delegates from twelve states. While praising the introduction of an FEPC law, the resolutions condemned the pending anti-labor bills as "an attack upon the liberties of the American working man and . . . move in the direction of dictatorship." The Conferences called upon the President to give such bills a "resounding veto" if passed.

The resolutions were sent to Senators and Congressmen from southern states as well as those from northern areas. Clarence Mitchell, Labor Secretary of the NAACP, pointed out that, in line with NAACP's program increasing the registration of voters in the South and gaining full use of the ballot, it is important that incumbent Congressmen and Senators know what their constituents want.

Clarence Mitchell
Labor Secretary

MS: NAACP II: A-528, DLC.

1. See 3/1 and 4/3/47.

Summary of Complaints against New Orleans Post Office, May 10, 1947

May 10, 1947

SUMMARY OF COMPLAINTS AGAINST NEW ORLEANS POST OFFICE

Affidavits filed by seventeen complainants against the New Orleans Post Office show that, although colored veterans received high averages in examinations for Clerk-Carrier, they were not appointed as regular substitute clerks. The affidavits also allege that two non-veterans were not appointed in spite of high averages.[1]

For the veterans, the averages ranged from a high of 100.2 which was the grade of Irvin V. McKendall, 1023 N. Liberty Street, to a low of 72.2 which was the grade of Henry R. Greene, a veteran with a ten-point preference. Most of the others are in the 90 or high 80 brackets. The two non-veterans earned averages of 87.2 and 85.6. These two men, Nathan N. Johnson who was formerly in the Merchant Marines and Earl R. Rousseau, Jr., were employed as war service appointees in the Post Office. Three of the veterans, Mr. Julius Bush, Mr. Maurice A. Fortin, and Mr. Flournoy L. Anthony, were also employed as war service appointees. At one time they received notices of dismissal which were retracted by the Post Office Department when the complainants showed that their rights under Section 14 of the Veterans Preference Act of 1944 had been violated. The twelve remaining veterans are seeking appointment in the Post Office and have not previously been employed there. They are

Mervin J. Ferrier
Alvin J. Lopez
Arthur J. Chapital, Jr.
Edward E. Meggs
Edgar H. Armstrong
Henry R. Greene
Joseph E. Kaufman
Morris M. Wilson
Alexander A. Moret
Irvin V. McKendall
Wilbur F. Ferrouillet
Paul M. Saizan

Mr. Rousseau contends that he was employed as a war service substitute on July 16, 1943. He states that his average was 87.2 in the examination for appointment as a regular substitute. However, he was sent a letter of termination instead of receiving regular appointment on the ground that he had a bad record. He contends that his efficiency rating was 97. Although he had 272 demerits, Mr. Rousseau contends that 100 of these were given because he did not report for duty on March 5 and 8, 1946. This 100 should not be considered, he contends, because they were in a period different from the period in which he received 172. These letter demerits were for tardiness and other minor violations. He contends the "I feel that I am being discriminated against because white persons have been appointed to probationary substitutes who have substantially larger amounts of demerits and lower efficiency ratings." He names Messrs. W. J. Collins, John Collins, and Charles Richaux as white persons who were below him.

Mr. Saizan, a ten-point veteran, contends that it is customary in the New Orleans Post Office to appoint white veterans with a ten-point preference. He also names W. J. Collins and Charles Richaux as white persons who have received numerous demerits but were appointed by the Postmaster.

Mr. Greene who also received a ten-point veterans preference for high blood pressure charges that at one point he was placed on a suspended appointment until his blood pressure was reduced. He states that about February 8, 1947, he was placed back on the list of eligibles. He also states that it is customary in the New Orleans Post Office to appoint white veterans who have ten-point preferences.

The basic complaint of all of the men which is contained in their affidavits is as follows: "The Postmaster at New Orleans has discriminated against me on account of my race and color in the selection of eligible applicants for positions for the following reasons: Several Negro veterans, one with an average of 100.2, another with a ten-point preference rating, have been passed over, like myself, for white applicants whose ratings are lower than mine. Two such white appointees, W. J. Collins and Charles Richaux, have more demerits than some of those passed over by the Postmaster. It has long been the policy, custom, usage, and practice to discriminate against Negroes in the New Orleans Post Office in the appointment, assignment, and promotion of Negro personnel."

Mr. Byrd also submitted a brief in which he charged that for sixty-five years Negroes have been employed in the Post Office in New Orleans but none have been upgraded beyond the automatic grade of special clerk for the last forty years. He charges that in the twelve years prior to 1941, not one Negro was appointed as substitute clerk although at least eleven were known to have passed the Civil Service examination in 1935 with averages between 90 and 96.5. This policy was changed slightly in 1942, Mr. Byrd states, when some colored clerks were appointed. However, discrimination still exists, he contends, in that of the twenty-seven Negro clerks currently employed seven are special clerks and two of these seven are senior to the last two white clerks who received supervisory appointments.

Negro clerks are also denied assignment in the following sections, he states: carrier section, general delivery, rated section, register section, supply section, stamp windows, letter stations, permit section, special delivery, and finance section. Letter carriers are also discriminated against, Mr. Byrd contends, in that none have been promoted in the past thirty years while white carriers with less seniority and fitness have been upgraded. Negroes are also denied certain preferred assignments, Mr. Byrd contends. Colored custodial employees are also denied upgrading, Mr. Byrd states.

These matters were presented to Mr. A. J. Leach, Regional Director of the 10th Civil Service Region. At the hearing on the specific cases, Mr. Leach denied that there had been evidence of discrimination because of race.

On the charge of passing over the eligibles to reach whites of lower ratings, Mr. Leach stated that "eligibles who received consideration on three separate occasions would not have to be considered further by the appointing officer."

Replying to the charge concerning the number of demerits of the white persons who were appointed, Mr. Leach said that "Richaux had only ten demerits at the time of his appointment. He had a 'much larger' number at one time but the time limit on some of them had expired and others were offset by merits. Collins had 385 demerits charged against him but since October 1, 1946, he received six for 'taking only twenty-four minutes for lunch instead of thirty.'"

The reply to Mr. Greene's charge states that there is considerable doubt about his ability to meet the physical requirements, but he is still on the list.

The Commission also takes the position that "it is not the practice of the Commission to take any action in appeals involving racial discrimination until the complainant has availed himself of all administrative channels and grievance procedures within his agency in an effort to secure a satisfactory solution. It appears that your charges of discrimination in connection with assignments, seniority, and promotions should first be taken up with the Post Office Department. The United States Official Postal Guide of July 1943 contains regulations governing such matters."

Three cases involving Messrs. Wilson, Saizan, and Johnson have not been decided as yet, according to the Washington Office of the Civil Service Commission.[2]

MS: NAACP WB-154, DLC.

1. See also 6/2 and 10/31/47; in appendix, 3/24/48.
2. On these cases, see also 1/1/47; in appendix, 3/24/48, 3/48, and 8/20/48.

Suggestions for Government Program against Employment Discrimination by Federal Agencies, November 7, 1947

November 7, 1947

SUGGESTION FOR GOVERNMENT PROGRAM AGAINST EMPLOYMENT DISCRIMINATION BY FEDERAL AGENCIES

The President's Committee on Civil Rights recommended that there be issued by the President a mandate against discrimination in government and that there also be created adequate machinery to enforce this mandate.[1]

To operate most effectively, any agency set up to enforce such a Presidential decree should have independent status. However, if it is not possible to work out independent status, a second choice would be location in the Bureau of the Budget. The President's Committee mentioned the possibility of including this function in the Civil Service Commission. The Commission, however, has consistently contended that in cases of discrimination it was hampered by certain legal restrictions in effecting redress for compliance.

There was nothing in the past history of the Bureau of the Budget to indicate that its policies on race relations could be considered either friendly or liberal. However, the fact that the Bureau is in the Executive Office of the President, and also exercises extensive control over the internal operations of all agencies of the Government, would make it a desirable place in which to locate the new agency. This would give those carrying out the requirements of the President's mandate prestige and a ready access to the President. Placing the agency in the Bureau of the Budget would also help to eliminate practices of discrimination which currently exist there.

The new agency would have as its major function the job of taking positive steps to ensure the full use of all persons in government without discrimination because of race, creed, color, or national origin. There has been considerable evidence that such a group should function on a fulltime basis, and, therefore, should be paid rather than voluntary officers of the Government. Three persons serving as a Board should be adequate if they are given sufficient personnel for immediate needs and the right to make use of personnel from other agencies as well as voluntary non-paid individuals. Although the agency would handle complaints brought in by individuals and make adjustments, its major function would be preventive work.

As a first step in a government program of eliminating discrimination, each agency should be required to issue a statement of policy to all department heads, personnel officers, and any other individuals concerned with hiring, transfers, promotions, or dismissals. This policy statement should spell out in clear terms the right of all qualified persons to positions in the Federal Government. It should make clear the fact that in the Federal Government there is no room for the operation of segregated facilities for employees nor is there any function of the Federal Government which is the exclusive property of any one racial or religious group. Copies of the statement should be posted in a conspicuous location in the offices of the agency. A second step should be the pooling of the best experiences of such agencies as the Housing and Home Finance, the War Department, and others which have used minority groups on a large scale for the purpose of working out techniques for preventing discrimination. When agencies report to the Bureau of the Budget on fiscal matters, the Board would have authority to request that they also report on the extent of compliance with the President's Order. Board members would be expected to give information on training programs for the implementing of the policy of no discrimination. However, agencies would also be expected to work out programs for their own use on this matter. A representative of the Board would be a member of the Council of Personnel Administration.

Executive Order NO. __________[2]

It is the policy of the Government of the United States to ensure the full utilization of all needed and qualified persons in or seeking government employment without regard to race, creed, color, or national origin.

By virtue of the authority vested in me by the Constitution and the Statutes, I now instruct the departments and agencies of the Federal Government to take positive steps to prevent discrimination in the hiring, promotion, transfer, or dismissal of employees because of race, creed, color, or national origin. The heads of departments and agencies are instructed to designate staff members who shall be responsible for the formulation and promotion of policies and programs to prevent discrimination in the aforementioned types of personnel action.

There is hereby established in the Bureau of the Budget a Board of ______ hereinafter referred to as the Board. The Board shall be composed of three persons appointed by the President. One member shall serve as chairman. The compensation of the chairman and members shall be fixed by the President at a sum not to exceed ______. The Board is also authorized to hire personnel for its immediate needs in carrying out the requirements of this Order. The Board shall meet with the heads of departments and agencies, or their authorized representatives, for the purpose of working out plans, policies, and programs to effectuate the provisions of this Order.

For the purpose of making investigations, reports, or obtaining compliance with the provisions of this Order, the Board may use the services of staff members of the Bureau of the Budget or of the United States Civil Service Commission by agreement with these agencies. For the purpose of developing personnel practices which will prevent discrimination because of race, creed, color, or national origin, the Board may use voluntary and uncompensated services of recognized experts in this field.

Members of the Board may be present at their discretion during hearings before agents of the Bureau of the Budget on fiscal matters of the various departments and agencies of the Federal Government. At the request of the Board transmitted by the Bureau of the Budget, the departments and agencies shall prepare reports on the progress of plans to eliminate discriminatory practices. Such reports may be submitted during hearings before the Bureau of the Budget on appropriation.

The Chairman of the Board shall designate a representative to serve on the Council of Personnel Administration for the purpose of incorporating safeguards against discrimination because of race, creed, color, or national origin in the regular personnel procedures of the departments and agencies of the Federal Government.

The Board may receive and investigate complaints of individuals who allege discrimination because of race, creed, color, or national origin in hiring, transfer, promotion, reinstatement, or dismissal. The Board shall take steps to adjust valid complaints and is authorized to hold hearings and call witnesses in connection with its investigations. Upon a finding of discrimination, the Board shall require that the offending agency take immediate steps to remedy the complaint by hiring, transferring, promoting, or reinstating the complainant involved. If the agency fails to take the proper action, the Board shall within 30 days after its initial request for remedy prepare for the signature of the President an order addressed to the department or agency head requiring corrective action.

Persons willfully violating the intent of this Order shall be dismissed from the Federal Service if charges are substantiated at a hearing before the appropriate board in the United States Civil Services Commission.

Provisions of any other Executive Order inconsistent with the provisions of this Order are hereby superseded.

The hearing by the Civil Service Commission shall be for the purpose of determining whether non-compliance with the director's request was willful.

MS: MP.

1. See 8/20 and 12/1/48, 6/29/54; in appendix, 11/7/47 and 6/8/49.

Mitchell sent this proposal to Walter White. According to a handwritten notation on the bottom of the first page of this text, copies were also sent to George L. P. Weaver, Dr. Frank Horne, and Evelyn Nesbitt Cooper. This text was used at 11/1/47; see also, among others, 5/2/47.

2. In January 1948, Mitchell forwarded to White a second proposed executive order. He stated that it was different from the first draft presented to White "some time ago" but "represented the thinking of a number of people in government and will most likely be what we will get if the president agrees to act." See Mitchell to White, 1/17/48, MP. The text of that order follows:

EXECUTIVE ORDER NO.________

In order to implement the policy of the United States that there shall be no discrimination in employment because of race, creed, color or national origin, as reaffirmed by Executive Order No. 8820 [8802], dated June 25, 1941, as amended by Executive Order No. 8823 of July 18, 1941, by Executive Order No. 9346 of May 27, 1943, and by Executive Order No. 9664 of December 20, 1945, I do hereby declare that it is the duty of all of the departments and agencies of the Federal Government to take positive measures to eliminate discrimination because of race, creed, color or national origin in the hiring, promotion, transfer and dismissal of Federal employees.

Now, therefore, by virtue of the authority vested in me by the Constitution and statutes, it is hereby ordered as follows:

1. The head of each department and agency of the Federal Government shall designate one or more staff members, as may be necessary, whose duties shall be to formulate and promote appropriate policies and programs for the elimination of discrimination because of race, creed, color or national origin in the hiring, promotion, transfer and dismissal of employees within their respective departments or agencies.

2. There is hereby established in the Department of Labor an Office of Fair Employment Practices which shall be administered by a Director to be appointed by the President. The Director shall receive such salary as shall be fixed by the President not exceeding $10,000 per year. Within the limits of funds available for that purpose, the Director shall hire such personnel and make provision for such supplies, facilities and services as may be necessary to carry out this Order. Wherever possible, however, the Director shall use the services, facilities and personnel of the several departments and agencies of the Federal Government, and he may use the voluntary and uncompensated services of persons, expert or competent in work useful to the Office.

3. The Director, together with the heads of the several departments and agencies or their authorized representatives, shall develop appropriate practices and programs to effectuate the provisions of this Order.

4. The Director shall be represented on the Council of Personnel Administration, and shall aid the Council in the establishment of safeguards against discrimination because of race, creed, color or national origin in the regular personnel procedures of the several departments and agencies of the Federal Government.

5. The departments and agencies of the Federal Government shall prepare reports on the progress of programs to eliminate discrimination in employment because of race, creed, color or national origin and shall submit such reports to the Bureau of the Budget during the annual hearings on appropriations.

6. The Director shall receive and investigate complaints of discrimination because of race, creed, color or national origin in the hiring, transfer, promotion, reinstatement or dismissal of Federal employees. The Director is authorized to conduct hearings and call witnesses, to make findings, and to take appropriate steps to secure the adjustment of valid complaints provided, however, that no finding shall be made against any agency, official, or employee thereof except after opportunity has been given that agency, official, or employee to appear and to he heard.

7. Upon making a finding of discrimination, the Director shall give notice thereof to the department or agency concerned and shall undertake to achieve a mutually satisfactory adjustment of the complaint. If the Director fails to achieve such an adjustment, he shall request the department or agency concerned to take specific steps to eliminate the discrimination. Such steps may include the hiring, transfer, promotion, or reinstatement of the complainant involved. If, within 30 days thereafter, the department or agency fails to take the action requested by the Director, the Director shall serve notice of such failure upon the United States Civil Service Commission for hearing before the Commission. Upon receipt of such notice of failure to comply, it shall be the duty of the Civil Service Commission to hold a hearing. At any such hearing before the Civil Service Commission, the findings of the Director shall not be subject to review by the Commission. At the conclusion of the hearing, the Commission shall take such action as in its opinion will effectuate the purposes of this order provided, however, that persons found by the Commission to be willfully violating this order shall be dismissed from the Federal Government.

8. The Director is authorized to attend hearings on appropriations of the several departments and agencies of the Federal Government before the Bureau of the Budget and to make such recommendations to the Bureau as he deems necessary to carry out the provisions of this Order.

9. The Director is authorized to promulgate such rules and regulations as may be necessary to carry out the provisions of this Order.

10. The Director shall be subject to the general supervision and direction of the Secretary of Labor.

11. The provisions of any other pertinent Executive Order inconsistent with this Order are hereby superseded.

Mitchell reported that this second version had been given to presidential adviser Clark Clifford and also had been seen by Oscar Ewing, administrator of the Federal Security Agency. He asked White not to mention it to David Niles because he did not know if Niles was aware of its existence. He also said he had discussed the need for an order with Labor Secretary Schwellenbach but did not ask him if he had seen a copy of "our" proposed order. Mitchell told White he believed "we can get this order through if it gets a real push from you in your meeting with the President." On January 28, 1948, White asked Truman to issue such an order, and, adopting the text of a letter Mitchell drafted, he wrote Truman again on April 7, 1948. See Mitchell's reports of 2/5, 4/30, and 8/31/48; see also Louis Wright's memorandum of 8/20/48 and the enclosed chronology of the NAACP's fight for the executive order, in appendix. For other texts discussing the content of the executive order, see: Howard Jenkins of Howard University to George M. Johnson, 2/10/48; Draft of Labor Department Press Release, 2/17/48; Mitchell to White, 2/17 and 4/5/48, enclosing the draft letter to Truman; Mitchell to Oscar Ewing, 4/9/48; Mitchell to Julius A. Krug, 4/16/48; Mitchell's memorandum to the files, 4/23/48, on his meeting with Krug; Mitchell to Charles S. Brannan, 4/28/48; White to Tom Clark, 4/20/48; and Clark's reply to White, 4/28/48, all in Personal and Outgoing folder, MP.

For the final Executive Order 990, signed by Truman on July 26, 1948, see 13 *Federal Register* 4311, 7/28/48. See also Wright's memorandum of 8/20/48; Mitchell's report of 8/31/48; and Watson, *Lion in the Lobby*, 159–61. On NAACP objections to placing the federal Fair Employment Board within the Civil Service Commission and the reasons it was nevertheless placed there, see Mitchell to Carl Murphy, 2/14/48; Mitchell to Evelyn Nesbitt Cooper, 8/18/48; Mitchell to C. Girard Davidson, assistant secretary of the Interior Department, 8/18/48; Davidson's reply to Mitchell, 8/23/48; and John A. Davis to Mitchell, 9/13/48, all in MP.

NAACP Legislative Program and Action Needed on Bills, March 16, 1948

WASHINGTON BUREAU, NAACP
100 MASSACHUSETTS AVENUE, N.W.
WASHINGTON 1, D.C.

March 16, 1948

NAACP LEGISLATIVE PROGRAM AND ACTION NEEDED ON BILLS IN THE 2ND SESSION

1. FEPC

S-984, known as the National Act Against Discrimination in Employment, introduced in the Senate by Senators Irving M. Ives (R., N.Y.), Leverett Saltonstall (R.,

Mass.), H. Alexander Smith (R., N.J.), Wayne Morse (R., Oreg.), Dennis Chavez (D., N.M.), James E. Murray (D., Mont.) and Francis J. Myers (D., Pa.). Favorably reported to the Senate by the Labor and Public Welfare Committee on February 26, 1948.[1]

Four companion bills have been introduced in the House: HR-2820 by Congresswoman Mary T. Norton (D., N.J.), HR-2824 by Congressman James G. Fulton (R., Pa.), HR-2902 by Congressman William L. Dawson (D., Ill.), and Congresswoman Helen Gahagan Douglas (D., Calif.) HR-2877.[2]

Action: Urge the leaders of the Senate and your own senators to bring the FEPC Bill to the floor for vote. Urge all senators to vote for the bill and for cloture in event of a filibuster.

To obtain public hearings in the House write Congressman Fred A. Hartley (R. N.J.), Chairman, House Committee on Education and Labor.

2. ANTI-LYNCHING

S-1352, introduced by Senators Robert F. Wagner (D., N.Y.) and Wayne Morse (R., Oreg.), provides heavy prison terms and fines for lynch mobsters and/or conspiring state officers. The bill has been referred to the Judiciary Subcommittee composed of:

Senator Homer Ferguson (R., Mich.), Chairman
Senator Chapman Revercomb (R., W. Va.)
Senator James O. Eastland (D., Miss.)

HR-5673, introduced in the House by Congressman Clifford P. Case (R., N.J.), was voted to be reported favorably by the House Judiciary Committee on March 2, 1948.[3]

Action: Write Senators Ferguson and Revercomb to report S. 1352 without amendment.

Urge your Congressman to vote for HR-5673 when it reaches the floor.

3. ANTI-JIM CROW TRAVEL

HR-280, a bill to prohibit segregation in trains, dining cars, buses, railroad and bus stations of passengers in interstate travel on account of their race and color, has been introduced in the House by Congressman A. Clayton Powell, Jr., (D., N.Y).[4]

A subcommittee of the House Foreign and Interstate Commerce Committee was appointed in June to consider this measure. Members are:

Congressman Marion T. Bennett (R., Mo.), Chairman
Congressman Edward J. Elsaesser (R., N.Y)
Congressman John W. Heselton (R., Mass.)
Congressman Robert Crosser (D., Ohio)
Congressman Dwight L. Rogers (D., Fla.)

Action: Urge Congressman Bennett and each member of his subcommittee to schedule full hearings on outlawing Jim Crow in interstate travel.

4. ANTI-POLL TAX

HR-29, the Bender Anti-Poll Tax Bill, passed the House July 21, 1947. It is now up to the Senate to pass HR-29 and thereby abolish the poll tax. This measure is now before the Senate Committee on Rules and Administration subcommittee.[5] Hearings are scheduled for March 22 through March 22 through March 25. Members of the subcommittee are:

Senator William E. Jenner (R., Ind.), Chairman
Senator John W. Bricker (R., Ohio)
Senator Francis J. Myers (D., Penna.)

Action: Urge subcommittee to report HR-29 favorably.
Get a promise from your senators to vote for the bill when it reaches the floor, and for cloture in event of a filibuster.

5. ANTI-FILIBUSTER RESOLUTIONS

The Senate Committee on Rules and Administration rejected resolutions to end filibusters by a majority vote on April 3, 1947. Instead it reported out an emasculated version of S. Res. 25 which would still require a two-third Senate vote to shut-off the filibuster.[6]

Action: Urge your Senator to offer an amendment from the floor to S. Res. 25 to provide for the invoking of cloture by a *simple* majority of the Senators voting.

6. HOUSING

S-866, introduced by Senators Robert A. Taft (R., Ohio), Allen J. Ellender (D., La.), and Robert F. Wagner (D., N.Y.), seeks to provide a comprehensive long range housing program for the construction of a total of one million units annually of privately built sale and rental homes and low rent public housing. It would construct approximately 500,000 units of public housing over a period of four years. Hearings in Senate Banking and Currency Committee completed and bill favorably reported on April 24, 1947.

A companion bill, HR-2523, was introduced in the House by Congressman Jacob K. Javits (R., N.Y.).[7]

Action: Present bill is wholly lacking in safeguards to assure equitable participation by racial minority groups. Every Congressman and Senator should be urged to sponsor and support non-discrimination amendments which have been drafted by the NAACP. Members of the House Committee on Banking and Currency should be particularly urged to support these amendments.

7. FEDERAL AID TO EDUCATION

S-472, introduced by Senators Robert A. Taft (R., Ohio) Elbert D. Thomas (D., Utah), and others, would appropriate $150 million for the fiscal year of 1948 to more nearly equalize opportunities in public elementary and secondary schools throughout the states. It seeks to establish a $ 40.00 a year minimum public school expenditure per child. The Senate Labor and Public Welfare Committee favorably reported S-472 raising minimum expenditures to $50.00 per child. The bill can now be brought to the Senate floor for vote.

In the House, HR-2953 has been introduced by Congressman Edward O. McCowen (R., Ohio). Hearings have been completed but neither the Committee nor the House leadership is considered favorable to federal aid.[8]

Action: Urge all members of the Senate to vote for S-472. Also, write Joseph W. Martin, Speaker of the House, Charles A. Halleck, Majority Leader, and every member of the House Education and Labor Committee to vote for HR-2953

8. EQUAL RIGHTS IN DISTRICT OF COLUMBIA

HR-231 and HR-805, bills to assure all persons regardless of race or color admission to places of public accommodation such as hotels, restaurants, theaters, hospitals, etc., were introduced by Congressmen William L. Dawson (D., Ill) and A. Clayton Powell, Jr. (D., N.Y.), respectively. These bills have been referred to the House District of Columbia subcommittee. Members are:

Congressman Joseph P. O'Hara (R., Minn.), Chairman
Congressman Gregory McMahon (R., N.Y.)
Congressman John J. Allen, Jr. (R., Calif.)
Congressman Oren Harris (D., Ark.)
Congressman Thomas G. Abernethy (D., Miss.)

Action: Urge Congressman O'Hara and each member of his subcommittee to hold hearings on these "first-class citizenship" bills.

9. DISPLACED PERSONS (European Refugees)

HR-2910, the Emergency Temporary Displaced Persons Admission Bill, was introduced by Congressman William G. Stratton (R., Ill.). It provides for the admission of

100,000 displaced persons annually for the next four years. A House Judiciary Subcommittee has completed hearings on this bill but will not act on the bill. Members are:

Congressman Frank Fellows (R., Maine), Chairman
Congressman Ed Gossett (D., Texas)
Congressman Louis E. Graham (R., Pa.)
Congressman Emanuel Celler (D., N.Y.)
Congressman Frank L. Chelf (D., Ky.)

S-2242, introduced by Senator Alexander Wiley (R., Wis.) and reported favorably by Senate Judiciary Committee on March 2 proposed to admit only 50,000 displaced persons a year.[9] It contains needless administrative complications.

Action: Ask each member of the House subcommittee to recommend enactment of HR-2910 in its present form.

Ask your senator to amend S-2242 from the floor so as to make it identical with the House Bill HR-2910.

10. MINIMUM WAGE BILL

S-1404, introduced by Senators Claude Pepper, Wayne Morse, and others, would amend the Fair Labor Standards Act so as to increase the minimum wage from the present 40c per hour to 65c. Said minimum would be automatically raised to 70c in 1949 and 75c in 1950.

A companion bill, HR-3764, has been introduced in the House by Congressman Ray J. Madden (D., Ind.). Hearings on minimum wage bills have been completed but the House Education and Labor subcommittee has not made its report.[10] Members are:

Congressman Samuel K. McConnell, Jr. (R., Pa.) Chairman
Congressman Wint Smith (R., Kan.)
Congressman Charles J. Kirsten (R., Wis.)
Congressman George MacKinnon (R., Minn.)
Congressman Thomas L. Owens (R., Ohio)
Congressman O. C. Fisher (D., Tex.)
Congressman Ray J. Madden (D., Ind.)
Congressman Arthur G. Klein (D., N.Y.)

Action: Urge fast action by Senate Labor and Public Welfare Committee.
Insist that House subcommittee make early favorable report.

11. SOCIAL SECURITY

S-1679, introduced by Senators James E. Murray (D., Mont.) Robert F. Wagner (D. N.Y.), and J. Howard McGrath (D., R.I.) would amend the Social Security Act so as to increase benefits and extend coverage to domestic workers, agricultural workers and other occupations not now protected by Social Security. This bill has been referred to the Senate Committee on Finance, Senator Eugene D. Milliken (R., Colo.), Chairman.

In the House, an identical bill, HR-4303, has been introduced by Congressman John D. Dingell (D., Mich.) and referred to the Ways and Means Committee, headed by Congressman Harold Knutson (R., Minn.).[11]

Action: Urge Senator Milliken and members of the Senate Finance Committee to hold hearings on the Murray-Wagner-McGrath Bill.

Write Congressman Knutson and members of the House Ways and Means Committee to do likewise on HR-4303.

12. *NATIONAL HEALTH INSURANCE BILL*

S-1320, introduced by Senator James E. Murray (D., Mont.) and others, sets up comprehensive health insurance program based on 1 _ per cent payroll deductions.[12] Hearings have not been completed by Senate Labor and Public Welfare subcommittee, who are:

Senator H. Alexander Smith (R., N.J.), Chairman
Senator Joseph H. Ball (R., Minn.)
Senator Forrest C. Donnell (R., Mo.)
Senator James E. Murray (D., Mont.)
Senator Claude Pepper (D., Fla.)

In the House a companion bill, HR-3548, has been introduced by Congressman John D. Dingell (D., Mich.) and referred to the Ways and means Committee.

Action: Urge that S-1320 be reported out. Oppose S-545, the Taft charity-state's rights bill, which would provide medical assistance *only* to persons financially unable to pay.

13. *VIRGIN ISLAND REVENUE*

S-1014, introduced by Senator Hugh Butler (R., Nebr.), would give the Virgin Islands greater financial independence by crediting to the Islands, and allowing them to spend, all taxes collected on articles produced and sent to the United States or consumed in the Islands. The bill passed the Senate July 23, 1947 and was sent to the House.

HR-4979, introduced by Congressman Fred L. Crawford (R., Mich.), is practically identical with S-1014 except that the money can be expanded only for projects approved by the President.[13]

Action: Urge Congressman Harold Knutson (R., Minn.), Chairman of the House Ways and means Committee, and committee members to act promptly and favorably on S-1014.

14. MISSOURI VALLEY AUTHORITY

S-1156, introduced by Senators James E. Murray (D., Mont.) William Langer (R., N.D.), Glen H. Taylor (D., Idaho), and others, would create a Missouri Valley Authority (similar to TVA) to prevent floods, irrigate and reclaim agricultural lands, and provide cheap hydro-electric power for 15,000,000 people living in the valley region.[14]

<u>*Action*</u>: Write Senator Chapman Revercomb (R., W.Va.), Chairman of the Senate Public Works Committee and committee members to hold hearings on this important bill.

NAACP *OPPOSES*

15. UNIVERSAL MILITARY TRAINING

HR-4278, introduced by Congressman Harry L. Towe (R., N.J.), provides that all able-bodied males upon reaching 18 years shall be recruited for 6 months of military training. This bill, which contains no provisions against racial segregation or discrimination, was reported favorably by the House Armed Services Committee on July 26, 1947. It is now before the House Rules Committee.

S-651 and S-652, requiring all males to undergo military training, were introduced by Senator Chan Gurney (R., S.D.). Hearings are scheduled before Senate Armed Services Committee March 16 through April 3, 1948.[15]

The 38th Annual Conference of the NAACP hold June 28, 1947, adopted the following resolution: "We oppose peacetime military conscription."[16]

<u>*Action*</u>: Write your congressman, senators and members of the Senate Armed Services Committee to oppose UMT.

16. SEGREGATED REGIONAL COLLEGES

S.J. Res. 191, introduced by Senator Spessard L. Holland (D., Fla.) on behalf of himself and 27 other southern senators, seeks congressional approval of a compact between 14 southern governors to set up segregated regional colleges. The first school to be taken over is Meharry Medical School in Nashville, Tennessee. Hearings on this resolution were held March 12 and 13, 1948 by a Senate Judiciary subcommittee consisting of Senators Alexander Wiley (R., Wisc.) and J. Howard McGrath (D., R.I.).

H.J. Res. 334, and identical resolution, introduced by Congressman Sam Hobbs (D., Ala.), was reported favorably on March 16 by the House Judiciary Committee without public hearings.[17]

Purpose of these resolutions is to (1) evade decisions of the U.S. Supreme Court in the Gaines[18] and Sipuel cases requiring states to give equal educational opportunity to Negroes _within_ the state and (2) entrench educational discrimination and segregation by congressional approval.

Action: Write all members of the Senate Judiciary Committee and the House of Representatives to vote against the resolution.

17. JIM CROW VETERANS HOSPITAL

S-1414, providing for the establishment of a hospital for Negro veterans in Franklin County, Virginia, the birthplace of Booker T. Washington, was introduced by Senator Chapman Revercomb (R.,W.Va.). A companion bill, HR-3814, has already passed the House.

All veterans should be hospitalized in governmental hospitals without regard to race. The enactment of this measure would extend the pattern of segregation with congressional approval.

Action: All members of the Senate Labor and Public Welfare Committee should be asked to vote against this bill. See, or write your senators to oppose it on the floor.

Leslie S. Perry

(See attached list of committee members.)

COMMITTEES OF THE SENATE

Labor and Public Welfare

Republicans	_Democrats_
Robert A. Taft, of Ohio	Elbert D. Thomas, of Utah
George D. Aiken, of Vermont	James E. Murray of Montana
Joseph H. Ball, of Minnesota	Claude Pepper, of Florida
H. Alexander Smith, of New Jersey	Allen J. Ellender, of Louisiana
Wayne Morse, of Oregon	Lister Hill, of Alabama
Forrest C. Donnell, or Missouri	
William E. Jenner , of Indiana	
Irving M. Ives, of New York	

Rules of Administration

C. Wayland Brooks, of Illinois	Carl Hayden, of Arizona
Kenneth S. Wherry, of Nebraska	Theodore Francis Green, of R.I.
Bourke B. Hickenlooper, of Iowa	Brien McMahon, of Connecticut
William F. Knowland, of California	Francis J. Myers, of Pa.
Henry Cabot Lodge , Jr. of Mass	Spessard L. Holland, of Florida
Williiam E. Jenner, of Indiana	
John W. Briker, of Ohio	
Irving M. Ives, of New York	

Finance

Eugene D. Millikin, of Colorado
Robert A. Taft, of Ohio
Hugh Butler, of Nebraska
Owen Brewster, of Maine
Harlan J. Bushfield, of S.D.
Albert W. Hawkes, of New Jersey
Edward Martin, of Pennsylvania

Water F. George, of Georgia
Alben W. Barkley, of Kentucky
Tom Connally of Tezas
Harry Flood Byrd, of Virginai
Edwin C. Johnson, of Colorado
Schoot W. Lucas, of Illiniois

Public Works

Chapman Revercomb, of W. Va.
John Sherman Cooper, of Kentucky
Harry P. Cain, of Washington
Edward Martin, of Pennsylvania
Arthur V. Watkins, of Utah
John J. Williams, of Delaware
George W. Malone, of Nevada

John H. Overton, of Louisiana
Dennis Chavez of New Mexico
Sheridan Downey, of California
W. Lee O'Daniel, of Texas
John L. McClellan, of Arkansas

Armed Services

Chan Gurney, of South Dakota
Styles Pridges, of New Hamsphire
Edward V. Robertson, of Wyoming
George A. Wilson, of Iowa
Leverett Saltonstall, of Mass.
Wayne Morse, Of Oregon
Raymond E. Baldwin of Connecticut

Milliard E. Tydings , of Maryland
Richard B. Russell of Georgia
Harry Flood Byrd, of Virginia
Lister Hill, of Alabama
Harley M. Kilgore, of W. Va.
Burnet R. Maybank, of S. C

Judiciary

Alexander Wiley, of Wisconsin, Chr.
William Langer, of North Dakota
Homer Ferguson, of Michigan
Chapman Reverocm, of W. Va.
E. H. Moore, of Oklahoma
Forrest C. Donnell, of Missouri
John Sherman Cooper, of Kentucky

Pat McCarran, of Nevada
Harley M. Kilgore, of West Va.
James O. Eastland, of Mississippi
Warren G. Magnuson, of Wash.
J. W. Fulbright, of Arkansas
J. Howard McGrath, of R.I.

COMMITTEES OF THE HOUSE:

Education and Labor

Fred A. Hartley, Jr., of N. J.
Gerald W. Landis, of Indiana
Clare E. Hoffman, of Michigan
Edward O. McCowen, of Ohio
Max Schwabe, of Mssouri

John Lesinski, of Michigan
Graham A. Barden, of N. C.
Augustine B. Kelley, of Pa.
O.C. Fisher of Texas
Adam C. Powell, Jr., of N. Y.

Samuel K. McConnell, of Pa.
Ralph W. Gwinn, of N.Y.
Ellsworth B. Buck, of N.Y.
Walter E. Brehm, of Ohio
Wint Smith, of Kansas
Charles J. Kersten, of Wisconsin
George MacKinnon, of Minnesota
Thomas L. Owens, of Illinois
Carroll D. Kearns, of Pa.
Richard M. Nixon, of California

John S. Wood, of Goergia
Ray J. Madden, of Indiana
Arthur G. Klein, of N.Y.
F. Kennedy, of Mass.
Wingate Lucas, of Texas

Banking and Currency

Jessee P. Wolcott, of Michigan
Ralph A. Gamble, of NY
Frederick C. Smith, of Ohio
John C. Kunkel, of Pa.
Henry O. Talle, of Iowa
Frank L. Sundstrom, of N.J.
Rolla C. McMillen of Illinois
Clarence E. Kilburn, of NY.
Albert M. Cole, of Kansas
Howard H. Buffett, of Nebraska
Merlin Hull, of Wisconsin
Wiliam G. Stratton, of Illinois
Hardie Scott, of Pa.
Parke M. Banta, of Missouri
Charles K. Fletcher, of California
Ellsworth B. Foote, of Conn.

Brent Spence, of Kentucky
Paul Brown, of Georgia
Wright Patman, of Texas
A.S. Mike Monroney, of Oklahoma
John H. Folger, of N.C.
Brooks Hays, of Arkansas
John J. Riley, of S.C.
Albert Rains of Alabama
Donald L. O'Toole, of N.Y.
Franck Buchanan, of Pa.
Hale Boggs, of La.

District of Columbia

Everett M. Dirksen, of Illinois
George J. Bates, of Mass.
Sid Simpson, of Illinois
J. Glenn Beall, of Maryland
Joseph P. O'Hara, of Minn.
Henry O. Talle, of Iowa
A.L. Miller, of Nebraska
James C. Auchincloss, of NJ
John McDowell, of Pa.
John J. Allen, Jr. of California
Gregory McMahon, of New York
Harold F. Youngblood, of Mich.
Robert N. McGarvey, of Pa.
Homer R. Jones, of Washington

John L. McMillan, of S.C.
Oren Harris, of Arkansas
F. Edward Hebert, of La.
Thomas G. Abernathy, of Miss.
Howard W. Smith, of Virginia
Arthur G. Klein, of N.Y.
Olin E. Teague, of Texas
Charles B. Deane, of N.C.
John F. Kennedy, of Mass.

Ways and Means

Harold Knutson, of Minnesota
Daniel A. Reed, of N.Y.
Roy O. Woodruff, of Michigan
Thomas A. Jenkins, of Ohio
Bertrand W. Gearhart, of Calif.
Richard M. Simpson, of Pa.
Robert W. Kean, of N.J.
Charles L. Gifford, of Mass.
Carl T. Curtis, of Nebraska
Noah M. Mason, of Illinois
Thomas E. Martin, of Iowa
Robert E. Grant, of Indiana
Hal Holmes, of Washington
Hubert S. Ellis, of W. Va.
John W. Byrnes, of Wisconsin

Robert L. Doughton, of N.C.
Jere Cooper, of Tenn.
John D. Dingell, of Michigan
Milton H. West, of Texas
Wilbur D. Mills, of Arkansas
Noble J. Gregory. of Kentucky
A. Sidney Camp, of Georgia
Walter A. Lynch, of New York
Aime J. Forand, of R.I.
Herman P. Eberharter, of Pa.

MS: NAACP II: A-203, DLC.
This is a Leslie Perry report.

1. This favorable action apparently resulted from continued NAACP lobbying over the recess. During the last days of the congressional session in 1947, the NAACP had sent out a "number of communications" urging the Senate Labor and Welfare Committee to report favorably on S. 984, but that did not happen. Instead, the committee urged "further study." Report of the Secretary for September, 1947, EC.

2. Even as southern Democrats were talking "revolt," three civil rights measures were nearing floor action: the antilynching, FEPC, and anti–poll tax bills. (*Congressional Quarterly Log for Editors* provides detailed summaries.)

The Fair Employment Practices Commission bill was approved by the Senate Labor and Public Welfare Committee. It provided (1) that discrimination by employers, unions, and the government was unlawful; (2) that a seven-man commission would be established to investigate complaints of unfair hiring practices; and (3) that the commission could ask courts to enforce decisions. "Status of Civil Rights Bills" (March 5, 1948), in *Congressional Quarterly Log for Editors*, 139.

3. The antilynching measure was the second civil rights item being considered by Congress. Ibid.

4. H.R. 2280 was the Powell anti–Jim Crow travel bill. A year earlier, the NAACP had urged Rep. Charles A. Wolverton (R-N.J.), chair of the House Interstate and Foreign Commerce Committee, to hold hearings on the measure. WB, 2/28/47, NAACP II: A-655, DLC. See also Alexander, "Recent Trends in the Law of Racial Segregation on Public Carriers."

5. An anti–poll tax bill was the third civil rights measure being considered by Congress. On April 30, 1948, the Senate Committee on Rules and Administration favorably reported out the bill. The House passed a similar measure in 1947. "Status of Civil Rights Bills" (March 5, 1948), *Congressional Quarterly Log for Editors*, 139. See also Leslie Perry, 7/8/47, *Hearings*, 125–33; 3/24/48, *Hearings*, 216–19; and the headnote on the Struggle to Abolish the Poll Tax.

6. Perry, 2/4/47, *Hearings*, 55–59.

7. The NAACP Annual Meeting on January 6, 1947, and the subsequent meeting of the board provided what Walter White called a mandate by approving the following resolution, which had been adopted at the 1946 NAACP Annual Conference in Cincinnati: "We endorse a bill for government assistance to a low-cost housing program similar to the Wagner-Ellender-Taft bill introduced in the 79th Congress, with proper safeguards for the rights of minorities."

White said the NAACP was "in substantial agreement with the public housing provisions" of the bill, except that the association believed the number of units was inadequate and should be increased to a minimum of 250,000 annually. Furthermore, the urban redevelopment section of the bill (Title 8) did not contain any safeguards against the misuse of governmental power to impose segregated patterns and in no way guaranteed participation of minorities in the benefits of the Urban Redevelopment Plan. Consequently, the NAACP proposed adding the following amendments:

(3) preference in the selection of tenants for dwelling units built in the project area be given to families displaced therefrom because of clearance and redevelopment activity, who desire to live in such dwelling units and who will be able to pay rents or prices charged other families for comparable dwelling units built as part of the same redevelopment.

(4) in disposing of land assembled with Federal aids provided herein, the redevelopment agency shall insert in all deeds, contracts, and leases a covenant running with the land prohibiting purchasers and lessees of that land from inserting covenants or conditions in deeds, contracts, and leases to all grantees, assignees or other subsequent holders to restrict its ownership, use, or occupancy by any racial, religious, or nationality group. (Memorandum from White to executive staff, 6/25/47, NAACP II: A-33, DLC)

See also Perry, 2/7/47, *Hearings*, 393–97.

8. Perry, 4/28/47, *Hearings*, 341–45; 5/14/47, *Hearings*, 394–405. See also related note at 11/30/46 and 4/3, 5/8, and 11/30/50.

Federal aid to education was included in the 1944 Democratic platform and subsequently recommended by President Truman. The 1948 Republican platform would merely favor "equality of educational opportunity for all and the promotion of education and educational facilities." *Congressional Quarterly Log for Editors* (July 6, 1948), 461.

9. "DP's: Are They Needed?" (March 12, 1948), *Congressional Quarterly Log for Editors*, 153. See also 4/3/50; *Congress and the Nation*, 219–21.

10. Proposals to increase the minimum wage eventually to 75¢ incited a barrage of public reaction that was second in intensity only to the debate over repeal of the Taft-Hartley law, according to the House Education and Labor Committee staff. *Congressional Quarterly Log for Editors* (April 1, 1949), 400.

11. For background on National Health Insurance, including counterproposals, see *Congressional Quarterly Log for Editors* (April 22, 1949), 509.

12. The only possible civil rights implication involved in the wrangling over the proposal to create a Missouri Valley authority for flood control was its likelihood of providing low-income jobs, as similar projects had done. For the background of this struggle, see *Congress and the Nation*, 807.

13. *Congressional Quarterly Log for Editors* (March 12, 1948), 152, and April 2, 1948), 194.

These bills were the next steps in implementing the findings and recommendations of Truman's Advisory Commission on compulsory military training. For the related story and findings, see *New York Times*, 6/2/47, 1, 5. A year later, on June 19, 1948, Congress passed a compromise draft bill after fierce battles in both the House and Senate.

On January 24, 1947, as debate over national security intensified, Jesse O. Dedmond Jr., NAACP secretary of veterans affairs, and William Hastie, also representing the NAACP, testified before the President's Committee on Universal Military Training that the association would be opposed to any UMT legislation unless it contained provisions for abolishing discrimination and segregation in the armed services. Report of the Secretary of Veterans Affairs, 2/47, EC. See also Hastie, 6/6/45, *Hearings*, 111–17; Dedmond, 3/30/48, *Hearings*, 662–68.

Given the rancorous debate that accompanied passage of the draft bill, there was absolutely no chance that including civil rights provisions in the law would be considered. *New York Times*, 6/20/48, 1, 34. See also *Congress and the Nation*, 250–52. But the efforts to establish a peacetime draft provided a new opportunity for other blacks similarly to protest segregation in the armed services. See A. Philip Randolph, 3/31/48, *Hearings*, 685–94; "Fighting the Jim Crow Army," editorial, *Crisis* 55 (May 1948): 136; "The Negroes and the Draft," editorial reprint from *PM* (April 11, 1948), in *Crisis* 55 (May 1948): 140, 154–55; headnote on Ending Segregation in the Armed Services; introduction.

14. While opposing UMT, the board, as it had done in 1940, urged the appointment of African Americans on draft boards. Minutes, 10/11/48, EC.

15. The resolutions sought congressional approval for a compact among fifteen southern states, drawn up in February, to provide education through regional professional and graduate schools in response to the NAACP's desegregation program that was progressing in the federal courts. Perry reported to the board that the Senate bill had twenty-nine sponsors, and a similar ratio, or one-quarter of the House, had sponsored H.J. Res. 334. Perry warned that if Congress passed the measures, the only recourse for defeating the new law would be a challenge before the Supreme Court. But, he said, the court could be influenced by the action in Congress. For a second time, the board therefore voted to

vigorously oppose the regional college plan. Minutes, 3/8/48, EC. It previously had expressed similar opposition at its meeting in February. Minutes, 2/9/48, 12/13/48, EC.

On May 13, 1948, the Senate voted to recommit the resolution ratifying the regional college plan. Walter White reported that the southerners had expected a victory in the Senate similar to the overwhelming vote the measure had received in the House on May 4, 1948. But the NAACP rallied the support of several national organizations, whose representatives testified against approval at hearings before a subcommittee of the Senate Committee on Judiciary. Sen. Wayne Morse, White said, had threatened to propose an amendment forbidding the establishment of separate institutions for white and black students and further to amend the resolution by adding civil rights measures, such as the anti–poll tax, antilynching, and fair employment bills. Report of the Secretary for June, 1948, EC. See also Report of the Washington Bureau, 4/30, 5/31/48, NAACP II: A-580, DLC.

Southern governors, nevertheless, continued to press for adoption of the plan, which the NAACP continued to oppose. Mitchell, however, was especially upset with Gov. William Preston Lane of Maryland. He told him that he was "angered and ashamed" that he had "been so active in identifying us with the most backward areas of the country by [his] activity in the Conference of Southern Governors." He told Lane that he knew the regional education plan was "Ku Kluxery" and the "brain child of an arrogant, stupid group of troublemakers" who were "attempting to circumvent Supreme Court decisions." Minutes, 12/12/48, 1/3/49; Mitchell's letter to Lane, 12/15/48, NAACP II: A-526, DLC; *New York Times*, 1/1/49, 12.

16. *Gaines*, 305 U.S. 337.

17. *Sipuel*, 332 U.S. 631.

18. A year earlier, the VA had announced that contracts had been let for the construction of a two-hundred-bed all-black hospital in Mound Bayou, Mississippi. The NAACP opposed that effort as well, fearing that if it were allowed to succeed, it would follow the World War I precedent, when an all-black hospital was built at Tuskegee, Alabama. Report of the Veterans Secretary, in Report of the Secretary for April, 1947, EC.

On February 19, 1948, White wrote to the members of the Senate Committee on Labor and Public Welfare, urging them to vote for an unfavorable committee report on S. 1414 and H.R. 3814, which sought to provide for the construction of a veterans' hospital for African American veterans at the birthplace of Booker T. Washington in Franklin County, Virginia. The NAACP said its opposition reflected the sentiments of the overwhelming majority of African Americans and "the most enlightened white persons." Report of the Secretary to the Board for February, 1948, EC. See also 10/31/47.

Although this proposal was defeated then, it subsequently resurfaced when, in 1951, Representative Rankin of Mississippi proposed another bill for the Jim Crow hospital. See, in appendix, 5/29/51.

Statement to the Civil Service Commission March 24, 1948

[STATEMENT TO THE CIVIL SERVICE COMMISSION]

March 24, 1948

Mr. Chairman and Members of the Commission, my name is Clarence Mitchell. I am Labor Secretary of the National Association for the Advancement of Colored People. Accompanying me is Mr. William C. Jason, Jr., Welfare Director of the National Alliance of Postal Employees. We represent seventeen colored persons who charge that they were denied employment as clerks in the New Orleans Post Office solely because of their race. The complaints were referred to us by local officers of our respective organizations in New Orleans.[1]

Pursuant to the request filed in a letter of November 13, 1947, we appear on appeal from a decision of the Board of Appeals and Review which held that there was no discrimination based on race in the failure of the Postmaster in New Orleans, Louisiana, to appoint these colored eligibles to the positions of regular substitute clerks.

Both Mr. Jason and I have recently been in the city of New Orleans to make a first hand review of the matters we now place before the Commission. There are six important points which we wish to develop in this presentation.

1. In these cases, the Board of Appeals and Review states that each of the eligibles was given three considerations, and, therefore, the Civil Service Rule on this was not violated. The Board further states that since this rule was not violated there was no evidence of discrimination. We contend that no information has been produced to show that the eligibles were given three separate considerations, and, even if they were, this does not release the Commission from providing a remedy for the violation of its rules which also provide that there shall be no discrimination because of race in the selection of eligibles.

2. The appointment and employment patterns in the New Orleans Post Office show discriminatory policies which result in the concentration of colored persons on certain jobs and white persons on other jobs. These patterns reflect a general policy of discrimination against colored persons which prevails in all of the Federal agencies in the city. Failure to halt them in the post office will strengthen such undemocratic practices in other agencies.

3. We contend that because these eligibles are veterans they were entitled to a written explanation of why they were not selected when the postmaster appointed nonveterans who were below them on the list. It is stated by the Board of Appeals and Review that since these men had received three considerations, the postmaster could

then pass over them to select a non-veteran and not be required to provide a reason for doing so. However, we charge that the failure to require that the postmaster give a written explanation of why he passed over these veterans for non-veterans defeats the intent of Congress as expressed in the Veteran's Preference Act.

4. The postmaster has not furnished any objective standards by which eligibles were judged before they were selected for appointment. Because of the elimination of persons who had qualified by written regular Civil Service examination, the eligible roster was exhausted in the latter part of 1947 and the postmaster, thereafter, appointed persons to serve on a temporary basis who had not taken any kind of examination.

5. In addition to those eligibles who qualified for appointment by examination but had no work experience in the post office, there were five war service indefinite employees who qualified for appointment on the examination. Three of these men are veterans. One was in the Merchant Marine during the war. The remaining man was in civilian status during the war. These eligibles were denied appointment by the postmaster on the ground that they had accumulated various demerits during their period of service.

We wish to show that white persons with a great number of demerits were appointed. In addition, we wish to offer positive evidence that the work records of the colored men show that they were desirable employees.

6. Because of the extensive pattern of discrimination which prevents the upgrading of colored persons who are already employed in the Post Office in New Orleans, we wish to submit information on the failure to promote both clerks and carriers in this post office because of their race.

I shall present a statement covering the first three points and Mr. Jason's statement[2] will cover the last three.

STATEMENT OF CLARENCE MITCHELL COVERING POINTS 1 THROUGH 3.

We appeared before the Civil Service Commission's Board of Appeals and Review on August 26, 1947. A copy of the summary of the complaints presented at that time in again submitted for the Commission's information. It contains the names of the complainants and a brief description of the charges they present.

Fifteen of these complainants are veterans of World War II. One of them, Irvin V. McKendall, 1023 North Liberty Street, New Orleans, had an average of 100.2. Most of the others were in the high 90 and 80 brackets.

The complainants allege that although they received high averages in the Civil Service examination, and, in some cases, were entitled to ten point preference, they were denied employment solely because of their race.

They also charge that the postmaster appointed white eligibles with lower grades who were not veterans. They cite as examples the appointment of W. J. Collins and Charles Richeaux, who are white and not veterans.

Point No. 1

Although we did not receive a written analysis of our charges presented to the Board of Appeals and Review, we did receive a letter which states that, because the Board felt that each eligible had received three considerations, there was no indication that there had been discrimination because of race.

Under its own regulations and the requirements of Executive Order 9346, the Commission must look beyond the questions of whether a single rule was violated. When all aspects of these cases are considered, racial discrimination is clear.

It is clear, of course, that it is entirely possible for an appointing officer to refrain from violating this rule and at the same time discriminate against eligibles because of their race. However, in this case there is no information before us to show that the eligibles were given three separate considerations.

The complete roster of eligibles was in the custody of a Mr. William C. Dering, Sr., who is an employee in the Post Office at New Orleans and also a member of the Board of Examiners of the Civil Service Commission in the Tenth Region. Thus, at all times the entire roster was in the hands of an employee of the Post Office Department.

Mr. Dering, in his capacity as a representative of the Civil Service Commission, furnished to the postmaster certificates of eligibles when the latter wished to make appointment. Under this system, it is entirely possible that the eligibles might receive their three considerations in one day and, thereafter, not be considered again.

We feel that, because the number of times that an eligible is considered has such an important bearing upon whether or not he is appointed, there should be some documentary evidence that a person entitled to three considerations actually did receive them.

Since this evidence does not exist in the New Orleans cases, we request that the defense of the postmaster that the eligibles were considered three times be disregarded by the Commission.

Point No. 2

The pattern of discrimination in the New Orleans Post Office was directed to the attention of the President's Committee on Fair Employment Practices in 1941. At that time, there were colored eligibles who, like the present complainants, had high averages on the roster for clerks. They were consistently passed over while approximately 175 white persons, many of whom had averages below the colored eligibles, were appointed. Eight of these colored eligibles in the 1941 group accepted jobs as laborers in the post office and another was appointed to the railway mail service. Thus, it was demonstrated that their character and physical conditions were such that they were eligible for employment in the postal service. Their grades ranged from 88.60 to 96.80. I am submitting these with their names for the Commission's information.

Because of the efforts of the Fair Employment Practice Committee and the manpower shortage, the New Orleans Post Office hired some colored clerks during the emergency, but, of course, they were war service appointees only.

The period during which the present complainants were discriminated against is from September 27, 1946 to March 24, 1947. During that time, there were five certificates submitted to the postmaster. From these certificates, 199 persons were appointed as regular substitute clerks. Of those appointed, 43 or 21.6% were colored and 156 or 78.4% were white. There were 44 persons not selected. Of these, 8 or 18.8% were white and 36 or 81.82% were colored. Of the total number of persons appointed, 28 were WSI employees. Of these, 21 were white and 7 were colored. Of 6 WSI's passed over, 4 were colored and 2 were white.

An illustration of how this system operated is furnished by the certificate of October 18, 1946. Of 5 persons not selected, 3 were colored. These three were Irvin McKendall, who served more than three years in the army and had an average of 100.2; Alvin J. Lopez, Jr., who served nearly four years in the army and had an average of 97.8; and Paul W. Saizan, a veteran with a ten point preference and an average of 81.6. White persons with averages as low as 70.6 were appointed from this certificate.

The postmaster selected 24 persons from the certificate of November 22. Of 8 persons not selected, 5 were colored. On the following certificate one of the white eligibles passed over on the November certificate was selected. Thus, it was actually 5 out of 7 persons rejected who were colored.

I wish to mention specifically the complaint of Mr. Henry R. Greene, a veteran with a ten point preference. Mr. Greene worked as a temporary employee in the post office, but his name was dropped from the eligible roster allegedly because of high blood pressure which was a service-connected disability. The Veterans Administration failed to find that he was unable to do the work required at the post office and his name was restored to the eligible roster. Thereafter, he continued to work as a temporary employee while white non-veterans below him on the register were appointed as regular employees.

The pattern of employment in the New Orleans Post Office tends to concentrate the colored employees in the carrier force and the white employees in the clerical force. Thus, there are 283 colored carriers and 66 white carriers. On the regular clerks roll, there are 451 white employees and 74 colored employees. It appears that this system not only deprives colored persons of employment as clerks, but also deprive white persons of employment as carriers. Colored persons also outnumber whites as mail handlers and custodial workers.

In the present cases, although the colored eligibles were denied appointment as clerks, some of them were offered an opportunity to be considered as temporary substitute carriers and others are now employed as mail handlers in the post office.

We know that a thorough investigation by the Civil Service Commission would reveal that this pattern of limiting the number of colored persons to certain jobs is typical of the policies followed by the seventy-six government agencies in the City of New Orleans. These agencies of the Federal Government, which employ some 9,000 persons, used colored persons in the least desirable jobs.

An illustration of the predicament into which a qualified colored person falls is furnished by instances affecting two colored stenographers who were eligible for jobs as clerk-typists. One of these women was a former employee of the War Department. At various times, they were first and second on the list of eligibles. One was certified for employment 16 times and the other 21 times. Each time the appointing officer rejected them. The agencies responsible for rejection included: the Naval Air Station, the Social Security Administration, the Railroad Retirement Board, the United States Public Health Service, the United States Customs House, the Veterans Administration, the Public Buildings Administration, and the Regional Office of the Civil Service Commission itself.

Failure of the Civil Service Commission to take corrective action on the complaints we have submitted will lend encouragement to the other agencies in New Orleans which carry on a shameful program of discrimination.

Point No. 3

The Veteran's Preference Act was passed for the purpose of providing protection to the veterans against appointing officers who would seek to give consideration to non-veterans in spite of preference provided on Civil Service examinations.

In the circumstances of this case, where the eligible roster was in the hands of an employee of the Post Office, the Civil Service Commission should require as a matter of simple justice that, when persons who are apparently the equals or superiors of non-veterans are passed over, the appointing officer should furnish a written reason for his act.

Here, the Commission's representatives in New Orleans hold that, because the postmaster considered the complainants three times, and, thereafter, appointed non-veterans, there is no requirement that a written explanation be given for passing over the veterans. As has been said previously, there is nothing to prove that the eligibles were considered three times. However, it was certainly not the intent of Congress to permit circumvention of the law by the technical device of giving applicants three considerations, and, thereafter, appointing non-veterans.

In addition, an investigation of the records in New Orleans will show that white persons who were given three consideration and presumably dropped into the status of the colored complainants were later appointed by the postmaster upon a fourth consideration.

If the postmaster had some objective standards by which he measured all eligibles, he should be willing to give them voluntarily in a case of this kind. If he does not have such standards, his method of selection is capricious and calls for a remedy. This remedy the Civil Service Commission has the power to provide. We, thereafter, ask that in these cases the Commission order the employment of the eligibles who were passed over, especially since following the exhaustion of the roster in the latter part of 1947, the postmaster appointed persons to serve on a temporary basis who had not taken any kind of an examination.

MS: MP.
Minor handwritten corrections to this text have been silently incorporated as directed.

1. On these cases, see also 1/1/47 and, in appendix, Mitchell's summary of complaints against the New Orleans Post Office, 5/10/47, his article, 3/48, Louis Wright's memorandum and the enclosed chronology on the NAACP fight against discrimination in the federal service, 8/20/48, and his statement, 6/28/49.

2. Jason's statement has not been printed.

"Demerits on Being Colored," by Clarence Mitchell, Labor Secretary, March 1948

"DEMERITS FOR BEING COLORED" BY CLARENCE MITCHELL, LABOR SECRETARY NAACP, WASHINGTON, D.C. OFFICE

[March 1948][1]

A Washington columnist recently quoted the Postmaster General as saying, "Any postal worker with interest, loyalty, initiative, and application can aspire to the highest position in our great service." Unfortunately, to this must be added the words "provided he is white."

The Post Office is one of the largest businesses in the country. It can and does set many important employment policies in communities throughout the land for private industry and other government agencies.

One can safely say that the best incentive any institution of this size and influence can offer to its thousands of employees is recognition of merit and efficiency. At present, thert [there] is some grumbling among white employees about failure to recognize and reward ability. I am not aware of the truth or falsity of such complaints in general, but I am acutely aware of the accuracy of the numerous complaints on this score which are registered by colored employees.

During my service with the Fair Employment Practice Committee, I had many meetings with various postal officials on the subject of discrimination in the Post Office Department. On one occasion when I met with Frank C. Walker, who was then the Postmaster General, he showed considerable interest in finding solutions to a great many complaints we had received from Texas, California, Louisiana, and Pennsylvania. A high official of the Department assured the Postmaster that he would make every effort to obtain correction of the complaints and to cooperate fully with the FEPC. We then went into a lengthy meeting with the hierarchy of the postal family.

This meeting could be summed up by saying those present spent most of the time trying to show that there was not discrimination in the Post Office Department, and, even if there was a little, it was "none of the business of outside groups." It seemed clear that the "outside groups" included the FEPC, although it was a Federal agency authorized by President Roosevelt to investigate complaints and "take corrective steps."

This example illustrates the stalemate we face in the Post Office Department. It is the total unwillingness to admit that a postmaster or any other appointing officer may have had the race of applicants in mind when he denied transfers, promotions, or appointments.

The artistry of deception is obvious when one reads a letter from the Department on this subject. It is willing to be tripped up on technicalities and seems to have respect for a foxy approach to settlements. However, it is unwilling to have above board discussions which would result in broad scale corrections of discriminatory policies.

We sincerely believe that such discussions with even a little planning would prevent many of the complaints which now arise and also would avoid the useless waste of time and paper in correspondence as is now the case. In addition, outside organizations would have a greater respect for the Department's decisions than they now have.

As the matters now stand, even when there may be just cause for Post Office action involving a complainant, the explanations of the Department sound hollow and unconvincing against the background of experience.

Discrimination in employment is not always clearly defined. The results are obvious but the methods of achieving them are usually devious. Thus, it was possible for the postal authorities in Los Angeles to deny discrimination for years until a forthright and fair-minded postmaster showed that, although [s]ome colored employees had been upgraded in a token fashion, actually the majority of higher jobs were closed to most of these employees because of their race.[2]

Currently, we are working to settle complaints of veterans and others in New Orleans who have been denied jobs as clerks. These men have been the victims of what appears to be an a[r]bitrary quota system established by the postmaster.

Those who served as war service appointees were turned down after they qualified by examination because they had demerits, although white eligibles with a greater number of demerits who were below them on the register were appointed. The colored eligibles who were not war service appointees were passed over without reason. Under the Veterans Preference Act, those who were ex-service men were entitled to a written explanation of why they were passed over in favor of persons who were not veterans. At this point, the Department protected itself by contending that the eligibles had been considered three times, and, therefore, it was not necessary to consider them any further. Also, it was stated that since the three considerations in effect dropped them from the list, the law no longer applied.

With William Jason, Welfare Director of the National Alliance of Postal Employees, the NAACP represented these men at a hearing before the Civil Service Board of Appeals and Review in Washington on August 26, 1947. We asked that the Post Office Department send a representative to this hearing, but this was not done.

Regrettably, the Board upheld the postmaster in this matter. A Commission representative also went further to contend that because a certain percentage of colored people had been appointed there was no evidence of discrimination.

The present New Orl[e]ans practices are not new in that city. In 1941, there was a similar complaint alleging that for the twelve preceding years no colored persons had been hired as clerks in that post office. Eight of the colored eligibles in the 1941 group accepted jobs as laborers in the post office and another was appointed to the railway mail service. Thus it was demonstrated that their character and physical fitness made them eligible for appointment. All of them had made high averages on the examination so their mental ability could not be challenged.

It was only great need for manpower during the war and the persistent efforts of local persons backed by the FEPC which caused the postmaster to hire any colored persons as clerks. Those who were employed were given war service appointments only. It is now apparent that the post office wishes to revert to its old practices in New Orleans and hold down the number of colored individuals appointed as clerks.

The New Orleans cases are among some of the most recent complaints, but they are by no means unique. The story is the same in other southern cities and is much worse in Knoxville and Memphis where colored clerks are not appointed at all.

In Memphis, the postmaster was quoted by one of the papers recently as saying that there had been no colored applicants for jobs as clerks, and, in any event, "it is not the custom to appoint them." At the same time, there were colored clerks working in Chicago who had left Memphis because they could not get jobs there.

The NAACP has fought discrimination in the postal service for a number of years. We feel that this problem could not exist if at the top there were people determined to do their duty and see that all persons have an equal opportunity for employment. Therefore, after repeated failures to obtain a remedy through Jesse M. Donaldson, who was then the First Assistant Postmaster General, we made an appearance at a hearing on his confirmation as Postmaster General before the Senate Civil Service Committee.

At this hearing, we asked that an investigation be made of the numerous practices which are so clearly discriminatory. We felt that the timing was proper because we consider the willingness to see that the principles of fair play are carried out in [is] a number one requisite of any one aspiring to the high office of Postmaster General.

It is pertinent here to quote a portion of the Association's testimony which was as follows: "For the record we wish to affirm our belief in the importance of rewarding qualified employees with promotions based on merit. There would be infinite improvement in all government services if every employee had the assurance that had work and devotion to duty would ultimately result in advancement. However, it is because this principle was too frequently ignored during Mr. Donaldson's administration as First Assistant Postmaster General that we now make an appearance."

The Senate Committee approved Mr. Donaldson's nomination, but it also authorized an investigation of the charges we made during the hearing. Mr. Donaldson himself, after denying knowledge of the complaints, pledged full cooperation in working against discrimination.

The investigation of the Post Office Department is now in progress and it is hoped that the airing of these wrongs will result in substantial correction. It must be kept in mind that such correction is possible only if we have the full cooperation of the Postmaster General and the top assistants in the Post Office Department. The need for legislative remedies may also be shown.

In addition to our appeal to the Congress, we have consistently urged the President to set up some kind of machinery to eliminate discrimination in government employment generally.

Walter White, Secretary of the Association, made this recommendation to President Truman and also urged the Civil Rights Committee to back up his recommendations. The Committee in its famous report did make this proposal and the NAACP has been taking follow up action which has resulted in a commitment in the President's message on Civil Rights that an executive order would be issued.

At the time of this writing, the order has not been issued but we have urged that it be a strong statement which will enable those who administer it to correct discriminatory hiring practices even without specific complaints.

The strength of the fight against discrimination, of course, will depend upon the strength of the organizations behind it. This means that there must be increased membership in the Alliance.

It also means that the present close working relationship which exists between the Alliance and the NAACP must continue and expand.

It will be valuable also to keep the ranks of the Alliance open to all regardless of race or creed. This will show that our fight for democracy is not selfish but rather is a struggle against wrong and injustice in the broadest sense.

In spite of the recent opening of a post office at the birthplace of Booker T. Washington and the issuance of a George Washington Carver stamp, color of skin is a demerit for thousands of postal employees. However, we do not propose that it can be remedied by giving any special advantages or merits to those who are colored. We ask only that color be of no importance in appointments, discipline, or promotions.

MS: NAACP II: A-526, DLC.

1. On March 1, 1948, Mitchell reported that his article would appear in the March issue of the *Alliance* magazine. He sent this copy in a note to Walter White of 4/5/48. See also, in appendix, 5/10 and 3/24/48.

2. See the section on Post Office Department in the headnote on Relationships with Federal Agencies in vol. I and, in vol. II, the numerous reports involving Joseph F. Gartland, chief of the Operations Board of the Post Office Department.

Report of Administrator's Committee on Negro Employment, Promotion, and Transfer in Bureau of Old-Age and Survivors Insurance in Baltimore, June 18, 1948

REPORT OF ADMINISTRATOR'S COMMITTEE ON NEGRO EMPLOYMENT, PROMOTION, AND TRANSFER IN BUREAU OF OLD-AGE AND SURVIVORS INSURANCE IN BALTIMORE

[June 18, 1948]

The Administrator of the Federal Security Agency [Oscar Ewing] late in April 1948 appointed a special committee to inquire into problems of Negro employment, promotion, and transfer in the Bureau of Old-Age and Survivors Insurance in Baltimore. This Committee was established following the receipt of protests against alleged discriminatory practices in that Bureau.[1]

The Committee assembled its information from material supplied by Management and by the employee union (Local 17, United Public Workers of America); from conferences with the Bureau Director, the Personnel Officer, the Accounting Operations Division Chief, Section Chiefs, and other officials; from meetings with union representatives; and from interviews with about 30 employees who responded to the Committee's invitation to discuss the Bureau's placement and promotion policies. The Committee also made first-hand observations of the Bureau's operations in the Candler and Paca-Pratt Buildings.

The Committee gave consideration to the following conditions:

1. The absence of Negro workers in the Guard Force.
2. The absence of Negro workers in the personnel office.
3. The effect of having segregated units.
4. The absence of Negroes in supervisory positions outside the segregated units.

The Committee undertook its assignment with the objective of finding the facts regarding employment and promotional opportunities in the Bureau and approached its job without attempting to become concerned with the motives of Management, union, or individual employees affecting the present situation.

I. BACKGROUND

Attention is centered in this report on the departmental offices of the Bureau of Old-Age and Survivors Insurance of the Federal Security Agency, located in Baltimore, Maryland. The outstandingly successful operation of this Bureau in the handling of 91,000,000 individual insurance accounts for wage-earners covered by old-age and survivors insurance has, during the twelve years of its existence, received international recognition. Its success in operation is of particular significance in view of the fact that it is one of the largest employers in the Federal Government of low paid clerical help.

The Bureau's largest single unit is the Division of Accounting Operations, with about 4,700 employees who work in the Candler and Paca-Pratt Buildings. Another 500 or so employees, in the several smaller divisions of the Bureau, are located principally in the Equitable Building. Out of a little over 5,200 employees, over 800 are Negroes, 182 of whom are located in 13 separate units in which there are only Negro employees. The other 629 colored employees are distributed throughout the Division of Accounting Operations (with a few in other divisions) without segregation. Nine of the Equitable Building's 500 employees are colored. The percentage of Negro employees exceeds 15%.

The Committee recognized that its concern was with the employment practices of a Federal agency, an agency which is subject to Civil Service rules that call for strict adherence to the merit principle as well as Federal Security Agency policy which states that: "There shall be no discrimination in favor of or against an employee of the Agency because of political or other affiliation (except as may be required by law) or because of race, sex, color, religion, or creed."

The Bureau states that, when the Division of Accounting Operations was established in Baltimore, it was necessary to make a determined effort not only to provide common washroom and eating facilities for both races, but even to employ Negroes at all. It indicated also that considerable opposition was encountered from building owners with respect to these points which was successfully overcome; however, as a result of the Bureau's handling of those situations, its operations have proceeded without serious incident and are continuing successfully. The union has also said that it has vigorously supported common facilities.

In the Bureau in Baltimore very few Negroes have attained intermediate level jobs and none are employed at the higher grades. All but a few of the colored employees are concentrated in grades CAF-1 (entrance salary $1,756) through CAF-4 (entrance salary $2,394). Those who are supervisors are on the lowest level of supervision. Under the present arrangement there are thirteen colored group leaders out of approximately 200 persons who perform this type of work. While white persons may be promoted from group leader to higher supervisory positions, colored persons cannot move any higher in the supervisory line under the present system. In addition, colored persons are trained as group leaders to fill vacancies in the colored group only. This means that there is in effect a quota system on the selection of colored supervisors. Training is not given to colored persons in excess of the number of supervisors required for such units.

There has been an increase over the years in the number of segregated units. The position of Management has been that this was necessary in order to provide supervisory job opportunities to colored workers, because it felt that the employment of colored supervisors over mixed groups was not feasible. There are, however, 52 colored employees in non-supervisory positions above the CAF-2 level (all but one are CAF-3 and CAF-4).

Management recognizes that Negro employment and promotion opportunities have been limited in the Bureau. However, it feels that better conditions and opportunities for "white collar" colored employees prevail there than in practically any other place of employment in Baltimore. Its hesitation at this time to take the step of permitting colored supervisors to supervise both races stems from a fear of adverse effects on its operations which are highly interdependent and on the Bureau's total employment situation a situation already made difficult by inadequate buildings in an undesirable section of the city, by the need for a night shift, by low pay, and by the already high turnover among lower grade employees. On the other hand, the union states that in 1942 a plan to double the number of exclusively colored units was thwarted because of the union's protects. It is also stated by the union that there has been a considerable "loss of superior Negroes who could not bear the frustrations of segregation and the denial of fair chances for promotion."

II. THE COMMITTEE'S OBSERVATION

The Federal Government is legally obligated to conform to merit principles and is expected to lead other employers in the matter of equality of opportunity. The Committee therefore considers it desirable to remove any practices in a Government agency which tend to treat colored workers as a group apart. We feel that all employees must be permitted to carry on their work and advance in their employment strictly on the basis of individual qualifications and merit. For this reason, local patterns relating to employment cannot be the determining factor in administration of a Government agency.

1. Guard Force–The Committee finds that one Negro worker has already been promoted to a position of Guard. While the fact that guard jobs are being reserved for veterans and have definite physical requirements somewhat narrows the field of selection for both colored and white persons, we have the assurance of Management that it has no reservations about the selection of colored employees for these positions. The positions, while not high in grade, have something of a symbolic and prestige value in emphasizing equality of opportunity for all employees. The Committee therefore assumes that these positions will continue to be filled strictly on the basis of merit without regard to race. The Committee and Bureau Management are therefore agreed on this point.

2. Personnel Office - The fact that the personnel office had no Negro employees at all when the inquiry began received the serious attention of the Committee.

As to the position of counselor, the personnel office reports that it has been interviewing colored candidates for some time and has now offered the position to a candidate from Boston, Massachusetts. Some members of the Committee feel that it was surprising that no suitable candidate could be found from among the 800 Negroes already in the Bureau in Baltimore. Other members of the Committee feel that, regardless of the racial issue, candidates for such positions are very difficult to find and that it is not at all unusual to have to go outside an organization even of this size to find a well qualified person. When the position is filled, the Bureau Director hopes to be able to use this counselor as an advisor to him on racial relations in the Bureau.

Since there are only three counseling positions at present (not counting the one to be added) an even more fruitful opportunity for employment for colored as well as white persons would be in the employment interviewing staff in which there are 12 interviewers. It would seem that every effort should be made to place colored employees in any appropriate capacity particularly in the personnel office because of the symbolic value. The Committee feels that the filling of vacancies in the personnel office with well qualified Negro applicants, when available, is an important requirement if discrimination or expressed feelings of the existence of discrimination is to cease.

The personnel officer states that the small number of colored persons in secretarial and stenographic positions throughout the Bureau has been because of their inability to pass the necessary tests. However, in the most recent test four colored employees qualified.

The Committee recognizes the validity of giving supervisors a choice among qualified candidates in filling a position. Management, however, has a definite responsibility to create attitudes that will prevent the exercise of this choice from becoming a means of racial discrimination.

The Committee has confidence that top Bureau Management is aware of the importance of correcting what appears to be discrimination against Negroes in the personnel office and in secretarial positions. It urges that this attitude be impressed upon the staff and that prompt action be taken.

3. Segregated Units - In some instances, particularly in the "Flexoline Files" (where there are four all-Negro units on both shifts), segregation is not obvious, because individual workers range over the total file floor and therefore appear to be on an intermixed basis. In other units, however, such as in the card punch unit in the Paca-Pratt Building, the segregated units are more obvious because colored employees are grouped together at separate rows of machines under their Negro supervisors, while adjoining units, under white supervisors, are composed chiefly of white employees. The Committee believes that the segregated unit is not a solution to racial employment issues. As one of the Committee members said, these units "serve more as a reminder than as a remedy."

4. Negro Supervisors Over Mixed Groups - Placing qualified colored employees in positions to supervise mixed groups seems to be a problem only in terms of timing.

Bureau Management fears difficulty if it took this step right now but recognizes that such a step "is definitely coming." The Committee realizes the limitations inherent in the short-term inquiry it has made. Also, it recognizes the importance of keeping the Bureau program operating without interruption. The Committee's conviction, however, is that there are little or no tangible grounds for fear of trouble that would arise if such supervisory opportunities were made available at once. It bases its conclusion on the following facts:

a. According to several members of the Committee who are long-time residents of Baltimore, the total situation in Baltimore does not preclude such action. They anticipate no serious difficulty from white workers.
b. Bureau employees have accepted Negro workers in the same units without difficulty.
c. The concensus of "Middle Management" (Section Chiefs) in the Division of Accounting Operations, while expressing doubts about the timing, seemed to be that such a step could be made successfully if it becomes Bureau policy.
d. Employees interviewed showed a healthy attitude toward accepting supervisory promotions based solely on merit. Certain employees reported occasions in the past when colored workers were temporarily in charge of mixed groups and in one instance on a regular basis. No difficulty was experience as a result of these occasions.
e. The recommendations of the Attitude Survey Committee in 1946 support the conclusion. This was a committee of employees which reviewed the results of a Bureau wide attitude survey and made a report on the subject. There was one "free lance" question asking "What do you like best about your job and what do you think are its worst features?" Out of 2,600 replies to this question only 68 made any reference to racial matters, 66 of which were protesting racial discrimination. This suggests that the racial issue was not predominant in employees' minds and that white employees were not resentful of employment and opportunities for Negroes. The Committee which reviewed the survey results made the positive recommendation that the all-Negro units be broken up and that some Negroes be placed in appropriate positions in the personnel office, particularly in interviewing and counseling work.

Accordingly the Committee concludes that this is not an inopportune time to introduce Negro supervision over mixed groups.

The Committee considered the possibility of trying out the supervision by Negroes over mixed groups by letting a colored employee act for a white supervisor during the latter's absence. After talking over this possibility with Section Chiefs the Committee concluded that such an approach would not be as successful as definite appointments, because it would be looked upon too widely as "experimental." A sounder approach would be to inform each employee in a work unit that a new supervisor had been chosen solely on the basis of being the best qualified person for the job.

III. RECOMMENDATIONS

The Committee recommends:

Guard Force

1. That the Bureau continue to seek and appoint qualified persons for the Guard Force without regard to race. It is especially important that this be done to avoid the impression that may be created that the one Negro appointment so far made is a "token."

Personnel Office

2. That the Bureau make every effort to give effect to its declared policy of seeking the best qualified persons without regard to race for positions in the personnel office; that it expedite its stated program of searching the qualifications of and interviewing colored employees in the Bureau for job eligibility for personnel jobs (a number of the employees contacted by the Committee seemed to be very able); and that at the first opportunity when colored employees become eligible for secretarial jobs the Bureau should select them for the first vacancies that occur. This is particularly applicable to the personnel office which is in strategic position to set the example.

Segregated Units

3. That the Bureau take steps to discontinue the segregated units by transferring white employees into those units in small groups and transferring Negro employees into other units. Whenever such changes offer opportunities for promotion of individuals it would facilitate this process.

Supervisory Opportunity

4. That the Bureau consider Negroes on an equal basis with white employees as candidates for the next vacancies in group leader positions regardless of the racial composition of the groups under such supervisory positions. It is urged that the next vacancy that occurs be filled in such manner. The Bureau should also consider the units in which colored supervisors could most readily be assigned, giving particular attention to mixed subunits that exist in the following units: Punching Unit, Flexoline Unit, Ledger and Wage-Card File Unit, Balancing (Operation 4) Unit, Tax Return File Unit, Adjustment Unit, Application and Correspondence Unit, and Photographic Unit. The units were offered by the union, at the Committee's request, as places in

which the attitudes of the employees ensure the greatest chances for success in the initial stages. Considering necessary time for normal turnover and the necessary administrative processes for internal placement, the Committee believes that the Bureau should have mixed units under colored supervisors within the very near future. The Committee further recommends that the Administrator, in consultation with the Bureau Management, establish a reasonable and definite time within which this can be accomplished. One committee member recommends strongly that the period be 30 days because he believes that unless an early time is fixed it will be difficult to achieve results.

5. That candidates for supervisory positions above that of group leader should be selected solely on the basis of merit. As a practical application every possible consideration should be given to filling the next vacancy of unit supervisor or assistant supervisor with a qualified colored employee. In addition, some members of the Committee strongly recommend that, at least for positions at these levels and above, vacancies be made known to employees by posting and other means.

Training

6. That the Bureau select candidates for the supervisory training course without regard to race, so that suitable material from both races for supervisory positions will be available as vacancies occur.

Transition

7. That the Bureau undertake these steps in a manner which indicates that they are a part of normal processes. As recommended in point 4 the Committee believes that the first examples of the new practice on supervisory selection should come immediately. In order to avoid the circulation of misinformation and unfounded rumors, the Committee recommends that the Administrator reaffirm in a memorandum to employees his insistence upon strict adherence to the merit principle without regard to race, creed, color, or national origin in appointments, promotions, and transfers throughout the Agency.

Subsequent Report

That a progress report within 90 days be made by the Bureau Director to the Administrator with copies to members of this Committee and that the Committee be given an opportunity to discuss this report with the Administrator.

Copies

9. That copies of the report of this Committee be sent by the Administrator to the Commissioner for Social Security, the Director of the Bureau of Old-Age and Survivors Insurance, and Local 17, United Public Workers of America.

COMMITTEE
Alexander J. Allen
Clarence Mitchell
Helen S. Pryor
O. Glenn Stahl
Dr. Ralph J. Young, M.D.

MS: NAACP II: A-526, DLC.

The date of this report is based on Mitchell's annual report of 12/20/48, in which he said that it was submitted to Oscar Ewing, administrator of the Federal Security Administration.

Mitchell served along with Alexander J. Allen, Helen S. Pryor, O. Glenn Stahl, and Dr. Ralph J. Young on the special committee that prepared this report. He enclosed this text in his letter of 7/21/48 to Gloster Current, director of NAACP branches. Both the letter and the report were stamped as received on 7/22/48. He suggested to Current that the technique used by the committee with the backing of the FSA administrator would be useful in meeting the employment problems of other large federal agencies. He noted that the material was not yet for publication but told Current he could share it with other NAACP members if he wished.

1. On the work of this committee and the responses to its report, see 5/28, 9/30, and 12/20/48.

The NAACP's Fight for an Executive Order against Discrimination in Federal Employment, August 20, 1948

MEMORANDUM

TO: All National Board Members and Branch Presidents
From: Dr. Louis T. Wright, Chairman of the Board
Subject: The NAACP's Fight for an Executive Order Against Discrimination in Federal Employment

[ca. August 20, 1948]

President Harry S. Truman issued an executive order forbidding discrimination in Federal employment on July 26, 1948. Behind his action lay nearly two years of effort by the NAACP to accomplish this objective. A chronological record of the major steps taken by the Association is attached. I hope that each Board member will personally read this record and I strongly recommend that it be read by branch presidents at the next board meeting after it is received. It is a clear reminder that the Association is battling for freedom on a broad front and that we make our gains because of determined and persistent effort.

The order is a long step forward by the Federal Government. Although it does not include some of the basic recommendations made by the NAACP, it provides an important tool with which to work against discrimination. It is the first action to implement the recommendation of the Civil Rights Report and will help to keep alive the national fight for a permanent fair employment practice commission for private industry.

Already, some hostile Congressmen and Senators are planning ways to destroy this new agency. Its life and usefulness will depend to a great extent on what we do in the NAACP to make it work.

The establishment of Federal machinery to combat discrimination within the government itself was one of the recommendations in the Final Report of the wartime FEPC. Our Labor Department began the fight for this program in 1946. Our National Conference of 1947 and 1948 went on record in favor of it.[1]

Among the persons who played an important part in helping to influence the President on the importance of taking this action are:

Mr. Oscar Ewing, Federal Security Administrator; the late Secretary Lewis B. Schwellenbach of the United States Department of Labor; Mr. C. Girard Davidson,

Assistant Secretary of the Interior; Mrs. Evelyn Cooper, Assistant to the Secretary of the Interior; Dr. Frank S. Horne, Assistant to the Administrator of Housing and Home Finance Agency; Mr. George L. P. Weaver, Director of the National CIO Committee to Abolish Discrimination, and other friends of the Association in government and labor organizations.

CHRONOLOGICAL ACCOUNT OF NAACP'S FIGHT FOR AN EXECUTIVE ORDER AGAINST DISCRIMINATION IN FEDERAL EMPLOYMENT

December 30, 1946: After describing cases of government discrimination handled during the year, the Annual Report of the NAACP Labor Secretary made the following statements:

"Whenever our flag flies over a Federal establishment there also do we find job discrimination. From occupied Germany to Japan, the American pattern of discrimination is in full force and effect. A conference with the President on this problem is most essential. The White House must issue, and provide for the policing of, a stern order against discrimination because of race."

January 21, 1947: The NAACP's Labor Department requested that the Civil Service Commission, because of weaknesses in regulations then in effect, devise a plan for overall action against discrimination in government employment. The Commission stated that it would handle individual cases, but declined to plan any overall strategy.

February 24, 1947: The United Public Workers of the CIO agreed with an NAACP proposal that the problem of discrimination in government be attacked on an overall basis by an executive order against discrimination in Federal employment.

April 17, 1947: Walter White appeared before the President's Committee on Civil Rights. He urged that the Committee recommend to President Truman that there be established an FEPC for Federal employees. The Committee's report issued on October 29, 1947 contained this recommendation.

April 21, 1947: In a letter to President Truman, Mr. White called for the issuance of an executive order to halt discrimination which he contended was forcing colored people back into pre-war discriminatory patterns in government employment.

May 21, 1947: Roy Wilkins wrote to President Truman reminding him of the communication of April 21 from Mr. White and offered as one example of treatment accorded Negroes the following:

"We have affidavits from fifteen honorably discharged veterans who charge that they were denied employment in the New Orleans Post Office solely because of their race. One had an examination average of 100.2. Others were in the high 90 and 80 brackets."

October 31, 1947: The NAACP Labor Department released a report on complaints involving more than two hundred persons who were the victims of discrimination because of race in twelve major government agencies. In addition to citing instances showing refusal to employ persons, the report also stated that "in one agency, colored employees were forced to work on a floor below the subbasement where they had considerable trouble battling rats."

November 14, 1947: The NAACP Labor Secretary met with government officials to draw up a proposed executive order which was circulated influencing the President.[2]

January 28, 1948: The President was asked by Walter White to include in his Civil Rights message to the Congress a statement against discrimination in the Federal government itself. Mr. White recommended that the President issue a strong executive order on this subject.

February 2, 1948: The President in his message to the Congress on civil rights legislation promised that he would issue an executive order.

February 10, 1948: The NAACP Labor Secretary met with Dean George Johnson of the Howard University Law School, and members of the faculty, to discuss a draft of the NAACP's proposal on what a Federal executive order against discrimination should include.

March 24, 1948: The NAACP Labor Secretary testified before the Civil Service Commission that in one southern city [New Orleans] 80% of the persons rejected by a Federal agency were colored. One applicant had been rejected sixteen times by various agencies in that city and another twenty-one times, although both were among the top people on the registers and each had extensive qualifying experience.[3]

April 1, 1948: The NAACP recommendations on the content of the executive order were submitted to the White House by the Labor Secretary during a conference.

April 7, 1948: Walter White in a letter to President Truman called upon him to issue a "ringing declaration prohibiting unfair practices in the Federal Government and underscore your determination to stand firm against those who are seeking to turn the fight for freedom into a retreat to reaction."

April 9, 1948: Oscar Ewing, Federal Security Administrator, was asked by Walter White to support the NAACP's effort to obtain the issuance of the executive order.

April 20, 1948: U.S. Attorney General Tom Clark was requested by Walter White to work for the immediate issuance of the order.

April 23, 1948: The NAACP Labor Secretary met with Julius A. Krug, Secretary of the Department of Interior, who pledged that he would urge the President to issue the order.

May 18, 1948: A meeting was arranged by Walter White with Oscar Ewing, Federal Security Administrator, and close advisor of the President. Those present were Channing Tobias, Director of the Phelps-Stokes Fund; Mrs. Mary McLeod Bethune, Presi-dent of the National Council of Negro Women; George L. P. Weaver, Director of the National CIO Committee to Abolish Discrimination; and Clarence Mitchell, NAACP Labor Secretary. Lester B. Granger, Executive Secretary of the National Urban League, was not present, but sent a letter urging issuance of the executive order. Mr. Ewing again stated his support of the order and assured the committee that it would be issued.

June 27, 1948: In the closing speech of the National Conference, Walter White called upon the President to take the first step to implement the civil rights report by issuing an executive order against discrimination in Federal employment.

MS: NAACP WB-69, DLC.

In a memorandum of 8/20, Mitchell informed Bobbie Branch of the NAACP national office that he was forwarding a copy of a summary "we prepared recently on work we have done to bring about the issuance of the President's executive order against discrimination in Federal employment. . . . The attached copy is yours because I like to have some of the key staff people know what we are doing from time to time." The text is stamped as received on 8/23. The following day, the NAACP board distributed this memorandum and chronology under Wright's signature. NAACP II: A-526, DLC.

1. As part of its drive for the establishment of machinery to combat employment discrimination, the convention urged Congress to enact a law to open up job opportunities on a merit basis. NAACP Annual Report, 1948, 71.

2. See 12/1/48, 6/29/54; in appendix, 11/7/47 and 6/28/49.

3. See, in appendix, 3/24/48.

Clarence Mitchell, "Notes on the Taft-Hartley Act," October 31, 1948

NOTES ON THE TAFT-HARTLEY ACT BY CLARENCE MITCHELL

[October 31, 1948]

In 1932, William Branson felt pretty good when he walked out of the office of the chemical company with a verbal promise that, because he had lost two fingers from his left hand in an accident on the job, he could count on working there for the rest of his life. He was only forty at the time and his big shoulders would have shaken with the force of his hearty laugh if anyone had told him that 15 years later Senator Robert A. Taft and Congressman Fred A. Hartley, Jr., men he had never heard of, would sponsor a law which in 1947 would make it possible for the company to fire him for doing his duty as a union shop steward. Yet that is exactly what happened. At fifty-five, minus two fingers, big Bill Branson picks up odd job to help earn his share of the family expenses.

Branson is a flesh and blood man. That is not his real name but the facts of his case are in the NAACP Labor Department's file. On the day he was fired from the job, he had protested to company officials because non-union white men were being used on the jobs which, under the contract between management and the union, belonged to both colored and white union members.

The dismissal of Bill Branson was a company triumph. Its management had long resented the growth of the local representing its employees under the Wagner Act. Most of the members are colored and many of them cannot read or write. Branson, with courage and natural leadership, was the chief target of management's dislike for the union. It is very possible that under the Wagner Act management would not have attempted to fire him. Even if he had been dismissed, however, there would have been an excellent chance for his reinstatement under the old law. Now his union cannot use the machinery of the National Labor Relations Board because, although its leaders fall in what is called the right wing labor group, they refuse to sign non-communist affidavits as required by the Taft-Hartley Act.

Purpose of Law

The sponsors of the new law, which officially bears the innocent title of Labor-Management Relations Act, have frequently said that it was designed to give greater protection to individual workers.[1] Bill Branson would undoubtedly feel a strong urge to punch somebody in the nose if he heard this because, when the NAACP assisted him in filing his complaint with the board, there were months of delay before it was investigated. Thereafter, he was asked whether he would withdraw it and when he did not do so it was tossed out by the regional office of the NLRB. An appeal was made to Robert N. Denham, the NLRB General Counsel, who said that there was an extensive file on the case showing that Branson did not have a complaint under the law. However, the General Counsel's Office has never revealed just what the evidence did show. Under the Taft-Hartley Act, Denham's word is final in cases of this kind. Prior to the passage of the new legislation, it could have been argued out before the board with both sides having a fair chance to state their case. Now, the General Counsel can arbitrarily shut off action without bothering to explain why he believes a case has no merit.

Branson does not fully understand how an Act of Congress transformed him from a useful worker into a man without a steady job. He no longer attends union meetings and those persons who formerly looked to him for leadership are fearful of what management will do to them if they "get out of line." For example, when one employee began circulating a petition urging that Branson be reinstated, some officials of the union halted it by saying that they could not offer protection to anyone who signed it.

When Branson's wife, who works in the garment industry, was asked to help organize her fellow employees she declined to do so. As the chief wage earner since her husband lost his job, she felt that she could not afford to take a chance.

This is a terrible part of the toll taken by the Taft-Hartley Law. By choking off remedies and making unions more vulnerable to attacks by employers, it has killed the enthusiasm which some people formerly had for organizing and participating in the affairs of trade unions. Of course the stalwarts have continued to fight, but in a free nation it should not be necessary for a man to have courage in order to be an active member of a union—no more than it is required that he be brave in order to read whatever newspaper he chooses, or vote according to his convictions in an election.

When the legislation which resulted in the Taft-Hartley Law was being considered by Congress, the NAACP testimony before the Senate Labor Committee pointed out that passage of it would adversely affect the organizing drives of the AFL and CIO in the South where colored workers would gain much by collective bargaining.

Apparently, this is exactly what the framers of the law intended it would do. Some inkling of how these members of Congress feel on racial matters may be gotten by reading the majority report of the Joint Committee on Labor-Management Relations headed by Senator Joseph A. Ball of Minnesota. This committee was established by the Taft-Hartley Act to keep an eye on how the law is working out. Of course Messrs. Taft and Hartley are key members, the latter being vice-chairman.

Typical Report

In discussing labor relations at the R. J. Reynolds Company in Winston Salem, North Carolina, the report states:

"The skill and dexterity of colored workers were peculiarily suited to the processing of hand made plugs of chewing tobacco and to filling cotton 'pokes' with finely shredded smoking tobacco. The tempo of the work was leisurely and unhurried . . . With the introduction of cigarettes making came a great increase in the number of white workers. They were engaged to operate the machines and to supply the higher skill that was deemed requisite to machine production of cigarettes."

The writers of the report evidently had had considerable experience in preparing minstrel show scripts for in discussing the type of grievances filed by employees, the following was stated:

"The grievances run the whole gamut of foibles, frailties, eccentricities, and superstitions. They may cover the complaint that 'there's a black cat running around our workroom,' or that one worker is 'hoaxing and jinxing' another worker.

"One of the frequent grievances confronting the company concerns employees who walked off the job without warning, and after a week or two of unexplained absence were severed from the pay roll. In demanding reinstatement through the union, the severed worker may say he went to 'visit his folks' in South Carolina or Georgia, and couldn't get back because 'his car broke down,' or 'the train didn't run.' Sometimes the explanation is 'the police picked him up.' In another instance, 'his wife beat him up."

The report also took several cracks at the union for working to get a colored man elected to the city council and "organizing the Negro population for political action along lines that are frictional and hostile in relation to the white population of the city." Of course the union's answers to these management inspired comments do not appear in the publication.

Four members of the committee, Senators Claude Pepper, James E. Murray, and Congressman John Lesinski, and Augustine E. Kelly, objected to the report stating that it, "indicates an anti-Negro bias and a lack of sympathy for the union's point of view."

In their dissent, the minority also stated that:

"Labor organizations report that since the passage of the Labor Management Relations Act, the process of organizing has become increasingly difficult, particularly in the South, because of employer resistance."

At the National Conference of the NAACP in 1947, a distinguished lawyer who works extensively in the field of labor relations remarked that the Taft-Hartley Act would be a great money maker for lawyers. He foresaw numerous court battles, particularly on the matter of injunctions against labor unions. It is interesting to note that during the first six months of the operation of the Act the NLRB reported 13 petitions for injunctions filed by its regional directors. Of these twelve were against unions.

Not only does the Act offer rosy prospects for the legal profession, but it offers wonderful opportunities for some politicians to spread confusion and get their names in the newspapers.

Washington Cafeteria Workers

In Washington, colored cafeteria workers have always had to struggle for recognition and bargaining rights. Nearly a thousand of them spent twelve weeks on the picket lines last winter because lawyers and congressmen were having a field day misinterpreting the requirements of the law.

The company for which these people worked refused to negotiate a new contract with them because their international leaders had not complied with what management said was the law. The Secretary of Labor, Lewis B. Schwellenbach, who, in addition to being a former Federal Judge, also had a deep sense of social justice, attempted to break the stalemate between management and labor. As soon as it appeared that management would have to yield and bargain with the union, Congressman Clare E. Hoffman of Michigan, a somewhat less imaginative northern version of Mississippi's Rankin, jumped into the fray. As chairman of a "special subcommittee" of the House Labor Committee, Mr. Hoffman regaled the public with an extensive harangue on the reason why management was right under the law. He also made spirited attacks on the Department of Labor for trying to promote a settlement. Under the stimulating glare of camera flash bulbs, the committee's record grew fatter and fatter while the colored employees grew thinner and thinner from missing meals and walking picket lines. Finally, the union gave in and met management's terms. Thereupon management insisted that it should have an election to determine whether the employees still wanted the union to represent them. Under management's plan, hundreds of strikebreakers who had been hired during the stoppage would also be eligible to vote. Since the union would obviously demand reinstatement of employees who had been replaced by strike breakers, one did not need a crystal ball to see which way the people on the job would vote.

Although it was clear that management was out to break the union at the outset, this detail became lost in the ensuing legal scuffle. As usual the wage earners with babies to feed and rent to pay suffered most. What is worse, a number of persons became embroiled in fist fights during the picketing and were subsequently sent to jail. Without condoning the actions of persons who resort to violence in labor disputes, one cannot forget that the employees were at best striking puny blows against people like themselves who were chiefly interested in making a living for their families. Management, on the other hand, was fighting both with the deadly weapon forged by the Congress in the form of the Taft-Hartley Law. Management knew that, once it had discredited and destroyed the union, it could thereafter leisurely separate from its payrolls any strike-breakers or former union members indiscreet enough to ask for pay raises or better working conditions.

Shortly after the Taft-Hartley Law was passed, a few people began saying that it had a little FEPC in it. Perhaps it would have been more accurate for them to say a microscopic FEPC or maybe even an invisible FEPC, because as yet this phase of the law has not been found nor has it revealed itself. There is no instance in which a single colored person has been able to keep or get a job because of the Taft-Hartley Act. On the other hand, numerous instances have arisen in which unions which exclude colored people have won bargaining rights or used the law to harass unions which do admit them. In other cases, employers have seized upon the race issue to weaken the organizing of workers.

AFL vs. CIO

In an Ohio Steel Plant, the law was made to order for a craft union which was seeking to oust an industrial union because the latter group, under the terms of its contract, had insisted that some colored members, who were also veterans, should be upgraded to jobs for which they were qualified. Some white employees staged a protest strike against the promotion of the colored employees, but it was unsuccessful.

The disgruntled white employees then asked that a craft union be allowed to represent them. Although the national policy of the craft union was against discrimination because of race, it was clear that those seeking to bring it in the plant intended to do so as a means of keeping their department all white. After extensive hearings and other legal maneuvers, the advocates of white supremacy lost their case. Had the persons who wanted to bring in a new union not had the encouragement of the Taft-Hartley Law they would hardly have pursued the matter as far as they did.

Far from squelching unions which bar colored people from membership, the present NLRB has actually reaffirmed its old stand of granting recognition to those unions which discriminate against colored employees. In the Texas and Pacific Motor Transport case, the NLRB refused to permit the insertion of evidence into the record by the AFL Teamsters that the International Association of Machinists would not properly represent colored employees, because it barred them from membership. The same attitude is expressed by the Board in the F. W. Wint Company and the Norfolk and Southern Bus Company Cases.

A great deal of Federal money is now being spent on taking cumbersome votes as required by Section 8 (a) (3) of the Act to determine whether employees want a union shop. The NLRB's own figures from April 1 to June 30, 1948, show that out of 11,882 elections held on the question of union shop, 11,568 resulted in the union's favor. In these elections, over a million valid votes were cast by employees. Even some of the most fervent supporters of the Act are beginning to admit this section is an expensive and complicated legislative device for proving that two plus two equal four.

The basic tragedy of the Taft-Hartley Act is that it has established a legislative pattern for whittling away valuable social legislation. The same people who rammed it through have also planned schemes for emasculating the Wage Hour Law and the Social Security Act. These persons did not favor anything which gives the employee the right to make himself heard and to obtain redress when he has a just grievance. They also include many who are against any protection for the victims of mobs, the persons who are denied a job because of his race and the man who get bashed in the face when he refuses to ride in a Jim-Crow car.

MS: "Notes on the Taft-Hartley Act," Crisis *55 (October 1948): 300–301, 313.*

For editorial purposes, this article has been assigned the date of 10/31/48. It was reprinted in the *Mid-West Labor Digest* (February 1949): 20–21, copy in MP.

1. The act was cosponsored by Rep. Fred A. Hartley Jr. (R-N.J.) and Sen. Robert A. Taft (R-Ohio). *Congress and the Nation*, 566–84. See 12/20/48, 4/1/49 for Mitchell's references to this article, and also introduction and the headnote on NAACP, the Taft-Hartley Act, and the National Labor Relations Board.

National Negro Publishers Association News Release ca. January 19, 1949

NATIONAL NEGRO PUBLISHERS ASSOCIATION NEWS RELEASE

[ca. January 19, 1949]

Washington, D.C. (NNPA)—Racial discrimination is widespread throughout the postal service, according to the report of a Senate Post Office and Civil Service subcommittee.

The report was the result of an investigation into complaints of discrimination made by Clarence Mitchell, labor secretary of the National Association for the

Advancement of Colored People, during a hearing on the nomination of Jesse M. Donaldson to be the Postmaster General.[1]

In addition to the findings regarding employment practices in the postal system, the report also covered a number of other Federal agencies, including the Civil Service Commission which has jurisdiction over inquiries in cases of discrimination.

A breakdown of employment of colored persons in the commission and in its regional offices, by grades, showed that that agency itself is practicing discrimination.

The findings of the subcommittee with respect to the postal system showed:

In Wilmington, Delaware, in fifty years, there is reported only one colored clerk and motor vehicle service employee. The report said the same thing was true of Atlantic City, New Jersey.

In Jacksonville, Florida, in 1942, ten colored eligibles were reported passed over for appointment at the post office.

In Knoxville, Tennessee, James G. Beck is reported as the only colored post office clerk. He was retired March 31, 1942. He had been appointed in 1908 after having served as a teacher in the local high school.

In Jackson, Tennessee, the entire force of custodians was at one time colored, but the report from that city disclosed that as rapidly as the incumbents were retired or died, they were replaced by white personnel until now no colored employees are found in the custodial force.

The subcommittee's investigator reported that for many years it was the "policy" of postmasters at Jackson, Mississippi, to maintain a carrier force composed entirely of colored men and a clerical force composed entirely of white persons.

This policy was effected by selecting only colored men for appointment as carriers and only white persons for appointment as clerks.

The investigator reported that this "policy" was abandoned in 1931, when E. C. Cloon was appointed postmaster. Mr. Cloon refused to appoint colored persons to any positions in the Jackson post office, restricting his appointments to the carrier force exclusively to white eligibles, though there are still nineteen colored carriers of a total of eighty-seven carriers.

Mr. Cloon, the investigator said, not only refused to appoint colored eligibles to any position but he instituted a system aimed at separating colored employees from the service, using various devious methods to accomplish this objective. As a result, during his administration, eleven colored employees were separated from the service from the time of his appointment in 1931 to the time he left the service in 1934.

The successor to Mr. Cloon, a Mr. Hederman, and the present postmaster, Aubrey C. Griffin, have maintained the policy of refusing to appoint colored persons to positions in the Jackson post office.

The subcommittee investigator also reported that colored employees are denied promotions beyond the automatic grades in the service and also are denied preferred assignments. The same practice of racial discrimination in indulged in by all of the other Federal agencies in Jackson, it was reported.

One witness at Jackson, a veteran of World War II, told the investigator that in 1946 he applied at the office of the Secretary of the Local Civil Service Board, who is a postal clerk, for application blanks to take an announced examination for clerk-carrier.

The secretary told him that all veterans get 100 on the examination but some never get appointed, the report said. On August 26, 1946, this veteran took the examination but aside from receiving notice of his rating he heard nothing from the examination, although he knew of white persons who took the same examination and received lower ratings but were appointed.

The report states that on August 14, 1947, this veteran passed a civil service examination for custodian-laborer, receiving a rating of 94.5. On February 2, 1948, he received a letter from the postmaster inquiring as to his availability for appointment. He stated that he immediately replied that he was available, but heard nothing further from the postmaster.

On November 19, 1947, the veteran passed a civil service examination for the position of mail handler, receiving a rating of 99.5. He heard nothing from this examination.

On February 6, 1948, the veteran took a civil service examination for clerk-carrier. The Secretary of the Civil Service Board repeated to him that all veterans get 100 but are not appointed. He requested the secretary of the board and the secretary to the postmaster to advise him of his position on the various civil service registers for the examinations he had taken and each refused to do so, telling him it was a violation of law to disclose such information.

Another colored veteran of World War II, who had served three and one-half years in the United States Marine Corps, a part of the time at Iwo Jima, applied to the secretary of the Civil Service Board at Jackson for the necessary blanks to take an announced examination for clerk-carrier.

He was told that no blanks were available. Later he saw the secretary furnishing blanks to a white applicant. She then gave him the blanks. He passed the examination, receiving a rating of 85, but heard nothing further from the examination.

The report stated that an examination of the civil service register disclosed that on certificate No. 21, dated January 29, 1947, this witness was No. 2 on the certificate for appointment as clerk and was passed over. On certificate No. 22 of the same date, he was No. 1 for appointment as clerk and he was again passed over, and on certificate No. 23, dated January 30, 1947, for the position of clerk, he was No. 1 with a rating of 85.2. The witness was again passed over, and the third eligible with a rating of 79.2 was appointed.

The witness, having been considered for three appointments and not having been selected, was disqualified from further consideration except at the discretion of the postmaster.

Another witness stated that he was on the following three civil service registers: clerk, carrier, and special delivery messenger. In June, 1947, he received a letter from the postmaster asking him to come to his office. He did so. The postmaster advised him that he could give him a temporary appointment as substitute carrier for few days' work and if he refused the appointment, which he did, it would not result in his name being removed from the register for declining.

Three days later the secretary of the Civil Service Board informed him that his name was off the register for declining the temporary appointment but upon offering evidence of his availability it would be restored.

He said he informed the secretary that he was available for permanent appointment but his name was not restored to the register of eligibles until January, 1948.

The report said that it appeared from an examination of the register that the suspension of eligibility is a device used in the Jackson office to disqualify colored eligibles for consideration when appointments are to be made. The reasons generally given are: Suspended pending furnishing of medical certificate, suspended pending investigation of availability, and suspended failure to reply to official communication.

This witness was certified for appointment to the position of probationary substitute carrier on January 27, 1947, and not considered. The subcommittee found that the only eligibles on the register on February 24, 1947, were this witness, who stood No. 1, and three others.

The report showed that an examination for clerk-carrier was held on February 15, 1930. Only sixteen eligibles received passing ratings and they, with two additions, constituted the register from which all appointments were required to be made.

Under an executive order of March 2, 1929, eligibles who had been allowed disability preference had their names entered at the top of the register, regardless of ratings attained in the examination. Audit of the register disclosed the following order of appointments:

The first appointment was made on November 17, 1930, and the first four eligibles on the register were colored. All four of them were appointed in the order of their standing on the register. There were no other appointments made from this register.

W. A. Freeman, who preceded Mr. Cloon, was postmaster at Jackson when these appointments were made. They were the last appointments of colored persons made to any position in the Jackson post office other than temporary appointments, with one exception.

MS: NAACP WB-154, DLC.

The approximate date of this National Negro Publishers Association news release is derived from references to its content in a memorandum of 1/19/49 from Gloster Current to Mitchell, which read as follows:

> Thanks for the Senate Report on Discrimination in Federal Service.
>
> I read with interest the press accounts of this report and noted that as usual, one Clarence Mitchell was the prime instigator of the action taken by the Federal Government.
>
> Congratulations on obtaining results.

The following handwritten note appears at the top of the story: "Not to be given out Lautier." The reason for excluding Lautier was that he and Mitchell had open differences over the lobbyist's aggressive style of pressing the Eisenhower administration for action. See 5/24/54 and 6/1/54 for their open exchange of views.

The National Negro Publishers Association, formed in 1940 as a federation of black community newspaper and magazine publishers, was renamed the National Newspaper Publishers Association in 1950. Louis Lautier, its bureau chief in Washington, was very likely a Republican who supported President Eisenhower.

1. Mitchell testified against Donaldson's appointment, 12/9/47, *Hearings*, 6–15. He reported on the problems of discrimination in the post office and stated that the principle of promotions based on merit was "too frequently ignored during Mr. Donaldson's administration as First Assistant Postmaster General." The Senate approved Donaldson's nomination but authorized an investigation into postal discrimination. See 12/23/47.

Thurgood Marshall, Memorandum to the President of the United States Concerning Racial Discrimination by the Federal Housing Administration, February 1, 1949

MEMORANDUM TO THE PRESIDENT OF THE UNITED STATES CONCERNING RACIAL DISCRIMINATION BY THE FEDERAL HOUSING ADMINISTRATION. [BY THURGOOD MARSHALL]

[February 1, 1949]

The shortage of housing is, today, a problem for every American. In addition to this barrier, however, minority groups as recognized by the President's Committee on Civil Rights are faced with a double handicap of "prejudice and discrimination. . . . which places them at a disadvantage in competing for the limited housing that is available."[1] The report of this committee found that these practices violated the basic principle that "equality of opportunity to rent or buy a home should exist for every American." The denial of equality of opportunity to secure housing has confined minority groups to congested and deteriorating racial ghettos, and the solution of the hosing problem of minorities is contingent upon procuring additional living space.

In spite of the growing pressure of racial population in Northern and Western urban centers, as the result of migration through the last thirty years, those swollen populations continued to be restricted to their already overcrowded areas by traditional real estate and financing discrimination, aided and abetted in recent years by the Federal Housing Administration. The overcrowding resulting from such constriction becomes apparent when the statistics on the urbanization of Negroes form the South is studied.

The number of Negroes living in urban areas rose to 48.6% in 1940, and increase of 21.3% over 1910. During the following seven years alone there was a continued increase of over two and one-half million non-white persons and a decline of more than a million non-whites in rural areas. The significance of this migration in terms of housing is illustrated by the fact that during these seven years the non-white population of Los Angeles increased almost 100%, with a similar increase in Detroit and a smaller increase such widely separated cities as St. Louis, Seattle, Akron.

During the same period, the money earnings of non-white workers doubled and the proportion of non-white, non-farm home owners rose by 40% as compared to 27% among whites. In 1947, one in every ten non-white households in non-farm areas was paying $40 or more for monthly rents.

In other words, the increased earning power of Northern Negroes, had produced a very real market for medium as well as low-priced housing. In 1947, many Negro veterans, had shelter been available at the price and quality they demanded, would have been willing and able to build their own homes. In Cleveland, the medium price these veterans were able to pay was $$5,000, in Detroit this amount was $5,500. The upper quartile in Detroit reported ability to pay $6,000 or more, and in Newark and Cleveland this group felt it could afford $7,000 or more. It is ironic indeed, that although the earning power of the desire for new and decent housing by Negroes is now a reality, the FHA-supported discriminatory tactics of real estate groups and interests constitute an impenetrable barrier towards better housing opportunities.

In the '30s with the initiation of a national housing program, the country embarked upon the solution of some of its major housing programs. For Negroes and other minorities some relief was afforded by access to low rent hosing. But with the growth in Negro urban population and the increased purchasing power of Negroes, the continued denial of the benefits to Negroes above the low income group eligible for public housing created greater hardships.

A. THE NATIONAL HOUSING ACT AND ITS ADMINISTRATION

The National Housing act is entitled, "An Act to encourage improvement in housing standards and conditions, to provide a system of mutual mortgage insurance and for other purposes", 48 STAT. 1246. The encouragement of the improvement of housing standards and conditions was undertaken not directly by building houses, but indirectly by encouraging private investment in housing through insuring the lenders against loss of funds (Sections 1703 and 1709). Neither the security of the lending institutions nor the profit of the builders thus financed was the objective of the legislation. Rather its aim is to improve the Hosing conditions of the nation.

The Federal Housing Administration has lost sight of this objective. Not only does the FHA deny its responsibility for a positive social policy but it now considers itself rather as a private business organization. Instead of contributing to the solution of the housing problems of minority groups, the FHA, as shown by the memorandum of the N.A.A.C.P. to the President of the United states in 1944,[2] embarked upon a program in which it followed traditional private real estate practice, fostered and spread race restrictive covenants, restricted mortgage insurance for Negroes to occupancy only in areas already occupied by Negroes and thus further curtailed needed living space and confounded the housing problems of racial minorities.

Following our protest, the FHA made certain revisions in their Underwriting Manual but continued in practice to deny insurance commitments for housing available to Negroes except in "Negro neighborhoods," or in sub-divisions generally contiguous to such neighborhoods, to insure properties encumbered by racial covenants and to require, in many cases, that such covenants be placed upon properties seeking to qualify for FHA insured mortgages.

While the revised Manual contains no direct reference to race, there are many references in the new Manual which are interpreted and applied to achieve the ends openly advocated by the old Manual.

In section 1104, the Manual requires the underwriter to make an estimate of "the probability of any change in occupancy relating to income *and other characteristics of occupancy* which would tend to change desirability for residential purposes. In section 1215 (4) (d), the underwriter is told to evaluate the degree of compatibility of the inhabitants of the neighborhood as "the presence of incompatible groups in a neighborhood tends to lessen or destroy owner-occupancy appeal." In section 1320, subdivisions (1) and (2), the underwriter is instructed to give weight to the "tendency of user groups to seek compatible conditions" and is admonished that "neighborhoods constituted of families that are congenial, physical conditions being acceptable, generally exhibit strong appeal and stability" and further he is instructed that his rating must reflect the degree of risk attendant upon change of occupancy of the neighborhood from one "user group" to another.

While no definition of the term "user group" and no analysis of compatibility of user groups is to be found in the Underwriting Manual, the FHA has elaborated its "underwriting philosophy" in letters to inquirers.

Thus in answer to a request for a statement of policy in regard to insuring mortgages on a proposed housing cooperative to be open to families of all racial groups, Mr. Foley, the Commissioner of FHA, wrote the Community Homes, Inc. on July 3, 1947 as follows:

> "This administration does not use the mortgage insurance system either to promote or to discourage any proposal on the ground that it involves interracial characteristics. Such aspects of a proposed transaction are given the same consideration as all other characteristics, such as transportation, taxes, community facilities, livability and design of structure. If the study on any of these points indicates probable adverse effect upon continued market acceptance to a degree significantly increasing the risk, we are not warranted in accepting the risk, regardless of the nature of the cause producing that effect."

The development of its philosophy is shown in a further letter dated November 19, 1948, sent by Mr. W. J. Lockwood, the Assistant Commissioner, to Mr. Herman Will, Jr. in connection with the York Center Community Cooperative, another proposed interracial housing project in Illinois as follows:

> "If it is therefore apparent, with respect to the particular neighborhood or property under analysis, that infiltration will be unacceptable to the local real estate market and desirability of properties will be reduced in the market's mind, then this Administration has no alternative but to so recognize the conditions in its valuation of specific properties within that sphere of influence."

The letter to Mr. Will is amplified by the annexed affidavit of Mr. Will setting forth the substance of a conference in which the FHA's representative in the area office located in Chicago, stated that "mixed" neighborhoods were a bad risk. As a result of this policy FHA approval was denied of the York Center Community Cooperative, because of its interracial membership.

It is an easy step from governmental disclaimer of any responsibility for the promotion of unrestricted housing to governmental participation in the perpetuation of restricted housing. That step the FHA has now taken, for Commissioner Franklin Richards has declared in a letter to Thurgood Marshall dated November 1, 1948, that FHA would and could, with complete freedom, insure mortgages for a veterans housing project known as Leavittown in New York where thousand of tenants are forced to sign leases containing a clause agreeing not to permit use of the premises by any person other than members of the Caucasian race. Contrasted with the vague language in which FHA's policy concerning unrestricted housing projects is couched, the Commissioner's statement of policy concerning housing projects restricted against Negroes is strong and clear:

> "I find nothing in the (restrictive covenant) decisions to indicate that in the absence of statutory authority the government, or any agency thereof, is authorized to withdraw its normal protection and benefits from persons who have executed but do not seek judicial enforcement of such covenants."

In sum, the FHA withdraws its "normal protection and benefits" from Negroes who wish to live outside the ghetto, yet contends it is not authorized to withdraws such benefits for persons who contract with their neighbors to discriminate against Negroes.

It is the thesis of this memorandum that support by the FHA of residential segregation in any shape or form is contrary and odious to the public policy of the United States as evidenced by the decisions of the United States Supreme Court last May prohibiting judicial enforcement of racial covenants and by the Report of the President's Committee on Civil Rights.

B. THE FHA POLICY OF CONDITIONING MORTGAGE INSURANCE FOR UNRESTRICTED HOUSING UPON APPROVAL BY THE LOCAL REAL ESTATE MARKET IS IN VIOLATION OF THE FIFTH AMENDMENT.

In their attempts to maintain residential segregation, property owners have secured government sanction for a series of devices which have been held unconstitutional. First, the Supreme Court struck down an ordinance of the City of Louisville with prohibited occupancy of homes by members of one race in any block where the majority of residences were occupied by persons of the opposite race. *Buchanan v. Warley*, 245 U.S. 60 Thereafter two ordinances from other cities were held similarly invalid, one where the ban on residence was based upon the Virginia miscegenation statute, *City of Richmond v. Deans*, 281 U.S. 704, and the other where the proposed resident of a block predominantly occupied by persons of the opposite race was required to secure the written consent of a majority of such person. *Harmon v. Tyler*, 273 U.S. 668.

These devices having failed, the Government was then asked to enforce racial residential segregation desired by white property owners through court enforcement of covenants, and again the United States Supreme Court intervened.

In striking down action by state courts which enforced private agreements barring Negroes form ownership or occupancy of real property, the Supreme Court stated:

> "It cannot be doubted that among the civil rights intended to be protected from discriminatory state action by the Fourteenth Amendment are the rights to acquire enjoy, own and dispose of property. Equality in the enjoyment of property rights was regarded by the framers of that Amendment as an essential pre-condition to the realization of other basic civil rights and liberties which the Amendment was intended to guarantee."
> Shelley v. Kraemer,——U.S.——(1948).

And in a companion case similarly striking down enforcement of such restrictions by a federal district court, Mr. Justice Franckfurther spoke of the rights of Negroes to legal equality in ownership and occupancy of property as:

> "so basic to our society that, after the Civil war, their protection against invasion by the states was safeguarded by the Constitution." Hurd v. Hodge——U.S.——(1948), concurring opinion.

Indeed, it is well established that the Constitution guarantees "the protection of equal laws". *Yick Wo v. Hopkins*, 118 U.S. 356, 369. Such principles apply to the granting of benefits or the imposition of penalties or burdens by any agency exercising governmental power in any form. *Virginia v. Rides*, 100 U.S. 313 (1880) *Civil Rights Cases*, 109 U.S. 3 (1883); *Brinkerhoff-Faris Trust & Savings Co. v. Hill*, 281 U.S. 673 (1930); *Shelley v. Kraemer*,——-U.S. (1948).

In the restrictive covenant decisions the Supreme Court found that "but for" the active intervention of the courts, the Negro petitioners would have been free to occupy the properties in question without restraint. The court stated, "These are not cases, as has been suggested, in which the states have merely abstained from action, leaving private individuals free to impose such discriminations as they see fit." *Shelley v. Kraemer*. What was unconstitutional in the restrictive covenant cases was that the states recognized and enforced the private discriminations. The Court stated:

> "And it would appear beyond question that the power of the State to create and enforce property interests must be exercised within the boundaries defined by the Fourteenth Amendment ." *Shelley v. Kraemer*

With the decisions in these cases it was hoped that the last source of government support for residential segregation was destroyed.

Yet the FHA continues to recognize, give weight to and lend its authority in support of the same private discriminations declared unenforceable by the Untied states Supreme Court. Just as the ordinance in *Harmon v. Tyler* did not prohibit absolutely occupancy by Negroes in blocks predominantly white, but conditioned such occupancy upon the will of a majority of the whites, so the FHA conditions the granting of benefits upon white "market acceptance." The action of FHA is unconstitutional for the same reason that the ordinance was unconstitutional.

In *Buchanan v. Warley*, supra, the Supreme Court examined in detail the objectives by which the ordinance was sought to be justified. Each of such reasons was found insufficient by the Court.

1. Even the police Power of the State in regard to maintaining Public Peace Cannot Sustain Residential Segregation by Government Action.

   "It is said such legislation tends to promote the public peace by preventing racial conflicts; that it tends to maintain racial purity; that it prevents the deterioration of property owned and occupied by white people, which deterioration, it is contended, is sure to follow the occupancy of adjacent premises by persons of color.

   "It is urged that this proposed segregation will promote the public peace by preventing race conflicts. Desirable as this is, and important as is the preservation of the public peace, this aim cannot be accomplished by laws or ordinances which deny rights created or protected by the Federal Constitution." (245 U.S. 60 at p. 81)

2. Race of the Occupants Is Not a Reasonable Measure of Depreciation of Property.

   "It is said that such acquisitions by colored person depreciate property owned in the neighborhood by white persons. But property may be acquired by undesirable white neighbors, or put to disagreeable though lawful uses with the like results." (245 U.S. 60 at p. 82)

3. Governmental recognition of the Racial Hostility Cannot Justify Depriving Citizens of Constitutional Rights."

   "That there exists a serious and difficult problem arising from a feeling of hostility, which the law is powerless to control and to which it must give a measure to consideration may be freely admitted. But its solution cannot be promoted by depriving citizens of their constitutional rights and privileges." (245 U.S. 80, 81)

The achievement of racial residential segregation is the purpose and the effect of the FHA's policy. The Supreme Court's interpretation of the Fifth Amendment has shown concern for the protection of the rights guaranteed from sophisticated as well as simple-minded violations. The most that can be said for the FHA's violation of constitutional rights is that it is the latest and the most sophisticated attempt to lend governmental aid to the imposition of racial residential segregation.

The decisions of the Supreme Court have thus established that state legislatures, state courts and federal courts are without authority to impose residential segregation. Congress itself has acted in this field through the adoption of Section 1978 of the Revised statues, Title, U.S.C. Section 42, reading as follows:

> "All citizens of the Untied States shall have the same right, in every state and Territory, as is enjoyed by white citizens thereof to inherit, purchase, lease, sell, hold, and convey real and personal property."

Despite these restraints the FHA has asserted an authority it does not possess, for its power cannot be greater than that of the federal government

C. IT IS UNLAWFUL FOR THE FEDERAL HOUSING ADMINISTRATION TO APPROVE PROJECTS FOR FHA INSURANCE WHERE IT IS ON NOTICE THAT SUCH PROJECTS WILL CONTAIN RACIAL RESTRICTIVE COVENANTS.

In *Shelley v. Kraemer*, supra, the Supreme Court found that the difference between governmental aid in enforcing the rights of private individuals to impose such discrimination as they see fit and non-enforcement of those covenants "is the difference to petitioners between being denied rights of property available to other members of the community and being accorded full enjoyment of those rights on an equal footing," and the Court said:

> "State action, as that phrase is understood for the purpose of the Fourteenth amendment, refers to exertions of state power in all forms. And when the effect of that action is to deny rights subject to the protection of the Fourteenth Amendment, it is the obligation of this Court to enforce the constitutional demands."

No distinction can be drawn between action of the Federal government aiding in the initiation of racial discrimination and governmental action in aid of the final achievement of racial discrimination.

Here, the FHA asserts its power to grant mortgage insurance to projects built by private builders which from the very beginning are limited by inclusion of a racial restrictive covenant to white residents only. We are not here concerned with the unexpressed intention of the builder of a project to choose among possible purchasers upon any basis which he may desire. We are concerned with the granting of Federal benefits to a private builder who openly announces his intention to refuse occupancy to Negroes and who, even further, seeks to bind by written agreement all future owners to a similar discriminatory policy.

If the government may not "by the active intervention of the . . . courts supported by the full panoply of state power" deprive a Negro of the right to occupy property, it is similarly true that the Federal government may not lend any portion of the panoply of governmental benefits to a project designed to deny Negroes the rights to occupancy granted to them by the Constitution.

FHA unashamedly attempts to justify this policy despite the fact that on November 4, 1947 FHA Administrator Foley wrote a letter to the Department of Justice explaining the damage to the National Housing Program resulting from restrictive covenants which said:

> "The existence of such covenants outside these constricted areas, makes it inordinately difficult and often impossible for prospective Negro buyers to qualify for FHA mortgage insurance. As a result, the middle income market among Negroes and similar racial minorities is largely excluded form the benefits of the mortgage insurance program."

The substitution of the words "policy of the FHA" for "covenants outside these constricted areas" in the letter written by Administrator Foley, gives an accurate description of the effect of the FHA's policy upon Negro citizens.

D. THE FULL INTEGRATION OF MINORITY GROUPS INTO AMERICAN LIFE IS AN ESSENTIAL PART OF THE NATIONAL HOUSING PROGRAM

The two preceding arguments have been devoted to the illegality of withholding FHA benefits from members of minority groups in response to the prejudices of a particular community. The response ability of the Federal Government, however, is based upon an even broader ground than the unconstitutionality of the actions of the FHA.

In a democratic society devoted to the proposition that all men are created equal even an overwhelming majority may not reach its objective at the expense of constitutional rights of a minority, however small it may be. Applying this basic principle to the program of the FHA, it is clear that within the democratic framework the housing problem of the nation cannot be resolved by denying to individuals who are members of minority groups the right to full and unrestricted participation in the housing program. This is true for the very practical reason that the housing problems of the minority groups are in a real sense the problems of the nation and will remain so until they are solved.

Housing, in our society today, is more than shelter. It includes the whole environment in which the home is maintained. A well-built house in a poorly planned, impoverished, slum area, without adequate schools, community facilities, etc., does not provide good housing. Nor does a well-built house in a ghetto provide good housing in a democratic society. The FHA has recognized that good neighborhoods are an integral part of good housing, but it has equated "good neighborhood" with a "racially homogenous" neighborhood. Any such concept can only frustrate the most important objective of the National Housing Act–which is to provide for Americans a healthful home environment, both physically and psychologically, in which they will develop into democratic citizens.

To achieve that end every agency administering the federal housing program is responsible for the encouragement of unrestricted housing. This is not the concern of any special interest, for the majority is as much damaged by ghetto living as the restricted minority. Such a program would improve the welfare of the whole nation and would contribute to the solution of the problems of our society.

The present program, on the other hand, is creating problems which must eventually be solved, and postponement only makes the solution more difficult. The acute nature of the problem was clearly stated by the Report of the President's Committee on Civil Rights, which found:

> "Today, many of our citizens face a double barrier when they try to satisfy their housing needs. They first encounter a general housing shortage which makes it difficult for any family without a home to find one. They then encounter prejudice and discrimination based upon race, color, religion or national origin, which places them at a disadvantage in competing for the limited housing that is available. The fact that many of those who face this double barrier are war veterans only underlines the inadequacy of our housing record. P. 67

Finally, the Justice Department in the U.S. brief *amicus curiae* in the covenant cases states: "The Federal Government has a special responsibility for the protection of the fundamental civil rights guaranteed to the people by the Constitution and laws of the untied States. The President of the United States recently stated:

> 'We must make the Federal Government a friendly, vigilant defender of the rights and equalities of all Americans...Our national Government must show the way.'"

The brief goes on to say, "It is fundamental that no agency of government should participate in any action which will result in depriving any person of essential rights because of race or color or creed." Apparently, the FHA is informed neither of the policy of the United States as interpreted by the Department of Justice and the Report of the President's Committee on Civil Rights nor of the policy of the Administrator of the Housing and Home Finance Agency, of which it is a constituent part.

RECOMMENDATIONS

In order to secure fair and equitable participation of Negroes in the benefits of FHA, it is necessary that the following steps be taken to eliminate discriminatory practices.

1. That the Underwriting Manual and regulations be revised and supplemented by explicit instructions that exclude all considerations predicated upon racial, religious or national distinctions for the purpose of making commitments for insurance under the National Housing Act.
2. That the FHA in the future refuse approval for insurance purposes of projects submitted for approval where it appears on the application that the occupancy of such project will be limited by race, religion or national origin.
3. That the FHA in the future refuse approval for insurance purposes of projects submitted for approval where it appears on the application that the occupancy of such project will be limited by race, religion or national origin.
4. That, wherever, after approval of a project for mortgage insurance, it is shown that racial or similar covenants or regulations are being invoked in deeds of sale or leases covering the project, FHA will withdraw further mortgage insurance until the practice is discontinued.
5. That explicit instructions be publicly amended and sent to all field officers and representatives of the FHA setting forth the above changes in policy.

Respectfully submitted,
Thurgood Marshall,
Special Counsel, National Association
for the Advancement of Colored People.

Dated: February 1, 1949

MS: MP.

In his cover letter to President Truman upon submitting the memorandum, Walter White said that despite the Supreme Court decisions in *Shelley v. Kraemer* and *Hurd v. Hodge* in May 1948 as well as the report of the President's Committee on Civil Rights, the Federal Housing Administration continued to "lend its full support to the perpetuation of ghettos." *Shelley* and *Hurd*, he noted, "established once and for all that private home owners and realtors who wished to exclude racial or religious minorities from a given neighborhood could not procure the aid of state or federal courts to enforce agreements for this purpose [segregation]." He added:

> In answer to protests against the granting of benefits to a veterans' housing project in which every tenant was required to sign an anti-Negro clause, F.H.A., in spite of the inclusion of race restrictive covenants in deeds or leases, stated that it would continue to give its support to such projects. On the other hand, requests for mortgage insurance for unrestricted housing were refused with the statement that unrestricted housing did not meet a favorable reaction on the part of prejudiced groups and consequently was a bad risk.

White asked the president for assurance that the federal government would cease giving its support to racial restriction in housing under the FHA. He said the NAACP was also seeking to have the FHA "establish through certain procedures outlined in our recommendations a wholly unbiased policy of mortgage insurance in which the granting of benefits will be determined solely on the basis of the individual applicant without regard to race, religion, color or national origin."

1. *To Secure These Rights*, 67.
2. Excerpts of the twelve-page memorandum, taken from Hastie, 12/12/45, *Hearings*, 759, are used in the headnote on Segregation in Federal Housing Programs.

Report on the NAACP Conference on the Filibuster March 10, 1949

[March 10, 1949]

NAACP CONFERENCE ON THE FILIBUSTER WASHINGTON, D.C.

At the request of the President,[1] I attended a conference of representatives of NAACP Branches and other Civil Rights organizations in Washington, D.C. on March 10, 11, 12, 1949. The purpose of this conference was to devise means of getting support for the proposed change in the rules of the Senate which would permit the invoking of cloture on a procedural question by a two-thirds vote.

On Thursday morning, March 10, 57 representatives from sections as far west as Missouri and Texas met at the Washington Office of the NAACP. After a thorough briefing by Mr. White on the issues involved, the delegates broke up into small groups by States to call on their Senators. A small select group was chosen to call on Senator Scott Lucas, Majority Leader, Senator Francis Myers of Pennsylvania and Senator McGrath, Chairman of the Democratic National Committee. Mr. Herbert Wright, President of the Illinois State Conference of Branches and I were members of this committee. This meeting took place at 11:15 AM. The committee informed the Democratic Leaders of the disappointment over the weak and ineffectual steps being taken by the administration leaders to break the filibuster. After some very heated exchanges between Mr. Lucas and several members of the committee, a promise was finally given by Senator Lucas that every effort would be put forth to break the filibuster and clear the way for the rules change. The remaining delegates called on their respective Senators, and in several cases effected a change of mind on the part of the Senators. This was true in the case of Senators Smith and Hendrickson of New Jersey, both of whom were reported as doubtful. The same was true of Senators Lodge and Saltonstall of Massachusetts, Tydings and O'Conor of Maryland, Frear of Delaware and Ferguson of Michigan.

Conferences were held with Capehart and Jenner of Indiana, Donnell and Kem of Missouri and Bricker of Ohio. In spite of the pressure applied on these gentlemen, any three of whom could have changed the voting, they all voted to override the Barkley ruling.

It s significant that all five of these men are Republican Senators from States all heavily populated by Negroes. Especially is this so, when viewed in the light of Senator Pepper of Florida and Senator Kefauver of Tennessee, both Southern Democrats who voted to uphold the Barkley ruling.

At six-o'clock Thursday, Senator Lucas presented a cloture petition signed by 17 Democrats and 16 Republicans. This petition provided for the shutting off of debate if 2/3 of the senators present and voting should so vote. At this point, Senator Russell of Georgia raised a point of order stating that cloture could not be applied to the situation now before the Senate because there was no pending measure. His position briefly was that the so-called cloture provision of rule 22 of the Senate adopted in 1917 could be applied only to a bill or a piece of legislation which was before the Senate for consideration. He contended that the present motion before the Senate was motion by Senator Lucas to bring before the Senate the resolution approved by the rules committee, known as the Hayden-Wherry resolution. This resolution would make rule 22 clear by amending to include not only a pending measure but all preliminary and procedural questions or motion introduced into the Senate. After about three hours of heated debate the Senators began to clamor for the Vice President to rule on the point of order raised by Senator Russell.

At this point, Mr. Barkley delivered what many thought to be one of the greatest decisions ever made by a Presiding Officer of the Senate. He clearly distinguished the present point of order form the one on which Senator Vandenberg ruled last August. He traced the history of all such rulings and gave a clear picture of what led the Senate in 1917 to adopt rule 22. He ended by stating that "in view of the obvious intention of the Senate in 1917, as the chair sees it, to close debate, as Senator Underwood said, on a Bill, resolution or any other parliamentary action that was before the Senate, and in view of the fact that the precedents which have been relied on do not in the opinion of the Chair apply to the present situation, the Chair cannot do otherwise than overrule the point of order, which he does." Senator Russell immediately appealed from the decision of the Chair after which Senator Lucas moved that the Senate recess until noon Friday. The motion carried.

After the usual preliminaries on Friday, Senator Vandenberg took the floor and attacked the Barkley ruling as "an ingenious devise". This was no surprise since Vice President Barkley's ruling in effect was a reversal of the ruling by Senator Vandenberg of last August 2nd.

From noon until 10 o'clock Friday evening, there was continuous debate, both pro and con. Notable of those in favor of the ruling were speeches by Pepper, Kefauver, Morse, and Knowland in favor of the ruling and Donnell, Long and Maybank against the ruling.

At this point, Senator Lucas made a magnificent speech upholding the ruling and at the completion, moved to lay the appeal from the decision of the Chair on the table.[2] This automatically closed debate and brought the question to a vote. This was probably one of the momentous occasions in the history of the Senate. No one was sure how the matter would ultimately be decided. Both sides claimed sufficient votes to win. To those of us who had worked hard for two days to line up support for this ruling it was indeed a tense moment. For we realized that the fate of the entire list of Civil Rights legislation rested on how 4 or 5 men, (whose positions were not clear) would vote.

The end of the roll call found 46 Senators opposed to the Barkley ruling and 41 in favor. (23 Southern Democrats and 23 Republicans against–25 Democrats and 16 Republicans in favor). At this point, Senator Lucas moved to recess until noon Saturday.[3] On Saturday morning a small group of us again called on Senator Lucas to urge him to continue the fight. He stated that there would be a meeting of the Democratic leaders of the Senate to determine what the strategy would be. Later, we were informed that the fight would go on, with <round> the clock sessions if necessary to break the filibuster.[4]

Later in the day, I talked at length with Senator Douglas and Frank McCullough his executive assistant on this and other civil rights issues. I believe we have a friend in Senator Douglas.

While Senator Lucas has appeared weak and ineffectual, he must be judged in terms of the task he is confronted with. To attempt to minimize difficulties facing the administration is to confess complete ignorance of the deep seated opposition to any change in the senate rules as well as the bitter opposition to Civil Rights legislation.

There is no question in my mind that the National office engineered one of the most tactically effective lobbies of all times Many of the Senators were astonished to see so many people, both Negro and white interested enough in Civil Rights to come from so many distant places on such short notice.

While the results my not be apparent, the efforts of National office under the dynamic leadership of Mr. White are definitely bearing fruit. There are others too of whom you don't hear too much but who are also doing a magnificent job of assisting Mr. White at the National level—-men like Leslie Perry, Clarence Mitchell and Gloster Current, all of whom participated in this effort.

My respect and admiration for the work of the National Office, which has always been considerable, has increased greatly. And in the words of Winston Churchill, "Never before in history have so many owed so much to so few".

It was a great honor and privilege to represent you. Mr. White asked me to thank you for sending a representative and urged me to urge you to keep on keeping on because in the end we must win, because right is on our side.

Respectfully submitted,
Henry W. McGee[5]

MS: NAACP WB-118, DLC.

1. This was Walter White, executive secretary.
2. *CR Digest*, 3/10/49, D111 of *CR*, 2125–59, 2166–75.
3. *CR Digest*, 3/11/49, D114 of *CR*, 2214, 2227–76.

4. *CR Digest*, 3/12/49, D117 of *CR*, 2321–55.

Full, progressive reports on the struggle to change the filibuster rule leading up to this conference were provided by Leslie Perry in his 1/49, 2/49, and 3/49 monthly reports. His 3/49 report on this conference reads as follows:

> From February 28, to March 17 resolutions to amend Senate Rule 22, limiting debate, were filibustered. As had been anticipated, Vice President Barkley ruled that cloture applies to procedural steps such as motions to consider, etc. On appeal from the ruling of the chair 23 Republicans joined 20 Dixiecrats and 3 Western Mountain States Democrats to override the Barkley ruling. This vote occurred on March 11.
>
> During the days immediately preceding, the NAACP arranged a conference in Washington attended by 60 persons from 16 states. These delegates had conferences with Majority Leader Lucas, Majority Whip Francis Myers, and the Chairman of the National Democratic Committee Senator Howard McGrath. They also talked to senators from their states. It is believed that they definitely influenced a number of votes including the senators from New Jersey and others who earlier had favored the Vandenberg ruling.
>
> After the defeat of the Barkley ruling the Republican-Dixiecrat coalition had control over the Senate. The Majority Leader did not have enough votes even to adjourn the Senate. Thereafter, Senator William F. Knowland (R., Calif.) began circulating a petition to amend the rule so as to require a constitutional two-thirds (64 senators) to shut-off debate on all matters before the Senate *excluding* further changes of the Senate rules. Such further changes of the Senate rules would not be subject to cloture on a motion to consider. This so-called compromise resolution, introduced by Senators Carl Hayden (D., Ariz.), Kenneth S. Wherry (R., Nebr.) on behalf of themselves and 50 other senators, was presented to the Senate. The Bureau personally urged approximately 30 senators to withdraw from the compromise resolution and to support the Myers-Morse resolution. When the vote came on March 17 on the Myers amendment, calling for a constitutional majority (49 senators) to shut off debate on all pending business, it was defeated by a vote of 69 to 17. Senator Morse's amendment, providing for a majority of those voting, was defeated 80 to 7. The Wherry-Hayden proposal, Senate Resolution 15 as amended, passed 63 to 23. The attempt to bring democracy to the Senate rules was defeated by active coalition of Dixiecrats and Republicans. (Reports of the Washington Bureau, 1/49, 2/49, 3/49, NAACP II: A-656, DLC)

See also the introduction for a summary of Perry's reports and the headnote on NAACP and the Filibuster.

5. The following is the text of the letter McGee sent Mitchell on 2/2/66 with his report on the NAACP Conference on the Filibuster, which apparently was prepared for representatives who attended:

> Enclosed is a copy of an NAACP conference held in Washington, D.C. on March 10, 11, and 12, 1949. I ran across this report while going through some old files.
>
> I am sending this to you because it seems to have relevance to the struggle carried on by you and other leaders of the Civil Rights movement to get the 1964 Civil Rights Act passed.
>
> I call your attention specifically to the one paragraph on Page 3 and the observations I made in this report on the job being done by you and other members of the NAACP staff. I thought you might be interested in this report because it seems to me to have some historical value. (NAACP WB-118, DLC)

Clarence Mitchell, Jr., "Education UAW Style," March 1949

EDUCATION UAW STYLE
BY CLARENCE MITCHELL

[March 31, 1949]

"I am opposed to segregation and all forms of discrimination because they are contrary to all the principles that have made America great. I am opposed to them regardless of geography because I don't think geography changes basic principles."

The foregoing words were part of the climax of Walter Reuther's testimony before the Senate committee on labor and public welfare in the 80th Congress.[1] As President of the United Automobile Workers, CIO, Mr. Reuther was testifying in favor of the proposed Federal Fair Employment Practice Act. He was answering a question put to him by Louisiana's cocky little Allen Ellender, an ardent foe of civil rights in general and of fair employment in particular.

May people have given an answer like that before, but only a few of them have an opportunity to put such beliefs into practice on the same scale as does Mr. Reuther. With its more than a million members in one of the county's most important industries the actions of the United Automobile Workers are bound to have considerable effect on American life.

At the UAW educational conference in Milwaukee during the month of January, I had an opportunity to get a firsthand view of how deeply the concept of democracy has penetrated into the mind of the average member of that union. With the repeal of the Taft-Hartley Act a major objective in the 81st Congress, it is important to take a look at this conference. That law was specifically designed to cripple such unions as the UAW.

Of course, it would be foolish to say that every person who pays his dues believes that every other member, regardless of race, creed, color, or national origin, is entitled to a square deal. There mere fact that a man or woman joins a union does not mean that over night this individual becomes subject to canonization. However, if the members are at all open-minded, the UAW will see that they are well informed on almost everything that touches the wage earner's daily life. This process of keeping members informed includes economics, politics, race relations, health, and recreation. I mention them in that order because that is the way they seem to line upon on the UAW's roster. About two cents of each member's dues go to the international union for educational purposes.

As an example of the UAW's approach to race relations, one might take a brief glance at two colored delegates who had just gotten to Milwaukee from Alabama. They were standing at the registration desk in the Schroeder hotel. At the time, the thermometer was sliding in the direction of ten degrees below zero. These men did not have a room, but they were not the least bit upset. Long before, they had leaned that their union had faced the issue of equal treatment of its members at conferences and conventions. They knew that this equal treatment includes hotel and restaurant accommodations.

PRACTICAL EXPERIENCE

When the UAW's President was telling Congress that there should bee a fair employment agency in the Federal Government, he was able to speak from very practical experience. He is the director of a smooth working department of men and women who administer the union's program in this field.

The co-director of this department is William H. Oliver, who has had extensive experience within the UAW from its beginning. With Bill Oliver and Harry Ross, Mrs. Carolyn Davis and Mrs. Lillian Hatcher. Not only do they keep a sharp eye on fair play for racial and religious groups, but they also look out for the interest of women workers. Proof that this fair practices idea is succeeding within the union comes from the delegates to the conference. The most eloquent speeches on fair play for racial minorities were made by white people and some of the most vigorous statements on behalf of women workers of all races came from colored men.

The union's fair practices program has helped to work out many problems in local plants. Success stories, and even unsuccessful efforts, were related with pride and frankness. They included a wide variety of things from upgrading on the job to the use of facilities in halls rented for union meetings.

It was interesting to talk with some of the delegates on the fair practice program as they saw it in their own plants and cities. One of these was Earl Zehring of Mishawaka, Indiana. It was not long before he was telling me of a town in Michigan where the underground railway had a terminus in the pre-Civil War period. He seemed to get increased satisfaction out of his pipe when he talked of how there was no segregation in the schools or churches and of how "white and colored people accept each other as a matter of course." It was clear that he wanted his own home town, his union, the nation, and the world to be the same way. In his spare time he writes poetry, but his aesthetic inclinations did not stop his demanding and getting skilled colored workmen in the Bendix plant where he is employed. He made short shrift of trouble-makers who threatened to quit by telling them that the union would not back them up in their undemocratic behavior. Looking at the breadth of his shoulders and the line of his chin, most people would think twice before trying to punch him in the nose for his views and statements.

MEMBERS HOLD NAACP CARDS

Roy Wilkins spoke at a morning meeting, and, later at a luncheon in his honor. One could have shut his eyes and fancied that he was at a convention of the NAAACP. His tart straight-from-the-shoulder language pleased these practical men and women. The coats of many delegates carried the union ribbon on their lapels and in their pockets were NAACP membership cards. Many greeted me with, "How is Brother Walter White?" Delegate William Jenkins of Racine Wisconsin, dropped by my room to talk over a housing problem in his home community. When I asked him what the local branch of the NAACP was doing about the matter, he said, "I am treasurer of the NAACP."

It is good to know that these two organizations have so much in common. There is not a piece of social legislation scheduled to come before the 81st Congress which does not include a booby trap on the race question. Federal aid to education, housing, minimum wage legislation, and, of course, the Taft-Hartley repeal contain the ingredients of a potential explosive which can blow up the "harmony house" in which those who favor human progress are drawing up the blue print for a new world.

No honest member of the UAW can say that he lacks information. At the conference were books with twenty per cent off, motion pictures, and numerous other educational suggestions which are a part of the UAW's drive to make its members the best informed trade union people in the country. There was a convincing speaker who talked on cooperatives and offered examples of how everything, from coal to fertilizer, could be bought cheaper under a program of this kind. Many of those who listened could have told about their own experiences in getting cheaper and better food through "coops" sponsored by the union. If they had any doubts about hospital costs, President Ruether could give them some firsthand knowledge from his game fight for life when his arm was nearly torn off by a shotgun blast.

There was some important talk on what happened during the 1948 campaign. Ten thousand workers were ringing door bells for the union to get out the vote. They even organized a baby sitting brigade for the purpose of getting mothers to the polling places. There was careful, systematic planning to get out the stay-at-homes in the various congressional districts. One congressman frankly told the delegates that he believed that estimates of how many persons would vote, which had been furnished him by the union, appeared to be far too optimistic, but when the returns were in the estimates were proved sound. He said he won, although none of the supporters of his opponent stayed at home. The actual count showed that his opponent received the same votes from the same areas as in 1946. The winner went to Washington in 1948 because persons who stayed home in the previous election were gotten out.

ICKES SPEAKS

Under the direction of Miss Olga Madar, the recreation department of the Union showed delegates how to make halls and meetings more attractive to the membership. Her department, with the help of Bill Oliver, carried on a fight to have colored persons participate in the America Bowling Congress.

After sessions on old age insurance, medical care, and many other things, the conference closed fittingly with a speech by Harold L. Ickes. He told the delegates that oil off the shores of Louisiana and Texas is probably worth about $27,510,000,000.00. He proposed that the Federal Government use the income from this vast supply to set up a trust fund which, among other things, could furnish badly needed federal aid to the nation's educational system. Set beside Mr. Ickes's estimate of billions of dollars in wealth beneath the sea, the UAW treasury of about three million dollars looks very small. However, if we are able to create the kind of political climate which will accept Mr. Ickes' proposal, the UAW will be one of the important forces in bringing it about.

MS: "Education UAW Style," Crisis *56 (March 1949): 73, 93.*

The date has been assigned for editorial purposes.

1. Reuther, 2/20/47, *Hearings*, 1275–1331. See 4/1/49 for Mitchell's reference to this article.

Clarence Mitchell, Jr., Statement on Behalf of Complainants against the New Orleans Post Office, June 28, 1949

STATEMENT OF CLARENCE MITCHELL, LABOR SECRETARY FOR THE NATIONAL ASSOCIATION FOR THE ADVANCEMENT OF COLORED PEOPLE, ON BEHALF OF COMPLAINANTS AGAINST THE NEW ORLEANS POST OFFICE, JUNE 28, 1949[1]

We appear before the Fair Employment Board in an effort to correct discriminatory practices based on race at the New Orleans Post Office. When these complaints were first filed, we represented seventeen persons. One of the men, Mr. Earl Rousseau, 2327 London Avenue, states that he has not changed his views about the discriminatory practices at the post office, but he is not a part of this appeal. One other has not been heard from. Those for whom we now seek redress are:

1.	Paul M. Saizan	-	1725 Urquhart Street
2.	Arthur J. Chapital, Jr.	-	1318 Columbus Street
3.	Edward Meggs	-	3945 Erato Street
4.	Henry R. Greene	-	548 Fourth Street
5.	Alexander Moret	-	2537 Annette Street
6.	Alvin J. Lopez	-	2007 LaHarpe Street
7.	Morris M. Wilson	-	1615 New Orleans Street
8.	Julius I. Bush	-	1819 Duel Street
9.	Irvin V. McKendall	-	1023 N. Liberty Street
10.	Maurice A. Fortin	-	1914 Ann Street
11.	Edgar H. Armstrong	-	1763 N. Miro Street
12.	Nathan J. Johnson	-	1112 S. Genois Street
13.	Wilbur Ferrouillet	-	2537 Pauger Street
14.	Mervin J. Ferrier	-	1558 N. Prieur Street
15.	Flournoy L. Anthony	-	1518 Columbus Street

These fifteen men have served their nation in time of war. They do not want special favors of their country. They seek for themselves and other applicants or employees fair treatment without regard to their race.

We ask that each of these men be offered employment as clerks in the New Orleans Post Office because such position have been wrongfully denied them. We request also that this Board require that personnel policies be established in the New Orleans Post Office which will eliminate existing practices of racial discrimination in the matter of promotions and preferred assignments.

BACKGROUND OF COMPLAINTS

During the twelve years prior to 1941, no colored men were appointed as substitute clerks although at least eleven were known to have passed the Civil Service examination, which was given in 1935, with averages ranging from 90 to 96.5. This policy of exclusion was changed to some extent in 1942 following inquiries by the President's Committee on Fair Employment Practice. As a result of the inquiries of this agency, some colored men were given appointments as clerks. It is the contention of the complainants that in the present situation an effort is being made to limit the number of colored men who are given regular assignments as clerks.

The complaints were first filed by the New Orleans branches of the National Association for the Advancement of Colored People and the National Alliance of Postal Employees. A summary of the contents of the brief drawn up at that time is as follows:

"For sixty-five years, Negroes have been employed in the Post Office in New Orleans but none have been upgraded beyond the automatic grade of special clerk for the last forty years. Of the twenty-seven Negro clerks currently employed, seven are special clerks and two of these seven are senior to the last two white clerks who received supervisory appointments.

"Negro clerks are also denied assignment in the following sections: carrier section, general delivery, rated section, registered section, supply section, stamp windows, letter stations, permit section, special delivery, and finance section. Letter carriers are also discriminated against in that none have been promoted in the past thirty years while white carriers with less seniority and fitness have been upgraded. Negroes are also denied certain preferred assignments. Colored custodial employees are also denied upgrading."[2]

EFFORTS TO OBTAIN SETTLEMENT

Efforts to settle the present cases began early in 1947 when the complaints were filed in the Tenth Regional Office of the United States Civil Service Commission, New Orleans, Louisiana. The Commission stated that the Postmaster had given each of the complainants three considerations, and, therefore, there was no proof of racial discrimination. The ruling of the regional office of the Commission was sustained by the Board of Appeals and Review in Washington. We then appealed to the full Civil Service Commission. The Commission granted a hearing and we were later advised by a member of the Commission that an effort was being made to settle the matter informally with the Post Office Department.

No settlement was made nor did the Commission make a ruling on the validity of the complaints. The entire case was referred back to Mr. Vincent C. Burke, Fair Employment Officer for the Post Office Department. Mr. Burke advised that the Post Office Department had investigated the matter and found that the complainants had been passed over "for good and sufficient reason." He concluded that there was no discrimination because of race. We then appealed to the Federal Fair Employment Board.

STATEMENT OF THE CASE

In 1948, a subcommittee of the Senate Committee on Post Office and Civil Service conducted an investigation of discrimination based on race in Federal agencies. This subcommittee found that the New Orleans Post Office employed 451 regular white clerks, 61 white substitute clerks, and 32 temporary white clerks, making a total of 544 persons of the white race employed as clerks. Among the colored employed, 74 were regular clerks, 28 were substitute clerks, and 28 were temporary indefinite substitutes, making a total of 130.

In the carrier force, the picture is somewhat reversed. The grand total for regular, substitute, and temporary carriers for white persons is 94; for colored persons it is 376. Among mail handlers which is an unskilled job, colored persons are 103 while white employees are 32.

As a practical matter, colored applicants in New Orleans and many other southern cities find it easier to obtain jobs in post offices as carriers than as clerks. This may be substantiated by reading the subcommittee's report dated December 31, 1948.

The pattern of limiting the number of colored persons employed as clerks is clear in these complaints. With a few exceptions, the colored men who were rejected as clerks received letters asking whether they were available for temporary indefinite work as carriers.

From November 16, 1946 to March 24, 1947, a total of 199 persons were appointed as clerks in the New Orleans Post Office. Of these, 156 were white and 43 were colored. Of those not selected during this period, 36 were colored and 8 were white.

On a certificate dated October 18, 1946, 5 persons were rejected. All of these were colored. Mr. Saizan's name is 17th on this list. Of the persons ahead of him, 11 were appointed. As a 10-point veteran, his average was 81.6. Mr. Saizan served in the army for 2 years and 3 months. He was wounded in a mine explosion during the Italian campaign. After Mr. Saizan was passed over by the Postmaster, persons with ratings from 80.8 down to 70.6 were appointed. Mr. Saizan is now working in the Railway Mail Service.

The other colored men rejected on this certificate were Messrs. McKendall, 100.2; Lopez, 97.8; Edward Lewis, and Joseph Arnaud. We are not authorized to act for Messrs. Lewis and Arnaud. All of these men are veterans of World War II. Mr. Lopez and Mr. McKendall were subsequently appointed to the Railway Mail Service on a different examination.

The certificate of November 22, 1946, shows that 8 persons not selected 6 were colored. One of the white persons rejected was selected from a subsequent certificate on January 7, 1947. The other white eligible declined appointment on the January 7 certificate. Thus there were only 6 eligibles who sought appointments but were not finally selected or offered jobs. All of them were colored. They were Messrs. Louis J. LaBaud, 92.8; Zenon, 91.6; Ferrier, 96.5; Wilson, 95.8; Ferrouillet, 95.4; and Theophile A. Saberre, 96.2. Mr. LaBaud and Mr. Zenon are 10-point veterans. We are not authorized to represent Mr. LaBaud, Mr. Zenon, and Mr. Saberre. Mr. Ferrouillet is serving as a temporary indefinite clerk in the New Orleans Post Office.

Mr. Ferrouillet's name appeared again on the certificates of January 7, 1947, but again he was not selected. Four other persons were also rejected. Two of these were colored. The colored persons not selected in addition to Mr. Ferrouillet were Messrs. Fortin, whose average was 93.0 and Chapital, whose average was 92.8. Mr. Chapital was offered temporary employment as a carrier. Mr. Fortin was already employed in the post office as a W.S.I. clerk.

On February 17, 1947, the Postmaster dismissed Mr. Fortin by reason of reduction in force. The records show that Mr. Fortin had worked for two years in the New Orleans Post Office. He had accumulated 412 demerits for minor latenesses and absences. However, he had completed what would have been a probationary period of service and had efficiency ratings of 89 and 84. Two other complainants, Mr. Bush and Mr. Anthony, joined Mr. Fortin in an effort to have the dismissal notice set aside.

Other white W.S.I. clerks, including W.J. Collins, who was not a veteran, and Charles Richaux, were appointed by the Postmaster. The Civil Service Commission in New Orleans sought to justify the Richaux appointment on the ground that he had a larger number of demerits at one time but at the time of his appointment he had only 10. The Commission said that the time limit on the others had expired. It was admitted by the Commission that Mr. Collins had 385 demerits.[3] Six of Mr. Collins' demerits were said to have been given him when he took *twenty-four minutes for lunch instead of thirty.*

In replying to the Commission on Mr. Fortin's behalf, Mr. Daniel Byrd, representing the NAACP in New Orleans, stated the following:

> "In discussing the case of Maurice Fortin, Jr., your letter did not disclose that Mr. Fortin had certain merits and it was also noted that great stress was laid upon the fact that the three Negroes involved were demerited for failing to report for duty, failing to notify the office of intended absence, etc., yet your letter did not disclose that W. J. Collins, white, for a long period of time was A.W.O.L. from the New Orleans Post Office and was guilty of the same offenses in a graver degree than any of the three Negroes involved.
>
> "We have been informed by Mr. Fortin that during the time he received a large number of demerits that his father was ill and he asked his immediate supervisor, Boltz, to move his reporting time up as he was forced to wait for the doctor due to the illness of his father. This request was made in the presence of a witness and while the supervisor knew of this condition he refused to grant a later reporting time saying in effect, 'that if I permit you to report later then all of the other men will want to report later.'
>
> "Much stress is also placed upon your letter in the last paragraph on Collins only having six demerits charged against him between October 1, 1946, and December 7, 1946. Nevertheless, in looking at Collins' record, it shows 391 demerits for a white, non-veteran and looking at Bush's record, it shows 316 demerits for a Negro, five-point veteran, and Fortin's record should show 412 demerits including thirty merits for a five-point Negro veteran, as compared against 391 demerits of Collins, a white non-veteran."

The Civil Service investigation in New Orleans revealed that the Postmaster had improperly dismissed the three men and the notice of separation was cancelled. However, they were never given regular appointments.

On the certificate of February 1, 1947, 15 persons were rejected. Of these, 11 were colored and 4 were white. The averages of these colored men ranged from 88.6 to 92.2. Those we represent are Messrs. Moret, Bush, Anthony, and Meggs. Mr. Anthony is a regular clerk in the Los Angeles Post Office while Messrs. Bush, Moret, and Meggs are working in the Railway Mail Service.

WAR SERVICE APPOINTEES

Five of the men we represent had War-Service appointments as clerks in the post office. We have already discussed the case of Mr. Fortin. Others are Messrs. Bush, Rousseau, Johnson, and Anthony. The Senate subcommittee found that the Postmaster appointed 28 W.S.I. clerks to regular positions. Of these, 21 were white and 7 were colored. Six W.S.I.'s were not appointed and five of these were colored. Of these five, only Mr. Johnson and Mr. Rousseau are still in the New Orleans Post Office. Mr. Rousseau is a regular carrier as a result of a new examination and Mr. Johnson[4] is a temporary indefinite special delivery messenger.

Because the situation affecting the W.S.I. appointees is somewhat different from that of the other men, we present in full the complaint of Mr. Bush. His case is typical of what happened to the others.

Mr. Bush was appointed to the post office on August 8, 1943. Prior to that time he was in the United States Navy. His first appointment in the post office was temporary, but, on October 23, 1943, he was given a war service indefinite appointment as clerk. He passed the clerk-carrier examination in August of 1946 with a rating of 91.2. He was certified for appointment on February 1, but was rejected by the Postmaster.

On February 17, the Postmaster advised Mr. Bush by letter that his services would be terminated because of reduction in force. The letter also stated that the dismissal was in accordance with post office and Civil Service regulations. As previously stated, Mr. Anthony and Mr. Fortin had received similar notices. As we have said before, their appeal also noted that white men below them, Mr. Collins and Mr. Richaux, had been given regular appointments. The Postmaster had violated the Civil Service rules in dismissing the men and the notices of separation were cancelled at that time.

Mr. Bush had been working for approximately three and one-half years. During the year of 1946, he had received 316 demerits. These were based on three absences, seven times being tardy, one time for failure to reply to an official communication, and two times for failure to file sick leave blanks. He had four efficiency ratings ranging from 90 to 94.[5]

As has been noted in the quotation from Mr. Byrd's letter, Mr. Collins had 385 demerits and was not a veteran. The demerits given Mr. Collins were for the same general reasons Mr. Bush was given demerits. Moreover, the whole process of giving demerits appears capricious in that Mr. Collins was given 6 demerits at one time for taking only 24 minutes for lunch when he should have taken 30. The system of granting demerits appears to be so flexible that it has little meaning. For example, this statement was made by the Civil Service Commission concerning Mr. Richaux, "It is true that he had a larger number of demerits at one time, but the time limit on some of his demerits had expired and he had offset other demerits by earning merits." This suggests a complicated arrangement in which picayune details may be used to reward or punish employees at the whim of supervisors.

However, even if we accept the system of merits and demerits as practiced by the post office, all persons should be treated alike under it. On the record, there are only two respects in which Mr. Bush and Mr. Collins differ. Mr. Bush is a veteran and colored. Mr. Collins is not a veteran and white. Apparently, the Postmaster thought that the fact that Mr. Collins was white was the most important factor in making his selection.

DISABILITY STATUS

We present a statement on the case of Mr. Greene as set forth on page 28 of the Senate subcommittee's report. Mr. Greene was not selected allegedly because of a service connected disability—high blood pressure. The Board will note that Mr. Greene was first appointed in 1944 as a mail handler which requires much physical activity. Later he worked as a temporary clerk. He was actually working in the post office at the time he was rejected for a permanent appointment. At present, he is employed by an insurance company. The duties he would have performed as a clerk in the post office are no more exacting than his present work. Mr. Greene's rating on the examination was 72.2. As we have previously stated, the Postmaster made appointments of persons whose grades went as low as 70.6. This information can be found on the certificate of October 18, 1946.

"Henry R. Greene, residing at 548 Fourth Street, New Orleans, La., served in the United States Army from September 12, 1942, to December 3, 1944, when he was honorably discharged. Greene is a 10-point disabled veteran of World War II and is, therefore, entitled to the benefits of the Veterans' Preference Act of 1944.

"In December 1944, Greene was appointed a war-service indefinite mail handler (formerly laborer) in the New Orleans post office. On March 6, 1945, Greene was appointed temporary clerk. On August 23, 1946, Greene passed a civil service examination for clerk-carrier, receiving a rating of 72.2. He received notice of his rating in the examination on October 21, 1946, and shortly thereafter his eligibility for appointment was suspended by the Commission because of hypertension.

"Greene was receiving treatment from the Veterans' Administration and on or about February 1, 1947, he presented evidence to the New Orleans Post Office setting forth that this physical condition was taken such that he could be considered for appointment. He was at this time actually working in the post office and had been so engaged since 1944. On or about March 14, 1947, Greene received a letter from the Postmaster at New Orleans inquiring as to his availability for appointment, to which he immediately replied in the affirmative. He received no further information from the Postmaster.

"On March 21, 1947, William C. Deering, Sr., of the personnel division of the New Orleans post office, stated that Greene's name was at that time on a certificates from the Civil Service Commission but had not been considered three times, and that the question of Greene's health would receive careful consideration by the Postmaster in connection with considering him for appointment.

"The following is taken from the report of Chief Investigator LeRay, who investigated the complaint of Greene for the Civil Service Commission:

'The matter of this appellant's physical condition was discussed with Dr. Ernest L. Mock, medical director of the tenth civil service region, who stated that his file disclosed that on approximately October 17, 1946, Mr. Greene had blood pressure of 190/120, whereas the requirement for appointment to the position of substitute clerk requires a blood pressure of not more than 160/100. On Approximately February 17, 1947, Dr. Mock received a communication from the Veterans' Administration indicating the complainant's blood pressure was 120/120. This blood pressure appeared to be an error to Dr. Mock who consulted the Veterans' Administration, where the appellant had been receiving treatment, and the Veterans' Administration reported that their last record indicated the appellant's blood pressure to be approximately 180/120.'

"Greene's name was certified for appointment on Civil Service certificates as follows:

Certificate No. 10, dated March 11, 1947
Certificate No. 11, dated March 26, 1947
Certificate No. 15, dated April 4, 1947

"Greene was not selected for appointment on either consideration and, having been considered three times, he was eliminated from further consideration."

THE REMEDY WE SEEK

1. For those men not now working in the New Orleans Post Office, it is clear that fair play requires that they be immediately offered employment with seniority dating from the time the discrimination occurred.
2. Those men working in the Railway Mail service and the one person employed in Los Angeles should be offered and opportunity to transfer to New Orleans with seniority dating from the time when the discrimination occurred.
3. The New Orleans Post Office should be required to review its policies of hiring, promotion, and transfer in order that racial discrimination shall be eliminated in that establishment.

We strongly urge that the Board study these policies at a later date to determine whether they are in fact operating in a non-discriminatory manner. We are ready to cooperate fully with the Board and the Post Office Department whenever our services are [missing text?]

MS: NAACP WB-154, DLC.

1. See also 3/28/48 in appendix for Mitchell's statement to the Civil Service Commission on problems with the New Orleans Post Office and other texts cited there.

2. Here, Mitchell appended the following handwritten notation: "We have letter from Donaldson indicating that senior employee meeting qualifications is usually selected P.M.G. letter to McGrath dated June 4."

3. Mitchell's handwritten note in the margin said: "400 demerits."

4. Here, Mitchell crossed out "Anthony" and replaced it with "Johnson."

5. Here, Mitchell added: "400 demerits considered good for grade 1 clerks and carriers."

[January 31, 1950]

Why Taft-Hartley Should be Repealed

In 1946 the Republican Party, for the first time in sixteen years, secured control of Congress. And, promptly, with the cooperation of Southern Democrats, it replaced the Wagner Act with the Taft-Hartley Act.[1]

The Republicans asserted that the Wagner Act was one-sided and unfair, because it conferred rights only upon employees and not upon employers.

Is there any truth to that charge?

The Wagner Act was passed because many employers tried to prevent workers from joining unions and refused to deal with unions. Such employers fired, or refused to hire, union members and refused to bargain with unions—except company unions. And employers promoted company unions and coerced their employees into joining them.

The Wagner Act was passed to stop employers from engaging in these abuses.

Unions, of course, were not engaged in any comparable abuses against employers.

Unions did not refuse to bargain with employers. Unions are formed for the very purpose of collective bargaining. Unions did not try to prevent employers from joining trade associations (the employers' unions)l or to make them join a particular trade association.

That is why the Wagner Act was directed only against employers, and not against unions. What was unfair about that? Employers need protection against unions about as much as motorists need protection against pedestrians.

PURPOSE OF TAFT-HARTLEY TO BREAK UNIONS

So the Republican 80th Congress passed the Taft-Hartley Act. But the purpose of that law was not to give management and labor equal rights: its purpose was to weaken and, if possible, destroy labor unions.

The Taft-Hartley Act contains not one but scores of union breaking provisions. The combined effect of these anti-union provisions is overpowering. That the unions of this country have survived under this law is a testimonial to their strength and to the determination of American workers to have unions. The Taft-Hartley Act is long and complicated. Here we can summarize only a few of its provisions.

UNION SECURITY CONTRACTS PROHIBITED

The Taft-Hartley Act outlaws any sort of real union security. The closed shop is prohibited. Only a special sort of union shop is permitted. (See definitions below.)

The closed shop was legal long before the Wagner Act was passed. Courts have held closed shops to be perfectly legal since almost the earliest days of the labor movement. The Wagner Act did not legalize the closed shop: it left the law as it found it.

The Taft-Hartley Act, in contrast, prohibits the closed shop and the type of union shop used before Taft-Hartley.

As long as there has been collective bargaining in America there have been closed and union shop contracts. Before the passage of the Taft-Hartley Act, approximately ten million American workers enjoyed the benefits of union security contracts in the steel industry, the clothing industry, fur, rubber, printing, maritime, electrical manufacturing, textile, and many other industries. The closed and union shops have contributed to industrial peace.

A study by Father Jerome L. Toner, formerly of Catholic University, draws the following conclusions with respect to the closed shop:

"1. Labor relations are considerably smoother as a result of the closed shop.

"2. trade unions have demonstrated genuine responsibility under closed shop contracts, and have contributed substantially to the improvement of production.

"3. The closed shop will probably be the rule rather than the exception within the next decade."[2]

Our labor history shows that employer opposition to the closed shop is a mask withch usually conceals a basic objective of destroying unionism. The same anti-labor employers who now claim to opposed the closed shop in principle did not, in the days before the Wagner Act, hesitate to sign closed shop contracts with company unions. As Father Toner's study pointed out:

Many of those employers who use the closed shop to frustrate genuine labor organization frown on it when they are asked to incorporate it into the standard union contract.

Under a Taft-Hartley union shop a union may seek the discharge of an employee who has been expelled from the union only if he was expelled for non-payment of dues. If he was expelled from the union because he was trying to undermine the union, or break its contracts, or was an employer spy or a Pinkerton man, the union may not, the Taft-Hartley Act provides, seek his discharge. And if a union does get such a person fired, the National Labor Relations Board will reinstate him and require the union to pay him back pay.

The Labor Board has recently gone even beyond the language of Taft-Hartley in destroying union security: it has held that a union may not, under a Taft-Hartley union shop, require even that an employee join the union, so long as he pays dues to it.

Thus, under the Taft-Hartley Act, a union can never obtain security against internal conflict, or attacks of employers, or rival unions. It is always "open season" on unions. Stability is eliminated from the collective bargaining relationship.

In addition, an employee may not under a Taft-Hartley union shop, be required to join a union until thirty days after he is hired. In many industries, such as longshoring and construction, jobs do not last thirty days. In such a situation a Taft-Hartley union shop is completely worthless. And how is a sailor to be brought into a union thirty days after his ship has left port?

Moreover, the Taft-Hartley Act, as it has been interpreted by the National Labor Relations Board and thus far by the courts, makes the hiring hall illegal if it is run by a union. Yet as everyone possessing the slightest familiarity with the long-shoring industry knows, the hiring hall is the only means for securing decent employment practices in that industry. The hiring hall is the answer, and the only answer thus far found to the shape-up.

The shape-up is the system by which men seeking work line up, say, at a pier where a ship is to be unloaded. A foreman for a stevedoring company picks from among the applicants men to unload a particular ship. The unsuccessful applicants then move on to the next pier, and so on. Kickbacks to the foremen are a regular and apparently inevitable accompaniment of this method of selecting a crew or work gang, and gangsterism is the regular companion of the kickback.

From the standpoint of the worker this system means that he must kick back part of his meager wage to foremen and gangsters. It means that he never knows whether or when he will have work. The more he kicks back or the better he stands in with the racketeers controlling the shape-up, the more likely he is to be hired. A union, of course, cannot exist under these conditions—unless it participates in the racketeering.

We are not alone in expressing this opinion. The same view was expressed by the Republican controlled Joint Congressional Committee on Labor-Management relations, established by the Taft-Hartley Act. *Fortune* magazine in its December, 1949, issue likewise condemns the shape-up and shakedown still employed in the longshore industry on the East Coast, and strongly condemns the union (AFL) and the employers for their refusal to establish hiring halls with rotational hiring. *Fortune* seems to be unaware that its favorite political party has outlawed the remedy to which it rightly points as the only cure for the evils of waterfront hiring practices.

Numerous employers in such industries as the construction, maritime, and longshore, in which unions have for many years served as employment agencies, have declared that Taft-Hartley's ban on the closed shop has destroyed access to a pool of skilled labor for the employer and regularity of employment for the employee.

Even the feeble Taft-Hartley union shop is not made freely available to unions. Even though a union is the certified bargaining representative, and even though the employer is perfectly willing to agree to a Taft-Hartley union shop, they are not permitted to unless the union wins a special authorization election. And in such an election the union is required to secure not merely a majority of those voting, as in the conventional elections, but a majority of those eligible to vote. Even when a union wins such an election, it has not achieved a unioin shop; it has only won the right to bargain with the employer for a union shop. And that right is subject to cancellation if it loses a de-authorization election.

It was obviously the hope of those who wrote the Taft-Hartley Act that this complicated and unfair election machinery would result in wiping out even limited union security. But that has not been the result. The Labor Board has reported from August 1947, to November, 1949, authorization elections were won by unions in 97.3 percent of the cases, and that 93.8 percent of those eligible voted in favor of union security. During the period in which these elections were conducted, 3,398,654 employees voted. The union authorization election thus has not served its purpose of preventing union security. On the contrary, many employers complain that it has promoted union security because it is more difficult to resist a demand for union security after the employees have voted in favor of it.

It has cost the government about 40 cents a vote to discover that employees want union security. The union security authorization election has also imposed a very heavy administrative burden upon the NLRB. During the fiscal year 1948–1949, the Board held no less than 30,000 union shop authorization elections. The result was that the Board was unable to process unfair labor practice cases with a reasonable degree of promptness, resulting, as a practical matter, in a denial of relief in many cases.

A further objection to the union authorization election provision is that it is completely unworkable in industries where employment is intermittent, such as construction, maritime, and longshore. The Labor Board has never been able to work out a method of conducting union security authorization elections in these industries.

Since union shop authorization elections have not operated as the authors of Taft-Hartley hoped, but instead have served to demonstrate union strength, and the desire of workers for union security, Senator Taft is now willing, and even anxious, to abolish these elections. That was one of the two changes which the Taft Bill, passed by the Senate at the last session of Congress, made in the union security provisions of Taft-Hartley.

The other Taft Bill change would allow a union to seek discharge for the following causes, in addition to non-payment of dues: (1) a strike in violation of a collective bargaining agreement, and (2) membership in the Communist Party. Unions would still be forbidden to seek the discharge of labor spies, company agents, or organizers of a rival union.

(Senator Taft, early in the 81st Congress, in January, 1949, proposed certain amendments to the Taft-Hartley Act which became known as the Taft Bill. Realizing that the 1948 election was a mandate from the voters of the country to the President and the Congress to repeal Taft-Hartley, Senator Taft was interested in preserving as much of the Taft-Hartley Act as possible. From time to time in this *Economic Outlook*, reference is made to the Taft Bill. It will become clear that that bill is no better than the original and represents only an attempt by Senator Taft to make the Taft-Hartley Act a little more palatable to the voters. However, to people informed on the nature of the proposed amendments, it will be clear that the Taft Bill offers no hope for a sound basis for collective bargaining.)

GOVERNMENT BY INJUNCTION

During the latter part of the Nineteenth Century, and up until 1932, federal court injunctions were a principal means of breaking strikes and unions. Sometimes these injunctions were obtained by employers, and sometimes they were secured by the federal government itself. Beginning with the infamous injunction against Eugene Debs in 1894, which broke the Pullman strike and the American Railway Union (and made a Socialist of Debs), the federal government broke many strikes, and destroyed several unions, by injunction.

In some instances the federal courts outlawed strikes outright, on the ground that their purposes were contrary to public policy. In the Debs case the strike was prohibited as interfering with the mails. In other cases the courts forbade picketing, or picketing by more than, say two pickets. Then, as now, the courts were staffed largely with judges who as lawyers had represented only employer interests.

Many of these injunctions purported to be issued under the general language of the Sherman Antitrust Act relating to restraints upon commerce. In 1914, early in the Wilson administration, Congress sought to put an end to this abuse of the anti-trust laws by providing, in the Clayton Act, that the labor of a human being should not be considered to be an article of commerce.

The federal courts showed little regard for the intention of Congress in passing the Clayton Act. Through the 1920s the United States Supreme Court, under the leadership of Chief Justice Taft, the father of the present Senator, continued to sanction the issuance of injunctions in all sorts of labor cases.

At the 1930 elections the Democrats regained control of Congress. Aided by insurgent Republicans, they made a further attempt, and this time a successful one, to restrict the use of injunctions in labor disputes except in certain unusual cases and subject to rigid restrictions. Labor unions thought that this law, the Norris-LaGurdia Act, had put an end for all time to the evil of government by injunction. While it had been passed by a Democratic Congress, it had been signed by a Republican President —Herbert Hoover.

But the Taft-Hartley Act brought back the evil of government by injunction in worse form than ever before. For the Taft-Hartley Act authorized the Labor Board to secure an injunction in each and every case in which it issues a complaint.

Under the practice established by the Wagner Act, after the Board issued a complaint, a hearing was held before a trial examiner and eventually the Board determined, upon the basis of the evidence at the hearing, whether the Act had been violated. If the Board found a violation, it could issue an order to correct the violation, but if enforcement of that order was necessary, the Board had to apply to a court.

Under the Taft-Hartley, in contrast, once the Board has issued a complaint it may ask a district court for a preliminary injunction pending the hearing before the Board's trial examiner. The result is that the injunction is issued first, and later the facts are heard by the Labor Board's trial examiner. The injunctive and contempt powers of the court are used to compel a union to cease practices with which it has merely been charged, and which it has not had an opportunity to refute.

After the injunction has been granted, and a trial examiner has heard the evidence, the Board may decide that the complaint was without merit. The Board's decision, however, may not come for a year or more after the injunction has been issued. Meanthile, the strike may have been broken and the union ousted from the plant. It was precisely such unfair and evil uses of the injunction which led to the Norris-LaGuardia Act. The damage to the union and the employees has been done. It makes no difference that ultimately the injunction may be shown to be erroneous and may be lifted.

It is worth noting that under the Wagner Act employees and unions neither asked nor received any remedy by injunction against employers. Relief had to await the outcome of Labor Board hearings and court proceedings. If an employee illegally discharged can forego emergency relief and can await the orderly and normal determination of his rights, one wonders why employers, with their greater resources, must have emergency relief.

The Taft Bill proposed no change in these injunction provisions of the Taft-Hartley Act. Evidently the Senator thought them perfect.

SECONDARY STRIKES AND BOYCOTTS

Almost as soon as labor unions started to develop in this country, the courts invented the theory that it was illegal for unions to engage in certain activities, called secondary strikes or boycotts. If, for example, members of a union refused to work on goods made under sweat shop conditions in a non-union plant which their union was trying to organize, that was declared to be an illegal secondary strike or boycott.

Union members, and liberals generally, have never accepted this judge-made-doctrine—and never will. Unions are morally entitled to protect union standards by refusing to handle non-union-made goods. Unions are morally entitled to support their organizing efforts by refusing to handle the products of non-union plants which they are seeking to organize.

One purpose of the Clayton Act, passed by Congress in 1914, was to stop the federal courts from prohibiting secondary strikes and boycotts.

But the United States Supreme Court ignored the language of the Clayton Act and the manifest intention of Congress, and continued to forbid secondary strikes and boycotts. In one such famous case, called the Bedford Stone case, members of a union refused to work on stone which had been cut at non-union quarries.[3] Over the protest of Justices Brandeis and Holmes, the Supreme Court upheld an injunction against the boycott.

Another such famous case was the Duplex Printing Press case. That case involved a manufacturer of newspaper printing presses. There were only four such manufacturers in the country, and all of the plants except that of Duplex were organized. Operating under sweat shop conditions Duplex was able to undersell its competitors. Two of them, therefore, notified the union that they would terminate their agreements with it unless it was able to organize Duplex. To aid the attempt to organize Duplex, members of the union refused to install presses which Duplex sold to newspapers.

The Court, again over the protest of the liberal Justices, held that the refusal to install Duplex printing presses was an illegal secondary boycott.

Eventually the unions secured relief from Congress. The Norris-LaGuardia Act, passed in 1932, deprived the federal courts of jurisdiction to issue injunctions in labor disputes, except in certain exceptional circumstances. The broad prohibition covered, of course, injunctions against secondary strikes and boycotts, and so long as the Norris-LaGuardia Act remained on the books unimpaired, no further injunctions against secondary strikes or boycotts were issued by the federal courts.

The Wagner Act, passed in 1935, did not specifically deal with secondary strikes or boycotts at all. However, its broad guarantee to employees of the right to engage in concerted activities for their mutual aid or protection no doubt covered secondary strikes and boycotts, and recognized them to be legal.

Taft-Hartley did two things with respect to secondary strikes and boycotts. First, it declared them to be unfair labor practices. Secondly, it directed that whenever an employer filed a charge that any person was engaging in a secondary strike or boycott, the General Counsel of the Labor Board should, if he had reasonable cause to believe the charge, secure an injunction from a federal district court pending the Board's decision with respect to the matter.

Thus Taft-Hartley created a situation more detrimental to labor, as regards secondary strikes and boycotts, than had existed even before Norris-LaGuardia. For Taft-Hartley directs that the government itself should secure an injunction in every secondary boycott case.

The Taft-Hartley Act thus adopted the reactionary and anti-union viewpoint, repeatedly rejected by Congress and by liberal Justices, that all secondary strikes or boycotts are improper and illegal. In addition, it provided, as had never been the law before, that the federal government must intervene on behalf of the employer in every secondary boycott situation, by securing an injunction against the union.

At the hearings before the Senate Committee at the First Session of the 81st Congress, CIO General Counsel [Arthur J.] Goldberg pressed Senator Taft as to whether he really believed that union members should be compelled by injunction to handle non-union, sweat-shop-made goods, as in the Bedford Stone and Duplex Printing Press cases. After some equivocation, the Senator acknowledged that he did believe that union members should be made to handle sweat-shop-made goods. "That may be a family prejudice," the Senator said, pointing out that his father had so held in the Bedford and Duplex cases. Surely a man's views of such a subject should have some basis other than that his father thought the same!

At the 1949 session of Congress Senator Taft proposed a single relatively unimportant modification to his sweeping prohibition of secondary strikes and boycotts. This modification would have given a union the right to refuse to work on goods which had been contracted out of a plant that was on strike. The Taft-Hartley Act had in fact already been given that interpretation by the courts.

In addition, the Taft Bill would have merged the requirement that the General Counsel of the NLRB seek an injunction in every secondary strike or boycott case into the general authorization to the Board to seek an injunction in any case.

EMPLOYER ANTI-UNION PROPAGANDA

Under the pretext of protecting the Constitutional rights of employers to freedom of speech, the Taft-Hartley Act has brought back the captive audience. Once more employers are free to require employees to listen to anti-union harangues.

No provision at all, of course, was needed to protect the Constitutional rights of employers. The Supreme Court had done that long before. "Freedom of Speech" was simply seized upon as a pretext for encouraging anti-union propaganda.

DENIAL OF VOTE OF STRIKERS

Perhaps the most outrageous single provision of Taft-Hartley is that which prohibits strikers from voting in Labor Board elections, if the strike concerns economic issues, such as wages, and if the employer has hired scabs to replace them.

Under the Wagner Act both striker and strike-breaker could vote. Anyone would have supposed that employers and scabs could not have asked more than that. But Senator Taft gave them more than that: he provided that only the strikebreakers could vote and that the strikers could not.

The Senator has been ready to abandon this provision since the election in 1948. Indeed, he now prefers not to talk about it at all.

INJUNCTIONS AGAINST NATIONAL EMERGENCY STRIKES

Under the Taft-Hartley Act, if the President finds that a strike threatens to create a national emergency, an injunction is issued for eighty days. It is issued without any inquiry by anyone as to whether the strike is the fault of the employer or the union. Even if a strike is caused by an unfair labor practice of the employer, it is the union which is restrained. There is no provision for plant seizure.

Since the Taft-Hartley Act also require that the union give the employer sixty days' notice before the end of the contract before striking, the total length of the prohibition against striking is actually almost five months. During that period the union is required by law to continue operations under the terms of the existing contract. And the employer has five months to get ready to break the strike.

Since these provisions of Taft-Hartley are manifestly unfair and indefensible, the Taft Bill attempted to created at least an appearance of fairness in the handling of national emergency disputes. In the first place, the Taft Bill would have shortened the eighty-day injunction period to sixty days. Together with the sixty-day notice period which the Taft Bill would have preserved, that would have meant a prohibition against striking for four months instead of nearly five, as under Taft-Hartley.

In the second place, the Taft Bill provided, in an attempt to make the bill look fair, that the President might apply to a court either for seizure or an injunction. However, the seizure was to be only a token one. For, the bill provided that the government might not during any period of seizure negotiate with a union for settlement of the dispute. Thus, Senator Taft clearly meant to have authorized only a fictitious seizure, during which the same management would continue in control but with the United States flag raised over the plant to make the union feel better about government strikebreaking.

We have discussed but a few of the crippling, union-breaking provisions of Taft-Hartley. Enumeration of the anti-labor provisions of that statute might be continued almost indefinitely. The effect of these provisions in combination is, of course, much greater than the single effect of any provision. These provisions working together, were carefully designed to enable an employer to break a union.

Business Week, a conservative publication of industry, has admitted as much. In a repentant editorial, which appeared immediately after the 1948 election, this periodical said:

> "What was wrong was that the Taft-Hartley Act went too far. It crossed the narrow line separating a law which aims only to regulate from one which could destroy.
>
> "Given a few million unemployed in America, given an administration in Washington which was not pro-union—and the Taft-Hartley Act conceivably could wreck the labor movement.
>
> "These are the provisions that could do it: (1) picketing can be restrained by injunction; (2) employers can petition for a collective bargaining election; (3) strikers can be held ineligible to vote—while the strike replacements cast the only ballots; and (4) if the outcome of this is a 'no-union vote, the government must certify and enforce it.
>
> "Any time there is a surplus labor pool from which an employer can hire at least token strike replacements, these four provisions, linked together, presumably can destroy a union."
>
> When industry admits that this is what the Taft-Hartley Act does, can labor be blamed for opposing it"

* * *

What was the purpose of employers and reactionary groups in the United States in passing the Taft-Hartley Act? That is the question that must be carefully analyzed in any discussion of Taft-Hartley or the substitute Taft Bill. . . .

The original Wagner Act made the function and place of trade unions in American life very clear. It stated in its declaration of policy that,

> "the inequality of bargaining power between employees . . . tends to aggravate recurrent business depressions, by depressing wage rates and the purchasing power of wage earners in industry and by preventing the stabilization of competitive wage rates and working conditions within and between industries."

This declaration of policy in the Wagner Act makes it clear that workers are to be permitted to organize into unions of their free choice without coercion and intimidation and to bargain collectively to improve their wages, working, and living conditions. . . .

UNION SECURITY DEFINITIONS

Closed Shop.

An agreement between an employer and a union which specifies that no persons shall be employed who are not members of the union and that all employees must continue to be members in good standing throughout their period of employment. Outlawed by the Taft-Hartley Act.

Union Shop.

An agreement between an employer and a union which requires all employees immediately after hiring or after a specified probationary period, to become and remain members of the union. Under the Taft-Hartley Act only a special type of union shop is permitted, and the employer and union may not negotiate a union shop until a majority of those eligible vote for it in a special NLRB election.

Open Shop.

A plant in which the employer recognizes no union organization. Open shop movements have appeared from time to time, disguised as an "American Plan," or claiming to preserve free enterprise.

MS: Published in the CIO's Economic Outlook *11 (January 1950), a copy of which is in NAACP WB-176, DLC. (Annotations are inserted by the editor.)*

1. The Taft-Hartley Act, formally the National Labor Relations Act of 1947, was sponsored by Sen. Robert A. Taft (R-Ohio) and Sen. Fred A. Hartley (R-N.J.) and finally passed by Congress on June 23, 1947. *Congress and the Nation*, 582.

For a layperson's explanation of the amendment, see "What Is This Taft-Hartley Act?" *U.S. News & World Report* 35 (October 16, 1953): 78, 80, 81, 83, 84.

2. Toner, *Closed Shop*, 1–15, 185–92.

3. *Bedford Cut Stone Co. v. Stone Cutters' Association*, 274 U.S. 37 (1927).

Memorandum from John A. Davis on Proposed Amendment for Changing the Method of Electing the President, February 28, 1950

[ca. February 28, 1950]

MEMORANDUM TO: Mr. Clarence M. Mitchell
Labor Secretary, NAACP

FROM: Dr. John A. Davis
Professor Political Science
Lincoln University, Pennsylvania

SUBJECT: Proposed Lodge Amendment for Changing the Method of Electing the President.

1. The Present Method of Electing the President. The Constitution of the United States takes no cognizance of parties and it is because of this that the present method of electing the President is not altogether satisfactory. The Constitution provides that the President shall be chosen by electors who are chosen by the various states. It was the intention of the founding fathers that these electors should use their own discretion in picking a man. However, the electors are nominated on a straight party ticket and always vote for their party's candidate (Dixiecrat electors sometimes do not follow this custom). It happens, therefore, that the presidential candidate in any state who gets more than one-half of the popular vote or a plurality of the popular vote gets all of the electoral votes. As a consequence, it is possible for a man to become President even though he has less than a majority of the popular votes and even though he has less popular votes than his unsuccessful competitors.[1]

In order to make this proposition clear, let us assume there are three states each with 100,00 popular votes and each with 10 electoral votes. Let us further assume that there are just two candidates for the President, whom we will call candidates A and B.

Candidate A wins the first state by 50,001 votes and wins 10 electoral votes. Candidate B loses the first state, receiving 49,999 popular votes but no electoral votes. In the second state, Candidate A wins in the same fashion and Candidate B loses in the same fashion. In the third state, Candidate B wins the entire state by a clean 100,000 popular votes and acquires ten electoral votes. It is clear that Candidate A wins the election with 100,002 popular votes and 20 electoral votes and Candidate B loses the election with 199,998 popular votes and only 10 electoral votes. In the history of the United States only two Presidents, Hayes and Harrison have won elections with less popular votes than their defeated opponents. In all other elections the winning candidate has had a majority or a respectable plurality.

2. The Lodge Proposal. The Lodge proposal aims to do away with the possibility of the President being elected by the minority or a small plurality of the popular votes by allotting electoral votes in each state in proportion to the popular votes. Thus in the state of Pennsylvania, the Republicans in the last election would have received approximately 19 electoral votes, the Democrats approximately16, and the Progressives approximately 1. As you know, what happened in the last election was that the Republicans got all of the electoral votes in Pennsylvania.

The Lodge proposal provides that in case no candidate gets at least 40% of the electoral votes, the election shall be determined by the House and Senate seated together and voting as individuals, not as states. This is certainly a more democratic method than the present arrangement which provides that if no candidate gets a majority of the electoral college, the House of Representatives shall decide the issue by a majority vote with each state delegation having one vote.

3. What the Lodge Proposal Means to the Negro, Minority Groups and Independent Voters. The Lodge proposal will effectively draw the political eye-teeth of all independent voters, including the Negro voter, as far as presidential elections are concerned. The political importance of independent voters exists in presidential, gubernatorial and senatorial elections. In these elections independent voters can swing the doubtful states into either one party column or the other. In New York in the last presidential election, the Progressive Party seceded from the Democratic Party and took enough votes to drop the state in the Republican ranks.

Since 1909, in ever increasing numbers, the Negro has been migrating out of the South to the large industrial states of the North where he has gone largely into heavy industry. He has migrated to those states with a heavy industrial population and consequently large electoral votes. It also happens that most of these states are doubtful states and pivotal states in presidential elections. A shift of from 2 to 4% of the votes in any one of these states will carry it for the Democratic or Republican candidate. It is possible to win a presidential election by carrying these large doubtful states. It is for this reason that Mr. Truman has been willing to stand up to the Dixiecrats. If the Lodge proposal goes through, the Negro vote and the vote of other minority, national, and religious groups will no longer be important in the great pivotal states of New York, New Jersey, Pennsylvania, Ohio, Indiana, Michigan, Illinois, California, West Virginia, Kentucky and Tennessee. Instead of being able to throw these great states to one column or the other, the Negro will be effective in only approximately 15 electoral votes (rough guess). Of course, the same is true of most independent voters and voters of religious and national groups who are for the most part liberal and espouse the Negro cause.

4. *Why the Lodge Proposal is Brought Forward.* First, it would appear that the Lodge proposal has been brought forward because Mr. Lodge and his following, if not Mr. Taft and his following, are convinced that the Republican Party is going to be a large minority party in the great pivotal industrial states. Mr. Lodge therefore hopes to pick up a proportionate share of the electoral votes in the big pivotal industrial states and to win by adding to these votes the electoral votes of the traditionally Republican states in the North and the West.

Secondly, Mr. Lodge expects the Democratic Party to be plagued by a large number of splinter groups such as the Dixiecrat party, the liberal party, the labor party, and so forth. It is for this reason that his proposal requires only *40%* of the electorial college for election. The Republican Party can get 40% of the popular vote.

Thirdly, the Lodge proposal undoubtedly seeks to destroy the Democratic Party. The Democratic Party has become a liberal party because of the influence of the big pivotal industrial states which have been falling into the Democratic column. As a result of this occurrence, Franklin Roosevelt in 1936 was able to get rid of the two-thirds rule for presidential nomination in the Democratic Party (a purely southern requirement). Under the Lodge proposal the electoral vote of the great northern states would be split but the Solid South would continue to deliver a solid Democratic vote. It must follow that the southern Democrats would again reestablish their power over the Democratic Party driving liberal and independent groups out of it. No more fortuitous happening could be envisaged by conservative Republicans.

5. *The Effect of the Lodge Proposal on the Northern and Larger States.* The Lodge proposal will result in a reduction of political influence for the North as a whole. Political representatives have had to pay attention to the needs of northern states and northern political, economic, religious and national groups because of the decisive effect of these groups in causing the blocks of electoral votes in the large northern states to fall to one party or the other. Under the Lodge proposal, each party would get its proportionate share of northern votes; consequently, the competition for the northern states as a whole will be reduced. But it should be remembered that the political influence of the South will still remain great since it will continue to vote solidly Democratic. The importance of the South will grow in the councils of the Democratic Party and in the nation as a whole.

For a long time persons concerned with politics have realized the essential danger of minority election inherent in the electoral college system, but they have thought that the present system of electing the President is the only possible political counterbalance to the Solid South.

6. *Is it "Democratic" to Oppose the Lodge Amendment?* A great many persons have admitted that the Lodge Amendment would have a bad effect on independent, liberal and Negro groups in the North as a whole and on the Democratic Party. But these

persons have felt that one cannot logically oppose more democracy in America. It is assumed that the Lodge proposal means more democracy.

First of all, we do not have a democratic system of Government but a republican system. The Senate of the Unite States represents each state equally. The people of New York, 13,000,000, have only two senators. The people of Delaware, 230,000, have two senators. Under the system of electing the President, the influence of the people of New York and of its independent groups is felt. Under the Lodge proposal the influence of the people of New York would be reduced and there would be no counterbalance to the equal representation of the small states in the Senate.

Secondly, we have a federal system of Government and the Lodge proposal fails to represent states in the election of the President. While the electoral votes are to be apportioned in accordance with the popular vote in each state, the real effect of the Lodge proposal, except for the loss of fractional popular votes in each state, is to cast the United States as one great elector<i>al district.

Thirdly, the Lodge amendment provides that a man may be elected President with only 40% of the <popular> electoral vote. We consistently do much better than this under our present system. It is hardly a democratic proposal.

Lastly, the only offset the Negro has had to disfranchisement in the South and the southern filibuster has been his political influence in the northern pivotal states. The Lodge proposal will rob him of this political influence without enfranchising him in the South and without proposing to stop the unconstitutional filibuster.

7. *The Cumulative Effect of the Lodge Proposal as Far As the Negro and other Independent Political National and Religious Groups are Concerned.* The Lodge Proposal would have a bad effect in a cumulative fashion. First of all, it will kill directly the political influence of the Negro and minority group votes in pivotal states. Secondly, it will reduce the importance of the northern states as a whole and the great industrial states specifically. Undoubtedly, it is in the North where the Negro and minority groups find most interest in their problems .Thirdly, it will destroy the liberal democratic party, for it will once again establish the power of the Solid South over the Democratic party. In the last twenty years most of the advancement of the Negro and other minority groups has come as a result of the interest of the liberal wing of the Democratic Party. Fourthly, many independent groups, liberal groups and even labor groups will begin to take less interest in the problems of the Negro and other minorities. As far as national politics are concerned, political groups in America are formed by accretion The Lodge proposal will have a disintegrative effect on the political groups with which the Negro and other minorities have been allied. Fifthly, the Lodge proposal will kill the influence of the great urban pivotal states. These states have had for the most part the most aggressive labor forces and have been the most powerful ones in presidential elections. They have been the doubtful states where a swerve from two to four percent of the vote on the average has been enough to carry the state for one presidential candidate or another.

8. *Why did the Administration Fail to Oppose the Lodge Amendment in the Senate?* It is difficult to understand why the opposition to the Lodge Amendment in the Sen-

ate came only from Mr. Taft and his followers and from a few Democrats. There are several possible explanations. First, it is possible that White House political leadership missed the significance of the whole move. Secondly, it is possible that Mr. Truman has been seriously hurt by splinter groups–Wallaceites, in the North and the Dixiecrats in the South–and is actually in favor of the Lodge move. There is no question that Mr. Truman is torn between Dixiecrates on one side and Negroes on the other. It might be that he is willing to get rid of these "splinters in his side" even at the cost of a less liberal Democratic Party. Lastly, there is evidently some feeling among labor groups that the Lodge proposal will allow labor for the first time to lump together all of its votes in the North, in presidential elections. It is true that the Lodge proposal is beneficial to all large minorities such as labor or the Republican Party. However, it seems to me that an immediate frontal political attack by labor will result in a general public reaction unfavorable to labor. Furthermore, I doubt if labor's influence under the Lodge system will be any greater than its influence under the present system. I also think that a multi, - party system for America will be disastrous. The political instability resulting from multi- party systems so weakened the French, Italian and German governments that they were unable to withstand aggression from the outside or revolution from within. The indecisive nature of our federal, separation of powers, check and balance system of government would be increased by a multiparty system.

9. *Why Did Mr. Taft Oppose The Lodge Amendment*? Mr. Taft probably opposed the Lodge Amendment because Mr. Lodge is a Young Turk in the Senate, leading a group which has generally been against Taft leadership. If the Lodge movement is successful, Mr. Taft will have to give way to the Young Turks. Moreover, Mr. Taft is probably not convinced that the Republican Party is a minority party in the great pivotal states.

10. *Why the Lodge Amendment must be Stopped in the House*. Should the Lodge amendment get past the House of Representatives, it has an excellent chance of being adopted by the states. The southern Democrats will vote for it as a block. Solid Republican or near solid Republican states will vote for it. Generally the rural states in America will vote for it since the effect of the Lodge proposal is to decrease the influence of the great urban states. It is also obvious that a great deal of conflict exists now between urban and rural population over the question of the cost of food and the farm price support program. The large urban states constitute only 12 of the nations 48 states. Of these, 3 are normally Republican. Constitutional ratification requires the adoption of ¾ of the states. The House of Representatives alone represents population and largely urban population. It is the best place, then, to fight the Lodge amendment which must be adopted by the House by a ⅔ vote.

11. *Can the South Steal the Presidency in 1952?* I am not impressed with the traditional arguments that the Dixiecrats are going to try to steal the presidency in 1952, by splitting up the electoral vote and throwing the election into the House of Representatives.

The Constitution requires that the President must be chosen by a clear majority of the electoral votes. If no candidates get this majority, the matter is decided by the

House of Representatives with each state delegation having one vote. If the Dixiecrats bolt the Democratic Party in 1952, they can perhaps prevent any candidate from getting a majority of the electoral vote. The election would then be thrown into the House of Representatives. Voting as states, the southern states would undoubtedly have more influence than if they had to rely on their electoral votes, but they cannot elect a President in the House of Representatives without the support of conservative Republicans. The Constitution requires a majority vote in the House of Representatives. If the conservative Republicans and the Dixiecrats should agree on a President, it would be the last election they would win for a long time. Exactly this kind of thing happened when the Clay and John Quincy Adams forces ganged up to take the election away from Jackson. The popular reaction was tremendous. The people took the attitude that the election had been stolen. At the next election Jackson was voted in overwhelmingly. The American people cannot be tricked except now and then.

It is far better to allow the southerners the opportunity now and then of an advantage when elections are thrown into the House of Representatives than to give them a consistent advantage by adopting the Lodge proposal.

It seems to me that at most the Dixiecrats can take only nine states in an election carried out in the House of Representatives. They will probably be able to take only three or four states. What they really would like to have is the Lodge proposal, as they have shown by their vote in the Senate. Their threat in a House election of the President, I think, is insignificant.

MS: copy, NAACP WB-126, DLC.

The date is estimated based on Mitchell's report of 3/8/55, vol. V.

1. See, among others, 3/3/50, 8/31/51, and, in appendix, 5/29/51.

Monthly Report of the Labor Secretary for June 7, 1950

STATEMENT OF JOSEPH C. WADDY, (ACCOMPANIED BY CLARENCE MITCHELL, LABOR SECRETARY, NAACP) ON H.R. 7789 TO AMEND THE RAILWAY LABOR ACT BEFORE THE HOUSE OF REPRESENTATIVES, COMMITTEE ON INTERSTATE AND FOREIGN COMMERCE, JUNE 7, 1950

My name is Joseph C. Waddy. I am an attorney at law with offices located in the District of Columbia. I am general counsel for the International Association of Railway Employees, the Association of Colored Railroad Trainmen and Locomotive Firemen, and the Colored Trainmen of America. These organizations have a combined membership of approximately 4,000 railroad employees. Accompanying me is Mr. Clarence Mitchell, Labor Secretary of the National Association for the Advancement of Colored People. By agreement this statement covers the position of all of the organizations mentioned. We appear on behalf of these organizations for the purpose of opposing H.R. 7789 as drawn but not in opposition to the principle of the union shop and dues check-off. Our opposition to H.R. 7789 as drawn grows out of the fact that in its present form the proposed amendment does not adequately protect the rights of minority railroad workers, and creates distinctions within the crafts based on race alone, contrary to the Constitution and the laws of the United States.

Under the Railway Labor Act as presently constituted the majority of a craft or class has a right to determine the representation of the entire craft or class and the railroad companies are forbidden to negotiate on a collective basis with any other organization or representative. There is no specific provision in the act which will compel the representatives chosen by the majority to permit the minority workers to membership in the union or to otherwise participate in the collective bargaining process. A correction of these deficiencies in the Railway Labor Act is a necessary concomitant to any amendment providing for a union shop and dues check-off.

As illustrative of the soundness of this conclusion we wish to call this Committee's attention to a few conditions as they now exist under the Railway Labor Act. For many years some railway labor organizations, particularly the Brotherhood of Locomotive Firemen and Enginemen, the Brotherhood of Railroad Trainmen, the Brotherhood of Locomotive Engineers, the Order of Railway Conductors and the Switchmen's Union of North America, have by constitutional provision barred Negroes from membership; have excluded them from all participation in the collective bargaining process under the Railway Labor Act and have used their positions as collective bargaining representatives to discriminate against Negro members of the crafts; to eliminate from the industry those presently employed therein and to prevent the hiring of any additional Negroes. Other railway labor organizations have shunted Negroes into Jim-Crow auxiliary locals that operate under the white locals, allowing to the Negroes only indirect, inadequate and pro forma participation in the affairs of the union and under which Negroes hold their jobs by sufferance rather than as a matter of right.

Until recently each of the "Big Four" railway labor unions had an absolute color bar in its constitution. However, some of them in order to technically meet the requirements of State FEP laws have now amended their constitutions to provide in effect that such restrictive provision shall not be operative in any jurisdiction where its application would be in violation of the laws of the jurisdiction. When, however, it is remembered that only ten states have FEP laws it becomes obvious that these changes offer no real departure from the exclusionary practices of the unions. Furthermore, even in states where FEP laws exist there is always the "black ball." It should also be remembered that in what is known as the "operating" crafts on the railroads Negroes are now employed only in the southern states where no FEP laws exist. For these employees, therefore, the color bar is still absolute.

Nor are the unions now under discussion content with barring Negroes from membership. In addition thereto they refuse to give the non-member Negro minority any notice or opportunity to be heard or chance to vote on propositions affecting the craft or class. The Negroes have no voice in the choosing of agents of the union who formulate the policies and carry on the collective bargaining; no means of censoring, removing or otherwise controlling these union agents and are thus precluded from any and all participation in the collective bargaining process. The hopeless situation which is thereby created for the Negro employees is graphically illustrated by the testimony given by Thad S. Lee, General Chairman of the Brotherhood of Locomotive Firemen and Enginemen on the Atlantic Coast Line Railroad, in the case of Rolax, et. al., vs. the Brotherhood of Locomotive Firemen and Enginemen, et al., United States District Court for the Eastern District of Virginia, Richmond Division, Civil Action No. 670.[1] During the course of that trial Mr. Lee testified under cross-examination as follows:

"BY MR. [THURGOOD] MARSHALL:

"Q. Getting back to the Brotherhood that you represent as chairman on the Atlantic Coast Line, am I correct that there are subordinate lodges that are more or less autonomous and they have each a local chairman?

"A. Yes, we have Local Lodges with local chairmen.

"Q. Is it not true your position is brought about by a vote of the local chairmen?

"A. That is correct.

"Q. And do you consider yourself responsive to those local chairmen?

"A. Yes, in the capacity of General Chairman.

"Q. Do you consider yourself responsive to the membership of those local chapters?

"A. I do and I might add to that I feel my responsibility to the firemen that are not members of this organization.

"Q. You said yesterday you not only did not notify the negro firemen as to some of your negotiations but you didn't always notify the white firemen, either?

"A. Yes, sir.

"Q. But you did consult with the general committee?

"A. Yes.

"Q. Is that an elected committee?

"A. Yes.

"Q. Who elects them?

"A. The membership.

"Q. Assuming that action is taken by you and/or the general committee that is considered to be objectionable to the local membership, what can the local membership do about it?

"A. If I took action as General Chairman—I think you said a member objected to it?

"Q. The majority of the membership objected to it, the rank and file members?

"A. The majority of the membership objected to it?

"Q. Yes.

"A. I would not take the action.

"Q. Assuming that under abnormal circumstances such action was taken—what I am trying to get at is what redress does rank and file membership have?

"A. Of course, under the laws of our Brotherhood a minority might have an opportunity to appeal over me probably to the International President but keep in mind if the majority of this railroad contemplated taking action he wouldn't get very far with his protest because we are governed by the majority.

"Q. Isn't it possible for each one of the subordinate lodges to vote out of office at the next election the local chairman?

"A. Yes, very definitely.

"Q. And wouldn't it therefore be possible that those local chairmen would be changed and new local chairmen would be put in and they would vote in a new General Chairman?

"A. That would be absolutely correct.

"Q. If the negro firemen on the Atlantic Coast Line objected to what you do as General Chairman, what redress under the sun do they have?

"A. Well, I think, first, if they was to file with me their objections and I thought their objections were well taken, I might agree with them.

"Q. Suppose you didn't?

"A. Well, I presume he would be in the same category as the minority group of white firemen. There wouldn't be much he could do.

"Q. Regardless of whether you consider him a minority group or anything else, the answer is there is nothing he could do? Isn't that the answer?

"A. I presume it is.

"Q. Are you familiar with the machinery of our organization?

"A. I think so.

"Q. Do you know anything in that machinery that would permit a Negro to do anything about what anybody in the Brotherhood under any circumstances did?

"A. No, offhand, I don't know what he could do.

"Q. By the way, negroes aren't eligible for admission to that organization? Is that correct?

"A. Yes, I think they are.

"Q. Negroes are eligible for admission into your Brotherhood?

"A. Yes.

"Q. Under what circumstances?

"A. Under the last action of the Convention. Have you read the late Constitution?

"Q. Certainly, I have.

"A. Doesn't it say in there—

"Q. It says where the State Laws require it.

"A. That is right.

"Q. And that was only passed after the case of Railway v. Causey—the New York case?[2] Isn't that correct?

"A. I don't know about that.

"Q. You were at the convention, weren't you?

"A. Yes, I was not a delegate.

"Q. But you don't know that is the reason that provision was put in there?

"A. No.

"Q. In the States in which your jurisdiction is, the Atlantic Coast Line, is a negro eligible for admission into your Brotherhood?

"A. No, I don't think so."

The harmful effect of this condition upon the Negro employees is by no means theoretical. For them it is immediate, real and cruel and the Brotherhoods have used its existence and are using it to squeeze the Negro out of the Railway industry. For instance, at its Thirty-Second Convention in 1931 the Brotherhood of Locomotive Firemen and Enginemen had before it for consideration the question of colored firemen. The Convention's action on this question is reported beginning at page 983 of the Convention proceedings as follows:

"SUBJECT: COLORED FIREMEN.

"Concerning this subject, we, your Special Committee, find the following matter referred to us for consideration and recommendation:

"From page 294, Eighth Day's Proceedings, we reproduce the following:

"'Motion by A.H. Allbright, Delegate Lodge No. 604.

"Seconded by J. T. Bryan, Delegate Lodge No 864.

"WHEREAS, There are employed on the railroads in the southern states and the railroads entering the southeastern district numerous Negro firemen, in some instances to the exclusion of white firemen and to the extent that they are highly discriminated against and

"WHEREAS, These negro firemen do not contribute to the maintenance of working conditions and rates of pay as secured by the white firemen through this great Brotherhood, and

"WHEREAS, There has been some progress made in the individual General Grievance Committee in the securing the white firemen a larger percentage of these desirable positions, this progress has not bee as great as could be desired, due, in some instances, to a lack of proper effort on the part of the General Grievance Committees and the members they represent, and

"WHEREAS, The General Grievance Committee on one Western railroad entering the Southwestern states has declined to take any further action on this paramount question advising, "that it is the opinion of this Committee that we have acquired all concessions possible on the negro question," and

"WHEREAS, We are informed that some thirty thousand experienced white firemen are at this time cut off of the working lists on the various railroads in the United States and the Dominion of Canada, unsuccessfully seeking employment elsewhere and in other lines, who would be glad to have these positions now held by the Negro firemen, therefore, be it

"*Resolved*, That this the Thirty-second Convention of the Brotherhood of Locomotive Firemen and Enginemen instruct the International President to take some immediate action to secure for the white firemen in the Southern states a greater percentage of the jobs now held by the negro firemen and to correct some of the rules and practices now in effect, whereby senior white firemen are cut off the working lists and seeking employment while junior negro firemen and holding regular assigned jobs at rates of pay and desirable working conditions secured by the white firemen; be it further

"*Resolved*, That this be referred to a Special Committee for investigation, and that all delegates from Southern states where Negro firemen are employed be requested to appear before the Committee.'

"The injustice to and discrimination against white firemen throughout the South is so glaringly outstanding, that this angle of the situation requires no extended comment on our part. Suffice to say, that while much has been accomplished through the efforts of our Committee on the lines where the colored fireman is an issue, the fact is, there are still a large number of colored men employed in engine service in the South, particularly in the Southeast. While on many lines new colored firemen are not hired, many of them remain in the service holding what may be properly termed "prior rights," and these rights are exercised in a manner that admits of gross discrimination against white firemen. As is well known, the character, habits, and general mental make-up of a negro are such as to, in practically all instances, disqualify him for a position of responsibility and trust. The very best evidence of the inferior qualities of the negro in general is the fact that railroads will not promote him to the position of locomotive engineer, yet, paradoxically as it may seem, they permit him to occupy a position that is tantamount to sharing the responsibilities of a locomotive engineer by assigning him to the left side of a locomotive on some of the best and fastest freight and passenger runs in the country. If the truth were told, it is probably not exaggerating the situation to state that the employment of negro locomotive firemen has been, at least, indirectly responsible for accidents; loss of life, and injury. Because of the fact that colored firemen are not promoted, coupled with the fact that many of them hold comparatively a great deal of seniority, they are at times in a position on the seniority roster where they can cover the very best runs available. One Delegate who appeared before our Committee pointed out that on his railroad some time ago a fleet of modern Mikado type, stoker-fired locomotives were placed in service, and that these locomotives, insofar as firemen are concerned, have been exclusively manned by negroes. Another Delegate who appeared before our Committee pointed out a situation that is typical of some seniority district down throughout the Southland. This Brother pointed out that of sixteen passengers runs, but one white fireman is employed; on twelve regularly assigned through freight runs, but three white firemen are employed; on fifteen chain-gang positions, but four white firemen are employed: on twenty seven yard crews, not a white fireman is employed; and on an extra board of twenty men, but five of them are white. In other words, out of ninety-nine firing positions, only fourteen white firemen are employed. The color line in this instance seems to be drawn quite decisively in favor of the colored man.

"While negroes are not eligible for membership in our Brotherhood, it should be remembered that practically every concession in the way of rates of pay, working conditions and general privileges now and in the past enjoyed by negro firemen have been secured by our organization. The fact is, that on some lines in the South committees of our organization handle grievances of colored firemen, thus guaranteeing them the same rights under the contract governing firemen and hostlers that while men enjoy, and on these lines negroes are now well represented. About the year 1918 colored firemen undertook to establish an organization of their own in the South, and went to Washington to get recognition, but our organization showed that they were already, in most instances, well represented.

"It should be kept in mind that certain publicity may do us considerable harm in handling the negro question. To have the impression go out that we are opposed to the use of negro firemen purely because of their race and color can do great damage, especially should we become involved in the courts, because this will be used to show that we are undertaking to handle the question purely on a class basis, and from a legal standpoint this is handicap.

"Many delegates who have appeared before our Committee expressed the opinion that this matter should be handled by individual General Grievance Committees on lines where the negro question is an issue; others believe a concerted movement should be organized, embracing all lines involved; others believe that the matter should be handled with the Interstate Commerce Commission, on the ground that the negro is an unfit subject to share the responsibilities of a locomotive engineman, while many of these delegates believe that the question should be handled through any and/ or all the methods just referred to. All of these delegates and General Chairmen share the opinion mutually with this Committee, that the negro is an undesirable in our particular vocation, therefore should be supplanted by a white man in all instances. The proper means to the desired end, of course, is the problem pressing for solution.

"However, we should not permit our anxiety to solve this question to overbalance our better judgment. It has been pointed out to our Committee by general officers of the Brotherhood, General Chairman, and Delegates to this Convention, that if we start a movement in a manner that in any way is indicative of a threat the reaction therefrom will damage our chances of accomplishing that which now seems to be possible and probable on some of the lines where negroes are now employed. We have been strongly advised by some against recommending any action that will in any manner indicate a threat. On the lines where the most has been accomplished to meet the situation, on these same lines, according to our information, the situation for the future is the most promising, and we are warned that if this Convention should authorize some action that might savor of a threat, the reaction therefrom would not only retard progress in a general way, but it would be particularly detrimental on the lines where the situation is partly solved, and on which lines hope for complete eliminating the negro is the most promising. Any action looking toward presenting the question to the Interstate Commerce Commission would necessarily have to be predicated upon the basis, not that the negro is undesirable as an engineman by reason of his race or color, but because of his inability to read and understand orders and instructions and by reason of his general mental deficiency, and, therefore, his use in this capacity is unsafe and creates a hazard. Undertaking to establish this claim might result in some sort of an examination or test applicable to all locomotive enginemen, which might tend (1) to disqualify some white men, and (2) establish the fitness of an occasional negro to act as engineer. In fact, the whole situation, obnoxious as it appears to us, is one that must be handled with the greatest degree of tact and diplomacy. It should be kept in mind that on some railroads existing rules will in time completely eliminate the employment of Negro firemen. This committee appreciates, to the fullest extent, the patience with which our members throughout the South have borne with this question. The Delegates who have appeared before our Committee have convinced us that the colored firemen question is a matter pressing for solution at the earliest possible time. However, we have also been impressed with the counsel and circumspection with which many of these Delegates have warned us to approach this question, pointing out the inadvisability of doing anything that will tend to destroy or impede progress already made, particularly calling attention to the different aspects of the matter on different lines in different localities. Although this Committee was rather impressed at the outset that with the idea that concerted action would bring about some desirable change in the situation more quickly than any other method, after giving careful consideration to the different witnesses who have appeared before and advised our Committee, we are rather of the opinion that for the time, at least, efforts should be confined to General Grievance Committees on the individual lines involved.

"RECOMMENDATION OF THE COMMITTEE

"After the most serious of this matter, the Committee recommends, that this matter be called to the attention of General Grievances Committees on lines where the subject forms an issue, by the International President, directing that such action as may appear to those Committees to be advisable be taken, furnishing assistance of Grand Lodge officers, if necessary, with the understanding that after efforts have been exhausted through this channel, General Grievance Committees on the lines involved are authorized to give consideration to the advisability of handling the matter at the time and in a manner that as may appear advisable to them, under our laws, and that such assistance, counsel and advice as may be needed and appear warranted will be furnished by the International President, upon request.

"It was moved and seconded that the recommendation of the Committee be adopted.

"Recommendation of Committee adopted."

By way of implementing the action of the Thirty-Second Convention, the Brotherhood on March 28, 1940, served a Notice on 21 railroads in the southeastern section of the country demanding the following:

> "1. Only promotable men will be employed for service as locomotive firemen or for service as helpers on other than steam power.
>
> "2. When new runs or jobs are established in any service, only promotable firemen or helpers will be assigned to them.
>
> "3. When permanent vacancies occur on established runs or jobs in any service, only promotable firemen or helpers will be assigned to them.
>
> "4. It is understood that promotable firemen or helpers on other than steam power are those in line for promotion under the present rules and practices to the position of locomotive engineer."

Under existing rules and practices in the railway industry colored men are not promoted from the position of locomotive fireman to that of locomotive engineer or from the position of trainman to that of conductor. Consequently, colored firemen are designated and known as non-promotable firemen and helpers on other than steam power and white firemen are designated and known as promotable firemen and helpers on other than steam power. Therefore, when the Brotherhood made its proposal for the employment and assignment of only promotable men it was requesting that only white firemen be employed and assigned for service on the railroads as locomotive firemen. Negotiations on this Notice resulted in the infamous Southeastern Carriers Conference Agreement of February 19, 1941, which was condemned by the United States Supreme Court in the cases of Steele v. L. & N. Railroad Co., 323 U. S. 192 and Tunstall v. the Brotherhood of Locomotive Firemen and Enginemen, 323 U. S. 210.

At its convention in 1941, Mr. David B. Robertson, International President of the Brotherhood of Locomotive Firemen and Enginemen reported to the convention on the progress that had been made by way of implementing the action of the Thirty-Second Convention as follows:

"CONCERTED MOVEMENT—SOUTHEASTERN RAILROADS: EMPLOYMENT AND ASSIGNMENT OF PROMOTABLE FIREMEN

"The Thirty-second Convention of our Brotherhood, held in 1931, thoroughly considered the situation existing on southeastern railroads generally involving the employment and assignment in engine service of employees not regarded as competent and qualified either to properly fill the position of locomotive firemen or to pass qualifying examination for promotion to the position of engineer. In its report upon this important subject, the Special Committee recommended that on railroad properties where such employment policy existed, general grievance committees undertake to effect an appropriate remedy; and in the event of failure of such effort, all committees concerned were authorized to give consideration to the advisability of further handling the matter under the laws of the organization at a time and in a manner that appeared most advisable. It was understood that such assistance, counsel, and advice as may be needed would be furnished by the International President.

"Recommendation of the Committee was adopted by the Convention and in line therewith the question was referred by the international president to general chairmen on railroads upon which non-promotable (Negro) firemen were employed. At that time, however, there was pending determination by the courts, litigation instituted by a Negro firemen against the Atlantic Coast Line Railroad seeking to invalidate an agreement consummated by and between the management and the B. of L. E. and B. of L. F. and E. general committees which restricted colored firemen on that property to fifty per cent of the runs in passenger and other road service, and on yard jobs. Officers of our Brotherhood and counsel cooperated with the Atlantic Coast Line Railroad Company in defending the agreement referred to. By decision of the court, said agreement was upheld, thus successfully concluding this litigation when no appeal was taken to a higher court by the plaintiff.

"In the light of this important and favorable development the entire subject was exhaustively discussed on a number of subsequent occasions by the Association of

> General Grievance Committees, District No. 3, out of which action was taken authorizing the inauguration of a concerned movement looking toward the ultimate employment and assignment only of promotable firemen on all locomotives in the service of all carriers concerned......................."

These organizations have also actively opposed the employment of any additional Negroes in the railway industry. In 1917 during the first World War the Brotherhood of Locomotive Engineers and the Brotherhood of Locomotive Firemen and Enginemen protested against the proposed employment of Negro locomotive firemen on the Baltimore & Ohio Railroad and the New York, New Haven and Hartford Railroad. In 1942, during World War II the Brotherhood of Locomotive Firemen and Enginemen issued a strike ballot on the Atlantic Coast Line Railroad and its members voted to strike to prevent the hiring of any additional Negro locomotive firemen on that carrier. This strike threat remained over the head of the Atlantic Coast Line Railroad until the fall of 1948. In 1928 the Brotherhood of Locomotive Firemen and Enginemen, the Brotherhood of Locomotive Engineers, the Brotherhood of Railroad Trainmen, and the Order of Railroad Conductors made a joint agreement with the St. Louis-San Francisco Railway Company providing that thereafter no more Negroes were to be employed on that carrier in train, engine, and yard service but not including train porters. This agreement remained in effect until 1949 when it was abrogated as a result of a $4,000,000.00 suit which the Negro employees on the Frisco filed against the Brotherhood. In 1943 the Brotherhood of Railroad Trainmen Grievance Committee on the St. Louis-San Francisco Railway Company protested the proposal of the carrier to hire Negro trainmen during World War II as being in violation of the 1928 agreement.

Largely as a result of this type of elimination and exclusion of Negroes from train and engine service the number of Negro locomotive firemen in ten Southern States decreased from a total of 5,636 in 1920 to 2,128 in 1940, and from a percentage of 41.6 to 29.5 of the total number of locomotive firemen in those States. During the same period of time the number of Negro trainmen in nine Southern States decreased from 5,083 in 1920 to 2,060 in 1940, and from a percentage of 29.8 to 15.1. The figures for the decade 1940 to 1950 are not yet known but we are painfully aware of the fact that the Brotherhoods have continued, and in some instances intensified, their efforts to eliminate Negroes from train and engine service on the nation's railroads.

In connection with the harmful effects of Negroes being excluded from membership in the Railway Labor unions, we wish to call the committee's attention to the anamolous situation that exists under the National Railroad Adjustment Board. Under section 3 of the Railway Labor Act, the National Railroad Adjustment Board is composed of 36 members, 18 of whom are selected by the carriers and 18 by labor unions national in scope. You begin to see at once what happens when you realize that the Negro workers are excluded from the unions national in scope when select the labor representatives on the board. Take for example Division No. 1 of the board which handles train, engine, and yard service employees. There are 10 members, 5 selected by the carriers and 5 by the unions. The 5 labor members are chosen one each from the Brotherhood of Locomotive Engineers, the Brotherhood of Locomotive Firemen and Enginemen, the Brotherhood of Railroad Trainmen, the Order of Railway Conductors, and the Switchmen's Union of North America. Every one of these 5 unions has a Negro color bar. Obviously, therefore, when a Negro fireman or a Negro brakeman is required to carry his grievance to the National Railroad Adjustment Board, First Division, he has little or no chance of securing fair and equitable adjudication of his claim. Particularly is this true where the grievance grows out of action on the part of one of the unions whose representatives sit on the Board.

Many other railway labor unions in the non-operating part of the industry have resorted to the device of segregating Negro workers in auxiliary and B-class locals. The National Association for the Advancement of Colored People has had many complaints from Negroes who have been segregated in these locals and it feels that the passage of H.R. 7789 as drawn would compel Negroes to join these auxiliaries and B-class locals which afford them no effective protection in their job rights.

The most dramatic illustration of the evils of auxiliaries came during the war when the Fair Employment Practice Committee, established by President Roosevelt, tackled this problem on the West Coast. A group of shipyards in that area had signed a closed shop contract with the Metal Trades Council of the American Federation of Labor. The International Brotherhood of Boiler-Makers, Iron, Shipbuilders, and Helpers of America as a member of the Council represented about 65% of the employees in the shipyards. This union refused to admit colored people to membership and opposed their employment just as the railway brotherhoods have done and are now doing.

After some persuasion, the union finally agreed to withdraw its opposition to the employment of colored people, but insisted that they become members of auxiliaries instead of the regular unions. After investigation and hearing, the Fair Employment Practice Committee had this to say:

> "The disadvantages inherent in the auxiliary device included the supervision of the auxiliaries by regular union locals, denying to the auxiliaries the right to select business agents or grievance committees, denial of the right to receive apprentices, denial to the auxiliary members of the right to change their job classification without the consent of the supervising locals, the denial of any voice in the formulation of the policies of the supervising locals and other advantages enjoyed by members of such locals, including the right of universal transfer, and the right to elect delegates to the international convention. Further, under the laws of the international, an auxiliary, unlike a regular local, could be abolished at any time by international officials.
>
> "When Negro employees refused to join or remain auxiliary members, the union demanded their discharge on the ground that they were not 'members in good standing.'"[3]

In the railroad industry, the Association has found that the pattern of forcing colored members to form segregated unions still persists. This question came before the Kansas Supreme Court in the case of *Betts v. Easley* in 1946. In order that this committee may have the exact circumstances as presented to the court, we quote from the decision a few paragraphs concerning the false promises made by the Brotherhood of Railway Carmen to colored men employed in the shops of the Santa Fe Railroad in Kansas City, Kansas, as follows:

> "The Grand Lodge Brotherhood Railway Carmen of America was chosen and officially designated as collective bargaining agent. Pursuant to the requirements of the law, the Mediation Board certified the result to the railway company and subsequent thereto the officers of the grand lodge sent their representative, Mott L. Fox, to Kansas City for the purpose of organizing a Local Lodge 'for and behalf of all the employees at the Argentine shops of the defendant railroad carrier.' The activities of said representative Fox resulted in the organization of Local Lodge No. 850 of the Brotherhood Railway Carmen of America. In soliciting memberships in the Local Lodge, Fox assured the plaintiffs and the other Negro employees that they would be entitled to full membership in Local Lodge No. 850. Pursuant to these promises, plaintiffs and those whom they represent in this action 'took out membership in the said Local Lodge No. 850.' In this connection the petition alleges:
>
> "As it subsequently developed, the defendants herein named, had no intention at the time they secured these plaintiffs' memberships, of admitting nor integrating these plaintiffs nor the rest of the Negro employees at the Santa Fe shops into the Brotherhood Railway Carmen of America.
>
> "Contrary to the assurances heretofore recital, Fox posted a notice on January 20, 1944, informing the employees of the Argentine shops that a meeting would be held on January 20, 1944, at a designated time and place 'to form a Santa Fe local for white employees only' and that a meeting would be held on January 25, 1944 'to form a separate local lodge for Negro employees only.'
>
> *"Since the organization of Local Lodge No. 850, the defendants have refused to admit the plaintiffs and other Negro employees to full membership in the Local Lodge, although they have paid their membership dues, and—-*
>
> *"Said defendants have insisted and still insist, and are determine to coerce and to force these plaintiffs and the other Negro employees who are members of said Local Unions, to accept membership in a separate, substandard organization known as a separate or auxiliary lodge for colored employees only."*

The court found that this type of trickery was "repugnant to every American concept of equality under the law."

Many other instances of the discriminatory practices carried on by these railway labor unions could be cited. Those mentioned are only typical of the consistent program carried on by the organizations for many years in their attempts to make the railway industry lily white. Other instances together with a complete statement concerning these practices may be found in the testimony of the late Charles H. Houston in hearings before a Special Subcommittee of the Committee on Education and Labor, House of Representatives, on H.R. 4453, pages 122–134, 197–220, 258–275, which we incorporate by reference herein.

The unions are firmly entrenched in their positions as collective bargaining representatives under the Railway Labor Act on the nation's railroads. By their discriminatory and exclusionary practices both in membership and employment they are now able to perpetuate themselves in office. The Negro railway workers are impotent to change the representation, and are equally impotent with respect to participation in the collective bargaining process. The sole protection now available is the long and costly process of litigation under the principles of the Steele and Tunstall cases and this is inadequate to meet many of the problems posed. To give to these unions the union shop and check off as proposed in H.R. 7789 without first providing safeguards and correcting the deficiencies that we have pointed out will result in relegating the Negro railway workers to a position similar to that of a defenseless minority in a Hitlerite county and will by Congressional Act facilitate the elimination of Negroes from a basic industry in America.

A further reason for our opposition to H.R. 7789 is our opinion that, as drawn, the bill is unconstitutional. The bill provides that carriers and authorized representatives of employees shall be permitted "(a) to make agreements requiring, as a condition of continued employment, . . . all employees shall become members of the labor organization representing the class or craft . . . ; _Provided_. That no such agreement shall require such condition of employment with respect to employees to whom membership is not available upon the same terms and conditions as are generally applicable to any other member or because of membership in any other labor organization." In other words the bill would permit the carriers and unions to require all white men to become members of the unions, but would not require Negroes to become members of any union that desired to exclude them. It would interfere with the internal affairs of the unions to the extent that it would compel the unions to accept undesirable white men while permitting and sanctioning by Federal law the exclusion of desirable Negroes. By Federal compulsion all white employees would be given the right to participate in the collective bargaining process while by the same Federal law the unions and their white members would be permitted to exclude all Negro employees from participation in that process. This would create distinctions within the craft based on race alone which the Supreme Court in the Steele case held to be "obviously irrelevant and invidious" and would constitute a denial of the equal protection of the laws.

On the basis of the foregoing we register our opposition to H.R. 7789 as drawn and proposed as a necessary concomitant of the union shop and dues check-off of the bill, and in lien of the provision contained in sub-section (a) thereof of H.R. 7789, a Paragraph "Twelfth," be added to Section Two of the Railway Labor Act as follows:

> "Notwithstanding any other provisions of this Act, or of any other statute or law of the United States, or Territory thereof, or of any State, any union, labor organization or labor representative that segregates members into separate or auxiliary locals or excludes any member of the craft or class from membership therein on the grounds of race, creed, color, or national origin, or denies membership therein to any member of the craft or class upon terms or conditions not generally applicable to all members of the craft or class; or excludes any member of the craft or class from participation in the collective bargaining process or that uses its position as a collective bargaining representative under this Act to discriminate against members of the

craft or class on the grounds of race, creed, color, or national origin; or that uses its position as such collective bargaining representative to bar the employment by the carrier of any person because of his race, creed, color, or national origin, shall not act as representative under this Act of any craft or class, and shall not be entitled to any of the provisions of the Act."

MS: NAACP WB-160, DLC.

Typescript of statement by Waddy, accompanied by Mitchell, on Railway Labor Act Amendments, 6/7/50, *Hearings*, 285–302. The testimony of Mitchell's former FEPC colleague Theodore E. Brown, representing the International Brotherhood of Sleeping Car Porters, precedes Waddy's (pp. 273–85). For similar testimony before a subcommittee of the Senate Committee on Labor and Public Welfare, see 5/18/50, *Hearings*, 242–309. See materials on Railway Labor Act in NAACP IX: 197, DLC; also see 5/31, 7/17, 8/31, and 12/21/50, 2/4/53.

1. This case is *Rolax et al. v. Atlantic Coast Line R. Co., et al.* Counsel for the plaintiffs—African American locomotive firemen employed by the Atlantic Coast Line—included Waddy; his partner, Charles Hamilton Houston; Oliver W. Hill of Richmond, Virginia; and Thurgood Marshall, NAACP special counsel. See http://web.lexis-nexis.com/universe/document?

For the background on the railroad cases and their relationship to union discrimination, see the introduction and the headnote on the FEPC and Unions in volume I.

2. The mention of "Railway v. Causey" was a reference to *Railway Mail Association v. Edward S. Corsi, Industrial Commissioner of the State of New York, et al., No. 691*, 326 U.S. 88, argued on April 3, 1945, and decided on June 18, 1945. It was brought before the Court on appeal from the New York Court of Appeals. William H. Hastie, Thurgood Marshall, and Leon A. Ransom had filed amicus curiae briefs on this case on behalf of the NAACP, and Arthur Garfield Hays and Walter Gordon Merrit had filed them on behalf of the American Civil Liberties Union. The Railway Mail Association, an organization of postal clerks in the U.S. Railway Mail Service, had challenged the applicability to the clerks of the state civil rights law prohibiting labor organizations from discriminating on the basis of race, creed, or color in the admission or treatment of members. The New York Court of Appeals and the Supreme Court affirmed the constitutionality of the state law and its applicability to the Railway Mail Association. See http://web.lexis-nexis.com/universe/document?m=357b . . . .

3. See Findings and Directives in Portland–Los Angeles Hearings, November 15–20, 1943, FEPC, HqR4, Office Files of George M. Johnson, Director, Dec. 1941–Nov. 1945, Boilermakers Union. See also George Johnson, Production in Shipbuilding Plants, H.R. 52, Subcommittee on Production in Shipbuilding Plants, Committee on the Merchant Marine and Fisheries, U.S. House of Representatives, 78th Congress, 2nd, 1/19/44, *Hearings*, 1173–77; Johnson's background report and "Digest of Hearing Held January 19, 1944," both in FEPC, HqR6, Office Files of George M. Johnson, Director, Dec. 1941–Nov. 1945, Johnson, Misc.; and Herbert R. Northrop's "Analysis of the Discrimination against Negroes in the Boilermakers Union," n.d., FEPC, HqR14, Records Related to Hearings, Dec. 1941–Mar. 1946, Shipbuilding: Boilermaker's Union—Exhibits (Part I), Herbert Northrop.

Clarence Mitchell, Jr., Statement on "State and Federal FEPC," June 21, 1950

Statement of Clarence Mitchell
Labor Secretary, N.A.A.C.P.
During Panel on "The Negro and the
Present Economic Situation"
Wednesday, June 21, 1950
41st Annual Convention of the
N.A.A.C.P. - Union Methodist Church
Boston, Massachusetts

STATE AND FEDERAL FEPC

The opponents of Fair Employment Practice legislation are whistling past a grave yard. They are making bold noises about defeating it, but inevitably it will become an accepted and respected part of AMERICAN law.[1]

TEN states have FEPC laws. If we had not been betrayed by old guard Republicans in Minnesota, Ohio, Pennsylvania and Illinois those states would have passed this legislation in 1949. I say old guard Republicans because the younger members of that party such as Senator Wayne Morse of Oregon, Governor Luther Younghdahl of Minnesota and Congressman Clifford Case of New Jersey, the more progressive type of G.O.P. leaders, stand squarely behind FEPC. The old guard gives lip service to FEPC but that is all.

If we are to win strong support from the Republican Party we must let the nation know that we are aware of the split within the G.O.P. on FEPC. This division is as clear and fundamental as the dividing line between the Northern Democrats and the DIXIEcrats.

We need the support of both major parties in the struggle we are making for FEPC. The courageous stand that President Truman has made for FEPC deserves the unstinted praise of everyone. But as a party the Democrats have failed miserably in the national fight for civil rights legislation in general. Their failure on FEPC has been due mainly to poor planning and a lack of enthusiasm. It is also true that the southerners are led by a tough shrewd crew of renegades who lost the national election in 1948, but win all of the major battles against progress in Congress.

There is no one in the Republican party top leadership in Washington who has matched President Truman's public stand on FEPC. Senator Taft of Ohio, whose influence is strongest in the capital among members of the Republican party, is the real author of the McConnell bill on FEPC. You will remember the McConnell FEPC bill as the legislation that is so weak that even Congressman John Rankin of Mississippi voted in favor of it.

From these remarks I am certain that you realize that I am charging both major parties with failure on FEPC. However, it is not enough simply to charge them with failure. We must begin a program of reaching those individual members of both parties who are responsible for the failure and remove them from office.

This is the only way we can give a real chance to the new leadership under people like Senator Humphrey of Minnesota, Senator Douglass of Illinois, Governor Driscoll of New Jersey and Governor Bowles of Connecticut. If we continue to return to power the Ohio compromisers and the Pennsylvania reactionaries we will always be the victims of the silly type of performance on the recent cloture vote in the Senate on FEPC. In that demonstration the Democrats made wonderful speeches but did not deliver the votes. The Republicans delivered a vote, but it was only a token and not the full strength that they can muster.

There is a great deal of talk these days about whether the major parties are sincere on FEPC. I do not know whether they are and I assure you that the question of sincerety is of no great importance at this time. But if we can engineer a few defeats of the malingerers in the November elections there will be a sharp upturn in our fortunes on FEPC. It will not be due to any increase in sincerety, but as long as public officials vote right we do not have to worry about whether they are sincere.

As colored people and non-colored people interested in civil rights we must make up our own minds that we really do want FEPC laws in our cities, states, and the Nation.

We must study the workings of the existing Fair Employment ordinances, laws and regulations. We must make better use of the machinery now available. There are not nearly enough persons filing complaints in the areas where FEPC laws exist.

There is a federal Fair Employment Board for Government workers, but its machinery is not being used to correct disgusting racial discrimination in the field offices of various federal agencies.

In Kansas City, Mo., for example, the Treasury Department has established a completely segregated work unit. This has been done in defiance of President Truman's Fair Employment Order. So far no employee of that office has filed a formal complaint against this discrimination.

It is amazing that in the whole state of New York only 315 verified complaints were filed in 1949. In the State of Washington only thirteen complaints were filed in 1949.

In the main the FEPC commissions are manned by capable and sincere people. They are doing a constructive job, but we must do more on our part to see that bona fide complaints are filed and processed.

Valuable FEPC agencies exist in New York, Massachusetts, Rhode Island, Connecticut, New Jersey, Washington, Oregon and New Mexico. The municipal FEPC groups in Philadelphia, Minneapolis and Cleveland provide effective ways of combatting job discrimination.

The urgency of passing national fair employment legislation is evident to anyone who looks at the Bureau of the Census data on unemployment.

During 1949 the percentage of unemployment among colored people rose from 6 per cent in January to a peak of 9.7 per cent in October. Among white people the unemployed were 4.3 per cent in January but even the highest percentage, which was reached in July, was only 6.2 per cent.

We need FEPC legislation to overcome the deadly effect of carefully organized campaigns to drive colored people out of certain industries.

A cruel example of such campaigns is furnished by the railroad industry. In 1931 the Brotherhood of Locomotive Firemen gave study to the best method of forcing colored men from that industry.

There was this interesting statement in the minutes of the meeting on how to get rid of colored railroad men. It is as follows:

> "Any action looking toward presenting the question (elimination of colored railway workers) to the Interstate Commerce Commission would necessarily have to be predicated upon the basis, not that the Negro is undesirable as an engineman by reason of his race or color, but because of his inability to read and understand orders and instructions and by reason of his general mental deficiency, and, therefore, his use in this capacity is unsafe and creates a hazard.
>
> "Undertaking to establish this claim might result in some sort of an examination or test applicable to all locomotive enginemen, which might tend (1) to disqualify some white men, and (2) establish the fitness of an occasional Negro to act as engineer."

Realizing that they could not win by direct action before the ICC, the Railway brotherhoods then began the negotiation of special agreements to accomplish by trickery the elimination of colored men. By this process they have suceeded in displacing nearly 6,000 colored railway employees.

We can attack these types of discrimination through the courts, as is now being done. We can attack them by seeking appropriate amendments to labor legislation, as we are doing. But in the final analysis the only broad scale attack that will be fully successful must be made through strong state and federal FEPC laws.

To win on FEPC we must return to our home communities in the spirit of the mobilization in Washington. We must begin at once to get from each candidate for office a pledge that he will work and vote for state legislation, if he is running for a state office, and national legislation if he is trying to get to Washington.

FEPC is a test of whether democratic concepts can survive in a world gone mad with atom bomb dictatorship. If we secure the right to work, it will be much easier to safeguard some of our other basic freedoms that are today threatened by those who trade in hunger and misery to achieve their ends.

MS: MP.

1. See, among others, 1/31 and 3/3/50 and the headnotes on Struggle for a Permanent FEPC, 1942–54.

Clarence Mitchell, Jr., Statement on "Migratory Workers," July 13, 1950

STATEMENT BEFORE THE PRESIDENT'S COMMISSION ON MIGRATORY WORKERS, JULY 13, 1950

My name is Clarence Mitchell. I am Labor Secretary of the National Association for the Advancement of Colored People.

We commend the President for appointment of this committee to investigate conditions affecting migratory workers.[1] We also wish to thank the members who have taken time out from their busy personal schedules to serve in this very important field. However, we are extremely disappointed that in the composition of this committee there is no colored member.

Colored citizens of the United States form a considerable proportion of the migratory workers of our country. The exclusion of them from membership of this committee shows that the United States Department of Labor and the Department of Agriculture are either unaware of or indifferent to the stake that we have in the problem which this committee is set up to study. We hope that one of the first official actions taken by the committee will be a recommendation to the President that a qualified colored member be appointed.

Most of the plans for meeting the nation's manpower needs in agriculture are geared solely to meet the requirements of the farmers. Very few if any of them take into consideration the needs of the people who perform the actual labor on the farms. Even in the communities which badly need agricultural workers, there is a distinct lack of friendliness toward the migratory workers who are brought in to plant or harvest the crops. Nevertheless, the number of migratory workers being used is steadily increasing.

The Governor's Interracial Commission of Minnesota published a study on August 15, 1948.[2] This study, which was under the direction of Father Francis J. Gilligan, Chairman of the Governor's Commission, reveals that there has been a steady growth in the use of foreign nationals for work in the sugar-beet fields and the canning companies in Minnesota.[3]

The National Farm Labor Union has prepared testimony dealing with the increasing use of Mexican nationals in the cotton farming in southern states.[4]

In a great country such as ours, we should always welcome new workers who are needed, but, at present, there are only three major reasons why foreign workers are imported for work on the farms of this nation.

The first reason is they are more easily exploited than our own citizens. The second is that nobody really knows how many unused farm workers there are in the United States. The third reason is southern land owners fear that if their workers move around too freely they may not return. Northern growers, on the other hand, fear that our own citizens from the South may decide to stay in northern communities after the work on the farms is at an end.

In 1948, the NAACP joined with the National Farm Labor Union, AFL, in suggesting that the Department of Labor use Arkansas and Southeastern Missouri as a testing ground to determine whether surplus agricultural labor could be found in that area for use in other parts of the country.[5] At about the same time, we submitted a case to the Department of Justice for investigation. The case submitted was that of a person who had been beaten by farmers in Missouri while he was recruiting farm laborers.

We contended that a careful investigation would show that many unused farm workers are kept idle in some areas of the country by force, subterfuge, and intimidation. So far as we know, the Department of Labor never made a real effort to recruit farm workers in the test area that we suggested.

Congress has used the function of recruiting agricultural labor as a kind of political bargaining point. This function properly belongs in the Department of Labor. However, that agency faces the constant threat that the function will be transferred to the Department of Agriculture if any liberal policies are adopted to better the lot of farm workers. It is well-known that the Department of Agriculture thinks almost entirely in terms of the employers needs and not of the needs of the farm laborers.

We hope that the committee will carefully explore the use of so-called labor contractors and other dubious systems used by the state employment services for recruiting farm workers.

The NAACP has joined with organized labor in urging that bona fide labor organization be used by the state employment services in filling orders for farm workers.

Local employment service offices rely very heavily upon labor unions for recruiting workers in other types of employment. The employment service officials are reluctant to use labor unions in getting farm workers, because it is feared that organized workers will not tolerate the hazardous transportation, terrible living conditions, and low wages that unorganized workers will accept.

This year, the State of California is making use of the Farm Labor Union's resources in recruiting some farm workers. We urge that the committee give study to this program and compare the results obtained under it with those obtained under other systems.

We ask that the committee review the legal barriers that interfere with interstate migration of our own citizens.

Herbert Roback published an interesting article on this subject in the Cornell Law Quarterly in 1943. On page 293, he tells of how an agent of the Fellsmere Sugar Production Association was arrested for soliciting laborers for work in Florida. Under South Carolina laws, he was required to have a license even though the State Employment

Service had approved the recruitment. In a footnote, Mr. Roback points out that six Florida farmers were jailed on the same type of charges in Georgia in 1942.[6]

We shall not give detailed statements on health, housing, and other conditions among migratory workers because we hope that this committee will get the latest information on these things by first hand on the spot investigations.

We hope that the work of this committee will reveal all of the shameful conditions that make pariahs of our citizens in the migratory labor force. We believe that once the American people know the true story Congress will be faced with a determined demand that appropriate legislation be passed to meet the problem.

MS: MP.

1. See 1/31, 3/30, 7/17, 8/31, and 12/21/50.

2. Records of the President's Commission on Migratory Labor, 220.7.13 Records, 10/28/2005, available at http://www.archives.gov/research/guide-fed-records/groups/220.html.

3. Mitchell first met and developed a very strong respect for Father Gilligan when he worked as executive secretary of the St. Paul Urban League from November 1937 to 1941. Watson, *Lion in the Lobby*, 105, 109; Watson, "Clarence Mitchell, Jr.," *American National Biography*, 594–95.

4. The National Farm Labor Union was formerly the Southern Tenant Farmers Union. See http://www.agclassroom.org/gantimeline/1940.htm.

5. Roback, "Legal Barriers to Interstate Migration."

NAACP WB Newsletter, December 20, 1950

NEWSLETTER

NATIONAL ASSOCIATION FOR THE ADVANCEMENT OF COLORED PEOPLE

December 20, 1950

WASHINGTON BUREAU
100 Massachusetts Avenue, N.W.
Washington, D.C.

This is the first regular news letter you will receive from the Washington Bureau. We are using this method to keep you informed on vital matters we are working on.[1] You are one of a few key people who are receiving it. Please let us know whether you want to be kept on the mailing list.

*****   *****   *****

The present national emergency requires the maximum employment of all available workers regardless of race, color, religion or national origin to build a solid defense program. By next year the country will need 1,500,000 new persons in the labor force. Yet qualified colored workers are being denied jobs in industries vital to our national defense.

Government action was necessary and effective to check unfair employment practices during World War II. Many of the gains made during the life of the President's Fair Employment Practices Commission were lost when that commission expired in 1946, and Congress failed to enact a permanent Fair Employment Practices Commission.

Government action is again necessary to check discriminatory employment practices. Therefore, the NAACP is working to get President Truman to issue a new executive order setting up an FEPC.[2]

The proposed executive order is broader in scope than the World War II order and contains enforcement powers.

The main issue delaying the order has been argument by some government officials that the Russell Amendment to the Independent Offices Appropriations Act of 19545 would prohibit the President from using his emergency funds to establish an FEPC.[3]

Expert legal analysis of the Russell Amendment shows that it does not prevent the President form acting now. Please write to the President and Secretary of Labor Maurice Tobin. Say we need FEPC.

* * * * *   * * * * *   * * * * *

Secretary of Labor Tobin has issued a directive known as General Order No. 48. It establishes three important committees to consider the problems in the defense employment picture. General Order No. 48 does not show that any of these committees will be concerned with the full use of minority group workers who are usually the victims of discrimination.

The NAACP has urged the Secretary of Labor to place qualified colored members on these committees to insure consideration of the problems of minority groups in the defense program. We also asked that racial designations be dropped from employment services application cards and that no discriminatory orders be accepted from Defense plant employers. Secretary Tobin has advised us that he is asking the states to drop the race tag on application cards. He favors nonacceptance of discriminatory orders but has not acted on it yet. You *can help by telling him action is needed now*. He has not acted on our request for representation on the key committees. We did get colored representation (not as much as we wanted) at important training conferences. These conferences are drawing up the blue prints for the defense training program.

* * * *   * * * *   * * * *

Down at the Los Alamos, New Mexico, Atomic Energy Project a colored employee (War Veteran of course) was denied a haircut by white barbers. It was the only shop on the project. Earle W. Fisher, Research Assistant in our D.C. Bureau, got the A.E.C. to order the barbers to serve the complainant. The barbers went on strike. *They were replaced*. The complainant (as soon as he gets his haircut) is going to start an NAACP branch.

The Atomic Energy commission is preparing to build an "H" Bomb project in South Carolina. Because of the important manpower problem involved, the Washington Bureau has asked the chairman of the A.E.C. to see hat the racial patterns of South Carolina are not imposed in the territory of that State where "H" Bombs will be produced.[4]

It has been pointed out to the A.E.C. that 42.9 per cent of the population of South Carolina is colored, and with any intelligent use of the local labor supply a large number of colored people will be employed.

The Washington Bureau has asked that definite assurance be given that there will be no discrimination or desegregation in housing facilities or job opportunities in the project. We have a meeting with A.E.C. on this scheduled for December 26, 1950.[5]

Walter White
Executive Secretary

Clarence Mitchell
Director
Washington Bureau

MS: NAACP II: A-655, DLC.

1. See also 12/21/50, where Mitchell announced the initiation of the newsletter.
2. See 12/5/51 for the issuance of EO 10308.
3. See Maslow, "FEPC—A Case History in Parliamentary Maneuver," and Maslow and Robinson, "Civil Rights Legislation and the Fight for Equality, 1862–1952."
4. See, particularly, 2/5/51.
5. See Earle Fisher's report on this meeting of December 26, 1950, which Mitchell also attended, in NAACP WB-8, DLC. See also, most immediately, 1/31, 2/2, 2/5, and 3/5/51 and, in appendix, 2/21/51.

Armed Forces, December 1950

ARMED FORCES

[ca. December 31, 1950]

The fighting in Korea brought into sharp focus the vital importance to our nation, both internally and externally, of the racial practices of our fighting forces. It revealed that full integration of Negro and white personnel promised soon to be an accomplished fact in the Navy and Air Force. It also revealed all too plainly that the Army was still sending segregated troops into battle on a fighting front where such racial practices were bound to cost us heavily in the eyes of our allies.[1]

Some progress, however, was made during the year in the Army. A directive was issued ordering assignment of personnel to all units without regard to race and the 10% Negro quota on enlistments was finally dropped.

In three states, Michigan, Oregon and Washington, executive orders were issued to end segregation in the National Guard.

1. In May, the President's Committee on Equality of Treatment and Opportunity in the Armed Services issued a comprehensive report of the steps taken to implement President Truman's Executive Order of July 26, 1948, directing the elimination of discrimination in the armed forces. The report showed considerable progress, indicating that segregation might be soon completely eliminated in the Navy and Air Force, much less progress was reported for the Army.[2]

   In the Navy all jobs and schools were said to be open to Negroes without restrictions or segregation. At the end of 1945 nearly 95% of the Negroes were in the messman's branch, but in 1950 over 40% were in general service, where they were completely integrated with whites in training, schools, jobs, messes and sleeping quarters, both on shore and at sea. Marine Corps advances were also reported but the Corps lagged somewhat.[3]

   In the Air Force about three-fourths of 25,000 Negroes were serving in non-segregated units and integration was continuing. All jobs and schools were open to Negroes without restriction or segregation in work, eating or sleeping arrangements.

   In the Army all racial quotas for school attendance were abolished in 1949. In January, 1950 a directive ordered that personnel would be assigned to all units without regard to race. In March the Army abandoned its 10% Negro quota in enlistments.

The Committee emphasized that no friction resulted from the integration of Negroes in the armed forces.

2. In June, the Secretary of the Navy banned participation by Navy men in activities sponsored by local groups which discriminate or segregate in offering their hospitality.

3. After protesting an advertisement appearing in a Hartford newspaper in September announcing "Openings in the Steward Branch of the Navy for Negroes," the Connecticut Inter-Racial Commission in December received assurances from the Navy Department that all men regardless of race, creed or color are held equally eligible for enlistment in any Navy rating available. The Office of the Secretary of the Navy reiterated Secretary Matthew's nondiscriminatory order of last year and advised the Connecticut Commission that it had corrected the erroneous understanding of the Hartford Naval recruiting office that the Navy maintained an all Negro service in the steward branch and that care had taken to prevent repetitions of the incident.

Early in the Korean war, the outstanding achievements of Negro troops called attention both to their fighting qualities and to the fact that segregation was still the general rule in the Army. In July, NAACP charged, in a letter to the Secretary of the Army, that while Negro combat troops were fighting in Korea, other Negro soldiers were being segregated and discriminated against by Army occupation authorities in Tokyo. An immediate investigation and elimination of discrimination was demanded.[4] In September, it was reported from Korea that Negro infantrymen were being assigned as replacement in previously all-white combat units.[5]

4. New York City's first draftees since the outbreak of the Korean war, including Negroes and whites, were given an impressive ceremony on the day of their induction in August but were promptly segregated by color when they arrived at Fort Dix, N.J.

5 Mobile, Alabama, NAACP officials in August protested to the Secretary of the Army that Negro draftees were forced to eat in the kitchen and backyards of a local white restaurant while white draftees ate in the main dining room. Investigations were promised by Army and Selective Service officials, but the practice was still in force a month later, according to local NAACP statements.[6]

7. NAACP announced in December that its Special Counsel would go to Korea and Japan to investigate charges of discrimination against Negroes in court-martial proceedings.[7]

8. Ensign Jesse P. Brown became the first Negro Naval officer ever to die in battle when his plane was shot down in December in the Changjin Reservoir Area of Korea. Ensign Brown was the first Negro officer permitted to fly a combat mission and the first commissioned officer of his race to die in Navy uniform in any war.[8]

8.5. A Negro Naval Air Station cadet at Pensacola, Fla., in October was named the top member of the graduating class at the preflight school.

9. In June, the Director of the Selective Service system announced that registrants under the draft law would no longer be asked any questions about race.[9]

9.5. In June, the U.S. Senate struck from the pending bill to extend the Selective Service Act a provision that all persons drafted should have the right to serve only in units of their own race. The provision had been proposed by Sen. Russell of Georgia and adopted by the Committee on Armed Services.[10]

10. Executive orders were issued in Michigan, Oregon and Washington forbidding discrimination and segregation in the National Guard.

11. In January, it was reported that Negroes in the New York National Guard were being integrated with white units under the terms of a 1949 statute which, at the time of its passage, was criticized as containing many loopholes.

12. A member of the Massachusetts legislature last winter introduced a bill calling for an investigation of the state National Guard's compliance with the 1949 non-segregation law. The Guard in March denied charges of racial discrimination.[11]

MS: NAACP WB-141, DLC.

1. See Mitchell, "Status of Racial Integration in the Armed Services"; MacGregor, *Integration of the Armed Forces, 1940–1965*, 430–34, 438–39.

2. This was the committee headed by Judge Charles Fahy. *New York Times*, 5/23/50, 1, 9. See http://www.trumanlibrary.org/hstpaper/fahy.htm#series5.

See also, among others, 8/31/48, and MacGregor, *Integration of the Armed Forces, 1940–1965*, 311–14, 331–33, 343–51, 348–58.

3. *New York Times*, 5/23/50, 9; MacGregor, *Integration of the Armed Forces, 1940–1965*, 348–60. For high points of Mitchell's struggle, for example, to end segregation of civilian facilities on navy bases, see 2/2/51; 6/5/52; 9/9, 10/6, 11/2, and 11/4/53; 6/29/54. For the Marine Corps policy of assigning blacks to the Stewards Branch, see 10/6/53.

4. Subsequently, the Army announced it would end segregation in the Eastern Theater. See 8/31/51; and MacGregor, *Integration of the Armed Forces, 1940–1965*, 430–34, 460.

5. On July 26, 1951, the army announced the integration of the Far East Command. MacGregor, *Integration of the Armed Forces, 1940–1965*, 444.

6. There is no item 6 in the manuscript.

7. At its September 11, 1950, meeting, the NAACP board adopted a resolution noting that the country would be unable "to win the support and loyalty of millions of non-white peoples as long as we retain any form of racial discrimination" in the armed forces. It therefore called for the end "of all forms of racial discrimination and segregation in our military and civilian life." Minutes, 9/11/50, EC.

"Legal," *Crisis* 58 (February 1951): 109–10; "Mr. Marshall Reports," *Crisis* 58(March 1951): 180–81; Marshall, "Summary Justice—The Negro GI in Korea," *Crisis* 58 (May 1951): 297–304, 350–55. See also, most directly, 12/21/50, where one of the problems highlighted involved Lt. Leon A. Gilbert, who initially was sentenced to death.

8. Regarding Brown's being commissioned, see also MacGregor, *Integration of the Armed Forces, 1940–1965*, 246.

9. Mitchell received assurances from Col. Campbell Johnson on October 26, 1950, that the Selective Service was eliminating racial designations on all its forms except one on which race was still being noted for the benefit of the FBI. Even this, however, might ultimately be eliminated. Mitchell's memorandum to the files, 10/26/50, NAACP WB-141, DLC. See also, among others, 12/4 and 12/21/50; 2/2/51; and, for broader aspects of the struggle, Dalfiume, *Desegregation of the U.S. Armed Forces*, 166–67.

10. See 7/17 and 12/21/50 and Dalfiume, *Desegregation of the U.S. Armed Forces*, 166.

11. For the beginning of the struggle related to the National Guard, see Dalfiume, *Desegregation of the U.S. Armed Forces*, 159–60.

NAACP WB Newsletter, February 21, 1951

NEWSLETTER

NATIONAL ASSOCIATION FOR THE ADVANCEMENT OF COLORED PEOPLE

February 21, 1951

Washington Bureau
100 Massachusetts Avenue, N.W.
Washington, D.C.

Visits to Paducah, Kentucky, and Aiken, South Carolina, made by the Director of the Washington Bureau recently, show the kind of actual and potential discrimination that colored people face in defense employment.[1]

These towns are the locations for new plants under the direction f the Atomic Energy Commission. In Paducah, the local Employment Service referred 400 persons for specialized work, but not one colored person although many were available. In South Carolina, colored janitors were the only persons observed on the job in temporary offices set up by AEC.

Fortunately, the AEC is sincerely working to correct such conditions. Some of its officials have shown that they are very fair in conferences with NAACP representatives.

There will be nearly 50,000 persons employed on these two sites for construction of the plants. Well over 10,000 may be employed for operation.

Copies of the full reports made by the Washington Bureau on the areas are available upon request. After you read them, write President Truman and urge him to issue an executive orders setting up a new FEPC on defense employment. The order is ready but it is being held up by a timid throng of bureaucrats who are trying to appease the southerners.

* * * * * * *   * * * * * * *   * * * * * * *

At least seventeen civil rights bills have been introduced in the House and Senate. The Administration has again sent its omnibus civil rights bill and a proposed anti-lynching statute to Congress. These were introduced by Chairman Celler of the Judiciary Committee in the House. In the Senate, Chairman McCarran of the Judiciary Committee has turned them over to a subcommittee headed by Senator Eastland of Mississippi.

A bill aimed at those who attempt to hold persons in involuntary servitude has also been sent to Congress by the Department of Justice. Senator McCarran has also referred this to the Eastland subcommittee. Other members of the subcommittee are Senators Kefauver, Langer, O'Conor, and Hendrickson.

Southerners are also inserting their versions of civil rights legislation. Congressman Brooks Hays of Arkansas, for example, has introduced an FEPC bill. Under his plan the government would investigate but not correct job discrimination. Mr. Hays has also introduced an anti-lynching bill which is just as weak as his FEPC bill.[2]

* * * * * * *   * * * * * * *   * * * * * * *

Examination of the Washington Bureau's files on the Veterans Administration reveals discriminatory policies and practices which result in shocking mistreatment and humiliation of colored veterans and extensive occupational segregation of colored employees.[3] Most of the complaints have arisen in southern states where there are close to a quarter of a million colored veterans.

At present, the laws relating to veterans have only been extended to cover those men who return from duty in this present conflict as casualties. The increased integration of colored men in all of the Services will mean a larger proportion of military casualties returning to civilian life for hospitalization and training for useful citizenship.

The primary sore spots are the hospitalization and training provision which are provided for veterans by Public law 346 and Public Law 16.[4]

The hospitals at Bonham, Texas; Augusta, Georgia; Gulfport, Mississippi; Tuscaloosa, Alabama; Marlin, Texas; and Durham, North Carolina, are operated on a segregated basis. We are advised that the VA discourages the admission of colored patients to the VA hospital in Bonham, Gulfport, and Tuscaloosa. There are 87,589 colored veterans in Texas who comprise 33.1% of the veteran population of that state.

The 81,465 colored veterans in Mississippi comprise 30.1% of the veteran population, and the 70,445 colored veterans in Alabama are 27.6% of the veterans in that state.

Because of the racial segregation in the VA Hospital at Fort Howard, Maryland, a colored veteran who needed immediate hospitalization nearly lost his life. We were advised on November 9, 1950, that the Fort Howard Hospital officials refused to admit this veteran because there was no "colored beds" available. There were, however, beds available for white patients. After a strenuous protest by the NAACP, the patient was finally admitted.

There are 32,689 colored veterans in Maryland who comprise 33.2% of the veteran population.

An account of the treatment given to colored patients in the VA Hospital at Wadsworth, Kansas, is given in a letter from a colored patient there. The report states, "The patients were seated in their respective places. It was noticed that the white patients were being served toast from a tray with the use of tongs by one employee. This same employee, after completing the serving of the white patients, put down her tray and tongs, went to the kitchen, returned with an arm load of plain light bread and began to toss it on the tables colored patients occupied." In Kansas, 41.2% of the veteran population is colored.

We have reason to believe that a large number of colored veterans are not getting the benefits due them by law. We believe that the large figure showing the numbers who have not participated in the veterans benefits does not reflect disinterest of colored veterans in the program, but a denial of the benefits to them by the VA officials in the South. We are asking our branches in the South to supply us with information concerning reports of denial of benefits to colored veterans by VA officials. This information will be presented to the Teague Subcommittee of the House Veterans Affairs Committee when it renews its investigation of the abuses of veterans benefits.[5]

Copies o f a memorandum on VA discrimination prepared by the Research Assistant are available upon request. You should read it and get indignant enough to write in a protest to the White House and the Veterans Administration.

Walter White
Executive Secretary

Clarence Mitchell
Director
Washington Bureau

Earle W. Fisher
Research Assistant
Washington Program

MS: NAACP II: A-655, DLC.

1. See, most immediately, 1/31, 2/2, 2/5, and 3/5/51 and, in appendix, 12/20/50.

2. This report complements 2/2/51.

3. See, among others, 5/3 and 6/4/51 and, in appendix, 5/29 and 6/29/51.

4. See, among others, 5/3, 6/4, and 8/31/53.

5. Olin E. Teague (D-Texas). See House Select Committee to Investigate Educational, Training, and Loan Guaranty Programs under GI Bill, CIS (82) H1385-1; or Digital Hearing-RD: HRG-1951-IET-0002.

NAACP WB Newsletter, September 21, 1951

NEWSLETTER

September 21, 1951

Washington Bureau
NAACP
100 Massachusetts Avenue, N.W.
Washington, D.C.

Because of the importance of the hearings on the Senate Cloture rule scheduled for October 2 and 3, this entire newsletter will be devoted to that subject.[1] Civil Rights bills will pass if we get a good rule.

Background

Cloture in parliamentary practice means ending debate. In 1917 the Senate by a vote of 76 to 3 adopted the cloture rule, rule number XXII.

Difficulty arose when rule XXII was interpreted so it would not apply to motions to take up legislation, but only to measures after they had been taken up.

This meant that a filibuster could continue against a motion to take up certain legislation.

The 1949 Battle for Cloture

The last all out effort to change rule XXII took place in the Senate in 1949.[2] During March of that year the Senate rejected a proposal to alter the interpretation of the rule as it applied to motions to take up legislation.

Senators Hayden (D. Ariz.) and Wherry (R. Neb.) proposed cloture on any matter by a simple two-thirds majority of those senators voting. However, Southern Senators filibustered against this proposal.

After this defeat Senator Lucas (D. Ill.) proposed that a straight two-thirds majority be sufficient to apply cloture on all matters except changing Senate rules. This proposal was also rejected.

A proposal was made by some senators that cloture could be invoked, with one exception, on any measure by two-thirds of the Senate or 64 Senators. The one exception being changes in the Senate Rules on which there could be no cloture. This last feature was an escape clause demanded by Southern Senators. This proposal was adopted and the Senate then became bound to this revision of rule XXII.

The problem now is getting 64 Senators at one time to vote that debate should be ended. So far it has been impossible to get this number.

The Rule Itself

Subsection II and III of Rule XXII of the Standing Rules of the Senate relating to Cloture reads as follows:

Notwithstanding the provision of rule III or rule VI or any other rule of the Senate, except subsection 3 of rule XXII, at any time a motion signed by sixteen senators, to bring to a close the debate upon any measure, motion, or other matter pending before the Senate, or the unfinished business, is presented to the Senate, the Presiding Officer shall at once state the motion to the Senate, and one hour after the Senate meets on the following calendar day but one, he shall lay the motion before the Senate and direct that the Secretary call the roll, and upon the ascertainment that a quorum is present, the Presiding Officer shall, without debate, submit to the Senate by a yea and nay vote the question.

"Is it the sense of the Senate that the debate shall be brought to a close?"

And if that question shall be decided in the affirmative by two-thirds of the Senators duly chosen and sworn, then said measure, motion, or the matter pending before the Senate, or the unfinished business shall be the unfinished business to the exclusion of all other business until disposed of.

Thereafter no Senator shall be entitled to speak in all more than one hour on the measure, motion, or other matter pending before the Senate, or on the unfinished business, the amendments thereto, and motions affecting the same, and it shall be the duty of the Presiding Officer to keep the time of each Senator who speaks. Except by unanimous consent, no amendment shall be in order after the vote to bring the debate to a close, unless the same has been presented and read prior to that time. No dilatory motion, or dilatory amendment, or amendment not germane shall be in order. Points of order including questions of relevancy, and appeals from the decision of the Presiding Officer, shall be decided without debate.

The Provisions of the last paragraph of rule VIII (prohibiting debate on motions made before 2 o'clock) and the subsection 2 of this rule shall not apply to any motion to proceed to the consideration of any motion, resolution, or proposal to change any of the Standing Rules of the Senate.

* * * * *   * * * * *   * * * * *

There have been four Senate Resolutions introduced in the 82nd Congress proposing to change rules XXII.

S. Res. 41 (Morse-Humphrey) January 18, 1951

The Morse-Humphrey Resolution seeks to change Rule XXII by permitting application of cloture by majority vote. A Senator may yield a part of all of the period of time he is entitled to speak to any other Senator. The Senator to whom the time has been yielded is then entitled to speak for the time yielded plus the period of the time he is allowed.

This Resolution repeals subsection 3 of Rule XXII which prohibits the application of the cloture rule to proposals to change any standing rule of the Senate.

This Resolution repeals subsection 3 of Rule XXII which prohibits the application of the cloture rule to proposals to change any standing rule of the Senate.

S. Res. 53 (Ives) January 25, 1951

The Ives Resolution seeks to change Rule XXII with respect to the number required for adoption of a cloture motion. This resolution changes the present requirements of a vote of two-thirds of the Senate (64 senators) to halt a filibuster to a vote by a majority of the authorized membership of the Senate (49 senators) to adopt a cloture motion.

S. Res. 105 (Lehman and others) March 22, 1951

The Lehman Resolution limits debate by a majority of the members of the Senate present and voting after 15 days of debate. The Lehman Resolution also provides that debate may be limited by a vote of two-thirds of the Senators present 48 hours after a cloture petition is filed.

S. Re. 203 (Wherry) September 10, 1951

The Wherry Resolution seeks to change Rule XXII with respect to the number required for adoption of a cloture motion. This resolution changes the two thirds vote of the Senate (64 Senators) to a vote by two-thirds of the Senators present and voting.

Organizations supporting the drive to limit debate are asking that the Lehman, Morse-Humphrey proposals be accepted as the minimum safeguards against filibuster.

Walter White
Executive Secretary

Clarence Mitchell
Director
Washington Bureau

Earle Fisher
Research Assistant
Washington Bureau

MS: NAACP II: A-655, DLC.

1. See also 10/4, 11/5, and 12/28/51 and the headnote on NAACP and the Filibuster.
2. See, in appendix, 3/10/49.

NAACP WB Newsletter, May 28, 1952

NEWSLETTER

NATIONAL ASSOCIATION FOR THE ADVANCEMENT OF COLORED PEOPLE

May 28, 1952

WASHINGTON BUREAU
100 Massachusetts Avenue, N.W.
Washington, D.C.

DON'T PUT A PIGMY IN THE WHITE HOUSE

"The times demand that the next President must be a giant in the civil rights field. Anyone who fails to support the full civil rights program set forth in the 1947 Report of the President's Committee on Civil Rights is a pigmy."[1] The foregoing quote is from the conversation of an NAACP friend. He concluded by saying, "*Don't put a pigmy in the White House*."

With the introduction, we give a brief summary on the positions of candidates' records.

Among the Democrats, Senators Hubert Humphrey (Minnesota) and Brien McMahon (Conn.) are the holders of perfect voting records on civil rights matters. Mr. W. Averell Harriman, Director for the Mutual Security Agency, has publicly endorsed an FEPC with enforcement powers.

Senators Estes Kefauver (Tenn.), Robert Kerr (Okla.), and Richard Russell (Ga.) all oppose FEPC with enforcement powers, although Kefauver and Kerr say they will support it if it is a part of the Party platform. All have voted to keep filibusters going at one time or another, but Kefauver now favors limitation of debate.

Senators Kefauver, Kerr, and Russell have voted to halt integration in the Armed Services, but Kefauver now says integration is working out satisfactorily. All three voted against the Lehman Amendment to protect members of the armed Services against violence.[2]

In the Republican camp, Senator Robert A. Taft (Ohio) has announced repeatedly that he opposes an FEPC with enforcement powers. He also opposed the Lehman Amendment to protect members of the Armed Services against violence. On the other hand, he voted against filibusters and he also voted to support integration in the Armed Services.

General Dwight Eisenhower's only record on civil rights is his testimony before the Senate Armed Services Committee in 1948 favoring "limited" segregation in the Armed Services. The General also said, "I do believe that if we attempt merely by passing a lot of laws to force someone to like someone else, we are just going to get into trouble." The unanswered question is what laws and what trouble did the General mean?

INTEGRATION IN THE ARMED SERVICES

In its annual report dated December 28, 1951, the Washington Bureau gave details on the action of the Association to speed up integration in the Armed Services. The report points out that integration got under way in the Far East following conferences at the Pentagon between friendly Senators and Defense Department officials.

A quote form the report states, "We have been assured that plans are under consideration for an announcement concerning integration of the Armed Services in the European Theater. Regrettably, full integration at home appears to be last on the list."

Although the order to integrate troops in Europe is now nearly two months old, it has not been officially released in Washington. NAACP prodding has jarred loose a statement for Heidelberg, Germany, confirming the plan of integration. We have also been assured that a full and official statement about this is being prepared at the Pentagon. Unfortunately, at the time of this Newsletter, it has not been received in writing. Nevertheless, integration is under way in Europe.

THE COX RESOLUTION

On April 4, 1952, by a vote of 194 to 158, the House approved the Cox Resolution to set up a special committee under the chairmanship of Eugene Cox (D., Ga.). The committee is to investigate tax-exempt charitable and educational organizations.[3]

Groups which might come under committee scrutiny are the Ford foundation, the Carnegie Foundation, the Rosenwald Foundation (which is now out of business), and many others. Part of the Cox attack is aimed at foundations that have made extensive contributions to colored schools in the South.

The House Ways and Means Committee, the House Un-American Activities Committee, and the House Committee on Education and Labor could handle such an inquiry if it is necessary. Ill-will seems assured since Mr. Cox wants a special committee to look into the matter.

The Committee does not yet have an appropriation. *Therefore, urge your Congressmen to vote against giving any money for this wasteful venture*.

THE WALTER-MCCARRAN IMMIGRATION BILLS

By a vote of 206 to 68, the House of Representatives on April 25, 1952 , passed the Walter Immigration Bill sponsored by Congressman Francis Walter (D.,Pa.). In brief, this bill, if enacted unto law, would make our immigration rules and practices even more restrictive than they are now, and they are now unfair to anyone outside the British Isles and Germany.

The even-more-restrictive McCarran Bill, introduced by Senator Pat McCarran (D., Nev.) passed by a simple voice vote on May 22. This action followed defeat of a motion to recommit the Bill to the Senate Judiciary Committee on May 19 by a vote of 44 to 28. Later amendment attempts also failed.

One of the chief objections of the NAACP is the limitation that the Bills placed on immigration from the British West Indies. It is estimated that under these Bills the number of British West Indians coming to the United States annually would be reduced form approximately 2,000 to 900.

House and Senate conferees will meet shortly to iron out differences between the two Bills. The result will be voted on by both Houses and, if passed as expected, the Bill will be sent to the President. McCarran's opponents hope and believe Mr. Truman will veto the measure and that they can gather enough Senate votes to make the veto stick.

A detailed statement on the Walter-McCarran Immigration bills, prepared by Mr. William C. Pryor, Jr., of the Washington Bureau, is available upon request.[4]

Be sure *to urge President Truman by wire or letter to veto the Walter-McCarran Bill. Urge your Senators to uphold the President's veto*.

* * * * *   * * * * *   * * * * *

If further information is needed, or additional copies of the Newsletter are desired, please write to the

WASHINGTON BUREAU, NAACP, 100 Massachusetts Ave., Washington, D.C.

MS: MP.

1. This newsletter, an extension of 6/5/52, has been cited at 12/28/51. See also, in appendix, 11/7/47.

2. See also, among others, 12/28/51, 2/6, 3/5, and 5/8/52; the headnote on Struggle for a Permanent FEPC, 1942–54; and Watson, *Lion in the Lobby*, 209, 210.

3. See also 11/5 and 12/28/51, 5/8, 6/5, 7/31, and 12/31/52; in appendix, 10/3/52.
4. See also, among others, 6/5 and 12/31/52; in appendix, 6/3/52 and 9/30/52.

Statement on McCarran Bill, June 3, 1952

STATEMENT ON MCCARRAN BILL

[June 3, 1952]

NAACP complaints against the McCarran Bill fall into six general groups.[1]

1. *Quotas*: Nations containing people most wanting to come here have the smallest quotas; for example, Italy, Turkey, and Japan. Much larger quotas are given to the British Isles and northwestern Europe where people are better off haven't the great need or desire to come here.
2. *Unused quotas*: The British Isles never uses even half its quota while other nations have borrowed on their quotas beyond the year 2000. We believe the unused quotas of one country should be given to a needy country to add to its own quota the next year.
3. *Quota basis*: Our present quotas are based on the population figures of 1920. Fairness and common sense dictate that they be automatically based on the latest census figures.
4. *Racial restrictions*: McCarran says his Bill has eliminated racial restrictions. Don't Let Him Fool You. It Hasn't. In a very subtle way, this Bill draws the racial line even more tightly for people from the Asia-Pacific area and the West Indies.
5. *Deportation*: The number of reasons for which a naturalized citizen may be deported are increased and many are vaguely defined. The Attorney General is given the power of deporting a naturalized citizen for any criminal offense committed during his first five years in this country. This can mean a parking ticket or nay petty misdemeanor. It can take effect in 1965 though the offense was in 1949 before the law was passed. And if the Attorney General believes that a naturalized citizen might cause trouble or become a public charge some time, he can order the person deported. So, if this Bill passes, we will have to have Attorney Generals who can see into the future. Lastly, the man deported under this law cannot appeal the decision and has only a very limited choice of places to go. Of course, he will be forced to leave home and family.

6. General Restrictions: According to this Bill, S. 2550, American consuls in all countries, at their discretion, may bar people from the Untied States for the same ridiculous reason for which the Attorney General can deport a citizen or alien. He, too, could be a sort of dictator. Also, immigrants would have to pass English literacy tests, not just those of their native language.

The items listed here only begin to scratch the surface of the facts for the Bills are very long and complicated. However, the facts presented give some indication of how unfair, how frightening, and yet how utterly asinine the two bills are.[2]

MS: NAACP WB-95, DLC.

1. The bill, S. 2055, sponsored by Sen. Pat McCarran (D.-Nev.), and another, H.R. 5678, sponsored by Rep. Francis E. Walter (D.-Pa.), embodied a complete codification and revision of immigration, naturalization, and nationality laws. *Congress and the Nation*, 222–23.

2. See also, among others, 6/5 and 12/31/52; in appendix, 5/28 and 9/30/52.

Clarence Mitchell, Jr., Statement on Government Contract Compliance, June 9, 1952

Statement of Clarence Mitchell, Director of the Washington Bureau, NAACP, Before The President's Committee on Government Contract Compliance, June 9, 1952, Washington, D.C.

Mr. Chairman and Gentlemen of the Committee on Government Contract Compliance, I am here today representing the National Association for the Advancement of Colored People. My presentation is stated briefly because I hope very much that each Committee member will read it.[1]

On December 3, 1951, the President issued Executive Order 10,308, establishing a Committee on Government Contract Compliance. The Committee was appointed on January 31, 1952.[2]

Six months have elapsed between the time the Executive Order was issued and the day of this hearing. During this period, no action has been taken to fulfill the requirements of the Executive Order. Hence, our first request of the Committee is that it take concrete action on discrimination in employment.

We have submitted to the Committee a complaint against the Washington Telephone Company. The Company has a Government contract. Its policies of discrimination are well-known. If this Company continues to evade the responsibilities that it has under its agreements with the United States Government, the effectiveness of Executive Order 10,308 will be open to serious question. On the other hand, if the Telephone Company complies with the non-discrimination clause in its contract and offers employment to qualified colored persons, particularly, as operators, there will be substantial reason for believing that this Committee is an effective instrument for combating employment discrimination.

As one who worked consistently for the issuance of an executive order in this field, I hope will all of my heart that the Committee will shortly announce that it has settled the specific complaint which we submitted against the Telephone Company operating in the Nation's capital.[3]

There are some specific procedures that the Committee should consider in carrying out its job. We recommend these in the January 1952 issue of our official organ, The *Crisis* magazine. The pertinent excerpts from the *Crisis'* article are as follows:

"A good Committee can get the member agencies to assign enough personnel from their staffs to make real investigations of discrimination. It can set the stage for the agencies to establish hearing panels to determine whether a complaint against a given company is bona fide.

"As an illustration of how the Committee can work, even under its present sharply restricted functions, let us consider a complaint against a company with an Air Force contract.

"The Committee could request that a panel of its members get and review the evidence in the case. If the panel included the Defense Department member, clearly the contractor would have to put in an appearance and give a full statement of the facts.

"Let us suppose that the Defense Department member of the panel agreed that there was discrimination, but refused to ask his agency to do anything about it. The Committee could review the panel's report and call upon the Air Force to take steps for the 'prevention and elimination of such discrimination.'

"If the Air Force refused to heed the Committee's request, the body could call upon the Director of Defense Mobilization. He, in turn, could get help from the President.

"Basically, of course, the Committee will get its signals from the White House. The President has said, 'In fulfilling a contract with the Federal Government a contractor should follow the national policy of equal treatment and opportunity. It is my belief that the Committee on Government Contract Compliance will show us the way.'

"The words 'equal treatment' have an ominous ring for colored people. We fear that some White House advisers still think it is possible to have segregation in employment without discrimination.'

"The great truth that segregation in employment inevitably leads to discrimination was dramatically established during the war. Companies found that they simply could not build separates restaurants and toilets each time they hired or transferred a colored employee to an all white department. Hence, those, who for one reason or another, maintained segregated facilities invariably determined against colored people in hiring, promotion, and transfers.

"Some companies deliberately maintain segregation in working arrangements because they know that this will make it possible to continue the use of colored people in unskilled jobs while saving the more desirable jobs for whites.

"One of the first jobs facing the Committee is taking a clear cut stand against segregation. Any vacillation on this will simply repeat the trouble encountered by the Wartime FEPC in the U.S. Cartridge Company of St. Louis, Missouri, the West Coast Shipyards, and numerous machine shops in the south. In all of these cases, failure to take a stand against segregation at the outset resulted in terrible wastes of manpower plus long and tedious actions to correct the problems that arose.

"A second job confronting the Committee is establishing rules which will convince employers and contracting agencies that mere volume of colored people on the payroll does not prove that there is no discrimination.

"The Government wartime files are full of letters from Army engineers who insisted that construction employment was fair on a given project because 'several thousand Negro laborers were employed.' Colored carpenters, electricians, and plumbers would be barred, but the Army engineer would insist that 'this was not discrimination.' The Committee must accept the principle that, even though a company may have a hundred colored laborers, it discriminates if it refuses to hire qualified colored skilled workers for existing openings.

"As a third responsibility, the Committee must obtain, through the contracting agencies, sufficient personnel to do the required job. This is not a routine assignment that can be handled by the run of the mill employees. Some of the agencies already employ persons who can handle these matters intelligently. Other experts in this field should be hired.

"The Committee needs an executive director who knows the problem of discrimination in employment. It is possible to hire an executive of this type and have one of the contracting agencies pay his salary.

"The Committee must avoid the mistake made by the Board which at present administers the President's Fair Employment Order on Government employment. This Board, now operating out of the Civil Service Commission, has a minuscule staff of whites only. Hence, it has difficulty persuading other Government agencies not to discriminate because it does not set the right example itself.

"The Committee should get the contracting agencies to agree upon what steps will be taken to enforce the non-discrimination clause if investigation shows that a given contractor is discriminating. There are several possibilities for workable program of enforcement. For example, there is a suggestion (made by Secretary Oscar Chapman of the Department of the Interior) that contracting agencies could ask the Department of Justice to seek court action against those who violate the clause.

"In many cases, clear cut compliance machinery will speed up the handling of complaints because agencies need not waste time in endless negotiations if they know that the problem can be settled by some orderly process. One of the great frustrations of the Wartime FEPC was knowledge that the President could take over a plant that refused to follow an FEPC Directive, but that the chance of getting him to take such an action was usually remote."

It is regrettable that the Committee has not yet selected personnel with experience in the field of fair employment practice. It is always good to bring in new recruits in the drive against job discrimination. Such additions frequently mean the bringing in of new skills and new ideas. However it must be remembered that much valuable time can be lost if the Committee staff does not have first hand knowledge of past successes and failures in efforts to correct discriminatory employment practices. Therefore, we urge that the Committee promptly add to its staff competent persons who have had experience in this field.

Finally, I wish to express appreciation for the time and energy that the members of this Committee are devoting to their work. There is no other job in the United States today more important that that of finding a formula for ending discrimination in employment. We are ready to assist you in every way that we can.

MS: NAACP II: A-208, DLC.

1. On June 29, 1952, Dwight Palmer, chair of the President's Committee on Government Contract Compliance, asked Walter White to testify at the committee's meeting on June 9, 1952, but the secretary responded that he could not do so because he had to attend two important meetings in New York. White therefore asked Palmer to allow Mitchell to testify in his stead. Palmer to White, White's response, and other related materials are in NAACP II: A-200, DLC. See also 6/5/52.
2. See 12/5 and 12/28/51.
3. See, among others, 12/28/51, 10/6/52.

Walter White, Testimony on Immigration and Naturalization, September 30, 1952

Testimony of Walter White
Secretary, National Association for the Advancement of Colored People
Before the President's Commission on Immigration and Naturalization
Federal Courthouse, Foley Square, New York, N.Y.
September 30, 1952

It is undoubtedly superfluous for me to begin my testimony before this distinguished committee by pointing out two important facts.[1] I ask the indulgence of the committee, however, because there are far too many Americans who either do not know the facts or fail to understand their grave significance to the present and future security and welfare of the United States.[2]

The first of these facts is that between two-thirds and three-fourths of the world's population is not white. Not only do men and women of black, brown or yellow skin constitute this overwhelming majority of the population of the world, but in the areas of the world where they live are to be found many, if not most, of the raw materials on which the highly industrialized civilization of the Western World is dependent. These include uranium, manganese, chrome, tungsten, cobalt, tin, rubber, diamonds, bauxite and molybdenum. Should the so-called white Western nations be deprived of these minerals, and should they go into the hands of the Soviet Union, it is most doubtful whether what we call the democracies can long continue to survive.

The second fact which I wish to emphasize is that one of the contributing factors to World War II and one which today lowers American prestige in Asia, Africa, the Caribbean and South America is the racially discriminatory immigration laws of the United States, Canada and Australia. Every nation, of course, has the right to determine for itself what its rules and regulations for the admission of immigrants shall be. But when a nation blatantly erects a color bar in its immigration policy, it immediately sows the dragon's teeth resentment.

As a result of a determined campaign at the beginning of the Twentieth Century in the United States about the "yellow peril," the Congress enacted so-called oriental exclusion laws which, along with such practices as that of extraterritoriality in Asia, have done irreparable harm all over the world to the prestige of the Untied States. Particularly since 1921 the indefensible criteria of race, color and national origin have been the principle bases for our immigration policies. These criterion were founded upon doctrines of racial superiority which were popular during the Twenties along with the revival of the Ku Klux Klan after World War I. The basic common sense of the American people soon put an end, temporarily at least, to the Klan's flagrant violation of the principles of American democracy. But this concept of racial superiority has continued to dominate the thinking of many congressmen, as is evidenced by the 1924 immigration law, the one enacted in 1929, and the McCarran-Walter Act of 1952.

The 1924 law excluded Japanese and other Asians from the United States. Japan, like Italy, was sorely plagued by overpopulation and meager natural resources. Italy was permitted to invade Ethiopia and to engage in what proved to be one of the most costly colonial expansion programs of contemporary history which led directly to World War II.

The 1924 American immigration law, the "white Australia" policy of the same period of Canada's exclusion policy not only aggravated Japanese economic difficulties which stemmed from overpopulation but, even more disastrously, cast a stigma of racial inferiority upon the Japanese and other orientals. The drive of Japan into Manchuria and later into the South Pacific was largely caused by her need to find an outlet for a constantly increasingly population.

But even more harmful to world security was the emotional drive—hatred of the white world–which dominated not only Japanese military policy by the thinking of Asians generally who bitterly resented the gratuitous insult of exclusion based solely upon color.

I submit that the McCarran-Walter Act, because of its racial implications against colored peoples from Asia, the Caribbean and other areas, may well prove equally harmful to the United States not only in Asia but in Latin America. It is true that there has been some slight modification restrictions against Japanese. But the basic evil of the color bar remains not only uncorrected by in some regards worse that it was before the McCarran-Walter Act was passed over President Truman's veto.

It is my understanding that the visa division of the State Department drafted those sections of the McCarran-Walter Act which cuts to one-tenth or less the number of dark-skinned human beings who may be admitted to the Untied States. If it be true that the State Department is responsible for these provisions, they constitute an act which contradicts all of the protestations by the State department regarding human dignity and human freedom. They constitute as well a contradiction of all of our nation's support of a human rights declaration and covenant in the Untied Nations.

Let me illustrate this specifically. During the past two months in the British West Indies I have seen the terrible consequences of colonial exploitation. In the island of Jamaica, for example, white European nations have ruled for the past 290 years. The cream of the wealth of Jamaica and other West Indian Islands have been siphoned off through the colonial system for the benefit of absentee landlords in Europe and, to a lesser degree in the United States. Most of the profits from sugar, rum, coffee, tobacco, citrus fruits and other products have gone to the colonial powers while the living standards of the native population have sunk lower and lower. Today in Jamaica 1,500,000 persons, of whom 98% are of Negro or Indian Blood, are forced, through no choice of their own, to live at incredibly substandard levels. Wages averaging fifty cents a day have continued while prices have trebled since World War II.

Your committee and the people of America may correctly retort that the Untied States as a whole is not responsible for these conditions and is not therefore obligated to be concerned about them. I venture to disagree most vigorously with any such opinion. If for no other reason, the justly celebrated humanitarianism of our nation should compel us to be concerned. But if one chooses not to be concerned for reasons of human decency, there is another and very practical reason for being aware of what is happening in the Caribbean.

A distinguished authority on Latin American affairs, who, because of his official position, wished to remain anonymous, put this in capsule form recently when I sought his assistance in gathering material for this hearing:

> "The importance of the Caribbean area as a major segment of the Western Hemisphere, and specifically as the gateway to the Panama Canal, must be obvious to all," he stated. "We are learning to our sorrow in Asia that the good will of peoples is essential to the effective cooperation of their governments. The degree of friendliness of the Caribbean community toward the United States is to be attributed in large part to the people from those areas who have been welcomed in the United States and have prospered here. The closing of the door of immigration is the one obvious gesture of hostility toward the entire areas which can quickly destroy all the goodwill that has been built up."

I encountered in the West Indies this summer many examples of anger mixed with shock at both the sharp reduction of immigration from certain West Indian islands and the racial implication of that action. Prior to enactment of the McCarran-Walter Act immigration to the United States from the British West Indies was included in Great Britain's annual quota of 65,000.

For many years the United Kingdom has used only half or less than half of its 65,000 quota. From Jamaica there has come during recent years approximately 1,000 persons annually. The McCarran-Walter Act reduces that number to "not to exceed 100 persons annually." Thereby in one fell swoop the hope of many Jamaicans and others from British, French and Dutch West Indian possessions of escape from economic bondage has been destroyed. That hope has been replaced by justified resentment that the exclusion is based primarily on skin color.

This inexplicable cruelty is matched only by its blindness. Our nation has grown to its present great power and prestige because the peoples of the world have come to our shores to make their contributions towards the building of a great civilization. Among those who have helped to make our nation strong are not only agricultural and industrial workers from the West Indies but those who have made notable contributions to the arts, sciences, business and sports.

Under the McCarran-Walter Act the great Alexander Hamilton, born in Nevis, might not have been allowed to come to the United States.

Here are some distinguished Americans who were either born in the West Indies or are of West Indian descent:

1. Bert Williams, believed by many to be the greatest of comedians.
2. Claude McKay, famous poet and novelist.
3. The late Judge James S. Watson, New York Civil Service commissioner.
4. Prince Hall, founder of colored Masonry.
5. Peter Ogden, founder of colored Odd Fellows
6. John Russwurm, fist Negro college graduate and publisher of the first Negro newspaper in the United States.
7. Hazel Scott, famous pianist.
8. Jan Matzeliger, inventor of the lasting machine which revolutionized the shoe industry.
9. Roy Campanella of the Brooklyn Dodgers, considered by many to be today's greatest catcher.
10. Lester B. Granger, executive director, National Urban League
11. Ashley Totten, secretary-treasurer, Brotherhood of Sleeping Car Porters.
12. Dean Dixon, distinguished orchestra conductor and composer.
13. Jersey Joe Walcott, until last week, world's heavyweight champion.
14. Sidney Poitier, famous moving picture actor.
15. Edward Margetson, composer.

16. Bishop C. C. Alleyne of the African Methodist Episcopal Zion Church.
17. The late Dr. William H. Crogman, university president.
18. A. A. Austin, real estate broker.
19. The late Canada Lee, actor.
20. Arthur A. Schomburg, creator of the Schomburg collection.
21. James Weldon Johnson and J. Rosamond Johnson.
22. Willaim Stanley Braithwaite, critic and anthologist.
23. Mabel Keaton Staupers, Spingarn Medalist and former president of the National Association of Colored Graduate Nurses.
24. P.H.M. Savory, physician and co-owner of the New York *Amsterdam News*.

These men and women, along with many others of West Indian descent have made notable contributions to the building of our nation.

Both with respect to a more just and sane immigration policy, free of dangerous racial connotations, I recommend strongly to your committee that it urge immediate revision of our immigration and naturalization laws to eliminate all distinctions based on race, sex, language or religion.

Particularly do I recommend that so-called colonial areas be not penalized for having been the victims of centuries of colonial and racial discrimination. Immigration from colonies and from trusts and non-self-governing territories should be included in the quotas of nations like the United Kingdom, France, Belgium and others which administer these colonies, trusts and non-self-governing territories.

Until this is done, all our talk about "good neighbor policy" is as sounding brass and tinkling cymbals.

MS: MP.

1. The commission was established in the Executive Office of the President by EO 10392 on September 4, 1952, following passage by Congress, which overrode a veto of the Immigration and Naturalization Act of 1952 on January 27, 1952. It was responsible for recommending immigration and naturalization policies in accordance with established foreign policy. Its chair was former U.S. solicitor general Philip B. Perlman. Following submission of its final report, *Whom Shall We Welcome*, on January 1, 1953, the commission was terminated on January 30, 1953. See http://www.archives.gov/research/guide-fed-records/groups/220.html.

2. See also 6/5 and 12/31/52; in appendix, 5/28 and 6/3/52.

NAACP WB Newsletter, October 3, 1952

NEWSLETTER

[October 3, 1952]

WASHINGTON BUREAU
100 Massachusetts Avenue, N.W.
Washington, D.C.

During the 1952 campaign, many candidates for Congress will try to confuse voters by saying that they supported certain measures when in reality they worked diligently to cut the heart out of such proposals.[1]

For example on September 18, 1952, the Director of the Washington Bureau shared the platform at Hartford, Connecticut, with Mr. Prescott Bush, candidate for the U.S. Senate on the Republican ticket.[2]

Mr. Bush said that the majority of the members of this party voted for FEPC in 1950 when it was before the House of Representatives. Actually, this is not true. The majority of the Republicans voted against the Powell FEPC Bill with contained enforcement powers. This vote came on February 22 and the Powell Bill was defeated. On February 23, the McConnell Bill, a weak measure with no enforcement powers, was passed with heavy Republican support.[3]

Since Mr. Bush was speaking from material sent out by his Party headquarters, it is likely that this statement is being made in many sections of the country. Therefore, we again remind you that when candidates for the House of Representatives say they voted for FEPC be sure to ask them whether they supported the Powell Bill on February 22 or the McConnell Bill. If they voted against the Powell [bill], they are no friends of FEPC.

***** ***** *****

Some Senate candidates for reelection are boasting about how they voted against the filibuster on May 19, 1950, and July 12, 1950.[4] These votes were fine but some of those who brag about them had earlier betrayed the cause of civil rights by voting against a ruling of Vice President Barkley which would have paved the way for dealing a death blow to filibusters. Therefore, be sure to ask candidates for the Senate whether they supported the Barkley Ruling on March 11, 1949.

The vote against the Barkley Ruling was 46 to 41. When the Barkley Ruling was defeated, a coalition of Northern and Southern Senators then teamed up to pass a rule that requires 64 votes to halt a filibuster. This rule was invoked to try to break a filibuster against FEPC on May 19, 1950. The vote was 52 for ending the filibuster and 32 against. On July 12, 1950, the vote was 55 to 33. Thus on both occasions, the filibuster group won because the pro-civil rights forces could not muster 64 votes.[5]

*****   *****   *****

BE SURE TO REGISTER AND VOTE ! TELL OTHERS TO DO THE SAME

*****   *****   *****

There is a great deal of excitement in Washington about a publication gotten out by the Republican National Committee giving information for speakers. Democrats are hopping mad about one section that charges "Navy integration is pure fiction." While this charge is an over-statement, the Administration is vulnerable on segregation in Navy Yards in Norfolk, Virginia, and Charleston, South Carolina. The Secretary of the Navy has flatly refused to correct these policies which require separate drinking fountains, separate lavoratories, and separate restaurants for colored and white persons.

The Army is also vulnerable because it has extended segregation in schools on military posts. Colored children at Fort Sill, Oklahoma, Fort Bliss, Texas, Fort Sam Houston, Texas, and Fort Belvoir, Virginia, are required to attend segregated schools.

The pamphlet also attacks the Housing policies of the Federal Government. Here, also, the agencies responsible for the program have failed miserably on civil rights. So far, all of the housing programs continue to give assistance to the development of projects both public and private for whites only. This is the exact opposite of Federal policy announced by the Solicitor General in the restrictive covenant cases.

*****   *****   *****

BE SURE TO REGISTER AND VOTE ! TELL OTHERS TO DO THE SAME

*****   *****   *****

The last newsletter described a select committee headed by congressman Eugene E. Cox of Georgia.[6] It was set up on April 4 by the House of Representatives for the purpose of investigating alleged subversive intent and influence by philanthropic foundations in the country. Cited as groups which might fall under the eye of the committee were the Rockefeller Foundation, the Rosenwald Foundation, the Ford Foundation, the Carnegie Foundation, the Guggenheim Foundation, and many others. All have aided Southerners educationally, including Negroes.

Owing to the anti-negro record of Cox, the NAACP vigorously opposed creation of this committee. So far, it has gotten $75,000 to hire investigators, and among other things, to take a trip to California. Why California was singled out is anyone's guess.

It is interesting to note that many Congressmen who often spearheaded economy drives to kill administration programs forsook economy to grant $75,000 for what bids fair to be a racebaiting witch-hunt.

The committee's lease on life expires with the 82nd congress on December 31, 1952. Urge your Congressman to deny further funds for this twentieth Century inquisition in the 83rd Congress.

* * * * *　　* * * * *　　* * * * *

BE SURE TO REGISTER AND VOTE ! TELL OTHERS TO DO THE SAME

* * * * *　　* * * * *　　* * * * *

MS: MP.

1. See also 7/31/52; in appendix, 5/28/52.

2. Prescott Bush was elected U.S. senator from Connecticut in 1952. He was the father of George Herbert Walker Bush, the forty-first president, and grandfather of George W. Bush, the forty-third president.

3. See 3/3 and 5/31/50.

4. *Congressional Record,* vol. 96, 5/19/50, 7292–7307; 7/12/50, 9976–82. On both occasions, the vote was on FEPC measures. They were defeated by failure to obtain the required two-thirds majority vote to end debate.

5. Leslie Perry provided the following background:

> After much wrangling in the Committee on Rules and Administration S. Res. 15, the Hayden-Wherry Resolution, was reported out on Feb. 17th. Earlier the Myers-Morse substitute was defeated by a vote of 11 to 2. By agreement the leadership brought this question to the floor on February 28th.
>
> The southern opposition proceeded to filibuster on the motion to consider the resolution. The Bureau has been contacting senators with two objects in mind: (1) to secure commitments to support the Myers-Morse majority resolution and (2) votes to sustain Vice President Barkley on appeal to the body if he rules that cloture is applicable to motions to consider. Among the senators from whom verbal commitments have been secured are J. Howard McGrath (D., R.I.), Elbert Thomas (D., Utah), Hubert H. Humphrey (D. Minn.), Glen Taylor (D., Idaho) and others. Senator Taft promised to support the Barkley ruling although there was evidence that a large part of the Republicans would vote to override principally for partisan considerations. Last minute tallies indicate that there are enough southerners and Republicans to override a favorable Barkley ruling in which event the filibuster can conceivably go on for weeks. (Report of the Washington Bureau, 2/49, NAACP II: A-656, DLC)

The next month, Perry reported:

> From February 28 to March 17 resolutions to amend Senate Rule 22, limiting debate, were filibustered. As had been anticipated, Vice President Barkley ruled that cloture applies to procedural steps such as motions to consider, etc. On appeal from the ruling of the chair 23 Republicans joined 20 Dixiecrats and 3 Western Mountain States Democrats to override the Barkley ruling. This vote occurred on March 11.
>
> During the days immediately preceding, the NAACP arranged a conference in Washington [see, in appendix, Report on the NAACP Conference on the Filibuster, 3/10/49] attended by 60 persons from 16 states. These delegates had conferences with Majority Leader Lucas, Majority Whip Francis Myers and the Chairman of the National Democratic Committee Senator Howard McGrath. They also talked to senators from their states. It is believed that they definitely influenced a number of votes including the senators from New Jersey and others who earlier had favored the Vandenberg ruling [see headnote on NAACP and the Filibuster].
>
> After the defeat of the Barkley ruling the Republican-Dixiecrat coalition had control over the Senate. The Majority Leader did not have enough votes even to adjourn the Senate. Therefore, Senator William F. Knowland (R., Calif.) began circulating a petition to amend the rule so as to require a constitutional two-thirds (64 senators) to shut-off debate on all matters before the Senate excluding further changes of the Senate rules. Such further changes of the Senate rules would not be subject to cloture on a motion to consider. This so-called compromise resolution, introduced by Senators Carl Hayden (Dr., Ariz.), Kenneth S. Wherry (R. Nebr.) on

behalf of themselves and 50 other senators, was presented to the Senate. The Bureau personally urged approximately 30 senators to withdraw from the compromise resolution and to support the Myers-Morse resolution. When the vote came on March 17 on the Myers amendment, calling for a constitutional majority (49 senators) to shut off debate on all pending business, it was defeated by a vote of 69 to 17. Senator Morse's amendment, providing for a majority of those voting, was defeated 80 to 7. The Wherry-Hayden proposal, Senate Resolution 15 as amended, passed 63 to 23. The attempt to bring democracy to the Senate rules was defeated by active coalition of Dixiecrats and Republicans. (Report of the Washington Bureau, 3/49, NAACP II: A-656, DLC)

See also 4/3/50, notes at 5/31/50, and 7/52 in appendix.

6. See 8/31, 11/5, and 12/28/51, 5/8, 6/5, and 12/31/52; in appendix, newsletters, 5/28 and 7/31/52.

NAACP WB Press Release, October 4, 1952

PRESS RELEASE **MR. WALTER WHITE**

WASHINGTON BUREAU
National Association for the Advancement of Colored People
100 Massachusetts Ave., N.W.
Telephone, National 5795

Washington, D.C., October 4, 1952–Abolition of segregation that forces colored children on Army posts to attend separate and inferior schools was asked by the Washington Bureau of the NAACP in a letter to Robert A. Lovett, Secretary of Defense, released for publication today.[1]

In the letter to the Secretary, Clarence Mitchell, Director of the Association's Washington Bureau, charged that colored children at Fort Bliss and Fort Sam Houston in Texas, Fort Sill in Oklahoma, and Fort Belvoir, Virginia, are shunted to inferior schools.

At Fort Sill, Mr. Mitchell charged, military officials boldly announced that white children will be given transportation to a new school on the post while colored children will not be given transportation by military authorities. At the white school, the NAACP letter stated, there will be a cafeteria where hot lunches will be served.

This practice, the NAACP said, is a shocking departure from the stand taken by President Truman in 1951 when he vetoed H.R. 5411, a school aid bill, because it contained language designed to introduce segregation in schools on military posts.

Speaking of the Commanders who have instituted these practices, the NAACP said that their's is "an unconscionable attempt by the military to subject the Government of the United States to the racial policies we were fighting against during World War II."

Referring to the effect this segregation has in the form of Communist propaganda, the letter said:

"It is well known that an important part of the Communist propaganda in the Far East is that our fight in Korea is for the purpose of promoting white supremacy rather than democracy. If the Armed Services, themselves, wantonly humiliate colored children and their parents in our own country, how can we answer this propaganda that the Communists use?"

A copy of the letter is attached.

October 2, 1952

Honorable Robert A. Lovett
Secretary of Defense
Department of Defense
Washington, D. C.

My dear Mr. Lovett:

We wish to place before you a very important question of policy affecting schools located on military posts. We have before us at this time complaints form Fort Bliss, Texas, Fort Sam Houston, Texas Fort Sill, Oklahoma, and Fort Belvoir, Virginia.

At Fort Sill, white children are given transportation to a new school building located on the post. Colored children not only are sent to an inferior school off the post, but also the military establishment has boldly announced that it will not provide transportation to the school for them. Among other advantages, the school for white children will have a cafeteria where hot lunches will be served.

In each of these instances, the post commanders have turned the schools on the posts over to local education authorities who, in turn, operate them on a segregated basis. This is a shocking departure from the stand taken by the President in 1951 when he vetoed H.R. 5411. That Bill, as you know, contained language which was designed to require segregation in schools on military posts. For some reason, members of the Department of Defense's Legal Staff have the opinion that H.R. 5411 was passed over the President's veto. This is not the case. Actually, there is not a shred of justification in committee hearings or otherwise for the present practice followed in these military installations in Texas, Oklahoma, and Virginia.

The system of allowing children of white service personnel to attend schools on the posts while shunting the Negro children to the inferior and inconveniently located schools is a disgraceful action, particularly, at a time when we are calling on so many young men and women to help preserve democracy in Korea and other parts of the world.

This practice of enforcing segregation by subterfuge on military reservations is an unconscionable attempt by the military to subject the Government of the United States to the racial polices that we were fighting against during World War II.

It is well known that an important part of the Communist propaganda in the Far East is that our fight with Korea is for the purpose of promoting white supremacy rather than democracy. If the Armed Services, themselves, wantonly humiliate colored children and their parents in our own country, how can we answer this propaganda that the Communists use?

In addition, the Attorney General and the Solicitor General of the Unitied States have both declared that the policy of our Government is against segregation on the basis of race. It is impossible to see how some of the legal minds in the Department of Defense are acting properly when they permit or encourage actions on military posts that are just the opposite of what the highest law officers of our Government have said in appearances before the United States Supreme Court.

Sincerely yours,
Clarence Mitchell

Clarence Mitchell
Director
Washington Bureau

MS: NAACP II: A-656, DLC.

1. See 10/6/52, where this press release is cited.

Broadcast

WLIB AND AFFILIATED STATIONS

Walter White

April 9, 1953

For a most important reason I shall this week forego having a guest on this program.

I do so because one of the most important—even critical—issues affecting human rights and the future of human freedom throughout the world is now pending before the Untied states Senate. Unless the American people let their senators know of their concern about this threat to constitutional government it is conceivable that this proposed alteration f the treaty-making power of the President may be made a reality because of pressure now being exerted on the Congress.

I shall return in a moment to this discussion.

* * * * * * * * * * *

The matter I wish to discuss on this program is the proposal of Senator John W. Bricker of Ohio and sixty-three other senators to amend the Federal Constitution and require that all treaties and conventions entered into by the United States government be formally approved not only by the Congress but by each state legislature before such treaties or conventions may apply to domestic law.[1]

Senator Bricker's proposal is elaborated upon by a second one now before the Senate. This one was drafted to follow recommendations of the America Bar Association and makes the additional provision that treaties, conventions and even executive agreements shall not be binding on citizens or states until such agreements have been ratified by passage of appropriated laws. In simple terms this means that the treaty-making powers of the United States government would now be vested in not *only* the Congress but in the legislatures of forty-eight separate states. Our entire national treaty-making machinery would be reduced to the moral and intellectual level of the most backward state of the nation. It would mean that as a nation we could take no higher moral ground than that permitted by states like Mississippi or South Carolina.

Because the public has not been furnished much information until recently on this issue, there is grave danger that both proposals may be approved by the Senate since sixty-four senators have joined in sponsoring them. Sixty-four is the number of senators required by the Constitution to approve a constitutional amendment.

Attorney general Hebert Brownell grimly warned the Senate Judiciary Committee on April 7 that nay such amendment will upset and possibly destroy the balance of power between the executive and legislative branches of government which has been one of the bulwarks of our democracy.[2]

Secretary o f State John Foster Dulles also tried to stop the Bricker amendment in his testimony before the Judiciary Committee on April 6.[3] But he did so through proposals which many Americans deplore. Mr. Dulles pledged the Senate that the Eisenhower administration would sign *no* treaty on human rights drafted under United Nations auspices nor would it ask approval of the already drafted convention on the political rights of women. He also pledged that the administration will not ask for ratification of the Untied Nations' Genocide Convention, which outlaws acts like those of Hitler and Russia against the Jew, intended to wipe out racial, national, ethnic or religious groups. The Genocide Convention has been pending before the Senate Foreign Relations Committee for almost five years. But even these pledges were not enough for Senator Bricker. Promptly and imperiously Bricker announced that he would not be appeased by the pledges of the Secretary of State.

Coming as it does when signs of hope of the ending of the Korean War appear on the horizon and on the eve of the meeting of the Human Rights Commission of the U.N. at Geneva, Mr. Dulles' pledges to the Senate have caused consternation at home and throughout the world. The distinguished Indian member o the Human Rights Commission promptly declared at Geneva that this "takes the bottom out of the work of this Commission."

Inevitably the widespread suspicion, whether it be justified or not, in many parts of the world that the United States is interested in human rights only as far as Soviet pressures force us, Mr. Dulle's surrender to the conservative pressures of the Senate and the American Bar Association will be interpreted as backtracking on human rights as soon as possibilities of ending the Korean war materialize.

Permit me to sketch the background of this issue. At the organizing convention of the Untied Nations in San Francisco in 1945, one of the most hotly contested issues was the Declaration of Human Rights. Hundreds of millions of peoples throughout the world who have been denied these rights were given hope and faith in the Untied Nations by the pledges of the Declaration even though those pledges were quite general in character. The United State, along with other member nations of the U.N., voted approval of the Declaration. That vote as much as any other action of the past half century caused the peoples of Asia, Africa and Latin America to believe in our sincerity and democracy.

In 1952 a California court ruled in a case involving the right of a Japanese-American to buy land that the United States in singing the Declaration of Human Rights had committed itself to respect and enforce those rights. Although the California Supreme Court reserved the lower court, there was consternation in conservative circles lest our international moral commitments require us to live up to those commitments here at home. Promptly two powerful forces in the United States moved into action. One of these was the conservative wing of the American Bar Association; the other the South. The latter feared that international agreement stop regulate labor, education, social security, legal procedure and other human rights would, according to the distinguished Washington correspondent, Doris Fleeson, "override the civil rights blockade set up in Congress by the South."

Here is an example of how the coalition operated. Our nation was one of the chief architects of the Bogota Convention. But powerful though quiet pressure of the State Department caused it to announce that the Untied States would sign the Bogota Convention only on condition that it was specifically and unmistakably freed form any and all obligations to comply with those sections of the Bogota Convention which affirmed equality of opportunity irrespective of race. This reservation immediately weakened almost to the point of destruction the effectiveness of the Bogota Convention..

It is this same kind of pressure which enables anyone reasonably familiar with today's Washington scene to understand why Secretary of State Dulles pledged the Eisenhower administration to abstain form singing any treaty on human rights such as the United Nations convention on the political rights of women or the one on human rights generally on which the U.N. Human Rights Commission has been working for several years. One can understand also why Mr. Dulles pledged, in an effort to stop the Bricker amendment, that the present administration will not press or ask for ratification of the Genocide Convention.

But you can't beat something with nothing. Americans who are concerned about our national prestige and integrity devoutly wish that Mr. Dulles had remembered the biblical statement: In the beginning was the word, and the was *with* God, and the word *was* God. We as a nation have grown great and strong because we are committed both to the *word* and the *way* of life which we call democracy. Our surrender will most certainly do exactly what Attorney General Brownell has said—it will limit the treaty-making authority of the President, upset the balance of power between the executive and legislative branches of the government, and will take the Soviet Union off the hook on the issue of civil rights. With characteristic amorality Communists throughout the world today rejoice that their embarrassment on the issue of anti-Semitism which has recently come to light will be glossed over. More, they will industriously quote Mr. Dulles' words to millions of desperate people in so-called undeveloped areas of the earth as evidence that the United States is not going to fight for human rights for oppressed peoples.

A few days ago I asked a high government official how we could effectively interpret United States policy to Asia and Africa—where social revolutions of vast importance against colonialism and racism sweep those parts of the world—in light of the pledge of our Secretary of state that we shall not support human rights covenants because we fear selfish and shortsighted opposition in the United States.

He replied with a cynical smile that the mandate of the people in the 1952 election required such action and added, somewhat cynically, "The first job of a statesman is to stay in office."

This commentator refuses to believe that last November's election can in any wise be interpreted as a mandate of fight and oppose human rights at home or abroad. Perhaps I am wrong. But I believe that the people of our nation do not want to stand in shame before the world preaching one doctrine and practicing another. I believe with equal fervor that if the people know the facts, they will let Senator Bricker and the other sixty-three senators who have joined with him in sponsoring this dangerous alteration of the constitution know that their action is not approved by those who really believe in freedom.

What do you think?

MS: MP.

1. See 6/15, 11/4, and 12/31/53, 9/29 and 12/31/54.
2. Brownell testimony, 4/7/53, before Senate Judiciary Committee.
3. Dulles testimony, 4/6/53, before Senate Judiciary Committee.

NEWSLETTER

NATIONAL ASSOCIATION FOR THE ADVANCEMENT OF COLORED PEOPLE

August 10, 1953

WASHINGTON BUREAU
100 Massachusetts Avenue, N.W.
Washington, D.C.

From the beginning when a Republican and Democratic Coalition defeated an anti-filibuster rules change offered by Senator Clinton Anderson (D., N.M.), by a vote of 70 to 21, the 83rd Congress made a determined and successful effort to avoid consideration of civil rights.

The Anderson motion was defeated when Senator Taft made a motion to table it on January 7. Taft was supported by 41 Republicans and 29 Democrats. Voting against Taft were 5 Republicans and 15 Democrats, and one Independent.

The decision to kill the rules change was firmly enforced as a matter of party discipline among the Republicans, according to the NAACP's Washington Bureau. New Republican senators who favored a rules change fell in line with policy decision of the leaders and voted to keep existing rules which permit endless talkathons.

On May 12, the Senate Rules Committee suddenly reported out S.Res. 20. This was during the Tidelands Oil Debate. However, no move has been made to schedule debate on this or any other anti-filibuster resolution. S. Res. 20 was introduced by Senator Jenner (R., Ind.) and is the least desirable. S. Res. 63 introduced by Senator Lehman (D., N.Y.), S. Res. 41 by Senator Morse (Ind., Ore.), and S. Res. 31 by Senator Ives (R., N.Y) offer workable plans for ending filibuster.[1]

***** ***** *****

In the House, the chief bottleneck on constructive legislation is the Rules Committee. On January 3, by a voice vote, the House adopted its old rules, thus, continuing the power of the Rules Committee, which is now headed by Congressman Leo Allen of Illinois.

Congressman Herman Eberharter of Pennsylvania was unsuccessful in getting consideration of a resolution which would allow committee chairmen to force House consideration of legislation which their committees approve but which the Rules Committee does not clear within twenty-one days after receiving it.[2]

***** ***** *****

Senator Irving Ives (R., N.Y.) set hearings on FEPC legislation, but postponed them until January 1954. No other committee of Congress definitely set hearings on civil rights bills.[3]

The late Senator Charles W. Tobey (R., N.H.) was studying Anti-Jim Crow Travel legislation in his committee on Interstate and Foreign Commerce and had agreed to hold hearings, but dates had not been set. Chairman Wolverton (R., N.J.) of the House Committee has pledged that he will hold hearings on the bill, but no date has been set.[4]

Although civil rights bills have been introduced in all major categories such as Fair Employment, Anti-Lynching, Anti-Jim Crow Travel, and Anti-Poll Tax, none of these is an Administration bill. Committee chairmen usually act on such legislation when the White House asks them to do so.

***** ***** *****

In the field of labor relations, all members of the Senate Labor Committee, except two, joined in sponsoring a vital amendment to the Taft-Hartley Act. This amendment (S. 1831) would prohibit segregation and discrimination in matters under the jurisdiction of the National Labor Relations Board.

Co-sponsors of S. 1831 are Mr. Smith of New Jersey, Mr. Aiken, Mr. Griswold, Mr. Purtell, Mr. Goldwater, Mr. Murray, Mr. Neely, Mr. Douglas, Mr. Lehman, and Mr. Kennedy.

Passage seems certain if the White House approves it in a forthcoming message on Taft-Hartley Amendments. The message is scheduled for September.[5]

***** ***** *****

House Appropriations Committee members singled out the racial relations service of the Housing Agencies for a cut when funds for the Agencies were under consideration. However, the Senate reversed this action.

The Banking and Currency Committees of the House and Senate extended the time limit for purchasing of mortgages by the Federal National Mortgage Association in order to benefit housing open to minority groups. However, the Appropriations Committee of the House dealt a deadly blow to minority groups by slashing Public Housing.

The House Committee led a successful fight to reduce the number of units authorized for construction form 35,000 to 20,000. It also obtained Congressional approval of a stipulation that no new units in excess of 20,000 could be built or planned without the consent of Congress.

This has the effect of halting construction of most of 55,000 public housing units the Government already has under contract. One-third of all existing public housing units in the country are occupied by colored people.[6]

***** ***** *****

The House has passed a bill to make Hawaii a state. The Senate may face a filibuster when the Hawaii Bill comes up because, during Senate hearings, Senator Smathers (D. Fla.) repeatedly dragged the race issue into the picture. In the House, it was supported by Congressmen from Texas, Georgia, Louisiana, and other anti-civil rights areas. The vote favored statehood by 274 to 178.[7]

* * * * *   * * * * *   * * * * *

The Senate passed a bill (S. 697) to give the District of Columbia a non-voting delegate in the House. However, the House buried the bill in committee. This and other Home Rule Bills for the District come under fire from some southern elements in Congress on the charge that colored people will out vote whites in the District.

* * * * *   * * * * *   * * * * *

The Senate Judiciary Committee on June 15, by a vote of 9 to 5, reported out a Constitutional amendment which would limit the Treaty making power of the President. Some of its supporters said the amendment was necessary to halt Civil Rights advances in the United States.[8]

* * * * *   * * * * *   * * * * *

For further information or additional copies, write the Washington Bureau of the NAACP at

100 Massachusetts Avenue, N.W., Washington, D.C.
Telephone National 8–5794

MS: NAACP II: A-656, DLC.

This is the closest that was found to the 8/6/53 report on legislative matters that Mitchell mentions in a footnote to 9/9/53. It is also an extension of 6/15/53.

1. See, among others, 4/30, 6/15, 11/2/53–2, 11/4/53.
2. See, among others, 2/4, 4/30, 6/15, and 11/4/53.
3. See, among others, 2/4, 4/3, 4/30, 5/4, 6/1, 6/15, 8/21, 9/9, 11/2/53–2, 11/4/53.
4. See, among others, 2/4, 3/3, 5/4, 6/1, 6/15, 11/2/53–2, 11/4/54.
5. See, among others, 2/4, 3/3, 4/3, 4/30, 5/4, 6/1, and 11/4/53.
6. See, among others, 3/3, 4/3, 4/30, 5/4, 6/1, 9/9, 11/2/53–2, 11/4/53.
7. See, among others, 2/4, 4/30, 6/15, 11/2/53–2, 11/4/53.
8. See, among others, 6/15 and 11/4/53.

PRESS RELEASE

Washington Bureau, NAACP
100 Massachusetts Ave., N.W.
Telephone National 8–5794

Washington, D.C. August 21, 1953—Climaxing a sustained drive by local branches and the national office of the NAACP, the Navy Department this week, announced that it would end segregation of civilian employees in all its shore establishments.

The major NAACP effort against Jim Crow policies of the Navy began in 1951 when Jerry O. Gilliam, President of the Norfolk, Virginia, NAACP, and Thaddeus G. Frazier, Secretary of the Charleston, South Carolina, branch, asked Clarence Mitchell, Director for the Washington Bureau, to work to end separate drinking fountain, Jim Crow wash-rooms, and other segregated facilities in Navy Yards of their cities.

The Navy resisted the NAACP's efforts, and, as one of his final acts while serving as acting Secretary of the Navy two days after the Eisenhower Administration took over, Under-Secretary Francis P. Whitehair of Florida affirmed the policy of segregation in a written order.

When Whitehair was replaced by Navy Secretary Robert B. Anderson, a Texan, the NAACP placed the question before him. When he failed to act,, the NAACP took the matter to Assistant Secretary of Defense, John Hannah. Mr. Hannah promised to end segregation. At the same time, he stated the Navy would study the extent of segregation in its shore establishments.

The NAACP and Congressman Adam Clayton Powell, Jr., also took the problem directly to the President.

Someone in the Navy Department anonymously released a story about proposed gradual changes in ending segregation on August 10. However, the official Navy announcement was made on August 20 by Secretary Anderson who said:

"In further pursuit of its objective of the elimination of segregated facilities, the Department of the Navy has completed a survey of 43 shore stations from Virginia through Texas. The study shows that segregated facilities for white and colored citizens are non-existent in approximately one-half of the activities; in the remainder, segregation practices range from minor in most instances to substantial in a few cases.

"Commanding officers have been requested to proceed steadily and expeditiously toward the complete elimination of all barriers to the free use of facilities on government owned shore stations and to report their progress in this regard to the Secretary of the Navy at sixty day intervals."

Mr. Mitchell said of the announcement: "The ending of segregation is long overdue. We hope that, at the end of the first sixty day interval, the commanders will report that all Jim Crow facilities have been eliminated. Even sixty days is too long to keep segregation anywhere—but especially on U.S. property."[1]

MS: WB-142, DLC.

1. See also 11/2/53 and Mitchell, "Negroes Now Eat Upstairs," 585–88, 638–39.

Memorandum

November 30, 1953

To: Members of the Committee on Government Contracts

From: The National Association for the Advancement of Colored People

We offer the following suggestions which we believe will be helpful to the Committee on Government Contracts in carrying out its mission to eliminate employment discrimination in those areas within its jurisdiction.[1]

1. Specific accomplishments are needed in the very near future if the committee is to win and hold public confidence. We suggest that it concentrate on successfully achieving the employment of colored operator in the Telephone Company in Washington. The Capital Transit Company, also represents a major unresolved problem which needs attention from the committee.[2]

   Committee action should bring an early end to the present practices of contractors at Atomic Energy installations in Paducah, Ky., and Aiken, S.C. At both of these locations colored people are currently barred from training programs solely because of race.[3]

   An excellent area for trial operation would be the State of West Virginia where many new industries hold government contracts. The NAACP has numerous complaints from this state alleging that there is wholesale discrimination against colored job applicants.

2. A procedure for obtaining compliance should be worked out by the committee. Unless this is done now future operations may be hampered by contractors who become defiant simply because they do not believe that the Government can require them to obey the non-discrimination clause in their contracts.

3. There are many organizations and individuals who desire to co-operate fully with the committee and to defend it when unfair attacks are made on its operations. However, those interested in the Committee's work should be kept informed through regular meetings at which they may discuss problems that the committee has under consideration.

   Regular press releases on the work and accomplishments of the committee will also be useful in establishing the committee's effectiveness.

4. Although the Committee can do a great deal of constructive work with its present resources and authority, it should always keep the public and the Congress

aware of the limitations on its effectiveness and the need for legislation in this field. Its work should reveal that an FEPC with enforcement powers is a practical and necessary Federal institution.

Walter White
Executive Secretary, NAACP

Clarence Mitchell
Director, Washington Bureau

MS: NAACP II A-208, DLC.

On January 11, 1953, White sent Mitchell a copy of a letter of 11/9/53 from Jacob Seidenberg inviting both of them to a meeting of the Subcommittee on Liaison with Interested Groups of the Government Contracts Committee on November 30. White told Mitchell: "I will come down early that day so we can get our howitzers properly loaded." Seidenberg told White that James P. Mitchell, secretary of labor and chair of the subcommittee, would "hold an informal, off-the-record, around-the-table meeting with representatives of eight other private, voluntary organizations to discuss ways and means by which the common objectives of the Committee of Government Contracts may be achieved." He said some of the topics to be covered were the "extent and scope of discrimination in employment; the nature and kind of discrimination practiced in employment; suggestions as to methods and procedures which would aid in obtaining effective compliance; the adequacy of the present non-discrimination clause—suggested revisions if any; sanctions; and the role and kind of publicity the Committee should use." The NAACP, he instructed White, should address itself to all or some of those topics. White responded that he would be accompanied by Clarence Mitchell. (Based on handwritten notes on White's 11/4/53 memorandum, the eight organizations Seidenberg referred to were the AFL, AJCom., AJCong., CIO, NAACP, NCCCA, NCRAC, NCWC, and NUL.)

Intense preparations for the meeting had begun earlier. In a memorandum of 11/4/53, White told Thurgood Marshall, NAACP special counsel, Channing Tobias, NAACP chair, Roy Wilkins, NAACP administrator, and Henry Lee Moon, NAACP director of public relations, that the committee had asked him "to gather information on targets and procedures from recognized agencies in the field of civil rights." Guided by Mitchell, White, in a memorandum of 11/5/53, provided suggestions from the Washington bureau director about issues for the group to discuss with Seidenberg that day in a preliminary meeting at the executive secretary's house in New York. Mitchell suggested:

1. The time has come for the committee to *get on the ball* with some concrete results. At the next meeting it should be prepared to say what it has done on the specific complaints submitted by NAACP on Washington Telephone Company and Atomic Energy Commission. Jake [Seidenberg] says they are active on these but, frankly, I think they should now be ready to say they have *corrected* these two. I think something specific in the way of achievement is *absolutely* essential if they are to keep public confidence.
2. The committee *must* have some regular way of keeping organizations informed on what they are doing. There is no excuse for the present procedure under which we must dig for information on what they are doing. Information could be given to us on an off-the-record basis, if necessary.
3. The committee should establish a procedure under which complaints may be filed.
4. We should have a clear picture of how the committee will enforce any finding that there has been discrimination by a given contractor.

   I think Jake needs this kind of firm talk personally. Sometimes I think he is not ready to move as fast as some members of the committee. Confidentially, I do not think he is the best choice for secretary of the committee. I understand he may leave to join the staff of the Ford Foundation, but I don't know whether it has jelled as yet.

Attached to this document was a typed note of 12/1/53 with the following names of persons who attended the meeting, which Mitchell had telephoned to Mabel D. Jackson, White's secretary: J. Ernest Wilkins; James C. Worthy, assistant secretary of commerce; William P. Rogers, deputy attorney general; Maxwell Rabb, associate counsel to the president; Ivan Willis, vice president, International Harvester Company; George Weaver (representing Walter Reuther of the UAW); Boris Shishkin; George McKibbin, consultant to the administrator, GSA; James P. Mitchell, secretary of labor; and Alvin Rucker and Jacob Seidenberg, both staff members. In his handwritten note, which also had those names, Mitchell listed these other attendees: Bill (William) Oliver, UAW-CIO; Julius Thomas, NUL; Will Maslow, AJCong.; Ed (Edwin J.) Lukas, AJCom.; Margaret Garrity, NCWC; Dick (Richard L.) Bennett, AFSC; Arnold Aronson, NCRAC; Bert Seidman, AFL; Sascha (Charles S.) Zimmerman, NCRAC; JLC MURATCHIC (Emanuel Muravchik, JLC); and Dr. (Earl F.) Adams, NCRAC. (These names were confirmed by the Report of the Subcommittee on Liaison with Interested Groups, 12/1/53, Committee—President's Committee on Govt. Contracts Compliance, DDEL.) All of the cited documents are to be found in NAACP, II: A-208, DLC.

The following statements, both dated 11/30/53, were also attached to this published document: "Non-discrimination under Government Contracts," with the AFL's recommendations, provided by Bert Seidman, staff economist, and "Outline of CIO's Position."

1. See Mitchell's statement before the committee, 6/9/52, in NAACP II: A-208, DLC; also see, among others, 9/9/53 and 9/29/54.

2. The Capital Transit Company would not begin to hire blacks as operators of streetcars and buses until 1955. See volume V.

3. An NAACP press release reported that, in presenting the requests to Vice President Richard Nixon, chair of the committee, Mitchell explained both the telephone and atomic energy cases had been pending before the committee since the Truman administration "and a considerable amount of work had been done on them." NAACP press release, 9/19/53, NAACP II: A-208, DLC.

Recommendations of the National Association for the Advancement of Colored People at the Conference on Minority Housing Problems Held in Washington, D. C., December 9–10, 1954

The role of Government in the national economy is to maintain a free and competitive market.[1] To fulfill this function in the field of housing, the Government must require that builders, lenders and any others who receive federal aid of any kind for housing programs agree that renters or buyers will not be denied such housing on the basis of race. This condition must apply to all Federal housing activities.

This policy will require the following:

1. All public housing must be open to tenants without regard to race. There will be no more "white" and "colored" projects. Tenant selection will be made on the basis of need for housing rather than on the basis of race.
2. There will be a contractual requirement that all housing and other facilities such as parks, playgrounds or hospitals erected or developed on land assembled through loans or grants under the Slum Clearance and Urban Redevelopment Program and the Urban Renewal Program would be open to all renters, buyers, or users without regard to race.

3. On all housing on which there is FHA insurance or VA guarantee or a commitment for such insurance or guarantee, there shall be a contractual agreement binding on those who own the property or control the sale or rental of such property that there shall be no discrimination against persons seeking to lease, rent or purchase such property on account of race, creed, color or national origin.

We believe that the above position is the only honorable and legal position that the Federal Government can take in this matter. It is also in line with President Eisenhower's policy of not permitting Federal funds to be used to promote racial discrimination.[2]

MS: NAACP WB-91, DLC.

1. See, among others, 9/29 and 11/4/54 and the headnote on Segregation in Federal Housing Programs.

For the NAACP's initial support for public housing with proper antisegregation safeguards, see Perry's Report of the Washington Bureau, 1/49, 2/49, 4/49, in NAACP II: A-656, DLC; Perry, 2/15/49, *Hearings*, 735–44.

APPENDIX 2

Biographical Directory

Acheson, Dean Gooderham (1893–1971), lawyer; assistant secretary of state (1941–45); undersecretary of state (1945–47); U.S. secretary of state (1949–53). In an amicus brief written in 1952 for the *Brown v. Board of Education* case, he denounced segregation and discrimination in terms of their effect upon diplomacy. In 1951, Mitchell conferred with him on ending employment discrimination within the State Department.

Adams, Earl Chester (1895–1971), "red cap" (baggage handler) for the Pennsylvania Railroad who became vice president, United Transport Service Employees of America, CIO; in July 1942, he represented UTSEA at the Conference of Cooperating Organizations.

Adams, Rev. Earl Frederick (1900–56), general secretary, NCRAC; executive director, Protestant Council of the City of New York. He represented the NCRAC at a 1953 meeting with a subcommittee of the CGC.

Adams, Maj. Gen. Emory Sherwood, Sr. (1881–1967), U.S. Army; veteran of Spanish-American War and World Wars I and II; U.S. adjutant general (1938–42). In 1940, he corresponded with Walter White of the NAACP concerning the U.S. Army's segregation policy.

Adams, John Wesley, Jr. (1913–89), foreign service officer and specialist on international political and security affairs, State Department (1941–73). He served on a department board investigating NAACP complaints against State Department hiring practices.

Adams, Llewellyn Sherman (1899–1986) (R-N.H.), business executive; New Hampshire state legislator (1941–44); U.S. representative (1945–47); governor of New Hampshire (1949–53); chief of staff to President Eisenhower (1953–58). He served as a formidable barrier between the president and the outside world before he was forced to resign due to a scandal.

Adams, Oscar William, Jr. (1925–97), attorney; associate justice, Alabama Supreme Court (1980–93). In 1953, he and other prominent Alabama figures visited HHFA head Albert Cole in order to protest the use of federal funds for segregated housing. During the 1960s, his firm became nationally prominent in handling civil rights litigation.

Addams, Jane (1860–1935), social reformer who pioneered the settlement house movement by opening up Hull House in Chicago; she was an active member of the Chicago branch of the NAACP. In 1915, she joined with Judge Edward O. Brown, Dr. Charles E. Bentley, and others in protesting the passage of the Immigration Act, particularly an amendment prohibiting the admission of "Negro aliens."

Agar, Herbert Sebastian (1897–1980), journalist and writer; sometime editor of the *Louisville Courier-Journal;* with a number of other influential people, including Wendell Willkie, Rex Stout, and Herbert Bayard Swope, he founded Freedom House in New York City; its goals were, during World War II, to prepare the country for peace once the war ended, and then to continue to defend peace and freedom throughout the world. In July of 1942, representing Freedom House, he attended the Conference of Cooperating Organizations.

Aiken, George David (1892–1984) (R-Vt.), Vermont state legislator (1931–35); lieutenant governor (1935–37); governor (1937–41); U.S. senator (1941–75). He supported the addition of a nonsegregation amendment to the National Labor Relations Act (Taft-Hartley Act).

Alexander, Kelly Miller, Sr. (1915–85), funeral home director; president, North Carolina State Conference of NAACP Branches (1948–85); member (1950–85), vice chair (1976–83), and chair (1983–85), NAACP National Board of Directors. He organized voting rights drives and campaigns for African American employment in the textile industry; in 1943, he was a witness to G. James Fleming's problems with whites on a Pullman sleeping car on a train running between North Carolina and New York City..

Allen, Alexander Joseph (1916–84), industrial secretary (1943) and executive director (1944–50), Baltimore Urban League; executive director, Pittsburgh Urban League (1950–60) and New York Urban League (1964–66); vice president, National Urban League (1979–84). He served as a member of a special committee formed in 1948 to inquire into problems of African American employment at the BOASI in Baltimore.

Allen, Fay Elizabeth (1901–87), vice president, NNC; president, Los Angeles chapter, NNC; member, executive board, Los Angeles branch, NAACP; head, Labor Committee, Los Angeles branch, NAACP (1947).

Allen, Leo Elwood (1898–1973) (R-Ill.), lawyer; U.S. representative (1933–61). A conservative Republican, he was a staunch critic of Roosevelt's and Truman's domestic policies. In 1952, he voted for a bill authorizing E. E. Cox of Georgia to investigate charitable organizations accused of fomenting class and racial strife in the South. In 1954, he blocked an anti–Jim Crow travel bill, and as Rules Committee chair (1947–49, 1953–55), he obstructed public housing and slum clearance legislation.

Allen, Rev. Thomas S., of the National Council of Churches; in 1950, as a member of the NECRM executive committee, he was a member of a delegation from the NECRM that met with President Truman; later that year Allen was named to the steering committee of the LCCR.

Allen, Wendel, member, Lansing, Michigan, NAACP branch. In 1951, he went to Washington, D.C., to protest the proposed Winstead amendment to the Universal Military Training bill.

Allen, Willard William (1888–1961), real estate broker, insurance broker, businessman; a native of tidewater Virginia, he came to Baltimore as a young man and started out in business selling real estate. He eventually owned the largest black-owned real estate firm in the city, as well as being president, Southern Life Insurance Company of Baltimore (1925–59), a member of the board of trustees of Morgan State College (now University), and a prominent Mason. In 1942, representing the National Negro Business League, he participated in the Conference of Cooperating Organizations.

Alleyne, Rev. Cameron Chesterfield (1880–1955), bishop, AME Zion Church, born Barbados, British West Indies. In 1952, Mitchell commented that, if the McCarran-Walter Act, with its severe restriction on immigration from the Caribbean and South America, had been in force when immigrants like Alleyne (who distinguished themselves in their adopted country) entered the United States, they would not have been able to make "notable contributions to the building of our nation."

Allinson, Thomas W. (1863–1940), social worker; for years he was the director of the Henry Booth Settlement House on Chicago's West Side; a member of the Chicago branch of the NAACP, his name appeared on a 1915 telegram protesting discriminatory language in legislation regulating immigration to the United States.

Altmeyer, Arthur Joseph (1891–1972), educator, economist, and statistician; executive director, WMC; member and then chair, SSB (1935–46); commissioner, SSA (1946–53). In 1946, he denied charges of widespread discrimination in the SSA, which at that time did not have a ban on employment discrimination by race.

Anderson, Beulah Dyson (1908–2004), member, Wilmington, Delaware, NAACP branch. In 1951, she went to Washington, D.C., to protest the proposed Winstead amendment to the Universal Military Training bill.

Anderson, Clinton Presba (1895–1975) (D-N.Mex.), journalist and businessman; New Mexico state treasurer (1933–34); U.S. representative (1941–45); U.S. secretary of agriculture (1945–48); U.S. senator (1949–73). In 1947, Mitchell successfully appealed to him to end discrimination at a federal hospital for migrant workers when it was turned over to the state of Florida. He also supported Mitchell in other civil rights battles.

Anderson, Marian (1897–1993), opera singer of international renown. Born in Philadelphia, she began her musical career at a young age at a local Baptist church. She became famous in 1939, when the Daughters of the American Republic barred her from singing at Constitution Hall in Jim Crow Washington because she was black. With the help of the NAACP, Harold Ickes, secretary of the interior, arranged for her to perform in concert on the steps of the Lincoln Memorial on Easter Sunday, April 9, 1939, for an audience of 75,000. Several weeks later, she gave a private concert at the White House for President Franklin Roosevelt and his guests, King George VI and Queen Elizabeth of Great Britain. In 1955, she became the first black person to debut at the New York Metropolitan Opera.

Anderson, Robert Bernerd (1910–89), secretary of the navy (1953–54); deputy secretary of defense (1954–55); secretary of the treasury (1957–61). In 1953, he disregarded NAACP requests to desegregate facilities on naval bases. The following year, however, he instructed shore stations of the navy and the Marine Corps that segregation in schools on military posts was prohibited.

Anderson, Wilbert "Will" (1891–1932), African American locomotive fireman shot and killed with fellow fireman Aaron Williams in Vicksburg, Mississippi, in March 1932, probably by whites who coveted their jobs.

Anthony, Flournoy L. (1926–), veteran and postal worker. He received a war service appointment to the post office in New Orleans but said the department sought to terminate him in violation of the Veterans Preference Act of 1944. In 1947, he became one of the NAACP's official complainants against the New Orleans Post Office.

Arens, Richard (1913–69), lawyer; staff director, Immigration and Naturalization Subcommittee, Senate Judiciary Committee (1947–52); drafter of McCarran-Walter Immigration Act of 1952; staff director and chief interrogator of Internal Security Subcommittee (1952–56) and of HCUA (1956–60); commissioner, U.S. Court of Claims (1960–69). In 1950, Mitchell complained that Arens deliberately elicited critical remarks about an American official in Germany and then emphasized that the official was African American. He was forced out of his congressional post in 1960 after it was revealed that he was a paid consultant for the multimillionaire Wickliffe Draper, whose foundation supported segregation and was issuing grants to prove the racial inferiority of blacks.

Armstrong, Edgar H. (1922–2002), veteran. He was a victim of employment discrimination at the New Orleans Post Office. In 1947, he became one of the NAACP's official complainants against that body.

Armwood, George (1911–33), farm laborer of Somerset County, Maryland; accused of raping the seventy-one-year-old widow of a local farmer, the feeble-minded Armwood was taken from the local jail in Princess Anne, Maryland, and dragged through the streets. He was beaten, tortured, shot, and set on fire, and his charred corpse was thrown into a lumberyard. Clarence Mitchell, then a reporter for the *Baltimore Afro-American*, was one of a team of reporters and photographers who reported on the atrocity.

Arnall, Ellis Gibbs (1907–92), (D-Ga.), lawyer and businessman; member, Georgia House of Representatives (1932–36); state attorney general (1938–42); governor (1943–47); director, U.S. Office of Price Stabilization (1949–50). A progressive and far-seeing chief executive, he led the fight to abolish the poll tax and promote other social and political improvements within the state. He supported Henry A. Wallace's candidacy for president on the Progressive ticket in 1948.

Arnaud, Joseph L. (1915–2001), veteran. Although claiming employment discrimination at the New Orleans Post Office, he declined to join those of his fellow postal workers and the NAACP in filing formal charges against that body.

Arnold, William J., represented the NAPE at the Conference of Cooperating Organizations in Washington on July 4, 1942.

Aronson, Arnold (1911–98), secretary, NCPFEPC (1943); executive director, BJEPC; consultant, Region VI, FEPC; director, NJCRAC (1945–76); member, Executive Committee, JCCR; secretary, NECRM of 1950; a founder and secretary of the LCCR (1950–80); a planner of the 1963 March on Washington; founder and president, Education Fund, LCCR (1980–98). A supporter of A. Philip Randolph's proposed 1941 March on Washington, he participated in a 1949 civil rights conference. In 1953, he attended a meeting between a subcommittee of the CGC and numerous interest groups.

Artemus, John Clarence (1885–1964), carpenter and insurance agent; business agent, UBC (1939–54); vice president at large, executive board, SCFL (1951–59). In 1951, he was a leader of NAACP efforts to ensure nonsegregation and nondiscrimination at a hydrogen bomb facility in South Carolina. He was also active in registering black voters and in working for black carpenters' access to jobs on major construction projects.

Atkinson, Glenn R. (1902–63), labor official; liaison officer, Railroad Labor Organization, OPA (1941–45); assistant to George M. Harrison, chair, Labor Division, Democratic National Committee (1945–50); labor attaché, U.S. Embassy, London (1950–53). In a 1948 letter to Edward J. Logue that was forwarded to Walter White, Atkinson told of Harrison's struggle to alter the constitution of the Brotherhood of Railway Clerks to remove the word *White* as a limitation to membership.

Austin, Augustine Alexander (1880–1960), real estate entrepreneur. A native of Antigua, he rose from Pullman porter to become the president of Antillean Holdings, Inc., of Manhattan, as well as the owner of vast expanses of New York City real estate. In 1952, Mitchell commented that, if the McCarran-Walter Act, with its severe restriction on immigration from the Caribbean and South America, had been in force when immigrants like Austin entered the United States, they would not have been able to make "notable contributions to the building of our nation."

Baber, George Wilbur (1897–1970), pastor, Ebenezer AMEC, Detroit (1934–44); bishop, Fourth Episcopal District (1948–56), First Episcopal District (1956–64), and Second Episcopal District (1964–70), AMEC. In 1953, he supported a Michigan FEPC law.

Badger, John Robert (1909–61), reporter and columnist for the *Chicago Defender* who, in 1943, accused BSCP and MOWM leader A. Philip Randolph of being a "'racist' for he finds the racial appeal an effective method for playing upon the national aspirations of his people. And although he beats his breast and shouts a thousand curses at Jim Crow, the very logic of his racism makes him a segregationist."

Bailey, Lester P. (1921–), executive secretary, Cincinnati NAACP branch (1945). He worked with Mitchell concerning the hiring of black telephone operators. In 1952, Bailey moved to San Francisco to become the NAACP West Coast field secretary.

Bailey, William J. (1890–1963), employee of the Standard Wholesale Phosphate and Acid Works of Baltimore. In 1946, he brought suit against the company as it was systematically reducing the number of its black workers in violation of its agreement with the UMW.

Baldinger, Mary Alice Negley (1908–82), legislative representative, Washington office, ACLU; executive director, NCLCH (1949–71). She assisted with planning and organizing the NECRM of 1950. The following year, she served on a committee working with Mitchell to prepare for hearings on Senate rules changes.

Baldwin, Raymond Earl (1893–1986) (R-Conn.), lawyer and jurist; Connecticut state legislator (1931–33); governor of Connecticut (1939–41, 1943–46); U.S. Senator (1946–49); justice,

Connecticut Supreme Court (1949–59). In 1945, Governor Baldwin was on record as endorsing proposed legislation to eliminate discrimination in employment. The bill, called the Aaron bill, after its primary sponsor, was based on the Ives-Quinn bill that was signed into law in New York State.

Baldwin, Roger Nash (1884–1981), director, ACLU (1920–50). He served on both the temporary executive board of the National Committee to Safeguard the FEPC (1943) and the executive board of the NCPFEPC. In 1942, he represented the ACLU at the Conference of Cooperating Organizations. Seven months before his death, he was awarded the Presidential Medal of Freedom by President Jimmy Carter.

Ball, Joseph Hurst (1905–93) (R-Minn.), journalist, writer, and businessman; U.S. senator (1940–42, 1943–49). He opposed FEPC legislation and headed a committee charged with overseeing implementation of the Taft-Hartley Act.

Bancroft, Harding Foster (1910–92), lawyer; staff member, OPA (1941–43); administrator, LLMNA and BUNA (1943–53); director, OUNPSA (1953); legal adviser, ILO (1953–56); executive, *New York Times* (1956–75). From 1949 to 1950, he was a member of a State Department board that reviewed that department's discriminatory employment policies. He later gained prominence for his role in the publication of the Pentagon Papers.

Bane, Frank (1893–1983), professor and lecturer; Virginia commissioner of public welfare (1926–32); director, APWA (1932–35); executive director, SSB (1935–38); executive director, CSG (1938–59); director of field operations, OPA (1941–42); chair, ACIR (1959–66). Mitchell appealed to him for assistance in preventing discrimination by USES offices after its units were returned to state control in 1946.

Banks, Barbara, of Paducah, Kentucky. In 1951, the Washington Bureau filed charges on her behalf, charging that AEC officials violated Executive Order 9980 by refusing to interview her for a clerical position at the AEC project in Paducah because she was African American.

Barden, Graham Arthur (1896–1967) (D-N.C.), lawyer and judge; North Carolina state legislator (1933); U.S. representative (1935–61). He opposed FEPC legislation and blocked many other measures that the NAACP supported. In 1949, he introduced a school-aid bill that did not include assistance for either parochial schools or schools for racial minorities, a measure that a colleague said "dripped with bigotry and racial prejudice." As chair of the House Education and Labor Committee (1949–53, 1955–61), he refused to appoint Adam Clayton Powell of Harlem as a subcommittee chair. That year (1949), he introduced a bill proposing that once a southern state raised expenditures for black students to a certain level, any money in the state budget that remained from the federal grant the state had received could be used exclusively for white schools. In 1952, Mitchell worked for his defeat in the congressional election in order to pave the way for a more liberal chair of the committee.

Barkley, Alben William (1877–1956) (D-Ky.), lawyer and judge; U.S. representative (1913–27); U.S. senator (1927–49, 1955–56); vice president of the United States (1949–53). Born in a log cabin, he was a liberal southerner who supported civil rights legislation. As president of the Senate, he tried unsuccessfully to impose cloture on filibusters against the FEPC and anti–poll tax legislation.

Barnes, Frank H. (1923–72), veteran and postal worker; president, Santa Monica branch, NAACP. In 1948, the post office raised disloyalty charges against him after he led an effort to obtain jobs for blacks at a Sears-Roebuck store. Following protests by the NAACP, the LRB cleared and reinstated him.

Barnes, Sam, African American locomotive fireman, who, with Turner Simms, on March 11, 1932 in McComb, Mississippi, was shot and wounded from ambush, probably by whites who coveted their jobs.

Barnett, Claude Albert (1889–1967), newspaperman, advertising executive, and entrepreneur; founder and president of the Associated Negro Press (ANP) (1919–67). Based in Chicago, the ANP supplied national news releases for black-owned-and-operated newspapers for a fee; in its heyday it supplied copy to fully 95 percent of the Negro press (almost two hundred newspapers). In 1943, Barnett was one of sixteen representatives of the Negro press who protested the cancellation of the FEPC's hearings into racial discrimination in the railroad industry and in its unions.

Baron, Samuel (1891–1969), union officer. He was the general manager of the Textile Workers Union–CIO when, in 1943, he was named to the executive board of the NCPFEPC.

Barrett, Robert J. (1902–66), superintendent, Washington, D.C., metropolitan police (1947–51). In 1950, Barrett attended a meeting regarding the arrest of African Americans seeking employment in the District. He denied that the arrests were improper.

Bass, Charlotta Amanda Spears (1874–1969), newspaper executive. Moving to Los Angeles from Rhode Island in 1910, she started out in the newspaper business by soliciting subscriptions for a small black-owned-and-operated newspaper, the *California Owl*. After the death of the owner three years later, she took over the business, hired an editor (whom she later married), and changed the name of the paper to the *California Eagle*. It soon became the largest black newspaper on the West Coast. Although a lifelong Republican, in 1950 she ran for Congress on the Progressive ticket, and two years later was nominated for vice president at the Progressive Party convention in Chicago. In 1942, the NAACP invited her to Washington for the Conference of Negro Newspaper Editors.

Bates, John Rosslyn (1882–1960), resident of U.S. Soldiers' Home. In 1954, Bates was a complainant against segregation at the Soldiers' Home. He had been assaulted by another black resident who supported segregation.

Battle, George Gordon (1869–1949), lawyer and politician; a native of South Carolina, he attended Columbia University Law School in New York City and remained there for most of the rest of his life. Affiliated with the New York Council against Intolerance, he attended the 1942 Conference of Cooperating Organizations.

Baxter, Julia E. (later Julia E. Baxter Bates) (1917–2003), first African American student admitted to New Jersey College for Women (now Douglass College, Rutgers University); national director of research and information, NAACP (1943–65). She gathered voting records and other information concerning African Americans. She also assisted in preparation of the "Brandeis Brief," a document tracing the history of civil rights in ten northern states. The brief was part of the plaintiff's argument in the *Brown v. Board of Education* case.

Beall, William Hayes, Jr. (1910–89), (D-Ill.), fair practice examiner, FEPC (1945–46); chief activist, U.S. Zone–Germany (1946–56); unsuccessfully ran for Congress from the Fourteenth District of Illinois (1960); director, Peace Corps training programs (1962–69). In 1946, he prepared a report for the FEPC that documented the number of nonwhites in the shipbuilding industry.

Beatty, Dr. Willard Walcott (1891–1961), superintendent of schools, Bronxville, New York (1926–36); president, PEA (1933–37); education director, BIA (1936–51); deputy director of education, UNESCO, Paris (1951–53). Responding in 1946 to complaints regarding Indian Service discrimination against African American teachers, he declared that certain tribes were prejudiced against blacks and objected to their employment. This prejudice allegedly stemmed from earlier misconduct by African American troops against Native Americans.

Beck, James Garfield (1881–1969), postal worker (1908–42). For a time, he was the only African American post office clerk in Knoxville, Tennessee.

Bell, Ulric (1892–1960), newspaperman; worked for the *Louisville Courier-Journal* as a reporter and editor from 1910 to 1921, when he became its national correspondent and moved to Washington, D.C., where he stayed until 1941. He served as executive director, Fight for Freedom (1941); assistant director, Office of Facts and Figures (1941–42); head, overseas branch, Office of War Information (1943–44). In 1942, Walter White suggested that Bell would be able to secure telephone service for the new NAACP Washington Bureau.

Bell, William Yancey, Sr. (1887–1962), Methodist minister; bishop in Colored (now Christian) Methodist Episcopal Church (CMEC). An ardent advocate of Marcus Garvey, he was involved in civil rights activity during the period of World War II.

Bennett, Lerone, Jr. (1928–), popular historian, magazine editor, author, and essayist. He attended Morehouse College where he edited the school newspaper; from there, he became a reporter and later city editor of the *Atlanta Daily World*. In 1953, he moved to Chicago to work for Johnson Publishing Company, where he was associate editor of *Jet* (1953–54) and *Ebony* (1954–57) before becoming *Ebony's* senior editor in 1957 and its executive editor in 1987. In 1962 he published his first historical study, *Before the Mayflower: A History of Black America 1619–1962*, and has since produced a number of well-received works including a controversial study of Abraham Lincoln and his relationship with African Americans.

Bennett, Richard Kistler (1916–92), assistant director, AFSC; grants manager (1955–79) and president (1979–80), William Penn Foundation. He represented the AFSC at a 1953 meeting with a subcommittee of the CGC.

Benson, Homer (1918–98), and his wife Laurajean (1918–2001), members of Terre Haute, Indiana, NAACP branch. In 1951, they went to Washington, D.C., to protest the proposed Winstead amendment to the Universal Military Training bill.

Bent, Don, clerk, NLRB, where he confronted counsel for the NAACP concerning segregated union locals.

Bentley, Dr. Charles Edwin (1859–1929), dentist; an 1887 graduate of the Chicago College of Dental Surgery, he was one of the first African American practitioners of dentistry and pioneered the promotion of dental hygiene "to preserve the health of the oral tissues and prevent tooth decay and other oral disease." He was also an active member of the Chicago branch of the NAACP, and a 1915 letter to him from Judge Edward Osgood Brown (which was subsequently published in the *Crisis*) describes the branch's actions in challenging discriminatory legislation.

Benton, William (1900–73) (D-Conn.), founder, Benton and Bowles advertising firm; publisher, *Encyclopedia Britannica* (1943–73); assistant secretary of state (1945–47); U.S. senator (1949–53). He supported Senate rules changes, antilynching and anti–poll tax legislation, FEPC measures, and bills to prevent violence against black service members. He was most prominent as a dogged critic of fellow senator Joseph McCarthy's anticommunist crusade. In 1952, Mitchell praised Benton for his support of cloture legislation.

Bergin, Maj. Gen. William Edward (1892–1978), adjutant general of the United States (1951–54). In 1954, he reported to Mitchell that the U.S. Army had no information as to the fate of two white soldiers at Fort Jackson, South Carolina, who had beaten Pvt. Jeff McGriff.

Bernard, Mrs. Willie, victim of discrimination. In 1947, she applied for a supervisory position at a Pentagon cafeteria run as a concession by the National Foods Corporation. She was at first refused employment on the grounds of race, despite having a BS in home economics and having served as an army hostess. After the NAACP protested, she was assigned to a marginal spot, and the staff was neither informed she was a supervisor nor encouraged to treat her with respect.

Bernstein, Meyer (1914–85), union official; organizer, Steelworkers Organization (1936–42); research assistant and national representative, United Steelworkers of America–CIO (1946–56); international affairs director, United Steelworkers of America–CIO (1950–80). In 1947, Mitchell conferred with Bernstein about the far-reaching effects of the Taft-Hartley Act.

Berry, Theodore Moody (1905–2000), lawyer; president, Cincinnati branch, NAACP (1943–46); member, OCCRL (1947–61); Cincinnati city councilman (1949–57, 1963–65, 1971–75); vice mayor (1955–57); mayor (1972–75). In 1951, he testified at a hearing of the Senate Committee on Banking and Currency. Speaking in support of nonsegregation provisions in the Defense Housing Act, he asserted that such federal support for nonsegregation would make it easier for local officials to adopt a similar position. In 1972, he became the first African American mayor of Cincinnati.

Best, Lee James, Sr. (1895–1979), lawyer; trial examiner, NLRB. In 1951, he ruled against several black employees of Young's Motor Freight of Houston, Texas, who had sued their employer for being dismissed from their jobs because they were black. The judgment was upheld on appeal.

Bethune, Mary Jane McLeod (1875–1955), teacher; founder (1904) and president (1904–42, 1946–47), Daytona Literary and Industrial School for Training Negro Girls (later Bethune-Cookman College); president, NACW (1924–28); president, NCNW (1935–49); director, Division of Negro Affairs, NYA (1939–44); vice president, NAACP (1940–55). One of seventeen children of former slaves, she attended a 1948 meeting as part of the NAACP's fight against federal employment discrimination.

Biddle, Francis Beverley (1886–1968), lawyer; U.S. solicitor general (1940–41); U.S. attorney general (1941–45); later chief U.S. representative at Nuremberg trials. President Roosevelt's letter to Biddle dated November 5, 1943, affirmed the mandatory nature of the nondiscrimination clauses in his executive orders.

Biddle, Maj. Gen. William Shepard (1900–81), deputy chief, Plans and Policy Group, Army General Staff (1947–53); commandant of cadets, Pennsylvania Military College (1962–66). In November of 1953, the NAACP protested General Biddle's dedication of a segregated primary school for the dependents of military personnel at Fort Hood in Killeen, Texas.

Bilbo, Theodore Gilmore (1877–1947) (D-Miss.), Mississippi governor (1916–20, 1928–32); U.S. senator (1935–47). A notorious racist, he once proposed an African colonization scheme for American blacks. In 1945, he participated in a filibuster against appropriations for the FEPC, and in the following year, he was investigated for taking gifts, services, and political contributions from military contractors and others seeking favors. Although he served as senator until his death in August 1947, he did not take the oath of office at the start of the 80th Congress earlier that year.

Billings, Dr. Richard A. (1906–68), social activist and fraternal leader. A native of Atlanta, Dr. Billings, a general practitioner as well as choir director at St. Paul's AME Church in Atlanta, mentored a number of young African Americans, including Vernon E. Jordan, the future president of the National Urban League. As president of Phi Beta Sigma fraternity (1941–44), Dr. Billings participated in the Conference of Cooperating Organizations on July 4, 1942.

Billingsley, Orzell, Jr. (1924–2001), lawyer and judge; member, Board of Directors, Alabama State Conference of NAACP Branches. He was part of a delegation from Alabama that visited HHFA head Albert Cole in 1953 to protest the use of federal funds for segregated housing. He was also one of the NAACP attorneys representing Martin Luther King Jr. during the latter's 1956 trial for coordinating the Montgomery bus boycott.

Black, Lucille (1909–75), staffer in NAACP National Office (1927–71); NAACP membership secretary (1947–71). She assisted in the organization of the LCCR, 1951.

Blackmon, Pvt. Gladys [married name Willis] (1920–2000), U.S. Army; a native of Oklahoma, she enlisted in the WAACs in Santa Fe, New Mexico, on December 10, 1942. Stationed at Camp Sibert, Alabama, in 1944, she was, with Private Roberta McKenzie, brutally beaten when she refused to give up her seat on a bus.

Blake, Charles W. (1917–92), railroad worker. In 1952, with two other plaintiffs, he filed suit in the U.S. district court in Washington, D.C., against the Brotherhood of Railway and Steamship Clerks, Freight Handlers, Express and Station Employees and the Baltimore and Ohio Railroad Company over a violation of the Railway Labor Act whereby the union forced its black members into segregated union locals.

Bloch, Emanuel Hirsch (1901–54), hearings examiner, Legal Division, wartime FEPC; staff member, Division of Field Operations, FEPC (1943–45); recruited to FEPC by Will Maslow; noted defense lawyer for leftist sympathizers and Trenton Six; defense counsel, along with his father, Alexander, in espionage trial of Ethel and Julius Rosenberg (1950–53); guardian of the Rosenberg children until his sudden death from a heart attack.

Bloom, Frank (1904–50), lawyer; chief trial examiner, NLRB (1937–47); general counsel, Telegraphers Union, AFL (1947–50); consultant to NAACP labor department; professor, Howard University School of Law. In 1950, Mitchell acknowledged his assistance in the civil rights cause.

Boehm, Albert Charles (1903–84), lawyer; manager, Pentagon cafeterias (1942–60). In 1947, he agreed to hire Mrs. Willie Bernard, who had complained about discrimination, and he implemented his decision when subordinates obstructed it.

Bond, Dr. Horace Mann (1904–72), educator; born in Tennessee; A.B., Lincoln University (Pennsylvania); M.A. and Ph.D., University of Chicago. He held positions at State Normal School in Montgomery, Alabama (1927–28), Fisk University in Nashville (1928–29, 1932–34, 1937–39), Dillard University in New Orleans (1935–37), and Fort Valley State College, Georgia (1939–45); president, Lincoln University (Pennsylvania) (1945–57); dean, Atlanta University School of Education (1957–66); director, Atlanta University Bureau for Educational and Social Research (1966–71). In 1937, Walter White used the results of a study Dr. Bond had performed that documented the gross disparity of spending by localities in New Deal programs on black and white education in the South to state the NAACP's position that federal aid to education in the various states be distributed on a nondiscriminatory basis.

Bonner, William (1905–98), gas station owner in Aiken, South Carolina. In 1951, Mitchell visited Bonner's filling station and noted that even though it was doing very well, having both black and white customers, it would have to close because the projected Savannah River Plant hydrogen bomb facility would encompass the station's location.

Booker, Ivan Albert (1901–85), educator. He was with the National Education Association for many years, serving in a number of positions including assistant director of research and assistant director of press relations. In July of 1942, representing the NEA, he was present at the Conference of Cooperating Organizations.

Booker, Joseph Robert (1893–1960), lawyer of Little Rock, Arkansas; president, NBA (1949–50); alternate delegate, RNC (1944, 1948). In 1950, with a number of representatives of civil rights and race-based organizations, met with President Truman to discuss expanding the scope and general effectiveness of the FEPC.

Boone, Adm. Joel Thompson (1889–1974), World War I and World War II veteran; White House physician (1922–33); chief medical director, Veterans Administration (1951–55). In 1951, he was questioned about discrimination and segregation at VA facilities.

Boston, Frank Dobson, Sr. (1919–87), veteran and postal worker in Baltimore. In 1949, with help from the NAACP, he was cleared of disloyalty charges filed by the U.S. Loyalty Review Board.

Bourne, James Franklyn (1917–72), lawyer; commissioner, Maryland Workmen's Compensation Commission (1967–71); judge, Prince Georges County (Md.) District Court (1971–72); president, Prince Georges County branch, NAACP. In 1949, as counsel for the NAACP, he successfully defended a Baltimore postal worker against a disloyalty charge. He was the first African American judge in Prince Georges County.

Bowles, Bryant William, Jr. (1920–97), founder (1954), NAAWP. As head of the NAAWP, the first of the prosegregation groups formed to combat school integration after the *Brown* decision, Bowles led anti-integration protests in Milford, Delaware; Baltimore; and Washington, D.C. During a Milford speech, he stated that "the Negro will not be satisfied until he moves into the bedroom of the white man's home." The NAACP exposed his previous criminal record, and he was arrested in Baltimore for violation of school laws. Eventually, he was imprisoned in Texas for killing his brother-in-law.

Bowles, Chester Bliss (1901–86) (D-Conn.), administrator, OPA (1943–46); chair, ESB (1946); Connecticut governor (1949–50); ambassador to India and Nepal (1951–53); U.S. representative (1959–61); ambassador to India (1963–69). In a 1950 statement, Mitchell said Bowles was part of a "new leadership" that could pave the way for a revitalized FEPC.

Boyd, Ralph F., Sr. (1920–), electrical worker and union representative; member, NAACP branch in Schenectady, New York; employed at General Electric in Schenectady; shop steward, Local 301, IUE-CIO (1963–71); delegate, Democratic National Convention (1968); vice president and public relations officer, Schenectady County Child and Family Services (1973–75). A community leader in Schenectady and environs for well over a half century, he went to Washington, D.C., in 1951 to protest the proposed Winstead amendment to the Universal Military Training bill. In 2001, his son and namesake was appointed by President George W. Bush to the post of assistant attorney general for civil rights.

Boyle, William Marshall, Jr. (1903–61), lawyer, stockbroker, and business executive; chair, DNC (1950–51). In 1950, the NAACP sent him a telegram expressing the organization's displeasure over the selection of Sen. Richard B. Russell (D-Ga.) as the Senate Democratic Party leader, due to his dismal record in the field of civil rights.

Bracey, John Henry, Jr. (1945–), historian and educator; taught at Northern Illinois University (1969–71), University of Rochester (1971–72), and University of Massachusetts–Amherst (1972–present), where he is the W.E.B. Du Bois Professor of Black Studies.

Bradshaw, Herbert Earl (1925–54), U.S. Air Force sergeant. Stationed at Lackland Air Force Base, San Antonio, he complained that he was beaten by white civilian police in Brownsville, Tennessee, while traveling with other service members to Sampson Air Force Base in Geneva, New York. The NAACP referred his case to the assistant secretary of the air force and cited his experience as evidence of the need for legislation to protect black service members from violence.

Braithwaite, William Stanley Beaumont (1878–1962), poet, essayist, and anthologist; although a native of Boston, Braithwaite's father was a native of British Guiana (now Guyana) who emigrated to the United States after the American Civil War. In 1952, Mitchell commented that if the McCarran-Walter Act, with its severe restriction on immigration from the Caribbean and South America, had been in force when immigrants like Braithwaite senior entered the United States, they would not have been able to make "notable contributions to the building of our nation."

Branch, Roberta "Bobbie" (1909–88), longtime manager of the NAACP office in New York City. In August 1948, Mitchell forwarded to her a copy of a memorandum summarizing the NAACP's role in facilitating the issuance of President Truman's executive order against discrimination in federal employment.

Branche, George Norman (1900–1972), insurance broker and businessman of Philadelphia; in July 1942, he represented the National Negro Insurance Association at the Conference of Cooperating Organizations.

Brannan, Charles Franklin (1903–92), lawyer; regional attorney, Office of the Solicitor, Department of Agriculture (1937–41); administrator, FSA (1941–44); assistant secretary of agriculture (1944–48); U.S. secretary of agriculture (1948–53). He consulted with the NAACP on discrimination complaints regarding African American access to training classes in science. He is most famous for his 1949 "Brannan Plan," which would have guaranteed farmer income while leaving commodities prices to the free market.

Brant, Irving (1885–1976), journalist and historian; a graduate of the University of Iowa, he was best known for his two-volume biography of James Madison. When Brant was asked for his thoughts on the constitutionality of the poll tax, he replied that he found it unconstitutional.

Braxton, Vivian L. (1892–1963), federal employee. In 1949, she was able, with the help of the NAACP, to make an arrangement with the FSA for a period of six months to "demonstrate her fitness as a supervisor" at St. Elizabeth's Hospital in Washington, D.C., where she was employed.

Breckinridge, Sophonisba Preston (1866–1948), social worker, educator, lawyer, and activist. The daughter of a Kentucky Confederate, and herself a graduate of Wellesley and the law school of the University of Chicago, she was a pioneer settlement house worker who lived and worked at Hull House (1907–20) and was actively involved in both women's suffrage and civil rights. A member of the Chicago branch of the NAACP, her name appeared on a 1915 telegram protesting discriminatory language in legislation regulating immigration to the United States.

Bresette, Linna Eleanor (1881–1960), social worker, investigator, author, and activist. A pioneer professional social worker in the Midwest, she worked with state governments to greatly extend the reach of state child labor laws before becoming field secretary for the NCWC (1921–55). She was named to the executive board of NCPFEPC, 1944.

Bricker, John William (1893–1986) (R-Ohio), lawyer; Ohio state attorney general (1933–37); governor (1939–45); Republican Party vice presidential candidate (1944); U.S. senator (1947–59). A staunch isolationist and anticommunist, he was best known for an amendment bearing his name, which would have restricted the treaty-making powers of the president. Southern conservatives supported the amendment because it would have prevented Congress from passing social legislation (such as civil rights bills) on the basis of carrying out the obligations of a treaty.

Brinsmade, Chapin (1885–1928), lawyer; in 1914, he was hired by the NAACP to staff its nascent Legal Bureau, becoming its first full-time lawyer; however, the next year, budget cutbacks eliminated his position. Before then, when it was discovered that proposed legislation provided no specific provision for black farmers to receive federal funding appropriated for agricultural extension work, he drafted an amendment to ensure them "a fair share of the moneys." After the NAACP persuaded Sen. Wesley L. Jones (R-Wash.) to introduce the amendment, Brinsmade and W.E.B. DuBois lobbied Congress for the passage of the bill with the amendment and attended hearings on the bill.

Britten, Gordon (1926–86), ACE representative. In 1951, he met with NAACP officials regarding efforts to ensure nonsegregation and nondiscrimination at the Savannah River Plant hydrogen bomb facility in Aiken, South Carolina.

Brooks, Robert Andrew (1904–68), businessman; president, Aiken, South Carolina, branch, NAACP. He was a leader of NAACP efforts to ensure nonsegregation and nondiscrimination at the Savannah River Plant hydrogen bomb facility in Aiken.

Brophy, John (1883–1963), labor leader, UMWA; director, Industrial Union Councils, CIO; member, FEPC (1941–45). A native of England, he wrote a letter of support for FEPC legislation in West Virginia in 1947.

Brown, Clarence James (1893–1965) (R-Ohio), publisher; Ohio lieutenant governor (1919–23); Ohio secretary of state (1927–33); U.S. representative (1939–65). A staunch anticommunist and foe of organized labor, he voted for the Taft-Hartley Act and opposed much of Truman's Fair Deal program. He did support civil rights measures, however, including an anti–poll tax bill (1944) and FEPC legislation (1950).

Brown, Edward Osgood (1847–1923), lawyer and jurist; the son of an antislavery activist, Brown, after the end of the Civil War, left Salem, Massachusetts, for Chicago, where he practiced law, involved himself in local politics, and ultimately sat on the state appellate court. He was also one of the founders of the NAACP branch in Chicago, where he served as branch president. In a 1915 letter that was subsequently published in the *Crisis*, he described the branch's active lobbying against legislation designed to discriminate against African Americans and others.

Brown, George E., president of the Hotel and Restaurant Workers Union; in 1943, he was named to the initial executive board of the NCPFEPC.

Brown, Harvey Winfield (1883–1956), vice president (1921–38), acting president (1938–39), and president (1940–48), IAM. He assisted with the settlement of FEPC cases involving discrimination by locals of the IAM.

Brown, Homer Sylvester (1896–1977), lawyer and judge; founder and first president, NAACP branch in Pittsburgh, Pennsylvania. He represented Allegheny County in the lower house of the state legislature (1934–50) and also was the first black on the Pittsburgh school board in 1943. In 1945, he authored state FEPC legislation and saw it become law. He later served as judge, Allegheny County Court of Common Pleas (1956–75) and served on the advisory board of UNESCO and the Pennsylvania state commission on education (1960). In 1943, Walter White contacted him and nine other branch secretaries representing the most effective branches to start protesting War Manpower Commissioner Paul V. McNutt's decision to cancel the FEPC hearings on racial discrimination in the railroad industry.

Brown, Jeanetta Welch (1910–2006), writer, newspaper columnist and editor, social worker, and activist; executive secretary, NCNW (1942–45, 1948–52); national public affairs director for Alpha Kappa Alpha sorority. Active in organizing black workers at the Ford Motor Company for UAW, she unsuccessfully ran for a seat in the Michigan State House of Representatives from the First District of Wayne County in 1946, being the first black to do so. She was a member of Michigan Democratic State Committee in 1947 and founded the National Association of Fashion and Accessory Designers (an affiliate of the NCNW) in 1949. Still later, she established the Cleveland, Ohio, chapter of the Job Corps with a grant from the U.S. Department of Labor. In 1953, she met with Mitchell and Albert M. Cole to review and discuss the federal government's housing policy.

Brown, Jesse LeRoy (1926–50), first African American navy pilot (1948) and first black naval aviator to die in combat. As part of Fighter Squadron 32 from the USS *Leyte*, he was shot down while providing close-air support for units of the Seventh Marines during fighting at the Chosin Reservoir in December 1950. He was posthumously awarded the Distinguished Flying Cross. In 1972, the navy named an ocean escort ship after him.

Brown, Oscar Cicero, Sr. (1895–1990), lawyer; a native of Arkansas, he taught school in Hinds County, Mississippi, before moving to Chicago, where he practiced law and was at one time an officer of the Chicago branch of the NAACP. In 1943, Walter White contacted him and nine other branch secretaries representing the most effective branches to start protesting War Manpower Commissioner Paul V. McNutt's decision to cancel the FEPC hearings on racial discrimination in the railroad industry. Brown's oldest son and namesake was internationally known as an innovative and versatile composer and performer who was at home in many musical genres, including jazz and blues.

Brown, Theodore E. (1915–83), economist; leader, MMWM; examiner in charge, St. Louis suboffice, FEPC (1943–45); administrative assistant to A. Philip Randolph (1946–56); assistant director, Civil Rights Department, AFL-CIO (1956–61); executive director, ANLCA (1962–68); special assistant on Africa, AID (1973–77). He testified on revision of the Taft-Hartley Act (March 1949) and amendments to the Railway Labor Act (May and June 1950) before the House Committee on Labor and Education and the House Committee on Interstate and Foreign Commerce, respectively.

Brown, Vashti Cravath Proctor (1905–95), complainant; in 1943, traveling south by train via the Southern Railway with her sisters Mrs. Lillian Falls and Mrs. Muriel Holcombe, all three refused to comply with the Jim Crow transportation laws and were arrested and fined. With the aid of the NAACP, they lodged a complaint with the Interstate Commerce Commission.

Brown, Warren Henry, Jr. (1905–92), educator and diplomat; director of Negro Relations, Council of Democracy (1941–47); assistant professor, City College of CUNY (1947–60); member, board of directors, ACLU (1949–60); foreign service officer, U.S. Government Council of Cultural Affairs (1960–70); adjunct associate professor, Department of Sociology, Catholic University of America (1971–72); professor (1972–75) and professor emeritus (1975–84) of urban affairs, Bowie State College (now University). He was named the executive secretary of the MOWC in 1941.

Brown, Willard L. (1911–78), lawyer; member, Charleston (West Virginia) branch, NAACP. In 1953, he reported to Mitchell on the state of employment opportunities for blacks in and throughout the Charleston metropolitan area.

Brownell, Herbert, Jr. (1904–96) (R-N.Y.), lawyer; New York state legislator (1933–37); presidential campaign manager for Thomas Dewey (1944, 1948); chair, RNC (1944–46); U.S. attorney general (1953–57). He played a key role in drafting the Civil Rights Act of 1957. He also filed an amicus curiae brief for the *Brown* case and in 1957 advised President Eisenhower to send troops to Little Rock, Arkansas.

Brownell, Samuel Miller (1900–90), professor; U.S. commissioner of education (1953–56); Detroit superintendent of schools (1956–66). As commissioner, he negotiated arrangements for the desegregation of schools run by local authorities for the children of personnel on military posts. He also conferred with NAACP representatives on school desegregation in anticipation of the Supreme Court decision in the *Brown* case.

Brownlow, James A. (1897–1981), secretary-treasurer, Metal Trades Department, AFL. In 1947, he appeared with Mitchell at the Catholic Conference on Industrial Problems in New York City.

Buck, Pearl Sydenstricker (1892–1973), novelist, essayist and activist; best known for her novels about pre-Revolution China, as well as for her advocacy of liberal and progressive causes.

Buckner, B. L., of Baltimore. A white parent of five school-age children who wrote a letter to the editor of the *Baltimore Sun*, published on October 6, 1954, decrying the appearance of segregationists around the public schools holding picket signs, observing that he felt that his children were in danger as long as they were there, and that "the law must be enforced to the extent that all must be quiet and peaceful around our schools."

Bunche, Ralph Johnson (1903–71), diplomat, educator, and author; member, U.S. delegation to the first UN General Assembly (1947); assistant director, UN Trusteeship Department (1947–48); undersecretary general, UN (1948–71). He accompanied Count Folke Bernadotte of Sweden to Israel in 1948 in an attempt to mediate between the Israelis and the Arabs; after Count Bernadotte was assassinated, Bunche took over and successfully negotiated a cease-fire and then an armistice and the subsequent end to that particular conflict. In 1950, Bunche received the Nobel Peace Prize as well as the NAACP's Spingarn Medal, the

U.S. Presidential Medal of Honor, and the U.S. Medal of Freedom. In 1954, with President Eisenhower, he spoke at the Freedom Fulfillment Conference.

Burke, Vincent C. (1887–1965), postal worker; postmaster of Washington, D.C. (1936–48); first assistant postmaster general (1948–49); deputy postmaster general (1949–52); fair employment officer, Post Office Department. He reported to the NAACP on the hiring of blacks as postal clerks in Memphis. He also denied racial discrimination in the New Orleans Post Office.

Burnett, Elias G. (1902–93), official, Houston, Texas, branch NAACP. In 1953, Mitchell reported to Burnett on lawsuits brought by the Baltimore and Washington branches of the NAACP to desegregate railroad unions.

Burnquist, Joseph Alfred Arner (1879–1961) (R-Minn.), lawyer; Minnesota lieutenant governor (1913–15); governor (1915–21); state attorney general (1939–55). As attorney general, he supported state FEPC legislation.

Burns, Harry Victory (1922–2000), civil servant and activist; treasurer and president, San Antonio branch, NAACP. A fixture at San Antonio City Council meetings, he worked tirelessly to hasten desegregation in that city. He was also the first black man hired as a clerk at Kelly Air Force Base, and he later led a challenge to the demotion of black staff at that facility. He served with the NAACP for a total of forty-seven years.

Burns, James MacGregor (1918–), educator; twice won the Pulitzer Prize in history for works on the public lives of the Roosevelt family; Woodrow Wilson Professor Emeritus of Political Science, Williams College. His writings on the concept of leadership have been held as seminal works in the study of that subject. A member of the ADA, he represented that organization when he appeared as part of the delegation from NECRM that met with President Truman in January 1950.

Busch, Sarah Halfacre (1897–1988), member of Aiken (South Carolina) Chamber of Commerce; in 1951 she authored a booklet outlining the city's plans for civic improvements financed with federal funds; these improvements would include parks, swimming pools, municipal buildings, and playgrounds, all segregated.

Bush, Julius (1922–83), veteran and postal worker. The New Orleans Post Office sought to terminate him in violation of the Veterans Preference Act of 1944. He then sought employment as a regular postal clerk–carrier but was denied a position despite his high Civil Service test score. In 1947, he became one of the NAACP's official complainants against the New Orleans Post Office.

Bush, Prescott Sheldon (1895–1972) (R-Conn.), business executive; U.S. senator (1952–63). He was the father of George H. W. Bush, the forty-first president of the United States, and grandfather of George W. Bush, the forty-third president. While campaigning for election to the Senate, Bush appeared on the same platform with Mitchell and gave out erroneous information concerning Republican congressional support of the FEPC.

Byrd, Charles E. (1909–2003), Baptist minister, U.S. Army Air Corps and U.S. Air Force chaplain, a veteran of World War II and Korea; pastor, Mt. Zion Baptist Church, Green Haven, New York (1936–52); pastor, Central Baptist Church, Clinton Corners, New York (1939–52). After serving as a chaplain in Burma, in 1946 Major Byrd was traveling north to his home in Dutchess County, New York, on a train of the Seaboard Air Line Road. While traveling in Virginia, he violated Jim Crow laws by not moving from his seat for a white person and was arrested and fined. With the help of the NAACP, he sued the railroad, but the Interstate Commerce Commission dismissed his claim.

Byrd, Daniel (1910–84), lawyer; president, Louisiana State Conference of NAACP Branches (1939–48). One of the leaders in the drive to integrate New Orleans schools, he also fought against employment discrimination by the New Orleans Post Office.

Byrd, Harry Clifton (1889–1970), president, University of Maryland (1936–54). He attempted to have the FAO located permanently at the University of Maryland. In 1949, the NAACP successfully opposed the plan on the grounds of the university's record of discrimination.

Byrnes, James Francis (1882–1972) (D-S.C.), court reporter, editor, and lawyer; U.S. representative (1911–25); U.S. senator (1930–40); U.S. Supreme Court associate justice (1941–42); head, OES (1942–43); director, OWM (1943–45); U.S. secretary of state (1945–47); South Carolina governor (1951–55). Although a moderate on most social issues, he opposed desegregation and a strong FEPC.

Cail, Lee Roy (1925–78), U.S. Army corporal; World War II and Korean War veteran. He was arrested in Richmond, Virginia, and jailed for 107 days after he attempted to give medical assistance to a soldier who was shot. He was later demoted to private because the army ruled he was AWOL while in prison.

Caldwell, Arthur Brann (1906–87), lawyer, Department of Justice (1941–68); chief, Civil Rights Section, Department of Justice. In 1953, he attended a meeting on civil rights between NAACP officials and U.S. attorney general Herbert Brownell. He also played an active role in the 1957 desegregation crisis in Little Rock, Arkansas.

Caldwell, Millard Fillmore (1897–1984) (D-Fla.), lawyer; Florida state legislator (1929–32); U.S. representative (1933–41); governor (1945–49); administrator, FCDA (1950–52); judge (1962–67) and chief justice (1967–69), Florida Supreme Court. The NAACP unsuccessfully opposed his nomination as FCDA administrator for several reasons, including: his expressed opposition to black voting rights in primary elections, his support of a southern regional university and professional education system that could continue segregated programs, his refusal to address African American men as "mister" in public correspondence, and his inaction as governor on lynching cases in his state.

Caldwell, Theodore Roosevelt (1910–75), member Lansing, Michigan, branch, NAACP. In 1951, he went to Washington, D.C., to protest the proposed Winstead amendment to the Universal Military Training bill.

Campaigne, Curtis, Jr. (1912–84), lawyer; national chairman, American Veterans Committee (AVC) (1950–53); in 1951, he was present at the organizational meeting of the LCCR.

Campanella, Roy (1921–96), professional baseball player (Brooklyn Dodgers) whose career was cut short as the result of a 1956 automobile accident that left him paralyzed. The son of an Italian American father from Pittsburgh and an African American mother from the state of Delaware, Campanella was erroneously thought by Mitchell to be of Caribbean ancestry and, in 1952, was included in a list of noted African Americans who were either born in or descended from the West Indies. Member of the Professional Baseball Hall of Fame.

Cannon, Poppy (1905–75), journalist and author; born Lillian Gruskin in South Africa of Lithuanian Jewish parentage, she emigrated to the United States as a child. She was food editor for *Ladies' Home Journal* and *House Beautiful* and writer for women's magazines as well as an author of cookbooks and popular histories. Married no less than five times, her fourth husband was Walter White, whom she married in 1950 after he divorced his wife of more than twenty years; this caused a scandal in the black community.

Capehart, Homer Earl (1897–1979) (R-Ind.), businessman; U.S. senator (1945–63). A fiscal conservative who supported the Taft-Hartley Act and opposed most social legislation, he nevertheless cosponsored an FEPC bill in 1951 and voted for the Civil Rights Act of 1957.

Carey, Archibald James, Jr. (1908–81), attorney, jurist, minister of the Gospel, and politician; alderman, Third District, Chicago (1948–55); alternate delegate to the United Nations (1953–56); chair, President's Commission on Government Employment Policy (1957–58). In 1953, he met with Mitchell and Albert M. Cole to review and discuss the federal government's housing policy.

Carey, James Barron (1911–73), chair, National CIO Committee to Abolish Racial Discrimination; national secretary, CIO (1938–42); secretary-treasurer, CIO (1942–55); member, PCCR (1946–47); president, IUERMW, CIO (1949–62); vice president, CIO (1955–65). A member of President Truman's CGCC, he also participated in a 1946 meeting with Secretary of Labor Lewis Schwellenbach on nondiscrimination by USES offices.

Carpenter, John Henry (1893–1954), Presbyterian minister, educator, and activist; instructor, New York University (1930–37); director of religious education, Brooklyn Federation of Churches (1926–32); executive secretary, Brooklyn Church and Mission Federation (1932–44); executive secretary, Protestant Council of City of New York (Brooklyn Division) (1944–54); secretary, Department of Urban Churches, National Council of Churches of Christ (1945–54); in 1945 named to reorganized board of directors of NCPFEPC.

Carr, Robert Kenneth (1908–79), professor, Department of Government, Dartmouth College (1937–60); executive secretary, President's Committee on Civil Rights (1945–48); president, Oberlin College (1960–70). In 1948, he wrote *To Secure These Rights*, which outlined the role the federal government should take to aggressively fight racial discrimination; the previous year, Carr had sought information from Walter White regarding the role of the federal government in protecting civil rights and in using the criminal sanctions in federal law to do so.

Carter, Ashby Bernard (1898–1953), Chicago postal clerk (1913–c. 1950); president, Chicago branch, NAPE; board member, NCPFEPC; national president, NAPE (1945–53). He protested discrimination in the post office system.

Carter, Eunice Roberta Hunton (1899–1970), lawyer and social worker; first black female assistant district attorney for New York County, under Thomas E. Dewey (1936–46). She was instrumental in linking prostitution to organized crime and successfully prosecuting mob boss Charles "Lucky" Luciano. She also was a member of the NCNW, worked with the UN, and served on the national board of the YWCA.

Carter, Herman Jefferson Davis (1909–78), veteran. In 1946, he was turned down for a clerical position at the U.S. Naval Gun Factory at the Washington navy yard despite the fact he was eligible for federal employment as a "permanent status person" and as a U.S. Army veteran with a ten-point disability.

Carter, Randall Albert (1865–1954), bishop, CME Church (1914–54); a native of Fort Valley, Georgia, after the 1920s he was based in Chicago. In 1942, he represented the church at the Conference of Cooperating Organizations in Washington.

Carter, Robert Lee (1917–), lawyer; legal assistant, NAACP (1944–45); assistant special counsel, NAACP (1945–56); general counsel, NAACP (1956–68); judge (1972–86) and senior judge (1986–), U.S. District Court for the Southern District of New York. As NAACP counsel, he was active in cases involving Jim Crow travel laws and the desegregation of AEC facilities. He played a key role in the NLRB's 1964 ruling that racial discrimination by a union was an unfair labor practice prohibited by the Taft-Hartley Act.

Carver, George Washington (1864–1943), biologist, botanist, agronomist, inventor, and innovator in the field of scientific agricultural experimental research; chair, Department of Agriculture, Tuskegee Institute (1891–1942). Nationally recognized for his work in soil conservation and the industrial utilization of agricultural products, Carver was best known for his work with the peanut, which he touted to southern farmers as a viable alternative to cotton; he then showed how the peanut could be used for many different purposes other than as a food. In January 1948, the U.S. Postal Service issued a commemorative stamp in his honor.

Case, Clifford Philip (1904–82) (R-N.J.), lawyer; New Jersey state legislator (1943–44); U.S. representative (1945–53); U.S. senator (1955–79). A liberal Republican, he was a supporter of antilynching, anti–poll tax, and FEPC legislation. In 1950, he opposed an electoral reform bill that opponents believed would enhance southern power in federal elections. During that same year, Mitchell listed him as one of the new, more progressive Republican leaders.

Cass, Millard (1916–2005), lawyer, NLRB (1941–46); assistant to the assistant secretary of labor (1946–47); assistant to the undersecretary of labor (1947–50); special assistant to the secretary of labor (1950–55); deputy undersecretary of labor (1955–71). In 1950, he conferred with the NAACP regarding nondiscrimination in government contracts.

Cavert, Rev. Samuel McCrea (1888–1976), Presbyterian minister; general secretary, Federal Council of Churches (1920–52). In 1944 he testified before the House Labor Committee in favor of S. 2048, a bill designed to strengthen the FEPC.

Celler, Emanuel (1888–1981) (D-N.Y.), lawyer; U.S. representative (1923–73). A consistent supporter of anti–poll tax bills and other civil rights legislation, he is credited with being one of the architects of the Civil Rights Act of 1957. He also opposed the Taft-Hartley Act, the McCarran Internal Security Act, and the postwar anticommunist crusade.

Chalmers, Allan Knight (1897–1972), minister, educator, social worker, and activist; YMCA worker in France during World War I; pastor, Broadway Tabernacle Congregationalist (now United Church of Christ) Church, New York City (1930–47); professor, Boston University Divinity School (1947–62). During the 1930s, he was active in the fight to free the Scottsboro Boys; he subsequently served as treasurer of the NAACP (1948–57), and also on the board of the NAACP Legal Defense and Education Fund. One of his students at Boston University was Martin Luther King Jr., whom he instructed, befriended, and mentored. In 1944, with A. Phillip Randolph, Chalmers served as cochairman of the NCPFEPC.

Chance, William Claudius, Sr. (1880–1970), educator; founder (1909), and principal of Parmele Industrial Institute, Parmele, North Carolina. In 1948 he challenged North Carolina's Jim Crow transportation laws, and, with the aid of the NAACP, was successful in having them overturned in *Chance v. Lambeth* (186 F. 2d 879 [1951]).

Chapital, Arthur Joseph, Jr. (1921–85), veteran. He was one of many black veterans who filed employment discrimination complaints against the New Orleans Post Office in 1947. Despite a high score on tests and veteran's preference, he was offered only temporary employment, whereas lower-scoring whites were hired for permanent positions. His father was Arthur J. Chapital Sr. (1901–72), a postal worker who was an NAACP leader for over forty years, acted as secretary and then president of the New Orleans branch, and organized the McDonogh Day Boycott of 1954, one of the city's first black protests of the civil rights era. Chapital Sr. was also later an organizer and officer of the ARPFE.

Chapman, Oscar Littleton (1896–1978), assistant secretary of interior (1933–46); undersecretary of interior (1946–50); U.S. secretary of interior (1950–53). A member of the Henry A. Wallace wing of the Democratic Party, he first gained fame in 1939 when he facilitated use of the Lincoln Memorial for a Marian Anderson concert. As secretary of interior, he was credited with making progress on desegregating Washington, D.C., facilities controlled by his department.

Chavez, Dennis (1888–1962) (D-N.Mex.), lawyer; member, New Mexico State House of Representatives (1923–24); U.S. representative (1931–35), U.S. senator (1935–62). He sponsored an FEPC bill in 1944 and a revision in 1947, but both efforts were defeated. In 1951, however, he voted to table an amendment to S. 1, the Universal Military Training bill that was designed to protect members of the armed forces against violence by civilians and peace officers.

Chelf, Frank Leslie (1907–82) (D-Ky.), lawyer; delegate to the Democratic National Convention (1936); U.S. representative (1945–67). In 1948, he served on a House judiciary subcommittee that heard testimony on the emergency temporary displaced persons bill of Rep. William G. Stratton (R-Ill.), which would have provided for the admission of 100,000 people annually for four years.

Cherne, Leo M. (1912–99), lawyer, business executive, and cofounder Research Institute of America, 1935. In 1943, while director of the National Citizens' Council on Civil Rights, he was named to the board of directors of NCPFEPC. He later served as chair, International Rescue Commission (1951–91) and member, President's Foreign Intelligence Advisory Board (1973–91). Although supporting Sen. Joseph R. McCarthy's (R-Wis.) antipathy toward Communists, Cherne debated him on the adverse effects the resulting witch hunt had on American society. President Ronald Reagan presented him with the Presidential Medal of Freedom in 1984.

Cherry, Robert Gregg (1891–1957) (D-N.C.), lawyer; North Carolina state legislator (1931–43); governor (1945–49). The NAACP sent him a letter of protest regarding discrimination by North Carolina's USES office. He insisted that no discrimination existed, even though the office restricted blacks to a separate basement section and required them to use an alley exit.

Christensen, Milo Frederick (1904–77), superintendent of recreation for the District of Columbia (1942–65). In 1951, Mitchell determined that the best way to have the D.C. Board of Recreation stop racial segregation in its parks was by filing a lawsuit; he came to this decision after receiving a letter from Christiansen stating that the board's policy regarding racial segregation was to move "at such rate of progression as may be consistent with the public interest, public order and effective administration."

Church, Robert Reed, Jr. (1885–1952), businessman and politician; the son of a wealthy African American businessman of Memphis, and the nephew of civil rights activist and club woman Mary Church Terrell, Church organized Memphis blacks into a significant voting bloc and became involved in national Republican politics to the extent that he gained access to the party's national organization and to immense patronage power. He was one of the earliest black supporters of the presidential candidacy of Gen. Dwight D. Eisenhower. In 1945, he was named to the reorganized board of directors of the NCPFEPC.

Churchill, Winston Leonard Spencer (1874–1965), prime minister of Great Britain (1939–45); in 1942, black American leaders were angered when he observed that the stipulations of the Atlantic Charter applied only to Nazi-occupied Europe and not to the free world as a whole. Black leaders felt that the Axis powers could be decisively overcome only by those people who were committed to extending democracy to the nonwhite world. As Roi Ottley warned in his *New World A'Coming*, the rest of the world was watching America "quite aware of the fact that a nation that is unable to solve its color problem at home will never be able to take the lead in creating a free world everywhere."

Clark, Gen. Mark Wayne (1896–1984), World War I, World War II, and Korean War veteran; chief of U.S. Occupation Forces in Austria; U.S. high commissioner for Austria; commander, UN Forces in Korea (1952–53); president, The Citadel (1953–65). In 1953, Mitchell referred to him as someone who could inform South Carolina of the propaganda damage done in Korea by reports of U.S. racial discrimination.

Clark, Tom Campbell (1899–1977), lawyer; special assistant to the U.S. attorney general (1937–43); assistant U.S. attorney general (1943–45); U.S. attorney general (1945–49); Supreme Court associate justice (1949–67). As attorney general, he supported the desegregation of public schools and argued against the judicial enforcement of restrictive covenants. He also participated in negotiations regarding executive orders against public employment discrimination and police violence against blacks. Although there was considerable opposition among liberals to his nomination to the Supreme Court—they felt that he was lukewarm on civil rights, despite his record as attorney general—as associate justice he endorsed the *Brown* decision and consistently supported desegregation.

Cleary, Ansel (1897–1978), assistant director, Apprentice Training Program, Department of Labor (1946). He consulted with Mitchell regarding the access of blacks to postwar training programs.

Clement, Arthur John Howard, Jr. (1908–86), businessman; president, Charleston branch, NAACP (1948–55). A leader in efforts to desegregate facilities at the Charleston Navy Yard (1953), he later served on NAACP boards in Newark, Los Angeles, Philadelphia, and again in Charleston, after returning in 1967.

Clifford, Clark McAdams (1906–98), lawyer; special counsel to the president (1946–50); U.S. secretary of defense (1968–69). Regarded for years as one of the most powerful men in Washington, he was the prime architect behind the Truman Doctrine and an adviser to several presidents. During the 1948 presidential campaign, he advised Truman to demand comprehensive health insurance and increased federal aid to housing and education, among other social programs. In later years, he was implicated in the BCCI banking scandal.

Cloon, Erskine Clibborn (1891–1960), postmaster, Jackson, Mississippi (1931–34). He instituted policies of no longer appointing blacks to any post office positions and dismissing previously hired black employees.

Clorety, Joseph Anthony (1912–82), vice chair, AVC. In 1948, he joined Mitchell in conferring with the FEB regarding the elimination of discrimination by government agencies.

Cobb, Julia, NAACP complainant. She charged the Bethesda Naval Hospital with discrimination.

Cobb, Dr. William Montague (1904–90), professor and later chair, Department of Anatomy, Howard University College of Medicine (1947–69); member, NAACP National Board of Directors (1951–82); president, NAACP (1976–82). A prominent opponent of segregation and discrimination in the health care field, he testified in favor of a national health bill (1946) and against segregation in psychiatric units of veterans' hospitals (1953).

Cohen, Felix Solomon (1907–53), lawyer; legal philosopher and educator; writer and essayist. Holding a doctorate from Harvard and a law degree from Columbia, as a solicitor in the Interior Department (1932–48) he drafted the 1935 Indian Reorganization Act, called the "Indian New Deal"; he taught legal philosophy at Yale, the City College of New York, and Rutgers. In 1950, representing AJComm, he was part of the delegation from NECRM that met with President Truman.

Cohen, Jules (1914–2003), lawyer, politician, of Brooklyn, New York. The longtime executive director of the JLC, he was also involved with the New York Council for a Permanent FEPC when he was part of the delegation from the NECRM that met with President Truman in January 1950.

Colborn, Fern M. (1905–92); social worker. She headed the Washington, D.C., office of the Department of Social Education and Action for the former United Presbyterian Church of the United States of America; at the same time, she was active in the National Federation of Settlements and Neighborhood Centers. In 1953, she met with Mitchell and Albert M. Cole to review and discuss the federal government's housing policy.

Cold, Ed (1887–1932), railroad brakeman killed by a shotgun blast from ambush on February 4, 1932, in Water Valley, Mississippi; the murderers, supposed to be whites who coveted Cold's job, were never apprehended. Cold left behind a wife and a large family.

Cole, Albert McDonald (1901–94) (R-Kans.), lawyer and businessman; Kansas state legislator (1941–45); U.S. representative (1945–53); administrator, HHFA (1953–59). In 1953, Mitchell questioned Cole's appointment to the HHFA because of the latter's previous opposition to public housing and his noncommittal statements on continuation of segregation therein. As HHFA administrator, Cole participated in discussions regarding the federal government's promotion of segregation.

Collins, Gen. Joseph Lawton (1896–1987), chief of staff, U.S. Army (1949–53). In 1951, he met in Washington with Mitchell, Walter F. White, Sen. Hubert H. Humphrey, and others to discuss discriminatory practices in the armed services.

Collins, W. J., postal worker, New Orleans Post Office, who in 1946 was appointed to a permanent position as a clerk over eligible African American applicants although he was not a veteran, scored lower on the clerk-carrier test than a significant number of African American applicants, and had amassed a large number of demerits during his stint as a temporary employee.

Collins, William (1893–1965), union official. In 1951, when he was the regional director of the AFL (1937–58), he participated in the organizational meeting of the LCCR.

Connell, John Gibbs, Jr. (1914–2004), personnel manager for the secretary of the army; administrative officer, Loyalty-Security Program, U.S. Army (1950–79); chair, ASSB (1953–66). He met with NAACP leaders to discuss army intelligence officials' negative comments about the NAACP.

Conyers, Henry, Jr. (1911–2002), veteran. As a civilian instructor employed by the U.S. Army Air Force in Japan after the end of World War II, Conyers complained of widespread discrimination he had faced in the military as a civilian instructor, including being forced to eat alone at a segregated table in the mess hall. He was subsequently assigned to the Sacramento Air Service Command in California and was dismissed from his job there because his superiors refused to give him work for which he was assigned. He asked the NAACP to intercede with the Department of the Army and get him reinstated.

Cooke, Edmund Douglas, Sr. (1913–2008), meteorologist. In 1947, Mitchell and the NAACP were instrumental in Cooke being offered a position as a meterological aide with the U.S. Weather Bureau.

Cooke, Raymond F., (1927–86), complainant. In 1954, he was notified that his apprenticeship in the U.S. Bureau of Engraving and Printing had ended and that he would not be able to continue in his field of employment.

Cooper, Evelyn O. Neilson (1914–80), attorney and hearings examiner, Legal Division, FEPC (1944–45); special assistant, Department of the Interior (1945–52). While in the Interior Department, she assisted Mitchell in the struggle to obtain permanent FEPC legislation and an executive order against discrimination in government employment.

Corning, Hobart Munson (1889–1970), Washington, D.C., superintendent of schools (1946–58). In 1950, he supported efforts to deny the use of school facilities for an interracial performance.

Corrothers [married name Webber], Rachel Victoria (1903–81), educator, newspaper reporter, clubwoman; in July 1942, with Geraldine Lensh, she represented the Union for Democratic Action at the Conference of Cooperating Organizations.

Corson, John Jay, III (1905–90), journalist, management consultant, and presidential advisor; assistant director, NYA (1935–38); assistant executive director, SSB (1936–38); director, OASI (1938–41, 1942–44); director, USES (1941–42); deputy director general, UNRRA (1944–45); executive, *Washington Post* (1945–50); as director of USES, he reported to the NAACP that only four of the states had passed FEPC legislation.

Cox, Edward Eugene (1880–1952) (D-Ga.), lawyer and judge; U.S. representative (1925–52). Known for his cantankerous and volatile nature—in 1949, he engaged in fisticuffs on the House floor with fellow representative Adolph J. Sabath—he was a vigorous foe of all civil rights legislation. Alienated by the Truman administration's civil rights measures, he supported the States' Rights (Dixiecrat) Party presidential nominee Strom Thurmond in the presidential election of 1948. Several years later, as chair of the Select Committee on Tax Exempt Foundations (informally known as the Cox Committee), he investigated charitable organizations that supported civil rights activities in the South.

Craft, Henry Kempton (1893–1974), longtime secretary of Harlem (135th Street Branch) YMCA (1932–58); a graduate of Harvard University, he had been involved with the YMCA in various capacities from 1916 on. He was an early participant in the MOWM and served as treasurer of the March on Washington Committee.

Cramer, Lawrence William (1897–1978), a native of New Orleans; instructor in government, Columbia University (1926–31); lieutenant governor of St. Croix, U.S. Virgin Islands (1931–35), then governor of the Virgin Islands (1935–41); first executive secretary, FEPC (1941–43); resigned after the FEPC was placed under the WMC, and its chairman Paul McNutt canceled hearings on discrimination in the railroad industry; later executive secretary of the Caribbean Commission.

Crigler, Jesse Rusia Burton (1901–94), employee, vice president, and general manager, Chesapeake and Potomac Telephone Company of West Virginia (1925–50); vice president and general manager, Chesapeake and Potomac Telephone Company of Washington (1950–66). He negotiated with the NAACP on the employment of African Americans; his lack of action led to efforts to enforce nondiscrimination provisions in government contracts.

Crockett, George William, Jr. (1909–97) (D-Mich.); African American lawyer, born West Virginia; senior attorney in the Solicitor's Office, Department of Labor (1939–43); 1943 appointed hearing examiner, FEPC; subsequently legal counsel, UAW; vice president, National Lawyers Guild; judge, Recorders Court, city of Detroit (1967–79); U.S. representative (1979–90).

Crogman, William Henry (1841–1931), college professor and president, Clark College, Atlanta (1903–10); born on St. Maarten, in the Leeward Islands. In 1952, Mitchell commented that, if the McCarran-Walter Act, with its severe restriction on immigration from the Caribbean and South America, had been in force when immigrants like Crogman entered the United States, they would not have been able to make "notable contributions to the building of our nation."

Croll, Rev. David Henry (1890–1983), Episcopal priest. A native of Jamaica, he pastored an Episcopal church in Annapolis, Maryland, and was active in the local NAACP branch. In 1951, he went to Washington, D.C., to protest the proposed Winstead amendment to the Universal Military Training bill.

Crosser, Robert (1874–1957) (D-Ohio), lawyer; Ohio state legislator (1911–12); U.S. representative (1913–19, 1923–55). A native of Scotland, he was a staunch labor advocate who supported Truman's Fair Deal programs and backed anti–Jim Crow travel legislation. In 1950, as chair of the House Committee on Interstate and Foreign Commerce, he presided over hearings on amendments to the Railway Labor Act that Mitchell and others felt would be detrimental to black employment in the railroad industry.

Crosswaith, Frank Rudolph (1892–1965), labor activist, author, and editor; a native of St. Croix in the (then Danish) Virgin Islands, Crosswaith was active in the recruitment of blacks into labor organizations, for example, working for A. Philip Randolph as an organizer for the BSCP, and as an organizer for the ILGWU. Crosswaith was best known for his work as the founder and organizer of the Negro Labor Committee in 1935; this later became the Harlem Labor Council. He worked with Randolph and others in planning for the 1941 March on Washington, which would culminate in President Franklin D. Roosevelt's signing of Executive Order 8802 and the establishment of the FEPC.

Cruikshank, Nelson Hale (1902–86), Methodist minister and labor lobbyist; executive assistant to labor members, WMC (1942–44); director of social insurance, AFL (1944–50); director, European Labor Division, ECA (Marshall Plan) (1951–52); director, Department of Social Security, AFL and AFL-CIO (1953–65); member, NAACP National Labor Board; president (1969–77) and president emeritus (1980–86), NCSC; chair, FCA (1977–80). He urged nondiscrimination in the USES and was influential in the passage of the Social Security Disability Act of 1956.

Crum, Bartley Cavanaugh, Sr. (1900–1959), liberal San Francisco lawyer; a founder of the National Lawyers Guild and of PM; special counsel for FEPC working on railroad cases, 1943;

member of NAACP National Legal Committee; in 1948, in conversation with James C. Evans, civilian assistant to the Defense Department, Mitchell mentioned Crum as a potential member of the new President's Committee of Equality of Treatment and Opportunity in the Armed Services established under Executive Order 9981. Crum was a lawyer for the "Hollywood 10" who refused to answer questions by the House Un-American Activities Committee; he was labeled as a "fellow traveler" by HUAC and kept under surveillance during investigations into the Communist party and associated organizations. He committed suicide in 1959.

Crump, Edward Hull (1874–1954) (D-Tenn.), machine politician and businessman; Memphis mayor (1910–16); U.S. representative (1931–35). Popularly known as "Boss" Crump, he was a power broker in Memphis and state politics for decades. Although blacks were a key component of his political machine, he opposed repeal of the poll tax, supported segregation, opposed Truman's civil rights policies, and supported Dixiecrat Strom Thurmond for president in 1948. He even opposed hiring blacks as postal clerks.

Crump, Mildred (1915–2001), staffer in the NAACP National Office; mentioned in 1942 correspondence between Walter White and Thurgood Marshall concerning the relationship between the new NAACP Washington Bureau, its Advisory Committee, and the national NAACP office in New York City.

Cullen, James Kevin (1901–88), lawyer and judge; judge, Supreme Bench, City of Baltimore (1952–70); on October 5, 1954, Judge Cullen presided over a legal action brought by the NAAWP against the city of Baltimore concerning the desegregation of the public schools; he found that the city had acted legally in desegregating the schools and dismissed the case.

Current, Gloster Bryant (1913–97), executive director, Detroit branch, NAACP (1941–46); director of branches and field administration, NAACP (1946–76); deputy executive director, NAACP (1976–78); member, NAACP National Board of Directors (1978–83); pastor, Westchester Community Church, Bronx, New York (1978–83). As director of branches, he supported state FEPC legislation and assisted the NAACP labor department. Following his career with the NAACP, Current—an ordained Methodist minister and accomplished musician—was an organist for the St. Paul United Methodist Church in Queens, New York.

Cuthbert, Marion Vera (1896–1989), educator, sociologist, poet, author, and activist. For her doctoral dissertation at Columbia, she studied the lives of black female college graduates; the resulting work, *Education and Marginality: A Study of the Negro Woman College Graduate*, was hailed as one of the first incisive studies in its field. Dean of women, Talladega College (1928–44); dean of women, Brooklyn College (1944–61). As a member of the NAACP National Board of Directors, she was present at the 1951 organizational meeting establishing the LCCR.

Dalton, Maj. Gen. Joseph Nicholas (1892–1961), U.S. Army; a graduate of VMI, he served as head of Military Intelligence to 1942, and afterward as head of department of military personnel; a member of the War Department's Advisory Committee on Negro Troop Policies from 1942. In 1944, he met with Walter White to discuss criticisms and recommendations in White's two reports on black troops in the European Theater and the North African Theater of Operations.

Daniels, Jonathan Worth (1902–81), newspaper reporter, editor, and author; presidential aide to President Franklin D. Roosevelt in charge of racial and labor problems and Southern politics (1943–45); press secretary to president (1945); U.S. member, UN Subcommittee on Prevention of Discrimination and Protection of Minorities (1947–53). He represented Roosevelt in discussions with FEPC on the Philadelphia transit strike and Los Angeles Railway case in 1944. In 1948, Mitchell castigated Daniels for his opposition to the strong enforcement provisions of a federal fair employment practice law.

Danley, Samuel Boba, Jr. (1897–1989), employee of the U.S. Department of Labor, first with USES and after January 1948 with the Apprentice Training Service. The NAACP had long been attempting to place a qualified individual in that position in order to facilitate the entry of more blacks into apprenticeships; Mitchell hailed Danley's selection as a step toward that goal.

Dann, Richard, member, NAAWP. He participated in picketing at Gwynn's Falls Junior High School in Baltimore to protest the implementation of the Supreme Court's *Brown* decision.

Dantzler, Capt. Tillman Trotter (1904–56), commander, Charleston Navy Yard. In 1953, he announced the desegregation of drinking fountains at the yard.

Davidson, Crowe Girard (1910–96), lawyer; assistant general counsel, WPB (1944–45); assistant secretary of the interior (1946–50). He aided the NAACP in the fight against federal employment discrimination.

Davidson, Eugene (1896–1976), board member, District of Columbia branch, NAACP (1927–57); senior field representative, FEPC (1941–43); assistant director of field operations, FEPC (1943–46). He was a leader in the movement to desegregate the nation's capital.

Davidson, Robert, member, NAAWP. He participated in picketing at Gwynn's Falls Junior High School in Baltimore to protest the implementation of the Supreme Court's *Brown* decision.

Davies, Dr. Arthur Powell (1902–57), clergyman (first Methodist, then Unitarian), activist, and author; pastor, Old Souls Unitarian Church, Washington, D.C. (1944–57). A native of Liverpool, he publicly proclaimed in 1953 that he would not eat in segregated Washington, D.C., restaurants. He was a staunch anticommunist and a promoter of aid to postwar Europe and Asia, but he opposed McCarthyism.

Davis, Brig. Gen. Benjamin Oliver, Jr. (1912–2002), U.S. Army Air Corps, son of the first African American general in the U.S. Army; USMA class of 1936. When the army finally allowed blacks into the Army Air Corps, he was selected to lead the first flight training program at Tuskegee Institute in Alabama, and subsequently commanded the 99th Pursuit Squadron and the 332nd Fighter Group, both all-black units. All told, during World War II, General Davis flew 60 missions in 224 combat hours and won a number of medals, including the Silver Star. After the end of the war, with the issuance of Executive Order 9981, which ended racial discrimination in the armed forces, Davis helped draft desegregation plans and was appointed to a number of command positions; he retired as a lieutenant general in 1970, and subsequently served as director of public safety in Cleveland, Ohio (1970–71), and assistant secretary, U.S. Department of Transportation (1971–75).

Davis, Carolyn (1913–89), UAW staffer. In 1948, she worked with William Oliver and Harry Ross in the Fair Practices and Anti-discrimination Department, UAW.

Davis, Dowdal Henry, Jr. (1913–57), artist, writer, and newspaper executive; editor and publisher, *Kansas City Call* (1950–57); chair, advertising department, NNPA (1941–47); member, board of directors, NNPA (1944–50), vice president, NNPA (1947–49); president, NNPA (1949–51). In 1952, Davis was one of a number of prominent businesspeople, labor leaders, and government officials named by President Truman to serve on his CGCC. Among their duties was overseeing Truman's FEPC.

Davis, Jack [John Aubrey?], assistant to Emanuel Lerner (director, NHA); in 1946 Mitchell reported to Walter White that Davis had been striving, to little avail, to protect the jobs of African Americans in shipyards, where a considerable reduction in force was anticipated with demand sharply falling off due to the end of World War II.

Davis, James Curran (1895–1981) (D-Ga.), lawyer; Georgia state legislator (1924–28); judge (1934–47); U.S. representative (1947–63). In 1951, he delayed efforts to integrate the Washington, D.C., fire department.

Davis, John Aubrey, Sr. (1912–2002), professor, City College of New York; head, Division of Review and Analysis, FEPC (1943–46); fair employment consultant, State Department (1952–53); member, NYSCAD (1957–61); member, CEEO (1961–66). He prepared a memorandum opposing the Lodge-Gossett bill, a measure designed to eliminate the role of the Electoral College in presidential elections. The paper argued that under the circumstances then prevailing, the measure would give undue political influence to the South and reduce the importance of blacks and other minorities as swing voters in states with large numbers of electoral votes. A pioneer in employing economic boycotts to achieve civil rights objectives, he also helped prepare the NAACP's brief in the *Brown* case.

Davis, John Warren (1888–1980), college administrator and president, West Virginia State College (now University) (1919–52); U.S. director of technical services to Liberia, U.S. Department of State (1952–54). He worked with the NAACP Legal Defense and Education Fund (1954–79) to assess the state of education for African Americans in the United States.

Davis, Oscar Lenard (1890–1940), farmer, of Pittsylvania County, Virginia. Shot and killed by Odell Waller, a young black sharecropper, over a dispute about pay. Waller claimed self-defense, but was eventually executed.

Davis, Maj. Steve Galbreth (1910–2000), U.S. Army. A native of Alabama, Davis moved to Chicago and was working for the U.S. Postal Service when he joined the Illinois National Guard in 1931. At the outbreak of World War II, he was commissioned, was placed on active duty, and served in Italy as the captain of an artillery unit. At the close of the war, he went to work in the Pentagon, eventually retiring as chief, Personnel Services Division, Office of the Deputy Chief of Staff Personnel, Headquarters, Department of the Army. After his retirement from active service (as a colonel) in 1967, he became executive director of the NNPA.

Dawson, H. A., of Rocky Mount, North Carolina. In 1943, he was named to the executive board of the NPCFEPC.

Dawson, William Levi (1886–1970) (D-Ill.), lawyer; Chicago alderman (1933–39); U.S. representative (1943–70). A Georgia native who graduated magna cum laude from Fisk University, he moved to Chicago as a young man and became the most powerful political broker of that city's South Side, acquiring the nickname "The Man" in the process. Elected to the U.S. House of Representatives in 1942—he was the only black member of Congress when he took his seat the following year—he became the first black chair of a major congressional committee (the House Committee on Government Operations) seven years later. Dawson supported anti–poll tax legislation and integration of the armed forces, and in 1944, he cosponsored legislation for a permanent FEPC. During the 1950s, however, he began to de-emphasize civil rights issues, believing that black advancement was more likely to be achieved through party loyalty rather than strident advocacy of civil rights. This strategy was symbolized by his arguments against strengthening the civil rights plank of the 1952 Democratic Party platform.

Dean, Gordon Evans (1905–58), lawyer and businessman; law professor, Duke University; member (1947–53) and chair (1950–53), AEC. The NAACP urged Chair Dean to desegregate schools run by the AEC.

Dedmon, Jesse Oscar, Jr. (1908–86), lawyer; captain, 366th U.S. Infantry (1941–45); secretary of veterans' affairs, NAACP (1945–48). He worked with Mitchell on those issues that affected returning black World War II veterans.

Delany, Hubert Thomas (1901–90), lawyer and judge; member, New York City Tax Commission (1929–37); assistant U.S. attorney for the Southern District of New York (1937–42); justice, New York City Domestic Relations Court (1942–55). He was a member of the NAACP National Board of Directors, the NAACP Legal Defense and Education Fund, and the National Urban League. In 1951, he resigned his position in the civil defense program in protest of the appointment of Millard F. Caldwell as civil defense director.

Delson, Max (1903–88), lawyer and activist. Although long identified with the Socialist Party in New York City, he also served as counsel to many labor organizations including the BSCP, and worked closely with A. Philip Randolph. Delson subsequently became a member of the NAACP National Board of Directors. In 1944, he was named to the executive board of the NCPFEPC.

Denham, Robert Newton (1885–1954), lawyer; special counsel to the comptroller of the currency (1933–34); trial examiner (1938–47) and counsel general (1947–50), NLRB. Labor leaders considered him to be antilabor and thus called for his removal from the NLRB. Truman requested and received his resignation in September 1950.

Dering, William Clouett, Sr. (1891–1954), postal worker; member, Board of Examiners, USCSC, Tenth Region. He was connected with employment discrimination at the New Orleans Post Office.

Detzer, Dorothy [married name Denny] (1893–1981), social worker, peace activist; working for the AFSC in post–World War I Europe convinced her of the folly of war, and as the national executive secretary of the Women's International League for Peace and Freedom (1924–46), she lobbied Congress on issues concerning peace as well as other matters calling for social reform; in July 1942, she participated in the Conference of Cooperating Organizations.

Dewey, Thomas Edmund (1902–71) (R-N.Y.), lawyer; chief assistant U.S. Attorney, Southern District of New York (1933–37); district attorney, New York County District Attorney's Office (1937–43); governor of New York (1943–55); Republican presidential candidate in 1944 and 1948. While governor, he signed the Ives-Quinn FEPC bill into law.

Dial, John H., Jr. (1917–2003), secretary, labor committee, Los Angeles branch, NAACP (1947). He reported to Mitchell on black employment in Los Angeles and branch membership drives.

Dickerson, Earl Burrus (1891–1986), lawyer; member, executive committee Chicago branch NAACP; member, NAACP national board of directors (1941–73); legal counsel, Supreme Life Insurance Company; first black Democratic alderman, city of Chicago (1938–43); member, FEPC (1941–43); president, National Bar Association (1945–47); president, National Lawyers' Guild (1951–59); president, Chicago Urban League (1939–47, 1950–55). He was called the "dean of Chicago's black lawyers."

Dickerson, John Maynard (1899–1976), lawyer and newspaper publisher; president, Ohio State Conference of NAACP Branches. A resident of Youngstown, Ohio, he supported state FEPC legislation.

Dillon, Brig. Gen. Joseph Vincent DePaul (1899–1971), air provost marshal, U.S. Air Force (1948–53). He attended a meeting in Washington, D.C., concerning the assault on a black corporal by military police.

Dirksen, Everett McKinley (1896–1969) (R-Ill.), businessman and lawyer; city government official (1927–31); U.S. representative (1933–49); U.S. senator (1951–69); Senate minority leader (1959–69). An occasional supporter of Fair Deal legislation, he voted for the Taft-Hartley Act and a fair employment bill without enforcement powers. His reputation was shaken by his support of Joseph McCarthy, but he was a consistent proponent of civil rights legislation from the mid-1950s onward.

Dixon, Dean Charles (1915–76), musician and conductor; in 1941 he was the first black (as well as the youngest musician to date) to conduct the New York Philharmonic Orchestra. Although he was a native of New York City, his parents were immigrants from the Caribbean who early exposed him to classical music. In 1952, Mitchell commented that, if the McCarran-Walter Act, with its severe restriction on immigration from the Caribbean and

South America, had been in force when immigrants like the Dixons entered the United States, they would not have been able to make "notable contributions to the building of our nation."

Doar, William Edward, Jr. (1911–82), social worker, state government employee and fraternity leader; national executive director, Phi Beta Sigma Social Fraternity (1949–78). He participated in the organization and establishment of the LCCR in 1951.

Dodson, Thurman L. (1904–85), lawyer, of Washington, D.C.; president, Washington Bar Association (1934–36); president NBA (1947–48); member, Council of Concerned Afro-American Republicans. In 1944, he was a member of the board of directors, NCPFEPC. In 1950, he was part of a delegation from the NECRM who met with President Truman.

Dombrowski, James Anderson (1897–1983), Methodist minister, educator, author and activist; World War I veteran of U.S. Army Air Corps. A native of Tampa, but educated in New Jersey, he was a cofounder of the Highlander Folk School in Grundy County, Tennessee; executive director, Southern Conference on Human Welfare (1942–46); executive director, Southern Conference Educational Fund (1946–66); founder and director, Southern Organizing Committee for Economic and Social Justice (1975–83); staunch opponent of the poll tax.

Donahue, Alphonsus Joseph, Sr. (1884–1949), business executive; World War I veteran. He rose from bellboy in the Waldorf-Astoria hotel in New York City to vice president of the American Fastener Company of Waterbury, Connecticut. He also served as chair, National Conference of Christians and Jews (NCCJ); in 1948, he was named to serve on the President's Committee for Equality in Training and Opportunity in the Armed Forces (Fahy Committee).

Donaldson, Jesse Monroe (1885–1970), postal worker; chief post office inspector (1943–45); first assistant postmaster general (1945–47); U.S. postmaster general (1947–53). The NAACP opposed his appointment to the latter position because of his failure as first assistant postmaster general to take action against discrimination in the postal system. In 1948, he apologized for the post office's categorization of AJCong and the AVC as subversive organizations.

Donaldson, Preston Thomas (1914–70), member NAAWP. He was involved in Baltimore public school antidesegregation activity in 1954.

Donnell, Forrest C. (1884–1980) (R-Mo.), lawyer; Missouri governor (1941–45); U.S. senator (1945–51). A conservative, he opposed federal aid to education and supported the Taft-Hartley Act. In 1949, he proposed that the word *race* be added to a section of a minimum wage bill that prohibited setting wage rates based on age or sex.

Doughton, Robert Lee (1863–1954) (D-N.C.), banker; North Carolina state legislator (1908–9); U.S. representative (1911–53). As Ways and Means chair (1933–47, 1949–53), he held hearings on coverage of domestic workers under the Social Security Act.

Douglas, Paul Howard (1892–1976) (D-Ill.), professor; Chicago alderman (1939–42); U.S. senator (1949–67). A strong anticommunist, he supported FEPC bills and legislation that would protect black service members from violence. He was also a leader in the unsuccessful fight to modify Senate Rule XXII, which southern senators used to filibuster against civil rights bills.

Douglass, Joseph Henry (1917–74), social worker and professor; assistant to the assistant secretary of HEW (1965–67). A great-grandson of Frederick Douglass, he published a well-received study of race relations in the nation's capital while acting as executive secretary of the National Urban League branch in Washington.

Douglass, Paul Franklin (1904–88), lawyer, minister, journalist, and professor; Vermont state legislator (1933–43); president, American University (1941–52). He made possible the integration of American University during the 1940s, despite the opposition of trustees. In 1948, Mitchell conferred with him on complaints of discrimination in training classes at the university. Douglass denied discrimination was university policy and promised action if such practices were found.

Drew, Dr. Charles Richard (1904–50), surgeon, educator, and pioneer in the development of blood plasma preservation.

Driscoll, Alfred Eastlack (1902–75) (R-N.J.), lawyer; New Jersey state legislator (1939–41); governor (1947–54). As governor, he integrated the National Guard and signed a bill prohibiting discrimination in any place of public accommodation. During his tenure, New Jersey became the first state to constitutionally outlaw segregation. Mitchell deemed him a promising leader in civil rights.

Du Bois, William Edward Burghardt (1868–1963), teacher, author, poet, scholar and Pan-Africanist; professor, classics, German and English, Wilberforce University (1895–97); professor, economics and history, Atlanta University (1897–1910); one of the original founders and incorporators of the NAACP; editor *Crisis* (1910–34); chairman, Department of Sociology, Atlanta University (1934–44); director of special research, NAACP (1944–48); co-chairman, Council on African Affairs (1948–51); American Labor party candidate for U.S. senator from New York, 1950. Thought of as "one of the most incisive thinkers and profound scholars of his time," DuBois penned the editorial "Closing Ranks," when editing the *Crisis* in 1918, calling for American blacks to join with white Americans to fight the Axis powers for the sake of saving democracy "while this war lasts."

Dudley, Edward Richard (1911–2005), lawyer, judge and diplomat; assistant attorney general, state of New York (1942–43); member, NAACP legal department (1943–45); active in lobbying efforts to insure the passage of the Ives-Quinn bill (New York State FEPC bill); legal counsel to governor of the U.S. Virgin Islands (1945–47). He was the first black to be appointed as U.S. ambassador (rather than as resident minister) to Liberia (1948–53); justice, domestic relations court, New York City (1953–61); president, borough of Manhattan (1961–64); judge, New York Supreme Court (1964–85); administrative judge for boroughs of Manhattan and the Bronx (1967–85).

Duff, James Henderson (1883–1969) (R-Pa.), lawyer; Pennsylvania attorney general (1943–47); governor (1947–51); U.S. senator (1951–57). A Republican with an independent streak, he supported FEPC legislation, desegregation measures, and modification of Senate Rule XXII. While governor, he signed a bill requiring equal pay for equal work, regardless of gender.

Duke, David Ernest (1950–), white supremacist; leader, NAAWP; Louisiana state legislator (1989–92). A former Klansman, but active in white nationalist groups for many years, he revived Bryant Bowles' old NAAWP; he sought to bring his group into mainstream politics, serving for a time in the Louisiana state legislature.

Dulles, John Foster (1888–1959) (R-N.Y.), lawyer and diplomat; representative to the General Assembly of the United Nations (1946–49, 1950); chair of the board, CEIP; member, NYSBB; U.S. senator (1949); consultant to the secretary of state (1951–52); U.S. secretary of state (1953–59).

Dunjee, Roscoe (1883–1965), journalist; editor and publisher, *Black Dispatch* (1915–65); president, Oklahoma Conference of NAACP Branches (1933–47); member, NAACP National Board of Directors (1940–61). He defied Oklahoma's Jim Crow travel law.

Dunnigan, Alice Allison (1906–83), journalist; chief, Washington bureau, ANP (1947–61). Daughter of a Kentucky sharecropper, she was the first black woman to obtain access to Capitol press galleries.

Durr, Virginia Foster (1903–99), activist; a native of Birmingham, Alabama who attended Wellesley College, she met Eleanor Roosevelt while living in Washington with her husband, Clifford Durr, a lawyer working for the Reconstruction Finance Corporation, and both Durrs became New Dealers. Mrs. Durr was a cofounder of the Southern Conference for Human Welfare and ran for senator from Virginia on the Progressive ticket in 1948. The Durr family moved to Montgomery, Alabama, in 1950 and supported the civil rights movement (she provided the cash bond to bail Rosa Parks out of jail, among other things) to the extent that her house was a home away from home for visiting activists while many native white Alabamians shunned her.

Dykstra, Clarence Addison (1883–1950), educator; chancellor, University of Wisconsin-Madison (1937–45); first director, U.S. Selective Service (1940–41); chancellor, UCLA (1945–50). When Dykstra took on the job as director of the Selective Service, black Washington lawyer and reserve Army officer Campbell C. Johnson was named to be the executive assistant to the director.

Early, Stephen Tyree, Sr. (1889–1951), press secretary for President Franklin D. Roosevelt (1933–45); vice president, Pullman Corporation (1945–49); deputy secretary of defense (1949–50). In 1940, Early announced that black leadership, including that of the NAACP, had agreed to have blacks serve in segregated units in the Armed Forces. He also was involved in an incident in New York City where, during a struggle, he kicked a African American policeman in the groin.

Eastland, James Oliver (1904–86) (D-Miss.), lawyer; Mississippi state legislator (1928–32); U.S. senator (1941, 1943–78); chair, Senate Judiciary Committee (1955–78); Senate president pro tempore (1971–78). He was a Dixiecrat and a rabid opponent of civil rights. In addition to voting against antilynching and anti–poll tax legislation in the 1950s, he believed that both the FEPC and the *Brown* decision were communistic. A signer of the anti-*Brown* "Southern Manifesto," he introduced a constitutional amendment that would nullify any Supreme Court decision outlawing segregation.

Edelsberg, Herman (1909–86), director, Washington office, ADL (1947–65); vice chair for civil rights, NCLCH; executive director, EEOC (1965–67); director, ICBB (1967–77). In 1951, he was a member of a committee working with Mitchell on Senate rules changes.

Edelstein, Julius Caesar Claude (1912–2005), journalist; aide to Adm. William Leahy (in World War II); executive assistant and chief of legislative staff for Sen. Herbert Lehman (1949–58); chief of staff for Governor Lehman (1959–61); executive assistant to Mayor Robert F. Wagner of New York City (1961–65); senior vice chancellor, City University of New York (1965–84). In 1951, as a senatorial assistant, he worked with Mitchell on Senate rules changes and measures to protect black service members from violence.

Edge, Walter Evans (1873–1956), (R-N.J.), newspaper owner and publisher; owner of an advertising agency; governor of New Jersey (1917–19, 1944–47); U.S. senator (1919–29); U.S. ambassador to France (1929–33). During his second term as governor (April 16, 1945), Edge signed into law New Jersey's state FEPC.

Edwards, Edward William (1878–1954), printing press operator and union official; secretary (1916–28) and president (1928–30), Allied Printing Trades Council; member, New York State Industrial Board (1927–45); commissioner (1945–53) and chair (1951–53), New York State Commission against Discrimination (1951–53). In 1947, Mitchell conferred with Edwards regarding the plight of black merchant marine officers who were forced out of particular vessels because the white officers did not wish to sail with them.

Edwards, India Taylor Walker (1895–1990), journalist and editor and Democratic national committeewoman; director, Women's Sector (1944–50) and vice chairman (1950–56), DNC. She was the first female candidate to have her name placed in nomination for office by a mainstream national political party (for vice president at the 1952 Democratic Convention); she also pressured President Truman to appoint a woman to the federal bench. In 1952, representing the DNC, she met with representatives from civil rights organizations interested in finding out more about how the federal government worked.

Edwards, Leverett (1902–89), lawyer and labor mediator; member, National Mediation Board (1950–70, with periods as chair). After his service, he became an arbitrator for the former Braniff Airlines and worked as a freelance labor management mediator well into his eighties. In 1952, Mitchell conferred with Edwards concerning any jurisdiction the National Mediation Board may have had over collective-bargaining contracts under the Railway Labor Act.

Eisenhower, Dwight David (1890–1969) (R-Kans.), head of operations to U.S. chief of staff (1939–42); commander, U.S. forces in Europe (1942–44); allied supreme commander (1944–45); chief of staff, U.S. Army (1945–48); president, Columbia University (1949–51); commander of NATO (1951–52); president of the United States (1953–61). Although he opposed the *Brown* decision, he otherwise supported civil rights. During his presidency, the desegregation of the armed services was completed when the army desegregated in 1954.

Elfenbein, Elsie (1899–1988), executive director of National Council of Jewish Women to 1957; in 1943, she served as a member of the executive board of the NCPFEPC.

Ellender, Allen Joseph (1890–1972) (D-La.), lawyer; city attorney, Houma, Louisiana (1913–15); district attorney, Terrebonne Parish, Louisiana (1915–16); delegate, Louisiana constitutional convention (1921); member, state house of representatives (1924–36); U.S. senator (1936–72). An avowed racist, Ellender was, surprisingly, anti-McCarthy and not a Dixiecrat.

Ellstein, Jack (1901–86), union official with the Amalgamated Clothing Workers; state legislator, serving the First District of Wayne County in the Michigan State Assembly (1945–46); executive director, Detroit Dry Cleaners and Laundry Institute; in 1946, he proposed legislation to create a four-main FEPC.

Embree, Edwin Rogers (1883–1950), sociologist, author and foundations executive; secretary (1917–24), director, Division of Studies (1924–27), and vice president (1927–28), Rockefeller Foundation; president, Rosenwald Fund (1928–48). He initiated programs designed to improve conditions in southern rural schools and worked to improve the plight of the black tenant farmer and sharecropper by focusing national attention on harmful effects of the system on both blacks and whites. In 1943, he was named to the executive board of NCPFEPC.

Emory (Emery), Gus (1890–1951), locomotive fireman who, on January 23, 1932 in Canton, Mississippi, was shot and wounded by whites coveting his job.

Engel, Irving Morris (1891–1978), lawyer; chair, Executive Committee of the American Jewish Committee. In 1952, Engel was one of a number of prominent businesspeople, labor leaders, and government officials named by President Truman to serve on his Committee on Government Contract Compliance. Among their duties was overseeing Truman's Fair Employment Practices program.

Epstein, Benjamin R. (1913–83), national director, ADL (1947–78); and prolific writer on topics involving cross-cultural and interracial interaction in American life, including a 1964 study of right-wing hate groups (*Danger on the Right*, with Arnold Forster) that highlighted Bryant Bowles' NAAWP. In 1950, Epstein was part of a delegation from the NECRM that met with President Truman.

Epstein, Henry (1895–1961), lawyer and judge; U.S. Navy veteran of World War I; New York state solicitor general (1932–42); chief counsel, FEPC (1942–43), resigning in protest of its policies; deputy mayor, City of New York (1953–55); New York state supreme court justice, First Judicial District (1955–61). In 1959, he ruled that the Arabian-American Oil Company

(Aramco) could not question job applicants about their religious affiliation or beliefs; upon appeal, his ruling was upheld.

Ericksen, Edward William (1901–74), tugboat operator in New York Harbor for over thirty years. In 1953, he wished to build and operate a six unit motel in La Plata, Maryland, but contracted with Bryant W. Bowles, Jr. of Bryant Roofing and Home Improvement of Baltimore to construct the units. Before the work was completed, Bowles defaulted to the tune of $5,000 and Ericksen won a judgment against him. However Bowles failed to adhere to the repayment schedule set by the court.

Estell, Ernest C., Sr. (1905–83), pastor, St. John's Baptist Church, Dallas, Texas; member, Dallas branch, NAACP; and advocate for the desegregation of public housing in Dallas. In 1943, he testified before a congressional subcommittee contemplating an anti-lynching bill.

Ethridge, Mark F. (1896–1981), publisher of the *Louisville Courier-Journal*; member and first chairman of FEPC, 1941. He was an observer of elections in Bulgaria and Romania in 1945, and he warned the world of undemocratic processes and Russian interference in Eastern Europe. He was also a native Southerner who was a moderate on desegregation.

Evans, James Carmichael (1900–88), electrical and construction engineer; vocational training associate, WMC (1941–43); assistant civilian aide to the secretary of war (1943–47); civilian assistant to the secretary of defense (1947–49). He composed a list of black scientists qualified to work for the AEC. He was also a source for information regarding black casualties during World War II and decorations awarded black service members during the Korean War.

Ewing, Oscar Ross (1899–1980), acting chair, DNC (1946); head, FESA (1947–52). During his tenure at the FESA, he appointed a committee to review discriminatory practices and segregation in the BOASI. He also ended the exclusion of black doctors from white hospitals in Washington, D.C., and led a fruitless effort for federally financed health insurance.

Fahy (Fahey), Charles (1892–1979), lawyer; counsel, NLRB (1935–40); U.S. solicitor general (1941–45); chairman, President's Committee on Equality of Treatment and Opportunity in the Armed Services (PCETOAS) (Fahy Committee) (1948–50); judge, U.S. Circuit Court of Appeals (1949-67).

Fairless, Benjamin Franklin (1890–1962), president (1938–52) and chair and CEO (1952–55), U.S. Steel Corporation. He opposed a wage increase in the steel industry as threatening profitability in the face of price regulations. The failure of negotiations with union representatives led to the steel strike of 1952 and President Truman's temporary seizure of the steel mills.

Falls, Lillian Steele Proctor (1899–1988), complainant. In 1943, traveling South by train via the Southern Railway with her sisters Mrs. Vashti Brown and Mrs. Muriel Holcombe, all three refused to comply with the Jim Crow transportation laws and were arrested and fined. With the aid of the NAACP, they lodged a complaint with the Interstate Commerce Commission. In 1950, she and her husband, Dr. Arthur G. Falls, attempted to purchase a home in an all-white suburb of Chicago, but the sale was blocked by their potential neighbors; it would take the Fallses three years of litigation, but they would ultimately be successful and move into their home, where they would live until Mrs. Falls' death thirty-five years later.

Fambro, Rev. William Henry (1884–1986), plasterer, paperhanger, and Baptist minister; member, Cleveland, Ohio, NAACP branch. In 1951, he went to Washington, D.C., to protest the proposed Winstead amendment to the Universal Military Training bill.

Farley, Rear Adm. Joseph Francis "Uncle Joe," Jr. (1889–1974), commandant, U.S. Coast Guard (1946–49). In 1947, Mitchell wrote him about black merchant marine officers who were barred from shipping out from seaports in the South.

Farmer, James Leonard, Jr. (1920–98), activist; race relations secretary, Fellowship of Reconciliation (1941–45); national chairman (1942–44, 1950) and national director (1961–66), CORE;

student field secretary, League of Industrial Democracy (1950–54); professor, social welfare, Lincoln University (Pennsylvania) (1966-68); assistant secretary, HEW (1969–71); executive director, Coalition of American Public Employees (1977–82); professor, Mary Washington College (1982–92). A student of Gandhi, Farmer, with his colleague Bayard Rustin, advocated nonviolent direct action to affect lasting social change.

Farrand, Brig. Gen. Edward Gilbert (1905–86), commander, Fort Hood, Texas (1953, 1960–61). He denied charges that he was failing to comply with President Eisenhower's program for ending segregation in the military.

Fassett, Elmer N. (1920–2002), veteran. In 1951, under Earle Fisher's direction, the NAACP won reinstatement for Fassett and other veterans receiving educational benefits under the GI Bill who had been removed from a plumbing course after a disturbance in class and forbidden to take any other training because of this incident.

Feinen, Herbert J. (1905–78), Du Pont Company representative. In 1951, he met with NAACP representatives regarding efforts to ensure nonsegregation and nondiscrimination at a hydrogen bomb facility in South Carolina.

Fenton, Francis Patrick (1895–1948), Boston labor leader; director of organization, CIO (1939–47); international labor representative, AFL (1947–48). He was a member of the NAACP National Labor Committee.

Ferebee, Dr. Dorothy Celeste Boulding (1890–1980), physician, educator, and administrator. She succeeded Mary McLeod Bethune as president of the NCNW (1949–53). As a young doctor, she established the Southeast Neighborhood House in Washington, D.C., to provide health care for the area's residents and the Southeast Neighborhood Society, with a playground and day care; her activism in the community was noted when she was appointed director of health services at Howard University Medical School (1949–68). In 1953, she met with Mitchell and Albert M. Cole to review and discuss the federal government's housing policy.

Ferguson, Garland Sevier, Jr. (1878–1963), lawyer; legal counsel for Southern Railway until appointed to the FTC by President Coolidge in 1929. In 1947, Ferguson met with Mitchell to discuss UPW charges that the FTC had racially discriminated against black and Jewish OPA employees.

Ferguson, Homer Samuel (1889–1982) (R-Mich.), lawyer and professor; U.S. senator (1943–55); ambassador to the Philippines (1955–56); judge (1956–71) and senior judge (1971–76), U.S. Court of Military Appeals. Although an opponent of most Fair Deal legislation, he introduced antilynching and anti–poll tax legislation while serving in the Senate.

Ferguson, Perry T. (1906–90), member, BCSP. He was involved in the organization of the MOWC, 1941.

Ferrier, Mervin J. (1919–2002), veteran and postal worker. He was an NAACP complainant against employment discrimination at the New Orleans Post Office (1947).

Ferrouillet, Wilbur F. (1923–84), veteran and postal worker. He was an NAACP complainant against employment discrimination at the New Orleans Post Office (1947).

Findley [Fendley], Elsworth (1914–85), member, NAAWP. He was involved in Baltimore public school antidesegregation activity in 1954.

Finletter, Thomas Knight (1893–1980), lawyer; special assistant on international communications to U.S. Secretary of State Cordell Hull; executive director, OFEC (1943–44); consultant at UN conference (1945); chairman, Air Policy Commission (1947–49); Secretary of the Air Force (1950–53); ambassador to NATO (1961–65). In 1951, Mitchell met with Finletter concerning the inability of black airmen at Walker Air Force Base in Roswell, New Mexico, to attend classes mandated by the Air Force but held off base at the New Mexico Military Institute where segregation was practiced.

Fisher, Adrian Sanford (1914–83), lawyer, diplomat, and law school dean; clerk for Supreme Court Justices Louis D. Brandeis and Felix Frankfurter; assistant chief, Foreign Funds Control Division, U.S. State Department (1940–42); member, Legal Affairs Section, U.S. War Department (1942, 1944–48); solicitor, U.S. Department of Commerce (1948–49); legal adviser, U.S. Department of State (1949–53); commissioner, President's Commission on Immigration and Naturalization (1952–61); department director, U.S. Arms Control and Disarmanent Agency (1961–68); dean, Georgetown University Law Center (1969–75); Francis Cabell Brown Professor of International Law, Georgetown (1977–80). In 1950, Fisher conferred with Mitchell and others regarding the wording of the civil rights provision of the Bogota Treaty with Latin America.

Fisher, Earle Wells (1920–), research assistant, NAACP Washington bureau (1950–53); regional director, OFHEO (1960–88). An army veteran and Boston University Law School graduate, he prepared newsletters, voting records, and other items for the Washington bureau.

Fleeson, Doris (1901–70), first nationally syndicated female newspaper columnist, writing for the *New York Daily News;* also served as a war correspondent for *Woman's Home Companion* magazine. Her comment that U.S. ratification of the Declaration of Rights as an international agreement would "override the civil rights blockade set up in Congress by the South" was approvingly quoted by Walter White in a 1950 radio broadcast.

Fleming, George James (1904–90), newspaperman, social scientist, educator and activist; born in (then Danish) Virgin Islands. He edited the traditionally Republican black newspaper the *Philadelphia Tribune,* was a member of Gunnar Myrdal's research group on race in America, and headed the first Chicago regional office of FEPC (1941–42). As an FEPC investigator in El Paso, Texas (1942–43), he investigated charges of discrimination against Chicanos in copper mines of New Mexico and Arizona. Examiner in charge, Detroit office, FEPC (1943); director, Region III [Philadelphia Office], FEPC (1943–45); race relations secretary, AFSC (1945–50); subsequently editor of the *Amsterdam News;* and professor of political science at Morgan State College (now University). In 1943, he reported to the NAACP about his experiences with several white people on a Pullman sleeping car on the run between Atlanta and Washington, D.C.

Flemming, Arthur Sherwood (1905–96), chief of labor supply, OPM; member, WMC; member, USCSC (1939–48); president, Ohio Wesleyan University (1948–51); assistant to director (1951–53) and director (1953–58), ODM; secretary, HEW (1958–60); chair, WHCA; chair, USCA. In 1951, the NAACP conferred with him on the enforcement of nondiscrimination clauses in government contracts.

Foley, Raymond Michael (1890–1975), commissioner, FHA (1945–47); head, HHFA (1947–53). He conferred with the NAACP on ending federal support for segregation and discrimination in federally supported housing.

Follin, James Wightman, Sr. (1892–1987), civil engineer and urban renewal and public housing expert. In 1954, as director of Slum Clearance and Redevelopment Section, HHFA, he challenged Mitchell's claim that people in Birmingham, Alabama would be adversely affected by an upcoming urban redevelopment project. Retired as director, Urban Renewal Agency.

Forbes, Russell LeRoy (1896–1957), college professor; secretary, National Municipal League (1928–33); commissioner, New York City Department of Purchasing (1934–41); deputy administrator, Defense Materials Procurement Agency, GSA (1949–53). In 1952, Forbes was one of a number of prominent businesspeople, labor leaders, and government officials named by President Truman to serve on his Committee on Government Contract Compliance. Among their duties was overseeing Truman's Fair Employment Practices program.

Ford, Rev. Jerry Wilburn (1921–79), minister, AMEC; president, Albuquerque, New Mexico, branch, NAACP (1947–50). In 1949, he successfully challenged right-to-work laws in New Mexico.

Ford, Peyton (1911–71), assistant and deputy U.S. attorney general (1947–53). He informed Mitchell on the investigation of killings of African Americans by police in Alabama.

Ford, Vernon (1924–94), regional director, UMWA, Baltimore area. Mitchell conferred with him on discriminatory staff reductions by Standard Wholesale, Phosphate, and Acid Works. These reductions were in violation of a union contract.

Fortin, Maurice A. (1926–), veteran. He was a postal worker in New Orleans whom the post office sought to terminate, in violation of the Veterans Preference Act of 1944. He then sought employment as a regular postal clerk or letter carrier but was denied a position despite his high civil service test score. In 1947, he became one of the NAACP's official complainants against the New Orleans Post Office.

Fox, Colonel, executive director, NYSCAD. In 1948, Mitchell requested information from Fox as to how NYSCAD handled situations where discrimination was alleged to have happened, specifically requesting how the agency determined discrimination in those instances.

Fox, Ida (1910–78), lawyer and activist; legislative assistant to Congressman Emanuel Celler (D-N.Y.) from 1938; legislative representative, NCPFEPC (1944–46); executive secretary, Committee for Racial Democracy (1946-48).

Fox, Mott Lavern (1891–1971), union representative. The NAACP accused Fox, a BRC representative, of misleading African American recruits regarding the BRC's policy on black membership.

Frank, Dr. Jerome David (1909–2005), psychiatrist; professor, Johns Hopkins School of Medicine. He supported the NAACP's position that segregation of mental patients in veterans' hospitals was unnecessary.

Frank, Murray (1908–77), writer and activist. As director of the NSWA, he was present at the organizational meeting of the LCCR in 1951.

Frankfurter, Felix (1882–1965), lawyer, educator, author, theorist and associate justice of the U.S. Supreme Court; professor of law, Harvard University (1920–38); associate justice, U.S. Supreme Court (1938–62); co-founder, ACLU (1920). Joseph L. Rauh, who drafted Executive Order 8802, and who would be prominent in civil rights activity during the 1950s and beyond, was one of Frankfurter's law clerks and would cite him as a positive influence on his future career.

Franklin, Chester Arthur (1881–1955), newspaper executive. From the age of eleven, he had worked in some fashion in the newspaper business; editor and publisher, (Denver, Colorado) *Statesman*, later *Star* (1901–13); editor and publisher, *Kansas City Call* (1919–55). In 1943, he was one of sixteen representatives of the black press who signed a telegram protesting the FEPC cancellation of hearings designed to review racial discrimination in the railroad industry.

Fraser, Thaddeus G. (1896–1976), secretary, Charleston, South Carolina, NAACP branch. He initiated action against segregated facilities in the Charleston Navy Yard.

Freeman, Emma, assistant to the director, NAACP to May of 1953 when she resigned; in 1951, she assisted in the organizing of the LCCR.

Freeman, James, complainant. In 1953, he boarded a bus in Leonardtown, Maryland, and was arrested for violating Jim Crow transportation laws.

Freeman, William A. (1865–1940), postmaster of Jackson, Mississippi (1928–31). He consistently hired blacks as carriers and whites as clerks.

Funk, John Benjamin (1905–93), Maryland state legislator (1935–46); Maryland secretary of state (1947); Maryland chief engineer. In 1949, he pledged nondiscrimination in employment on public projects.

Gaddis, Callaway (1885–1964), of Houston, Texas. He was a railroad worker employed by the Texas and New Orleans Railroad who was forced by the International Association of Machinists to join a segregated union. Gaddis lodged a complaint with the NAACP, but they were unable to do anything about it at that time, despite attempts by Mitchell to bring up the topic before a congressional committee concerning the Taft-Hartley Act.

Gaines, Lloyd Lionel (1911–39?), named plaintiff in *State ex rel. Gaines v. The University of Missouri,* where the U.S. Supreme Court ruled that, as the states must accord equal protection of the laws to all citizens within their jurisdiction, racial discrimination could not be enforced under state law unless equal facilities were provided (the "separate but equal" doctrine as found in *Plessy v. Ferguson*). Lloyd Gaines had applied to the university's law school and was turned down due to his race. As there was no state-supported law school for black Americans in Missouri, the court determined that he would have to be admitted to the university. Soon after the decision, Gaines left his home to buy stamps and was never seen again. Although rumors abounded that he was abducted by a carful of whites and subsequently killed, no hard evidence was ever submitted to either support or dismiss that story.

Galarza, Ernesto, Jr. (1905–84), educator, author and activist. He was born in the state of Nayarit in Mexico and, with his family, emigrated to California, where they worked as migrant farm laborers. He won a scholarship to Stanford University and would eventually earn a doctorate from Columbia. Chief, labor section, Pan-American Union (1936–47); vice president, National Farm Laborers Union, AFL (1947–63). He is best known today for his 1971 autobiography *Barrio Boy.* In 1944 he testified before the House Labor Committee in favor of S. 2048, a bill designed to strengthen the FEPC.

Gallagher, Dr. Buell Gordon (1904–78), Congregationalist minister, professor, and author; president, Talladega College (1933–43); member, NAACP National Board of Directors (1934–76); vice chair, NAACP (1971–76); assistant commissioner, USOE (1950–52); president, City College of New York (1952–61, 1962–69). He attended a February 1954 meeting with U.S. commissioner of education Samuel M. Brownell on the impending *Brown* decision.

Gallon, James, Sr. (1900–80) and James Gallon Jr. (1924–2003), victims of mob violence. In 1951, both men, black residents of Greensboro, Florida, were beaten by a mob after a dispute with a white store owner. The NAACP obtained employment for them in the Washington, D.C., area and sent data on the case to the Florida NAACP for use in its antilynching campaign.

Galvin, Maj. Gen. Michael Joseph (1907–63), U.S. undersecretary of labor (1949–53). In 1952, he was one of a number of prominent businesspeople, labor leaders, and government employees named by President Truman to serve on his Committee on Government Contract Compliance. Their duties included overseeing Truman's Fair Employment Practices program.

Gandhi, Mohandas Karamchand "Mahatma" (1869–1948), lawyer and activist. He was the well-known advocate of nonviolent protest and civil disobedience whose tactics were utilized by A. Philip Randolph in his planning for the proposed March on Washington in 1941.

Gantt, John P. (1926–81), complainant against Bryant W. Bowles, Jr., in a civil action in Baltimore, Maryland, in 1953.

Garfinkel, Herbert (1920–2003), educator; professor of political science at the University of Michigan who wrote about the work of the NAACP in the time of World War II and the postwar world in order to insure equal legal rights under the law for all.

Garrity, Margaret (1918–83), social worker; executive secretary, Catholic Conference on Industrial Problems (1941–48); subsequently director of research project studying the plight of migrant farm workers for the Office of Economic Opportunity, as well as staff member, President's Committee on Government Contracts (1954–56); president, National Association of Intergroup Relations (1957–58). She represented the National Catholic Welfare Conference at a meeting of a subcommittee of the Committee on Government Contracts in November 1953.

Gartland, Joseph Francis (1881–1949), postal worker and postal inspector; chief, Operations Board, Post Office Department; director of budget and administrative planning, Post Office Department. He participated in negotiations to resolve FEPC complaints against various post offices.

Garvey, Marcus Moziah (1887–1940), black nationalist, orator and author. A native of St. Ann's Bay, Jamaica, Garvey rose from humble beginnings to become the president of and the motivating force behind the Universal Negro Improvement Association (UNIA), a political and social organization that advocated black self-determination and provided blacks with a sense of nationalism.

Gates, Ralph Fensler (1893–1978) (R-Ind.); governor of Indiana (1941–47). Mitchell appealed to him for assistance in preventing discrimination by USES offices after its units were returned to state control in 1946.

Gibbs, William Brown, Jr. (1909–87), African American schoolteacher and acting principal in Montgomery County, Maryland. In 1936, with support of the NAACP, he sued the county school administration for pay equal to other school principals in the county. Although he did win (1938), the school authorities found some "irregularities" with Gibbs' license to serve as an acting principal and removed him from his position. He never again taught school in Maryland.

Gibson, Truman Kella, Jr. (1912–2005), African American lawyer from Chicago; member of executive committee, Chicago Branch, NAACP; assistant to Judge William H. Hastie, civilian aide to the U.S. secretary of war (1940–43); succeeded Judge Hastie in February 1943 and served to November 1945. In 1944, as a member of the War Department's Advisory Committee on Negro Troop Policies, Gibson met with Walter White to discuss criticisms and recommendations in his two reports on black troops in the European Theater and the North African Theater of Operations. He was later member of Truman's Advisory Committee on Universal Military Training (1946); winner in 1947 of Medal of Merit Award for Civilians; boxing manager and promoter and director and secretary of Joe Louis Enterprises.

Gilbert, Leon Aaron, Jr. (1920–99), army lieutenant. A member of the all-black 24th U.S. Infantry Regiment during the Korean War, he was sentenced to death for refusing to obey the command of a white officer to return with his men to a dangerous position. Following legal challenges by the NAACP, his sentence was reduced by President Truman to twenty years, of which he served five before being released on parole.

Gill, Warren Calavan (1912–87) (R-Ore.), lawyer, businessman, and Oregon state legislator. His appointment as a U.S. attorney in 1953 was successfully opposed by the NAACP, which noted his opposition to state civil rights legislation.

Gillem, Maj. Gen. Alvan Cullem, Jr. (1887–1973), U.S. Army. He headed a committee that in 1948 would submit the *Gillem Report* (*War Circular Number 124*), a policy review of the role of the African American in the post-World War II U.S. Armed Forces.

Gillette, Guy Mark (1879–1973) (D-Iowa), lawyer; Iowa state legislator (1912–16); U.S. senator (1936–45, 1949–55). A veteran of the Spanish-American War and World War I, he was an independent-minded Democrat known for his oratorical skills. As chair of the Senate Subcommittee on Privileges and Elections, he informed Mitchell that there would be an effort to investigate red- and race-baiting tactics in Democratic primaries for 1950 senatorial elections in North Carolina and Florida. He also supported changes in the cloture rule.

Gilliam, Jerry Othenia (1888–1968), real estate broker; railway postal clerk (1913–47); president, NAPE (1934–36); executive secretary, Norfolk, Virginia, branch, NAACP. He facilitated desegregation of facilities at the Norfolk navy yard and other naval shore establishments in the South. In 1948, he was a Progressive Party candidate for Congress.

Gilligan, Fr. Francis James (1898–1997), Roman Catholic priest and author; chair, GICM (1943–55); member, Board of Directors, St. Paul Urban League; member, NAACP National Labor Committee. He was a leader in the drive for the passage of state fair employment practice legislation. He befriended Mitchell when the latter was executive director of the St. Paul Urban League.

Gingrich, Adm. John Edward (1897–1960), chief of security, AEC. The NAACP conferred with him on the establishment of fair hearings procedures for persons accused of disloyalty.

Givens, Willard Earl (1885–1971), educator; executive secretary, National Education Association (1935–52). In 1951, Givens invited Mitchell to appear at a National Education Association conference on federal aid to education. After attending the conference, Mitchell noted that representatives from a number of other organizations attended and that some of those organizations would oppose the NAACP's advocacy of a "no segregation clause" in legislation involving federal aid to education.

Goldberg, Arthur Joseph (1908–90), lawyer and judge; general counsel, CIO; U.S. secretary of labor (1961–62); associate justice, U.S. Supreme Court (1962–65); U.S. ambassador to the United Nations (1965–68). In 1950, he challenged Sen. Robert A. Taft (R-Ohio) at a Senate committee hearing concerning whether union workers would be forced to accept "sweatshop made work" (that is, work produced by nonunion shops) under injunction.

Goldberg, Dorothy Kurgans (1910–89), artist, author, lecturer and clubwoman; she married Arthur J. Goldberg in 1931 and they had two children. In 1944, as the legislative representative of the National Women's Trade Union League of America, she appeared before the House Labor Committee to testify in favor of S. 2048.

Goldstein, Sidney Emanuel (1879–1955), religious leader; assistant (1907–49) and chief rabbi (1949–55), the Free Synagogue, New York City. He was a well-known pacifist and social activist who was at one time chairman of the War Resisters League. He was a pioneer in the field of marriage counseling and family planning, and at one time served as a member of the national board of directors of Planned Parenthood. In 1943, he was named to the first executive board of the NCPFEPC.

Goldwater, Barry Morris (1909–98) (R-Ariz.), businessman; Phoenix city councilman (1949–52); U.S. senator (1953–65, 1969–87); Republican Party presidential nominee (1964). He believed that federal civil rights legislation violated both states' rights and the individual's freedom to discriminate. He also opposed federal aid to education, minimum wage laws, and tax reductions for low-income families. However, he ended segregation in his department stores, and he helped eliminate segregation in Phoenix schools and restaurants and in the Arizona National Guard.

Goodgame, John Washington, Jr. (1894–1962), pastor, Sixth Avenue Baptist Church, Birmingham, Alabama (1938–62). He was one of a group of Alabama civic and religious leaders who traveled to Washington in 1953 to express their disapproval of the use of federal funds for a segregated health center.

Goodwin, Robert Clifford (1906–99), director, Region V (Cleveland), WMC (1942–45); executive director, WMC (1945); director, USES (1945–48); director and later administrator, BES, Department of Labor (1948–69); executive director, ODMA (1950–53); associate manpower administrator for unemployment insurance, Manpower Administration (1969–74); associate vice president, ICES (1974–79). Mitchell conferred unsuccessfully with him on preventing discrimination by the USES after its return to state control. He was a consistent roadblock to ending discrimination in employment in the defense industry and government.

Gordon, Arnold (1889–1963), immigrant, born in Nassau, Bahamas, British West Indies. In 1951, the Boston branch of the NAACP asserted that his naturalization petition was delayed by the government because of his NAACP membership.

Gordon, George C. (1912–94), chair, ECRC (1948); president, NAACP New England Regional Conference. He reported on the investigation of complaints about discriminatory recruitment in Pennsylvania by companies based in Connecticut.

Gordon, Walter Arthur (1894–1976), lawyer and judge. A graduate of the University of California at Berkeley and of its law school at Boalt Hall, he, at times, served as a Berkeley city policeman, a college football coach, and as counsel for the Golden State Insurance Corporation, while maintaining a private legal practice in Oakland, California. He served as an officer of the Berkeley branch of the NAACP and, in 1943, Walter White contacted him and nine other branch secretaries representing the most effective branches to start protesting War Manpower Commissioner Paul V. McNutt's decision to cancel the FEPC hearings on racial discrimination in the railroad industry. Gordon subsequently served as governor of the U.S. Virgin Islands (1955–58) and as judge of the U.S. district court for the Virgin Islands (1958–76).

Gossett, Ed Lee (1902–90) (D-Tex.), lawyer and judge; U.S. representative (1939–51). He cosponsored the Lodge-Gossett resolution, which sought to amend the Constitution to abolish the Electoral College and split the electoral vote of each state in accordance with the popular vote. The NAACP opposed the resolution on the grounds that one of its chief purposes was to destroy the political effectiveness of blacks and other minorities holding a "balance of power" in pivotal states. He also called for tougher immigration restrictions.

Graham, Frank Porter (1886–1972) (D-N.C.), educator, college administrator, and lawyer; professor of history (1915–30) and president (1930–49), University of North Carolina; U.S. senator (1949–50); mediator, UN (1951–67). Mitchell quoted Graham as saying in 1950, as defense manpower administrator, that 8 million workers would be needed in defense plants; to meet that challenge, he called for a greater utilization of the national workforce.

Granger, Lester Blackwell (1896–1976), social worker and professor; assistant executive secretary, National Urban League (1941–61). The son of a doctor from Barbados, he promoted trade unionism among African American workers and desegregation of the military.

Grant, David Marshall (1903–85), lawyer; leader, SLMWM (1942–45); leader, ICSL (1945–c. 1960). In the 1930s, he pioneered African American picketing against stores accused of economic discrimination. During the postwar years, he challenged Jim Crow in interstate transportation and served as a lawyer for the NAACP in desegregation cases.

Granville, Robert Richey (1916–2005), army officer; FBI agent (1940–52); field supervisor for Soviet espionage (1946–52); executive director, President's Commission on Government Contract Compliance (1952–53). As an FBI agent, Granville arrested accused spies Ethel and Julius Rosenberg, David Greenglass, and Judith Coplon. As executive director of the Committee on Government Contract Compliance, Granville received a letter from Mitchell mentioning the possibility that a "colored" resident of another country could be subjected to the officially sanctioned segregation of the Norfolk navy yard.

Graves, Lemuel Eugene, Jr. (1915–), journalist, *Pittsburgh Courier.* In 1949, he criticized Mitchell's refusal to appear at a brief hearing on the repeal of the Taft-Hartley Act.

Gray, Maj. Gen. Carl Raymond, Jr. (1889–1955), as brigadier general, in charge of railway transportation, Allied European Theater (1942); made major general in 1945; administrator, Veterans Administration (1947–53). Gray's impending resignation was rumored in 1950.

Upon hearing this rumor, Mitchell was determined to quickly present reports of discrimination in the VA to President Truman so that Gray's successor would be prepared to act immediately.

Green, Dwight Herbert (1897–1958) (R-Ill.), lawyer; U.S. district attorney for Chicago (1932–35); Illinois governor (1941–49). He was one of the governors to whom Mitchell sent letters in 1946, urging them to end discrimination in USES offices when they were returned to state control. He pledged a special study of the issue.

Green, John (1896–1957), president, IUMSWA (1935–51); board member, NCPFEPC; founding member, ADA. In 1947, he expressed his appreciation of the NAACP's support of the union during its strike against the Bethlehem Steel Shipbuilding Co.

Green, Theodore Francis (1867–1966) (D-R.I.), lawyer and businessman; Rhode Island state legislator (1907); governor (1933–36); U.S. senator (1937–61). A supporter of the Fair Deal, he backed anti–poll tax legislation, Senate rules changes that would limit filibusters, and legislation to protect service members from violence.

Green, William (1873–1952), Ohio leader of UMWA and AFL; president, AFL (1924–52); member, FEPC (1941–46). He helped secure passage of New Deal labor legislation, including the Norris–La Guardia Act of 1932, the National Labor Relations Act of 1935, and the Fair Labor Standards Act of 1938. In 1950, Mitchell urged that he be contacted to oppose legislation seeking to block integration of the Treasury Department's Bureau of Engraving.

Greenberg, Jack (1920–), lawyer; assistant counsel (1949–61) and director-counsel (1961–84), NAACP, Inc.; professor of law, Columbia University School of Law (1984–). Among the many NAACP/NAACP LDF cases he handled or in which he participated, he was on the brief in *Brown v. Board of Education of Topeka.* He represented plaintiffs in, among others, *Griggs v. Duke Power Company,* where decisions in getting employment and job promotion based on the results of tests with discriminatory impact were held to be unconstitutional, and *Furman v. Georgia,* where the death penalty was held to be cruel and unusual punishment under the Eighth Amendment.

Greene, Dr. Harry J. (1900–84), president, Philadelphia branch, NAACP (resigned in 1940); president, Pennsylvania State Conference of NAACP Branches; member, executive committee, Philadelphia branch, NAACP; member, NAACP National Board of Directors (elected in 1950); member, NAACP National Health Committee (appointed in 1953). In 1949, he was the NAACP representative on the Pennsylvania State Committee for FEPC.

Greene, Henry R. (1905–?), veteran. He was dropped from his temporary job in the New Orleans Post Office, allegedly because of high blood pressure incurred during his war service. Reinstated, he was denied permanent employment despite good test scores, even as whites scoring lower were being hired. In 1947, he became one of the NAACP's complainants against the New Orleans Post Office.

Greene, Walter Leigh (1891–1981), deputy commissioner and chair of finance committee, FHA (1934–52); commissioner, FHA (1952–54). In 1952, the NAACP conferred with him on desegregation of public housing.

Gregg, John Andrew (1877–1953), African Methodist Episcopal minister; bishop, AMEC (1924–53); declined appointment as president, Howard University (1926). In 1943 he was selected by the Fraternal Council of Negro Churches to travel in the war zones to preach and visit black troops; in 1945 he was named to serve on the reorganized board of directors of NCPFEPC.

Grey, John, complainant against Bryant W. Bowles, Jr., in a civil action in Baltimore, Maryland (1953).

Griffin, Aubrey Chester, Sr. (1886–1975), postmaster of Jackson, Mississippi (1938–56). He maintained a policy of refusing to appoint blacks to any post office positions.

Griffith, Thomas Lee, Jr. (1902–86), lawyer and judge; president, Los Angeles NAACP branch (1935–50); later judge, municipal court of Los Angeles (1953–69); and California superior court judge for Los Angeles County (1969–75). He was involved with court decisions and the passage of legislation barring the use of restrictive covenants on deeds of sale of real estate. He was also successful in forcing the Pasadena Department of Parks to change their policies so that blacks and Mexicans were allowed in the municipal pools every day and not just on Wednesdays. In 1943, Walter White contacted him and nine other branch secretaries representing the most effective branches to start protesting War Manpower Commissioner Paul V. McNutt's decision to cancel the FEPC hearings on racial discrimination in the railroad industry.

Grigsby, Ralph Deloss (1913–86), member, Terre Haute, Indiana, NAACP branch. In 1951, he went to Washington, D.C., to protest the proposed Winstead amendment to the Universal Military Training bill.

Grimke, Archibald Henry (1849–1930), attorney, civil servant, activist, writer, newspaper editor; U.S. consul, Dominican Republic (1894–98); president, American Negro Academy (1903–19); president, Washington D.C. branch, NAACP (1913–25); recipient, Spingarn Medal (1919). Born a slave in Charleston, South Carolina, and a graduate of Lincoln University and Harvard Law School, Grimke built the Washington D.C. branch into the largest in the country. He was the leader in the NAACP's lobbying efforts in Congress and other federal agencies attempting to retard the progress of segregation due to the policies of the Woodrow Wilson administration, as well as fighting discrimination in the nation's capital itself.

Grove, Rev. Eugene T. (1912–87), member, Baltimore NAACP branch. In 1951, he went to Washington, D.C., to protest the proposed Winstead amendment to the Universal Military Training bill.

Grovey, Richard Randolph (1890–1961), barber, educator, union organizer and activist. A graduate of what is now Huston-Tillotson College, Grovey taught school and served as a school principal before moving to Houston, Texas, and opening a barber shop. He was involved in the organization of the Third Ward Civic Club and the Harris County Negro Democratic Committee, and would soon challenge the segregated state Democratic primary. In *Grovey v. Townsend* (*295 US 45* [1935]), the U.S. Supreme Court, in a unanimous decision, held that the exclusion of blacks from the Democratic primary by party resolution did not qualify as state action under either the Fourteenth or Fifteenth Amendments to the Constitution. In 1943, he testified before a congressional committee regarding an anti-lynching bill.

Gruening, Ernest (1887–1974) (D-Ark.), journalist and editor; official, Department of the Interior (1934–39); member, AIHC (1938–42); governor, Alaska Territory (1939–52); elected senator from Alaska Territory in 1955, acting as advocate of Alaska statehood (1955–59); U.S. senator (1959–69). Known as "the father of Alaska statehood," he responded to NAACP complaints made in 1950 on discrimination in Alaska.

Guernsey, George Thomas (1909–79), associate director of education, CIO (1945–55). In 1952, he corresponded with Roy Wilkins concerning federal funding for segregated public school systems.

Gunther, John Joseph (1925–97), leader, ADA; executive director, USCM (1961–87). In 1951, he served on a committee working with Mitchell on Senate rules changes.

Gunther, Violet Megrath (1912–88), official (1947–60) and national director (1960–63), ADA; vice chair for government and civil liberties, NCLCH; member, Washington Conference Committee, NCRM of 1950; writer and organizational liaison, LCCR (1963–64); executive secretary, CCAP (1964–66). She participated in a February 1949 civil rights meeting that established the JCCR. In 1951, she served on a committee working with Mitchell on Senate rules changes.

Guttmacher, Dr. Manfred Schanfarber (1898–1966), author and associate professor of clinical psychiatry, University of Maryland; chief medical officer to the Supreme Bench of Baltimore (1930–66). He conducted a psychiatric examination of white supremacist Bryant W. Bowles for the latter's 1954 trial. Years later, he testified during Jack Ruby's murder trial that Ruby was legally insane when he shot Lee Harvey Oswald.

Haas, Rev. Monsignor Francis Joseph (1889–1953), born, educated and ordained in Wisconsin; Ph.D. from Catholic University, 1922; labor mediator; dean, School of Social Sciences, Catholic University; supporter of New Deal and holder of various New Deal posts; chairman of FEPC (1943), resigned October 1943 when appointed bishop of Grand Rapids, Michigan. In 1946, Bishop Haas was appointed to Truman's Committee on Civil Rights and signed the 1947 report *To Secure These Rights.*

Hague, Rear Adm. Wesley McLaren (1897–1982), chief, OIR (1949–52); commandant, ICAF (1952–55). In 1952, as OIR chief, he issued a statement of naval policy on the segregation of naval facilities, asserting that local laws and customs would be followed if to do otherwise would "in the judgment of the Commanding Officer result in definite impediment to productive effort."

Hall, Alvin William (1888–1969), accountant and government employee; senior cost accountant, U.S. Bureau of Ordnance (1918–20); accountant and investigator, U.S. Bureau of Efficiency (1920–22); chief, planning unit, Bureau of Engraving and Printing (1922–25); director, Bureau of Engraving and Printing (1925–50). A native of the Pennsylvania coal regions, Hall worked as a bookkeeper for a grocery store and as paymaster in a coal mine before entering government service during World War I. After World War II, the Bureau of Engraving and Printing constantly discriminated against black apprentice-trainees by denying them the opportunity to continue in the line of work they had been trained for, once they had completed their apprenticeships.

Hall, Cameron Parker (1898–1987), Presbyterian minister and activist. He was serving as executive director of the department of Church and Economic Life of the National Council of Churches of Christ in 1943 when he was named to the board of directors of the NCPFEPC.

Hall, Prince (1735?–1807), abolitionist and organizer of the Masonic order amongst African Americans. He was long thought to have been a native of Barbados, although current scholarship finds no convincing evidence about his place of birth. In 1952, Mitchell commented that, if the McCarran-Walter Act, with its severe restriction on immigration fromthe Caribbean and South America, had been in force when immigrants like Hall entered the United States, they would not have been able to make "notable contributions to the building of our nation."

Halleck, Charles Abraham (1900–86) (R-Ind.), lawyer; U.S. representative (1935–69); House majority leader (1947–49, 1953–55); House minority leader (1959–65). A prime mover behind the Taft-Hartley Act, he was a strong foe of organized labor and a noted conservative. In 1954, however, the majority leader agreed to suspend House rules so that an anti–Jim Crow travel bill could be considered.

Hallock, Adney Lowell (1892–1977), bank executive, educator, and Unitarian layman from Hempstead, N.Y. As president of the Unitarian Fellowship for Social Justice, he was present at the organizational meeting of the LCCR in 1951.

Hamilton, Albert, represented the WDL at the Conference of Cooperating Organizations on July 4, 1942.

Hamilton, Alexander (1758–1804), merchant, lawyer, businessman, and soldier; U.S. secretary of the treasury (1789–1797); born on the island of Nevis. In 1952, Mitchell commented that, if the McCarran-Walter Act, with its severe restriction on immigration from the Caribbean and South America, had been in force when immigrants like Hamilton entered the United States, they would not have been able to make "notable contributions to the building of our nation."

Hannah, John Alfred (1902–91), president, Michigan State University (1941–69); assistant secretary of defense (1953–54); member, PJBDCUS (1954–63, 1969–73); commissioner and chair, USCCR (1955–69). As assistant secretary of defense for manpower, he supported the desegregation of schools on military posts and the desegregation of facilities at naval bases.

Hannegan, Robert Emmet (1903–49) (D-Mo.), local party leader and Truman supporter; commissioner of Internal Revenue (1943–44); Democratic National Committee chairman (1944–45); U. S. postmaster general (1945–47). In 1945, in response to President Truman's seeming lack of support of the FEPC, the NAACP National Board of Directors voted that the Association would hold its next big meetings in St. Louis and Kansas City, the home bases of Hannegan and Truman, respectively.

Hard, James Henry, Jr. (1886–1963), personnel director, Jefferson County, Alabama (1935–42); director of personnel, Treasury Department; fair employment officer, Treasury Department. In 1949, he opposed NAACP efforts to end segregated work arrangements in Treasury Department offices that were moved to Kansas City, Missouri.

Hardin, Walter T., African American organizer for UAW in Chicago and Detroit; subsequently director, interracial commission, UAW (1944–48). He was formerly a member of the IWW and of the Communist Party of the United States as well as an organizer for the UMW in Johnstown, Pennsylvania before World War I. He was considered an especially effective speaker and organizer, and was a featured speaker at the annual National Urban League conference in 1943. He was briefly considered as a potential member of the temporary national executive board of what would eventually become the NCPFEPC.

Hardy, Henry J. (1905–80), farmer and agronomist; county extension agent for Aiken County, South Carolina. Known as a soil conversation expert, he was a member of the Aiken NAACP branch in 1951 when Mitchell visited the area.

Hargrove, John R. (1923–2003), lawyer and judge; first black to receive an appointment as assistant U.S. attorney in Maryland (1955–67); subsequently served as associate justice of the Baltimore municipal court (1968–71); administrative judge, district court of Maryland #1 (1971–74); and associate justice, supreme bench, city of Baltimore (1974–93). In 1951, with Juanita Jackson Mitchell and others, he represented members of the Baltimore branch of the NAACP who filed suit in the United States district court in Washington, D.C. against the Brotherhood of Railway and Steamship Clerks, Freight Handlers, Express and Station Employees, and the Baltimore & Ohio Railroad Company over a violation of the Railway Labor Act where the union forced its black members into segregated union locals.

Harmon, Fred, African-American railroad brakeman, who, on November 7, 1931, in Aberdeen Junction, Mississippi, was shot from ambush and severely wounded, probably by whites who coveted his job.

Harold, James Linwood (1920–2003), veteran and government worker in the War Department Building (Pentagon) in 1942 when he was beaten by Theodore Lee, a guard hired by John McShain Company, a construction firm based in Philadelphia contracted to complete construction and perform renovations on the building. Harold was attacked as he left the War Department cafeteria where he had been refused service. One of the first official acts of the NAACP Washington Bureau was to file Harold's complaint against Lee and the John McShain Company.

Harper, Charles Lincoln (1877–1955), professor; principal, Booker T. Washington High School, the first black high school in Atlanta (1924–42); founder and president, Atlanta branch, NAACP; president, Georgia State Conference of NAACP Branches; national vice president, NAACP; head, GTEA. In 1949, he sent information to the Washington bureau regarding obstacles to black employment in Atlanta at General Motors, Ford, and the Southern Bell Telephone Company. Three years later, he protested a proposed segregated public housing project in Atlanta.

Harper, Fowler Vincent (1898–1965), lawyer and educator; general counsel, FSA (1940–42); deputy chairman, WMC (1942–43), resigning in protest over the committee's tendency to favor management over labor in policy decisions; visiting professor of law, Yale University (1947–48); Simeon E. Baldwin Professor of Law, Yale (1948–65). An advocate of free speech as well as an opponent of the House Un-American Activities Committee, he represented the Planned Parenthood League of Connecticut against the state of Connecticut before the U.S. Supreme Court; the disposition of the case *(Poe v. Ullman* 387 US 497 [1966])was pending at his death.

Harris, Arthur J. (1891–1980), and his wife, Ella Mae (1901–91), members, NAACP branch in LaMott, Pennsylvania, just north of Philadelphia. In 1951, they went to Washington, D.C., to protest the proposed Winstead amendment to the Universal Military Training bill.

Harris, Thomas Everett (1913–96), lawyer; associate general counsel, CIO (1948–55); associate general counsel, AFL-CIO (1955–75); member, Federal Election Commission (1975–87). He actively worked with congressmen and members of the NECRM of 1950 in order to schedule meetings on the FEPC bill.

Harrison, Byron Patterson "Pat" (D-Miss.) (1881–1941), lawyer; U. S. representative (1911–19); U.S. senator (1919–41). He was an early advocate of federal aid to local school districts.

Harrison, George McGregor (1895–1968), president (1928–63) and chief executive officer (1963–65), BRSC; assistant to the director, ODM (1951–53). A staunch opponent of the 1943 FEPC railroad hearings, he conferred with Mitchell in 1951 on segregation in his union. When no action was taken, the NAACP initiated a lawsuit.

Harrison, Gilbert Avery (1915–2008), magazine publisher; a World War II veteran of the U.S. Army Air Corps. In 1948, he was recently named national vice chairman, AVC (1948–50), when, in correspondence between Walter White and Roy Wilkins, he was mentioned as a potential participant in a proposed conference on civil rights. Harrison subsequently became the owner and publisher of the *New Republic* magazine (1953–74).

Harten, Thomas Samuel (1887–1968), Baptist minister and Garveyite. He pastored Western Avenue Baptist Church, Cambridge, Massachusetts (1913–22), and Holy Trinity Baptist Church in Brooklyn, New York (1922–68), and was best known for his fiery sermons and his advocacy of the teachings of black nationalist Marcus Garvey. In 1951, representing the National Baptist Convention, he participated in the creation of the LCCR.

Hastie, William Henry (1904–76), lawyer; chair, NAACP National Legal Committee; assistant solicitor, Department of the Interior (1933–37); judge, U.S. District Court for the Virgin Islands (1937–39); dean, Howard University School of Law (1939–46); civilian aide to the secretary of war (1940–43); governor, Virgin Islands (1946–49); judge (1950–68) and chief justice (1968–71), U.S. Court of Appeals, Third Circuit. Winner of the 1943 Spingarn Medal, Hastie resigned his position as civilian aide to the secretary of war in protest of the army's decision to set up a segregated Air Corps technical training school in Missouri.

Hatcher, Lillian (1915–98), factory worker and union executive; UAW representative to the WPD; member, Advisory Council to the Woman's Bureau of the U.S. Labor Department. She was the first black woman appointed to the UAW staff as an international representative. In 1948, she worked with William Oliver and Harry Ross in the Fair Practices and

Anti-discrimination Department, UAW. In 1961, she was a delegate to the Michigan state constitutional convention, where she introduced a civil rights proposal that, once accepted, established the Michigan State Civil Rights Commission.

Havenner, Franck Roberts (1882–1967) (P, D-Calif.), journalist; member, San Francisco Board of Supervisors (1926–36); U.S. representative (1937–41, 1945–53); member, CRC (1941–44). A protégé of California progressive Hiram Johnson, he sponsored legislation to protect service members from violence.

Hayden, Carl Trumbull (1877–1972) (D-Ariz.), businessman; county treasurer (1904–6); county sheriff (1907–12); U.S. representative (1912–27); U.S. senator (1927–69). Although considered a liberal regarding most domestic issues, he had a mixed record on civil rights, flip-flopping on both the poll tax and the filibuster issues. From 1949 to 1953, he was chair of the Senate Rules and Administration Committee.

Hayden, Frances F. (1894–1988), social worker. In 1944, representing the Paseo Branch of the YWCA in Kansas City, Missouri, she testified before the House Labor Committee in favor of S. 2048, a bill designed to strengthen the FEPC.

Hayes, George Edward Chalmers (1894–1968), lawyer and educator; president, Washington, D.C., NAACP branch; lead counsel in *Bolling v. Sharpe*, a companion case to *Brown v. Board of Education of Topeka;* later, the first black to sit on the District of Columbia Public Utilities Commission. In 1946, Mitchell sent him a letter from the U.S. Department of Labor describing USES's responsibility for its racially discriminatory actions against nonwhites.

Hayes, Owen Bernard (1923–73), member, NAAWP. He participated in picketing at Gwynn's Falls Junior High School in Baltimore to protest the implementation of the Supreme Court's *Brown* decision.

Hayes, Roland Willsie (1887–1976), internationally known concert singer who gained fame as one of the great singers of the twentieth century. Born in a two-room Georgia shack, he rose from poverty to world acclaim, performing with the great orchestras and leading conductors of his day. In 1924, the NAACP awarded him the Spingarn Medal. In 1946, his wife and daughter were forcibly removed from a shoe store in Rome, Georgia, where they had sat down in the "white" section. When Hayes came to protest, the store clerk claimed that he had attacked him, and Hayes was arrested and beaten by four policemen.

Haynes, George Edmund (1880–1960), pioneer in religious programs and social work education for blacks; secretary, Colored Men's Department, International YMCA (1905–08); involved in the organization and formation of what would become the National Urban League (1909–18); special assistant to U.S. Secretary of Labor (1918–21); executive secretary, department of Race Relations of the Federal Council of the Churches of Christ in America (1921–47); consultant on Africa for World Committee of YMCAs (1948–55). On August 27, 1942, he attended a meeting of A. Philip Randolph's March on Washington Committee in Harlem.

Haynes, John K. "J. K.," Sr. (1907–97), teacher and school administrator; president, Louisiana Colored Teachers Association (1941–47); executive secretary, Louisiana Education Association (1947–78). He was a pioneering civil rights leader in Louisiana. As president of the Louisiana Colored Teachers Association, he fought for equal salaries for all public school teachers in the state. In 1950, he personally escorted to the gates of Louisiana State University the first black applicant, in an attempt to integrate the university. The next year, he contended that he was being denied an opportunity to operate a trade school for veterans; his complaint was being handled by Earle Fisher, the research assistant for the NAACP's labor department.

Hays, Arthur Garfield (1881–1954); lawyer. He filed an amicus brief for the ACLU in *Railway Mail Association v. Corsi* in 1945.

Hederman, Ellen Jane (1880–1964), postmaster, Jackson, Mississippi (1934–38). Like her predecessor, E. C. Cloon, and her successor, Aubrey Griffin, Hederman refused to hire blacks for any position in the Jackson post office.

Hedgeman, Anna Arnold (1899–1990), activist; staff member, YWCA in Springfield, Ohio (1924–27) and Harlem (1927–34, 1936–37); consultant on racial matters to New York City municipal government (1934–36); executive secretary, NCPFEPC (1944–46); dean of women, Howard University (1946–49); assistant to administrator, FSA (1949–54); assistant to Mayor Robert F. Wagner, Jr. of New York City (1954–58); member, commission of religion and race, National Council of Churches (1963–67). She was the only woman on the planning committee of the August 1963 March on Washington. In February 1944, she participated in a mass meeting dedicated to save the FEPC.

Height, Dorothy Irene (1912–2010), clubwoman and activist. The executive secretary of the Phillis Wheatley branch of the YWCA in Washington, D.C. (1937–44), she participated in the Conference of Cooperating Organizations on July 4, 1942. After serving on the YWCA national board (1944–47), she served as president, Zeta Phi Beta sorority (1947–56), and would later succeed Mary McLeod Bethune as president, NCNW (1956–94), and emeritus and chairperson (1994–2010). Upon her retirement as NCNW president in 1994, President Bill Clinton awarded her the Medal of Freedom.

Heller, Robert (1899–1973), management engineer and consultant; principal, Robert Heller & Associates, Inc. (1935–63); chairman, National Committee for Strengthening Congress (c. 1945–50).

Henderson, Elmer William (1913–2001), attorney, administrator, and educator; director, American Council for Human Rights (1948–55); general counsel, House Government Operations Center (1955–82). He was a civil rights activist best known for his role as the plaintiff in *Henderson v. United States* (338 U.S. 816), where the Supreme Court outlawed segregated accommodations on trains in interstate commerce. In 1953, he met with Mitchell and Albert M. Cole to review and discuss the federal government's housing policy.

Henderson, Susie, complainant. In 1952, she was fired from her job as a custodian at Fort McPherson, Georgia, after having her job classification changed, thus dropping her into a lower pay grade; then she was reassigned to other duties before being dismissed.

Hendricks, Mae Bean (1911–60), secretary in Washington bureau. She joined the bureau after working in the U.S. Department of Labor. According to Mitchell, she performed far above and beyond the requirements of her job; in 1958, she returned to her home in Indiana on a year's leave of absence and never went back to Washington.

Hendrickson, Robert Clymer (1898–1964) (R-N.J.), lawyer; New Jersey state legislator (1934–40); state treasurer (1942–48); U.S. senator (1949–55); ambassador to New Zealand (1955–56). Known primarily for his opposition to Joseph McCarthy's anticommunist crusade, he supported antifilibuster resolutions, legislation to protect service members from violence, and desegregation of schools on military posts.

Hermann, Albert Bartholomew (1899–1980), professional baseball player and congressional aide; infielder, Boston Braves (1923–24); aide to Senators H. Alexander Smith (R-N.J.) and Clifford P. Case (R-N.J.); executive director, RNC (1949–52, 1957–61). He was one of the founders of the National Republican Heritage Council, designed with the intent to discover and address the needs of members of minority groups within the Republican party. In 1952, he met with a delegation of representatives from civil rights organizations.

Herzog, Paul M. (1906–86), assistant to the secretary, NLB (1933–35); member (1937–42) and chair (1942–44), NYSLRB; chair, NLRB (1945–53). In 1949, he conveyed the NAACP's views on provisions of the Taft-Hartley Act to the NLRB.

Hester, Richard Arthur (1888–1983), jeweler and merchant, of Dallas. In 1950, he was serving as the supreme chancellor of the Supreme Lodge of the Knights of Pythias when he was part of a delegation from the NECRM who met with President Truman.

Hickey, Edward Joseph, Jr. (1912–2000), lawyer. Representing the BRC in a 1953 case, he said that a local white union could admit blacks despite the union's ban on black members because the union constitution did not bar membership when the restriction was contrary to law.

Hickman, Emily Gregory (1880–1947), historian, educator and activist. One of the first women to earn the PhD in history (Yale, 1911), she taught history at Wells College (1911–27) and at what is now Douglass College of Rutgers University (1928–47). An adherent of progressive causes, she was best known as an advocate for world peace. In 1944 she testified before the House Labor Committee in favor of S. 2048, a bill designed to strengthen the FEPC.

Higley, Harvey Van Zandt (1892–1986), businessman; administrator, Veterans Administration (1953–57). He was involved in the desegregation of Veterans Administration facilities.

Hill, Herbert (1924–2004), labor organizer who succeeded Clarence Mitchell as labor secretary of NAACP (1951–77); Evjue-Bascom professor (and professor emeritus) of African American Studies and Industrial Relations, University of Wisconsin-Madison (1977–2004). In 1951, Hill was one of the NAACP staffers assisting in the organizing and establishment of the Leadership Conference for Civil Rights (LCCR).

Hill, Dr. James Otto (1894–1961), (R-N.J.), general practitioner of Newark, New Jersey; member New Jersey State Assembly (1943–47). In 1945, he proposed legislation calling for the end of employment discrimination in New Jersey as well as creating a "Division Against Discrimination" with enforcement powers in the state department of education; the division would consist of seven non-salaried members and would be headed by the state commissioner of education. Governor Walter E. Edge threw his support behind the bill and on April 16, 1945, he signed it into law, after it passed both houses of the state legislature.

Hill, Joseph Lister (1894–1984) (D-Ala.), lawyer; U.S. representative (1923–38); U.S. senator (1938–69). Although he supported the New Deal and opposed the Taft-Hartley Act, he was an ardent segregationist who opposed Senate rules changes, nondiscrimination amendments to Taft-Hartley, and enforcement powers in fair employment bills. He also filibustered against the creation of a permanent FEPC and opposed an amendment to his hospital bill that would bar aid to hospitals that discriminated in the employment of doctors.

Hill, Oliver White (1907–2007), lawyer; chair, NAACP Virginia Legal Committee (1940–61); first African American on Richmond, Virginia, city council (1949); member, CGCC (1952–53). During his legal career, he worked on railroad discrimination, school equalization, and desegregation cases. These cases included *Davis v. County School Board of Prince Edward County*, which, along with others, was consolidated into the *Brown v. Board of Education* case. In 1951, he was offered a position as assistant general counsel in the ODM, but he declined.

Hill, Thomas Arnold, Sr. (1888–1947), assistant to the executive secretary, National Urban League (1914–16); assistant to the executive secretary, Chicago Urban League (1917–25); director, department of industrial relations (1925–40) and acting executive secretary (1933–36), National Urban League; member, executive staff, NYA (1940–47); special assistant to the administrator on racial matters, OPA (1943). In 1940, with Walter White and A. Philip Randolph, he met with President Franklin D. Roosevelt to urge "the immediate and total abolition in the armed services of segregation based on race and color."

Hill, William Allyn (1908–60), poet, veteran, and engineer; member, Washington, D.C., NAACP branch. In 1947, Mitchell forwarded a report to Hill discussing his (Mitchell's) attempt to get the Bell Telephone Company in Atlantic City to hire a qualified black woman as a telephone operator.

Hillman, Sidney (1887–1946), Lithuanian-born Jewish labor leader who served as president of Amalgamated Clothing Workers Union (1939–43), as well as a member of various New Deal and wartime boards including the OPM and WPB and as labor adviser to President Roosevelt as of 1943. In June 1941, he attended a meeting with President Roosevelt, Walter White of the NAACP, and A. Philip Randolph of the BSCP and others concerning attempts to desegregate the armed forces.

Hines, Lewis Graham (1888–1960), metal polisher, electroplater, and union official; president, Metal Polishers International Union (1921–27); director, USES (1930–33); director of Department of Labor and Industry for the Commonwealth of Pennsylvania (1939–43); legislative representative, AFL (1944–50). In a congressional hearing, he and Mitchell gave testimony regarding FEPC.

Hinton, James Myles, Sr. (1891–1970), businessman; president, South Carolina State Conference of NAACP Branches (1941–58); pastor, Second Calvary Baptist Church, Columbia, South Carolina (1960–70). A leader of NAACP efforts to ensure nonsegregation and nondiscrimination at a hydrogen bomb facility in South Carolina, he was also active in school desegregation (including *Briggs v. Elliott*, the Clarendon County school case) and voting rights campaigns. He was kidnapped by the Ku Klux Klan in the early 1950s and threatened on numerous other occasions.

Hitler, Adolf (1889-1945), leader of Germany's Third Reich (1933–45) and of the Axis alliance that challenged the free world in World War II.

Hobby, Oveta Culp (1905–95), lawyer, and journalist; publisher, *Houston Post*; director, WAAC (1942–45); head, FESA (1953); secretary, HEW (1953–55). As head of HEW, she was criticized both for being slow in implementing the desegregation of schools on military posts and for supporting federal grants to segregated facilities.

Hoffman, Clare Eugene (1875–1967) (R-Mich.), lawyer; U.S. representative (1935–63). A staunch conservative known for his isolationism and opposition to social reform, he opposed FEPC legislation and the abolition of the poll tax. He also voted to authorize the Cox Committee to investigate charitable organizations in the South that were supportive of civil rights.

Holcombe, Muriel Morgan Proctor (1897-1983), complainant; in 1943, traveling South by train via the Southern Railway with her sisters Mrs. Vashti Brown and Mrs. Lillian Falls, all three refused to comply with the Jim Crow transportation laws and were arrested and fined. With the aid of the NAACP, they lodged a complaint with the Interstate Commerce Commission.

Holifield, Chester Earl (1903–95), (D-Calif.), men's apparel manufacturer; U.S. representative (1943–74). He was known as an ardent supporter of the use of atomic power. In 1950, he arranged a meeting between certain members of Congress and the NAACP concerning the effect of the proposed Lodge-Gannett resolution on the civil rights movement.

Holland, George L. (1914–81), Veterans Administration official (1946–54, 1956–65, 1966–71); State Department adviser (1954–56); director, EEOC (1965–66). He was involved in the issue of desegregating veterans' hospitals.

Holland, Spessard Lindsey (1892–1971) (D-Fla.), lawyer and judge; Florida state legislator (1932–40); governor (1941–45); U.S. senator (1946–71). He opposed most civil rights legislation, but on numerous occasions (beginning in 1949), he introduced a constitutional amendment to abolish the poll tax in federal elections. This goal was accomplished in 1964 with the ratification of the Twenty-fourth Amendment.

Hollander, Sidney (1881–1972), pharmaceutical manufacturer in Baltimore; president, Maryland Pharmaceutical Company, and The Rem Company (1900–56); president, National Council Jewish Federations and Welfare Funds (1938–46); board member, National Urban League (1945–72). He was active on the governing boards of numerous community relations and social welfare organizations; although a candidate for membership on the FEPC (1943) he was not appointed. He subsequently served on the board of directors of the NCPFEPC.

Holliday, Presly (1872–1954), "Buffalo Soldier" (retired as Sergeant Major, 10th U.S. Cavalry) and Spanish-American War veteran. A resident of the Old Soldiers' Home, he became a life member of the NAACP in 1953. Earlier in life, he had participated in the Battle of San Juan Hill.

Hollis, Everett L. (1914–94), lawyer; general counsel, AEC (1953). In 1952, Hollis was one of a number of prominent businesspeople, labor leaders, and government officials named by President Truman to serve on his Committee on Government Contract Compliance. Their duties included overseeing Truman's Fair Employment Practices program.

Holsey, Albon Lewis (1893–1950), secretary to the principal of Tuskegee Institute; founder and president of the Colored Merchants' Association (1928–34); and the National Negro Business League (1936–50). In 1943, he participated in the Emergency Conference on the Status of the Negro in the War for Freedom.

Hoover, Herbert Clark (1874–1964) (R-Calif.), mining engineer, civil servant; secretary, U.S. Department of Commerce (1925–29); U.S. president (1929–33). In 1930, his nomination of Judge John J. Parker to be associate justice of the United States Supreme Court went down to defeat primarily through the efforts of the NAACP.

Hope, Clifford Ragsdale (1893–1970) (R-Kans.), lawyer; Kansas state legislator (1921–27); U.S. representative (1927–57). During his first term as chair of the House Committee on Agriculture (1947–49), he conferred with the NAACP on migrant farm labor bills.

Horkan, Maj. Gen. George Anthony, Sr. (1899–1974), U.S. Army officer. In 1952 Mitchell conferred with him concerning segregated burial areas in national cemeteries.

Horne, Edward A. (1922–92), veteran. In 1948, he was the first black hired as a substitute postal clerk in the Memphis post office.

Horne, Dr. Frank Smith (1899–1974), optometrist and poet; assistant director, Division of Negro Affairs, NYA (1936–38); staff member (1938–40) and director (1940–46), Office of Race Relations, USHA; assistant to the administrator, HHFA (1946–53). He aided the NAACP in the fight against federal employment discrimination.

Houghteling, James Lawrence (1883–1962), banker and editor; U.S. commissioner of immigration and naturalization (1937–40); special assistant to the secretary of the treasury (1940–47); chair, FEB (1947–52). He was praised by Mitchell as having a broader understanding of the work at the FEB than Guy Moffatt, the previous chair.

Houston, Charles Hamilton (1895–1950), lawyer and columnist; resident vice dean (1929–32) and dean (1932–35), Howard University School of Law; special counsel, NAACP (1935–40); member (1940–50) and chair (1948–50), NAACP National Legal Committee; vice president, ACRR (1940–50); member, FEPC (1944–46). In 1948, he testified before the U.S. Senate on antilynching legislation.

Houston, John Mills (1890–1975) (D-Kansas), lawyer; U. S. representative (1935–43); member, NLRB (1943–53), where he confronted counsel for the NAACP concerning segregated union locals.

Howard, Hillard (1897–1946), woodworker and lather, of Chicago. A native of Birmingham, Alabama, he moved to Illinois after the end of World War I and attempted to join the

Wood, Wire and Metal Lather's International Union and was turned down based on his race.

Howard, Joseph Clifton (1894–1985) woodworker and lather, of Chicago. A native of Birmingham, Alabama, he moved to Illinois after the end of World War I and attempted to join the Wood, Wire and Metal Lather's International Union and was turned down based on his race.

Howard, William H., African American dismissed by the FSA in 1951. Despite Howard's claims that he was dismissed due to his attempts to stop racial discrimination in the area he worked, and despite the aid of research assistant Earle W. Fisher of the Washington bureau in making his appeals, Howard's dismissal was upheld by a hearing board called to review his appeal, and afterwards, the board's ruling was upheld by the head of the FSA.

Hughes, William Andrew (1895–1986), telephone company executive and assistant director, Industrial Personnel Relations, Army Service Forces, War Department in 1944 when he testified before the House Labor Committee in favor of S. 2048, a bill designed to strengthen the FEPC.

Huiet, Benjamin Tillman (1895–1987), commissioner, GPSC (1933–36); commissioner, GDOL (1938–67). In 1948, he conferred with the NAACP on the denial of unemployment compensation to black veterans in Georgia.

Humelsine, Carlisle Hubbard (1915–89), assistant secretary and deputy undersecretary of state, State Department (1946–53); executive, Colonial Williamsburg Foundation (1953–85); chair, NTHP (1973–80). He promised to continue efforts to increase black employment in the State Department.

Humphrey, George Magoffin (1890–1970), lawyer and businessman; U.S. secretary of the treasury (1953–57). President Eisenhower's most trusted adviser, he became embroiled in a controversy involving the admission of blacks to apprenticeship programs of the BPE.

Humphrey, Hubert Horatio, Jr. (1911–78) (D-Minn.), Minneapolis mayor (1945–48); U.S. senator (1949–65); vice president of the United States (1965–69); Democratic Party presidential nominee (1968). He was a longtime collaborator with the NAACP on civil rights and social legislation. As mayor of Minneapolis, he presided over the enactment of the first fair employment practices city ordinance in the country. He also supported the NAACP's struggle for Senate rules changes, enforcement provisions in fair employment bills, antilynching legislation, nonsegregation amendments to the Taft-Hartley Act, and the desegregation of schools on military posts.

Hunton, George Kelly (1888–1967), social worker; director, Catholic Interracial Council of New York City. In 1950, he met with Mitchell and W. Stuart Symington, chair of the NSB, to discuss how nonwhites and other racial minorities could aid the war effort during the Korean conflict.

Hurley, Ruby (1909–80), secretary, NAACP National Youth Program (1943–51); director, NAACP Southeast Region (1952–78). A civil rights pioneer, she led the effort to establish NAACP branches in the Deep South—for several years, she was the only full-time professional civil rights worker in that region. As regional director, she investigated a number of racial crimes, including the 1955 lynching of Emmett Till.

Hurok, Solomon Isaievitch (1888–1974), impresario. A native Ukrainian, he was credited with the discovery of African American singer Marian Anderson. Well known as the "King of Ballet," he arranged for a number of Soviet musicians and performers (including the Bolshoi Ballet in 1959) to perform in the United States.

Ickes, Harold Le Claire (1874–1952), lawyer and government official; president, Chicago branch, NAACP (1922–25); U.S. secretary of the interior (1933–46); director, PWA (1933–41); columnist, *New Republic* (1946–52). In 1939, he arranged for Marian Anderson to sing at the Lincoln Memorial when the Daughters of the American Revolution barred her from performing at Constitution Hall in Washington. He was a strong supporter of civil rights, including President Truman's FEPC. In 1949, he appeared at the UAW education conference and delivered a speech calling for federal government funding of public education.

Illig, William Frederick (1905–89), lawyer, of Erie, Pa.; partner in what is presently (2010) the firm of McDonald, Illig, Jones & Britton. In 1976, he reported to the Warren Commission that he represented Dr. George G. Burkley, the personal physician to President Kennedy; the doctor (who had signed the death certificate and who also contended that he had information leading to the premise that Lee Harvey Oswald was not the only assassin) had not yet been interviewed by the commission. In 1942, as the NAACP struggled to find funds with which to open and subsequently operate the Washington bureau, Walter White contacted Illig as a potential donor.

Imes, William Lloyd (1889–1986), Presbyterian minister, author, educator, community organizer and activist; pastor, St. James Presbyterian Church, New York City (1938–43); president, Knoxville College (1943–47); director of social and adult education for the New York State Council of Churches (1947–55). In 1941, he was one of the first to call for a March on Washington and served on the sponsoring committee of the MOWM.

Issa, Abdullahi (1922–88), first prime minister of Somalia (1953–60); Somali foreign minister (1960–64). In 1953 Issa was the leader of the Somali Youth League in what was then the territory of Italian Somaliland; he wished to enter the United States to go before the United Nations with a plea for independence for his people, However, he was unable to enter the United States and turned to the NAACP for help. After several weeks where Mitchell and the Washington bureau cut through mounds of red tape, Issa was able to enter the United States. Once Somalia achieved independence, Issa became prime minister of the new country.

Ives, Irving McNeil (1896–1962) (R-N.Y.), businessman; New York state legislator (1930–46); chair, NYSCAD (1944–45); sponsor, New York State fair employment law (1945); U.S. senator (1947–59). While serving in the U.S. Senate, he supported anti–poll tax legislation, anti–Jim Crow travel laws, nondiscrimination amendments to the Taft-Hartley Act, legislation to protect service members from violence, Senate rules changes, and nonsegregation amendments to housing legislation.

Ives, John Hull (1909–2001), motivational speaker, author; insurance executive of Bridgeport, Connecticut; administrator of and lay preacher in Congregationalist and Universalist churches (later United Churches of Christ). Representing the Federal Council of Churches of Christ, in 1950, he met with Mitchell and W. Stuart Symington, chairman of the NSB to discuss how nonwhites and other racial minorities could aid the war effort during the Korean conflict.

Ivy, James Waldo (1901–74), journalist, editor, educator, polylinguist and essayist; professor of literature, Hampton Institute (1942–46); assistant editor (1946–50) and editor (1950–66), *Crisis.* He was one of a number of NAACP staff members involved in the formation of the LCCR, 1951.

Jackson, Emory Overton (1908–75), managing editor, *Birmingham World* (1941–75); board member, Birmingham Urban League; founder and first president, Alabama State Conference of NAACP Branches (1944–47). He participated in numerous civil rights activities in Alabama, including struggles for antisegregation measures, equal pay for African American teachers, and voting rights. He also reported cases of police violence in Alabama to the NAACP Washington bureau.

Jackson, John G., serviceman. His British wife of Japanese descent (he was black) was initially denied admission to the United States by the U.S. consulate in London. She was granted admission following investigation and intervention by the NAACP.

Jackson, Lawrence "Larry," member, Cordale, Pennsylvania (near Uniontown), NAACP branch. In 1951, he went to Washington, D.C., to protest the proposed Winstead amendment to the Universal Military Training bill.

Jackson, Lillie Mae Carroll (1895–1971), mother of Juanita Jackson Mitchell and mother-in-law of Clarence Mitchell Jr.; president, Baltimore NAACP branch (1935–70). In 1931, she assisted Juanita in organizing the City-Wide Young People's Forum, an organization for social education, uplift, and protest. Her organizing of a "Buy Where You Can Work" boycott of A&P food stores in Baltimore in 1935 brought her to the attention of Carl Murphy, publisher of the *Baltimore Afro-American,* who asked her to become chair of the reorganizing committee of the local NAACP. She then led a successful membership drive and later organized the Maryland NAACP State Conference of Branches. She also became a member of the NAACP National Board of Directors. Under her leadership and in conjunction with Juanita, who became a lawyer, Maryland was desegregated by 1954. The Baltimore NAACP branch's most significant contribution to this effort was its sponsorship in 1935 of *Murray v. Maryland,* which resulted that year in the desegregation of the University of Maryland Law School, the first in the series of cases that built to the landmark *Brown v. Board of Education* decision in 1954.

Jackson, Luther Porter, Jr. (1925–2008), journalist and educator. Son of the president of Virginia State College, he served in the U.S. Marines during World War II and, during that time, challenged Jim Crow travel arrangements in Virginia. He subsequently graduated from Columbia University's School of Journalism; reporter, (Newark, New Jersey) *Newark Evening News* (1951–58); reporter, *Washington Post* (1959–63); associate director of public relations NAACP and editor of *Crisis* (1968); professor, Columbia University School of Journalism (1968–92).

Jackson, Mabel D. [married name Smith] (1921–2003), staffer, NAACP national office, New York City; personal secretary to Walter White. In 1953, Mitchell forwarded to her a list of members of the President's Committee on Government Compliance who were present at a meeting of other organizations designed to help the committee achieve its goals; the list also included participants who were not members of the committee.

Jason, William Charles, Jr. (1898–1988), welfare director, NAPE. In 1948, he testified before the USCSC on discrimination against African Americans in the New Orleans Post Office.

Javits, Jacob Koppel (1904–86) (R-N.Y.), lawyer; U.S. representative (1947–54); New York state attorney general (1954–57); U.S. senator (1957–81). A liberal Republican, he supported nonsegregation and nondiscrimination amendments in military training, labor and housing legislation, desegregation of schools on military posts, and the abolition of the poll tax.

Jefferson, Thomas (1743–1826), lawyer; patriot; signer of Declaration of Independence, 1776; governor of Virginia (1779–81); U.S. ambassador to France (1785–89); U.S. secretary of state (1789–93), vice president of the U.S. (1797–1801); president of the U.S. (1801–09).

Jenkins, Howard, Jr. (1915–2003), lawyer; professor Howard University School of Law (1946–56); special assistant to the solicitor general, U.S. Department of Labor (1956–59); deputy commissioner, office of regulation, Bureau of Labor Management Relations (1959–62); assistant commissioner, Bureau of Labor Management Relations (1962–63); member NLRB (1963–83), being the first black to sit on that board. In 1951, with Juanita Jackson Mitchell and others, he represented members of the Baltimore branch of the NAACP who filed suit in the United States district court in Washington, D.C. against the Brotherhood of Railway and Steamship Clerks, Freight Handlers, Express and Station Employees, and the Baltimore & Ohio Railroad Company over a violation of the Railway Labor Act where the union forced its black members into segregated union locals.

Jenkins, William J. (1916–99), treasurer, Racine, Wisconsin, NAACP branch. In 1949, he was a delegate to the UAW education conference, where he met Mitchell and discussed a situation affecting housing for blacks in Racine.

Jenner, William Ezra (1908–85) (R-Ind.), lawyer; Indiana state legislator (1934–42); U.S. senator (1944–45, 1947–59). A conservative Republican and anticommunist, he was noted for his strong criticism of George C. Marshall. In 1951, he cosponsored an FEPC bill, but in the following year, he voted against an antifilibuster measure.

Jernagin, Rev. William Henry (1869–1958), Baptist minister and educator; president, National Peace Conference (1916–17); president, National Fraternal Council of Churches (1938–58); president, National Sunday School Union and Baptist Youth Congress. A native of Mississippi, he pastored churches in Oklahoma City and Mound Bayou, Mississippi, before establishing Mount Carmel Baptist Church in Washington, D.C., in 1912. In 1946, he was present at a meeting with Mitchell and U.S. secretary of labor Lewis Schwellenbach, where the latter pledged that segregation would end in the Washington offices of the Department of Labor by September 30 of that year.

John, Eardlie T. S. (1894–1975), lawyer; assistant corporation counsel, City of New York; a native of St. Vincent's, British West Indies, and a graduate of McGill University and New York University Law School. He was actively involved in planning for the proposed June 1941 MOWM.

Johnson, Campbell Carrington (1895–1968), lawyer and army officer; executive assistant, Selective Service (1940–55). In 1951, Mitchell met with him to discuss preventing the segregation of black draftees and enlisted men in the South. He ultimately achieved the rank of colonel.

Johnson, Carl Roman (1894–1960), lawyer; president, Kansas City branch, NAACP (1950–51); member, NAACP National Board of Directors (1949–51). In 1949, he protested the segregation of Treasury Department offices in Kansas City, Missouri.

Johnson, Dr. Charles Catlett, Jr. (1906–87), pharmacist. He was a leader in the effort to ensure nonsegregation and nondiscrimination at the Savannah River Plant hydrogen bomb facility in Aiken, South Carolina. With his brothers Free Mason Johnson (1908–95) and Ladeveze Wilson Johnson (1912–68), he owned and operated Johnson Brothers Drug Store in Aiken (closed in 1986); their youngest brother, Reed Poindexter Johnson, MD (1916–2003), had his office in the same building.

Johnson, Dr. Charles Spurgeon (1893–1956), educator, social scientist, author and editor; director of research and records, Chicago Urban League (1917–19); associate executive director, Chicago Commission on Race Relations (1919–21); director, department of research and investigations, National Urban League (1921–28); chair, social science department (1928–46) and president, Fisk University (1946–56). In 1951, with Walter White and A. Philip Randolph, he attended a meeting with President Harry S. Truman commemorating the three year anniversary of his first civil rights message to Congress.

Johnson, Clarence R. (1903–83), rose from dining car chef to the assistant general chairman of the Dining Car Employees Union (an affiliate of the Hotel and Restaurant Employees International Alliance) in 1938; from there he became minorities consultant, Negro Employment and Training Branch, WMC (1942–44). He was serving as regional director of the Federal Public Housing Authority when he was considered for the newly minted post of NAACP labor secretary in 1945.

Johnson, Dagney [married name Krantz] (1925–2004). In 1954, she investigated the desegregation of public schools in Baltimore, Maryland and Washington, D.C. with J. Francis Pohlhaus of the NAACP's Washington bureau.

Johnson, Earl Dallam (1905–90), businessman; assistant secretary of the army (1950–52); undersecretary of the army (1952–54). Mitchell met with him to discuss preventing segregation of black draftees and enlisted men in the South.

Johnson, George Marion (1900–87), lawyer; member, NAACP National Legal Committee; assistant executive secretary (1941–43) and deputy chair (1943–46), FEPC; acting general counsel and director, Legal Division, FEPC (1943–45); associate professor and dean, Howard University School of Law (1946–58). In 1948, the NAACP consulted with him on the proposed content of Truman's executive order against employment discrimination by the federal government.

Johnson, Brig. Gen. Hugh Samuel (1882–1942), U.S. Army and chief of staff to President Franklin D. Roosevelt. In early 1941, he tried to dissuade A. Philip Randolph from planning and organizing his proposed March on Washington.

Johnson, James B., complainant. In 1953, he boarded a train in Richmond, Virginia, and ran afoul of Jim Crow transportation laws when he refused to move his seat and was arrested and fined.

Johnson, James Weldon (1871–1938), poet, teacher, U.S. consul, author, editor, and civil rights activist, and his brother John Rosamond Johnson (1873–1954), composer and actor, were the sons of a woman of French and Haitian ancestry born in Nassau, Bahamas. In 1952, Mitchell commented that, if the McCarran-Walter Act, with its severe restriction on immigration from the Caribbean and South America, had been in force when immigrants like Helen Dillet Johnson entered the United States, they would not have been able to make "notable contributions to the building of our nation."

Johnson, Louis Arthur (1891–1966), lawyer; West Virginia state legislator (1917); assistant secretary of war (1937–40); U.S. secretary of defense (1949–50). In 1950, he and Mitchell discussed a Pentagon exhibit on black service members.

Johnson, Lyndon Baines (1908–73) (D-Tex.), teacher (1928–31); congressional secretary (1931–35); state director, NYA of Texas (1935–37); U.S. representative (1937–49); U.S. senator (1949–61); Senate minority leader (1953–55); Senate majority leader (1955–61); vice president of the United States (1961–63); president of the United States (1963–69). Although a supporter of Franklin Delano Roosevelt and the New Deal, he moved to the right during the Truman years, aligning himself with conservative senator Richard Russell of Georgia. He voted for the Taft-Hartley Act, opposed outlawing state poll taxes, and opposed a new FEPC.

Johnson, Nathan N. (1910–91), postal worker. A war service appointee to the New Orleans Post Office, he filed an employment discrimination complaint against that institution in 1947.

Johnson, Reginald A. (1903–81), housing expert. He was with the National Urban League from 1930 to 1968, working in bureaus in St. Louis, Pittsburgh, and Atlanta as director of field services before going to New York City to serve as the league's first national director of housing (1952–61); subsequently, he was the NUL's associate director and assistant director (1965–81). In 1953, he participated with Clarence Mitchell and Albert M. Cole in a meeting discussing the federal government's housing policy.

Johnson, Thelma R. (1912–), chemist. With the NAACP's help, she successfully challenged the segregation of the restaurant at Mount Alto Veterans Hospital in Washington, D.C.

Johnson, Thomasina Tempie Walker (1908–2002), journalist and lobbyist. While director of the non-partisan council of the Alpha Kappa Alpha sorority (1942–46), in 1943 she was named to the initial executive board of the NCPFEPC; she later served as chief, division of minority affairs, USES (1946–53). After her marriage to George E. Norford (the first black television network producer [NBC, 1958] who subsequently served as vice president and general executive of Group W [Westinghouse Broadcasting Corporation]), she became women's editor of the black-owned newspaper, the *Amsterdam News*.

Johnston, Olin DeWitt Talmadge (1896–1965) (D-S.C.), lawyer; South Carolina state legislator (1923–24, 1927–30); governor (1935–39, 1943–45); U.S. senator (1945–65). Although he supported labor legislation and measures for the poor, he was a rabid segregationist and white supremacist. Over the course of his political career, he opposed civil rights measures such as the FEPC and anti–poll tax bills. A stalwart anticommunist, he once advocated waging an atomic war against the Soviet Union.

Jones, Donald A. (1905–87), postal clerk, newspaperman, NAACP staffer; clerk in New Orleans Post Office from 1926. An active member of the NAACP branch in New Orleans, he was editor of the *Louisiana Weekly* and publicity director for Dillard University, New Orleans, to 1943 when he was named NAACP assistant field secretary for Louisiana; he would later become the NAACP southwest regional secretary. In 1942, the NAACP invited him to Washington for the Conference of Negro Newspaper Editors at the time of the opening of the NAACP Washington bureau.

Jones, Edmund L. (1894–1980), lawyer. In 1954, he represented the Capital Transit Company of Washington in defending the discrimination suit from the Washington bureau of the NAACP.

Jones, Fleming Adolphus, Jr. (1895–1961) (D-W.Va.), lawyer, of Welch, West Virginia, and the first African American to serve in the West Virginia state legislature (1935–43; 1945–47). In 1945, he proposed legislation to end employment discrimination and create a state FEPC with enforcement powers, but the legislature adjourned without acting on it.

Jones, Madison Sumner, Jr. (1909–2002), NAACP youth director (1940–43); examiner, New York office, FEPC (1943–45); administrative assistant, NAACP national office (1945–51); racial relations adviser, FHA (1951–55). As administrative assistant, he helped in negotiations with AT&T regarding discrimination complaints against telephone companies. He also participated in the effort to desegregate restaurants in Washington, D.C.

Jones, Roger W. (1908–83), attorney and educator; assistant director for legislative reference, U.S. Bureau of the Budget (1953–59); chair, U.S. Civil Service Commission (1959–61); deputy undersecretary of state for administration (1961–62); special assistant to the director (1962–63) and assistant director (1963–75), U.S. Bureau of the Budget. In 1953, he gave Mitchell a memo discussing segregated schools located on federal property for dependents of military personnel.

Jones, Toussaint L. [L'Ouverture?] (1920–91), teacher. Hired to teach for the Indian Service in Montana, he was subsequently denied employment due to alleged American Indian prejudice against blacks. He was reinstated after his case was taken up by the NAACP Washington bureau.

Jordan, Mortimer (1911–80), collector of internal revenue. An Alabaman, he was dismissed from his collector position in 1948 after refusing to follow federal nondiscrimination policy.

Jurney, Chesley Webb (1877–1947), lawyer of Waco, Texas; secretary to Sen. Charles A. Culberson (D-Tex.) (1909–33) and subsequently appointed U.S. Senate sergeant-of-arms. Outfitted with striped trousers, a cutaway coat, and a ten-gallon Stetson, Jurney enforced the rules of the senate from 1933 to 1943. Senator Robert F. Wagner (D-N.Y.) requested Jurney to make a full investigation of the incident where A. Philip Randolph and Rev. Adam Clayton Powell, Jr., along with a group of ministers from New York, were kept from entering the senate public galleries, and were insulted and otherwise harassed by capitol police, with the further request to bring strong disciplinary action against the policemen if the charges were found to be true.

Kamler, John (1911–68) of Baltimore. Complainant against white supremacist Bryant W. Bowles, Jr., 1953, Kamler brought suit against Bowles for wages due him for a job. Bowles pled guilty on all charges.

Kampelman, Max M. (1920–), lawyer; legislative counsel to Sen. Hubert H. Humphrey (D-Minn.) (1948–54); counsel, U.S. Department of State (1978–80); ambassador and head of U.S. delegation to the negotiations with the Soviet Union on nuclear and space arms (1980–83); vice chair, U.S. Institute of Peace (1992–2001). While serving as counsel to Senator Humphrey, Kampelman received a letter from Mitchell together with a request that it go out under Humphrey's signature to Anna Rosenberg, assistant secretary of defense; the letter asked if Humphrey and the NAACP could meet with her regarding the existence of segregated schools located on federal property.

Kane, Irving (1908–97), lawyer and businessman. A native of Kiev, he and his family came to the United States when he was five years old; he subsequently moved to Cleveland where he practiced law; owner, Hospital Speciality Company, Cleveland (1941–62). He was one of the founders of the Jewish Community Relations Commission of Cleveland in 1947; chair, NCRAC (1943–53); vice-president, AJCong (1956–58). Representing NCRAC, he was a member of the delegation from the NECRM that met with President Truman in January of 1950.

Kaufman, Joseph E. (1911–99), veteran and postal worker. He was an NAACP complainant against employment discrimination at the New Orleans Post Office (1947).

Kaye, Betty [married name Taylor] (1925–), political activist; organizer, ILGWU (1946–48); assistant director, JLC (1948–81); executive secretary, Ad Hoc Commission on Human Rights and Genocide (1948–81). She sat on the executive committee of the NECRM of 1950.

Keating, Kenneth Barnard (1900–75) (R-N.Y.), lawyer; U.S. representative (1947–59); U.S. senator (1959–65); judge, New York State Court of Appeals (1965–69); ambassador to India (1969–72); ambassador to Israel (1973–75). He was a supporter of social welfare and civil rights measures who also had strong anticommunist credentials. While in the House, he introduced antilynching legislation and helped draft what became the Civil Rights Act of 1957.

Keenan, Edward Louis, Jr. (1911–89), regional representative for Ohio, Michigan and Kentucky, BES, Department of Labor (1937–42); acting chair, Regional Labor Supply Committee, Region V (Cleveland), WPB (1942); deputy regional director, Region V, WMC (1942–43); Ohio state director, WMC (1943–45); director, Region V, WMC (1945); deputy director, USES (1945–48); deputy director, BES, Department of Labor (1949–58); assistant executive director, ODM (1951). As assistant executive director of the ODM, he negotiated the employment of blacks at the Capital Transit Company. He continued to hold similar manpower posts through the 1970s.

Keenan, Joseph Daniel (1896–1988), Chicago leader of IBEW-AFL; labor adviser, OPM (1940–41); associate director, Labor Production Board (1942); vice chair, Office of Labor Production, WPB (1943–45); aided in reorganization of German labor movement in War Manpower Division, Germany (1945–48); special assistant for labor, ODM (1953–58); international secretary, IBEW (1954–74); vice president, AFL-CIO. In January of 1950, he was a part of a delegation from the NECRM who met with President Truman.

Kefauver, Carey Estes (1903–63) (D-Tenn.), lawyer; Tennessee state commissioner of finance and taxation (1939); U.S. representative (1939–49); U.S. senator (1949–63); Democratic Party vice presidential candidate (1956). Most famous for heading a Senate committee investigating organized crime, he had a mixed civil rights record. Although he opposed FEPC and antilynching legislation, he supported the abolition of the poll tax and refused to sign the "Southern Manifesto," the 1955 statement by southern members of Congress declaring their opposition to the *Brown v. Board of Education* decision.

Kelly, Harry Francis (1895–1971), (R-Mich.), lawyer and businessman; governor of Michigan (1943–47); justice, Michigan Supreme Court (1954–71). In 1946, he announced that he supported the national Republican party plank calling for a permanent FEPC, but Mitchell reported that he hadn't yet taken a stand on proposed legislation in his state calling for the creation of a four-man FEPC.

Kelly, Rev. Msgr. William Francis (1908–84), Roman Catholic priest; member of the Social Action Department, National Catholic Welfare Council; affiliated with the Association of Catholic Trade Unionists. In 1947, he appeared with Mitchell at the Catholic Conference on Industrial Problems in New York City.

Kemnitz, Milton Neumann (1911–2005), social worker, artist, and activist. A graduate of the University of Michigan who served in the merchant marine during World War II, he was the secretary for the Conference for the Protection of Civil Rights, and remained in that position when it became the National Federation for Constitutional Liberties; he was serving in that post when, as a member of the delegation from the NECRM, he met with President Truman in January of 1950.

Kennedy, Hunter (1909–88), AEC official. In 1951, he served as a coordinator with the NAACP to help prevent segregation and discrimination at the Savannah River Plant hydrogen bomb facility in Aiken, South Carolina.

Kennedy, John Fitzgerald (1917–63) (D-Mass.), author and journalist; U.S. representative (1947–53); U.S. senator (1953–60); president of the United States (1961–63). While in Congress, he supported nondiscrimination amendments to the Taft-Hartley Act and a fair employment bill with enforcement powers.

Kido, Saburo (1902–77), lawyerand journalist; founder of Japanese-American Citizens League and leader of that organization during World War II. In 1946, he was present at a meeting with Mitchell and U.S. secretary of labor Schwellenbach, in which the latter pledged that segregation would end in the Washington offices of the Department of Labor by September 30 of that year.

Kilgore, Harley Martin (1893–1956) (D-W.Va.), educator, lawyer, and judge; U.S. senator (1941–56). A liberal Democrat, he supported legislation to protect service members from violence and held hearings on antilynching legislation.

Kimball, Dan Able (1896–1970), businessman; undersecretary of the navy (1949–51); secretary of the navy (1951–53). In 1952, the NAACP urged him to end segregation in the Charleston and Norfolk navy yards. As president of the Aerojet-General Corporation, he constructed a factory in the Watts section of Los Angeles following the 1965 riot, giving priority employment at the facility to those who had not graduated from high school and/or those who had police records.

Kincaid [Kimcaird], Frank (1897–1931), locomotive fireman of Canton, Mississippi, who was shot and wounded on August 31, 1931. After he recovered and returned to work, he was shot and killed on November 10, 1931 in Canton; the perpetrators were thought to have been whites who coveted his job during the early days of the Depression.

King, Rev. Martin Luther, Jr. (1929–68), Baptist minister; social activist; president, SCLC (1957–68); mentioned, along with A. Philip Randolph, as one who sought racial justice by challenging the government from outside, whereas the NAACP challenged it from inside.

Kingdon, Rev. Frank (1894–1972), pastor, Brick Church Presbyterian Church, East Orange, New Jersey when he served as the president of the New Jersey Independent Citizens' League. The League supported legislation calling for the end of employment discrimination and the establishment of a commission against discrimination with enforcement powers. Governor Walter Edge was not in favor for the establishment of "a costly new separate agency."

Kingman, Harry Lees (1892–1982), baseball player, New York Yankees (1914–16); served in China for the International YMCA (1921–27); head, West Coast office, Region XII, FEPC (1943–45); cofounder and head, CCFFP (1957–70). Mitchell considered him to be the most effective of the FEPC regional leaders. He campaigned for state FEPC legislation in California before retiring in 1956. Shortly after his retirement—and at Mitchell's urging—he returned to Washington, D.C., where he and his wife created the CCFFP.

Klein, Maj. Gen. John A. (1897–1991), deputy adjutant general of the United States (1950–54). In 1953, he informed Mitchell that two white army privates had been court-martialed and sentenced to prison for their assault on a black army private.

Knight, Felix Harrison (1874–1952), union official; assistant general president (1913–35) and president (1935–52), Association of Railway Carmen; vice president, AFL (1936–52). He attempted to have the Association of Railway Carmen remove the Jim Crow section of their constitution and admit blacks to membership as early as 1946; this would not occur until after his death.

Knowland, William Fife (1908–74) (R-Calif.), publisher; California state legislator (1933–39); U.S. senator (1945–59); Senate majority leader (1953–55); Senate minority leader (1955–59). His conservative reputation was based in large part on his backing of Nationalist China, but Mitchell won his support on civil rights legislation. During the Truman years, he opposed prosegregation amendments to draft and housing legislation and offered a bill to invoke cloture by a simple majority. He committed suicide in 1974.

Knox, William Franklin "Frank" (1874–1944), newspaper reporter, businessman, newspaper owner, and diplomat; veteran, Spanish-American War (served with Theodore Roosevelt's "Rough Riders") and World War I; owner of *Chicago News*; ran on Republican presidential ticket as vice president in 1936; U.S. secretary of the navy (1940–44). He met with President Roosevelt and the NAACP about desegregation of the U.S. Navy in 1942.

Knudsen, William Signius [Signius Wilhelm Paul] "Big Bill" (1879–1948), automobile company executive (Danish born); president of Chevrolet division, General Motors (1926–37); president of General Motors (1937–40); director of production, Office of U.S. Undersecretary of War (1942–44); director, Army Air Forces Material and Service (1944–45). In June 1941, he participated in a meeting with President Roosevelt, Walter White of the NAACP and A. Philip Randolph of the International Brotherhood of American Sleeping Car Porters and others concerning attempts to desegregate the armed forces.

Konvitz, Milton Ridvas (1908–2003), lawyer, educator, author and activist; counsel, NAACP Legal Education and Defense Fund (1930–33); professor, New School of Social Research (1942–46); professor, Cornell Law School (1946–73) and founding faculty member, Cornell School of Industrial and Labor Relations (1946–73); internationally known legal authority on civil rights, human rights, constitutional law, and labor law. In 1943, he published a review of court cases involving Jim Crow travel.

Kriegsfeld, Irving M. (1920–2004), housing advocate; staff member, National Federation of Settlements and Neighborhood Centers; executive director, PATH, a nonprofit housing group in Cleveland, Ohio (1960–68); director, Cuyahoga Metropolitan Housing Authority (1968–71). Longtime advocate of affordable and safe public housing in urban areas. In 1953, he met with Mitchell and Albert M. Cole to review and discuss the federal government's housing policy.

Krock, Arthur (1886–1974), newspaperman, magazine writer and editor, and book author. A native of Glasgow, Kentucky, he was the Washington correspondent and bureau chief for the *New York Times* for over twenty years. In late 1952, Mitchell responded to a column

Krock had written on the Electoral College, stating in part that, in his (Mitchell's) opinion, most advocates of changing the voting procedures are not as much interested in reforming the process but are trying to transfer influence from larger and more populated states to "less enlightened areas of the country."

Kroll, Jack (1925–2000), writer, essayist, critic and editor, *Newsweek* magazine (1965–2000). In 1950, when the NAACP suggested that those groups that had participated in the National Emergency Civil Rights Mobilization meet again to devise political action against particular congressmen, Phillip Murray of the CIO, citing his regrets, designated Jack Kroll to attend such a meeting. When it was determined that most of the groups would be unable or unwilling to attend, Murray suggested to Mitchell that it might be more effective if the voting records of these congressmen be made available to interested parties.

Krug, Julius Albert (1907–70), public utilities expert, FCC (1935–37); chief power engineer, TVA (1938–40); chief power consultant, OPDM (1941); official (1942–44) and chair (1944–45), WPB; U.S. secretary of interior (1946–49). In 1948, the NAACP consulted with him on Executive Order 9980, which banned discrimination in public employment.

Kuchel, Thomas Henry (1910–94) (R-Calif.), lawyer; California state legislator (1936–45); state controller (1946–53); U.S. senator (1953–69). He voted for the Bricker amendment and opposed censure of Joseph McCarthy, but his voting record became more liberal over time. In 1953, he supported a Senate rules change that would have hampered filibusters.

Kyes, Roger Martin (1906–71), lawyer; deputy secretary of defense (1950–53). He was succeeded by Robert B. Anderson. Kyes' resignation was noted by Mitchell in a 1953 speech.

LaBaud (Lebeaud), Louis J. , veteran. Although claiming employment discrimination at the New Orleans Post Office, he declined to join those of his fellow postal workers and the NAACP in filing formal charges against that body.

LaFarge, Rev. John, S.J. (1880–1963), Catholic priest and member of the Society of Jesus; journalist, educator, missionary, and activist; founded and operated Cardinal Gibbons Institute in Ridge, Maryland, a school for blacks based on Tuskegee Institute, to 1921 when he joined the editorial staff of *America*, "a weekly journal of opinion"; he served as executive editor (1942–44), editor-in-chief (1944–48) and associate editor (1948–65). He organizedthe Catholic Interracial Council of New York City in 1934 and in 1944 he testified before the House Labor Committee in favor of S. 2048, a bill designed to strengthen the FEPC.

LaFollette, Charles Marion (1898–1974) (R-Ind.), lawyer; Indiana state legislator (1927–29); U.S. representative (1943–47); deputy chief of counsel for war crimes, Nuremberg, Germany (1947); national director, ADA (1949–50); member, SACB (1950–51). A liberal Republican, he supported FEPC and anti–poll tax legislation while serving in Congress. He also amassed a strong labor record, including a vigorous defense of UAW head Walter Reuther during the 1946 General Motors strike. As ADA director, he wrote a letter to President Truman urging complete civil rights for African Americans in the armed forces.

LaGrone, Hobart Lee (1897–1966), board member, NAACP southwest region; president, Albuquerque branch, NAACP; president, New Mexico State Conference of NAACP Branches. He was a leading supporter of state FEPC legislation in New Mexico. He also opposed that state's right-to-work law.

La Guardia, Fiorello Henry (1882–1947), attorney and politician; U.S. House of Representatives (1916–17, 1919–20, 1922–33); president, New York City Board of Aldermen (1920–21); mayor, New York City (1933–45); director, Office of Civilian Defense (1941); director general, UN Relief and Rehabilitation Administration (1946–47); member, NAACP National Labor Board (1946–47). In 1947, he accepted an offer to chair an informal group of nonlabor organizations brought together to defeat the Taft-Hartley bill.

Laidler, Harry Wellington (1884–1970), newspaper reporter, writer, magazine editor, and politician. He joined the Socialist party in 1903 while an undergraduate at Columbia University and two years later founded the Intercollegiate Socialist Society; in 1921, as the organization's focus changed, its name was changed to the League for Industrial Democracy, and he was named its executive director (1921–57). He represented the organization at the Conference of Cooperating Organizations in July of 1942.

Lampkin, Daisy Elizabeth Adams (1884-1965), suffragette, newspaper executive and civil rights activist; involved in circulation sales for the *Pittsburgh Courier* (1913-29); vice president, *Courier* corporation (1929-65); regional field secretary (1929-35), national field secretary (1935-47), NAACP, and member NAACP National Board of Directors (1947-65). On February 12, 1954, she appeared, with President Eisenhower, Dr. Ralph Bunche and others, at the Freedom's Fulfillment Conference in New York City.

Lampkin, Daisy Elizabeth Adams (1884–1965), newspaper publisher and civic leader; vice president, *Pittsburgh Courier* (1925–65); regional field secretary (1930–35), national field secretary (1935–47), and member, NAACP National Board of Directors (1947–65).

Lancaster, John Wesley, Jr. (1901–89), civic leader; president, Bridgeport-Stratford, Connecticut, NAACP branch (1936–49). In 1947, Mitchell met with him and other community and labor leaders to settle a strike by the United Construction Workers of District 50, UMWA.

Land, Adm. Emory Scott (1889–1971), U.S. Navy; assistant chief, Bureau of Aeronautics, Department of Navy (1932–37); commander (1937–38) and chairman (1938–46), U.S. Maritime Commission. Staffer Daniel Ring represented the Maritime Commission and Admiral Land when he (Ring) went before a congressional committee to testify in favor of S. 2048, which would have strengthened the FEPC.

Lane, Layle (1893–1976), teacher, union leader and activist; officer, American Federation of Teachers; a leader of the March on Washington Movement, New York City; supporter of complainant in a FEPC case.

Lane, William Preston, Jr. (1892–1967) (D-Md.), Maryland attorney general (1930–34); governor (1947–51). In 1947, he informed the NAACP that nondiscriminatory standards for USES offices under state control were being considered.

Langer, William (1886–1959) (R-N.Dak.), North Dakota attorney general (1916–20); governor (1933–34, 1937–39); U.S. senator (1941–59). An isolationist, he backed a constitutional amendment to abolish the poll tax (1954) and introduced an antisegregation amendment to education legislation (1949).

Langhorn, Herman (1922–91), complainant. In 1954, he was notified that his apprenticeship in the U.S. Bureau of Engraving and Printing had ended and that he would not be able to continue in his field of employment.

Langlie, Arthur Bernard (1900–66) (R-Wash.), Seattle city councilman (1935–38) and mayor (1938–41); Washington governor (1941–45, 1949–57); chief executive officer (1957–61) and chair of the board (1961–65), McCall Corporation. Mitchell believed that he was not in favor of state FEPC legislation.

Langsen, James, general chairman, Brotherhood of Railway Carmen in 1953, when it was noted by Mitchell in a letter to Langsen that the Brotherhood's constitution still had a provision requiring that black members join segregated locals under the control of white union locals.

Larsen, Roy Edward (1899–1979), magazine executive; circulation manager (1923–29) and vice president (1929–79), Time, Inc.; chair, National Citizens' Commission for the Public Schools (1949–56); member, Board of Trustees, Ford Foundation (1957–79). In 1951, when the National Citizens' Commission for the Public Schools endorsed the segregated public school system of Arlington County, Virginia, Mitchell sent Larsen a letter protesting the decision, stating that it was a waste to maintain a dual school system, with the resulting state of public education due to segregation.

Lausche, Frank John (1895–1990) (R-Ohio), lawyer; businessman; mayor of Cleveland (1942–45); governor of Ohio (1945–47, 1949–57); U.S. senator (1957–69). In 1945, Will Maslow reported that Lausche, in his annual message to the state legislature, asked it to consider the creation of "a non-salaried Race Relations Committee without coercive powers to develop a program to eliminate discrimination."

Lautier, Louis Robert (1896–1962), journalist; assistant to the civilian aide to the secretary of war (1941–43); Washington bureau chief, NNPA (1943–61). In 1947, as a reporter for the *Atlanta Daily World,* he became the first African American to obtain credentials to the Capitol press galleries. Eight years later, he was the first African American to be admitted to the NPC.

Lawson, Belford Vance, Jr. (1901–85), lawyer and activist; with N. Franklin Thorne and John A. Davis, Sr., in 1933, he founded the National Negro Alliance in Washington, D.C. With its slogan "Don't Buy Where You Can't Work," the NNA was a militant response to discrimination. When challenged, Lawson joined with fellow attorney Thurman L. Dodson to successfully defend the NNA before the U.S. Supreme Court (*National Negro Alliance v. Sanitary Grocery Co.,* 303 US 552 [1938]). It was as president of the Alpha Phi Alpha fraternity that Lawson participated in the 1942 Conference of Cooperating Organizations.

Lawton, Frederick J. (1900–75), director, U.S. Bureau of the Budget (1950–53). In 1950, Maurice J. Tobin, U.S. secretary of labor, wrote a letter to Lawton explaining the difference between Executive Order 9346, which established a wartime FEPC, and the proposed Executive Order 10308, which called for a more far-reaching FEPC—broader in scope than the previous one and, moreover, with enforcement powers.

Layton, Elton Jesse (1890–1971), clerk, House Committee on Interstate and Foreign Commerce. In 1951, he received a letter from Mitchell and Joseph Waddy concerning their joint testimony before the committee on the subject of proposed amendments to the Railway Labor Act, stating that they were "in favor of the principles embodied in the bill but in opposition to the bill as drawn."

Leach, Aloysius Joseph (1909–53), the director of the Tenth U.S. Civil Service Region in 1947. When charges of employment discrimination were brought against the New Orleans Post Office, Leach, a native of the city, denied that there had been evidence of discrimination based on race.

Lee, Canada (1907–52), actor; was born Lionel Cornelius Canegata in New York City, the son of Barbadian immigrants. In 1952, Mitchell commented that, if the McCarran-Walter Act, with its severe restriction on immigration from the Caribbean and South America, had been in force when immigrants like the Canegatas entered the United States, they would not have been able to make "notable contributions to the building of our nation."

Lee, Maj. Gen. John Clifford Hodges, Sr. "Jesus Christ Himself" (1887–1958), U.S. Army; second-in-command to General Dwight D. Eisenhower in the European Theater of Operations. In December 1944, he issued a directive calling for black soldiers, who were primarily in service battalions behind the front lines, to volunteer to serve with white troops in rifle companies, stating "it is planned to assign you without regard to color or race to the units where assistance is most needed, and give you the opportunity of fighting shoulder to shoulder to bring about victory. . . . Your relatives and friends everywhere have been urging that you be given this privilege." Over forty-five hundred black soldiers volunteered, were trained for combat duty, and served in sixty man platoons embedded in two-hundred-man rifle companies, fighting in France, Germany and Italy.

Lee, Rev. Julius (1916–92), member, Hudson, New York, NAACP branch. In 1951, he went to Washington, D.C., to protest the proposed Winstead amendment to the Universal Military Training bill.

Lee, Thaddeus Shuptrine, Sr. (1898–1960), locomotive engineer; general chair, Brotherhood of Locomotive Firemen and Enginemen. In 1950, he testified in the case of *Rolax et al. v. Atlantic Coast Line Railway Company et al.*, and under cross-examination by Thurgood Marshall, representing the plaintiffs, Lee testified as to why very few black firemen were members of the union.

Lee, Theodore (1901–88), employed as a guard by the John McShain Company of Philadelphia in 1942; the company was finishing construction on the "War Department Building" (Pentagon) in Arlington, Virginia. Lee was accused by War Department employee James Harold of assaulting him when he was leaving the War Department cafeteria where he (Harold) had been refused service.

LeFlore, John Luzine, Sr. (1903–76), journalist and editor; executive secretary, Mobile, Alabama, branch, NAACP (1926–56); chair, NAACP Regional Conference of Southern Branches (1936–45); vice president (1945–51) and member (1952–53), Board of Directors, Alabama State Conference of NAACP Branches. A longtime post office employee, he was disciplined for being involved in civil rights activities and was eventually forced to retire early. In 1953, he informed the NAACP of post office discrimination in Mobile.

Lehman, Herbert Henry (1878–1963) (D-N.Y.), banker; New York lieutenant governor (1929–32); governor (1933–42); director general, UNRRA (1943–46); U.S. senator (1949–57). A persistent civil rights advocate in the Senate, he supported Senate rules changes, nondiscrimination amendments to labor and housing legislation, desegregation of schools on military bases, fair employment laws with enforcement powers, and legislation to protect service members from violence.

Leland, Wilfred Chester, Jr. (1908–96), college professor, administrator, and grandson of the founder of the Lincoln Automobile Company (later acquired by Ford); teaching assistant (1937–39) and instructor in business administration (1940–48), University of Minnesota; executive secretary, Mayor's Council on Human Relations, Minneapolis (1945–49); executive director, Minneapolis FEPC (1948–55). He worked closely with Hubert Humphrey and Clarence Mitchell in implementing both state and federal FEPC mandates. In 1952, Leland was interviewed for the post of executive director of the Committee on Government Contract Compliance, but he was not selected for the position.

Lennartson, Nils Andrew (1915–77), deputy director of public relations, Department of the Air Force (1948–52); special assistant to the secretary of the air force (1951–52); director of public information, Department of Commerce (1952–53); assistant to the secretary of the treasury (1953–61); deputy assistant secretary of defense for public affairs (1961–65). He attended a 1950 meeting in Washington concerning an assault on a black corporal by military police in Fort Worth, Texas.

Lenroot, Katharine Fredrica (1891–1982), investigator, assistant chief (1915–34), and chief (1934–51), Children's Bureau, Department of Labor. In 1947, Mitchell successfully appealed to her to prevent discrimination at a Belle Glade, Florida, hospital for migrant workers following its reversion from federal to state control.

Lensh, Geraldine [married name Lenvin] (1910–98), social worker and educator. In July of 1942, with Rachel Corrothers, she represented the Union for Democratic Action at the Conference of Cooperating Organizations, where she spoke of her organization's efforts to end discrimination in the armed services. She would later turn to teaching, retiring as chair of the English department at Falls Church High School in Virginia; after retirement, she would pen charming essays and "letters to the editor" on various subjects to local publications including the *Washington Post.*

Leonard, Col. Joseph Stephens (1888–1963), U.S. Army; USMA class of 1910; secretary, War Department's Advisory Committee on Negro Troop Policies from 1942; he had previously been involved in military personnel matters for the army. In 1944 he met with Walter White to discuss criticisms and recommendations in his (White's) two reports on black troops in the European Theater and the North African Theater of Operations. Leonard is buried at Arlington National Cemetery.

LeRay, Nelson Ludwig, Sr. (1903–74), chief investigator, Tenth U.S. Civil Service Region in 1947 when he investigated New Orleans postal worker Henry R. Greene's complaint of employment discrimination for the U.S. Civil Service.

Lerner, Emanuel Richard (1908–2002), economist; labor director, NHA (1942–47). In 1946, he conferred with Mitchell on utilization of nonwhite labor in postwar federal housing programs.

Lesinski, John (1885–1950) (D-Mich.), businessman; U.S. representative (1933–50). Known primarily for his prolabor views, he offered an amendment to the Taft-Hartley Act that would have forbade segregation and discrimination in unions seeking to use NLRB facilities.

Leskes, Theodore J. (1908–64), lawyer, author, and activist. He is best known in recent times for monographs on the civil rights movement and the history of racial and religious discrimination in the United States. In 1951, representing the AJCong, Leskes attended a meeting of concerned organizations discussing Senate rules change.

Levy, Herbert Monte (1923–), ACLU lawyer. In 1951, he participated in a meeting in Washington whose purpose was to seek changes to the Senate rules.

Levy, Nettie S. (1896–1987), known professionally as Mrs. I. Lee Levy, was the wife of the owner of Isidore Levy & Company, a Manhattan producer of ladies wear. Mrs. Levy was active in many social and charitable activities, including the National Council of Jewish Women, and, as its representative, she was part of a delegation from the NECRM that met with President Truman in January of 1950.

Lewis, Alfred Baker (1897–1980), lawyer, businessman, and author; secretary, Boston branch, NAACP; member, NAACP National Board of Directors (1939–80); national treasurer, NAACP (1958–72). An insurance company executive, he supported state FEPC legislation.

Lewis, Edward A. (1921–2010), veteran. Although claiming employment discrimination at the New Orleans Post Office, he declined to join those of his fellow postal workers and the NAACP in filing formal charges against that body.

Lewis, Rev. Forrest H. (1891–1973), clergyman. A resident of Charleston, West Virginia, he organized local labor committees in 1948.

Lewis, Ira Foster (1883–1948), newspaper executive. He joined the *Pittsburgh Courier* in 1914 as a sportswriter, but soon moved into advertising sales and, with the help of local businesspeople like Daisy Lampkin, built up circulation and revenue from advertising and was eventually made business manager of the paper. In 1943, he was one of sixteen members of the black press who protested the cancellation of the FEPC's hearings on racial discrimination in the railroad industry.

Lewis, John Llewellyn (1880–1969), coal miner and labor leader; president, United Mine Workers (UMW) (1920–60). Known as a hard-nosed negotiator and fighter, capable of calling out miners to strike at the drop of a hat, he was also a firm supporter of President Roosevelt, the New Deal and the Wagner Act. When the UMW sent organizers into heavy industry and the AFL hesitated to include unskilled workers, Lewis led the UMW and other unions away from the AFL and founded the CIO. In 1964, President Lyndon B. Johnson awarded Lewis the Medal of Freedom.

Lewis, Peter (1900–81), railroad brakeman, of Holmes County, Mississippi. In January 1931, in McComb, Mississippi, Lewis was shot and seriously wounded by whites who coveted his job.

Lincoln, Abraham (1809–65) (R-Ill.), lawyer; U.S. representative (1847–49); unsuccessful candidate for Whig nomination for U.S. senator from Illinois (1858); president of the U.S. (1861–65). The first Republican presidential candidate elected president, his tenure encompassed the American Civil War. Due to his work to save the Union, free the slaves, and lay the groundwork for the eventual passage of the Thirteenth and Fourteenth Amendments, the Republican party has often been called the "Party of Lincoln" when civil rights are discussed.

Liveright, Alexander Albert (1907–69), professor; executive director, WMC (1943–45); executive director, ACRR (1945–47); director, CSLEA (1956–68). He attended a 1946 conference about racial discrimination in USES offices.

Lockwood, Warren Jay (1884–1961), architect, real estate manager, and government official; chief underwriter, FHA (1933–35); assistant deputy commissioner, Mortgage Insurance Division, FHA (1935–36); deputy commissioner, FHA for the Rocky Mountain and Pacific Coast regions (1936–38); deputy commissioner, FHA, for the midwestern states (1938–41); director, New Jersey Division, FHA (1941–46); assistant commissioner, FHA (1946–53). In 1948, in a letter to housing advocate Herman Will Jr. that was ultimately forwarded to Mitchell, Lockwood outlined how a proposed interracially populated housing project in Chicago could be deemed unacceptable to the neighborhood due to the "infiltration" of blacks into the neighborhood and thus should be avoided.

Lodge, Henry Cabot, Jr. (1902–85) (R-Mass.), Massachusetts state legislator (1933–36); U.S. senator (1937–44, 1947–53); U.S. representative to the United Nations (1953–60); ambassador to the Republic of Vietnam (1963–64, 1965–67); ambassador to Germany (1968–69). He was a cosponsor of the Lodge-Gossett bill, which would have amended the Constitution to abolish the Electoral College and split the electoral vote of each state in presidential elections in accordance with the popular vote. Mitchell and the NAACP opposed the resolution on the grounds that one of its chief purposes was to destroy the political effectiveness of African American and other minority voting districts in pivotal states.

Loeb, James Isaac, Jr. (1908–92), newspaper editor, educator, and diplomat; national director of UDA (1945–47) and of its successor, ADA (1947–51); consultant to Charles S. Murphy, special counsel to President Truman (1951–52); executive assistant to Gov. W. Averell Harriman of New York (1952–53); U.S. ambassador to Peru (1961–62); U.S. ambassador to Guinea (1963–65). In 1950, an article Loeb wrote for the *ADA World* criticizing the proposed Lodge-Gossett resolution was used by Dr. John A. Davis in preparing a memorandum outlining the reasons why the NAACP opposed the resolution.

Loescher, Frank Samuel (1911–76), sociologist, author, and peace activist; associate professor, Department of Sociology, Temple University, Philadelphia (1943–49); chair, Philadelphia FEPC (1949–53); AFSC (1960–70). In later years, he actively promoted closer ties with South Africa and, to bring that about, organized the United States–South Africa Leadership Exchange. In 1946, he was present at a meeting with Mitchell and U.S. secretary of labor Schwellenbach, in which the latter pledged that segregation would end in the Washington offices of the Department of Labor by September 30 of that year.

Logan, Rayford Whittingham (1897–1982), historian, author, and activist. He was a World War I veteran who remained in France after the end of the war, becoming a Pan-Africanist and a close colleague of W.E.B. DuBois; professor of history, Virginia Union University (1925–30); assistant to Carter G. Woodson at the Association for the Study of Negro Life and History (1930–33); professor of history, Atlanta University (1933–38); professor of history, Howard University (1938–74); recipient of the Spingarn Medal, 1980. He was actively involved in the organization of MOWM and was named to its sponsoring committee in 1941.

Logue, Edward Joseph (1921–2000), lawyer. In a 1948 letter to Loge that was forwarded to Walter White, Glenn Atkinson, then assistant to George M. Harrison (chair of the Labor

Division of the Democratic National Committee), told of Harrison's struggle to alter the constitution of the Brotherhood of Railway Clerks to remove the word *White* as a limitation to membership.

Long, Herman Hodge (1912–76), sociologist and author; professor, Department of Sociology, Fisk University (1944–64); director, Race Relations Institute, Fisk University (1947–64); president, Talladega College (1964–76). During the 1940s and 1950s, Long wrote a number of monographs on segregation in housing and in public transportation. One of those publications, *Segregation in Interstate Railway Coach Travel,* was deemed by Mitchell in 1954 as "very useful" despite the fact Long erroneously assumed that the Maryland Jim Crow legislation affecting railway travel within its borders was still in force.

Looby, Zephaniah Alexander (1899–1972), born in Antigua; educated at Howard University and Columbia University Law School, with advanced degrees in law from New York University; moved to Memphis in 1923, and then to Nashville three years later; instructor, Fisk University (1926–28); founder and president, Kent College of Law, Nashville (1932–41); with Robert E. Lillard, first black elected to Nashville City Council since Reconstruction (1951–71); active in civil rights activity for nearly a half century; called the dean of African American lawyers of Nashville, Tennessee; member of NAACP National Board; member of NAACP National Legal Committee; assisted with many NAACP cases; home bombed in 1960. In 1942, representing Omega Psi Phi fraternity, he attended the Conference of Cooperating Organizations in Washington.

Lopez, Alvin J., Jr. (1919–80), veteran. He sought employment in the New Orleans Post Office but was denied a job despite his high civil service test score. In 1947, he became one of the NAACP's official complainants against the New Orleans Post Office.

Lourie, Donold Bradford (1899–1990), president (1947–53, 1954–56), chief executive officer (1956–62), and chair (1962–70), Quaker Oats Company; undersecretary of state for administration, State Department (1953–54). A former All-America quarterback at Princeton University, he reported on personnel issues during the struggle to integrate the State Department.

Lovett, Robert Abercrombie (1895–1986), assistant secretary of war for air (1941–45); undersecretary of state (1947–49); deputy secretary of defense (1950–51); U.S. secretary of defense (1951–53). In 1952, the NAACP appealed to him to end segregation of schools on military posts.

Lucas, Charles Payne (1911–89), executive secretary, Cleveland branch, NAACP (1945–54); member, CTB; member, OBE. He fought for state and local FEPC legislation. In 1950, he secured passage of such a law for Cleveland in place of an ineffective voluntary plan.

Lucas, Scott Wike (1892–1968) (D-Ill.), lawyer; chair, ISTC (1933–35); U.S. representative (1935–39); U.S. senator (1939–51); Senate majority leader (1949–51). The NAACP sought his assistance as majority leader in moving FEPC legislation and an antisegregation amendment to draft legislation.

Luckman, Charles (1909–99), architect, designer and business executive; rose from draftsman in the advertising department of Colgate-Palmolive (1930–35) to national sales manager for Pepsodent toothpaste (1935–46) to president of the parent company Lever Brothers (1946–50), before returning to southern California to establish an architectural firm. In 1948, he was named to President Truman's Committee on Equality of Treatment and Opportunity for Negro Troops in the Armed Forces.

Lukas, Edwin Jay (1902–73), lawyer and criminologist; general counsel and head, Civil Rights and Social Action Department, AJCom (1950–68). He represented AJCom at a 1953 meeting concerning the CGC.

Mabry, Thomas Jewett (1884–1962) (D-N.Mex.), lawyer and publisher; New Mexico state legislator (1912–17); member, Albuquerque City Commission (1926–27); Albuquerque district attorney (1932–36); Albuquerque district judge (1937–39); chief justice, New Mexico Supreme Court (1939–46); governor (1947–51). Although Mitchell believed that he was not a supporter of state FEPC legislation, such a commission was established while he was governor.

MacArthur, Gen. Douglas (1880–1964), U. S. Army. As supreme commander of U.S. Pacific forces during World War II, he corresponded with Walter White concerning the disposition of black troops in the Pacific Theater.

MacGregor, Morris J., Jr. (1931–), historian and author; staff member, Historical Division, U.S. Joint Chiefs of Staff (1957–68); historian (and acting chief historian), U.S. Army Center of Military History (1968–92).

MacKinnon, George Edward (1906–95) (R-Minn.), lawyer and jurist; Minnesota state legislator (1935–42); U.S. representative (1947–49); consultant to the administrator, GSA (1952–53); U.S. attorney for the District of Minnesota (1953–58); judge, U.S. Court of Appeals, District of Columbia Circuit (1969–83); senior judge (1983–95). In 1953, as consultant to the administrator of GSA, MacKinnon was present at a meeting of the Committee for Government Compliance and governmental agencies and other voluntary organizations designed to help the committee achieve its goals.

MacLean, Dr. Malcolm Shaw, Sr. (1893–1964), of Virginia, educator; president, Hampton Institute (1940–42); chairman, FEPC (1942–43); head, planning section, Office of Occupied Areas, U.S. Navy (1943–45). In 1948, in conversation with Mitchell, James C. Evans, civilian assistant to the Department of Defense, mentioned MacLean as a possible member of the President's Committee on Equality of Treatment and Opportunity in the Armed Services, established through President Truman's Executive Order 9981.

Madar, Olga Marie (1915–96), physical education teacher and union executive; chair, Recreation Committee, UAW (1940–66); commissioner, Detroit Municipal Parks and Recreation Commission (1958–66); member at large (1966–70) and international vice president (1970–74), UAW International Executive Board. As a member of the union Recreation Committee, Madar's goal was to encourage physical fitness, personal hygiene, and good health among union members. She was also instrumental in desegregating bowling leagues in which black and white union members participated, and she worked to ensure that playgrounds and other public places would be integrated. At the 1948 UAW education conference, she presented a seminar on how to make halls and meetings more attractive for delegates who attended those meetings.

Madison, James (1751–1836) (D-R-Va.), lawyer, planter, businessman, and author; U.S. representative (1789–97); U.S. secretary of state (1801–09); president (1809–17). Irving Brant, who wrote an award-winning biography describing Madison's life and career, declared that in his opinion, the poll tax was unconstitutional.

Magnuson, Warren Grant (1905–89) (D-Wash.), lawyer; Washington state legislator (1933–34); U.S. district attorney (1934); U.S. representative (1937–44); U.S. senator (1944–81). "Maggie," as the popular senator was affectionately known, was noted for his ability to steer congressional pork to his constituents. He also compiled a liberal voting record, including support for anti–poll tax legislation and opposition to the Taft-Hartley Act.

Malin, Patrick M. (1903–64), economist, educator, and activist; professor, Department of Economics, Swarthmore College (1930–50); executive director, ACLU (1950–63). In 1951, he testified before the Senate Committee on Rules and Administration concerning the use of the filibuster.

Manley, Michael James (1896–1973), lawyer and jurist of Baltimore; associate justice (1945–63) and chief justice (1963–66), Supreme Bench of Baltimore City; in 1954, he officiated over the various trials of Bryant W. Bowles, Jr.

Manly, Milo Alexander (1903–91), of La Mott, Pennsylvania, just north of Philadelphia. He was a former Philadelphia parole officer and investigator and supervisor with the Pennsylvania Department of Public Assistance who was appointed examiner, Region III, FEPC in 1943. He was later examiner in charge of the Pittsburgh sub-office, FEPC; he played a major role in negotiating settlement of work stoppage at Clairton Byproducts Plant of the Carnegie-Illinois Steel Corporation. He served as field director, NCPFEPC (1947–48) and subsequently as executive director, Pennsylvania Human Relations Commission.

Margetson, Edward Henry (1891–1962), composer and lyricist; born St. Kitts, B.W.I. In 1952, Mitchell commented that, if the McCarran-Walter Act, with its severe restriction on immigration from the Caribbean and South America, had been in force when immigrants like Margetson entered the United States, they would not have been able to make "notable contributions to the building of our nation."

Markle, Harry Carl (1896–1971), lawyer; executive director, Michigan Unemployment Compensation Commission. In 1951, Mitchell cited Markle's testimony before the Michigan State House of Representatives as to the level of employment discrimination in the state of Michigan.

Marmion, Fr. Charles Gresham, Jr. (1905–2000), Episcopal priest. When Congress held hearings concerning an anti-lynching bill, Father Marmion, then pastor of St. Albans' Protestant Episcopal Church in Washington, D.C., testified concerning a lynching he witnessed in Texas. He later served as Episcopal Bishop of Kentucky (1954–74).

Marr, Col. Jack Franklin (1915–81), staff member, Office of Director of Personnel Planning, Department of the Air Force. He authored a 1948 study depicting waste and inefficiency in the air force resulting from that institution's segregation policy. In 1950, he attended a meeting on the assault of a black corporal by military police.

Marshall, Dr. Charles Herbert, Jr. (1898–1983), president, National Medical Association (1946–48). A graduate of Howard University and a general practitioner in Georgetown, D.C., he represented the NMA at the Conference of Cooperating Organizations in July of 1942, stating that the chief surgeon of the U.S. Army should endorse the construction of black VA hospitals because "about the only advantage of a segregated union [unit] is that it gives credit to the Negro, whereas in a mixed unit, the colored doctor gets lost."

Marshall, George Catlett (1880–1959), army officer; U.S. secretary of state (1947–49); U.S. secretary of defense (1950–51). As secretary of defense, he worked on protecting service members from violence and securing nonsegregation of draftees and inductees under postwar military service legislation.

Marshall, Thurgood (1908–93), lawyer; assistant special counsel, NAACP (1936–38); special counsel, NAACP (1938–61); director-counsel, NAACP Legal Defense and Educational Fund, Inc. (1940–61); judge, U.S. Second Circuit Court of Appeals (1961–65); U.S. solicitor general (1965–67); associate justice, U.S. Supreme Court (1967–91). Active in railroad and school desegregation cases during Truman's presidency, he also traveled to Japan and Korea in 1951 to investigate convictions of black soldiers by army courts. Later that year, the NAACP published his *Report on Korea: The Shameful Story of the Court Martial of Negro GIs.*

Martin, Edward (1879–1967) (R-Pa.), businessman, author, and newspaper executive; veteran of the Spanish-American War, World War I, and World War II and retired Major General, Pennsylvania National Guard; governor of Pennsylvania (1943–46); U.S. senator (1947–59). While governor, he opposed the creation of a separate state FEPC due to added expense and requested the sponsors of the bills calling for the end of employment discrimination and the establishment of some commission to oversee that it occur to come to a compromise. He would later sign into law a state FEPC law originally introduced by African-American state legislator Homer S. Brown of Pittsburgh.

Martin, Rear Adm. Farar Benjamin Conner "Pepper" (1905–89), World War II naval commander; commanding officer, USS *Toledo* (1952–53); director, Distant Early Warning Line (1957–70). As head of the navy's recruitment division, he met with Mitchell in 1950 on segregation in the armed forces.

Martin, Haywood T. (1913–87), at one time director of personnel, U.S. State Department. In 1951, Secretary of State Dean Acheson referred Martin to Mitchell and others attempting to have more black employees serving in the department of state.

Martin, Joseph William, Jr. (1884–1968) (R-Mass.), journalist and publisher; Massachusetts state legislator (1912–17); U.S. representative (1925–67); House minority leader (1940–47, 1949–53, 1955–59); Speaker of the House (1947–49, 1953–55); chair, RNC (1940–42). Although he opposed most Fair Deal legislation, he supported anti–poll tax and antilynching measures. In 1948, he backed an antidiscrimination amendment to a Selective Service bill.

Martin, Louis Emanuel, Jr. (1912–97), journalist and editor; editor-in-chief, (Detroit) *Michigan Chronicle* (1936–47); editor-in-chief (1947–59), editor (1969–78), and columnist (1987–97), *Chicago Defender*; deputy chairman, DNC (1960–69); special assistant to President Jimmy Carter (1978–81); assistant vice president of communications, Howard University (1981–87). In 1943, he was one of sixteen black newspaper owners, publishers, and editors protesting the FEPC's cancellation of hearings concerning racial discrimination of blacks in the railroad industry. In 1951, he was present at the organizational meeting of the LCCR.

Marvin, Cloyd Heck (1889–1969), president, George Washington University (1927–59). In 1950, he refused to commit to admitting African American students and to ending segregation at his school.

Masaoka, Mike Masuru (1915–91), newspaper editor and publisher and public relations executive; national secretary (1940–42) and Washington, D.C., representative (1945–72), Japanese-American Cultural League. He helped organize and ultimately enlisted in the 442nd U.S. Regimental Combat Team in World War II. In 1946, he was present at a meeting with Mitchell and U.S. secretary of labor Schwellenbach, in which the latter pledged that segregation would end in the Washington offices of the Department of Labor by September 30 of that year.

Maslow, Will (1907–2007), lawyer and editor; trial examiner and administrative law judge, NLRB (1937–43); director of field operations, FEPC (1943–45); counsel (1945–56) and executive director (1960–72), AJCong. A native of Kiev, he participated in a 1946 conference with Labor Secretary Schwellenbach on ending discrimination by USES offices. Five years later, he was a member of a strategy group working for Senate rules changes.

Mason, Myron (1900–88), carpenter, of Aiken, South Carolina; member of the Carpenters' Union of Columbia, South Carolina, a predominately white union local. In 1951, he reported to Mitchell and the Aiken NAACP branch that the union had referrals for work on the Savannah River Plant hydrogen bomb facility in Aiken.

Mather, Anne (1920–), sociologist, social worker, and administrator; director, Committee to Support the Ives-Quinn Law (1944–49); executive secretary, Consumers League of New York City (1946–51); delegate to the Democratic National Convention (1972). A descendant of the Puritan divine Cotton Mather and a graduate of Smith College and the Columbia University School of Social Work, she shocked white New York society in 1950 by marrying black social worker and activist Frank C. Montero (1909–98), who was then associate executive director of the National Urban League. They had two daughters but divorced after twenty-five years. In 1949, Anne Mather sent a draft report from the Committee to Support the Ives-Quinn Law to Marian Wynn Perry of the NAACP Legal Defense and Educational Fund, Inc.

Matthews, Francis Patrick (1887–1952), member, PCCR (1947); secretary of the navy (1949–51); ambassador to Ireland (1951–52). In 1951, he ordered that members of the navy could not participate in activities sponsored by groups that discriminated.

Matthews, Rev. Malcom M. (1909–93), president, Missouri State Conference of NAACP Branches. He approved a NAACP labor department letter to the governor of Missouri calling for an end to discrimination by a USES office once it was returned to state control.

Matzeliger, Jan Earnst (1852–89), inventor of a number of patented works, including a shoe lasting machine which revolutionized the shoe making industry; a native of Dutch Guiana (now Suriname), he worked his way to the United States as a deckhand on a freighter. In 1952, Mitchell commented that, if the McCarran-Walter Act, with its severe restriction on immigration from the Caribbean and South America, had been in force when immigrants like Matzeliger (who distinguished themselves in their adopted country) entered the United States, they would not have been able to make "notable contributions to the building of our nation."

Maxwell, Oscar Clay (1885–1973), Baptist minister; a native of St. Louis, he was best known for his tenure as pastor, Mount Olivet Baptist Church in Harlem (1929–67). In 1941, after A. Philip Randolph had spoken at the church concerning the proposed March on Washington, Reverend Maxwell presented him with $114.40 that had been collected from the congregation.

Maybank, Burnet Rhett (1899–1954) (D-S.C.), businessman; Charleston mayor (1931–38); South Carolina governor (1938–41); U.S. senator (1941–54). A conservative senator who specialized in public housing matters, he opposed integration of such housing. He also opposed a permanent FEPC and the elimination of the poll tax. In 1951, he threatened to cut appropriations for the AEC after that body issued an antisegregation policy.

Mayor, Beatrice, represented Zeta Phi Beta sorority at the Conference of Cooperating Organizations on July 4, 1942.

Mays, Benjamin Elijah (1894–1984), educator and clergyman; dean, Howard University School of Religion (1934–40); president, Morehouse College (1940–67); vice president, Federal Council of Churches of Christ (1944–48); member, Atlanta (Georgia) Board of Education (1969–73; president from 1970). In 1945, he was traveling from Atlanta to New York by rail when he was refused service in the dining car. When the examiner for the ICC found no discrimination was involved, the NAACP filed exceptions to the report, but the scheduled rehearing was indefinitely postponed. In 1951, with Walter White and A. Philip Randolph, he attended a meeting with President Harry S. Truman commemorating the three year anniversary of his first civil rights message to Congress.

McCarran, Patrick Anthony "Pat" (1876–1954) (D-Nev.), lawyer and district attorney; associate (1913–17) and chief justice (1917–18), Nevada Supreme Court; state government official (1913–32); U.S. senator (1933–54); chair, Senate Judiciary Committee (1943–47, 1949–53). He was a sponsor of the Internal Security Act of 1950, the McCarran Immigration Act, and other security-related measures.

McCarthy, Eugene Joseph (1916–2005) (D-Minn.), teacher and professor; U.S. representative (1949–59); U.S. senator (1959–71). A liberal with a strong prolabor voting record, he opposed legislation that provided aid for segregated schools on military posts.

McClendon, Sarah Newcomb (1910–2003), journalist; president and owner of McClendon News Service. As a single mother, she had served as Washington correspondent for the *Philadelphia Daily News* during World War II but was fired from her position in order to make room for returning veterans; thereupon, she started her own syndicated news service. She was a fixture at Washington news conferences from the fourth administration of Franklin D. Roosevelt to the first administration of George W. Bush.

McCloy, John Jay (1895–1989), lawyer, business executive and diplomat; World War I veteran; assistant secretary of war (1936–40); deputy secretary of war (1941–45); president, World Bank (1945–49); military governor and high commissioner for West Germany (1949–52). He corresponded with the NAACP about the role of blacks in the American Army during World War II. He was a member of the President's Committee for the Equality of Treatment and Opportunity in the Armed Forces (PCETOAS), or Fahy Committee, at the close of World War II.

McCone, John Alex (1902–91), president, Bechtel-McCone Corporation (1937–46), California Shipbuilding Corporation (1941–46), and Joshua Hendy Iron Works Corporation (1945–69); assistant to the secretary of defense (1948–50); undersecretary, U.S. Air Force (1950–51); chair, AEC (1958–60); director, CIA (1961–65). While serving as acting secretary of the air force, he issued a statement that arranged for air force training for black service members in New Mexico.

McConnell, Samuel Kerns, Jr. (1901–85) (R-Pa.), investment banker; U.S. representative (1944–57); executive director, UCPAI (1957–61). As an alternative to an FEPC bill sponsored by Adam Clayton Powell, he introduced a watered-down version that lacked enforcement powers, did not apply to the AEC or its contractors, and had other provisions designed to limit its force. This bill, with amendments, was backed by conservative Republicans and southern Democrats and led to the defeat of Powell's measure. McConnell also voted to authorize E. E. Cox of Georgia to investigate charitable organizations accused of fomenting class and racial strife in the South.

McCormack, John William (1891–1980) (D-Mass.), lawyer; Massachusetts state legislator (1920–22, 1923–26); U.S. representative (1928–71); House majority leader (1939–47; 1949–61); Speaker of the House (1961–71). Known as "the Fighting Irishman" for his aggressive political style, he was a pro–Fair Deal anticommunist with a strong labor and civil rights record. He opposed the Cox Committee, authorized in 1952 to investigate charitable organizations that supported civil rights activities in the South.

McCormick, Col. John Halliday (1903–92), U.S. Army Air Corps; retired as Major General, U.S. Air Force. In 1944, as a member of the War Department's Advisory Committee on Negro Troop Policies, he met with Walter White to discuss criticisms and recommendations in White's reports on black troops in the European Theater and the North African Theater of Operations.

McCready, Esther (1932–), nurse, musician, concert singer and activist; first African American to successfully enroll in the University of Maryland School of Nursing, with help from the Baltimore chapter of the NAACP. After graduation, she went to New York City where, while working as a private duty nurse, she pursued a career in music. She received a master's degree from the Manhattan School of Music and would eventually sing in the chorus of the Metropolitan Opera. For a time, she was the music teacher and voice tutor for the actress Raven-Symone.

McCulloch, William Moore (1901–80) (R-Ohio), lawyer; Ohio state legislator (1933–44); U.S. representative (1947–73). Although known as a staunch conservative, he was a prime mover behind the Civil Rights Acts of 1960 and 1964.

McCune, Wesley (1916–2003), journalist and author; executive assistant to the secretary of agriculture (1948–53); assistant to the deputy chair, DNC (1953–56); director of public relations, NFU (1956–62); president, Group Research Incorporated (1962–96). His Group Research Incorporated newsletter kept tabs on right-wing organizations. He also served as fair employment officer for the Department of Agriculture.

McDonald, Louise J. (1899–1982), educator and sorority leader. A longtime teacher in the metropolitan New York City school system, she was also active in the Alpha Kappa Alpha sorority, serving in a number of administrative positions over a thirty-year period. She represented the sorority at the Conference of Cooperating Organizations on July 4, 1942.

McDonald, Willard Floyd (1891–1969), meteorologist and administrator. A native of Indiana, he started at the U.S. Weather Bureau as an observer and steadily rose through the ranks, serving as acting chief of the Weather Service in 1951. Nearing the end of his career with the bureau, he served as assistant chief of personnel, and in that capacity, he met with Mitchell to assure him that Edmund D. Cooke would be offered a position as meterological aide with the bureau.

McFadyen, Gen. Bernice Musgrove (1896–1954), World War I and World War II veteran; chief, MPMD, Army General Staff. In 1951, he conferred with Mitchell on discrimination in the armed forces. He ultimately achieved the rank of major general.

McFarland, Ernest William (1894–1984) (D-Ariz.), lawyer; U.S. senator (1941–53); Senate majority leader (1951–53); Arizona governor (1955–59); associate (1964–68) and chief justice (1968–70), Arizona Supreme Court. As senator, he specialized in communications matters. A states' rights sympathizer, he nevertheless supported antilynching legislation while serving as majority leader.

McGee, Henry Wadsworth (1910–2000), postal worker; president, Chicago branch, NAACP (resigned in 1948); Chicago postmaster (1966–72). Mitchell corresponded with him on relations between the Chicago branch and the PHWU. In 1966, he became the first black postmaster in the history of Chicago.

McGowan, Fr. Raymond A. (1892–1962), Roman Catholic priest and activist. He joined the Social Action Department of the NCWC in 1919 and succeeded Monsignor John A. Ryan as director in 1945, serving until his retirement in 1954. In 1943, he was a member of the Citizens' Committee to Save Colored Locomotive Firemen's Jobs.

McGrath, Earl James (1902–93), professor and college administrator; commissioner, PCHE (1946–47); U.S. commissioner of education (1949–53). In 1953, he advised the Department of Defense that segregation in schools on military posts could be eliminated.

McGrath, James Howard (1903–66) (D-R.I.), lawyer and businessman; Rhode Island governor (1941–45); U.S. solicitor general (1945–46); chair, DNC (1947–49); U.S. senator (1947–49); U.S. attorney general (1949–52). A strong supporter of civil rights, he ended the segregation of DNC headquarters while serving as that body's chair. During his brief Senate tenure, he introduced FEPC, antilynching, and anti–poll tax legislation, and as attorney general, he actively challenged the constitutionality of segregation.

McGraw, Booker Tanner (1899–1978), accountant; professor of economics, Lincoln University (in Missouri) (1936–46); principal housing analyst, NHA (1946–49). In 1946, Mitchell sent a memorandum to McGraw and Frank Horne outlining questions concerning the FHA's continued role in the postwar world as it concerned the plight of black Americans.

McGriff, Jeff (1917–96), serviceman. In 1954, he was abused by white soldiers at Fort Jackson, South Carolina.

McGuire, Charles H. (1901–84), head, Division of Contract Evaluation, Maritime Administration (1946–51); director, NSA (1951–53); director, Office of the National Shipping Authority and Government Aid, Maritime Administration (1953–55). In 1951, NAACP research assistant Earle Fisher met with him on the issue of employment of black merchant marine officers.

McIntire, Dr. Ross T. (1889–1959), White House physician (1933–38); surgeon general and chief of Bureau of Medicine and Surgery, U.S. Navy (1938–46); chair, PCEPH (1947–54). Mitchell encouraged him to hire black disabled veterans for the staff of the PCEPH.

McIntyre, Marvin Hunter (1878–1943), journalist; special assistant to the U.S. secretary of the Navy (1918–21); traveling secretary for President Roosevelt (1933–37); corresponding secretary for President Roosevelt (1941–43). In 1942, a letter to Walter White of the NAACP was sent out under McIntyre's signature reassuring White that the FEPC was safe in the hands of Paul V. McNutt, the head of the War Manpower Commission, and the ultimate responsibility for the FEPC's continued existence still rested with the president.

McKay, Claude (1889–1948), poet and novelist; born Jamaica. In 1952, Mitchell commented that, if the McCarran-Walter Act, with its severe restriction on immigration from the Caribbean and South America, had been in force when immigrants like McKay entered the United States, they would not have been able to make "notable contributions to the building of our nation."

McKay, Douglas (1893–1959) (R-Ore.), businessman; Oregon state legislator (1935–42, 1943–48); governor (1949–53); U.S. secretary of the interior (1953–56). In 1952, Mitchell asked him to continue the desegregation of Washington, D.C., facilities that were administered by the Department of the Interior.

McKellar, Hugh Clinton (1875–1953), Memphis, Tennessee, postmaster. A brother of Tennessee senator Kenneth D. McKellar, he opposed the hiring of blacks as postal clerks. His discriminatory policy was ended following a 1948 Senate investigation of discrimination by the Post Office Department.

McKellar, Kenneth Douglas (1869–1957) (D-Tenn.), lawyer; U.S. representative (1911–17); U.S. senator (1917–53); president pro tempore of the Senate (1945–47, 1949–53). An ally of Ed "Boss" Crump, he was a master at obtaining patronage plums for his state. He was best known in the immediate postwar years for accusing David Lilienthal (Truman's nominee to head the AEC) of communist sympathies.

McKendall, Irvin V. (1921–73), veteran. He sought employment in New Orleans as a postal clerk or letter carrier but was denied a position despite his high civil service test score. In 1947, he became one of the NAACP's official complainants against the New Orleans Post Office.

McKenzie, Pvt. Roberta (1921–), U.S. Army; a native of Blytheville, Arkansas, she enlisted in the WAACs in Little Rock March 26, 1943. With Pvt. Gladys Blackmon, she was severely beaten on a bus on the way to Camp Sibert, Alabama, when both refused to give up their seats on the bus for white people.

McKnight, Robert. One of a group of black teenagers who, in 1953, challenged Jim Crow transportation laws and refused to move to the back of a bus in Richmond, Virginia.

McLaurin, Benjamin Franklin (1906–89), union leader and social activist. A member of BSCP from 1926, he served as national secretary, MOWM from 1941. A member of the ADA, WDL and the president of the Professional Household Workers Association, in the administration of New York City Mayor John V. Lindsay, he served on the Mayor's Commission on Exploitation of Workers.

McLaurin, George Washington (1887–1968), educator; at one time instructor, foreign languages, Arkansas Baptist College and professor of foreign languages, Langston University; named plaintiff in segregation case *McLaurin v. Oklahoma State Regents for Higher Education* (339 US 637). After being admitted to the University of Oklahoma's graduate school, he had been required to sit in a special seat in the classroom and at designated separate tables in the cafeteria and the library because of his race. The United States Supreme Court ruled that McLaurin must receive the same treatment as any other student and could not be segregated from them.

McMichael, Rev. Jack Richard (1917–84), Methodist minister, educator and activist. In 1951, while serving as executive secretary for the Methodist Federation for Social Action (1945-53), he was present at the organization of the LCCR.

McMillan, John Lanneau (1898–1979) (D-S.C.), lawyer; U.S. representative (1939–73). He sponsored a 1950 bill that would have transferred six swimming pools in the District of Columbia from the control of the Department of the Interior to the D.C. Recreation Board, a measure that would have ensured continued segregation of those facilities. He also opposed home rule for the District, accusing that measure's proponents of being "communist sympathizers."

McMurdy, Robert (1860–1940), lawyer, jurist, Illinois state legislator, novelist, and essayist. A wealthy and influential Chicago lawyer and a power in Republican politics, McMurdy was a staunch supporter of equal treatment of all people and was an active member of the Chicago branch of the NAACP. In 1915, he joined with Judge Edward O. Brown, Jane Addams, and others in protesting the passage of the Immigration Act, particularly an amendment prohibiting the admission of "Negro aliens."

McNutt, Paul Vories (1891–1955) (D.-Ind.), governor of Indiana (1933–38); high commissioner to the Philippines (1939–45); administrator, FSA (1942–45); chairman, WMC (1942–45). He was criticized as "Adolph McNutt" by the NAACP and black press for arbitrary and dictatorial procedures when the FEPC was placed under his control in 1943.

McSherry, Brig. Gen. Frank Johnson (1892–1980), U.S. Army. He served as chief of operations, WMC from May to December 1943, and was involved with the revamping of USES *Bulletin C-45* that allowed employers to search for applicants who were "white," "Christian," and "Protestant," thus violating President Roosevelt's Executive Order 8802.

Meany, George (1894–1980), plumber and union official; business agent, Local 463, New York City Plumbers' Union (1922–34); president, New York State Federation of Labor (1934–39); secretary-treasurer (1939–52) and president (1952–55), AFL; president, AFL-CIO (1955–79). In 1952, Meany was one of a number of prominent businesspeople, labor leaders, and government officials named by President Truman to serve on his Committee on Government Contract Compliance. Among their duties was overseeing Truman's Fair Employment Practices program.

Medford, Hampton Thomas (1881–1964), minister, educator, and Bishop, AME Zion Church, for the Fourth District (Virginia and North Carolina). On July 4, 1942, he participated in the Conference of Cooperating Organizations.

Meggs, Edward Eugene (1915–94), veteran and postal worker. He was an NAACP complainant against employment discrimination at the New Orleans Post Office (1947).

Meier, August (1923–2003), educator, historian, and social activist; one of the most prominent chroniclers of the African-American experience in the United States; taught at Tougaloo College (1945–49), Fisk University (1952–57), Morgan State College (now University) (1957–63), Roosevelt University (1963–66), and Kent State University (1967–2003); secretary, Newark (New Jersey) branch, NAACP (1951–52, 1956–57).

Meiklejohn, Dr. Alexander (1872–1964), teacher and philosopher; dean of students, Brown University (1901–12); president, Amherst College (1912–24); professor, Department of Philosophy, University of Wisconsin (1924–38). Born in England of Scottish parentage, he was involved in the formation and organization of the ACLU and, in 1943, he was a member of the Citizen's Committee to Save Colored Locomotive Firemen's Jobs. In the 1950s, he also formed the National Commission to Abolish the House Un-American Activities Committee. In December of 1963, President Lyndon B. Johnson presented him with the Presidential Medal of Freedom.

Mercke, James W. (1907–96), Du Pont Company representative. In 1951, he met with an NAACP committee on efforts to ensure nonsegregation and nondiscrimination at the Savannah River Plant hydrogen bomb facility in Aiken, South Carolina.

Merriam, Robert E. (1918–88), business executive, author, and politician; director, Chicago Metropolitan Housing Council (1946–47); alderman from the Second District of Chicago

(1947–55); assistant director (1955–58) and deputy director (1958), U.S. Bureau of the Budget; deputy assistant to the president (1958–61). In 1953, he met with Mitchell and Albert M. Cole to review and discuss the federal government's housing policy.

Merritt, Walter Gordon (1880–1967), lawyer. In 1945, he filed an amicus brief for the ACLU in the case *Railway Mail Association v. Corsi.*

Metzenbaum, Howard Morton (1917–2008) (D-Ohio), lawyer and businessman; Ohio state legislator (1943–51); U.S. senator (1974, 1976–95). In 1945, he proposed legislation to eliminate discrimination in state agencies as well as in unions and private employers; reporting on it, Will Maslow stated that this bill, as well as others pending did not appear "to have a chance of passage."

Metzger, Stanley David (1916–), author and law professor; fair practice examiner, Division of Field Operations, FEPC (1944); assistant to the legal adviser, State Department (1948–60). He served on a board dealing with personnel issues in the State Department.

Miles, Evelyn, of Paducah, Kentucky. In 1951, the Washington Bureau filed charges on her behalf, charging that AEC officials violated Executive Order 9980 by refusing to interview her for a clerical position at the AEC project in Paducah because she was African American.

Milgram, Morris (1916–97), activist; home builder specializing in integrated housing and owner of and investor in real estate. He graduated from what is now Rutgers University's Newark campus in 1939 and joined the WDL, rising to national secretary by 1949. He then moved to the Philadelphia area where he bought up derelict housing stock, made needed repairs and made them available for blacks and other racial minorities; he soon owned a construction company where he built homes and apartments where all who could afford it were encouraged to buy or rent.

Milici, Louis Victor (1912–83), at one time acting chief, protective section, U. S. Public Buildings Administration. In 1953, he was detailed to work with Earle Fisher, the research assistant for the NAACP Labor Department to attempt to solve problems involving the guards at the Pentagon, some of whom contended that they were not being promoted fairly, and black taxi drivers who claimed that they were being forced from their stands at the Pentagon because of "Virginia interests."

Miller, Edward Godfrey, Jr. (1911–68), lawyer, business executive, and diplomat; U.S. assistant secretary of state in charge of Western Hemisphere affairs (1949–52); chair, New York City Commission for Puerto Rican Affairs (1952–55). The son of an engineer who was employed looking after the machines that refined sugar in factories and on plantations, Miller was born in Puerto Rico and brought up in Cuba. In 1950, he conferred with Mitchell and others regarding the wording of the civil rights provision of the Bogota Treaty with Latin America.

Miller, Irving (1903–80), rabbi, of Woodmere, Long Island, New York. He represented AJComm in 1950 when he was part of the delegation from NECRM that met with President Truman.

Miller, Leo L. (1901–69), executive assistant to the administrator (1945–49) and fair employment officer (1949–53), FSA; fair employment officer, SSA (1953–61); fair employment officer, FDA (1961–66). In 1949, upon hearing (and subsequently approving) Vivian Braxton's request for six months to "demonstrate her fitness" as a supervisor at St. Elizabeth's Hospital in Washington, Miller directed all FSA employment officers to make every effort to assist complainants in a friendly matter.

Miller, Loren, Sr. (1903–67), journalist, lawyer, and judge; city editor (1931–51) and owner-publisher, (Los Angeles) *California Eagle* (1951–67). As a board member of the ACLU and cochair of NAACP's West Coast Legal Committee, he was an outspoken opponent of federal support of racial discrimination in housing, particularly situations where mortgages funded by the FHA and VA secured properties where the deeds of sale included restrictive covenants that racially discriminated against blacks and members of other minority groups. In light of the U.S. Supreme Court decision in *Shelley v. Kraemer*, he won a number of court cases that struck down these restrictive covenants, including *Barrows v. Jackson* (346 US 249) He served as justice, California superior court for the county of Los Angeles (1963–67); his son and granddaughter have succeeded him on the state superior court bench.

Milton, Hugh Meglone, II (1897–1987), president, New Mexico A&M (1938–48); assistant secretary of the army (1953–58); undersecretary of the army (1958–61). While serving as assistant secretary, he helped investigate the abuse of a black serviceman at Fort Jackson, South Carolina.

Ming, William Robert, Jr. (1911–73), lawyer and law professor; member, NAACP National Legal Committee (1940–43); assistant general counsel (1943–46) and associate general counsel (1947), OPA; member, NAACP National Board of Directors (1958–73). He was a member of the NAACP's *Brown v. Board of Education* litigation team. In 1952, the NAACP backed him as a candidate for the CGC. The organization's William Robert Ming Advocacy Award, the highest legal honor the NAACP bestows, is named after him.

Minkoff, Isaiah (1901–83), labor leader and activist. The founding executive vice president of NJCRAC, he was named to the executive board of directors of NCPFEPC in 1943.

Minkoff, Nathaniel M. (1893–1984), labor leader with the ILGWU, he also served as a New York State Assemblyman from the Bronx (1939–41). He was named to the executive board of directors of the NCPFEPC in 1943.

Mitcham, James Aaron, Jr. (1915–2003), analyst. Working in the legislative research service of the Library of Congress, he turned out a number of monographs and statistical studies on various topics, including the 1952 "Fair Employment Practices Legislation: A Summary of Its History and Development on Both Sides." He would later attend Princeton Theological Seminary, be ordained a Presbyterian minister and service a number of churches, including the Cadillac Presbyterian Church in Cadillac, Michigan (1961–67).

Mitchell, Arthur Wergs, Sr. (1883–1968) (D-Ill.), lawyer and businessman; U.S. representative (1935–43), and the first black Democrat to sit in Congress. In 1937, he was traveling from Memphis, Tennessee, to Hot Springs, Arkansas, when he was compelled to leave his seat in a first-class carriage and go to a separate Jim Crow car once the train crossed into Arkansas. He brought suit against the railroad company to the Interstate Commerce Commission, who dismissed the complaint, whereupon he brought suit in federal court. The case eventually reached the U.S. Supreme Court as *Mitchell v. United States* where the court found in his favor, declaring Jim Crow travel illegal.

Mitchell, Harry Bremner (1867–1955), newspaper editor and publisher; president (1933–49) and chair (1949–51), U.S. Civil Service Commission. In 1947, he ensured that qualified black candidates would be hired by the U.S. Postal Service in Winston-Salem, North Carolina. A native of Scotland.

Mitchell, Harry Leland (1906–89), founder and executive secretary, STFU (1934–39, 1941–44); president, NLFU (1945–55); president, NAWU (1955–60). He cooperated with the NAACP on limiting importation of foreign agricultural workers until the domestic supply was fully utilized.

Mitchell, James Paul (1899–1964), staff member, NJRA (1931–36); staff member, WPA (1936–40); director, Industrial Personnel Division, Army Service Forces, War Department (1941–45); department store executive (1945–53); assistant secretary of the army (1953); secretary of labor (1953–61); vice chair, CGC (1953–61). Early in his tenure as labor secretary, he gave assurance that all contracts with the District of Columbia would ban discrimination. In 1954, he met with NAACP officials to discuss federal aid to segregated housing.

Mitchell, Juanita Jackson (1913–92), lawyer, wife of Clarence Mitchell Jr., and mother of their four sons; special assistant to Walter White, NAACP executive secretary; and NAACP national youth director (1935–38). She married Clarence Mitchell in 1938 and worked at home until entering the University of Maryland Law School in 1946. She was the first African American student to be elected to the law school's editorial board, and the school's dean presented her with the *Maryland Law Review* scroll of honor at the annual alumni banquet in April 1950, the year in which she graduated. Also in that year, she won admission to the state bar, thus becoming the first black woman to practice law in Maryland. She was also admitted to practice law before the Court of Appeals of Maryland and the U.S. District Court for the District of Maryland, and in 1950, she was admitted to practice before the U.S. Supreme Court. As chair of the NAACP Legal Redress Committee of Maryland, she directed the state's legal program.

Mitchell, Keiffer Jackson, Sr. (1941–), surgeon and second son of Clarence Mitchell Jr. and Juanita Jackson Mitchell. While in junior high, he was assaulted by an NAAWP-led group of whites who were protesting the desegregation of Baltimore public schools. He later walked picket lines with his father and fought for equal access to health care in Baltimore.

Mitchell, Parren James (1927–2007) (D-Md.), youngest brother of Clarence Mitchell, Jr. In 1954, after the University of Maryland was forced to admit blacks after the Supreme Court decision in *Brown v. Board of Education of Topeka,* he applied to the graduate school to study for his master's degree in sociology. Although he was accepted, he was barred from attending the College Park campus, so with the help of the Baltimore NAACP branch, he sued the university for the right to go to classes on that campus and won. He would later go into politics, ultimately representing his Baltimore district in Congress (1971–87).

Mitchell, Timothy (1903–66), complainant against Bryant W. Bowles, Jr., whom he had to sue to recover wages owed him.

Mock, Dr. Ernest Leighton (1919–2007), medical director for the Tenth U.S. Civil Service Region, who performed a medical examination on veteran Henry R. Greene as to his physical capacity to perform his duties as a postal worker in the New Orleans Post Office.

Moffatt, Guy (1882–1963), administrative and personnel expert; official, USCSC (1909–29); secretary (1930–31) and executive (1931–41), Spelman Fund of New York; chair, FEB (1948–49). He asked the NAACP to appear before the FEB to discuss recommendations to end segregation and discrimination.

Monroney, Almer Stillwell "Mike" (1902–80) (D-Okla.), journalist and businessman; U.S. representative (1939–51); U.S. senator (1951–69). An independent Democrat, he supported filibuster rules changes but voted for the Taft-Hartley Act and against FEPC legislation.

Monson, Charles Harold (1933–2010), machinist; a native of Fresno, California, who spent his later years in San Antonio. In 1953 he was employed at the Charleston (South Carolina) Navy Yard and witnessed the desegregation of the cafeteria, as well as of other areas in the facility. His opinions and comments on the process were subsequently printed in the local newspaper, the *Charleston News-Courier.*

Montague, Edwin Newell (1900–84), army officer; bureau chief, Bureau of the Budget (1947–51); director, Office of Personnel, State Department (1951–55); personnel director, IRS (1955–60). He was involved with the NAACP's efforts to improve the minority hiring practices of the State Department.

Montgomery, Eugene A. R. (1923–96), businessman and social worker; executive secretary, South Carolina State Conference of NAACP Branches (1948 to 1952 or 1953); treasurer, Orangeburg, South Carolina, branch, NAACP. A leader in the struggle to ensure nonsegregation and nondiscrimination at the Savannah River Plant hydrogen bomb facility in Aiken, South Carolina.

Moore, E. Earl (1894–1965), vice president for industrial relations (1940–53) and vice president and assistant to the president (1953–59), U.S. Steel; member, Board of Directors, NAM. In 1952, he promised that there would be no new job discrimination at U.S. Steel's new Pennsylvania plant.

Moore, Harry Tyson (1905–51), schoolteacher and administrator; president, Brevard County, Florida, NAACP branch; NAACP state organizer. His wife, Harriette Vyda (Sims) Moore (1902–52), was a schoolteacher, insurance agent, and storekeeper. Both were killed in the bombing of their home on Christmas night 1951. Harry Moore had fought for equal pay for all Florida public school teachers, whether white or black, and had been leading the NAACP drive to register black Floridians to vote after the U.S. Supreme Court, in *Smith v. Allwright*, had struck down the state's all-white primary; in March 1951, after an incident in which the local sheriff had shot two handcuffed black prisoners, Moore loudly called for the sheriff's removal. On Christmas night that year, the couple's twenty-fifth wedding anniversary, a bomb planted under their bedroom window exploded. Harry Moore died the next day; his wife lived eight more days before succumbing to her injuries. Harry Moore was posthumously awarded the NAACP's 1952 Spingarn Medal. In 2005, Florida finally reopened the case and determined that the most likely perpetrators were members of the Ku Klux Klan.

Moore, T. W., officer, BSCP; with A. Philip Randolph, he represented the BSCP at the Conference of Cooperating Organizations on July 4, 1942.

Moret, Alexander A. (1918–2006), veteran and postal worker. He was an NAACP complainant against employment discrimination at the New Orleans Post Office (1947).

Morgan, Irene (1917–2007), Baltimore native who successfully fought Jim Crow travel in the 1940s. The mother of two, she left her home in Gloucester County, Virginia, on a Greyhound bus heading north to Baltimore, and refused to move to the back of the bus when ordered to do so by the bus driver. She was then arrested and subsequently tried and convicted under Virginia's Jim Crow statutes. When she reached Washington, she contacted the NAACP and filed suit against the commonwealth of Virginia. The case eventually reached the United States Supreme Court and Thurgood Marshall and William H. Hastie successfully pleaded her case. Mrs. Morgan subsequently moved to Brooklyn, New York, finished college and graduate school and, with her second husband, Stanley Kirkaldy, owned and operated a day care center in Queens County, New York.

Morris, Alberta, of Philadelphia, who represented the Committee on Race Relations, AFSC, at the Conference of Cooperating Organizations on July 4, 1942.

Morris, Dr. David Gladstone (1893–1986), president of Bayonne, New Jersey NAACP branch. A native of Tampa, Florida, Dr. Morris graduated from Lincoln University (Pennsylvania) and the medical school of the University of Vermont and settled in Bayonne in 1926, where he led the fight to desegregate the schools, parks and other public buildings, before he stepped down in 1980. In 1942, Mitchell corresponded with Dr. Morris concerning the creation of the NAACP Washington Bureau.

Morse, David Abner (1907–90), lawyer; general counsel, NLRB (1945–46); assistant secretary of labor (1946–47); undersecretary of labor (1947–48); acting secretary of labor (1948); director general, ILO (1948–70). While in the Department of Labor, he conferred with Mitchell on several issues, including agricultural labor and an executive order against discrimination in public employment.

Morse, Wayne Lyman (1900–74) (R, I, D-Ore.), dean and professor of law, University of Oregon (1931–44); member, NWLB (1942–44); U.S. senator (1945–69). An authority on labor relations, he was sympathetic to civil rights and supported FEPC and antilynching legislation, nonsegregation amendments to the Taft-Hartley Act, and desegregation of schools on military posts. Although he and Mitchell had their differences, Mitchell regarded him as one of the more progressive Republican politicians.

Morton, Thruston Ballard (1907–82) (R-Ky.), businessman; U.S. representative (1947–53); assistant secretary of state for congressional relations (1953–56); U.S. senator (1957–68). A supporter of most civil rights legislation—including the Civil Rights Act of 1957—he nevertheless voted in 1952 to authorize the Cox Committee to investigate charitable organizations that supported civil rights activities in the South.

Moser, M. Peter (1928–2008), lawyer of Baltimore. He was working as an assistant state's attorney when, in 1954, he received a letter from attorney Edward F. Shea, Jr. concerning Bryant W. Bowles, Jr., who had not complied with a court-ordered payment schedule in conjunction with a judgment against him.

Moss, Richard Maurice (1897–1958), associate director, National Urban League, when he was present (as an observer) at the organizational meeting of the LCCR in 1951.

Motley, Constance Baker (1921–2005), attorney, NAACP Legal Defense and Educational Fund, Inc. (1945–65); New York state legislator (1964–65); president, Borough of Manhattan, New York (1965–66); judge (1966–82), chief judge (1982–86), and senior judge (1986–2005), U.S. District Court for the Southern District of New York. In 1952, she participated in a meeting with U.S. Steel executives on black employment and housing of workers. Fourteen years later, she became the first black woman to serve as a federal judge.

Muir [Fullarton], Jean (1911–96), actress. A Screen Actors Guild member, her career was cut short because she was blacklisted by the movie and television industry. In 1950, the NAACP National Board of Directors, on Walter White's recommendation, adopted a resolution condemning General Foods for refusing to employ Muir on a television program merely because she was listed in the publication *Red Channels*, which named alleged members of the Communist Party or those who were not members but were sympathetic to its aims and goals.

Mulzac, Capt. Hugh Nathaniel (1886–1971), merchant seaman. A native of the British West Indies, Captain Mulzac commanded the SS *Booker T. Washington* with an interracial crew from early 1943 to the end of World War II. In 1948, Mitchell noted that, after the war's end, Captain Mulzac, along with other black officers and sailors in the merchant marine, could not find work on ships commensurate with their training.

Mundt, Karl Earl (1900–74) (R-S.D.), teacher, professor, and; businessman; member, South Dakota State Game and Fish Commission (1931–37); U.S. representative (1939–48); U.S. senator (1948–73). He rose to prominence in 1948, when he presided over the HCUA investigation that led to the indictment of Alger Hiss. That same year, he cosponsored (with Richard M. Nixon) legislation that in part required the registration of groups named by the attorney general as communist or communist fronts; many of the provisions of this bill were included in the McCarran Act of 1950. Although known as a staunch conservative, Mundt was a committed conservationist, and he supported civil rights legislation.

Murdock, Orrin Abram "Abe," Jr. (1893–1979) (D-Utah), lawyer and farmer; U.S. representative (1933–41); U.S. senator (1941–47); member, NLRB (1947–57). In 1951, as a member of the NLRB, he upheld the decision in the *Young's Motor Freight* case in which all of the company's black truck drivers were summarily dismissed.

Murphy, Dr. Carl James (1889–1967), of Baltimore. One of five sons of John H. Murphy, Sr., later president, *Afro-American* newspapers, he was educated at Howard University, Harvard University, and University of Jena in Germany; professor of German and chairman of German department, Howard University (1913–18); joined *Baltimore Afro-American* staff in 1918 and subsequently became editor-publisher (1922–61) of the newspaper which had been run by his father. He was a member of the NAACP National Board of Directors (1931–67) and helped develop the Baltimore NAACP branch and the Maryland state conference of NAACP branches into the country's largest branches. He was one of a number of black newspaper owners, publishers, and editors who protested the cancellation of FEPC hearings on racial discrimination in the railroad industry, 1943.

Murphy, Charles S. (1909–83), lawyer and administrative aide; administrative assistant to the president of the United States (1947–50); special counsel to the president of the United States (1950–53); undersecretary of agriculture, U.S. Department of Agriculture (1960–65); chair, Civil Aeronautics Board (1965–68). In 1950, Mitchell suggested that a telegram should be sent to Murphy denouncing the attempt of Sen. Scott Lucas (D-Ill.) to schedule discussion on a natural gas bill before a discussion was held on the FEPC bill.

Murray, Donald Gaines, Sr. (1914–98), who in 1935, brought suit against the University of Maryland Law School after he was barred from attending because he was an African American. His fraternity, Alpha Phi Alpha, financed the suit, and he was represented by the NAACP with Charles H. Houston as lead attorney. After hearing the case in Baltimore city court, Judge Eugene O'Dunne issued a writ of mandamus ordering the university to admit Murray at once. After graduating from law school and passing the Maryland state bar, Murray practiced law in Baltimore.

Murray, James Edward (1876–1961) (D-Mont.), lawyer; U.S. senator (1934–61). A liberal Democrat, he supported nondiscrimination amendments to the Taft-Hartley Act, legislation to protect service members from violence, modification of the filibuster, and a fair employment bill with enforcement powers. He also introduced the nation's first Medicare bill in 1943; the Wagner-Murray-Dingell bill added health insurance to the Social Security system.

Murray, Philip (1886–1952), union leader; vice president, UMWA (1920–42); president, USWA (1942–52); vice president (1938–40) and president (1940–52), CIO; member, FEPC; member, NAACP National Board of Directors. He was a staunch supporter of the NAACP and was a member of the executive board of the NCPFEPC.

Myers, Esther Pauline (1909–98), activist; she was involved with a number of social and civil rights movements including serving as executive secretary, MOWM (1941–43); lauded as one of those folks who shunned the limelight but who worked behind the scenes to keep programs and activities moving along.

Myers, Francis John (1901–56) (D-Pa.), teacher and lawyer; U.S. representative (1939–45); U.S. senator (1945–51). A former high school teacher, he backed anti–poll tax measures and other civil rights legislation.

Myers, James (1882–1967), Presbyterian minister and labor advocate; personnel director, Dutchess Bleachery, Wappingers Falls, New York (1918–25); secretary for Industrial Relations, Federal Council of Churches (1925–47). He lobbied for legislation that would profit the workingman, including the Wagner Act (1935). He served as a member of the Citizens' Committee to Save Colored Firemen's Jobs and also was a member of the initial executive board of the NCPFEPC.

Myers, Robert L. (1910–78), farmer of Aiken, South Carolina. In 1951, Mitchell visited his farm and lumber business and approvingly noted how prosperous the business was.

Myrdal, Karl Gunnar (1898–1987), sociologist, economist, researcher, educator, and lecturer; director, Study of American Negro Problem for the Carnegie Corporation (1938–42). Swedish born, he was sent to the southern United States to study the plight of the African American because it was felt, as a foreigner, he would be able to give an informed, yet detached opinion about how things were. The results of his study were published in his *The Negro Problem and Modern Democracy* (New York: Harper & Brothers, 1944).

Nathanson, Jerome (1908–75), president, New York Ethical Society, and chairman, committee on Federal Aid to Public Education. In a 1947 letter to Mitchell he emphasized the division between church and state in the matter of public education.

Neely, Matthew Mansfield (1874–1958) (D-W.Va.), lawyer; U.S. representative (1913–21, 1945–47); U.S. senator (1923–29, 1931–41, 1949–58); West Virginia governor (1941–45). A Spanish-American War veteran, he was a strong ally of organized labor. He also supported nonsegregation amendments to the Taft-Hartley Act, desegregation of the Washington, D.C., fire department, home rule for the District, progressive Senate rules changes, and a fair employment bill with enforcement powers.

Nehru, Jawaharlal (1889–1964), barrister and activist; first president of India (1947–64). In 1951, Mitchell mentioned President Nehru in his testimony on the India Emergency Act before a Congressional committee.

Nelson, Donald Marr (1888–1959), business executive; starting as a chemist for Sears Roebuck in 1912, by 1930, he had risen to the position of executive vice president. In 1942, President Roosevelt appointed him director of priorities, OPM (1941–42); after that agency was abolished, Nelson was appointed chair, WPB (1942–47), where, as Walter White observed, he was placed "in charge of the whole war production machinery."

Nelson, Harold Sidney (1914–2009), lawyer. In 1952, he represented black employees of Kelly Air Force Base near San Antonio before the Civil Service Commission.

Niles, David K. (1890–1952), assistant director and director, Ford Hall Forum, Boston (1921–52); assistant administrator, WPA (1936–39); special assistant to the U.S. secretary of commerce (1939–40); administrative assistant to the president of the United States (1942–51). Born David Neyhaus of Russian Jewish parentage in Boston, he worked for the establishment of Israel as an independent state. In 1950, at the request of President Truman, Niles sent Mitchell a telegram explaining why S. 1728, the FEPC bill, had been postponed and expressing his intention to have the bill brought back up for consideration and a vote in the near future.

Nimitz, Rear Adm. Chester William (1885–1966), U.S. Navy, retired as Fleet Admiral of the Navy and Chief of Naval Operation in 1947 after a forty-five year career. In 1940, he corresponded with the NAACP about the segregation policy for black uniformed naval personnel.

Nixon, Richard Milhous (1913–94) (R-Calif.), lawyer; U.S. representative (1947–50); U.S. senator (1950–53); vice president of the United States (1953–61); Republican Party presidential nominee (1960, 1968, 1972); president of the United States (1969–74). After achieving notoriety for his role in the Alger Hiss controversy, he served from 1953 to 1961 as chair of the CGC, a body that oversaw compliance with nondiscrimination provisions in government contracts.

Norman, Dorothy Stecker (1905–97), photographer, graphic artist, writer, editor, essayist and researcher; she was a member of the boards of Planned Parenthood, New York City Urban League and the National Urban League, as well as a founding member of New York's Liberal Party and was active in a number of progressive causes. In 1945, she was a member of the board of directors of the NCPFEPC.

Norton, Mary Teresa (1875–1959) (D-N.J.), lawyer; U.S. representative (1925–51); member House Committee on Labor; a sponsor of permanent FEPC legislation.

Norvell, Col. Frank C. (1913–2000), executive assistant in the Office of the Secretary of Defense. In 1953, he reported to Mitchell that the U.S. Army was "taking steps" to integrate schools for the dependents of military personnel on army bases.

Nunn, William Goldwin, Jr. (1925–), newspaperman and sports figure. The son of the editor of the *Pittsburgh Courier*, he followed in his father's footsteps on the paper, eventually becoming a sportswriter and, subsequently, editor of the *Courier*'s sports page. He would later become a scout for the Pittsburgh Steelers. In 1949, he interviewed Walter White of the NAACP, who informed him that, with the proliferation of civil rights organizations seeking to ameliorate the plight of the oppressed, civil rights had become "big business."

O'Conor, Herbert Romulus (1896–1960) (D-Md.), lawyer; Maryland attorney general (1935–39); governor (1939–46); U.S. senator (1947–53). As a senator, he was known almost exclusively for his strong anticommunist views, at one point accusing the Truman administration of being soft on communism.

O'Donnell, William Joseph (1917–76), lawyer and judge, of Baltimore, Maryland. He represented Bryant W. Bowles, Jr., noted white supremacist, in a number of civil actions in and around the city and county of Baltimore in 1953 and 1954. He lost the election for Maryland states attorney in 1954, but would eventually sit as a trial judge on the Baltimore city circuit court (1964–74) and subsequently as associate justice, Maryland state court of appeals (1974–76).

Ogden, Peter (?–1852), ship's steward and organizer of the Grand United Order of Odd Fellows, a fraternal order. In 1952, Mitchell commented that, if the McCarran-Walter Act, with its severe restriction on immigration from the Caribbean and South America, had been in force when immigrants like Ogden entered the United States, they would not have been able to make "notable contributions to the building of our nation."

O'Hara, Joseph Patrick (1895–1975) (R-Minn.), lawyer; U.S. representative (1941–59). A former halfback at Notre Dame, he was a strict isolationist who never supported a foreign aid measure. In 1952, he voted to authorize the Cox Committee to investigate charitable organizations that supported civil rights activities in the South.

Oliver, William Henry (1915–94), union official; codirector, Fair Practices and Anti-discrimination Department, UAW (1946–80); alternate, NAACP National Labor Committee; member, NAACP National Board of Directors. He represented the UAW at civil rights–related meetings.

Ornburn, Ira M. (1889–1950), labor organizer, newspaper editor and publisher, and freelance writer; secretary-treasurer, Label Trades Department, AFL. In 1946, he was present at a meeting with Mitchell and U.S. secretary of labor Schwellenbachin which the latter pledged that segregation would end in the Washington offices of the Department of Labor by September 30 of that year.

Osthagen, Clarence Hillman (1904–75), special assistant, Department of the Air Force. He attended a meeting on the assault of a black corporal by military police.

Ottilie, Marvin Julius (1908–66), U.S. Navy veteran of World War II. He subsequently was employed by the Navy Department in a number of civilian capacities, particularly in the Office of Industrial Relations; in 1953, Mitchell, in a letter to Maxwell Rabb, stated that Ottilie was the actual author of official letters endorsing segregation at the Norfolk and Charleston navy yards. Mitchell wished that the response to his letter clearly endorsed a policy of no segregation at any and all U.S. Navy installations, including those at Norfolk and at Charleston.

Ottley, Vincent Lushington "Roi" (1906–60), journalist and author; reporter, sports editor, and columnist, *Amsterdam News* (1932–38); freelance writer (1938–41, 1946–52); director, public relations, CIO, National War Relief (1943); war correspondent *PM* (newspaper) and *Liberty Magazine* (1943–45); war correspondent, *Pittsburgh Courier* and *Overseas News Agency* (1944–45) as one of the few black World War II war correspondents; *Chicago Tribune* (1953–60). A perceptive commentator on contemporary affairs, in 1941, he recorded the energizing effect of A. Philip Randolph's March on Washington on black Americans.

Owlett, Gilbert Mason (1892–1957) (R-Pa.), lawyer and businessman; Pennsylvania state legislator (1932–40). He was a leading opponent of FEPC legislation in Pennsylvania.

Oxnam, Garfield Bromley (1892–1963), Bishop of the Methodist Episcopal Church (1934–63); president, DePauw University (1928–36); member of Federal Council of Churches of

Christ. He was named as a member of a proposed delegation to meet with President Truman concerning the FEPC.

Pace, Frank C., Jr. (1912–88), lawyer; special assistant to the attorney general (1946); executive assistant to the postmaster general (1946–48); assistant director (1948) and director (1949–50), Bureau of the Budget; secretary of the army (1950–53); executive, General Dynamics Corporation (1953–63); chair, CPB (1968–72); chair, NESC (1977–88). Mitchell negotiated with him on racial designations on military forms, excessive sentences for blacks in courts-martial, and desegregation of the military.

Packard, George (1868–1949), lawyer and politician; a member of the Chicago branch of the NAACP, his name appeared on a 1915 telegram protesting discriminatory language in legislation regulating immigration to the United States.

Padmore, George (1903–59), journalist and activist; born in Trinidad as Malcolm Ivan Meredith Nurse, in 1924, he emigrated to the United States to attend college. He changed his name after joining the Worker's (Communist) Party and worked with C. L. R. James at the International African Services Bureau after the Italian invasion of Ethiopia in the 1930s. He published many newspaper articles and essays decrying colonialism and exhorting the oppressed to rise. After the country of Ghana became independent in 1957, he became a close adviser to President Kwame Nkrumah.

Palmer, Dwight Rupert Glyndon (1886–1980), president, chair of the Executive Committee, and board member, General Cable Corporation (1933–52); member, PCETOAS (Fahy Committee) (1948–50); chair, CGCC (1952–53). As CGCC chair, he worked with the NAACP in investigating the Chesapeake and Potomac Telephone Company's hiring practices.

Parker, John Johnston (1885–1958); lawyer; judge of the United States court of appeals for the Fourth Circuit (1925–58). His nomination to the Supreme Court was blocked in 1930 as a result of the objections of the NAACP and the AFL to his statements against black voting rights and his decisions on labor issues.

Parrish, Richard Franklin (1918–83), teacher in the New York City school system and trade union activist. As a youth group leader for the BCSP, he was involved in the early preparations for the proposed 1941 March on Washington. He later served as assistant treasurer of the United Federation of Teachers' New York City local and ran for office as councilman-at-large on the Socialist party ticket in 1963.

Pasqua [Posqua], Charles Francis (1924–94), complainant against Bryant W. Bowles, Jr. In 1953, Pasqua brought suit against Bowles on the grounds of false pretenses (a check returned for insufficient funds). Bowles was found guilty and sentenced to a year in the Maryland House of Corrections but sentence was suspended on account of Bowles' good behavior and on the condition that he make restitution to Pasqua within a reasonable time.

Pastore, John Orlando (1907–2000) (D-R.I.), lawyer; Rhode Island state legislator (1935–37); governor (1945–50); U.S. senator (1950–76). A liberal Democrat, he endorsed FEPC legislation while serving as governor. During his tenure as senator, he was a reliable supporter of civil rights measures, including legislation to protect black service members from civilian violence. He was also the first U.S. senator of Italian descent.

Patterson, Robert Porter, Sr. (1891–1952), lawyer; judge, U.S. District Court, Southern District of New York (1930–39); judge, U.S. Court of Appeals for the Second Circuit (1939–40); assistant secretary of war (1940); undersecretary of war (1940–45); U.S. secretary of war (1945–47). In 1946, he denied the existence of discrimination in his department.

Payne, Ethel Lois (1911–91), newspaper reporter and columnist, freelance writer, and radio commentator; reporter and foreign correspondent, *Chicago Defender* (1951–78); radio commentator on the program *Spectrum* on CBS Radio (1972–78). A hostess in a U.S. Army Special Services club in Japan after World War II, she recorded her experiences and those of the soldiers she met in a daily journal; a reporter from the *Defender* read her accounts and opinions and took the journal back to Chicago, where its pages provided a basis for a number of front-page stories. From that start, she became a reporter for the *Defender* and subsequently became its White House correspondent; she would also file reports from Vietnam, Biafra, and Indonesia.

Pearson, Andrew Russell "Drew" (1896–1969), journalist and radio commentator. A self-proclaimed liberal, he was a noted foe of the Ku Klux Klan and Joseph McCarthy during the postwar years. In 1948, he announced the inclusion of Memphis among the places being investigated by the Senate Civil Service Committee on charges of discrimination by the Postal Service.

Penney, Marjorie (1908–83), social worker. She attended the Conference of Cooperating Organizations on July 4, 1942 as director of the Young People's Interracial Fellowship (now Freedom Farm of Pottstown, Pennsylvania) of the Society of Friends (1936–68).

Pepper, Claude Denson (1900–89) (D-Fla.), lawyer; Florida state legislator (1929–30); state government official (1931–33); U.S. senator (1936–51); U.S. representative (1963–89). Known primarily for his work on behalf of the elderly, he also supported progressive Senate rules changes and cosponsored a bill to repeal the poll tax. Unlike many of his southern colleagues in the Senate, he abstained from filibusters against civil rights measures. In 1950, he lost a bitter, racially charged Democratic senatorial primary to George Smathers.

Perkins, Frances (1880–1965), teacher and professor; executive secretary, CSCNY (1912–17); member, NYSIC (1919–23); member (1923–26) and chair (1926–29), NYSIB; New York State industrial commissioner (1929–33); U.S. secretary of labor (1933–1945); member, USCSC (1946–52). The first woman to hold a federal cabinet post, she requested NAACP suggestions for guidelines regarding employment discrimination.

Perlman, Philip Benjamin (1890–1960), newspaper reporter and lawyer; solicitor general of the United States (1947–52). A native of Baltimore, Perlman went from newspaper work into the law and was known for his handling of a number of civil rights cases while in private practice. During his tenure as solicitor general, the first Supreme Court cases challenging restrictive covenants were heard and adjudicated.

Perry, Jennings (1900–87), newspaperman best known as the longtime editor of the *Nashville Tennesseean*. He was a Southern moderate on race and a leading foe of the poll tax in Tennessee.

Perry, Leslie S. (1907–64), lawyer; FEPC complainant (1942); administrative assistant, NAACP Washington bureau (1942–50); member, strategy committee, NCPFEPC (1943). He established several of the legislative initiatives that Mitchell inherited, but he seemed to have had difficulty winning respect as leader of the bureau from Walter White, Roy Wilkins, and Thurgood Marshall. He resigned in July 1950 after a widely publicized alienation of affection suit initiated by his first wife, Olive Perry, against his second wife, NLRB lawyer Ruth Weyand, who was white. He then returned to private practice and apparently lost interest in NAACP affairs.

Perry, Marian Wynn (1919–94), attorney, Wage and Hour Division, U.S. Department of Labor (1943–45); NAACP Legal and Educational Defense Fund (1945–49); secretary, National Lawyers Guild (1945–50). She was involved in much of the early civil rights agitation on the federal level immediately after World War II. She subsequently remarried and, under the name Marian Yankauer, became a sociologist specializing in urban themes.

Persons, Wilton Burton (1896–1977), deputy assistant (1953–58) and assistant to the president (1958–61), Eisenhower administration. An opponent of integration, he corresponded with the NAACP about the desegregation of schools on military posts.

Peterson, Frederick Valdemar Erastus "Val" (1903–83) (R-Neb.), Nebraska governor (1947–53); head, FCDA (1953–57); ambassador to Denmark (1957–61); ambassador to Finland (1969–73). The NAACP welcomed his appointment as head of the FCDA.

Peterson, Ivar H. (1911–80), lawyer; member, NLRB (1952–56) where he confronted counsel for the NAACP concerning segregated union locals.

Pettis, Oliver Thomas (1905–80), mechanic, longshoreman, and dockworker.. In 1934, Pettis organized a local of the ILA at the port of Brownsville, Texas, but when job opportunities in the port increased, the charter was rescinded; white dockworkers organized a new union local and barred blacks from membership, thus effectively keeping them from work.

Pickens, William, Sr. "Dean" (1881–1954), educator and civil rights activist. He taught classics and sociology at Talladega College (1904–14), Wiley University, Marshall, Texas (1914–15), and Morgan College (later Morgan State University) in Baltimore (1915–20), where he also served as dean of students; field secretary and director of branches, NAACP (1920–41); director, Interracial Section of U.S. Treasury Department's Savings (later War) Bonds division (1941–50), where he and his staff sold an estimated one billion dollars of war bonds to African-Americans. While director of branches, Pickens was asked by Thurgood Marshall to ask the NAACP branches to urge seventy-five senators previously contacted by Walter White to support a nondiscrimination clause added to what would become the Selective Service Act of 1940.

Pickett, Clarence Evan (1885–1965), minister of the Society of Friends and activist; executive secretary, AFSC (1929–50). He worked to protect the civil rights of Japanese-Americans during World War II. In 1944 he testified before the House Labor Committee in favor of S. 2048, a bill designed to strengthen the FEPC.

Pike, Sumner Tucker (1891–1976), geologist and business executive; member, SEC (1940–42); chief, Price Division, OPA (1942–46); chair, AEC (1946–52). In 1950, when Mitchell lodged complaints against the AEC for racial discrimination against blacks in both housing and employment, Pike ducked responsibility.

Pinn, Howard William (1917–51), merchant seaman. In 1951, he was removed from his position as deck steward on the SS *America*, as he was thought to be a poor security risk; upon being cleared by an investigation mounted by the U.S. Coast Guard, he asked the NAACP to intercede with both the Coast Guard and the National Maritime Union and request that he be reinstated.

Plummer, Louis Andrew (1891–1971), farmer of Huntingtown, Charles County, Maryland, who sued white supremacist Bryant W. Bowles, Jr. in Baltimore County in 1953, on the grounds of false pretenses (check returned due to insufficient funds); Bowles was found guilty.

Pohlhaus, John Francis (1918–81), a graduate of Western Maryland College and Georgetown University Law School; was a member of the bar of Maryland and the District of Columbia. Practiced law in Baltimore, Maryland, and served as an attorney there with the Federal Security Agency; left in 1951 to join the Civil Rights Section of the Department of Justice; in 1954 he joined the NAACP Washington bureau staff as counsel, serving until 1981, when he retired. He helped organize the Catholic Interracial Council of Baltimore and served as an officer of the council; he was active with the St. Peter Claver Center, the Washington branch of the Friendship House movement. Pohlhaus was active in labor union affairs with the United Steelworkers and the Government and Civic Employees Organizing Committee.

Poitier, Sidney (1924–), Academy Award-winning actor; was born in Miami, but was taken as a child back to his ancestral home in the Bahamas, where he stayed until he was fifteen. In 1952, Mitchell commented that, if the McCarran-Walter Act, with its severe restriction on immigration from the Caribbean and South America, had been in force when immigrants like Poitier and his family entered the United States, they would not have been able to make "notable contributions to the building of our nation."

Pope, Henry Washington (1899–1953), social worker and union official; his final appointment was as field secretary, NUL (1950–53). In 1941, while preparing for the March on Washington, A. Philip Randolph asked Walter White to work with Pope (then with the BSCP), Frank Crosswaith, and Lester Granger to prepare a list of demands for the MOW to submit to government officials requesting that they pressure President Roosevelt to issue an executive order abolishing discrimination in the federal government and in the defense industries.

Popel, Esther (1896–1957), poet and schoolteacher. A native of Harrisburg, Pennsylvania, and a Phi Beta Kappa graduate of Dickinson College, she taught modern languages in the Washington D.C. public school system for many years. In the August 1934 issue of the *Crisis*, her poem, "Flag Salute," a cry against the racial injustices and neglect American blacks suffered, was published.

Porter, George Francis (1876–1951), educator; member Dallas, Texas, NAACP branch. In 1938, while president of what is now Wiley University in Marshall, Texas, he was beaten up and thrown down the stone stairwell of the Dallas County Court House when he attempted to register for jury duty. The resulting injuries would eventually cause blindness. In 1943, he testified before a congressional committee considering an anti-lynching bill.

Porter, Maj. Gen. Ray Edison (1891–1963), U.S. Army. In 1944, as a member of the War Department's Advisory Committee on Negro Troop Policies, he met with Walter White to discuss criticisms and recommendations in his two reports on black troops in the European Theater and the North African Theater of Operations.

Powell, Adam Clayton, Jr. (1908–72) (D-N.Y.), minister, journalist, publisher, and editor; U.S. representative (1945–67, 1967–71). A flamboyant and controversial figure, he once referred to himself as the "first bad nigger in Congress." In the 1950s, he worked closely with Mitchell, repeatedly introducing amendments that banned discrimination in federal spending bills. These measures, drafted by Mitchell, came to be known as Powell amendments.

Powell, Dr. Clilan Bethany (1894–1977), physician and newspaper executive. A 1920 graduate of Howard University Medical School, Dr. Powell moved to New York City and, in 1935, with Dr. P.M.H. Savory, purchased the black newspaper, the *Amsterdam News*, where he served as both editor and publisher until he sold the paper in 1971. During his tenure, the *Amsterdam News* explored the relationship between blacks and Jews, advocating the formation of an alliance as oppressed peoples fighting for a fair share, as well as supporting the civil rights struggle and the fight for equal opportunity in the armed forces and the defense industry during World War II. In 1941, Dr. Powell was one of sixteen representatives of the black press who signed a telegram protesting the FEPC cancellation of hearings designed to review racial discrimination in the railroad industry.

Price, Charles Melvin (1905–88) (D-Ill.), journalist; U.S. representative (1945–88). He was a sportswriter and newspaper correspondent before entering the political arena. In 1951, he helped defeat the Winstead amendment, a measure that would have continued segregation in the armed services.

Proskauer, Joseph Meyer (1877–1971), lawyer and judge; judge, New York State Supreme Court (1923–27); associate justice, Appellate Division, First Department (1927–36); president, Federal of Jewish Philanthropies (1931–35); president, American Jewish Committee (1943–49). In 1948, in correspondence between Roy Wilkins and Walter White, Judge Proskauer was named as a potential participant in a proposed conference on civil rights.

Pryor, Helen Sloman (1901–87), author; employee counselor, SSS; personnel officer, ECA (Marshall Plan); personnel officer, U.S. Foreign Aid Mission, Seoul. She was a member of a special committee that looked into problems of African American employment at the BOASI in Baltimore.

Pryor, William Clayton, Jr. (1926–), assistant to the director, NAACP Washington bureau (1951–54). In 1953, he assisted the NAACP in investigating segregation in the Marine Corps and the hotel industry. He also contributed to the Washington bureau's unsuccessful 1952 struggle to defeat the McCarran immigration bill. In May 1954, he resigned to take a government post in Indochina.

Pusloskie [Puss Loskie], Nick [Nicholas], Jr. (1927–74), member, NAAWP. He participated in picketing at Gwynn's Falls Junior High School in Baltimore to protest the implementation of the Supreme Court's *Brown* decision.

Quigley, Martin (1890–1974), newspaper reporter, publisher and coauthor of the Motion Picture Production Code. In 1953, he was involved with the merger of the NCPFEPC and the NECRM of 1950.

Quinn, Elmer Francis (1895–52) (D-N.Y.), New York state legislator (1934–52). With Irving M. Ives, he authored the Ives-Quinn Fair Employment Practices Act, which was enacted in 1945.

Rabb, Maxwell Milton (1910–2002), lawyer; White House counsel (1954–58); secretary to the Eisenhower cabinet (1954–58); ambassador to Italy (1981–89). He acted as the Eisenhower administration's chief adviser on race matters, attending meetings on civil rights and serving on the CGC. He also met with naval officials to promote the elimination of discrimination at the Charleston and Norfolk naval bases.

Rabkin, Sol (1911–2003), lawyer and activist. In 1951, representing the anti-defamation league of B'Nai B'Rith, Rabkin attended a meeting of concerned organizations discussing Senate rules changes; later that year, he was present at the organization and establishment of the LCCR.

Randolph, Asa Philip (1889–1979), labor leader; editor, *Messenger* (1918–27); founder, BSCP (1925); president, NNC (1936–40); founder, NCPFEPC (1943); member, NAACP National Board of Directors; member, NAACP National Labor Committee from 1946. He spearheaded the March on Washington Movement, which led President Roosevelt to issue EO 8802 in 1941. He also pressured President Truman to issue EO 9981 (in 1948), which outlawed segregation in the armed forces.

Raney, Everett P. (1926–), complainant; a U. S. Navy reservist. In 1949, while a student at what is now Norfolk State University, he was on a bus leaving Norfolk, Virginia, when he sat next to a white woman and refused to change his seat in compliance with Jim Crow laws. He was arrested and fined. With the help of the NAACP, he sued the carrier and lost.

Rankin, James Lee (1907–96), lawyer; U.S. assistant attorney general (1953–56); U.S. solicitor general (1956–61); general counsel, Warren Commission (1963–64); corporation counsel, New York City (1966–72). A strong supporter of civil rights, he testified amicus curiae for the *Brown v. Board of Education* case. He later joined Thurgood Marshall in urging the immediate integration of Arkansas high schools. In 1962, he argued for the ACLU in *Gideon v. Wainwright*, the landmark Supreme Court case that established the right of the indigent to legal representation at public expense.

Rankin, John Elliott (1882–1960) (D-Miss.), lawyer; U.S. representative (1921–53). First elected to Congress in 1920 on a white supremacist platform, he was a segregationist who consistently opposed civil rights legislation. His congressional district had the highest poll tax in the country.

Ransom, Leon Andrew, Sr. (1899–1954), lawyer and educator; professor of law, Howard University (1930–54); acting dean (1940–44). One of the leading legal minds in the black community, Ransom either appeared for or was on the brief in a number of landmark civil rights cases in the period before *Brown v. Board of Education of Topeka*. In 1945, with Thurgood Marshall and William H. Hastie, on behalf of the NAACP, Ransom filed *ami-*

cus curiae briefs in the Supreme Court case *Railway Mail Association v. Edward S. Corsi, Industrial Commissioner of the State of New York, et al.* (326 US 88).

Raper, Arthur Franklin (1899–1979), sociologist; research secretary, Committee on Interracial Cooperation (1926–39); staff, Study of the American Negro Problem, Carnegie Corporation (1939–40); social scientist, U.S. Department of Agriculture, Bureau of Agricultural Economics (1940–52). A native of North Carolina, he went to Georgia in 1926 as a member of the Commission on Interracial Cooperation to study sociology, but soon found himself studying the lives and folkways of black Georgians. His studies and reports were invaluable in providing a clear and accurate picture of the state of blacks in Georgia and elsewhere. In 1944 he testified before the House Labor Committee in favor of S. 2048, a bill designed to strengthen the FEPC.

Rauh, Joseph Louis, Jr. (1911–92), founder, Americans for Democratic Action (ADA) (1947); civil rights vice chairman (1952–55) and chairman (1955–57), ADA; general counsel of the Leadership Conference on Civil Rights. He played a major role in drafting and lobbying for civil rights legislation and was involved with the issue of nonsegregation provisions for national guard programs. In June 1941, while working in the U.S. Office of Emergency Management, he drafted Executive Order 8802 which barred discrimination in the defense industries and created the Fair Employment Practice Committee (FEPC).

Raushenbush [Rauschenbusch], Winifred (1894–1979), educator, social worker, activist, and author. The daughter of the Reverend Walter Rauschenbusch, one of the leading purveyors of the "Social Gospel" of the early twentieth century, she was internationally known for her work as a social worker and activist. In 1943, she was named to the executive board of the NCPFEPC. She married newspaperman James Rorty; their son, Dr. Richard Rorty of Princeton University, was a leading modern American philosopher.

Ray, Lt. Col. Marcus Hanna (1906–88), army officer. He commanded an artillery battalion in Italy during World War II and then left the service to be civilian aide to Robert P. Patterson, secretary of war (1945–47). He reentered the service and joined the U.S. Army European Command of Gen. Lucius D. Clay, serving as his aide in matters concerning black troops (1947–57). In 1947, Ray met with Mitchell in regard to Henry Conyers, who had been terminated from his position as a civilian instructor for the U.S. Army Air Force in Japan due to his complaints about widespread discrimination in the service.

Ray, Rev. Sandy Frederick (1898–1979), Baptist minister. A classmate (Morehouse College) and lifelong friend of Martin Luther King, Sr., after 1930 Rev. Ray would pastor churches in Macon and LaGrange, Georgia, before becoming the pastor of Shiloh Baptist Church of Columbus, Ohio (1940–44). Ohio state legislator (1943–44); pastor, Cornerstone Baptist Church, Brooklyn, New York (1944–79); president, Empire State Baptist Convention (1954–79), the New York state affiliate of the National Baptist Convention (NBC); vice president, NBC (1968–79). He represented the NBC when he was part of a delegation from the NECRM who met with President Truman in January 1950.

Rayburn, Samuel Taliaferro (1882–1961) (D-Tex.), lawyer; Texas state legislator (1907–13); U.S. representative (1913–61); House majority leader (1937–40); House minority leader (1947–49, 1953–55); Speaker of the House (1940–47, 1949–53, 1955–61). Although a highly partisan Democrat who usually sided with the Truman administration, he was lukewarm on civil rights issues. Thus, though he opposed the Dixiecrat movement, he only supported a voluntary FEPC. In 1954, as House minority leader, he refused to consent to a rules change that would have allowed a vote on an anti–Jim Crow travel bill.

Read, Harry Cyril (1892–1957), newspaperman and union official; he was employed as a reporter on newspapers in Cheyenne, Wyoming, and in Chicago (1912–45), and involved in union activity during that time; assistant to secretary treasurer, CIO (1945–57). He was present at the formation and organization of the LCCR in 1951, later serving on its steering committee.

Reber, Gen. Miles (1902–76), engineer; instructor, USMA (1932–36); assistant chief (1944–45) and deputy chief (1947–50), Legislative and Liaison Division, OCS; chief, Office of Legislative Liaison, OCS (1950–53); commanding general, Western Area Command, U.S. Army Europe (1953–55). A grandson of Maj. Gen. Nelson A. Miles, he attended a 1951 meeting on discriminatory practices in the armed services.

Redd, Rev. Albert C. (1917–), minister; executive director of the South Carolina State NAACP Chapter until 1956. -He is probably best known for his participation in the Tallahassee, Florida, bus boycott of 1957.

Redmond, Sidney Revels (1902–74), lawyer. The grandson of the first African American to sit in the U.S. Senate, he attended Harvard Law School and practiced law in St. Louis where he participated in a number of civil rights cases including *Missouri ex rel. Gaines v. Canada*. He served as president, St. Louis branch NAACP (1938–44) and, while he was in that post, in 1943, Walter White contacted him and nine other leaders of NAACP branches (representing the most effective branches) to start protesting War Manpower Commissioner Paul V. McNutt's decision to cancel the FEPC hearings on racial discrimination in the railroad industry.

Reed, Charles C. (1906–85), chair, NAACP labor committee, Knoxville, Tennessee. In 1949, he assisted in enforcing nondiscrimination measures in military contracts.

Reed, Thomas C. (1931–51), serviceman. After a private Phoenix cemetery refused to bury him (he was black), his family secured his burial in a nonsegregated section of a veterans' cemetery. His case raised awareness of continued segregation at military cemeteries.

Reeves, Frank Daniel (1916–73), lawyer; legal research assistant, NAACP national office (1940–42); administrative assistant, NAACP Washington bureau (1942); professor, Howard University School of Law (1942–43); trial attorney, Legal Division, FEPC (1942–45); attorney, OPA (1945–46); member, NAACP National Legal Committee; consultant, NAACP Washington bureau; chair, Washington, D.C., branch, Legal Redress Committee. During his work with the NAACP, he assisted in many civil rights and loyalty investigation cases. In 1960, he became the first African American to serve on the DNC.

Reid, Dr. Ira De Augustine (1901–68), sociologist and author. He succeeded W. E. B. DuBois as chair of Atlanta University and later taught at several other institutions. Rep. E. E. Cox of Georgia labeled him a "communist fronter."

Reid, Dr. Leon Asbury, Sr. (1893–1965), dentist, of Richmond, Virginia. Representing the National Dental Association, he participated in the Conference of Cooperating Organizations on July 4, 1942. He was also an active member of the NAACP branch in Richmond.

Reilly, Gerard Denis (1906–95), Harvard-educated lawyer and Labor Department solicitor; member, NLRB (1941–46) where he confronted counsel for the NAACP concerning segregated union locals. He later helped draft the Taft-Hartley Act of 1947 and subsequently served as a judge for the U.S. court of appeals for the District of Columbia (1970–76; senior status, 1976–80).

Reitman, Alan (1921–), activist; director of public relations, Political Action Group, CIO (1945–49); director of public relations and editor of monthly publications (1949–57) and assistant executive director (1957–89), ACLU. In the 1950s, he was a member of the LCCR's steering committee.

Reuther, Roy (1909–68), labor organizer; labor information specialist, WPB; administrative assistant to the president, UAW (1948–49). He was among the NECRM of 1950 delegates who visited President Truman.

Reuther, Walter Philip (1907–70), union leader; director, General Motors Division, UAW (1939–42); vice president (1942–46) and president (1946–70), UAW; president, CIO

(1952–55); vice president, AFL-CIO (1955–58). A member of the NAACP National Labor Committee, he was a consistent civil rights supporter. As a student at Detroit City College, he protested the institution's leasing of a segregated swimming pool. In 1948, he helped found the anticommunist ADA. That same year, he was the victim of an assassination attempt.

Reynolds, Grant (1908–2004), business executive; sometime New York commissioner, Department of Corrections. He was not successful in his run for Congress on the Republican ticket against Adam Clayton Powell Jr. (D-N.Y.) in 1946 and 1948, despite the endorsement of a number of influential blacks, including Joe Louis. In 1947, with A. Phillip Randolph, he formed the Committee against Jim Crow in Military Service and Training, which sought to end such discrimination.

Reynolds, Hobson Richmond (1898–1981), funeral home owner of Philadelphia, Pennsylvania; Philadelphia city magistrate and ward leader; president of Improved Benevolent Protective Order of the Elks. In January 1950, he was part of a delegation from the NECRM who met with President Harry S. Truman.

Rhodes, Lewis B., Jr. (1893–1964), engineer and sales representative; personnel director, National Foods Corporation, which at one time held the concession to provide food services for the Pentagon. In 1947, he placed an advertisement in the Washington papers for a supervisor for the Pentagon cafeteria. When Mrs. Willie Bernard applied for the job, she was told she was fully qualified for the position, but once it was determined that she was black, she was told she would not be hired.

Rice, John Inglis (1893–1967), lawyer; city recorder (municipal judge), Columbia, South Carolina. He was the named defendant in *Elmore v. Rice* (72 F. Supp. 516), which challenged and overruled South Carolina's "white" primaries. In 1950, he tried and convicted black soldiers who had refused to move their seats on a bus, one sitting next to a white woman.

Richards, Franklin Dewey (1900–87), lawyer and banker; commissioner, FHA (1947–52). The NAACP asked him for help in ensuring fair employment practices in FHA projects built by private companies.

Richeaux, Charles, postal worker, New Orleans Post Office. In 1946, he was appointed to a permanent position as a clerk over other eligible African American applicants although he was not a veteran, scored lower on the clerk-carrier test than a significant number of African American applicants, and had amassed a large number of demerits during his stint as a temporary employee.

Richman, Col. Milton Herbert (1895–1974), U.S. Army; lawyer and World War II veteran; national commander, Jewish War Veterans (1947–48); member of the executive board, NCPFEPC (1943).

Richmond, 1st Lt. K. M., U.S. Air Force. In 1953, Lt. Richmond complained to the Washington bureau that, during a discussion about segregation in the post barber shop at Chanute Field in Illinois, the commanding general called Richmond a "Communist." Although the general later withdrew the "Communist" statement, Mitchell contended that none of that would ever have arisen if the Air Force had actively pursued a non-discrimination policy at post barber shops.

Ridgely, Brig. Gen. Reginald Heber, Jr. (1902–79), U.S. Marine Corps. In 1953, Mitchell consulted General Ridgely concerning the use of black Marines as stewards and servants of high-ranking officers.

Riley, Edward John (1892–1965), manager of employee relations, General Electric, Schenectady, New York. In 1951, the NAACP conferred with him on a program to increase black employment in General Electric.

Riley, William Henry (1879–1955), railroad engineer, labor leader, and state official. He was New Hampshire commissioner of labor in 1947 when the NAACP contacted him concerning the wife of a veteran who, as the only black employee in her office, faced continuous efforts by the other workers to have her resign or be fired.

Ring, Daniel S. (1899–1982), lawyer. He represented Admiral Emory Land of the U.S. Maritime Commission when he (Ring) went before a congressional committee to testify in favor of S. 2048, which would have strengthened the FEPC.

Riordan, Arthur D. (1905–59), publicity director, IUERMW, CIO (1949–59); editor, *IUE-CIO News* (1949–52). In 1950, he assisted the Washington bureau in developing a press relations program. Four years earlier, while working as an assistant telegraph editor, he led a strike against the *Philadelphia Record.*

Roback, Herbert (1914–77), lawyer and government official. In 1950, Mitchell quoted an article Roback had written for the *Cornell University Law Journal* describing how interstate travel of migrant workers was hindered by legal barriers set up by the various states they traveled through.

Roberts, Maurice Aaron (1910–2001), examiner/investigator/counsel, INS (1941–55) and Immigration Litigation Unit, Department of Justice (1955–68); chair, BOIA (1968–74); editor/editor emeritus, *Interpreter Appeals* (1974–2001). In 1951, he investigated the delay of Arnold Gordon's naturalization, a delay based on Gordon's membership in the NAACP. He is popularly known as the "dean of immigration law."

Robertson, David B. (1876–1961), locomotive engineer on the Erie Railroad (1898–1913); general chair (1905–13) and international president, Brotherhood of Locomotive Firemen and Enginemen (1913–22, 1929–60). He led the brotherhood in an attempt to completely eliminate black firemen from railroads where white union members worked, in violation of the Railway Labor Act.

Robinson, Sgt. Aubrey Eugene, Jr. (1922–2000), U.S. Army. A native of Madison, New Jersey, he was, along with twelve other black servicemen from Camp Gordon, Georgia, arrested for violating South Carolina's Jim Crow laws after an altercation on a bus traveling to Aiken, South Carolina. Robinson and the others were convicted and sentenced to thirty days on the chain gang. After the war, he graduated from Cornell University Law School and practiced law in Washington, D.C. before being appointed by President Lyndon B. Johnson to the U.S. district court for the District of Columbia in 1966. In 1982, he became chief judge and served in that position until he took senior status in 1992. Among the cases he presided over was that of accused spy Jonathan J. Pollard in 1987.

Robinson, Col. Bernard L. (1901–94), U.S. Army Corps of Engineers and commissioner of the District of Columbia (1949–52). He retired as a major general. In 1951, Mitchell conferred with him about racial segregation in the public parks and playgrounds of Washington, D.C.

Robinson, Florence, one of a group of black teenagers who, in 1953, challenged Jim Crow transportation laws and refused to move to the back of a bus in Richmond, Virginia.

Robinson, George Oscar (1907–81), author; public relations official, AEC. In 1951, he met with NAACP officials regarding efforts to ensure nonsegregation and nondiscrimination at the Savannah River Plant hydrogen bomb facility in Aiken, South Carolina.

Robinson, James, one of a group of black teenagers who, in 1953, challenged Jim Crow transportation laws and refused to move to the back of a bus in Richmond, Virginia.

Robinson, Spottswood William III (1916–98), lawyer and judge; Virginia representative, NAACP LDEF (1948–50); southeast regional counsel, NAACP (1950–59); member, U.S. Commission on Civil Rights (1961–63); professor of law and dean (1960–63), Howard University Law School; judge, U.S. district court for the District of Columbia (1964–66); judge, U.S. court of appeals for the District of Columbia (1966–89; chief judge, 1981–86; senior status, 1986–1989). In 1944, he was one of the NAACP attorneys defending Irene Morgan when she brought suit against the commonwealth of Virginia due to her arrest and conviction of violating the state segregation laws by refusing to move to the back of a Greyhound bus en route to Baltimore.

Robison, Joseph B. (1919–1983), lawyer. In 1951, he was director, Committee on Law and Social Action, AJCong, when he was present at the organization of the LCCR; he also collaborated with William Maslow in the work "Civil Rights Legislation and the Fight for Equality, 1862–1952," which has been cited as a companion for volume 3 of this work.

Rockefeller, Nelson Aldrich (1908–79) (R-N.Y.), businessman and philanthropist; director, OIAA (1940–44); assistant secretary of state (1944–45); member and chair, PACGO (1953–58); undersecretary of HEW (1953–54); special assistant to the president (1954–55); New York governor (1959–73); vice president of the United States (1974–77). He was a liberal Republican, and as undersecretary of HEW, he conducted an investigation to determine whether federal funding would be eliminated for Howard University on the grounds that a number of its faculty members belonged to the allegedly subversive National Lawyers Guild.

Rogers, William Pierce (1913–2001), lawyer; New York State assistant attorney general (1938–42); deputy U.S. attorney general (1953–57); U.S. attorney general (1957–61); U.S. secretary of state (1969–73). In 1953, he attended an Eisenhower administration meeting on civil rights and a meeting of a subcommittee of the CGC. He is credited with helping strengthen what became the Civil Rights Act of 1957.

Roosevelt, Anna Eleanor (1884–1962), wife of Franklin D. Roosevelt and activist; first lady of the United States (1933–45); member, NAACP National Board of Directors (1945–62). While serving as first lady, she pushed for antilynching legislation and corresponded regularly with NAACP executive secretary Walter White (she joined the NAACP in 1939). Following her husband's death, she urged President Truman to uphold civil rights and maintain the FEPC. Roy Wilkins once referred to her as "the Negro's true friend."

Roosevelt, Franklin Delano (1882–1945), (D-N.Y.), U.S. president (1933–45), who signed Executive Orders 8802 and 9346 which established and strengthened FEPC. He also was actively involved in attempts to desegregate the armed forces during World War II, although full desegregation did not come until 1948.

Rose, Alex (1898–1976), lawyer, union leader and activist; president, United Hatters, Cap and Millinery Workers International Union (1950–76); one of the founders of the American Labor Party (1938) and the Liberal Party of New York State (1939). In 1943, he was named to the initial executive committee of the NCPFEPC.

Rosenberg, Anna Marie Lederer (1902–83), public relations executive; assistant New York regional director (1934–36) and New York regional director (1936–39), NRA; regional representative, SSA (1937–43); director, New York State SSB (1940); director, Region II, WMC (1942–45); assistant secretary of defense (1950–53). One of Mitchell's favorites, she supported permanent FEPC legislation. As assistant secretary of defense, she was involved with the development of universal military service legislation, desegregation of the armed forces, and increasing the role of women in the military. In 1962, she married Paul G. Hoffman and was subsequently known as Anna Rosenberg Hoffman.

Ross, Harry Earl (1901–93), UAW staffer; treasurer, UAW Local 3, Dodge Brothers Automobile Company, Detroit (1938–39); codirector, Fair Practices and Anti-discrimination Department, UAW (1946–65). In 1949, he participated in the UAW Educational Conference in Milwaukee.

Ross, Malcolm (1895–1965), author and editor. A native of Newark, New Jersey and a graduate of Yale, he served in the U.S. Army Air Corps in World War I. He served as director of information, NLRB (1936–42) and subsequently as deputy chair, then chair, FEPC (1943–46).

Rothschild, Jerome Joseph (1884–1964), lawyer. Co-founder of the Philadelphia law firm Fox Rothschild, he was prominent in both the American Jewish Committee and the National

Council of Christians and Jews. In July of 1942, he attended the Conference of Cooperating Organizations.

Rousseau, Earl R., Jr. (1925–2002), postal worker. A war service appointee to the New Orleans Post Office, he filed an employment discrimination complaint against that institution in 1947.

Royall, Kenneth Claiborne (1894–1971), lawyer; North Carolina state legislator (1927); chief of legal section (1942–43) and deputy fiscal director (1943–45), Army Service Forces; special assistant to the secretary of war (1945); undersecretary of war (1945–47); U.S. secretary of war (1947); secretary of the army (1947–49). He opposed desegregating the military, leading the NAACP to call for his resignation as secretary of the army. During his tenure, however, it was established that there would be no new segregated areas in national cemeteries.

Rubenstein, Leon A. (1905–89), lawyer and jurist of Baltimore; Maryland state legislator who in 1945 introduced a FEPC bill that Will Maslow said "has no chance of passage."

Ruch, Judson E. (1911–89), lawyer. In 1950, he represented Lt. Leon A. Gilbert at his trial after he was sentenced to death for refusing to obey the command of a white officer to return with his men to a dangerous position. Following legal challenges by the NAACP, Gilbert's sentence was reduced by President Truman to twenty years.

Russell, Richard Brevard, Jr. (1897–1971) (D-Ga.), lawyer; Georgia state legislator (1921–31); governor (1931–33); U.S. senator (1933–71). A Dixiecrat, he consistently opposed civil rights legislation. He also supported federal funding of black migration to northern cities, the retention of the poll tax, and a segregation amendment to draft legislation. He was once quoted as saying that "if they [blacks] overcome us you'll find me in a last ditch."

Russwurm, John Browne (1799–1851), newspaper editor, abolitionist, and colonizationist; Liberian government official, born in Port Antonio, Jamaica. In 1827, with Rev. Samuel E. Cornish, he produced the first newspaper issued by blacks, *Freedom's Journal.* In 1952, Mitchell commented that, if the McCarran-Walter Act, with its severe restriction on immigration from the Caribbean and South America, had been in force when immigrants like Russwurm entered the United States, they would not have been able to make "notable contributions to the building of our nation."

Rustin, Bayard (1910–87), activist; youth organizer, MOWC (1940–42); field secretary, CORE (1941–45); race relations director, Fellowship of Reconciliation (1941–53); executive secretary, War Resisters' League (1953–55); special assistant to Rev. Dr. Martin Luther King, Jr., SCLC (1955–60); national coordinator, March on Washington (1963); executive director, A. Philip Randolph Institute (1964–85); chairman, executive committee, LCCR (1951–53). He was recruited by A. Philip Randolph to formulate plans for the MOWC and served as its youth organizer; he also worked with Randolph in 1947 when the latter commenced opposition to universal military training and a segregated military. Rustin, a known pacifist as well as a student of the teachings of Mohandas K. Gandhi, was an influence on Randolph in promoting nonviolent social protest when the latter devised the MOWM.

Ryan, Rev. Msgr. John Augustine (1869–1945), the Roman Catholic Church's expert on economic and social questions during the first half of the twentieth century. Born and educated in Minnesota, he earned a Ph.D. in Sacred Theology from Catholic University of America in 1906 and taught in Washington, D.C. at Catholic University and Trinity College. He served in a number of New Deal federal posts, and from 1920 to 1945, he headed the Social Action Department of the National Catholic Welfare Council (NCWC). He was considered for a position on FEPC, but did not serve. He testified before a congressional committee in favor of permanent FEPC legislation (Chavez-Norton Bill) in 1944. He was also a member of the executive committee of NCPFEPC.

Ryan, Joseph Patrick (1884–1963), union leader; vice president, NYSFL (1926–46); president, ILA (1927–53); president, CLCGNY (1928–38). In 1947, NAACP officials contacted him regarding discrimination by a white ILA local in Brownsville, Texas.

Saberre, Theophile A., Jr. (1921–2005), veteran. Although claiming employment discrimination at the New Orleans Post Office, he declined to join those of his fellow postal workers and the NAACP in filing formal charges against that body.

Saizan, Paul Morin (1923–2000), veteran. A victim of employment discrimination at the New Orleans Post Office, he became (in 1947) one of the NAACP's official complainants against that body.

Saltonstall, Leverett (1892–1979) (R-Mass.), lawyer; Massachusetts state legislator (1923–36); governor (1939–45); U.S. senator (1945–67). A liberal Republican supportive of civil rights, he voted in 1950 against Richard Russell's segregation amendment to draft legislation. In 1947, he introduced a resolution to break filibusters by a majority vote.

Sarnoff, David (1891–1971), of New York; Russian-born president of Radio Corporation of America (RCA) (1930–47), and chairman of the board (1947–69). He was a career employee of Marconi Wireless Telegraph Company who rose through the ranks of RCA after it took over the Marconi firm. A member of FEPC, he resigned in 1943 after Paul McNutt cancelled hearings on railroad cases.

Savory, Dr. Philip Marcowen Hugh (1889–1965), physician and newspaper executive; a native of Georgetown, British Guiana (now Guyana) who emigrated to New York City before World War I. In 1935, with Dr. C. B. Powell, he purchased the black newspaper the *Amsterdam News.* In 1952, Mitchell commented that, if the McCarran-Walter Act, with its severe restriction on immigration from the Caribbean and South America, had been in force when immigrants like Savory entered the United States, they would not have been able to make "notable contributions to the building of our nation."

Sawyer, Charles (1887–1979), lawyer; Cincinnati city councilman (1911–15); Ohio lieutenant governor (1933–35); ambassador to Belgium and minister to Luxembourg (1944–45); U.S. secretary of commerce (1948–53). In 1951, he assured Mitchell that there would be no segregation at Dulles Airport.

Scanlon, Thomas Edward (1896–1955) (D-Pa.), pressman for Pittsburgh newspapers (1914–36) and delegate to Pittsburgh Central Labor Union (1920–40); U.S. representative (1941–45). He was a cosponsor of a permanent FEPC bill, known as the Dawson-Scanlon-La Follette Bill.

Schieffelin, William Jay (1866–1955), chemist and corporate executive; chairman of the board, Schieffelin & Co., wholesale pharmaceutical firm of New York City. A Spanish-American War and World War I veteran, in 1917, he was appointed Colonel of the replacement Fifteenth New York National Guard after the original regiment had been federalized as the 369th U.S. Infantry Regiment and sent to France. As president, Citizens Union of New York (1921–55), he was a staunch supporter of the NAACP and of many liberal causes; in 1945 he was named a member of the board of directors of a revamped NCPFEPC.

Schoeneman, George Jeremiah (1889–1966), official, BIR (1920–44); assistant commissioner of internal revenue (1944–45); administrative assistant to the president (1945); special executive assistant to the president (1945–47); commissioner of internal revenue (1947–51). In 1947, he stated that the BIR did not have a policy of discrimination and would enact corrective measures if discriminatory practices were found.

Schoeppel, Andrew Frank (1894–1962) (R-Kans.), lawyer; chair, Corporation Commission of the State of Kansas (1939–42); Kansas governor (1943–47); U.S. senator (1949–62). A fiscal and social conservative, he voted against anitfilibuster legislation (1949) and against a bill to protect servicepeople from violence (1951). While governor, he gained notoriety for his antilabor views. In 1950, he questioned the loyalty of Secretary of the Interior Oscar L. Chapman.

Schomburg, Arthur Alfonso (1874–1938), bibliophile, curator, writer and archivist, whose vast collection of Afro-Americana provided the foundation of the New York City Public Library's Schomburg Center for Research in Black Culture; was a native of San Juan, Puerto Rico. In 1952, Mitchell commented that, if the McCarran-Walter Act, with its severe restriction on immigration from the Caribbean and South America, had been in force when immigrants like Schomburg entered the United States, they would not have been able to make "notable contributions to the building of our nation."

Schroeter, Leonard W. (1924–), lawyer and activist; staff member NAACP LDEF (1951–52) where he was present at the organization of the LCCR in 1951. He then moved to Seattle where he was the director of B'Nai B'Rith for the northwestern United States (1952–55) before going into private practice. He is a staunch advocate of free speech and civil rights and has been actively involved in ameliorating the plight of Jews in the former Soviet republics.

Schuyler, George Samuel (1895–1977), journalist, essayist, editor, columnist, satirist and author. A World War I veteran, he wrote for various publications including the *Crisis, The Nation, Opportunity,* and A. Philip Randolph's magazine *Messenger* and did publicity for the NAACP. However, he was best known as a columnist and editor for the *Pittsburgh Courier* (1925–75). His writings would eventually exhibit a tendency to conservatism to the extent that it was rumored that he was a member of the John Birch Society. His daughter was the child prodigy Philippa Duke Schuyler, concert pianist and composer. In June of 1943, he participated in the NAACP-sponsored Emergency Conference on the Status of the Negro in the War for Freedom, held in Detroit.

Schusterman, Rabbi Abraham (1907–85), chief rabbi, Har Sinai Congregation (Reformed), Baltimore (1941–72). A member of the National Conference of Christians and Jews, as well as the Interfaith Council of Metropolitan Baltimore and the Central Committee of Rabbis, in 1943, he was a member of the Citizens' Committee to Save Colored Locomotive Firemen's Jobs.

Schwartz, Jonas Gillis (1903–66), lawyer; secretary to Gov. Luther W. Youngdahl (D-Minn.). In 1951, Mitchell wrote Schwartz to commend the governor on his support of black Minnesota National Guard troops.

Schwellenbach, Lewis Baxter (1894–1948) (D-Wash.), lawyer; U.S. senator (1935–40); delegate, Interparliamentary Union at The Hague (1938); judge, U.S. District Court for the Eastern District of Washington (1940–45); U.S. secretary of labor (1945–48). As secretary, he participated in conferences with civil rights leaders, ended segregation in USES offices in Washington, D.C. (1946), and conferred with Mitchell on access of blacks to training programs.

Scott, Hazel Dorothy (1920–81), pianist and singer; born Port-of-Spain, Trinidad, she was brought to New York City by her parents when she was four years old. In 1952, Mitchell commented that, if the McCarran-Walter Act, with its severe restriction on immigration from the Caribbean and South America, had been in force when immigrants like the Scotts entered the United States, they would not have been able to make "notable contributions to the building of our nation."

Scott, James Edward (1895–1968), lawyer; grand polemarch, Kappa Alpha Psi social fraternity (1939–40). In 1953, representing the American Council for Human Rights, he met with Mitchell and Albert M. Cole to review and discuss the federal government's housing policy.

Scott, Jeanne Simmons (1898–1966), manager, Pittsburgh branch, Pennsylvania State Employment Service; secretary, Pennsylvania State Conference of NAACP Branches. In the late 1940s, she labored for state FEPC legislation in Pennsylvania.

Scott, John Thad, Jr. (1918–2005), lawyer; chair, National Mediation Board (1948–53). In a letter to Mitchell, Scott reaffirmed that the function of the National Mediation Board was to "mediate labor disputes."

Scott, William T. (1909–92), employee of the Washington (D.C.) Railroad Terminal. In 1953, the NAACP successfully upheld his right not to join a segregated chapter of the Brotherhood of Railway Carmen.

Scruggs, H. W., Baptist minister; pastor, Thankful Baptist Church, Birmingham, Alabama, and leader of a local organization called the Home Owners Protection League. He was one of a group of Alabama civic and religious leaders who traveled to Washington in 1953 to express their disapproval of the use of federal funds for a segregated health center.

Seidenberg, Jacob (1914–96), lawyer and labor arbitrator; staff member, CGCC (1951–53); executive director, CGC (1953–60). In 1953, he invited Mitchell to attend a CGC subcommittee meeting regarding employment discrimination.

Seidman, Bertrand Russell (1919–2004), economist, Research Department, AFL (1948–62); delegate, ILO (1958–76); European representative, AFL-CIO (1962–66); head, Social Security Department, AFL-CIO (1966–90). During his tenure as an economist for the AFL, he attended a meeting of a subcommittee of the CGC regarding employment discrimination.

Seitz, Peter M. (1905–83), lawyer and labor arbitrator. He was best known as an arbitrator for Major League Baseball, where in 1975, he ruled that the reserve clause was illegal and that those major league baseball players who played a year for their team without a new contract became free agents. In 1951, Seitz was the assistant to Assistant Secretary of Defense Anna Rosenberg and sponsored a meeting attempting to facilitate the desegregation of the armed forces.

Seligman, Daniel (1925–), writer and editorial columnist, *Fortune* (1949–96) and *Forbes* (1996–). In 1950, in a letter to Seligman, Mitchell explained why he and Joseph C. Waddy prepared a joint statement for their testimony about the Railway Labor Act before the Senate Subcommittee of the Committee of Labor and Public Welfare.

Sengstacke, John Herman Henry (1912–97), publisher, *Chicago Defender* (1934–97); founder (1940) and president, NNPUA; member, PCETOAS (Fahy Committee) (1948–50). He supported a conference with Secretary of Labor Schwellenbach on nondiscrimination by USES offices. Along with Rep. William L. Dawson, he is often credited with having facilitated Richard Daley's rise to power in Chicago politics.

Shane, Francis C. (1905–99), union officer. In 1951, he was the civil rights coordinator for the United Steelworkers Union-CIO when he was present at the meeting to organize and establish the LCCR.

Shaw, Gardiner Howland (1893–1965), diplomat and "nationally known specialist in field of criminal rehabilitation and youth problems." He joined the U.S. Department of State in 1917, and was initially assigned to postings in Turkey. While there he became interested in the plight of incarcerated youth and continued this interest while serving as chief, Near Eastern Affairs (1926–29); chief, Division of Foreign Service Personnel (1937–41); assistant secretary of state (1941–44); member, board of trustees and board of visitors, National Training School; member, board of directors, American Correctional Association. In 1945, he was named to the board of directors of a revamped NCPFEPC.

Shea, Edward Francis, Jr. (1925–96), lawyer; in 1954, as an associate with the Baltimore firm of Sherbow & Sherbow, Shea reported to Maryland State's Attorney M. Peter Moser that Bryant W. Bowles, Jr., who had been ordered by the court to comply with a payment schedule set up in lieu of him going to jail, had not yet done so.

Shepard, Marshall Lorenzo, Sr. (1899–1967), pastor, Mt. Olivet Baptist Church in Philadelphia (1931–67); Philadelphia County Recorder of Deeds (1951–55). In 1941, Reverend Shepard was part of a delegation of blacks (including Walter White) who met with Sidney Hillman of the OPM to discuss racial discrimination in defense plants.

Shields, Augustus G., journalist and businessman. He was an African-American newspaperman who served as business manager of a number of Midwestern newspapers including the *Memphis World* (1930–40) and the *Arkansas Post* of Little Rock (1940–57). In 1943, he was one of sixteen representatives of the black press who signed a telegram protesting the FEPC cancellation of hearings designed to review racial discrimination in the railroad industry.

Shipp, Lawrence R. (1925–), veteran and engineer. In 1949, he complained to the NAACP that the U.S. Public Health Service in Bethesda, Maryland, had denied him employment solely on the basis of race. The charge was investigated and found to be accurate, and Shipp was subsequently hired.

Shishkin, Boris Basil (1906–84), economist; secretary, Housing Committee, AFL (1939–55) and AFL-CIO (1955–71); member, FEPC (1943–45); director, European Labor Division, ECA (Marshall Plan) (1948–52); secretary, Social Security Committee, AFL (1951–53); director, Civil Rights Department, AFL-CIO (1955–64); member, NAACP National Labor Committee from 1946. As a member of the CGC, he assisted the NAACP in obtaining apprenticeships for minority workers in the construction industry.

Shorter, Charles A. (1909–2000), official, Philadelphia branch NAACP. In 1953, he met with Mitchell and officials from U. S. Steel concerning segregation in company housing in Bucks County, Pennsylvania.

Sibley, Georgiana Farr (1887–1980), known professionally as Mrs. Harper Sibley, of Rochester, New York, she was married to the heir of the Western Union telegraph company fortune and had six children. She was also a supporter of liberal causes and served as longtime president of the United Council of Church Women. In 1943, she served as member of the executive board of NCPFEPC.

Sifton, Paul Field (1897–1972), journalist and playwright; official, NYSDL; official, Wage and Hour Division, U.S. Department of Labor; legislative representative, UAW (1948–62); legislative director, NCPFEPC (1946–48). In 1951, he worked with Mitchell on Senate rules changes.

Silver, Dr. George A. (1913–2005), doctor and activist. He served in the U.S. Army Medical Corps during World War II; chief, social medicine division, Montefiore Hospital, New York City (1951–65); deputy assistant secretary for health and scientific affairs, HEW (1965–68), where he oversaw the implementation of Medicare and Medicaid as well as the desegregation of American hospitals under Title VII of the 1964 Civil Rights Act. In 1951, representing the JLC, he worked with Mitchell and others on Senate rules changes.

Simmons, Le Roy J. (1905–73) (D-Wis.), postal clerk of Milwaukee; Wisconsin state assemblyman (1945–52); the only African American in the state legislature. In 1945, he joined with state senator Robert E. Tehan to sponsor a bill forbidding discriminatory employment practices by private employers or trade unions and establishing a FEPC having enforcement powers; although supported by labor, religious groups, blacks and Jews, the legislation was opposed by state and local Chambers of Commerce. A compromise bill, calling for an FEPC without enforcement powers, was subsequently signed into law.

Simmons, lst Lt. Thomas J., II (1919–2003), U.S. Army (he retired as a colonel). In 1952, he worked in the Office of the Secretary of Defense and sent Mitchell a copy of a wartime directive from the War Department mandating that equal opportunity for all service members to enjoy recreational facilities in all military facilities was to be obtained through inspection by responsible commanders and inspectors general.

Simms, Cleve (1882–1945), locomotive fireman. With fellow fireman Jack Taylor, he was shot from ambush on September 7, 1931 in Durant, Mississippi because he and Taylor had jobs coveted by unemployed whites.

Simms, David M. (1933–), Baptist minister; a native of Pittsburgh, Pennsylvania, but later a resident of Richmond, Virginia, he was a graduate of Virginia Union University and the Episcopal Theological Seminary in Alexandria, Virginia. In 1953, while president of the Virginia State Conference of NAACP Youth Councils, he violated Jim Crow transportation laws by refusing to move his seat for a white person, and was arrested and fined.

Simms, Samuel Turner (1892–1971), locomotive fireman, farmer, and day laborer; of Holmes County, Mississippi. On March 11, 1932, in McComb, Mississippi, Simms and fellow fireman Sam Barnes were shot from ambush and wounded; the perpetrators were thought to have been whites coveting their jobs during the early days of the Depression.

Singleton, John A. (1910–88), president, NAACP branch, Jamaica, N.Y. In 1941, Roy Wilkins contacted Singleton to assure him that the NAACP fully supported the proposed MOWM.

Sipuel, Ada Lois (1924–95), lawyer; professor, Langston University (1957–87); member, Board of Regents, University of Oklahoma (1992–95). A plaintiff in *Sipuel v. Board of Regents of the University of Oklahoma*, an NAACP-backed case that went all the way to the Supreme Court in 1948. She sought and ultimately obtained admission to the University of Oklahoma Law School, which had been segregated. This decision opened the nation's law schools and graduate schools to blacks and established legal precedents used in the *Brown v. Board of Education* case. Her married name was Fisher.

Skinner, Floyd Howard (1919–), attorney; president, NAACP branch, Grand Rapids, Michigan; subsequently, the first African American to join the Grand Rapids Bar Association. In 1953, he reported to Mitchell about Janie Spaulding's resignation from her post at HEW.

Small, John D. (1893–1960), businessman; executive officer, War Production Board (1943–46); administrator, Civil Production Administration (1946–50); chair, Munitions Board, U.S. Department of Defense (1950–54). In 1952, Small was one of a number of prominent businesspeople, labor leaders, and government officials named by President Truman to serve on his Committee on Government Compliance. Their duties included overseeing Truman's Fair Employment Practices program.

Smalls, Emma Ophelia Pringle (1921–2007), of Charleston, South Carolina. In 1953, she wrote a letter to the *Charleston News and Courier* expressing her displeasure at the desegregation process of the cafeteria of the Charleston Navy Yard, essentially complaining about the alleged bad conduct of some of the African American workers who first used the cafeteria, once restricted to "whites only."

Smathers, George Armistead (1913–2007) (D-Fla.), lawyer; assistant U.S. district attorney (1940–42); U.S. representative (1947–51); U.S. senator (1951–69). He first achieved prominence through his bitter 1950 Democratic senatorial primary campaign against incumbent Claude D. Pepper. During that contest, Smathers accused Pepper of being a Stalinist and asserted that the FEPC (which Pepper supported) was a communist-inspired plot to eliminate segregation. As senator, he continued to pound on the anticommunist theme, seeking in 1953 to deny Hawaii statehood because of alleged communist influence there. During his first year in office, he offered to defend gratis any police officer indicted for violation of civil rights. He later asserted that a Supreme Court decision banning segregation would "set the situation in the South back fifty years."

Smith, Alfred Edgar (1903–86), journalist. A writer for *Chicago Defender*, he criticized Mitchell for not testifying at a brief 1949 hearing on the proposed repeal of the Taft-Hartley Act.

Smith, Arthur V. (1922–97), veteran. The NAACP successfully challenged his dismissal from the RMS on the grounds of discrimination.

Smith, Howard Alexander (1880–1966) (R-N.J.), lawyer; executive secretary (1919–27) and lecturer (1927–30), Princeton University; U.S. senator (1944–59). He opposed nondiscrimination amendments to the Taft-Hartley Act and fair employment bills with enforcement powers.

Smith, Howard Worth (1883–1976) (D-Va.), lawyer and judge; U.S. representative (1931–67); sponsor, Alien Registration Act (Smith Act, 1940) and War Labor Disputes Act (Smith-Connolly Anti-strike Act, 1943); chair, Select Committee to Investigate Executive Agencies (Smith Committee) (1943–44); chair, House Rules Committee (1955–67). A consistent opponent of the FEPC, he supported segregation, the Taft-Hartley Act, and the "Southern Manifesto." As early as 1945, however, he endorsed an equal rights amendment for women.

Smith, John Lee (1894–1963), lawyer and judge; Texas state legislator (1941–43); lieutenant governor (1943–47). The NAACP opposed his nomination as U.S. attorney for the Northern District of Texas because of his support of segregation.

Smith, Lillian Eugenia (1897–1966), author and editor. Author of *Strange Fruit* (1944) and *Killers of the Dream* (1949), she was also the editor of the journal *The South Today.* An opponent of segregation and a supporter of the NAACP Legal Defense and Education Fund, she was accused by Rep. E. E. Cox of Georgia of being a "communist fronter."

Smith, Margaret Chase (1897–1995) (R-Maine), businesswoman and air force reservist; U.S. representative (1940–49); U.S. senator (1949–73). An independent-minded Republican who often voted with Democrats on domestic issues, she supported Senate rules changes.

Snyder, John Wesley (1895–1985), banker; national bank receiver, controller of the currency (1930–37); manager, St. Louis office, RFC (1937–43); director, OWMR (1945–46); U.S. secretary of the treasury (1946–53). In 1947, he negotiated with the NAACP on ending segregation in the Treasury Department.

Soll, George (1920–80), lawyer; staff counsel, ACLU as well as a member of its executive board; member, executive committee, NECRM of 1950.

Solomon, David (1893–1957), building contractor and business executive of Brooklyn, New York. A veteran of World War I, he was serving as national commander, JWV, when he was part of a delegation from the NECRM that met with President Truman in January 1950.

Sparkman, John Jackson (1899–1985) (D-Ala.), lawyer; U.S. representative (1937–46); U.S. senator (1946–79); Democratic Party vice presidential nominee (1952). One of the more liberal members of the South's congressional delegation, he supported Truman's Taft-Hartley veto, rent control, and federal aid to education and housing. Yet he was a strong critic of civil rights measures, opposing anti–poll tax and antilynching legislation and voting against liberalization of the cloture rule. He also backed the Dixiecrat ticket in 1948, condemned the *Brown* decision, and said that Truman's civil rights program was a "colossal blunder."

Spaulding, Jane [or Janie] Eloise Morrow (1897–1965), assistant secretary, HEW (1953–54). The first African American woman to hold a subcabinet position, she was forced to resign from her assistant secretary post. Mitchell suspected that she was a victim of employment discrimination.

Spaulding, Theodore O. (1903–72), lawyer and judge; a native of Cabarrus County, North Carolina, he moved to Philadelphia in 1930 and soon became involved with the NAACP, being active in most civil rights litigation in Philadelphia; judge, Philadelphia County court of common pleas (1958–66); judge, Pennsylvania Superior Court (1966–72). In 1943, Walter White contacted him and nine other branch secretaries representing the most effective branches to start protesting War Manpower Commissioner Paul V. McNutt's decision to cancel the FEPC hearings on racial discrimination in the railroad industry.

Spears, Jacob Franklin, Sr. (1893–1946) (D-Texas), lawyer of San Antonio and Texas state legislator, serving in the state House of Representatives (1934–36) and state Senate (1937–46). In 1945, he proposed a bill forbidding discrimination in employment and in places of public accommodation designed to protect Mexicans and other Latinos only. The civil rights of Blacks, Jews, Catholics, and Asians were not covered under that bill.

Speight, Lillian A. (1899–1978); schoolteacher and activist, of Washington, D.C.. Representing the MOWM, she attended the Conference of Cooperating Organizations on July 4, 1942.

Spellman, Francis Joseph (1889–1967), Roman Catholic priest; auxiliary bishop of Boston (1932–39); Archbishop of New York (1939–67), named Cardinal (1946). He was named as a possible participant in a proposed conference on civil rights in correspondence between Walter White and Roy Wilkins in 1948.

Spencer, Mabel W. (1901–84), secretary to Ruby Hurley, director, NAACP southeast region. In 1953 she reported to Mitchell about Ms. Hurley's activities in Birmingham, Alabama, concerning discrimination in public housing there, and the federal housing program overall.

Spencer, Samuel (1910–97), lawyer; president, D.C. Board of Commissioners (1952–54). He insured that the board of commissioners ordered the desegregation of the nation's capital, therefore bringing it in line with the remainder of the federal government. This order was instituted, exempting only the D.C. Fire Department and the D.C. Department of Recreation, and certain other "public welfare" organizations as the board of commissioners felt that they did not have the authorization to command them to desegregate.

Spicely [Specely], Pvt. Booker Thomas (1909–44), U.S. Army. A native of Nottoway County, Virginia, Spicely was the assistant business manager for Tuskegee Institute when he enlisted in the U.S. Army in Philadelphia, Pennsylvania, on December 31, 1943. After finishing basic training, he was to receive further training as a cook and was sent to Camp Butner in North Carolina. On July 8, 1944, near Durham, North Carolina, he refused to move to the back of a bus and the bus driver, Herman Lee Council, pulled out a pistol and fired two times, hitting Spicely in the liver and through the heart; Spicely died on the spot. Although the incident was investigated by the NAACP, Council was tried by an all-white jury on a murder charge, and was acquitted.

Spingarn, Arthur Barnett (1878–1971), lawyer. With his brother Joel, he was one of the earliest supporters of the NAACP; both men gave financial support to the organization. Arthur Spingarn became the first head of the NAACP Legal Defense Fund, and subsequently, he served as president (1940–65). In 1954, he appeared with President Eisenhower, Dr. Ralph Bunche, and others at the Freedom Fulfillment Conference in New York City.

Spingarn, Hope E. (1906–88), actress, activist, daughter of Joel E. Spingarn, and niece of Arthur Spingarn. In 1946, she promised to find ways to make the projected *NAACP Labor Manual* "simple and attractive."

Spingarn, Stephen Joel (1908–84), lawyer and government official; younger son of Joel E. Spingarn and nephew of Arthur Spingarn. Longtime employee of the U.S. Treasury Department, where he served as assistant attorney (1934–39), special assistant (1937–38), assistant general counsel (1946–49), and deputy director, Office of Contract Settlement (1947–49); administrative assistant to President Truman (1949–50); commissioner (1950–53) and acting chair (1952–55), FTC. In 1942, before he went to serve in World War II, Spingarn was named to the advisory board to the fledgling NAACP Washington bureau.

Spottswood, Rev. Stephen Gill (1897–1974), minister and later bishop, AME Zion Church; president, Washington, D.C., branch, NAACP (1947–52); leader, NECRM of 1950; member, NAACP National Board of Directors (1955–61); chair of the board, NAACP (1961–74). He was prominent in the movements for Washington, D.C., home rule and desegregation.

St. Claire, Darrell M. (1906–), Senate staff member (1933–77). As chief clerk for the Senate Committee on Rules and Administration, he assisted the NAACP during hearings on rules changes.

Stahl, Oscar Glenn (1910–2002), administrator and author. A member of a special committee to inquire into problems of African American employment at the BOASI in Baltimore, he later authored a popular text on public personnel administration.

Starr, Frederick (1878–1951), businessman. Starting as a teacher in the New York City public schools, he became the owner of a company that sold coal and heating oil (Frederick Starr Coal Company) in the Bronx. In 1942, as the NAACP attempted to raise funds to open and operate the Washington bureau, Walter White contacted Starr, requesting a donation.

Staupers, Mabel Doyle Keaton (1890–1989), registered nurse and civil rights activist. A native of Barbados, she emigrated to Harlem with her family at the age of thirteen and subsequently graduated from what is now Howard University College of Nursing. She was active in the National Association of Colored Graduate Nurses, as well as a number of community-oriented activities; she worked to integrate black nurses into the mainstream medical world. In 1948, the American Nursing Association admitted black nurses to membership and in 1951, for her efforts, the NAACP awarded her the Spingarn Medal. In 1944, she was one of the members of the initial executive committee of the NCPFEPC. In 1952, Mitchell commented that, if the McCarran-Walter Act, with its severe restriction on immigration from the Caribbean and South America, had been in force when immigrants like Staupers entered the United States, they would not have been able to make "notable contributions to the building of our nation."

Steele, Julian D. (1906–70), activist; Massachusetts state coordinator, Model Cities program; commissioner, Massachusetts Department of Community Affairs (1965–70). As secretary of the Boston branch of the NAACP, he was successful in mounting a letter-writing campaign to force through both houses of the state legislature a law permitting blacks who graduated from medical or nursing schools the opportunity to apply for positions in public institutions within the commonwealth of Massachusetts. In 1943, Walter White contacted him and nine other branch secretaries representing the most effective branches to start protesting War Manpower Commissioner Paul V. McNutt's decision to cancel the FEPC hearings on racial discrimination in the railroad industry.

Steiner, Richard Lewis (1913-89), educator, administrator, and housing expert; program planner, USHA (1938-41); director, Baltimore Redevelopment Commission (1946-54); deputy commissioner (1954-57) and commissioner (1957-59), Urban Renewal Administration, HHFA; director, Baltimore Urban Renewal and Housing Agency (1959-67); professor, city planning, Howard University (1968-70). In 1954, Steiner testified before a Congressional subcommittee that although he had been the director of the Redevelopment Commission for eight years that he had never met Clarence Mitchell. Mitchell rejoined that Steiner must have met his wife, Juanita Jackson Mitchell, who had appeared as counsel on behalf of the NAACP in a number of matters concerning public housing in Baltimore during that period.

Stennis, John Cornelius (1901–95) (D-Miss.), lawyer; Mississippi state legislator (1928–32); judge (1937–47); U.S. senator (1947–89). He was a staunch opponent of civil rights measures. During the Truman years, he filibustered against an anti–poll tax bill, helped defeat antifilibuster legislation, and voted against a bill that forbade segregation in public housing.

Stephens, Roderick, Sr. (1885–1975), owner of heating oil company in the Bronx; president, Bronx Board of Trade; vice chairman, New York Triborough Bridge Commission. In 1943, he was named to the executive board of the NCPFEPC and several years later to the executive committee of the NECRM of 1950. His sons would become known as designers and builders of yachts and other pleasure craft.

Stevens, Harold Arnoldus (1907–90), lawyer and judge; counsel, BSCP; counsel, Provisional Commission to Organize Colored Locomotive Firemen; counsel, FEPC (resigned in 1943 from the latter in protest of its policies); World War II veteran; represented Thirteenth Assembly District in New York State Assembly (1947–50); judge, New York court of general sessions (1950–55); judge, New York State Supreme Court (1955–58); associate justice

(1958–69) and presiding justice (1969–74, 1975–77), appellate division, New York Supreme Court, First Department; acting justice, New York State Court of Appeals (1974–75).

Stevens, Lawrence N. (1915–99), administrative analyst, U.S. Office of Indian Affairs. In 1946, Mitchell conferred with Stevens about the case of Toussaint L. Jones.

Stevenson, Adlai Ewing (1900–65) (D-Ill.), lawyer; special assistant to the secretary of the Navy (1941–44); special assistant to the secretary of state (1945); alternate U.S. delegate to the United Nations (1947–48); Illinois governor (1949-53); Democratic Party presidential nominee (1952, 1956); ambassador to the United Nations (1961–65). As governor he compiled a solid civil rights record, including a proposal for a state FEPC. When riots broke out in Cicero, he won praise by sending troops to protect black families in the area.

Stevenson, William Edwards (1900–85); lawyer, educator and athlete; won the gold medal in the 1924 Paris Olympics for the United States as the anchor man on the 1600 (4 x 400) meter relay; president, Oberlin College (1947–62); U.S. ambassador to the Philippines (1962–65). In 1948, he was named to serve on the President's Committee for Equality in Training and Opportunity in the Armed Forces (Fahy Committee); cousin of Adlai Stevenson.

Stewart, James Edward, Sr. (1912–97), businessman and civic leader; president, Oklahoma City branch, NAACP (1946–57); member, NAACP National Board of Directors (1957–?). He reported on discrimination by USES offices in Oklahoma.

Stickgold, Simon (1911–84), lawyer, of Chicago; trial attorney, legal division, FEPC (1945); author of *Memorandum #1: Specific Methods for Promoting Good Will among Racial Groups in Illinois,* published by the Illinois Interracial Commission (1945).

Stimson, Henry Lewis (1867–1950), lawyer; U.S. district attorney, Southern District of New York (1906–9); U.S. secretary of war (1911–13, 1940–45); diplomat; governor general of the Philippines (1928–29); U.S. secretary of state (1929–33). Perhaps best known for his recommendation to President Truman that the United States use the atomic bomb against Japan, he also supported federal legislation for protecting service members from violence.

Stone, Gertrude (1902–76), writer and social activist involved in the Washington D.C. chapter of the NAACP. In 1942, she turned down a position as clerk-stenographer in the new Washington bureau.

Stone, Kimbrough (1875–1958), lawyer; judge, Sixteenth Circuit Court of Missouri (1913–17); judge, U.S. Court of Appeals, Eighth Circuit (1917–47). In 1950, the NAACP opposed his appointment as chair of a commission investigating conditions of agricultural workers.

Straight, Michael Whitney (1916–2004), publisher. While at Cambridge University, he became a Communist and fell in with the infamous spy ring that included Kim Philby and Donald Maclean; in later years, he repudiated his involvement with the Communists and provided information that led to the discovery of Sir Anthony Blunt as a Russian spy. Speechwriter for FDR; U.S. Army Air Corps veteran of World War II; publisher of the magazine *New Republic* to 1953; national chair, American Veterans Committee (1948–50); served for a time on the NAACP Washington bureau advisory committee; was also a member of the NECRM delegation that met with President Truman in January 1950.

Strauss, Anna Lord (1899–1979), magazine editor and activist; great-granddaughter of nineteenth-century feminist and abolitionist Lucretia Mott. After serving as managing editor of *Century Magazine* (1923–29), she was the president of the New York chapter of the League of Women Voters (1937–43) and was subsequently elected the organization's national president (1944–50). In 1941, she was named as a participant in a proposed conference on civil rights.

Strauss, Lewis Lichtenstein (1896–1974), businessman and banker; member (1947–50) and chair (1953–58), AEC; U.S. secretary of commerce designate (1958–59, nomination rejected by the Senate). The NAACP contacted him regarding desegregation of schools run by the AEC.

Studebaker, John Ward (1887–1989), educator and administrator; superintendent of schools, Des Moines, Iowa (1920–34); U.S. Commissioner of Education (1934–48); vice president and chairman of editorial board, *Scholastic Magazine* (1948–68).

Styles, Paul Lafayette, Sr. (1907–), lawyer; member, NLRB (1950–53). With other members of the board, he upheld the decision confirming management's firing of the black truck drivers at Young's Motor Freight Company in Houston, Texas, all of whom were summarily dismissed because they were black.

Sugar, Maurice (1891–1974), lawyer, activist, and songwriter; longtime general counsel, UAW. As a member of the National Lawyers' Guild, he attended the Conference of Cooperating Organizations on July 4, 1942.

Suitt, Eversley Vincent, Sr. (1913–72), social worker and educator. He was involved with National Urban League affiliates in Newark, New Jersey, Kansas City, Missouri, and Atlanta, Georgia. While with the Kansas City Urban League, in 1944 he testified before the House Labor Committee in favor of S. 2048, a bill designed to strengthen the FEPC.

Summers, Clyde Wilson (1918–), lawyer, educator and activist; associate professor (1949–54) and professor (1954–56) of law, University of Buffalo; professor of law, Yale University (1957–75); Jefferson B. Fordham Professor of Law, University of Pennsylvania (1975–88, emeritus from 1988). One of his law review articles was utilized by Roy Wilkins in a discussion concerning the plight of the black worker and his or her inability to become a member of certain trade unions.

Swanson, Mabel, staffer in office of the Washington Bureau. In 1954, Mitchell commended Miss Swanson and Mrs. Mae Hendricks for their work in organizing and taking care of "many, many details" connected with the Freedom Fulfillment Conference, as well as providing temporary help for the Bureau office while the staff attended the Conference.

Sweatt, Heman Marion (1912–82), black postal worker who applied to the University of Texas School of Law in 1946 and was refused admittance solely on the basis of his race. Although the state of Texas, in an attempt to provide "substantially equal" segregated facilities opened a temporary law school in a basement in the capital city of Austin, in June 1950, the United States Supreme Court ruled in Sweatt's favor, stating that the equal protection clause of the Fourteenth Amendment to the Constitution was violated because Sweatt would not be able to get the same quality law school education at the temporary law school than he would at the law school of the University of Texas, and would have to be admitted there.

Sweetland, Monroe Mark (1910–2006), lawyer, Oregon state legislator, author and activist. A practicing Socialist, he also served as a member of the initial executive board of the NCPFEPC (1943).

Symington, William Stuart (1901–88) (D-Mo.), businessman; chair, SPB (1945–46); assistant secretary of war for air (1946–47); secretary of the air force (1947–50); chair, NSRB (1950–51); administrator, RFC (1951–52); U.S. senator (1953–76). As secretary of the air force, he participated in an investigation of violence against African Americans by military police. In 1951, Mitchell met with him as part of an effort to persuade President Truman to issue an FEPC executive order.

Tackman, Arthur Lester (1916–2004), official (1950–65) and personnel director (1959–65), AEC; personnel director, HUD (1965–70). In 1951, he met with an NAACP committee on efforts to ensure nonsegregation and nondiscrimination at the Savannah River Plant hydrogen bomb facility in Aiken, South Carolina.

Taft, Charles Phelps II (1897–1983) (R-Ohio), lawyer and diplomat; World War I veteran; younger brother of Robert A. Taft. He served as Hamilton County (Ohio) prosecutor (1927–28); councilman (1938–42, 1948–51, 1955–57) and mayor (1955–57) of Cincinnati. He was cofounder and first lay president of the Federal Council of Churches of Christ in America (1947–48) and actively encouraged the Republican party to end any appearance of racial discrimination.

Taft, Robert Alphonso (1889–1953) (R-Ohio), lawyer; Ohio state legislator (1921–26, 1931–32); U.S. senator (1939–53). Known best for his isolationist foreign policy views and his cosponsorship of the Taft-Hartley Act, he was inconsistent on civil rights legislation. He supported antilynching and anti–poll tax bills, yet he opposed a strong FEPC with enforcement powers. He also disagreed with the NAACP's view that the Taft-Hartley Act aided segregation in unions.

Taggart, Dr. Ernest William (1892–1968), dentist of Birmingham; also sometime president, Birmingham NAACP; in 1937 was one of the co-founders of the Birmingham Urban League; in 1965, he donated $50,000 to Miles College in Birmingham. In 1941, Dr. Taggart was asked by the NAACP to launch an independent investigation to determine the truth of the rumor that war training for African-Americans had been stopped in Alabama.

Talbott, Harold Elstner, Jr. (1888–1957), construction engineer and the owner of a construction company; U.S. Secretary of Air Force (1953–55). While secretary, he corresponded with Walter White and Roy Wilkins concerning the plight of service members traveling through the Jim Crow South.

Talmadge, Herman Eugene (1913–2002) (D-Ga.), lawyer; Georgia governor (1947, 1948–55); U.S. senator (1957–81). Son of Eugene Talmadge, a Georgia governor and white supremacist, he was a diehard segregationist. As governor, he oversaw the establishment of educational requirements for voting and tried (unsuccessfully) to revive the state poll tax, which had been repealed in 1945. During his 1950 gubernatorial reelection campaign, he said that the proposed FEPC posed a threat to white supremacy.

Tappis, Samuel (1917–92), member, AVC. In 1951, he attended a meeting of organizations interesting in changing the rules of procedure for the U.S. Senate.

Taylor, Abner Graham (1891–1967), funeral home director of Statesville, North Carolina. In 1943, he was riding on a train traveling through North Carolina and witnessed G. James Fleming's troubles with whites while he attempted to get a night's rest in a Pullman sleeping car.

Taylor, Howard (1916–90), railroad worker. In 1952, with two other plaintiffs, he filed suit against the Brotherhood of Railway and Steamship Clerks, Freight Handlers, Express and Station Employees and the Baltimore and Ohio Railroad in the U.S. district court in Washington, D.C., over a violation of the Railway Labor Act whereby the union forced its black members into segregated locals.

Taylor, Jack. African American railroad brakeman who, on September 7, 1931, in Durant, Mississippi, with Cleve Simms, was shot and wounded from ambush by whites who coveted their jobs.

Taylor, James P. (1919–96), railroad worker. In 1952, with two other plaintiffs, he filed suit against the Brotherhood of Railway and Steamship Clerks, Freight Handlers, Express and Station Employees and the Baltimore and Ohio Railroad in the U.S. district court in Washington, D.C., over a violation of the Railway Labor Act whereby the union forced its black members into segregated locals.

Taylor, Maj. Gen. Maxwell Davenport (1901–87), U.S. Army; superintendent, U.S. Military Academy (1945–49); commander, Allied troops in occupied Germany (1949–51); U.S. Army chief of staff (1955–59); military assistant to President John F. Kennedy (1961–62); chairman,

Joint Chiefs of Staff (1962–64); U.S. ambassador to South Vietnam (1964–65). In 1951, he attended a meeting with Mitchell in the office of Senator Herbert Lehman (D-N.Y.) where Lehman and nine other senators introduced an amendment calling for the protection of black servicemen from the brutality inflicted on them by peace officers and civilians.

Tehan, Robert Emmet (1905–75) (D-Wis.), lawyer and jurist; Wisconsin state legislator (1936–49), chairman, state Democratic committee (1944–49); judge, U.S. District Court (E.D.-Wis.) (1949–75). In 1945, as a state senator, he joined with assemblyman Le Roy J. Simmons of Milwaukee to sponsor a bill forbidding discriminatory employment practices by private employers or trade unions and establishing an FEPC having enforcement powers; although supported by labor, religious groups, blacks and Jews, the legislation was opposed by state and local Chambers of Commerce. A compromise bill, calling for an FEPC without enforcement powers, was subsequently signed into law.

Teller, Emil Albert, member, NAAWP. He participated in picketing at Gwynn's Falls Junior High School in Baltimore to protest the implementation of the Supreme Court's *Brown* decision. Probably the same person as Emil Albert Cella (1903–68), the owner of a "sea food" house in Baltimore's Third Ward in 1930 and subsequently a tavern (and other businesses) in South Baltimore from approximately 1935 to 1965.

Terry, Evelyn (1902–86), secretary; was active in the Philadelphia branch of the NAACP. In 1942, she was offered a position as staffer of the new NAACP Washington bureau.

Teverbaugh, Sgt. Jesse (1904–66), U.S. Marine Corps. In 1952, he was blocked from a segregated movie theater showing a film about his unit.

Thomas, Charles Sparks (1897–1983), businessman; undersecretary of the navy (1953); assistant secretary of defense (1953–54); secretary of the navy (1954–57); president, Trans World Airlines (1958–60). It was during his tenure as secretary of the navy that naval shore installations in the South were desegregated.

Thomas, Everett C. (1916–93), resident of New York City, but a native of Charlotte, North Carolina, who was riding in a Jim Crow train between Atlanta and New York City in 1943 when he was a witness to the tribulations G. James Fleming encountered while attempting to sleep in a Pullman car.

Thomas, Julius Albert (1896–1973), director, Department of Industrial Relations, National Urban League (1943–61); industrial relations consultant (1961–73). During his tenure with the Urban League, he focused on obtaining postwar employment for African Americans. His 1946 report, "Study of Negro Job Performances in 300 War Plants," played a major role in securing job gains for blacks in the industrial field. In 1949, he arranged for General Electric and General Cable Corporation executives to recruit at the Howard University School of Engineering, the first time in American history that white recruiters visited a black college.

Thomas, Norman T. (1928–99), TVA employee. In 1951, he was dismissed from his TVA position because of his NAACP activity.

Thomas, P., of the NAACP LDEF, who, in 1947, was considered as a possible candidate for the post of NAACP labor secretary.

Thomas, Rolland Jay "R.J." (1900–67), Detroit union leader; president of UAW (1939–46), serving at the same time as a CIO vice-president. He was a member of various wartime boards, including the WLB and was involved with NAACP efforts to better organize its branches and chapters.

Thompson, Dr. Charles Henry (1896–1980), professor; member, NAACP National Board of Directors; dean of the College of Arts and Sciences (1938–43) and dean of the Graduate School (1944–64), Howard University. He attended an important meeting of NAACP officials with U.S. commissioner of education Samuel Brownell on the *Brown v. Board of Education* case.

Thompson, Eugene Charlesworth (1893–1955), executive secretary and chief mediator, National Mediation Board. In 1952, he reported to Mitchell that the board had no jurisdiction to oversee or control the operation of collective-bargaining agreements under the National Railway Act.

Thompson, William (1892–1977), longshoreman of Houston, Texas. In 1948, he met with Mitchell and O. T. Pettis regarding employment discrimination against blacks in the port of Brownsville, Texas.

Thornton, Mary H. (1903–78), executive secretary, Bridgeport, Connecticut, branch, NAACP. In 1946, she reported that the branch's labor director had received the *NAACP Labor Manual* and had reported favorably on it.

Thurmond, James Strom (1902–2003) (D, R-S.C.), teacher and lawyer; South Carolina state legislator (1933–38); governor (1947–51); States' Rights Party (Dixiecrat) presidential nominee (1948); U.S. senator (1954–56, 1956–2003). As governor, he compiled a moderate civil rights record by leading a repeal of the poll tax, appointing a respected lawyer to prosecute a lynch mob, and naming the first African American to the state's board of medical examiners. Still, he was a segregationist and states' rights advocate who opposed federal antilynching legislation and often linked integration with communism. Running for president under the Dixiecrat banner in 1948, he declared that "on the question of social intermingling of the races, our people draw the line." He was also one of the initiators of the anti-*Brown* "Southern Manifesto."

Thye, Edward John (1896–1969) (R-Minn.), farmer; Minnesota deputy commissioner of agriculture (1939–42); lieutenant governor (1943–44); governor (1944–47); U.S. senator (1947–59). A liberal Republican, he supported civil rights legislation, including antisegregation bills. Mitchell did criticize him, however, for a 1949 vote against a cloture ruling. In 1950, he was one of the seven cosigners of the "Declaration of Conscience" against Joseph McCarthy.

Tobey, Charles William (1880–1953) (R-N.H.), businessman; New Hampshire state legislator (1915–16, 1919–20, 1923–24, 1925–26); governor (1929–30); U.S. representative (1933–39); U.S. senator (1939–53). During his brief tenure as chair of the Senate Committee on Interstate and Foreign Commerce (1953), he was contacted several times by the NAACP concerning anti–Jim Crow travel legislation. He also favored a change in the filibuster rule.

Tobias, Channing Heggie (1882–1961), student secretary, International Committee of the YMCA (1911–23); senior secretary, Colored Work Department, YMCA (1923–46); director, Phelps-Stokes Fund (1946–53); member, PCCR (1946–47); member (1943–53) and chair (1953–59), NAACP National Board of Directors. He attended a 1948 meeting as part of the NAACP's fight against federal employment discrimination. At the 1953 NAACP Annual Convention, he called for an end to discrimination by January 1, 1863, the centennial of the final Emancipation Proclamation.

Tobin, Maurice Joseph (1901–53) (D-Mass.), Boston mayor (1938–44); Massachusetts governor (1945–47); U.S. secretary of labor (1948–53). As secretary of labor, he met with the NAACP to discuss job discrimination, importation of foreign agricultural workers, and the forcing of workers to join segregated unions. Massachusetts enacted a fair employment practice law during his tenure as governor.

Toner, Fr. Jerome Leo, O.S.B. (1899–1974), Roman Catholic priest, member of the Oblates of Saint Benedict, labor organizer, and college professor. A labor organizer in Brooklyn, he was selected by President Truman as a delegate to the International Labor Organization.

He also authored a number of writings on the labor movement, most notably *The Closed Shop in the American Labor Movement* (1942). He was president of St. Martin's College (now University) in Lacey, Washington from 1959 to 1965.-

Totten, Ashley Leopold (1884–1963), a native of St. Croix, (Danish) Virgin Islands, who worked with A. Philip Randolph and others to organize the BSCP, and would serve as its international secretary-treasurer (1932–63). In 1952, Mitchell commented that, if the McCarran-Walter Act, with its severe restriction on immigration from the Caribbean and South America, had been in force when immigrants like Totten entered the United States, they would not have been able to make "notable contributions to the building of our nation."

Towers, William Henry (1895–1959), lawyer of Kansas City, Kansas, and Kansas state legislator (1937–39, 1941–47). One of the first African-American lawyers in Kansas City, he was active in both the local NAACP and the Kansas City Urban League. In 1945, legislation he sponsored calling for the establishment of a state FEPC was killed by the Kansas State House Judiciary Committee.

Townsend, Willard Saxby, Jr. (1895–1957), president, IBRC (1937–40); international president, UTSEA (1940–57). He was a board member of the NCPFEPC, secretary for the National CIO Committee to Abolish Racial Discrimination, and a member of the NAACP National Labor Committee.

Tracy, Estelle R. (1917–), claims examiner, board of appeals of the U.S. Civil Service Commission. In May 1947, Mitchell met with her regarding the complaints of veterans and others against the New Orleans Post Office Department, requesting that an informal meeting be scheduled in an attempt to resolve the situation without a formal hearing.

Trager, Bernard Harold (1906–92), lawyer and activist; longtime chairman, NCRAC. Although Roy Wilkins has commonly been listed as the founder of the LCCR, Trager's statement on the matter gives the credit to Walter White.

Trager, Frank Newton (1905–84), educator and activist; national labor secretary, Socialist party of the U.S. (1936–37); program director, AJComm (1938–43); assistant to president, NCCJ (1945–46); program director, Anti-Defamation League (1946–51); director, AID mission to Rangoon, Burma (1951–53); research professor (1953–58) and professor, international affairs (1958–81), New York University; named to executive board of the NCPFEPC, 1944.

Trent, William Johnson, Jr. (1910–93), educator and economist; advisor on Negro Affairs to Harold L. Ickes, U.S. Secretary of the Interior (1938–42); race relations officer, Federal Works Agency (1942–44); executive director, United Negro College Fund (1944–64); assistant personnel director, Time, Inc. (1964–75). Trent's government positions were amongst those cited by Walter White as the modest gains made by blacks in government service that could be wiped out if the "Southern bloc" in Congress implemented budget cuts to eliminate these gains.

Truitt, Willie James (1897–1968), Pullman porter. In 1943, he assured G. James Fleming that he would not be removed from his berth in a Pullman sleeping car by whites who were upset that Fleming, a black, would be sleeping in the same car as they.

Truman, Harry S. (1884–1972) (D-Mo.), businessman and judge; U.S. senator (1935–45); vice president of the United States (1945); president of the United States (1945–53). During his presidency, he issued Executive Order 9980, which established the FEB, and Executive Order 9981, which desegregated the armed forces. He also appointed the PCCR and supported antilynching, anti–poll tax, and permanent FEPC legislation. Following his election in 1948, he strengthened the Department of Justice's Civil Rights Division, leading to an increase in the filing of briefs against restrictive covenants and segregation in public schools. His loyalty program, however, drew criticism from civil libertarians.

Turnbull, Alexander Alan, Jr. (1908-2000), statistician; he was serving as the head of the Accident Analysis and Injury Compensation Section, Office of Industrial Relations, U.S. Department of the Navy in 1947, when he responded to Mitchell's query as to why the U. S. Navy continued to designate race on forms for reporting injuries or occupational diseases. A native of Scotland, he served in the U.S. Navy during World War II and is buried in Arlington National Cemetery.

Turner, Edward M. (1907–64), lawyer; president, Detroit branch, NAACP (1949–57); president, Michigan State Conference of NAACP Branches (1952–64); member, NAACP National Board of Directors. He was a prominent advocate of state FEPC legislation in Michigan.

Tyson, William Sherrod (1903–78), lawyer; assistant solicitor (1943–45) and solicitor (1945–53), Department of Labor. He attended a 1950 meeting concerning arrests of unemployed black job seekers near USES offices in Washington, D.C.

Tyus, Randall Lee (1903–73), teacher; secretary, Washington branch, NAACP. In 1943, Walter White contacted him and nine other branch secretaries representing the most effective branches to start protesting War Manpower Commissioner Paul V. McNutt's decision to cancel the FEPC hearings on racial discrimination in the railroad industry.

Valentine, Wellington C. (1926–51), U.S. Army corporal. He was arrested and assaulted by civilian and military police in Fort Worth, Texas, in November 1949. His case was taken up by the NAACP and cited as an example of the need to protect black service members from violence. A native of Pennsylvania, he died in Korea in 1951 of "other causes."

Van Arkel, Gerhard Peter (1907–84), lawyer; general counsel, NLRB (1946–47); counsel for Senate Committee on the District of Columbia (1950). He arranged a meeting regarding the arrests of unemployed blacks who had gathered near the Washington, D.C., USES office.

Van Devander, Charles (1902–86), newspaperman; chief, Washington bureau of the *New York Post* (1941–50); public relations director, DNC (1950–53). In 1946, Mitchell sent him a copy of a report outlining instances of widespread racial discrimination throughout the federal government.

Vann, Jessie Matthews (1885–1967), widow of *Pittsburgh Courier* publisher Robert L. Vann. She took over the *Courier* upon her husband's death in 1940. In 1951, Walter White recommended her as a person to contact for the purpose of exerting press influence on Republican members of Congress.

Vardaman, James Kimble (1861–1930) (D-Miss.), lawyer; member, Mississippi House of Representatives (1890–96); major, U.S. Volunteers, Spanish-American War; governor of Mississippi (1904–08); U.S. senator (1913–19). A virulent racist, Vardaman fought the passage of legislation designed to help African Americans.

Vessels, Alma Elizabeth [married name John] (1906–86), nurse practitioner and educator. A native of Philadelphia, and a graduate of New York University and Harlem Hospital's school of nursing, she was later fired from Harlem Hospital after attempting to organize the nurses in a union. Subsequently, executive director, National Association of Colored Graduate Nurses; in that capacity, she was a member of a delegation from the NECRM who met with President Truman in January 1950. In her later years she hosted radio programs discussing current events and ways to improve the health of African Americans.

Vivian, John Charles (1887–1964) (R-Colo.), journalist and poet; Colorado lieutenant governor (1939–43); governor (1943–47). Responding to an NAACP letter to governors regarding discrimination by USES offices placed under state control, he opposed a request to have his state's USES refuse to accept discriminatory work orders. He further asserted that having the USES actively promote the full utilization of minority groups would itself be discriminatory.

Vorys, John Martin (1896–1968) (R-Ohio), lawyer; Ohio state legislator (1923–26); U.S. representative (1939–59); regent, Smithsonian Institution (1949–59). A staunch anticommunist—in 1951, he called the Soviet foreign minister a "skunk"—he focused on foreign affairs while serving in Congress. In 1952, he discussed with Walter White and Mitchell the inclusion of language they sought in the mutual security bill that would assure Dependent Overseas Territories of Point IV assistance in public health, industrial production, economic development, and agriculture.

Waddy, Joseph Cornelius (1911–78), lawyer; associate judge, Domestic Relations Bar, Municipal Court of the District of Columbia (1962–67); adjunct professor, Howard University School of Law (1966–67); judge, U.S. district court for the District of Columbia (1967–78). As counsel for black railroad unions, he argued the *Steele* and *Tunstall* cases before the U.S. Supreme Court. In 1950, he testified with Mitchell against an amendment to the Railway Labor Act that would permit union shop and dues checkoffs without first ensuring nondiscrimination. Three years later, he assisted the NAACP in a hearing on regulations requiring black workers to join segregated unions.

Wade, James Edward (1932–69), U.S. Army private. In 1953, he was beaten by police in Leesville, Louisiana.

Wailes, Edward Thompson (1903–69), assistant secretary of administration, State Department (1953–54); ambassador to South Africa (1954–56), Iran (1958–61), and Czechoslovakia (1961–62). He conferred with the NAACP on improving State Department employment practices.

Waites, Royce G. (1919–2002), building contractor and business owner; secretary, Columbia (South Carolina) Building and Trades Council. In 1951, Waites proposed that the South Carolina Federation of Labor charter the Columbia Building and Trades Council to represent individuals (black and white) who would be working on the Savannah River Plant hydrogen bomb facility in Aiken, South Carolina.

Walcott, "Jersey Joe" (1914–94), boxer (heavyweight champion of the world, 1951–52); referee; sheriff, Camden County, New Jersey (1972–75); chair, New Jersey State Athletic Commission (1975–84). Born Arnold Raymond Cream in Camden, New Jersey, the son of a Barbadian immigrant, he turned to boxing after his father's death. In 1952, Mitchell commented that, if the McCarran-Walter Act, with its severe restriction on immigration from the Caribbean and South America, had been in force when immigrants such as Walcott's father entered the United States, they would not have been able to make "notable contributions to the building of our nation."

Walker, Cora Thomasina (1922–2006), pioneer black female attorney in Harlem, where she practiced for over fifty years; partner in firm Walker & Bailey (1976–99), the junior partner being her eldest son, Lawrence Bailey, Jr. She also served as a New York state Republican committeewoman and was an unsuccessful candidate for public office. Active in the NBA, she established its Corporate Section, and it was as a representative of the NBA that, in 1951, she participated in the formation of the LCCR.

Walker, Frank Comerford (1886–1959), lawyer and businessman; director, NEC (1933–34); U.S. postmaster general (1940–45); chair, DNC (1943–44). Mitchell met with him to discuss employment discrimination in the postal service.

Walker, William Otis (1896–1981), journalist and editor; publisher, *Cleveland Call and Post* (1932–81); Cleveland city councilman (1940–45); Ohio director of industrial relations (1963–71). Mitchell believed that he might be useful in pressuring Republican members of Congress to vote for legislation to protect service members from violence.

Wallace, Henry Agard (1888–1965) (D, P-Iowa), agronomist; U.S. secretary of agriculture (1933–40); vice president of the United States (1941–45); U.S. secretary of commerce

(1945–46); editor, *New Republic* (1946–48); Progressive Party presidential nominee (1948). A proponent of engagement with the Soviet Union, he was removed as secretary of commerce following a speech in which he criticized the Truman administration's foreign policy. A strong civil rights advocate, he supported an end to discrimination and segregation in USES offices. He also issued calls for racial equality while touring the South for his 1948 presidential campaign.

Waller, Odell (1917–42), sharecropper of Pittsylvania County, Virginia, who shot and fatally wounded his white landlord, Oscar Davis, over a dispute concerning payment for work performed by Waller's wife and his mother. Waller escaped to Ohio, was captured and brought to trial in Virginia, where a jury, composed of those whites who had paid their poll taxes, took twenty minutes to convict him of first-degree murder. Waller claimed self-defense, saying he shot Davis when the latter reached into his pocket where he was known to carry a firearm. Despite pleas for clemency from President Roosevelt on down, Waller was executed.

Walter, Noah Charles Archibald, Jr. (1905–84), labor activist; ran for a seat in the New York State Assembly from the Twenty-first District (New York County) 1934 and 1938 on the Socialist Party ticket; member executive board, American Labor Party; president of Laundry Workers Union, CIO. Active in MOWM as well as the NCPFEPC, he received an appointment as deputy commissioner, U.S. Department of Labor, in 1964.

Wanger [Feuchtwanger], Walter (1894–1968), motion picture producer; known as a socially conscious movie executive and a friend of Walter White. In 1942 Wanger received notice of the opening of the NAACP's Washington Bureau.

Ware, James Lowell (1912–92), Baptist minister; pastor, Trinity Baptist Church, Birmingham, Alabama (1941–72). He was one of a group of Alabama civic and religious leaders who traveled to Washington in 1953 to express their disapproval of the use of federal funds for a segregated health center.

Waring, Julius Waties (1880–1968), lawyer; judge of the U.S. district court for South Carolina (1942–52). Judge Waring heard a number of landmark cases in his courtroom that struck down various laws upholding segregation and other discriminatory acts; such cases would be used as precedent in subsequent civil rights litigation. For his efforts, his home in Charleston, South Carolina, was firebombed.

Warren, Earl (1891–1974) (R-Cal.), lawyer and jurist; California state attorney general (1939–43); governor of California (1943–53); chief justice, U.S. Supreme Court (1953–69); unsuccessful candidate for Vice President on the Republican ticket 1948. As governor of California, in his 1945 annual message to the legislature, he urged establishing a "Commission on Political and Economic Equality" to, as Will Maslow stated, "report on the necessity of new laws against discrimination."

Washington, Booker Taliaferro (1856–1915), educator, author, and race leader; president, Tuskegee Institute (1881–1915). At one time, he was the most influential African American in the United States. In 1948, the U. S. Postal Service opened a post office at his birthplace in Franklin County, Virginia.

Washington, George (1732–99) (Federalist-Va.), soldier and statesman; commander in chief, Continental Army (1775–83); U.S. President (1789–97). At the beginning of the American Revolution, General Washington barred blacks from serving in the Continental Army, but was forced to modify his stand once the Royal Governor of Virginia, Lord Dunmore, promised all blacks who deserted their masters to fight for the British would be freed. Washington allowed free blacks to sign up, although a significant number of the 5,000 blacks who did serve were themselves slaves who were allowed in by recruiters seeking to meet their monthly quotas.

Washington, George Willie (1890–1978), pawnbroker; vice chair, Labor Relations Committee, Dallas, Texas, NAACP branch. In 1947, he reported to Mitchell that his group was undertaking an employment survey of the black community in order to determine the number of blacks who had marketable skills or were otherwise employable.

Watkins, Maude S. (1913–75), librarian employed in the New York Public Library system. A member of Delta Sigma Theta sorority, it was as its representative that she was present at the formation of the LCCR, 1951.

Watson, Brig. Gen. Edwin Martin (1883–1945), U.S. Army; secretary and military attaché to President Roosevelt. He met with Walter White concerning the introduction of blacks into the military.

Watson, James Samuel (1882–1952), lawyer and jurist; with Charles E. Toney was the first black elected to a judicial post in New York City; judge, New York City Municipal Court (1930–50); president, New York City Municipal Civil Service Commission (1950–52); born Spanish Town, Jamaica. In 1952, Mitchell commented that, if the McCarran-Walter Act, with its severe restriction on immigration from the Caribbean and South America, had been in force when immigrants like Watson entered the United States, they would not have been able to make "notable contributions to the building of our nation."

Watts, Lyle Ford (1890–1962), chief, U.S. Forest Service (1943–52). In 1951, he asserted that segregation regulations for the Pisgah National Forest in North Carolina were established upon requests from African Americans.

Weaver, George Leon Paul (1912–95), union leader; member, UTSEA; national director, Committee to Abolish Discrimination (later the Civil Rights Committee), CIO (1942–55); assistant to secretary-treasurer, CIO (1942–55); executive secretary, Civil Rights Committee, AFL-CIO (1955–58); assistant to the director and director, political education program, IUERMW (1958–61); assistant secretary of labor for international affairs (1961–69). A member of the NAACP National Labor Committee, he supported antidiscrimination amendments to the Taft-Hartley Act and conferred with the FEB.

Weaver, Dr. Robert Clifton (1907–97), author, economist, and professor; administrator and minority affairs adviser in various New Deal agencies (1933–40); chief, Negro Training and Employment Branch, Labor Division, OPDM and WPB (1942–43); chief, Negro Manpower Service, WMC (1943–44); director of community services, ACRR (1945–48); director, Opportunity Fellowships program, John Hay Whitney Foundation (1949–55); New York State rent commissioner (1955–59); chair, NAACP National Board of Directors (1960–61); administrator, HHFA (1961–66); secretary, HUD (1966–68). He assisted the NAACP in its push against segregated housing. In 1966, he became the first African American to hold a cabinet post.

Weber, Frederick Palmer (1914–86), financial adviser and investment banker; research director, Political Action Committee, CIO (1944–47); member, NAACP National Board of Directors (1946–51); southern regional director, Progressive Party (1948); member, Advisory Committee, ACLU. While a student at the University of Virginia in the 1930s, Weber petitioned the state legislature to end segregation at the school. He later became the first southern white member of the NAACP National Board of Directors. Still later, he was instrumental in opening the doors of Wall Street and business concerns to the NAACP and its fund-raising efforts.

Webster, Milton Price (1887–1965), of Chicago, Illinois; dining car waiter on railroads and union officer. While first international vice president, BSCP, in 1943, he was appointed as a member of FEPC. He was also known as an outspoken critic of the NAACP.

Weightman, Philip Mitchell, Jr. (1902–91), union leader; vice president, PHWU, Chicago (1943–48); member, Board of Directors, NCPFEPC (1943–45); vice president, Chicago branch, NAACP (elected in 1948); field director, Political Action Committee, CIO

(1948–55); field director, then assistant national director, Committee on Political Education, AFL-CIO (1955–67); labor-management relations specialist, OEO (1967–80). During a 1946 CIO convention, he discussed with Mitchell cooperation between the PHWU and the Chicago branch of the NAACP.

Welsh, William Brownlee (1924–), government official; president, National Student Association (1946–49); chief researcher for Sen. Herbert H. Lehman (D-N.Y.) (1949–57); research director, DNC (1957–58); administrative assistant to Sen. Philip A. Hart (D-Mich.) (1959–66); administrative assistant to Sen. Hubert H. Humphrey (D-Minn.) (1966–69); executive director, DNC (1969–71); director for government affairs, AFSCME (1972–79); assistant secretary for legislation and intergovernmental affairs, HUD (1979–80); assistant secretary for legislation and intergovernmental affairs, HHS (1980–83); staff director, Post Office and Civil Service Committee (1983–85); legislative director, AFSCME (1985–88). In 1952, Welch informed Mitchell that Senator Lehman had decided to make a motion to change the rules that the Senate worked under on the first day of the new legislative session.

Werner, Ludlow Weymouth, Sr. (1907–67), newspaper editor and public relations executive; editor and publisher of the *New York Age* (1943–48), succeeding his maternal grandfather and longtime publisher of the paper, Fred R. Moore. Werner was also active in local politics, having, in 1938, managed Thomas E. Dewey's bid for New York District Attorney in Harlem, and four years later unsuccessfully running for state senator on the Republican ticket. In 1943, he was one of sixteen representatives of the black press who signed a telegram protesting the FEPC cancellation of hearings designed to review racial discrimination in the railroad industry.

Wesley, Carter Walker (1892–1969), lawyer; owner, publisher and sometime editor, *Houston* (Tex.) *Informer* (1927–67). An overseas veteran of World War I, Wesley was a graduate of Fisk University and the law school of Northwestern University. Returning to his hometown of Houston, Wesley was active in civil rights activity, both as an advocate (he was directly involved in pleading the cases of *Grovey v. Townsend* and *Smith v. Allwright* before the U.S. Supreme Court, as well as providing advice and monetary support to Heman M. Sweatt in his attempt to enroll at the University of Texas) and as a newspaper editor. In 1942, he was invited by the NAACP to participate in a Conference of Negro Newspaper Editors concerning the opening of the Washington bureau.

Wheeler, Margaret, member, NAAWP. She participated in picketing at Gwynn's Falls Junior High School in Baltimore to protest the implementation of the Supreme Court's *Brown* decision.

Wherry, Kenneth Spicer (1892–1951) (R-Neb.), businessman and lawyer; Nebraska state legislator (1929–32); U.S. senator (1943–51); Senate minority leader (1949–51). Perhaps best known for his malapropisms—he once referred to Indochina as "Indigo China"—he was a conservative Republican who opposed most Fair Deal legislation. In 1946, he introduced a bill for an anti–poll tax constitutional amendment. Three years later, he brokered a deal on the Senate cloture rule that helped preserve filibusters against civil rights bills.

Whitby, Beulah Tyrrell (1897–1990), social worker, educator and activist; staff member, YWCA, Detroit (1922–27); social worker, women's division, Detroit Police Department (1927–31); social worker (1931–41) and chief (1941–43), Alfred District of Wayne County Department of Public Welfare; assistant director, Detroit Commission on Community Relations (1943–62); chairman, Department of Sociology, Mercy College (1962–68). As national president of the Alpha Kappa Alpha sorority (1941–46), in 1943 she testified before the House Labor Committee in favor of S. 2048, a bill designed to strengthen the FEPC.

White, Rev. E. W., of Baltimore. In 1943, he was the president of the Citizens' Committee for Justice that protested the cancellation of FEPC hearings designed to discuss racial discrimination in the railroad industry.

White, Harris Lee (1912–69), lawyer, businessman, and U.S. Navy commander; assistant secretary, U.S. Air Force (1953–54). As assistant secretary, he worked on the case of Thomas E. Williams, an African American lieutenant in the U.S. Air Force who was dismissed from service for violating segregation rules in interstate travel.

White, Leah Gladys Powell (1894–1975), first wife of Walter White and mother of his two children; their 1949 divorce, and his subsequent marriage to journalist Poppy Cannon produced a scandal in the black community.

White, Brig. Gen. Miller Grieve (1895–1987), U.S. Army. A native of Macon, Georgia, he fought in World War I as a member of a National Guard unit and after his return, he remained in the National Guard while working as a Macon policeman and as the manager of a dairy until the outbreak of World War II. He served as assistant chief of staff, personnel division, U.S. Army (1942–44); assistant chief of staff for personnel matters, U.S. Army North African Theater of Operations (1944–45); deputy chief of staff, personnel division, U.S. Army European Theater (1945–48).

White, Walter Francis (1893–1955), author and columnist; secretary, Atlanta branch, NAACP (1916–18); assistant secretary, NAACP (1918–31); acting secretary, NAACP (1929–31); executive secretary, NAACP (1931–55); director, NAACP Washington bureau (1942–50). He was the nation's most prominent civil rights leader during the postwar years. Among other activities, he pushed for desegregation of the armed forces, military installations, and federal housing; the protection of service members from violence; and Senate rules changes. He was best known for his crusade against lynching. In 1952, he founded the LCCR, which absorbed the NECRM and the NCPFEPC. He was chair of the LCCR from 1952 to 1955.

Whitehair, Francis Preston (1900–77), lawyer, citrus grower, and World War I and World War II veteran; undersecretary of the navy (1951–52); acting secretary of the navy (1952–53). He opposed ending segregation of schools on military posts. In 1953, he issued a written order affirming the policy of segregation in naval facilities.

Whiteman, Marjorie Millace (1898–1986), lawyer and international law expert; research associate, Columbia University Research Committee on Latin America (1927–28); special assistant to legal adviser, U.S. Department of State (1928–46); legal counsel to Eleanor Roosevelt as U.S. representative to the UN Commission on Human Rights (1948); legal assistant adviser for American Republic affairs, U.S. Department of State (1949–65); counselor, international law, Office of Legal Adviser, American Republic affairs (1965–70); honorary vice president, American Society of International Law (1985–86). In 1950, she conferred with Mitchell and others regarding the wording of the civil rights provision of the Bogota Treaty with Latin America.

Whitney, Alexander Fell (1873–1949), author; president, BRT (1928–49). The NAACP contacted Whitney on the admission of black stewards to the BRT.

Whitney, Samuel G. (1905–83), complainant. In 1947, he was fired from a custodial position at the AEC in Richland, Washington, because he was unjustly accused of being a communist.

Wilborn [Willburn], William Henry (1888-1966), retired U.S. Postal Service employee; official, Augusta, Georgia, branch, NAACP. He participated in NAACP efforts to ensure nonsegregation and nondiscrimination at the Savannah River Plant hydrogen bomb facility in Aiken, South Carolina.

Wilkes, William Reid, Sr. (1902–76), minister, AMEC; elected bishop (1948) and served the Sixth Episcopal District (1948–52), Twelfth Episcopal District (1952–60), Sixteenth Episcopal District (1960–64), Third Episcopal District (1964–72), and Thirteenth Episcopal District (1972–76). As a member of the board of trustees of his alma mater, Morris Brown College in Atlanta, he facilitated the transfer of the Turner Theological Seminary to the

Interdenominational Theological Seminary system of Atlanta University. He was also, at one time, secretary of the NAACP branch in Atlanta, and in 1943, Walter White contacted him and nine other branch secretaries representing the most effective branches to start protesting War Manpower Commissioner Paul V. McNutt's decision to cancel the FEPC hearings on racial discrimination in the railroad industry.

Wilkins, Jesse Ernest (1894–1959), lawyer; vice chair, CGC (1953); assistant secretary of labor (1954–58); member, USCRC (1958–59). In 1953, he attended a meeting between a CGC subcommittee and various interest groups. The following year, he became the first African American to serve as assistant secretary of labor.

Wilkins, Roy Ottoway (1901–81), managing editor, *Kansas City Call* (1923–31); assistant national secretary, NAACP (1931–49); editor, *Crisis* (1934–49); acting national secretary, NAACP (1949–50); administrator for internal affairs, NAACP (1950–55); national secretary and executive director, NAACP (1955–77); chair, LCCR (1955–77). He led the organization of the NECRM of 1950 in Washington, D.C., a coalition that became the fulcrum of the NAACP's lobbying arm for civil rights laws. In 1952, NECRM and the NCPFEPC were merged with the LCCR.

Wilkinson, Kenneth Lawrence (1890–1976), assistant vice president, Personnel Relations Department, AT&T (1937–50). In 1948, he negotiated with the NAACP on the employment of blacks at telephone companies. Mitchell described the negotiations as not very encouraging.

Will, Herman, Jr. (1915–2003), lawyer, social worker, and peace activist; staff executive, United Methodist Church Board of Church and Society. He was instrumental in the organization of CORE in 1942 and later served as administrative secretary for the Board of World Peace. In 1949, he reported to Mitchell about the discriminatory tactics employed by the FHA in Chicago.

Willburn [more correctly Wilborn], William Henry (1888–1966), retired U.S. Postal Service employee; official, Augusta, Georgia, branch, NAACP. He participated in NAACP efforts to ensure nonsegregation and nondiscrimination at the Savannah River Plant hydrogen bomb facility in Aiken, South Carolina.

Williams, Aaron (1877–1932), locomotive fireman shot dead in Vicksburg, Mississippi, in March of 1932, along with fellow fireman Wilbert "Will" Anderson, probably by whites who coveted their jobs during the days of the Great Depression.

Williams, Aubrey Willis, Sr. (1890–1965), educator and administrator; director, NYA. In June 1941, he participated in a meeting with President Roosevelt, Walter White of the NAACP, A. Philip Randolph of the BSCP. and others concerning attempts to desegregate the armed forces. He also attempted to convince Randolph to call off the proposed March on Washington later that year.

Williams, E. E., union officer; president of Local 29, Blasters and Drillers Union in New York City, when in 1941, he was named to the sponsoring committee of the MOWC.

Williams, Egbert Austin "Bert" (1873–1922), entertainer, actor, comedian, and author; born Nassau. A fixture in vaudeville and on Broadway, starting in 1910, he was a featured headliner in various editions of the Ziegfeld Follies. In 1952, Mitchell commented that, if the McCarran-Walter Act, with its severe restriction on immigration from the Caribbean and South America, had been in force when immigrants like Williams entered the United States, they would not have been able to make "notable contributions to the building of our nation."

Williams, Eugenia N. (1925–2003), official, El Paso, Texas, branch, NAACP. She was active in the desegregation of schools designed for the education of military dependents at Fort Hood in 1954.

Williams, Franklin Hall (1917–90), special counsel, NAACP legal department (1945–50); regional director, NAACP West Coast (1951–56); California assistant attorney general (1959–61); assistant to the director, Peace Corps (1961–63); regional director for Africa, Peace Corps (1963); U.S. representative to UNESCO (1963–64) and UNESC (1964–65); ambassador to Ghana (1965–68); director, Columbia University Urban Affairs Center (1968–70); president, Phelps-Stokes Fund (1970–90). In 1953, he implemented the NAACP's housing programs in San Francisco.

Williams, Gerhard Mennen (1911–88) (D-Mich.), Michigan governor (1949–61); ambassador to the Philippines (1968–69); justice (1971–83) and chief justice (1983–86), Michigan Supreme Court. He was a strong supporter of state FEPC legislation.

Williams, Cdr. Raleigh Corwin (1886–1972), U.S. Navy officer. In 1947, he conferred with Mitchell regarding the navy's policy of designating race on occupational injury forms.

Williams, Roberta J., assistant office manager (1943–67) and office manager (1967–83) of NAACP's national office in New York City. In July of 1948, David K. Niles, senior White House advisor on minority affairs, dictated to Williams the near-final draft of President Truman's Executive Order 9981 which abolished segregation in the U.S. Armed Forces.

Williams, Lt. Thomas Eldridge (1925–55), air force pilot. He was dismissed from service in 1953, allegedly for violating segregation rules in interstate travel. Following his dismissal, he testified before the House Interstate and Foreign Commerce Committee on legislation to end segregation. In 1955, he died in a jet crash while serving in the New Jersey National Guard.

Willis, Ivan L. (1897–1974), business executive and industrial relations expert. He worked for the Mayo Clinic, Standard Oil of New Jersey, and Curtiss-Wright/Wright Aeronautical in the field of industrial relations; after 1946, he was vice president for industrial relations at International Harvester. Willis worked closely with Mitchell in developing procedures to recruit and retain qualified black workers; he was also instrumental in working with management and the unions to ensure that black workers were welcomed and accepted as equals.

Willkie, Phillip Herman (1919–74), banker, businessman, stockman, and politician. The son of Wendell Willkie, Phillip Willkie, then serving the first of his three terms in the Indiana House of Representatives, in 1951 testified before the Senate Committee on Rules and Administration concerning the use of the filibuster.

Willkie, Wendell Lewis (1892–1944), lawyer and businessman; Republican candidate for U.S. president (1940). In 1942, he received notice of the opening of the NAACP's Washington Bureau.

Wilson, Boyd L. (1911–90), labor leader. He was an officer of the United Steelworkers of America–CIO, based in Pittsburgh. He was a member of the delegation from the NECRM that met with President Truman in January 1951 as well as being present at the 1951 organizational meeting of the LCCR.

Wilson, Charles Edward (1886–1972), consultant; president, General Electric (1939–42, 1944–50); member, WPB (1942–44); chair, PCCR (1946–47); director, ODM (1950–52); executive, then chair, W. R. Grace and Company (1952–56); president, People to People Foundation (1956–58). He was popularly known as "Electric Charlie." In 1948, he investigated NAACP charges of discrimination against his company's Kentucky plant. He also conferred with Mitchell on the enforcement of nondiscrimination clauses in military contracts and was involved with efforts to desegregate the armed services. In 1951, he agreed to support Mitchell in seeking an executive order (what became EO 10308) to establish a committee to police nondiscrimination clauses in defense contracts.

Wilson, Charles Erwin (1890–1961), engineer; vice president (1928–39), executive vice president (1939–41), and president (1941–52), General Motors; U.S. secretary of defense (1953–57).

He was popularly known as "Engineer Charlie." In 1954, he issued an order ending segregation of schools on military posts.

Wilson, Harold. One of a group of black teenagers who, in 1953, challenged Jim Crow transportation laws and refused to move to the back of a bus in Richmond, Virginia.

Wilson, James Finley "The Grand" (1881–1952), newspaperman, historian and fraternal leader; grand exalted ruler of the Improved Benevolent Protective Order of the Elks of the World (I.B.P.O.E. of W.) (1922–52). In 1941, he was named to the sponsoring committee of the March on Washington Committee by A. Philip Randolph.

Wilson, Morris M. (1910–2006), veteran and postal worker. He was an NAACP complainant against employment discrimination at the New Orleans Post Office (1947).

Wilson, Thelma. One of a group of black teenagers who, in 1953, challenged Jim Crow transportation laws and refused to move to the back of a bus in Richmond, Virginia.

Wilson, Wilbert, serviceman. In 1951, the NAACP went to Wilson's aid after his Asian wife was denied admission to the United States.

Winant, John Gilbert, Sr. (1889–1947) (D-N.H.), lawyer and diplomat; governor of New Hampshire (1925–27, 1931–35); director, SSB (1935–37); U.S. ambassador to Great Britain (1941–46). During World War II, he met with Walter White while the latter reviewed the plight of black troops fighting in the European theatre.

Winstead, William Arthur (1904–95) (D-Miss.), farmer and county executive; U.S. representative (1943–65); commissioner, MDPW (1968–71). He authored a 1951 amendment for continued segregation of the armed forces. He also signed the "Southern Manifesto," written in protest against the *Brown v. Board of Education* decision.

Wise, Stephen Samuel (1874–1949), senior rabbi and founder, Free Synagogue of New York City (1906–49); president, AJCong. In 1944 he testified before the House Labor Committee in favor of S. 2048, a bill designed to strengthen the FEPC.

Withers, Garrett Lee (1884–1953) (D-Ky.), lawyer; commissioner, KDH (1947–49); U.S. senator (1949–50); Kentucky state legislator (1951); U.S. representative (1952–53). He advocated a constitutional amendment to ban poll taxes.

Wogan, William W., Jr. (1909–80), lawyer. In 1950, he represented Lt. Leon A. Gilbert at his appeal after he was sentenced to death for refusing to obey the command of a white officer to return with his men to a dangerous position. Following legal challenges by the NAACP, Gilbert's sentence was reduced by President Truman to twenty years.

Wolchok, Samuel (1894–1979), labor leader. In 1942, as president of the United Retail, Wholesale and Department Store Employees union, he participated in a rally dedicated to the support of a permanent FEPC.

Wolverton, Charles Anderson (1880–1969) (R-N.J.), lawyer; New Jersey state legislator (1915–18); U.S. representative (1927–59). As chair of the House Committee on Interstate and Foreign Commerce (1947–49, 1953–55), he held hearings on (and supported) anti–Jim Crow travel legislation.

Woodard, Isaac, Jr. (1919–92), veteran. He was beaten and blinded by police in Batesburg, South Carolina, after he reportedly violated Jim Crow travel laws on a Greyhound bus. He moved to New York City and spoke at NAACP meetings about his ordeal, inspiring the organization to protest on his behalf and establish a fund to assist in his support. His case became a focal point in the campaign to protect black service members from civilian violence.

Woodring, Harry Hines (1890–1967) (D-Kan.), lawyer; governor of Kansas (1931–33); Assistant U.S. Secretary of War (1933–36); U.S. Secretary of War (1936–40). In 1940 he corresponded with NAACP about the U.S. Army's policy of segregated units.

Woodward, Robert Forbes (1908–2001), U.S. foreign service officer and diplomat; U.S. vice consul in Rio de Janeiro (1938–40), Lima, Peru (1940–43), and La Paz, Bolivia (1943–45);

chief of division, U.S. Foreign Service Personnel (1950–54); U.S. ambassador to Costa Rica (1954–58); U.S. ambassador to Uruguay (1958–60); U.S. ambassador to Chile (1960–61); assistant secretary of state for Latin American Affairs (1961–62); U. S. ambassador to Spain (1962–65). In 1953, he conferred with the NAACP on improving State Department employment practices.

Woofter, Thomas Jackson, Jr. (1893–1972), sociologist. A relative of Stonewall Jackson and Ty Cobb and the son of the president of the University of Georgia, T. J. Woofter, Jr. performed invaluable field work for the WPA in studying the lives of black sharecroppers and other workers in the American South, including a study of how local municipalities in the South apportioned federal monies in segregated school systems.

Worthy, James Carson (1910–98), assistant deputy administrator, NRA (1933–36); executive, Sears Roebuck and Company (1938–53, 1953–61); assistant secretary of commerce (1951–53); professor (1972–98). He was a member of the CGC.

Wrenn, John Joseph (1906–96), lawyer of Providence, Rhode Island; longtime Rhode Island state legislator who would serve as Speaker of the House (1965–69). In 1945, a bill he sponsored eliminating discrimination and employment and establishing a state FEPC had the support of Black and Jewish groups throughout the state.

Wright, Fielding Lewis (1895–1956) (D-Miss.); lawyer and businessman; governor of Mississippi (1944–52); vice presidential candidate, States' Rights ("Dixiecrat") Party, 1948. He was an avowed segregationist and foe of the FEPC. Mitchell reportedly stated that that the only ones who benefited from Congress' consideration of FEPC legislation in 1947 were the railroads that collected fares from persons who went to Washington to testify and Governor Wright who endeared himself to his supporters by claiming to have blocked passage of the act.

Wright, Herbert L. (1925–), activist; national youth leader, NAACP (1949–63); he was later the manager for popular singer Brook Benton (1963–68). Wright was present at the formation of the LCCR, 1951.

Wright, Dr. Louis Tompkins (1891–1952), surgeon and medical researcher; chair, NAACP National Board of Directors (1935–52). He established the NAACP National Medical Committee to oppose discrimination in medicine.

Yeagley, John Walter (1909–90), special agent, FBI (1942–48); director, Security and Investigation Division, BECA, State Department (1948–51); associate general counsel, RFC (1952–53); deputy assistant attorney general (1953–59) and assistant attorney general (1959–70), Department of Justice; associate judge (1970–79) and senior judge (1979–85), D.C. Court of Appeals. In 1953, he attended an LCCR-sponsored meeting on strengthening both the Department of Justice's Civil Rights Division and the CGC.

Young, Consuelo C. [married name Megahy] (1907–77), one time professor of journalism, Lincoln University (Missouri) and reporter and editor of "women's features" for the *Chicago Defender.* Representing the NAACP, she also sat on the initial executive board of the NECRM of 1950.

Young, Plummer Bernard, Sr. "P.B." (1884–1962), publisher and editor of the *Norfolk Journal and Guide* (1910–46), called at one time "the best edited Negro newspaper in America"; a leader of Southern Conference on Race Relations; member of second FEPC, 1943-44.

Young, Dr. Ralph Jonathan (1893–1968), physician. He was a member of a special committee formed in 1948 to inquire into problems of African American employment at the BOASI in Baltimore.

Young, Thomas White (1908–67), newspaper publisher, younger son of P. B. Young, Sr. of the *Norfolk Journal and Guide*; under his father's tutelage, he worked as the newspaper's business manager. After his father retired in 1946, he took up the day-to-day operation of the newspaper and continued until his death in an airplane crash. In 1943, he was one of sixteen representatives of the black press who signed a telegram protesting the FEPC cancellation of hearings designed to review racial discrimination in the railroad industry.

Youngdahl, Luther Wallace (1896–1978) (R-Minn.), lawyer; associate justice, Minnesota Supreme Court (1942–46); governor (1947–51); judge, U.S. district court for the District of Columbia (1951–78). He was a supporter of FEPC legislation, and Mitchell considered him one of the more progressive Republican Party leaders.

Zanuck, Darryl Francis (1902–79), motion picture executive; leaving his native Nebraska for Hollywood after service in World War I, he started out sending in unsolicited scripts to various studios until he was able to get a position as a scriptwriter. Zanuck rose through the ranks until 1933 when he co-founded what would become Twentieth Century Fox, which would become one of the major motion picture studios producing hit movies during Hollywood's "Golden Age." In 1942, Zanuck received notice of the opening of the NAACP's Washington Bureau.

Zaritsky, Max (1885–1959), labor leader; president, Cloth Hat, Cap and Millinery Workers Union (1919–36); president, United Hatters, Cap and Millinery Workers International Union (1936–50). In 1943, he was named to the executive board of the NCPFEPC.

Zehring, Earl Winton (1911–61), machinist at the Bendix plant in Mishawaka, Indiana. In 1949, Mitchell met him at the UAW Education Convention in Milwaukee and was favorably impressed by Zehring's efforts to welcome and retain black workers at his place of employment.

Zenon, John A. (1920–2005), veteran. Although claiming employment discrimination at the New Orleans Post Office, he declined to join those of his fellow postal workers and the NAACP in filing formal charges against that body.

Zimmerman, Charles Sascha (1896–1983), union leader; representative, NJCRAC. Active in Communist Party and Socialist Party circles, he represented the NJCRAC at a 1953 meeting with a subcommittee of the CGC.

Zuckert, Eugene Martin (1911–2000), lawyer; legal staffer, SEC (1937–40); assistant secretary of the air force (1947–52); member, AEC (1952–54); secretary of the air force (1961–65). In 1951, Mitchell negotiated with him on the nonsegregation of inductees into the military.

APPENDIX 3

Congressional Directory

ALP—American Labor Party
D—Democratic Party
FL—Farm Labor
I—Independent
L—Liberal
P—Progressive
R—Republican Party
S—Silver Republican Party

Abernethy, Rep. Thomas Gerstle (1903–98) (D-Miss.)
Aiken, Sen. George David (1892–1984) (D-Vt.)
Allen, Rep. John Joseph, Jr. (1899–1995) (R-Calif.)
Allen, Rep. Leo Elwood (1898–1973) (R-Ill.)
Andersen, Rep. Herman Carl (1897–1978) (R-Minn.)
Anderson, Rep./Sen. Clinton Presba (1895–1975) (D-N.Mex.)
Anderson, Rep. John Zuinglius (1904–81) (R-Calif.)
Andresen, Rep. August Herman (1890–1958) (R-Minn.)
Andrews, Rep. Walter Gresham (1889–1949) (R-N.C.)
Arends, Rep. Leslie Cornelius (1895–1985) (R-Ill.)
Auchincloss, Rep. James Coats (1885–1976) (R-N.J.)
Austin, Rep. Warren Robinson (1877–1962) (R-Vt.)
Bailey, Rep. Cleveland Monroe (1886–1965) (D-W.Va.)
Baldwin, Rep. Joseph Clark (1897–1957) (R-N.Y.)
Baldwin, Sen. Raymond Earl (1893–1986) (R-Conn.)
Ball, Sen. Joseph Hurst (1905–93) (R-Minn.)
Banta, Rep. Parke Monroe (1891–1970) (R-Mo.)
Barbour, Sen. William Warren (1888–1943) (R-N.J.)
Barden, Rep. Graham Arthur (1896–1967) (R-N.C.)
Barkley, Sen. Alben William (1877–1956) (D-Ky.)
Barrett, Rep./Sen. Frank Aloysius (1892–1962) (R-Wyo.)
Bates, Rep. George Joseph (1891–1949) (R-Mass.)
Beall, Rep. James Glenn (1894–1971) (R-Md.)
Beamer, Rep. John Valentine (1896–1964) (R-Ind.)
Bender, Rep./Sen. George Harrison (1896–1961) (R-Ohio)
Bennett, Rep. Marion Tinsley (1914–2000) (R-Mo.)
Benton, Sen. William (1900–73) (D-Conn.)

Bible, Sen. Alan Harvey (1909–88) (D-Nev.)
Biemiller, Rep. Andrew John (1906–82) (D-Wisc.)
Bilbo, Sen. Theodore Gilmore (1877–1947) (D-Miss.)
Bishop, Rep. Cecil William (1890–1971) (R-Ohio)
Black, Sen. Hugo La Fayette (1886–1971) (D-Ala.)
Blackney, Rep. William Wallace (1876–1963) (R-Mich.)
Boggs, Rep./Sen. James Caleb (1909–93) (R-Del.)
Boggs, Rep. Thomas Hale (1914–72) (D-La.)
Bramblett, Rep. Ernest King (1901–66) (R-Calif.)
Brehm, Rep. Walter Ellsworth (1892–1971) (R-Ohio)
Brewster, Rep./Sen. Ralph Owen (1888–1961) (R-Maine)
Bricker, Sen. John William (1893–1986) (R-Ohio)
Bridges, Sen. Henry Styles (1898–1961) (R-N.H.)
Briggs, Sen. Frank Parks (1894–1992) (D-Mo.)
Brooks, Sen. Charles Wayland (1897–1957) (R-Ill.)
Brown, Rep. Clarence James (1893–1965) (R-Ohio)
Brown, Rep. Paul (1880–1961) (D-Ga.)
Brown, Rep./Sen. Prentiss Marsh (1889–1973) (D-Mich.)
Buchanan, Rep. Frank (1862–1930) (D-Ill.)
Buck, Sen. Clayton Douglass (1890–1965) (R-Del.)
Buck, Rep. Ellsworth Brewer (1892–1970) (R-N.Y.)
Buffett, Rep. Howard Homan (1903–64) (R-Neb.)
Bulow, Sen. William John (1869–1960) (D-S.D.)
Burke, Rep. Thomas Henry (1904–59) (D-Ohio)
Burton, Sen. Harold Hitz (1888–1964) (R-Ohio)
Bush, Sen. Presccott Sheldon (1895–1972) (R-Conn.)
Bushfield, Sen. Harlan John (1882–1948) (R-S.D.)
Butler, Sen. Hugh Alfred (1878–1954) (R-Neb.)
Butler, Sen. John Marshall (1897–1978) (R-Md.)
Byrd, Sen. Harry Flood (1887–1966) (D-Va.)
Byrne, Rep. William Thomas (1876–1952) (D-N.Y.)
Byrnes, Rep./Sen. James Francis (1882–1972) (D-S.C.)
Byrnes, Rep. John William (1913–1985) (R-Wis.)
Cain, Sen. Harry Pulliam (1906–79) (R-Wash.)
Camp, Rep. Albert Sidney (1892–1954) (D-Ga.)
Cannon, Rep. Clarence Andrew (1879–1964) (D-Mo.)
Cannon, Rep. Joseph Gurney "Uncle Joe" (1836–1926) (R-Ill.)
Capehart, Sen. Homer Earl (1897–1979) (R-Ind.)
Capper, Sen. Arthur (1865–1951) (R-Kans.)
Carrigg, Rep. Joseph Leonard (1901–89) (R-Pa.)
Carroll, Rep./Sen. John Albert (1901–83) (D-Colo.)
Case, Rep./Sen. Clifford Philip (1904–82) (R-N.J.)
Celler, Rep. Emanuel (1888–1981) (D-N.Y.)
Chandler, Sen. Albert Benjamin "Happy", Sr. (1898–1991) (D-Ky.)
Chapman, Rep./Sen. Virgil Munday (1895–1951) (D-Ky.)
Chavez, Rep./Sen. Dennis (1888–1962) (D-N.Mex.)

Chelf, Rep. Frank Leslie (1907–82) (D-Ky.)
Chiperfield, Rep. Robert Bruce (1899–1971) (R-Ill.)
Church, Rep. Marguerite Stitt (1892–1990) (R-Ill.)
Clapp, Sen. Moses Edwin (1851–1929) (R-Minn.)
Clements, Rep./Sen. Earle Chester (1896–1985) (D-Ky.)
Clevenger, Rep. [Everett] Cliff (1885–1960) (R-Ohio)
Cole, Rep. Albert McDonald (1901–94) (R-Kans.)
Cole, Rep. William Sterling (1904–87) (R-N.Y.)
Connally, Rep./Sen. Thomas Terry "Tom" (1877–1963) (D-Tex.)
Cooper, Rep. Jere (1893–1957) (D-Tenn.)
Cooper, Sen. John Sherman (1901–91) (R-Ky.)
Cordon, Sen. Guy (1890–1969) (R-Ore.)
Cox, Rep. Edward Eugene (1880–1952) (D-Ga.)
Cravens, Rep. William Fadjo (1899–1974) (D-Ark.)
Crawford, Rep. Fred Lewis (1888–1957) (R-Mich.)
Crosser, Rep. Robert (1874–1957) (D-Ohio)
Crumpacker, Rep. Shepard J., Jr. (1919–98) (R-Ind.)
Curtis, Rep./Sen. Carl Thomas (1905–2000) (R-Neb.)
Curtis, Rep. Thomas Bradford (1911–93) (R-Mo.)
Dague, Rep. Paul Bartram (1898–1974) (R-Pa.)
Danaher, Rep. John Anthony (1899–1990) (R-Conn.)
Darby, Sen. Harry (1897–1987) (R-Kans.)
Davis, Rep. Glenn Robert (1914–88) (R-Wisc.)
Davis, Rep. James Curran (1895–1981) (D-Ga.)
Dawson, Rep. William Levi (1886–1970) (D-Ill.)
Deane, Rep. Charles Bennett (1898–1969) (D-N.C.)
Delaney, Rep. James Joseph (1901–87) (D-N.Y.)
Derounian, Rep. Stephen Boghos (1918–2007) (R-N.Y.)
Devereux, Rep. James Patrick Sinnott (1903–88) (R-Md.)
Devitt, Rep. Edward James (1911–92) (R-Minn.)
D'Ewart, Rep. Wesley Abner (1889–1973) (R-Mont.)
Dingell, Rep. John David, Sr. (1894–1955) (D-Mich.)
Dirksen, Rep./Sen. Everett McKinley (1896–1969) (R-Ill.)
Dollinger, Rep. Isidore (1903–2000) (D-N.Y.)
Dolliver, Rep. James Isaac (1894–1978) (R-Iowa)
Donnell, Sen. Forrest C. (1884–1980) (R-Mo.)
Doughton, Rep. Robert Lee (1863–1954) (D-N.C.)
Douglas, Rep. Helen Gahagan (1900–80) (D-Calif.)
Douglas, Sen. Paul Howard (1892–1976) (D-Ill.)
Downey, Sen. Sheridan (1884–1961) (D-Calif.)
Doxey, Rep./Sen. Wall (1892–1962) (D-Miss.)
Duff, Sen. James Henderson (1883–1969) (R-Pa.)
Dulles, Sen. John Foster (1888–1959) (R-N.Y.)
Dworshak, Sen. Henry Clarence (1861–1962) (R-Idaho)
Eastland, Sen. James Oliver (1904–86) (D-Miss.)
Eberharter, Rep. Herman Peter (1892–1958) (D-Pa.)

Ecton, Sen. Zales Nelson (1898–1961) (R-Mont.)
Eliot, Rep. Thomas Hopkinson (1907–91) (D-Mass.)
Ellender, Sen. Allen Joseph (1890–1972) (D-La.)
Ellis, Rep. Hubert Summers (1887–1959) (R-W.Va.)
Ellsworth, Rep. Matthew Harris (1899–1986) (R-Ore.)
Elsaesser, Rep. Edward Julius (1904–83) (R-N.Y.)
Elston, Rep. Charles Henry (1891–1980) (R-Ohio)
Feighan, Rep. Michael Aloysius (1905–92) (D-Ohio)
Fellows, Rep. Frank (1889–1951) (R-Maine)
Fenton, Rep. Ivor David (1889–1986) (R-Pa.)
Ferguson, Sen. Homer (1889–1982) (R-Mich.)
Fisher, Rep. Ovie Clark "O. C." (1903–94) (D-Tex.)
Flanders, Sen. Ralph Edward (1880–1970) (R-Vt.)
Fletcher, Rep. Brooks (1879–1945) (D-Ohio)
Fletcher, Rep. Charles Kimball (1902–85) (R-Calif.)
Folger, Rep. John Hamlin (1880–1963) (D-N.C.)
Foote, Rep. Ellsworth Bishop (1898–1977) (R-Conn.)
Forand, Rep. Aime Joseph (1895–1972) (D-R.I.)
Frear, Sen. Joseph Allen, Jr. (1903–93) (D-Del.)
Fulbright, Rep./Sen. James William (1905–95) (D-Ark.)
Fulton, Rep. James Grove (1903–71) (R-Pa.)
Gallinger, Sen. Jacob Harold (1837–1918) (R-N.H.)
Gamble, Rep. Ralph Abernethy (1885–1959) (R-N.Y.)
Gavagan, Rep. Joseph Andrew (1892–1968) (D-N.Y.)
Gavin, Rep. Leon Harry (1893–1963) (R-Pa.)
Gearhart, Rep. Bertrand Wesley (1890–1955) (R-Calif.)
George, Sen. Walter Franklin (1878–1957) (D-Ga.)
Gerry, Rep./Sen. Peter Goelet (1879–1957) (D-R.I.)
Geyer, Rep. Lee Edward (1888–1941) (D-Calif.)
Gillette, Rep./Sen. Guy Mark (1879–1973) (D-Iowa)
Golden, Rep. James Stephen (1891–1971) (R-Ky.)
Goldwater, Sen. Barry Morris (1909–98) (R-Ariz.)
Goodwin, Rep. Angier Louis (1881–1975) (R-Mass.)
Gore, Rep./Sen. Albert Arnold, Sr. (1907–98) (D-Tenn.)
Gorski, Rep. Martin (1886–1949) (D-Ill.)
Gossett, Rep. Ed Lee (1902–90) (D-Tex.)
Graham, Sen. Frank Porter (1876–1962) (D-N.C.)
Graham, Rep. Louis Edward (1880–1965) (R-Pa.)
Granahan, Rep. William Thomas (1895–1956) (D-Pa.)
Grant, Rep. Robert Allen (1905–98) (R-Ind.)
Green, Sen. Theodore Francis (1867–1966) (D-R.I.)
Gregory, Rep. Noble Jones (1897–1971) (D-Ky.)
Griswold, Sen. Dwight Palmer (1893–1954) (R-Neb.)
Gurney, Sen. John Chandler "Chan" (1896–1985) (R-S.Dak.)
Gwinn, Rep. Ralph Waldo (1884–1962) (R-N.Y.)
Hale, Rep. Robert (1889–1976) (R-Maine)

Halleck, Rep. Charles Abraham (1900–86) (R-Ind.)
Harris, Rep. Oren (1903–97) (D-Ark.)
Harrison, Rep./Sen. Byron Patton "Pat" (1881–1941) (D-Miss.)
Harrison, Rep. William Henry (1896–1990) (R-Wyo.)
Hart, Rep. Edward Joseph (1893–1961) (D-N.J.)
Hartley, Rep. Fred Allan, Jr. (1902–69) (R-N.J.)
Havenner, Rep. Franck Roberts (1882–1967) (P, D-Calif.)
Hawkes, Sen. Albert Wahl (1878–1971) (R-N.J.)
Hayden, Rep./Sen. Carl Trumbull (1877–1972) (D-Ariz.)
Hays, Rep. Lawrence Brooks (1898–1981) (D-Ark.)
Hebert, Rep. Felix Edward (1901–79) (D-La.)
Hendrickson, Sen. Robert Clymer (1898–1964) (R-N.J.)
Hennings, Rep./Sen. Thomas Carey, Jr. (1903–60) (D-Mo.)
Herter, Sen. Christian Archibald (1895–1966) (R-Mass.)
Heselton, Rep. John Walter (1900–62) (R-Mass.)
Hickenlooper, Sen. Bourke Blakemore (1896–1971) (R-Iowa)
Hill, Rep./Sen. Joseph Lister (1894–1984) (D-Ala.)
Hill, Rep. William Silas (1886–1972) (R-Colo.)
Hillings, Rep. Patrick Jerome (1923–94) (R-Calif.)
Hinshaw, Rep. John Carl Williams (1894–1956) (R-Calif.)
Hobbs, Rep. Samuel Francis (1887–1952) (D-Ala.)
Hoey, Rep./Sen. Clyde Roark (1877–1954) (D-N.C.)
Hoffman, Rep. Clare Eugene (1875–1967) (R-Mich.)
Hoffman, Rep. Elmer Joseph (1899–1976) (R-Ill.)
Holifield, Rep. Chester Earl (1903–95) (D-Calif.)
Holland, Sen. Spessard Lindsey (1892–1971) (D-Fla.)
Holmes, Rep. Oliver Halbert "Hal" (1902–77) (R-Wash.)
Hope, Rep. Clifford Ragsdale (1893–1970) (R-Kans.)
Horan, Rep. Walter Franklin "Walt" (1898–1966) (R-Wash.)
Hull, Rep. Merlin (1870–1953) (R-Wisc.)
Humphrey, Sen. Hubert Horatio, Jr. (1911–78) (D-Minn.)
Hunt, Rep. Lester Callaway (1892–1954) (D-Wyo.)
Ives, Sen. Irving McNeil (1896–1962) (R-N.Y.)
Jackson, Rep. Donald Lester (1910–81) (R-Calif.)
Jackson, Rep./Sen. Henry Martin "Scoop" (1912–83) (D-Wash.)
James, Rep. Benjamin Franklin (1885–1961) (R-Pa.)
Javits, Rep./Sen. Jacob Koppel (1904–86) (R-N.Y.)
Jenkins, Rep. Thomas Albert (1880–1959) (R-Ohio)
Jenner, Sen. William Ezra (1908–85) (R-Ind.)
Jensen, Rep. Benton Franklin (1892–1970) (R-Iowa)
Johnson, Rep. Edwin Carl (1884–1970) (D-Colo.)
Johnson, Sen. Hiram Warren (1866–1945) (R-Calif.)
Johnson, Rep. Justin Leroy (1888–1961) (R-Calif.)
Johnson, Rep./Sen. Lyndon Baines (1908–73) (D-Tex.)
Johnston, Sen. Olin De Witt Talmadge (1896–1965) (D-S.C.)
Jonas, Rep. Charles Raper (1904–88) (R-N.C.)

Jonas, Rep. Edgar Allan (1885–1965) (R-Ill.)
Jones, Rep. Homer Raymond (1893–1970) (R-Wash.)
Jones, Rep. Paul Caruthers (1901–81) (D-Mo.)
Jones, Sen. Wesley Livsey (1863–1932) (R-Wash.)
Judd, Rep. Walter Henry (1898–1994) (R-Minn.)
Kean, Rep. Robert Winthrop (1893–1980) (R-N.J.)
Kearns, Rep. Carroll Dudley (1900–76) (R-Pa.)
Keating, Rep./Sen. Kenneth Barnard (1900–75) (R-N.Y.)
Kefauver, Sen. Carey Estes (1903–63) (D-Tenn.)
Kelley, Rep. Augustine Bernard (1883–1957) (D-Pa.)
Kem, Sen. James Preston (1890–1965) (R-Mo.)
Kennedy, Rep./Sen. John Fitzgerald (1917–63) (D-Mass.)
Kerr, Sen. Robert Samuel (1896–1963) (D-Okla.)
Kersten, Rep. Charles Joseph (1902–72) (R-Wisc.)
Kilburn, Rep. Clarence Evans (1893–1975) (R-N.Y.)
Kilgore, Sen. Harley Martin (1893–1956) (D-W.Va.)
Klein, Rep. Arthur George (1904–68) (D-N.Y.)
Knowland, Sen. William Fife (1908–74) (R-Calif.)
Knutson, Rep. Harold (1880–1953) (R-Minn.)
Kuchel, Sen. Thomas Henry (1910–94) (R-Calif.)
Kunkel, Rep. John Crain (1898–1970) (R-Pa.)
La Follette, Rep. Charles Marion (1898–1974) (R-Ind.)
Landis, Rep. Gerald Wayne (1895–1971) (R-Ind.)
Lane, Rep. Thomas Joseph (1898–1994) (D-Mass.)
Langer, Sen. William (1886–1959) (R-N.Dak.)
Lanham, Rep. Henderson Lovelace (1888–1957) (D-Ga.)
Latham, Rep. Henry Jepson (1908–2000) (R-N.Y.)
Leahy, Sen. Edward Lawrence (1886–1953) (D-R.I.)
Lehman, Sen. Herbert Henry (1878–1963) (D-N.Y.)
Lennon, Rep./Sen. Alton Asa (1906–86) (D-N.C.)
Lesinski, Rep. John (1885–1950) (D-Mich.)
Lewis, Sen. James Hamilton (1863–1939) (D-Ill.)
Lodge, Sen. Henry Cabot, Jr. (1902–85) (R-Mass.)
Long, Sen. Russell Billiu (1918–2003) (D-La.)
Lovre, Rep. Harold Orrin (1904–72) (R-S.Dak.)
Lucas, Rep. Scott Wike (1892–1968) (D-Ill.)
Lucas, Rep. Wingate Hezekiah (1908–89) (D-Tex.)
Lynch, Rep. Walter Aloysius (1894–1957) (D-N.Y.)
Machrowicz, Rep. Thaddeus Michael (1899–1970) (D-Ill.)
Mack, Rep. Peter Francis, Jr. (1916–86) (D-Ill.)
MacKinnon, Rep. George Edward (1906–95) (R-Minn.)
Madden, Rep. Ray John (1892–1987) (D-Ind.)
Magnuson, Rep. Donald Hammer (1911–79) (D-Wash.)
Magnuson, Rep./Sen. Warren Grant (1905–89) (D-Wash.)
Malone, Sen. George Wilson (1890–1961) (R-Nev.)
Mann, Rep. James Robert (1856–1922) (R-Ill.)

Marcantonio, Rep. Vito Anthony (1902–54) (R, ALP-N.Y.)
Martin, Sen. Edward (1879–1967) (R-Pa.)
Martin, Rep. Joseph William, Jr. (1884–1968) (R-Mass.)
Martin, Rep. Thomas Ellsworth (1893–1971) (R-Iowa)
Mason, Rep. Noah Morgan (1882–1965) (R-Ill.)
Maybank, Sen. Burnet Rhett (1899–1954) (D-S.C.)
McCarran, Rep. Patrick Anthony (1876–1954) (D-Nev.)
McCarthy, Rep./Sen. Eugene Joseph (1916–2005) (D-Minn.)
McCarthy, Sen. Joseph Raymond (1908–57) (R-Wisc.)
McClellan, Rep. John Little (1896–1977) (D-Ark.)
McConnell, Rep. Samuel Kerns, Jr. (1901–85) (R-Pa.)
McCormack, Rep. John William (1891–1980) (D-Mass.)
McCowen, Rep. Edward Oscar (1877–1953) (R-Ohio)
McCulloch, Sen. William (1901–80) (R-Ohio)
McDonough, Rep. Gordon Leo (1895–1968) (R-Calif.)
McDowell, Rep. John (1902–57) (R-Pa.)
McFarland, Sen. Ernest William (1894–1984) (D-Ariz.)
McGarvey, Rep. Robert Neill (1888–1952) (R-Pa.)
McGrath, Sen. James Howard (1903–66) (D-R.I.)
McKellar, Rep./Sen. Kenneth Douglas (1869–1957) (D-Tenn.)
McMahon, Rep. Gregory (1915–89) (R-N.Y.)
McMahon, Sen. James O'Brien "Brien" (1903–52) (D-Conn.)
McMillan, Rep. John Lanneau (1898–1987) (D-S.C.)
McMillen, Rep. Rolla Coral (1880–1961) (R-Ill.)
McNary, Sen. Charles Linza (1874–1944) (R-Ore.)
McSweeney, Rep. John (1890–1969) (D-Ohio)
Mead, Rep./Sen. James Michael (1885–1964) (D-N.Y.)
Miller, Rep. Arthur Lewis (1892–1967) (R-Neb.)
Miller, Rep. Edward Tylor (1895–1968) (R-Md.)
Milliken, Sen. Eugene Donald (1891–1958) (R-Colo.)
Mills, Rep. Wilbur Daigh (1909–92) (D-Ark.)
Mitchell, Rep. Arthur Wergs (1883–1968) (D-Ill.)
Mitchell, Rep./Sen. Hugh Burnton (1907–96) (D-Wash.)
Monroney, Rep. Almer Stillwell "Mike" (1902–80) (D-Okla.)
Moody, Sen. Arthur Edson Blair (1902–54) (D-Mich.)
Moore, Sen. Edward Hall (1871–1950) (R-Okla.)
Morrison, Rep. James Hobson (1908–2000) (D-La.)
Morse, Rep. Wayne Lyman (1900–1974) (R, I, D-Ore.)
Morton, Rep./Sen. Thruston Ballard (1907–82) (R-Ky.)
Moulder, Rep. Morgan Moore (1904–76) (D-Mo.)
Multer, Rep. Abraham Jacob (1900–1986) (D-N.Y.)
Mundt, Rep./Sen. Karl Earl (1900–1974) (R-S.Dak.)
Murdock, Rep./Sen. Orrin Abram, Jr. "Abe" (1893–1979) (D-Utah)
Murray, Sen. James Edward (1876–1961) (D-Mont.)
Myers, Rep./Sen. Francis John (1901–56) (D-Pa.)
Neely, Rep./Sen. Matthew Mansfield (1874–1958) (D-W.Va.)

Neuberger, Sen. Richard Lewis (1907–60) (D-Ore.)
Nicholson, Rep. Donald William (1888–1968) (R-Mass.)
Nixon, Sen. Richard Milhous (1913–94) (R-Calif.)
Norris, Rep./Sen. George William (1861–1944) (R, I-Neb.)
Norton, Rep. Mary Teresa (1875–1959) (D-N.J.)
Nye, Sen. Gerald Prentice (1892–1971) (R-N.D.)
O'Conor, Sen. Herbert Romulus (1896–1960) (D-Md.)
O'Daniel, Sen. Wilbert Lee (1890–1969) (D-Tex.)
O'Hara, Rep. Barratt (1902–64) (D-Ill.)
O'Hara, Rep. Joseph Patrick (1895–1975) (R-Minn.)
O'Mahoney, Sen. Joseph Christopher (1884–1962) (D-Wyo.)
O'Toole, Rep. Donald Lawrence (1902–64) (D-N.Y.)
Outland, Rep. George Elmer (1906–81) (D-Calif.)
Overton, Rep. John Holmes (1875–1948) (D-La.)
Owens, Rep. Thomas Leonard (1897–1948) (R-Ill.)
Pastore, Sen. John Orlando (1907–2000) (D-R.I.)
Patman, Rep. John William Wright (1893–1976) (D-Tex.)
Pelly, Rep. Thomas Minor (1902–73) (R-Wash.)
Pepper, Sen. Claude Denson (1900–1989) (D-Fla.)
Peterson, Rep. James Hardin (1894–1978) (D-Fla.)
Phillips, Rep. John (1887–1983) (R-Calif.)
Poulson, Rep. Charles Norris (1895–1982) (R-Calif.)
Powell, Rep. Adam Clayton, Jr. (1908–72) (D-N.Y.)
Powers, Rep. David Lane (1896–1968) (R-N.J.)
Price, Rep. Charles Melvin (1905–88) (D-Ill.)
Priest, Rep. James Percy (1900–56) (D-Tenn.)
Purtell, Sen. William Arthur (1897–1978) (R-Conn.)
Radcliffe, Sen. George Lovic Pierce (1877–1974) (D-Md.)
Rains, Rep. Albert (1902–91) (D-Ala.)
Ramey, Rep. Homer Alonzo (1891–1960) (R-Ohio)
Ramsay, Rep. Robert Lincoln (1877–1956) (D-W.Va.)
Ramspeck, Rep. Robert C. Word (1890–1972) (D-Ga.)
Rankin, Rep. John Elliott (1882–1960) (D-Miss.)
Rayburn, Rep. Samuel Taliaferro (1882–1961) (D-Tex.)
Reece, Rep. Brazilla Carroll (1889–1961) (R-Tenn.)
Reed, Rep. Chauncey William (1890–1956) (R-Ill.)
Reed, Rep. Daniel Alden (1875–1959) (R-N.Y.)
Rees, Rep. Edward Herbert (1886–1969) (R-Kans.)
Revercomb, Sen. William Chapman (1895–1979) (R-W.Va.)
Richards, Rep. James Prioleau (1894–1979) (D-S.C.)
Riley, Rep. John Jacob (1895–1962) (D-S.C.)
Robertson, Rep./Sen. Absalom Willis (1887–1971) (D-Va.)
Robertson, Sen. Edward Vivian (1881–1963) (R-Wyo.)
Rodino, Rep. Peter Wallace, Jr. (1909–2005) (D-N.J.)
Rogers, Rep. Byron Giles (1900–83) (D-Colo.)
Rogers, Rep. Dwight Laing (1886–1954) (D-Fla.)

Rooney, Rep. John James (1903–75) (D-N.Y.)
Roosevelt, Rep. Franklin Delano, Jr. (1914–88) (L&D-N.Y.)
Root, Sen. Elihu (1845–1937) (R-N.Y.)
Russell, Sen. Richard Brevard (1897–1971) (D-Ga.)
Sabath, Rep. Adolph Joachim (1866–1952) (D-Ill.)
Saltonstall, Sen. Leverett (1892–1979) (R-Mass.)
Scanlon, Rep. Thomas Edward (1896–1955) (D-Pa.)
Schenck, Rep. Paul Fornshell (1899–1968) (R-Ohio)
Schoeppel, Sen. Andrew Frank (1894–1962) (R-Kans.)
Schwabe, Rep. Max (1905–83) (R-Mont.)
Scott, Rep. Hardie (1907–99) (R-Pa.)
Scrivner, Rep. Errett Power (1898–1978) (R-Kans.)
Shafer, Rep. Paul Werntz (1893–1954) (R-Mich.)
Shafroth, Sen. John Franklin (1854–1922) (D, S-R, R-Colo.)
Sherman, Sen. Lawrence Yates (1858–1939) (R-Ill.)
Shipstead, Sen. Henrik (1881–1960) (FL, R-Minn.)
Short, Rep. Dewey Jackson (1898–1979) (R-Mo.)
Simpson, Rep. Richard Murray (1900–1960) (R-Pa.)
Simpson, Rep. Sidney (1894–1958) (R-Ill.)
Sittler, Rep. Edward Lewis, Jr. (1908–78) (R-Pa.)
Smathers, Rep./Sen. George Armistead (1913–) (D-Fla.)
Smith, Rep. Frederick Cleveland (1884–1956) (R-Ohio)
Smith, Sen. Howard Alexander (1880–1966) (R-N.J.)
Smith, Rep. Howard Worth (1883–1976) (D-Va.)
Smith, Rep./Sen. Margaret Chase (1897–1995) (R-Maine)
Smith, Sen. Michael Hoke (1855–1931) (D-Ga.)
Smith, Sen. William Alden (1859–1932) (R-Mich.)
Smith, Rep. Wint (1892–1976) (R-Kans.)
Sparkman, Rep./Sen. John Jackson (1899–1985) (D-Ala.)
Spence, Rep. Brent (1874–1967) (D-Ky.)
Springer, Rep. William Lee (1909–92) (R-Ill.)
Staggers, Rep. Harley Orrin (1907–91) (D-W.Va.)
Steed, Rep. Thomas Jefferson (1904–83) (D-Okla.)
Stennis, Sen. John Cornelius (1901–95) (D-Miss.)
Stratton, Rep. William Grant (1914–2001) (R-Ill.)
Sundstrom, Rep. Frank L. (1901–80) (R-N.J.)
Symington, Sen. William Stuart (1901–88) (D-Mo.)
Taber, Rep. John (1880–1965) (R-N.Y.)
Taft, Sen. Robert Alphonso (1889–1953) (R-Ohio)
Talle, Rep. Henry Oscar (1892–1969) (R-Iowa)
Talmadge, Sen.Herman Eugene (1913–2002) (D-Ga.)
Taylor, Sen. Glen Hearst (1904–84) (D-Ind.)
Teague, Rep. Olin Earl (1910–81) (D-Tex.)
Thomas, Sen. Elbert Duncan (1883–1953) (D-Utah)
Thomas, Rep. Elmer (1876–1965) (D-Okla.)
Thompson, Rep. Ruth (1889–1970) (R-Mich)

Thurmond, Sen. James Strom (1902–2003) (D-S.C.)
Thye, Sen. Edward John (1896–1969) (R-Minn.)
Tobey, Rep./Sen. Charles William (1880–1953) (R-N.H.)
Tolan, Rep. John Harvey (1877–1947) (D-Calif.)
Towe, Rep. Harry Lancaster (1898–1991) (R-N.J.)
Truman, Sen. Harry S. (1884–1972) (D-Mo.)
Tunnell, Sen. James Miller (1879–1957) (D-Del.)
Twyman, Rep. Robert Joseph (1897–1976) (R-Ill.)
Tydings, Sen. Millard Evelyn (1890–1961) (D-Md.)
Umstead, Sen. William Bradley (1895–1954) (D-N.C.)
Underwood, Sen. Thomas Rust, Sen. (1898–1956) (D-Ky.)
Upton, Sen. Robert William (1884–1972) (R-N.H.)
Vandenberg, Sen. Arthur Hendrick (1884–1951) (R-Mich.)
Van Nuys, Sen. Frederick (1874–1944) (D-Ind.)
Van Zandt, Rep. James Edward (1898–1986) (R-Pa.)
Vardaman, Sen. James Kimble (1861-1930) (D-Mississippi)
Velde, Rep. Harold Himmel (1910–85) (R-Ill.)
Voorhis. Rep. Horace Jeremiah (1901–84) (D-Calif.)
Vorys, Rep. John Martin (1896–1968) (R-Ohio)
Wagner, Sen. Robert Ferdinand, Sr. (1877–1953) (D-N.Y.)
Walter, Rep. Francis Eugene. (1884–1963) (D-Penn.)
Warburton, Rep. Herbert Birchby (1916–83) (R-Del.)
Watkins, Sen. Arthur Vivian (1886–1973) (R-Utah)
Weichel, Sen. Alvin F. (1891–1956) (R-Ohio)
Werdel, Rep. Thomas Harold (1905–66) (R-Calif.)
West, Rep. Milton Horace (1888–1948) (D-Tex.)
Wherry, Sen. Kenneth Spice (1892–1951) (R-Neb.)
White, Rep./Sen. Wallace Humphrey, Jr. (1877–1952) (R-Maine)
Wier, Rep. Roy William (1888–1963) (D-Minn.)
Wiley, Sen. Alexander (1884–1967) (R-Wis.)
Williams, Rep. John Bell (1918–83) (D-Miss.)
Williams, Sen. John James (1904–88) (R-Del.)
Wilson, Sen. George Allison (1884–1953) (R-Iowa)
Winstead, Rep. William Arthur (1904–95) (D-Miss.)
Withers, Sen./Rep. Garrett Lee (1884–1953) (D-Ky.)
Wolcott, Rep. Jesse Paine (1893–1969) (R-Mich.)
Wolverton, Rep. Charles Anderson (1880–1969) (R-N.J.)
Wood, Rep. John Stephens (1885–1968) (D-Ga.)
Woodruff, Rep. Roy Orchard (1876–1953) (R-Mich.)
Works, Sen. John Downey (1847–1928) (R-Cal.)
Yates, Rep. Sidney Richard (1909–2000) (D-Ill.)
Young, Sen. Milton Ruben (1897–1983) (R-N.D.)
Youngblood, Rep. Harold F. (1907–83) (R-Mich.)
Younger, Rep. Jesse Arthur (1893–1967) (R-Calif.)

APPENDIX 4

List of Reports of the Washington Bureau
with Subjects Covered

by Leslie Perry

1942

Monthly Report, October 1942 (10/31/42)[1]

Congress and Congressional Legislation: Poll Tax, Manpower, FEPC, OPA, War Department, Civil Rights, Miscellaneous

Monthly Report, November 1942 (11/30/42)

Congress and Congressional Legislation: Poll Tax, Manpower, Federal Housing, National Youth Administration, War Department, Civil Rights, Miscellaneous

1943

Monthly Report (August 11, 1943)

Congress and Congressional Legislation: Civil Rights, Miscellaneous, FEPC, Post Office

Report for the Week of August 19–26, 1943, August 28, 1943

Housing Situation in Evansville, Indiana, Baltimore Housing Situation, National Labor Relations Board

Report for the Week of September 9–16, 1943, September 23, 1943

F.E.P.C., War Department, Poll Tax, Red Cross, Conference with Post Office, F.E.P.C., Housing

Monthly Report, September (9/30/43)

Permanent FEPC, Surplus War Property Bill, Protection of Members of Armed Forces, Public Health Service, Government Printing Office, War Department, New Iberia, GI Bill, Congressional Voting Record, Query for Congressional Candidates

1944

Monthly Report, August 1944 (8/31/44)

Congress and Congressional Legislation: Murray-Kilgore War Mobilization and Adjustment Bill, Surplus Government War Property Bill, Permanent FEPC

Government Department and Agencies: United States Employment Service, Farm Security Administration, Navy Department, War Department, Miscellaneous

Monthly Report, November 1944 (11/30/44)

Congress and Congressional Legislation: GI Assault Bill, Permanent FEPC, Government Departments and Agencies: OPA, War Shipping Administration, FEPC, Armed Forces, GI Bill of Rights, Camp Investigation

Miscellaneous: Employer Survey, West Virginia FEPC

1945

Monthly Report, January 1945 (1/31/45)

Anti-lynching Legislation, Anti–Poll Tax Bill, Fair Employment Practice Committee, Federal Aid to Education, Bill to Prohibit Segregation in Interstate Travel, Select Committee to Investigate Executive Agencies, GI Assault Bill.

Departments and Agencies: Post Office, Veterans Administration, United States Civil Service Commission, FEPC Hearings on Capital Transit, Meetings

Monthly Report, February 1945 (2/28/45)

Legislation: Anti-lynching Bill, Anti–Jim Crow Travel Bill, Anti–Poll Tax Bill, Permanent FEPC Bill, May-Bailey Work-or-Fight Bill, GI Assault Bill

Government Departments and Agencies: National Housing Agency, Federal Works Administration, War Shipping Administration, Miscellaneous

Monthly Report, March 1945 (3/31/45)

Anti-lynching Bill, Anti–Poll Tax Bill, FEPC, Extension of Price Control Act, Federal Hospital Bill, Confirmation of Aubrey Williams

Government Departments and Agencies: National Housing Agency (continued), Discrimination in the Armed Forces, Miscellaneous

Monthly Report, April 1945 (4/30/45)

Congress and Congressional Legislation: Anti-lynch Bill, Permanent FEPC, Anti–Jim Crow Travel Bill, Anti–Poll Tax Bill, Discrimination in Armed Forces, Miscellaneous

Monthly Report, June 1, 1945

Congress and Congressional Legislation: Anti-lynching Bill, Anti–Poll Tax Bill, FEPC, Peacetime Military Conscription, Lesinski Housing Bill

Government Departments and Agencies: Department of Justice, USES, War Department, Miscellaneous

Monthly Report, June 28, 1945

Congress and Congressional Legislation: FEPC Appropriation, Permanent FEPC, Federal Aid to Education, Full Employment Bill, Miscellaneous, Action Letter No. 10

Monthly Report, September 1945 (9/30/45)

Congress and Congressional Legislation: Full Employment Bill, Unemployment Compensation, S. 1274, Lucas Amendment, Anti–Poll Tax Bill, FEPC, Pepper Minimum Wage Bill, Miscellaneous

Monthly Report, October 1945 (10/31/45)

Congress and Congressional Legislation: Full Employment and Unemployment Compensation Bills, Minimum Wage Bill, Ball-Burton-Hatch Bill, Daughters of the American Revolution, Anti–Poll Tax Bill, Miscellaneous

Monthly Report, November 1945 (11/30/45)

Congress and Congressional Legislation: FEPC, National Housing Bill, Minimum Wage Bill, Federal Aid to Education, Anti-labor Bills, Statute of Limitations, Miscellaneous, Action Letter to the Branches

1946

Monthly Report, February 1946 (2/28/46)

Congress and Congressional Legislation: FEPC, School Lunch Bill, Peacetime Military Conscription, Housing, Anti-lynching

Government Agencies: Department of Justice, Wage Ceilings on Cotton Pickers, Miscellaneous

Monthly Report, March 1946 (3/31/46)

Congress and Congressional Legislation: Minimum Wage Bill, Housing, Anti–Poll Tax, Hastie Nomination for Governor of the Virgin Islands

Monthly Report, April 1946 (4/30/46)

Congress and Congressional Legislation: National Health Bill, Housing Bill, Emergency Housing Bill, Price Control

Government Agency: National Housing Agency, Federal Reserve Board, Miscellaneous

Monthly Report, July 1 to August 15, 1946 (8/15/46)

Congress and Congressional Legislation: Anti–Poll Tax Bill, OPA, Minimum Wage Bill, Wagner-Ellender-Taft Housing Bill, Changing Rules of Senate, Anti-lynching Bill, Questionnaire for Congressional Candidates, Voting Record for September NAACP Bulletin

Monthly Report, September 1946 (9/30/46)

Departments and Agencies: Federal Communications Commission, OPA, the Council of Economic Advisors to the President, Housing, Police Training in Race Relations,

Discrimination Platform of the D.C. Chapter of the American Veterans Committee, Speaking Engagement

Monthly Report, October 1946 (10/31/46)

Federal Communication Commissions, Navy Department, Conferences

Monthly Report, November 1946 (11/30/46)

Conference with Editors of Washington Newspapers, Federal Aid to Education, State Department, Department of Justice, Political Action, Speaking Engagements

Monthly Report, October 1945 to December 1946 (12/30/46)

FEPC, Anti-lynching, Anti–Jim Crow Travel, Minimum Wage, Continuation of USES, School Lunch Program, National Health, Continuation of Price Control and the Anti–Poll Tax

1947

Monthly Report, January 1947 (1/31/47)

Congress and Congressional Legislation: Anti-filibuster Resolutions, Anti–Poll Tax Bill, Anti-lynching, Conferences with Speaker Martin and Republican Majority-Whip Wherry, Housing, Federal Public Housing, Miscellaneous

Monthly Report, February 1947 (2/28/47)

Congress and Congressional Legislation: Testimony in Support of Rent Control, Anti-filibuster Resolutions, Anti–Jim Crow Travel Bill, Anti–Poll Tax Bill

Government Agencies: the President's Committee on Civil Rights, State Department, Miscellaneous

Monthly Report, March 1947 (3/31/47)

Congress and Congressional Legislation: Rent Control, Housing, Anti–Jim Crow Travel Bill, School Lunch Program, the Hobbs Bill to Nullify the McNabb Decision, Exclusion of Negro Reporters from the Capitol Press Galleries, Exclusion of Negro Employees from the Senate Restaurant, Query to Senator Langer re: Federal Employment Policies, Miscellaneous, Speaking Engagement

Monthly Report, April 1947 (4/30/47)

Congress and Congressional Legislation: Federal Aid to Education, Appropriations for the Department of Labor, School Lunch Deficiency Appropriation, D.C. Equal Rights Bill, Taft-Ellender-Wagner Bill, Anti–Poll Tax Bill, Anti-filibuster Resolution, Rent Control, Segregation in Senate Cafeteria, Conference with Commissioner of the Federal Public Housing Authority, Legislative Program

Miscellaneous: Civil Rights, Speaking Engagements

Monthly Report, May 1947 (5/31/47)

Congress and Congressional Legislation: Anti-lynching Bill, Federal Aid to Education, Civil Rights for the District of Columbia, Housing Legislation, FHA Underwriting Manual, Publication of *FASCISM IN ACTION*, Anti-labor Legislation

Miscellaneous: Speeches

Monthly Report for July 1– August 15, 1947 (8/15/47)

Congress and Congressional Legislation: Anti-ynch Discharge Petition #9, Anti–Poll Tax, Anti–Jim Crow Travel Bill, School Lunch Appropriations, Senate Cost of Living Study, Congressional Probe of Real Estate Interests, Legislative Letter to NAACP Branches, Voting Record Issue of the Bulletin

Government Agencies: Federal Bureau of Investigation, Discrimination in the Admission of Negro Tourists to Guatemala and Panama, Speaking Engagements

Monthly Report, November, 1947 (11/30/47)

Congress and Congressional Legislation: Anti-lynching Bill, House, Senate, School Lunch Program, Federal Aid to Education

International: State Department, Panama and Guatemala, Miscellaneous

1948

Monthly Report, January 1948 (1/31/48)

Congress and Congressional Legislation: Anti-lynching Bill, Legislation to Establish Jim-Crow Booker T. Washington Hospital, Housing Hearings, Price Control, Rent Control, Miscellaneous

Monthly Report, February 1948 (2/28/48)

Congress and Congressional Legislation: Anti-lynching Bill, Anti–Poll Tax, a Bill to Create Permanent Units of WACS and Waves, School Lunch Appropriation, Housing and Home Finance Agency, Miscellaneous

Monthly Report, April 1948 (4/30/48)

Congress and Congressional Legislation: Anti–Poll Tax, Anti-lynching Bill, Regional Education, WAVE-WAC Bill, Taft-Ellender-Wagner Bill, Miscellaneous

Monthly Report, May 1948 (5/31/48)

Congress and Congressional Legislation: Regional College Proposal, Anti-lynching Bill, Anti–Poll Tax, Mundt-Nixon Bill, Taft-Ellender-Wagner Housing Bill

Miscellaneous: State Department, Meetings, Speaking Engagements

Monthly Report, November 1948 (11/30/48)

Congress and Congressional Legislation: Housing, Discrimination against Fiancée of Negro Soldier, School Lunch Program, Newly Elected Congressmen and Senators, Miscellaneous

1949

Monthly Report, January 1949 (1/31/49)

Congress and Congressional Legislation: Anti-filibuster Resolution, Federal Aid to Education, Housing, Anti–Jim Crow Travel, Miscellaneous

Monthly Report, February 1949 (2/28/49)

Congress and Congressional Legislation: Anti-filibuster, Housing, Rent Control, Miscellaneous, Speaking Engagements

Monthly Report, March 1949 (3/31/49)

Congress and Congressional Legislation: Anti-filibuster, Anti-lynching Bill, Anti–Jim Crow Travel, D.C. Sales Tax, Rent Control, Miscellaneous

Monthly Report, April 27, 1949

Senator Morse, the Administration's Civil Rights Bills, Anti-lynching Bill, Anti–Poll Tax Bill, Housing Bill

Monthly Report, April and May 1949 (5/31/49)

Congress and Legislation: Housing, Federal Aid to Education, Anti–Poll Tax, Civil Rights Legislation, Anti-lynching, FEPC, Query to Senators Regarding Cloture, D.C. Home Rule Bill, Miscellaneous, Speaking Engagements

Report for October and November 1949 (11/30/49)

Voting Record Bulletin, Washington Planning Committee for the National Civil Rights Mobilization, Swearing In of Mr. Justice Minton, UN Day, Housing, Speaking Engagements

1950

Monthly Report, January 1950 (1/31/50)

Congress and Congressional Legislation: Civil Rights Mobilization, Anti-lynching Bill, Repeal of the Oleomargarine Tax, Vote on Changing House Rules, FEPC

Government Agencies: State Department, Housing

Miscellaneous: Gloucester, Virginia, Branch Election, Speaking Engagements

Monthly Report, March 1950 (3/31/50)

Congress and Congressional Legislation: Abolition of the Poll Tax, Striking Dixiecrats from Federal Payrolls, Federal Aid to Education, Resident Commissioner for the Virgin Islands, Rent Control, Bureau Engraving Employees, Housing Agency, State Department, Speaking Engagements

Monthly Report, March and April 1950 (4/30/50)

Congress and Congressional Legislation: Abolition of the Poll Tax, Barring from the Federal Payroll Persons Practicing Discrimination, Federal Aid to Education, Resident

Commissioner for the Virgin Islands, Rent Control, Apprentice Training for Bureau of Engraving Employees, Displaced Person Act, Ratification of Genocide Convention, Pepper-Smathers Senatorial Race

Government Departments and Agencies: Housing, State Department, Speaking Engagement

Monthly Report, May 1950 (5/31/50)

Congress and Congressional Legislation: Rent Control, Point Four Program, Strengthening Public Support for UN and Its Specialized Agencies, Home Rule for the District of Columbia, Federal Aid to Education, Barring from the Payroll Persons Practicing Discrimination

Miscellaneous: Housing, Speaking Engagements

Notes

MS: NAACP II: A-656, DLC.

1. Leslie Perry was an administrative assistant in the NAACP Washington bureau from 1942 to 1950. The day/month dates in brackets are added for editorial purposes.

APPENDIX 5

Statements and Testimonies

STATEMENTS AND TESTIMONIES OF NAACP REPRESENTATIVES BEFORE CONGRESSIONAL COMMITTEES, 1916–49

1916

(64) H144-19:[1] Intermarriage of Whites and Negroes in D.C. and Separate Accommodations in Street Cars for Whites and Negroes. H.R. 12+. Committee on the District of Columbia, U.S. House of Representatives, 64th Cong., 1st sess., February 11, 1916, *United States Congressional Committee Hearings*, 3–19 (Archibald H. Grimke).
(Digital Collection, Hearing-ID: HRG-1916-DCH-0005)[2]

1920

(66) H234-Pt.2-1: Part I, Segregation. Part II, Antilynching. H.J. Res. 75; H.R. 250; H.R. 4123; H.R. 11873. Committee on Judiciary, U.S. House of Representatives, 66th Cong., 2nd sess., January 15, 1920, *United States Congressional Committee Hearings*, 8–10 (Part I, Neval H. Thomas, representing the NAACP).
(Digital Collection, Hearing-ID: HRG-1920-HJH-0004)

(66) H234-Pt.2-1: Part I, Segregation. Part II, Antilynching. H.J. Res. 75; H.R. 259; H.R. 4123; H.R. 11873. Committee on Judiciary, U.S. House of Representatives, 66th Cong., 2nd sess., January 29, 1920, *United States Congressional Committee Hearings*, 32–36, 45–62, 62–66, 68–72 (Part II, Arthur B. Spingarn, 32–36; James Weldon Johnson, field secretary, NAACP, 45–62; Archibald H. Grimke, president, Boston NAACP branch, 62–66; Neval Thomas, member, NAACP executive board, 68-72)
(Digital Collection, Hearing-ID: HRG-1920-HCH-0004)

(66) H249-2: Apportionment of Representatives. H.R. 14498; H.R. 15021; H.R. 15158; H.R. 15217. Committee on Census, U.S. House of Representatives, 66th Cong., 3rd sess., December 28, 30, 1920, *United States Congressional Committee Hearings*, 35–42, 42–67, 68–80 (December 28, 1920, William Pickens, field secretary, NAACP, 35–42; December 30, 1920, Walter F. White, assistant secretary, NAACP, 42–67; James Weldon Johnson, secretary, NAACP, 68–80).
(Digital Collection, Hearing-ID: HRG-1920-HCH-0002)

1926

(69) S253-7: To Prevent and Punish the Crime of Lynching. S. 121. Subcommittee on S. 121, Committee on Judiciary, U.S. Senate, 69th Cong., 1st sess., February 16, 1926, *United States Congressional Committee Hearings*, 6–37 (James Weldon Johnson).
(Digital Collection, Hearing-ID: HRG-1926-SJS-0003)

1932

(72) H618-1: D.C. Appropriation Bill for 1933. H.R. 11361. Subcommittee on D.C. Appropriations, Committee on Appropriations, U.S. House of Representatives, 72nd Cong., 1st sess., March 3, 1932, *United States Congressional Committee Hearings*, 1123–35 (Emma F. G. Merritt, with John A. Lankford and Emory B. Smith, representing the Bethel Literary and Historical Association; William H. Lewis and W. W. Hall, representing the Federation of Civic Associations; Ethel H. Grubbs, representing the College Alumnae Club; Nellie H. Skinner, representing the Alpha Kappa Alpha Sorority; E. P. Lovett, representing the Kappa Alpha Psi Fraternity; Henry W. Sweet; and the Rev. E. R. Barnum).
(Not in the Digital Collection)

(72) S387-1: D.C. Appropriation Bill for 1933. H.R. 11361. Committee on Appropriations, U.S. Senate, 72nd Cong., 1st sess., May 18, 1932, *United States Congressional Committee Hearings*, 184–85 (Emma F. G. Merritt).
(Digital Collection, Hearing-ID: HRG-1932-SAP-0008)

1934

(73) S435-5-A: Punishment for the Crime of Lynching, Part 1. S. 1978. Subcommittee of the Committee on Judiciary, Committee on Judiciary, U.S. Senate, 73rd Cong., 2nd sess., February 20, 1934, *United States Congressional Committee Hearings*, 62–67 (Arthur B. Spingarn, chairman, NAACP National Legal Committee).[3]
(Digital Collection, Hearing-ID: HRG-1934-SJS-0002)

(73) S435-5-A: Punishment for the Crime of Lynching, Part 1. S. 1978. Subcommittee of the Committee on Judiciary, Committee on Judiciary. U.S. Senate, 73rd Cong., 2nd sess., February 20, 1934, *United States Congressional Committee Hearings*, 82–93 (Charles H. Houston, dean, Howard University Law School).
(Digital Collection, Hearing-ID: HRG-1934-SJS-0002)

(73) S435-5-A: Punishment for the Crime of Lynching, Part 1. S. 1978. Subcommittee of the Committee on Judiciary, Committee on Judiciary, U.S. Senate, 73rd Cong., 2nd sess., February 20, 1934, *United States Congressional Committee Hearings*, 93–102 (Herbert K. Stockton, member, NAACP National Legal Committee).
(Digital Collection, Hearing-ID: HRG-1934-SJS-0002)

1935

(74) H699-0: Economic Security Act. H.R. 3977; S. 1130+. Committee on Ways and Means, U.S. House of Representatives, 74th Cong., 1st sess., February 1, 1935, *United States Congressional Committee Hearings*, 796–98 (Charles H. Houston).
(Digital Collection, Hearing-ID: HRG-1935-WAM-0001)

(74) S476-0: Economic Security Act. S. 1130. Committee on Finance, U.S. Senate, 74rd Cong., 1st sess., February 9, 1935, *United States Congressional Committee Hearings*, 640–47 (Charles H. Houston).
(Digital Collection, Hearing-ID: HRG-1035-FS-0002)

1937

(75) H800-6: Federal Aid to the States for the Support of Public Schools. H.R. 5962. Committee on Education, U.S. House of Representatives. 75th Cong., 1st sess., April 1, 1937, *United States Congressional Committee Hearings*, 185–197 (Charles H. Houston).
(Digital Collection, Hearing-ID: HRG-1937-EDH-0002)

(75) S-547-5: Assistance to States and Territories in Providing Programs of Public Education. S. 419. Committee on Education and Labor, U.S. Senate, 75th Cong., 1st sess., July 10, 1937, *United States Congressional Committee Hearings*, 151–176 (Charles Hamilton H., Houston).
(Digital Collection, Hearing-ID: HRG-1937-EDS-0021)

(75) S592-0-C: Investigation of the Tennessee Valley Authority. Joint Committee on Investigation of the Tennessee Valley Authority, 75th Cong., 3rd sess., August 17, 18, 1945, United States Congressional Committee Hearings, 2347–54, 2356–90 (Charles H. Houston).
(Digital Collection, Hearing-ID: HRG-1938-ITV-0006)

1939

(76) S585-5: Federal Aid to Education Act of 1939. S. 1305. Subcommittee of Committee on Education and Labor, Committee on Education and Labor, U.S. Senate, 76th Cong., 1st sess., March 3, 1939, *United States Congressional Committee Hearings*, 178–184 (Charles H. Houston).
(Digital Collection, Hearing-ID: HRG-1939-EDS-0001)

1940

(76) H887-1: Selective Compulsory Military Training and Service. H.R. 10132. Committee on Military Affairs, U.S. House of Representatives, 76th Cong., 2nd sess., July 1, 1940, *United States Congressional Committee Hearings*, 589–90 (Charles H. Houston).
(Digital Collection, Hearing-ID: HRG-1940-MAH-0004)

(76) H920-0-B: Interstate Migration, Part 8. Washington, D.C. Hearings. Select Committee to Investigate Interstate Migration of Destitute Citizens, U.S. House of Representatives, 76th Cong., 2nd sess., July 29, 1940, *United States Congressional Committee Hearings*, 3154–74 (Charles H. Houston, associate counsel, NAACP; member, NAACP National Legal Committee, participating as a panel of testimony with Mrs. John J. O'Connor, chairman, Transient Committee, Council of Social Agencies; Mrs. Frank A. Linzel, chairman, Family Welfare Division, Council of Social Agencies; Miss Alice Elizabeth Junes, executive secretary, Washington Travelers' Aid Society; and Maj. Charles H. Dodd, Divisional Commander of the Salvation Army).
(Digital Collection, Hearing-ID: HRG-1940-IIM-0008)

(76) S620-10: Crime of Lynching. H.R. 801. Subcommittee on H.R. 801, Committee on Judiciary, 76th Cong., 2nd sess., February 7, 1940, *United States Congressional Committee Hear-*

ings, 75–95 (Arthur B. Spingarn and William H. Hastie, in the order in which they appeared. See also statement of Walter White).
(Digital Collection, Hearing-ID: HRG-1940-.SJS-0001)

(76) S622-3: Construction of Hospitals. S. 3230. Subcommittee on S. 3230, Committee on Education and Labor. U.S. Senate, 76th Cong., 2nd sess., March 19, 1940, *United States Congressional Committee Hearings*, 83–87 (Charles H. Houston).
(Digital Collection, Hearing-ID: HRG-1940-EDS-000)

1941

(77) S663-8: Educational Finance Act of 1941. S1313. Senate Subcommittee on S. 1313, Committee on Education and Labor, U.S. Senate, 77th Cong., 1st sess., April 29, 1941, *United States Congressional Committee Hearings*, 218–25 (Charles H. Houston).
(Digital Collection, Hearing-ID: HRG-1041-EDS-0008)

1943

(78) S708-5: Education Finance Act of 1943. S. 637. Committee on Education and Labor, U.S. Senate, 78th Cong., 1st sess., April 7, 1943, *United States Congressional Committee Hearings*, 239–42 (Charles H. Houston).
(Digital Collection, Hearing-ID: HRG-1943-EDS-0004)

(78) S716-14: Poll Taxes. H.R. 7. Committee on Judiciary, U.S. Senate, 78th Cong., 1st sess., October 26, 1943, *United States Congressional Committee Hearings*, 60–69 ("Statement submitted by Leslie Perry on behalf of the counsel for the National Association for the Advancement of Colored People on the constitutionality of H.R. 7." Dated October 1943. Of counsel: William H. Hastie, Leon A. Ransom, George W. Crockett, Jr.)
(Digital Collection, Hearing-ID: HRG-1943-SJS-0007)

1945

(79) H1091-1-A: Universal Military Training. H. Res. 465. Select Committee on Postwar Military Policy, U.S. House of Representatives, 79th Cong., 1st sess., June 6, 1945, *United States Congressional Committee Hearings*, 111–17 (William H. Hastie).
(Digital Collection, Hearing-ID: HRG-1945-PMP-0001)

(79) S759-4: Low-cost Housing in D.C. S. 13; S. 610. Subcommittee on Housing, Committee on District of Columbia, U.S. Senate, 79th Cong., 1st sess., March 7, 1945, *United States Congressional Committee Hearings*, 192–96 (William H. Hastie, representing the Washington, D.C., NAACP branch).
(Digital Collection, Hearing-ID: HRG-1945-DCS-0001)

(79) S765-3: Fair Employment Practice Act. S. 101; S. 459. Committee on Education and Labor, U.S. Senate, 79th Cong., 1st sess., March 14, 1945, *United States Congressional Committee Hearings*, 170–73 (William H. Hastie, as dean of Howard University Law School and chairman, Legal Committee, NAACP, March 14, 1945).
(Not in Digital Collection)

(79) S787-1-B: General Housing Act of 1945, Part 2: Revised. S. 1592. Committee on Banking and Currency, U.S. Senate, 79th Cong., 1st sess., December 12, 1945, *United States Congressional Committee Hearings*, 755–68 (William H. Hastie).
(Digital Collection, Hearing-ID: HRG-1945-BCS-0013)

1947

(80) H1151-4: Federal Aid to Education, Volume 1. H.R. 140; H.R. 156; H.R. 1722+. Subcommittee No. 1, Committee on Education and Labor, U.S. House of Representatives, 80th Cong., 1st sess., May 14, 1947, *United States Congressional Committee Hearings,* 401 (Thurgood Marshall, mentioned in testimony by Leslie Perry, NAACP administrative assistant working out of the NAACP Washington Bureau).
(Digital Collection. Hearing-ID: HRG-1947-EDL-0015)

(80) S840-1: Antidiscrimination in Employment. S. 984. Subcommittee on Antidiscrimination, Committee on Labor and Public Welfare, U.S. Senate, 79th Cong., 1st sess., June 11, 1947, *United States Congressional Committee Hearings,* 101–37 (A. Philip Randolph).
(Digital Collection, Hearing-ID: HRG-1947-LPW-0019)

1948

(80) S860-9: Universal Military Training. Committee on Armed Services, U.S. Senate, 80th Cong., 2nd sess., March 30, 1948, *United States Congressional Committee Hearings,* 662–68 (Jesse O. Dedmond, Jr.).
(Not in Digital Collection)

(80) S862-3: Regional Education Interstate Compact. S.J. Res. 191. A Subcommittee of the Committee on the Judiciary, U.S. Senate, 80th Cong., 2nd sess., March 13, 1948, *United States Congressional Committee Hearings,* 69–99 (Thurgood Marshall).
(Digital Collection, Hearing-ID: HRG-1948-SJS-0004)

1949

(80) H1173-A.68: Hearing on H.R. 6274 and H.R. 6401, to Provide for the Common Defense by Increasing the Strength of the Armed Forces of the U.S., and for Other Purposes. Committee Serial No. 265, U.S. House of Representatives, 80th Cong., 2nd sess., April 16, 1948, *United States Congressional Committee Hearings,* 6317–6327 (Jesse O. Dedmond, Jr.).
(Not in Digital Collection)

(81) S965-5: Civil Rights. S. 1725; S. 1734. Subcommittee of the Committee on Judiciary, U.S. Senate, 81st Cong., 1st sess., July 14, 1949, *United States Congressional Committee Hearings,* 30–36 (Thurgood Marshall).
(Digital Collection, Hearing-ID: HRG-1949-SJS-0021)

STATEMENTS AND TESTIMONIES OF LESLIE S. PERRY BEFORE CONGRESSIONAL COMMITTEES, 1943–50

1942

(77) Providing for full investigation of the manpower resources of the nation and the most advantageous use thereof in the war effort. S.R. 291. Subcommittee on Senate Resolution 291, U.S. Senate, 77th Cong., 2nd sess., November 28, 1942 (NAACP Statement, NAACP II: A-661, DLC).
(Not in Digital Collection)

1943

(78) S722-5: George Washington Carver National Monument. S. 37; S. 312; H.R. 647. Committee on Public Lands and Surveys (and House Committee on Public Lands), U.S. Senate, 78th Cong., 1st sess., February 5, 1943, *United States Congressional Committee Hearings*, 56.
(Digital Collection, Hearing-ID: HRG-1943-PLV-0005)

1945

(79) H1083-2: Proposed Amendments to the Fair Labor Standards Act, [Part 1].[4] Committee on Labor, U.S. House of Representatives, 79th Cong., 1st sess., November 1, 1945, *United States Congressional Committee Hearings*, 441–48.
(Not in Digital Collection)

(79) S758-3: Extending the Emergency Price Control and Stabilization Acts of 1942, as Amended. S.J Res. 30. Committee on Banking and Currency, U.S. Senate, 79th Cong., 1st sess., March 9, 1945, *United States Congressional Committee Hearings*, 359–60.
(Not in Digital Collection)

(79) S757-7: National War Agencies Appropriation Bill for 1946. H.R. 3368. Committee on Appropriations, U.S. Senate, 79th Cong., 1st sess., June 16, 1945, *United States Congressional Committee Hearings*, 150-52.
(Digital Collection, Hearing-ID: HRG-1945-SAP-0013)

(79) S777-2-A: Federal Aid for Education, Part 1. S. 181. Committee on Education and Labor, U.S. Senate, 79th Cong., 1st sess., January 31, 1945, *United States Congressional Committee Hearings*, 270–83.
(Not in Digital Collection)

1946

(79) H109-2-B: Universal Military Training, Part 2. H.R. 515. Committee on Military Affairs, U.S. House of Representatives, 79th Cong., 2nd sess., February 20, 1945, *United States Congressional Committee Hearings*, 940–48.
(Digital Collection, Hearing-ID: HRG-1946-MAH-0004)

1947

(80) H1149-1: Anti-Poll Tax Legislation. H.R. 29+. Subcommittee on Elections, Committee on House Administration, U.S. House of Representatives, 80th Cong., 1st sess., July 8, 1947, *United States Congressional Committee Hearings*, 125–33.
(Digital Collection, Hearing-ID: HRG-1947-ADH-0001)

(80) H1151-4: Federal Aid to Education, Volume 1. H.R. 140+. Subcommittee No. 1 (Education and Labor), Committee on Education and Labor, U.S. House of Representatives, 80th Cong., 1st sess., May 14, 1947, *United States Congressional Committee Hearings*, 394–405.
(Digital Collection, Hearing-ID: HRG-1947-EDL-0015)

(80) S815-1: Rent Control. S. 415+. Subcommittee on Housing and Rents, Committee on Banking and Currency, U.S. Senate, 80th Cong., 1st sess., February 7, 1947, *United States Congressional Committee Hearings*, 393–97.
(Digital Collection, Hearing-ID: HRG-1947-BCS-0001)

(80) S816-14: Amending Senate Rules Relating to Cloture. S. Res. 25+. Subcommittee on Rules, Committee on Rules and Administration, U.S. Senate, 80th Cong., 1st sess., February 4, 1947, *United States Congressional Committee Hearings*, 55–59.
(Not in Digital Collection)

(80) S819-1: Housing. S. 287, S. 866+. Committee on Banking and Currency, U.S. Senate, 80th Cong., 1st sess., March 19, 1947, *United States Congressional Committee Hearings*, 560–61 (Statement submitted for the record).
(Digital Collection, Hearing-ID: HRG-1947-BCS-0005)

(80) S823-2: Federal Aid to Education. S. 81+. Subcommittee on S. 81, S. 170, S. 199, and S. 472, Committee on Labor and Public Welfare, U.S. Senate, 80th Cong., 1st sess., April 28, 1947, *United States Congressional Committee Hearings*, 341–45.
(Digital Collection, Hearing-ID: HRG-1947-LPW-0007)

1948

(80) H1173-A-41: Subcommittee Hearings on S. 1641, to Establish the Women's Army Corps in the Regular Army, to Authorize the Enlistment and Appointment of Women in the Regular Navy and Marine Corps and the Naval and Marine Corps and the Naval and Marine Corps Reserve, and for Other Purposes. Subcommittee No. 3, Organization and Mobilization (Armed Services), U.S. House of Representatives, 80th Cong., 2nd sess., February 18, 1948, *United States Congressional Committee Hearings*, 5603–16.
(Digital Collection, Hearing ID: HRG-1948-ASH-0006)

(80) H1188-0-B: Department of Agriculture Appropriation Bill for 1949, Part 2. Subcommittee on Department of Agriculture Appropriations, Committee on Appropriations, U.S. House of Representatives, 80th Cong., 2nd sess., February 24, 1948, *United States Congressional Committee Hearings*, 717–19.
(Digital Collection, Hearing-ID: HRG-1948-HAP-0009)

(80) S853-0-A: National Stabilization, Part 1. S. 1873+. Committee on Banking and Currency, U.S. Senate, 80th Cong., 2nd sess., January 23, 1948, *United States Congressional Committee Hearings*, 394–95.
(Not in Digital Collection)

(80) S866-3: Study and Investigation of Housing, Part 5: Proceedings at Washington, D.C. S. 866; S. 1543. Joint Committee on Housing, U.S. Senate, 80th Cong., 2nd sess., January 19, 1948, *United States Congressional Committee Hearings*, 5479–82.
(Not in Digital Collection)

(80) S858-0-D: Poll Tax. H.R. 29. Committee on Rules and Administration, U.S. Senate, 80th Cong., 2nd sess., March 24, 1948, *United States Congressional Committee Hearings*, 216–19.
(Not in Digital Collection)

1949

(81) H1247-1: Housing Act of 1949. H.R. 4009; S. 1070. Committee on Banking and Currency, U.S. House of Representatives, 81st Cong., 1st sess., April 26, 1949, *United States Congressional Committee Hearings*, 218–32.
(Not in Digital Collection)

(81) HHad-T.9: Anti-Poll Tax. H.R. 3044; H.R. 3199. Subcommittee on Elections, Committee on Administration, U.S. House of Representatives, 81st Cong., 1st sess., May 5, 1949, *United States Congressional Committee Hearings*, 197–210.
(Digital Collection, Hearing-ID: HRG-1949-ADH-0020)

(81) H1269-1: Antilynching and Protection of Civil Rights. H.R. 115+. Subcommittee No. 3 (Judiciary), Committee on Judiciary, U.S. House of Representatives, 81st Cong., 1st sess., June 22, 1949, *United States Congressional Committee Hearings*, 145–50.
(Digital Collection, Hearing-ID: HRG- 1949-HJH-0017)

(81) S887-4: General Housing Legislation. H.R. 1376+. Subcommittee on Housing and Rents, Committee on Banking and Currency, U.S. Senate, 81st Cong., 1st sess., February 15, 1949, *United States Congressional Committee Hearings*, 735–44.
(Digital Collection, Hearing-ID: HRG-1949-BCS-0003)

1950

(81) H1299-0-C: Lobbying, Direct and Indirect, Part 6: Americans for Democratic Action. Select Committee on Lobbying Activities, U.S. House of Representatives, 81st Cong., 2nd sess., July 11, 1950, *United States Congressional Committee Hearings*, 71. (Although the Digital Collection lists this *Hearings* record with Perry, it properly belongs with the Roy Wilkins listings because the hearing on lobbying required the NAACP executive secretary, as chairman of the National Emergency Civil Rights Mobilization also, to come to the defense of the ADA's liberal activities versus those of the Communists.)
(Digital Collection, Hearing ID: HRG-1950-LAS-0006)

(81) S034-8: Extension of Rent Control. S. 3181; S. 3464; and S. 3492. Committee on Banking and Currency, U.S. Senate, 81st Cong., 2nd sess., April 26, 1950, *United States Congressional Committee Hearings*, 245 (statement submitted).
(Digital Collection, Hearing ID: HRG-1950-BCS-0009)

STATEMENTS OF CLARENCE MITCHELL JR. BEFORE CONGRESSIONAL COMMITTEES, 1934–54

1934

(73) S435-5-A: Punishment for the Crime of Lynching. S. 1978. Subcommittee of the Committee on Judiciary, Committee on Judiciary, U.S. Senate, 73rd Cong., 2nd sess., February 20, 1934, *United States Congressional Committee Hearings*, 168–69 (Baltimore, *Afro-American* newspaper).
(Digital Collection, Hearing-ID: HRG-34:-SJS-0002)

1944

(78) H1037-1-C: Production in Shipbuilding Plants. H. Res. 52. Subcommittee on Production in Shipbuilding Plants, Committee on Merchant Marine and Fisheries, House of Representatives, 78th Cong., 2nd sess., January 19, 1944, *United States Congressional Committee Hearings*, 1181–84.
(Digital Collection: Hearing-ID: HRG-1943-MMF-0020)

1947

(80) S817-O-B: Labor Relations Program, Part 3. S. 55; S.J. Res. 22. Committee on Labor and Public Welfare, U.S. Senate, 80th Cong., 1st sess., February 20, 1947, *United States Congressional Committee Hearings*, 1254–64.
(Digital Collection, Hearing-ID: HRG-1947-LPW-0004)

(80) S818-3: Labor-Federal Security Appropriation Bill for 1948. H.R. 2700. Committee on Appropriations, U.S. Senate, 80th Cong., 1st sess., April 17, 1947, *United States Congressional Committee Hearings*, 892–97.
(Digital Collection, Hearing-ID: HRG-1947-SAP-0005)

(80) S846-5: Nomination Confirmations—Jesse M. Donaldson. Department of Post Office; Paul Aiken; Nominations. Committee on Civil Service, U.S. Senate, 80th Cong., 1st sess., December 9, 1947, *United States Congressional Committee Hearings*, 6–15.
(Digital Collection, Hearing-ID: HRG-1947-SCV-0032)

1948

(80) H1197-1: Supplemental Federal Security Agency Appropriation Bill for 1949. Committee on Appropriations, U.S. House of Representatives, 80th Cong., 2nd sess., April 7, 1948, *United States Congressional Committee Hearings*, 724–35.
(Digital Collection, Hearing-ID: HRG-1948-HAP-0014)

(80) H1201-2: Investigation of GSI Strike. Special Subcommittee to Investigate GSI Strike, Committee on Education and Labor, U.S. House of Representatives, 80th Cong., 2nd sess., February 2, 1948, *United States Congressional Committee Hearings*, 158–61.
(Digital Collection, Hearing-ID: HRG-1948-EDL-0004)

1949

(81) H1242-0: National Labor Relations Act of 1949. H.R. 2032. Special Subcommittee on Labor-Management Relations Act, Committee on Education and Labor, U.S. House of Representatives, 81st Cong., 1st sess., March 15, 1949, *United States Congressional Committee Hearings*, 799–818.
(Digital Collection, Hearing-ID: HRG-1949-EDL-0003)

(81) H1246-0: Social Security Act Amendments of 1949, Part 2: Old-Age, Survivors, and Disability Insurance. H.R. 2893. Committee on Ways and Means, U.S. House of Representatives, 81st Cong., 1st sess., April 21, 1949, *United States Congressional Committee Hearings*, 2144–48.
(Digital Collection, Hearing-ID: HRG-1949-WAM-0004)

(81) H1253-8: Federal Fair Employment Practice Act. H.R. 4453. Special Subcommittee on Fair Employment Standards Act, Committee on Education and Labor, U.S. House of Representatives, 81st Cong., 1st sess., May 19, 1949, *United States Congressional Committee Hearings*, 293–300.
(Digital Collection, Hearing-ID: HRG-1949-EDL-0005)

(81) S898-5-B: Labor Relations, Part 6 and Appendix. Committee on Labor and Public Welfare, U.S. Senate, 81st Cong., 1st sess., February 23, 1949, *United States Congressional Committee Hearings*. Statement submitted to the Senate Committee on Labor and Public Welfare on the Repeal of the Taft-Hartley Law. February 10, 1949 (NAACP II: A-337, DLC).
(Digital Collection, Hearing-ID: HRG-1949-LPW-0007)

(81) S906-6: Fair Labor Standards Act Amendments of 1949. S. 653. Subcommittee on Fair Labor Standards Act Amendments, Committee on Labor and Public Welfare, U.S. Senate, 81st Cong., 1st sess., April 12, 1949, *United States Congressional Committee Hearings*, 225–33.
(Digital Collection, Hearing-ID: HRG-1949-LPW-0015)

1950

(81) H1291-3: Railway Labor Act Amendments. H.R. 7789. Committee on Interstate and Foreign Commerce, U.S. House of Representatives, 81st Cong., 2nd sess., June 7, 1950, *United States Congressional Committee Hearings*, 285–302 (Mitchell was accompanied by Joseph C. Waddy).
(Digital Collection, Hearing-ID: HRG-1950-FCH-0006)

(81) H1299: Lobbying, Direct and Indirect. H.Res. 298. Part 6: Americans for Democratic Action. Select Committee on Lobbying Activities, U.S. House of Representatives, 81st Cong., 2nd sess., July 12, 1950, *United States Congressional Committee Hearings*, 119 (Telegram of April 17, 1950, sent to Sen. Scott Lucas, majority leader, cosigned by Mitchell).
(Digital Collection, Hearing-ID: HRG-1950-LAS-0006)

(81) S932-5: Social Security Revisions. H.R. 6000. Part 3. Committee on Finance, U.S. Senate, 81st Cong., 2nd sess., March 15, 1950, *United States Congressional Committee Hearings*, 1928–32.
(Digital Collection, Hearing-ID: HRG-1950-FNS-0003)

(81) S949-1: To Amend the Railway Labor Act—Providing for Union Membership and Agreements for Deductions from Wages of Carrier Employees for Certain Purposes. Subcommittee on Railway Labor Act Amendments. S. 3295. Committee on Labor and Public Welfare, U.S. Senate, 81st Cong., 2nd sess., May 18, 1950, *United States Congressional Committee Hearings*, 242–309 (Mitchell was accompanied by Joseph C. Waddy).
(Digital Collection, Hearing-ID: HRG-1950-LPW-0003)

1951

(83) 1311-11: 1951 Extension of the Reciprocal Trade Agreements Act. H.R. 1612. Committee on Ways and Means, U.S. House of Representatives, 82nd Cong., 1st sess., January 25, 1951, *United States Congressional Committee Hearings*, 625 (Mitchell letter of January 25, 1951, supporting the agreement extension submitted to Robert L. Doughton, chair, House Ways and Means Committee).
(Digital Collection, Hearing-ID: HRG-1951-WAM-0001)

(82) H1313-7: India Emergency Act of 1951. H.R. 2692+. Committee on Foreign Affairs, U.S. House of Representatives, 82nd Cong., 1st sess., February 21, 1951, *United States Congressional Committee Hearings*, 103–05.
(Digital Collection, Hearing-ID: HRG-1951-FOA-0007)

(82) H1333-8: Amend the Constitution to Abolish the Electoral College System. H.J Res. 11; H.J. Res. 14; H.J. Res. 19+. Subcommittee No. 1 of the Committee on the Judiciary, U.S. House of Representatives, 82nd Cong., 1st sess., April 18, 1951, *United States Congressional Committee Hearings*, 310 (in conjunction with the submission of a statement opposing H.J. Res. 19, prepared at the request of the NAACP by John A. Davis, professor of political science, Ohio State University, 308–10).
(Digital Collection, Hearing ID: HRG-1951-HJH-0007)

(82) H1453-0.4: Universal Military Training. H.R. 1752. Committee on Armed Services, U.S. House of Representatives, 82nd Cong., 1st sess., March 8, 1951, *United States Congressional Committee Hearings*, 844–56.
(Digital Collection, Hearing-ID: HRG-1951-ASH-0010)

(82) S960-9: Universal Military Training and Service Act of 1951. S. 1. Preparedness Subcommittee, Committee on Armed Services, U.S. Senate, 82nd Cong., 1st sess., January 24, 1951, *United States Congressional Committee Hearings*, 861–73.
(Digital Collection, Hearing-ID: HRG-1951-SAS-0001)

(82) S961-4-A: Defense Housing Act, [Part 1]. S. 349. Committee on Banking and Currency, U.S. Senate, 82nd Cong., 1st sess., February 20, 1951, *United States Congressional Committee Hearings*, 477–81.
(Digital Collection, Hearing-ID: HRG-1951-BCS-0003)

(81) S963-2: Nomination of Millard Frank Caldwell, Jr., to be Federal Civil Defense Administrator. Committee on Armed Services, U.S. Senate, 82nd Cong., 2nd sess., January 15, 1951, *United States Congressional Committee Hearings*, 1–10.

(82) S964-3-A: Trade Agreements Extension Act of 1951. H.R. 1612. Part 1. Committee on Finance, U.S. Senate, 82nd Cong., 1st sess., February 27, 1951, *United States Congressional Committee Hearings*, 403 (Mitchell letter of February 27, 1951, supporting the agreement extension submitted to Walter F. George, chair, Senate Committee on Finance).
(Digital Collection, Hearing-ID: HRG-1951-FNS-0003)

(82) S996-11: Limitation of Debate in the Senate. S. Res. 41; S. Res. 52; S. Res. 105; S. Res. 203 (Resolutions Relative to Amending Senate Rule XXII Relating to Cloture). Committee on Rules and Administration, U.S. Senate, 82nd Cong., 1st sess., October 2, 1951, *United States Congressional Committee Hearings*, 34-63 (Walter White, NAACP executive secretary, testified, accompanied by Mitchell).
(Digital Collection, Hearing-ID: HRG-1951-RAS-0003)

1952

(82) H1368-5: Federal Assistance for School Construction and Aid to Education. H. Res. 73: A Resolution Authorizing the Committee on Education and Labor to Conduct Studies and Investigations Relating to Matters within its Jurisdiction. Special Subcommittee on Education and Labor, U.S. House of Representatives, 82nd Cong., 2nd sess., April 3, 1952, *United States Congressional Committee Hearings*, 352[5] (Mitchell letter, May 21, 1952, submitted for the record).
(Digital Collection, Hearing ID: HRG-1952-EDL-0003)

(82) H1454-0.2: Universal Military Training. H.R. 5904. Committee on Armed Services, U.S. House of Representatives, 82nd Cong., 2nd sess., January 30, 1952, *United States Congressional Committee Hearings*, 2982–99.
(Digital Collection, Hearing-ID: HRG-1952-ASH-0005)

(82) S1002-9: National Security Training Corps Act. S. 2441. Committee on Armed Services, U.S. Senate, 82nd Cong., 2nd sess., February 14, 1952, *United States Congressional Committee Hearings*, 502–10.
(Digital Collection, Hearing-ID: HRG-1952-SAS-0002)

(82) S1018-2: Discrimination and Full Utilization of Manpower Resources. S. 1732; S. 551. Subcommittee on Labor and Labor-Management Relations, Committee on Labor and Public Welfare, U.S. Senate, 82nd Cong., 2nd sess., April 17, 1952, *United States Congressional Committee Hearings*, 141–63 (Testified with Walter White).
(Digital Collection, Hearing-ID: HRG-1952-LPW-0006)

(82) S1021-1-A: Migratory Labor, Part I. S. 984. Subcommittee on Labor and Labor-Management Relations, Committee on Labor and Public Welfare, U.S. Senate, 82nd Cong., 2nd sess., February 27, 1952, *United States Congressional Committee Hearings*, 458–68. (Digital Collection, Hearing-ID: HRG-1952-LPW-0007)

(82) S1032-5: Washington Metropolitan Area Transit Problem. S. 1868; S.J. Res 135. Committee on Interstate and Foreign Commerce, U.S. Senate, 82nd Cong., 2nd sess., May 21, 1952, *United States Congressional Committee Hearings*, 8-9. Letter of May 16, 1952, from Mitchell to Sen. Edwin C. Johnson, chairman, Interstate and Foreign Commerce Committee, affirming the statement of Don S. Willner, Greater Area Council, American Veterans Committee (AVC), of May 21, 1952, which was made on behalf of the Washington, D.C. NAACP branch, 4–8. (Digital Collection, Hearing ID: HRG-1952-ISF-0010)

1953

(83) H1402-1-A: Labor-Management Relations, Part 6. Committee on Education and Labor, U.S. House of Representatives, 83rd Cong., 1st sess., March 31, 1953, *United States Congressional Committee Hearings*, 2055–78 (Testified with Walter White). (Digital Collection, Hearing-ID: HRG-1953-EDL-0006)

(83) H1409-7: Housing Amendments of 1953. S. 692. Committee on Banking and Currency, U.S. House of Representatives, 83rd Cong., 1st sess., June 23, 1953, *United States Congressional Committee Hearings*, 203–05. (Digital Collection, Hearing-ID: HRG-1953-BCU-0003)

(83) 83 HVet-T.1: To Amend the Veterans Readjustment Assistance Act of 1952, with Respect to the Number of Non-Veteran Students Required in Approved Schools. H.R. 2827. Subcommittee on Education and Training, Committee on Veterans Affairs, U.S. House of Representatives, 83rd Cong., 1st sess., July 30, 1953, *United States Congressional Committee Hearings*, 28–34. (Digital Collection, Hearing-ID-HRG-1953-VAH-0021)

(83) S1036-2-A: Nomination of Albert M. Cole, [Part 1].[6] Committee on Banking and Currency, U.S. Senate, 83rd Cong., 1st sess., March 2, 1953, *United States Congressional Committee Hearings*, 27–34. (Digital Collection, Hearing-ID: HRG- 1953-BCS-0002)

(83) S1037-14: First Independent Offices Appropriations, 1954. H.R 4663. Committee on Appropriations, U.S. House of Representatives, 83rd Cong., 1st. sess., April 25, 1953, *United States Congressional Committee Hearings*, 488–97. (Digital Collection, Hearing-ID: HRG-1953-SAP-0003)

(83) S1050-1-B: Taft-Hartley Act Revisions, Part 4 [continuation of hearings]. S. 225+. Committee on Labor and Public Welfare, U.S. Senate, 83rd Cong., 1st sess., April 29, 1953, *United States Congressional Committee Hearings*, 2186–96. (Digital Collection, Hearing-ID: HRG-1953-LPW-0005)

(83) S1046-1: Housing Act Amendments of 1953. S. 1621; S. 1848; S. 1864; S. 2103. Committee on Banking and Currency, U.S. Senate, 83rd Cong., 1st sess., June 18, 1953, *United States Congressional Committee Hearings*, 264–67. (Digital Collection, Hearing-ID: HRG-1953-BCS-0003)

(83) S1061-6-A: Statehood for Hawaii. Committee on Interior and Insular Affairs, U.S. Senate, 83rd Cong., 1st sess., July 9, 1953, *United States Congressional Committee Hearings*, 429–30. (Digital Collection, Hearing-ID: HRG-1953-INS-0052)

1954

(83) H1456-7: Amending Interstate Commerce Act (Segregation of Passengers). H.R. 563+. Committee on Interstate and Foreign Commerce, U.S. House of Representatives, 83rd Cong., 2nd sess., May 13, 1954, *United States Congressional Committee Hearings*, 39 (in conjunction with Lt. Thomas Williams, Camden, N. J., 40–55; Robert L. Carter, assistant special counsel, NAACP, with Mitchell, 96–118).
(Digital Collection, Hearing-ID: HRG-1954-FCH-0014)

(83) S1070-1: Taft-Hartley Act Revisions, Part 6. Committee on Labor and Public Welfare, U.S. Senate, 83rd Cong., 2nd sess., January 29, 1954, *United States Congressional Committee Hearings*, 3177–84.
(Digital Collection, Hearing-ID: HRG-1954-LPW-0001)

(83) S1072-6-A: Housing Act of 1954, Part 1. S. 2889; S. 2938; S. 2949. Committee of Banking and Currency, U.S. Senate, 83rd Cong., 2nd sess., March 25, 1954, *United States Congressional Committee Hearings*, 893–900.
(Digital Collection, Hearing-ID: HRG-1954-BCS-0004)

(83) S1078-2: Independent Offices Appropriations, 1955. H.R. 8583. Committee on Appropriations, U.S. Senate, 83rd Cong., 2nd sess., April 21, 1954, *United States Congressional Committee Hearings*, 686–92.
(Digital Collection, Hearing-ID: HRG-SAP-0009)

(83) S1079-8-C: President's Health Recommendations and Related Measures, Part 3. S. 2758+. Subcommittee on Health, Committee on Labor and Public Welfare, U.S. Senate, 83rd Cong., 2nd sess., April 21, 1954, *United States Congressional Committee Hearings*, 847–56.
(Digital Collection, Hearing-ID: HRG-1954-LPW-0016)

(83) S1085-1: Construction of School Facilities. S. 359; S. 2601; S. 2779. Subcommittee on Education, Committee on Labor and Public Welfare, U.S. Senate, 83rd Cong., 2nd sess., May 20, 1954, *United States Congressional Committee Hearings*, 248–52.
(Digital Collection, Hearing-ID: HRG-1954-LPW-0017)

(83) S1101-1: Commission on Civil Rights. S. 1; S. 535. Subcommittee of the Committee on Judiciary, Committee on Judiciary, U.S. Senate, 83rd Cong., 2nd sess., January 26, 1954, *United States Congressional Hearings*, 41–50, 75–77.
(Digital Collection, Hearing-ID: HRG-1954-SJS-0012)

STATEMENTS AND TESTIMONIES OF CLARENCE MITCHELL JR. BEFORE NONCONGRESSIONAL COMMITTEES, 1949–54

Statement on Minimum Wage for Western Union Messengers, December 28, 1949.

Statement before the President's Commission on Migratory Workers, July 13, 1950 (text in appendix).

Statement before the National Conference on Federal Aid to Education, November 13, 1950, Washington, D.C. (NAACP WB-70, DLC).

Presented Statement of Thurgood Marshall, NAACP Special Counsel, in Support of the Petition of the Pyramid Lake Paiute Tribe for the Right to Counsel of Their Choosing, January 3, 1952. (NAACP WB-3, DLC).

Statement before the President's Committee on Government Contract Compliance, June 9, 1952. (NAACP II: A-208, DLC [text in appendix]).

STATEMENTS OF WALTER WHITE BEFORE CONGRESSIONAL COMMITTEES, 1930–54

1930

(71) H573-4: Investigation of Communist Propaganda, Part 3: Volume No. 4. Special Committee to Investigate Communist Activities in the United States, U.S. House of Representatives, 71st Cong., 2nd sess., September 27, 1930, *United States Congressional Committee Hearings*, 199–204.
(Digital Collection, Hearing-ID: HRG-1930-ICA-0009)

(71) S331-12: Confirmation of Hon. John J. Parker to be Associate Justice of the Supreme Court of the U.S. Subcommittee of Committee on Judiciary, Committee on Judiciary, U.S. Senate, 71st Cong., 2nd sess., April 5, 1930, *United States Congressional Committee Hearings*, 74–79.
(Digital Collection, Hearing-ID: HRG-1930-SJS-0006)

1934

(73) S435-5-A: Punishment for the Crime of Lynching. S. 1978. Subcommittee of the Committee on Judiciary, Committee on Judiciary, U.S. Senate, 73rd Cong., 2nd sess., February 20, 1934, *United States Congressional Committee Hearings*, 9–37.
(Digital Collection, Hearing-ID: HRG-1934-SJS-0002)

1935

(74) S474-7: Punishment for the Crime of Lynching. S. 24. Subcommittee on S. 24, Committee on Judiciary, U.S. Senate, 74th Cong., 1st sess., February 14, 1935, *United States Congressional Committee Hearings*, 32–64.
(Digital Collection, Hearing-ID: HRG-1935-SJS-0001)

1936

(74) S519-2: U.S. Housing Act of 1936. S. 4424. Committee on Education and Labor, U.S. Senate, 74th Cong., 2nd sess., April 24, 1936, *United States Congressional Committee Hearings*, 207–09.
(Digital Collection, Hearing-ID: HRG-19360-EDS-0002)

1940

(76) S620-10: Crime of Lynching. H.R. 801. Subcommittee on H.R. 801, Committee on Judiciary, U.S. Senate, 76th Cong., 2nd sess., February 7, 1940, *United States Congressional Committee Hearings*, 51–74. (See also statements of William H. Hastie and Arthur B. Spingarn.)
(Digital Collection, Hearing-ID: HRG-1940-SJS-0001)

1942

(77) S699-8-A: Poll Taxes, [Part I]. S. 1280. Subcommittee of the Committee on Judiciary, Committee on Judiciary, U.S. Senate, 77th Cong., 2nd sess., July 30, 1942, *United States Congressional Committee Hearings*, 335–38.
(Digital Collection, Hearing-ID: HRG-1942-SJS-0010)

1943

(78) S718-0-P: Manpower (National War Service Bill), Part 16. S. 666. Committee on Military Affairs, U.S. Senate, 78th Cong., 1st sess., April 1, 1943, *United States Congressional Committee Hearings*, 641–58.
(Digital Collection, Hearing-ID: HRG-1943-MAS-0045)

1944

((78)H1032-3-A: To Prohibit Discrimination in Employment, Volume 1. H.R. 3986; H.R. 4004; H.R. 4005. Committee on Labor, U.S. House of Representatives, 78th Cong., 2nd sess., June 13, 1944, *United States Congressional Committee Hearings*, 163–69.
(Not in Digital Collection)

(78) S739-2: Fair Employment Practices Act. S. 2048. Subcommittee of Committee on Education and Labor, Committee on Education and Labor, U.S. Senate, 78th Cong., 2nd sess., September 8, 1944, *United States Congressional Committee Hearings*, 196-202 (letter, September 6, 1944, to Dennis Chavez, chairman, Senate Subcommittee on S. 2048, and statement).
(Digital Collection, Hearing-ID: HRG-1944-EDS-0004)

1945

(79) S763-0: Full employment Act of 1945 [Revised].[7] S. 380. Subcommittee on Full Employment, Committee on Banking and Currency, U.S. Senate, 79th Cong., 1st sess., August 29, 1945, *United States Congressional Committee Hearings*, 615–21.
(Digital Collection, Hearing-ID: HRG-1945-BCS-0010)

1948

(80) H1187-8 [same as S854-0-A]: Antilynching. H.R. 41+. Subcommittee No. 4, Committee on Judiciary, U.S. House of Representatives, 80th Cong., 2nd sess., February 4, 1948, *United States Congressional Committee Hearings*, 48–67.
(Digital Collection, Hearing-ID: HRG-1948-HJH-0001)

(80) S850-0-B: European Recovery Program, Part 2. Committee on Foreign Relations, U.S. Senate, 80th Cong., 2nd sess., January 27, 1948, *United States Congressional Committee Hearings*, 952–54.
(Digital Collection, Hearing-ID: HRG-1948-FOR-0004)

(80) S854-0-A [same as H1187-8]: Crime of Lynching. H.R. 4528; S. 42+. Subcommittee on S. 42, S. 1352, and S. 1465, Committee on Judiciary, U.S. Senate, 80th Cong., 2nd sess., February 2, 1948, *United States Congressional Committee Hearings*, 97–121.
(Digital Collection, Hearing-ID: HRG-1948-SJS-0001)

(80) S857-0-A: Veterans Hospital Program—Proposed Booker T. Washington Hospital—Continued. Subcommittee on Veterans Affairs, H. Con. Res. 54; S. 1414+. Committee on Labor and Public Welfare, U.S. Senate, 80th Cong., 2nd sess., February 3, 1948, *United States Congressional Committee Hearings*, 100–121.
(Digital Collection, Hearing-ID: HRG-1948-LPW-0004)

1951

(82) S992-3: Establishing of a Commission on Ethics in Government. Special Subcommittee on the Establishment of a Commission on Ethics in Government, Committee on Labor and Public Welfare, U.S. Senate, 82nd Cong., 1st sess., July 6, 1951, *United States Congressional Committee Hearings*, 394–400.
(Digital Collection, Hearing-ID: HRG-1951-LPW-0005)

(82) S996-11: Limitation of Debate in the Senate. S. Res. 41; S. Res. 52; S. Res. 105; S. Res. 203. Committee on Rules and Administration, U.S. Senate, 82nd Cong., 1st sess., October 2, 1951, *United States Congressional Committee Hearings*, 34–64 (accompanied by Clarence Mitchell Jr.).
(Digital Collection, Hearing-ID: HRG-1951-RAS-0001)

1952

(82) S1018-2: Discrimination and Full Utilization of Manpower Resources. S. 1732; S. 551. Subcommittee on Labor and Labor-Management Relations, Committee on Labor and Public Welfare, U.S. Senate, 82nd Cong., 2nd sess., April 17, 1952, *United States Congressional Committee Hearings*, 141–58 (White and Mitchell testified together).
(Digital Collection, Hearing-ID: HRG-1952-LPW-0006)

1954

(83) S1071-10: Antidiscrimination in Employment. S. 692. Committee on Labor and Public Welfare, U.S. Senate, 83rd Cong., 2nd sess., February 25, 1954, *United States Congressional Committee Hearings*, 176–91.
(Digital Collection, Hearing-ID: HRG-1954-LPW-0012)

STATEMENTS OF ROY WILKINS BEFORE CONGRESSIONAL COMMITTEES, 1932–54

1932

(72) S391-4: Federal Emergency Measures to Relieve Unemployment. S. 4076. Committee on Manufacturers, U.S. Senate, 72nd Cong., 1st sess., June 20, 1932, *United States Congressional Committee Hearings*, 20–21.
(Digital Collection, Hearing-ID: HRG-1932-MFS-0003)

1945

(79) S765-3: [same as (80) S840-1] Fair Employment Practice Act. S. 101; S. 459. Committee on Education and Labor, U.S. Senate, 79th Cong., 1st sess., March 14, 1945, *United States Congressional Committee Hearings,* 128–30.
(Digital Collection, Hearing-ID: HRG-1945-EDS-0003)

1947

(80) S840-1: [same as (79) S765-3] Antidiscrimination in Employment. S. 984. Subcommittee on Antidiscrimination, Committee on Labor and Public Welfare, U.S. Senate, 80th Cong., 1st sess., June 12, 1947, *United States Congressional Committee Hearings,* 182–95. (This was Walter White's testimony, as presented by Wilkins; see typescript with explanation in NAACP II: A-272, DLC.)
(Digital Collection, Hearing-ID: HRG-1947-LPW-0019)

1949

(81) S965-5: Civil Rights. S. 1725; S. 1734. Subcommittee of the Committee on Judiciary, U.S. Senate, 81st Cong., 1st sess., July 14, 1949, *United States Congressional Committee Hearings,* 36–40.
(Digital Collection, Hearing-ID: HRG-1949-SJS-0021)

OTHER RELATED STATEMENTS BEFORE CONGRESSIONAL COMMITTEES, 1947–54

1947

(80) H1173-0.28: Full Committee Hearings on Universal Military Training. Committee on Armed Services, U.S. House of Representatives, 80th Cong., 1st sess., June 11, 1947, *United States Congressional Committee Hearings,* 4363–66 (Rep. Adam Clayton Powell, Jr.).
(Digital Collection, Hearing-ID: HRG-1947-ASH-0068)

(80) S817-0-B: Labor Relations Program, Part 3. S. 55; S.J. Res. 22. Committee on Labor and Public Welfare, U.S. Senate, 80th Cong., 1st sess., February 20, 1947, *United States Congressional Committee Hearings,* 1275–1330 (Walter Reuther, president and director of Fair Practices and Antidiscrimination Department, UAW).
(Digital Collection, Hearing-ID: HRG-1947-LPW-0004)

1948

(80) H1187-8: Antilynching. H.R. 41+. Subcommittee No. 4, Committee on Judiciary, U.S. House of Representatives, 80th Cong., 2nd sess., February 4, 1948, *United States Congressional Committee Hearings,* 96–98 (Rep. Adam Clayton Powell, Jr.).
(Digital Collection, Hearing-ID: HRG-1948-HJH-0001)

(80) S859-0-A: Home Rule and Reorganization for D.C. S. 1968; H.R. 4902. Joint Committee on District of Columbia, U.S. Senate; U.S. House of Representatives, 80th Cong., 2nd sess., February 2, 1948, *United States Congressional Committee Hearings*, 3 (Rep. Adam Clayton Powell, Jr.).
(Digital Collection, Hearing-ID: HRG-1948-DCS-0001)

(80) S860-9: Universal Military Training. Committee on Armed Services, U.S. Senate, 80th Cong., 2nd sess., March 31, 1948, *United States Congressional Committee Hearings*, 685–94 (A. Philip Randolph, national treasurer, Committee against Jim Crow in the Military Service and Training; president, Brotherhood of Sleeping Car Porters).
(Digital Collection, Hearing-ID: HRG-1948-SAS-0003)

1949

(81) H1242-0: National Labor Relations Act of 1949. H.R. 2032. Special Subcommittee on Labor-Management Relations Act, Committee on Education and Labor, U.S. House of Representatives, 81st Cong., 1st sess., March 15, 1949, *United States Congressional Committee Hearings*, 1015–1117 (Theodore E. Brown on behalf of A. Philip Randolph, president, Brotherhood of Sleeping Car Porters).
(Digital Collection, Hearing-ID: HRG-1949-EDL-0003)

(81) H1253-8: Federal Fair Employment Practice Act. H.R. 4453. Special Subcommittee on Fair Employment Standards Act, Committee on Education and Labor, U.S. House of Representatives, 81st Congress, 1st sess., May 19, 1949, *United States Congressional Committee Hearings*, 300–09 (Lewis G. Hines, national legislative representative, AFL).
(Digital Collection, Hearing-ID: HRG-1949-EDL-0005)

(81) S885-1: Limitation on Debate in the Senate. Committee on Rules and Administration, U.S. Senate, 81st Cong., 1st sess., January 24, 1949, *United States Congressional Committee Hearings*, 1–6 (Sen. Carl Hayden).
(Digital Collection, Hearing-ID: HRG-1949-RAS-0001)

(81) S965-5: Civil Rights. S. 1725; S. 1734. Subcommittee of the Committee on the Judiciary, U.S. Senate, 81st Cong., 1st sess., July 14, 1949, *United States Congressional Committee Hearings*, 30–36 (Thurgood Marshall).
(Digital Collection, Hearing-ID: HRG-1949-SJS-0021)

1950

(81) H1299-0-C: Lobbying, Direct and Indirect, Part 6: Americans for Democratic Action. H. Res. 298. Select Committee on Lobbying Activities, 81st Cong., 2nd sess., July 11, 1950, *United States Congressional Committee Hearings*, 11–55 (Francis Biddle, national chairman, ADA).
(Digital Collection, Hearing-ID: HRG-1950-LAS-0006)

1951

(82) S996-11: Limitation on Debate in the Senate. S. Res. 41; S. Res. 52; S. Res. 105; S. Res. 203. Committee on Rules and Administration, U.S. Senate, 82nd Cong., 1st sess., October 2,

1951, *United States Congressional Committee Hearings*, 19–34 (Hubert H. Humphrey, U.S. senator, typescript of statement, NAACP WB-33, DLC).
(Digital Collection, Hearing-ID: HRG-1951-RAS-0003)

(82) S996-11: Limitation on Debate in the Senate. S. Res. 41; S. Res. 52; S. Res. 105; S. Res. 203. Committee on Rules and Administration, U.S. Senate, 82nd Cong., 1st sess., October 3, 1951, *United States Congressional Hearings*, 125–73 (Walter Reuther, president and director of Fair Practices and Antidiscrimination Department, UAW).
(Digital Collection, Hearing-ID: HRG-1951-RAS-0003)

(82) S996-11: Limitation on Debate in the Senate. S. Res. 41; S. Res. 52; S. Res. 105; S. Res. 203. Committee on Rules and Administration, U.S. Senate, 82nd Cong., 1st sess., October 3, 1951, *United States Congressional Committee Hearings*, 234–49 (Carl Hayden, U.S. senator).
(Digital Collection, Hearing-ID: HRG-1951-RAS-0003)

1952

(82) H1454-0.2: Universal Military Training. H.R. 5904. Committee on Armed Services, U.S. House of Representatives, 82nd Cong., 2nd sess., January 30, 1952, *United States Congressional Committee Hearings*, 2982–99 (Rep. Adam Clayton Powell, Jr.). (Text is in NAACP WB-184, DLC.)
(Digital Collection, Hearing-ID: HRG-1952-ASH-0005)

1953

(83) S1036-2-A: Nomination of Albert M. Cole, [Part 1].[8] Committee on Banking and Currency, U.S. Senate, 83rd Cong., 1st sess., March 2, 1953, *United States Congressional Committee Hearings*, 1–26. (Albert M. Cole)
(Digital Collection, Hearing-ID: HRG-1953-BCS-0002.)

(83) S1038-11: Treaties and Executive Agreements. S.J. Res. 1; S.J. Res. 43. Subcommittee on Constitutional Amendments, Committee on Judiciary, U.S. Senate, 83rd Cong., 1st sess., April 7, 1953, *United States Congressional Committee Hearings*, 823–900, 901–47. (Herbert Brownell, Jr.)
(Digital Collection, Hearing-ID: HRG-1953-SJS-0014)

1954

(83) H1456-7: Amending Interstate Commerce Act (Segregation of Passengers). H.R. 563+. Committee on Interstate and Foreign Commerce, U.S. House of Representatives, 83rd Cong., 2nd sess., May 13, 1954, *United States Congressional Committee Hearings*, 55–65 (Rep. Adam Clayton Powell, Jr., testimony January 28, 1953).
(Digital Collection, Hearing-ID: HRG-1954-FCH-0014)

Notes

1. The foundation of this search was *CIS U.S. Congressional Committee Hearings Index.*

2. This search was aided by LexisNexis Congressional Hearings Digital Collection.

3. Charles Hamilton Houston became NAACP special counsel in 1935 and served until 1940. (Report of the secretary for the September 1935 board meeting, minutes, October 14, 1940, EC.)

4. As inserted in *CIS U.S. Congressional Committee Hearings Index.*

5. Taken from a very preliminary list prepared by J. Francis Pohlhaus, counsel, NAACP Washington Bureau, for Robert L. Carter, NAACP general counsel, August 14, 1957 (NAACP WB-151, DLC).

6. As inserted in *CIS U.S. Congressional Committee Hearings Index.*

7. As inserted in *CIS U.S. Congressional Committee Hearings Index.*

8. As inserted in *CIS U.S. Congressional Committee Hearings Index.*

BIBLIOGRAPHY

PRIMARY SOURCES

Manuscript Collections

Henderson, Elmer W. Collection. Privately held by family, Washington, D.C.
LexisNexis Congressional Hearings Digital Collection
Mitchell, Clarence, Jr. Papers. Privately held by family, Baltimore, Md.
Papers of the National Association for the Advancement of Colored People (NAACP). Library of Congress, Washington, D.C.
President's Committee on Fair Employment Practice. Records. FEPC Papers. RG 228. National Archives, Washington, D.C.

Microform Publications

Kirby, John B., ed. *New Deal Agencies and Black America in the 1930's.* 25 reels. Frederick, Md.: University Publications of America, 1984.
Microfilm Record of Selected Documents of the Committee on Fair Employment Practice in the Custody of the National Archives. Glen Rock, N.J.: Microfilming Corporation of America, 1970.
National Association for the Advancement of Colored People Papers. Frederick, Md.: University Publications of America, 1982–.

Oral Histories

Selected interviews conducted by Denton L. Watson
Mitchell, Clarence, Jr. December 28, 1981; June 17, August 12, October 1, 1982; April 1, 9, October 1, 21, December 2, 1983; November 22, 1984, Baltimore, Md.
Mitchell, Juanita Jackson. April 7, 1982; August 3, 1983; April 20, 21, October 5, 6, 1984; March 8, 1985; July 10, 1987; September 27, 28, 1987; August 3, 1988, Baltimore Md.
Rauh, Joseph L., Jr. November 30, December 12, 1981; April 15, December 1, 1983; July 8, 1988; May 9, 1990, Washington, D.C.

Other Interviews and Oral Histories

Kingman, Harry L. "Citizenship in a Democracy: An Interview Conducted by Rosemary Levenson." University of California at Berkeley, Bancroft Library, Regional Oral History Office, 1973.
Mitchell, Clarence, Jr. Interview by Merl Reed, August 24, 1978, Baltimore, Md. In the private collection of Merl Reed.

Newspapers

Black Worker
Boston Globe
Bridgeport (Conn.) Post
Chicago Defender
Chicago Sun-Times
Cincinnati Enquirer
Guardian (London)
Minneapolis Star Tribune
New York Times
Philadelphia Inquirer
Pocono (Pa.) Record
San Antonio Express-News
San Francisco Chronicle
Tulsa World
Virginia Pilot (Virginia Beach, Va.)
Washington Post
Washington Times
Youngstown (Ohio) Vindicator

Government Reports and Documents (Published)

Annual Report of the Federal Trade Commission for the Fiscal Year Ended June 30, 1950. Washington, D.C.: U.S. Government Printing Office, 1951.

"Brief Sketch of the History and Functions of the Public Employment Service," n.d. (Previously, Acc. No. 64A–249, Box 6, National Records Center, NRA). RG 182, FEPC, National Archives and Records Administration, Washington, D.C.

Congressional Information Service (CIS), Serial Set 114887-2. Calendar No. 182. Defense Housing and Community Facilities Development Act of 1951. Report of the Committee on Banking and Currency to accompany S. 349. U.S. Senate, 82nd Cong., 1st sess. Report No. 189, 3/21/51.

———. Serial Set. Calendar No. 1187. Amending the Cloture Rule with Respect to the Number Required for Adoption of a Cloture Motion. Report of the Committee on Rules and Administration to accompany S. 203. U.S. Senate, 82nd Cong., 2nd sess. Report No. 1256, 2/25/52.

———. Serial Set 11675. Doc. 15. Employment and Economic Status of Negroes in the United States. Staff Report to the Subcommittee on Labor and Labor-Management Relations of the Committee on Labor and Public Welfare, February 18, 1953. U.S. Senate, 82nd Cong., 2nd sess.

———. State and Municipal Fair Employment Legislation. Staff Report to the Subcommittee on Labor and Labor-Management Relations of the Committee on Labor and Public Welfare, February 20, 1953. U.S. Senate, 82nd Cong., 2nd sess.

Congressional Record. 80th Cong., 2nd sess., 1948. Vol. 72.

———. 81st Cong., 1st sess., 1949. Vol. 95.

———. 81st Cong., 2nd sess., 1950. Vol. 96.

Congressional Record Daily Digest. 81st Cong., 1st sess., 1949. Vol. 95.

Fair Employment Practice Committee. *First Report, July 1943–December 1944*. Washington, D.C.: Government Printing Office, 1945.

———. *Final Report*. Washington, D.C.: Government Printing Office, 1946.

Mitchem, James A. "Fair Employment Practices Legislation: A Summary of Its History and Development with Statements on Both Sides." Library of Congress Legislative Reference Service, Government Section, 1952, a copy in NAACP II: A-264, DLC.

"The Public Employment Service, an Instrument for Full Employment," September 21, 1945. (Previously, Acc. No. 64A-249, box 6, National Records Center, NRA). RG 182, FEPC, National Archives and Records Administration, Washington, D.C.

Public Papers of the Presidents of the United States, 1945–54. Washington, D.C.: Government Printing Office, 1960–66.

U. S. Congress. House of Representatives. Subcommittee on Appropriations. *Supplemental Federal Security Appropriations for 1949*. 80th Cong., 2nd sess. Washington, D.C.: Government Printing Office, 1948.

U. S. Congress. Senate. Committee on Appropriations. H.R. 2700. *Labor-Federal Security Appropriations Bill for 1948*. 80th Cong., 1st sess. Washington, D.C.: Government Printing Office, 1947.

———. Committee on Armed Services. S. 2441. *National Security Training Corps Act*. 82nd Cong., 2d sess. Washington, D.C.: Government Printing Office, 1952.

Other Published Primary Sources

NAACP. *Annual Reports*, 1914, 1915, 1916, 1917, 1918, 1922, 1923, 1935, 1947, 1948, 1949, 1950, 1951, 1952, 1953, and 1954. New York: NAACP.

Scott, Foresman. *Robert's Rules of Order*. 1990 ed. Glendale, Ill.: Scott, Foresman Company, 1990.

SECONDARY SOURCES

Books and Articles

Adams, Stephen B., and Orville R. Butler. *Manufacturing the Future: A History of Western Electric*. Cambridge: Cambridge University Press, 1999.

Alexander, Raymond Pace. "Recent Trends in the Law of Racial Segregation on Public Carriers." *National Bar Journal* 5 (December 1947): 401–13.

"The American Negro in World War I and World War II." *Journal of Negro Education* 12 (Summer 1943): 263–578.

Anderson, Jervis. *A. Philip Randolph: A Biographical Portrait*. New York: Harcourt Brace Jovanovich, 1972.

Anderson, J. W. *Eisenhower, Brownell, and the Congress: The Tangled Origins of the Civil Rights Bill of 1956–57*. Tuscaloosa: University of Alabama Press, 1964.

Ashby, Warren. *Frank Porter Graham: A Southern Liberal*. Winston-Salem, N.C.: John F. Blair, 1980.

Askin, Kelly D., and Dorean M. Koenig, eds. *Women and International Human Rights Law*. Vol. 1. Ardsley, N.Y.: Transnational Publishers, 1999.

"Attitude of National Association for Advancement of Colored People in Regard to Organized Labor." *Monthly Labor Review* (July–December 1924): 678–79.
"Back the Tolan Committee." *Nation*, January 2, 1943, 6–7.
Bailey, Lloyd H. "Organized Labor and Racial Minorities." *Annals of the American Academy of Political and Social Sciences* 274 (March 1951): 101–7.
Bailey, Robert. "Theodore G. Bilbo and the Fair Employment Practice Controversy: A Southern Senator's Reaction to a Changing World." *Journal of Mississippi History* 42 (1980): 27–42.
Bartley, Numan V. *The Rise of Massive Resistance: Race and Politics in the South during the 1950s.* Baton Rouge: Louisiana State University Press, 1969.
Baxter, Julia E. "New York State Bars Economic Jim Crow." *Crisis* 52 (April 1945): 98–99, 116.
Bell, Daniel. "Taft-Hartley, Five Years After." *Fortune* 46 (July 1952): 171–72.
Bell, Derrick A., Jr. *Race, Racism, and American Law.* Canada: Little, Brown and Company Law Book Division, 1980.
Bendiner, Robert. "Battle of Filibuster: New Round Opens." *New York Times Magazine*, September 14, 1952, 17, 26, 28.
Bennett, Lerone, Jr. *Confrontation: Black and White.* Chicago: Johnson Publishing, 1965.
Benton, William. "Need for a Suitable Cloture Rule." *Crisis* 59 (February 1952): 83–88.
Berman, William C. *The Politics of Civil Rights in the Truman Administration.* Columbus: Ohio State University Press, 1970.
Bernstein, Barton J., ed. *Politics and Policies of the Truman Administration.* Chicago: Quadrangle Books, 1970.
Billington, Monroe. "Freedom to Serve: The President's Committee on Equality of Treatment and Opportunity in the Armed Forces, 1949–1950." *Journal of Negro History* 51 (October 1966): 262–374.
Binder, Sarah A., and Steven S. Smith. *Politics or Principle? Filibustering in the United States Senate.* Washington, D.C.: Brookings Institution Press, 1997.
Binkin, Martin, and Mark J. Eitelberg, with Alvin J. Schexnider and Marvin M. Smith. *Blacks and the Military.* Washington, D.C.: Brookings Institution, 1982.
Blantz, Thomas E. *A Priest in Public Service: Francis J. Haas and the New Deal.* Notre Dame, Ind.: University of Notre Dame Press, 1982.
Bluford, Lucile. "Missouri 'Shows' the Supreme Court." *Crisis* 46 (August 1939): 231–32, 242, 246.
Bontecou, Eleanor. *Federal Loyalty-Security Program.* Ithaca, New York: Cornell University Press, 1953.
Borklund, Carl W. *Men of the Pentagon.* New York: Praeger, 1966.
Brazeal, Brailsford. *The Brotherhood of Sleeping Car Porters: Its Origin and Development.* New York: Harper and Brothers, 1946.
———. "The Present Status and Programs of Fair Employment Practices Commissions—Federal, State and Municipal." *Journal of Negro Education* 20 (Summer 1951): 378–97.
Breezer, Bruce. "Black Teachers' Salaries and the Federal Courts before *Brown v. Board of Education:* One Beginning for Equity." *Journal of Negro Education* 55 (Spring 1986): 200–213.
Broady, T. Rupert. "Poll Tax: Symbol of Oppression." *Crisis* 48 (June 1941): 192, 204–5.
Brock, Clifton. *Americans for Democratic Action: Its Role in National Politics.* Washington, D.C.: Public Affairs Press, 1962.
Brooks, Thomas R. *Walls Come Tumbling Down: A History of the Civil Rights Movement, 1940–1970.* Englewood Cliffs, N.J.: Prentice-Hall, 1974.
Brownell, Herbert, and John P. Burke. *Advising Ike: The Memoirs of Attorney General Herbert Brownell.* Lawrence: University Press of Kansas, 1993.
Burdette, Franklin L. *Filibustering in the Senate.* Princeton, N.J.: Princeton University Press, 1940.

Burk, Robert F. *The Eisenhower Administration and Black Civil Rights.* Knoxville: University of Tennessee Press, 1984.

Burkart, J. Austin. "Yonder Sits the Rocking-Chair." *Crisis* 59 (December 1952): 619–25.

Caplan, Marvin. "Virginia Schools: A Study in Frustration." *Crisis* 58 (January 1951): 5–11, 61–63.

Carr, Robert K. *Federal Protection of Civil Rights: Quest for a Sword.* Ithaca, N.Y.: Cornell University Press, 1947.

Carter, Robert L. "Legal Background and Significance of the May 17th Decision." *Social Problems* 2 (April 1955): 215.

"Census." *Jet,* July 21, 1997, 18.

Chen, Anthony S. "The Strange Career of Federal Fair Employment Policy, 1941–1963." Paper presented at the Miller Center for Public Affairs, University of Virginia, Charlottesville, May 26, 2001.

———. "Rethinking the Origins of Affirmative Action in Employment, 1941–1972." Paper presented at the Graduate Student Research Conference, Institute for Labor and Employment, University of California at Santa Cruz, January 9, 2002.

"The Civil Rights Mobilization." *Crisis* 57 (February 1950): 100–101.

Clark, Kenneth B. "The Civil Rights Movement: Momentum and Organization." *Daedalus* 95 (Winter 1966): 240–47.

The Commonweal. The week of April 4, 1947.

Congress and the Nation, 1945–1964. Washington, D.C.: Congressional Quarterly, 1965.

Congressional Quarterly Log for Editors. Washington, D.C.: Congressional Quarterly News Features, 1948.

Congressional Quarterly Weekly Report. Washington, D.C.: Congressional Quarterly News Features, 1951–54.

"The Country's Defense." *Guardian,* reprinted in *Crisis* 47 (December 1940): 387.

"Crisis in the Making: U.S. Negroes Tussle with Issue . . . of Resisting Draft Law Because of Racial Segregation." *Newsweek,* June 7, 1948, 28–29.

Cronon, Edmund D. *Black Moses: The Story of Marcus Garvey and the Universal Negro Improvement Association.* Madison: University of Wisconsin Press, 1957.

Crosby, Alexander L. "America's Segregated Cities." *Negro Digest* 9 (August 1951): 82–94.

Current, Gloster B. "Martyr for a Cause." *Crisis* 59 (February 1952): 73–81, 133–34.

Dabney, Virginius. "Shall the South's Poll Tax Go?" *New York Times Magazine,* February 12, 1939, 9, 20.

Dalfiume, Richard M. *Desegregation of the U.S. Armed Forces: Fighting on Two Fronts, 1939–53.* Columbia: University of Missouri Press, 1969.

"Dangerous Federal School Aid." *Crisis* 44 (February 1937): 41–42, 50.

Daniel, Clete. *Chicano Workers and the Politics of Fairness: The FEPC in the Southwest.* Austin: University of Texas Press, 1991.

Daniels, Roger. *Prisoners without Trial: Japanese Americans in World War II.* New York: Hill and Wang, 1993.

Davis, John A. "Negro Employment: A Progress Report." *Fortune,* July 1952, 102–3, 158, 161–62.

Davis, John P. "NRA Codifies Wage Slavery." *Crisis* 41 (October 1934): 298–99, 304.

———. "The Maid-Well Garment Case." *Crisis* 41 (December 1934): 356–57.

Delgado, Richard. "Explaining the Rise and Fall of African American Fortunes—Interest Convergence and Civil Rights Gains." *Harvard Civil Rights–Civil Liberties Law Review* 37 (2002): 369–87.

Dierenfield, Bruce J. *Keeper of the Rules: Congressman Howard W. Smith of Virginia.* Charlottesville: University Press of Virginia, 1987.

"Discrimination by Labor Union Bargaining Representatives against Racial Minorities." *Yale Law Journal* 56 (April 1947): 731–37.

"Disenfranchisement by Means of the Poll Tax." *Harvard Law Review* 53 (February 1940): 645–52.

Dittmer, John. "Rising Expectations." In *The American Civil Rights Movement: Readings and Interpretations*, ed. Raymond D'Angelo, 78–92. Blacklick, Ohio: McGraw-Hill/Dushkin, 2001.

DuBois, W. E. B. "Segregation." *Crisis* 41 (January 1934): 20.

———. "The NAACP and Race Segregation." *Crisis* 41 (February 1934): 52–53.

Duram, James C. *A Moderate among Extremists: Dwight Eisenhower and the School Desegregation Crisis.* Chicago: Nelson-Hall Publishers, 1981.

Durr, Virginia Foster. *Outside the Magic Circle: The Autobiography of Virginia Foster Durr.* Tuscaloosa: University of Alabama Press, 1985.

Eby, Kermit. "The Labor Issue." *Current History* 27 (October 1954): 235–40.

Finkle, Lee. *Forum for Protest: The Black Press during World War II.* Rutherford, N.J.: Farleigh Dickinson University Press, 1975.

Fite, Gilbert C. *Richard R. Russell, Jr.: Senator from Georgia.* Chapel Hill: University of North Carolina Press, 1991.

Fleming, Harold C. "Resistance Movements and Racial Desegregation." *Annals of the American Academy of Political and Social Sciences* 304 (March 1956): 44–52.

Flemion, Jess, and Colleen M. O'Connor, eds. *Eleanor Roosevelt: An American Journey.* San Diego, Calif.: San Diego State University Press, 1987.

Foner, Philip S. *Organized Labor and the Black Worker, 1619–1973.* New York: Praeger, 1974.

Foner, Philip S., and Ronald L. Lewis. *The Black Worker from the Founding of the CIO to the AFL-CIO Merger, 1936–1955.* The Black Worker: A Documentary History from Colonial Times to the Present 7. Philadelphia: Temple University Press, 1983.

Forster, Arnold, and Benjamin R. Epstein. *Danger on the Right.* New York: Random House, 1964.

"Fortune Management Poll." *Fortune* 27 (February 1943): 144.

Franklin, John Hope. *From Slavery to Freedom: A History of African Americans.* Boston: McGraw-Hill, 2000.

Friend, Bruce I. *Guide to the Microfilm Record of Selected Documents of the Committee on Fair Employment Practice in the Custody of the National Archives.* Glen Rock, N.J.: Microfilming Corporation of America, 1970.

Galloway, George B. *History of the House of Representatives.* 2nd ed. New York: Thomas Y. Crowell, 1976.

———. *Limitation of Debate in the United States Senate.* Washington, D.C.: Library of Congress Legislative Reference Service, 1951.

Gardner, Michael R. *Harry Truman and Civil Rights: Moral Courage and Political Risks.* Carbondale: Southern Illinois University Press, 2002.

Garfinkel, Herbert. *When Negroes March: The March on Washington Movement in the Organizational Politics for FEPC.* Glencoe, Ill.: Free Press, 1959.

Garvey, Amy Jacques. *Garvey and Garveyism.* New York: Macmillan, 1970.

Gelfand, Mark. *A Nation of Cities: The Federal Government and Urban America, 1933–75.* New York: Oxford University Press, 1975.

Geyer, Lee E. "The Poll Tax Can Be Abolished." *Crisis* 48 (February 1941): 41, 60–61.

Glenn, A. L., Sr. *History of the National Alliance of Postal Employees, 1913–1955.* Washington, D.C.: National Alliance of Postal Employees, 1955.

Gloster, Hugh M. "The Southern Revolt." *Crisis* 55 (May 1948): 137–39, 155–56.

Godson, Ray. *American Labor and European Politics: The AFL as a Transnational Force.* New York: Crane, Russak, 1976.

Gooden, Karen Lesla Williams. *A Cross Borne: A Biography of Judge James Franklyn Bourne, Jr.* Marceline, Mo.: Walsworth Publishing, 1995.

Granger, Lester B. "The President, the Negro, and Defense." *Opportunity* 19 (July 1941): 204–7, 220.

Grant, Philip A. "Illinois Congressional Leaders, 1945–1984." *Illinois History: A Magazine for Young People* 47 (April 1994): 49–51.

Grantham, Dewey W. *Hoke Smith and the Politics of the New South.* Baton Rouge: Louisiana State University Press, 1958.

Graves, John Temple. "The Southern Negro and the War Crisis." *Virginia Quarterly Review* 18 (Autumn 1942): 500–517.

Green, Ben. *Before His Time: The Untold Story of Harry T. Moore, American's First Civil Rights Martyr.* New York: Free Press, 1999.

Greenberg, Jack. *Crusaders in the Courts: How a Dedicated Band of Lawyers Fought for the Civil Rights Revolution.* New York: Basic Books, 1994.

Gregory, T. Montgomery. "The 'Jim Crow' Car." *Crisis* 11 (December 1915): 87–89.

———. "The 'Jim Crow' Car." *Crisis* 12 (January 1916): 137–38.

———. "The 'Jim Crow' Car." *Crisis* 12 (February 1916): 195–98.

Gressman, Eugene. "The Unhappy History of Civil Rights Legislation." *Michigan Law Review* 50 (1952): 1323–58.

Hall, Kermit L., ed. *The Oxford Companion to the Supreme Court of the United States.* New York: Oxford University Press, 1992.

Hamilton, Charles V. *Adam Clayton Powell, Jr.: The Political Biography of an American Dilemma.* New York: Atheneum, 1991.

Harrison, William. "First Martyr to American Independence." *Crisis* 54 (December 1947): 386, 397–98.

Hastie, William H. "A Look at the NAACP." *Crisis* 46 (September 1939): 262–64, 274.

Haynes, George H. *Senate of the United States, Its History and Practice.* New York: Russell and Russell, 1960.

Hedgeman, Anna Arnold. "Make the FEPC Permanent." Letters to the Editor. *Nation* 159 (July 15, 1944): 83.

Hill, Herbert. *Black Labor and the American Legal System: Race, Work, and the Law.* Madison: University of Wisconsin Press, 1985.

Horne, Frank. "A Long Ways from Home: Review of *The Negro Ghetto,* by Robert C. Weaver." *Crisis* 55 (August 1948): 244, 253.

Houston, Charles H. "Educational Inequalities Must Go!" *Crisis* 42 (October 1935): 300–301, 316.

———. "Cracking Closed University Doors." *Crisis* 42 (December 1935): 364, 370, 372.

———. "Foul Employment Practice on the Rails." *Crisis* 56 (October 1949): 269–71, 284–85.

Houston, Charles H., and John P. Davis. "TVA: Lily-White Reconstruction." *Crisis* 41 (October 1934): 290–91, 311.

Hughes, Langston. *Fight for Freedom: The Story of the NAACP.* New York: W. W. Norton, 1962.

Hunt, A. Bruce. "The Proposed Fair Employment Practice Act: Facts and Fallacies." *Virginia Law Review* 32 (December 1945): 1–38.

Hunt, D. Bradford. "How Did Public Housing Survive the 1950s?" *Journal of Policy History* 17, no. 2 (2005): 193–216.

Hutchinson, Dennis J. "Unanimity and Desegregation: Decisionmaking in the Supreme Court, 1948–58." *Georgetown Law Journal* 68 (1979): 1–96.

Hyman, Sidney. *The Lives of William Benton.* Chicago: University of Chicago Press, 1969.
Ickes, Harold. "To Have Jobs or to Have Not." *Negro Digest* 4 (January 1946): 73.
Indritz, Phineas. "Racism in the Nation's Capital." *Crisis* 59 (October 1952): 355–57.
"In the Second Year." *Business Week,* January 11, 1947, 86, 88.
Ivey, John E., Jr. "Facts about Regional Education." *Crisis* 57 (November 1950): 628–32, 674–75.
Ivy, James W. "Editors Speak on the Senate Filibuster." *Crisis* 56 (June 1949): 170–73, 189–90.
Johnson, Clarence R. "Negro Labor in Public Housing." *Crisis* 48 (February 1941): 44–45, 61–62.
Johnson, Ernest E. "Reconversion: America's No. One Problem." *Crisis* 52 (October 1945): 282–83, 301–2.
Kahn, Elinor. "Abolition of the Poll Tax, a War Measure: The Case for Immediate Passage of Anti–Poll Tax Legislation Pending in Congress." Memorandum no. 3, August 20, 1942, National Federation for Constitutional Liberties, New York.
Katznelson, Ira, Kim Geiger, and Daniel Kryder. "Limiting Liberalism: The Southern Vote in Congress, 1933–1950." *Political Science Quarterly* 108 (Summer 1993): 282–306.
Kellogg, Charles Flint. *NAACP: A History of the National Association for the Advancement of Colored People,* vol. 1. Baltimore, Md.: Johns Hopkins University Press, 1967.
Kemper, Donald. *Decade of Fear: Senator Hennings and Civil Liberties.* Columbia: University of Missouri Press, 1965.
Kenneally, James J. "Black Republicans during the New Deal: The Role of Joseph W. Martin, Jr." *Review of Politics* 55, no.1 (1993): 117–39.
Kennedy, Stetson. *Jim Crow Guide to the U.S.A.* Westport, Conn.: Greenwood Press, 1959.
Kersten, Andrew E. *Race, Jobs, and the War: The FEPC in the Midwest, 1941–46.* Urbana: University of Illinois Press, 2000.
Kesselman, Louis C. *The Social Politics of FEPC: A Study in Reform Pressure.* Chapel Hill: University of North Carolina Press, 1948.
Key, V. O. *Southern Politics in State and Nation.* New York: Knopf, 1949.
King, Desmond S. *Separate and Unequal: Black Americans and the U.S. Federal Government.* New York: Oxford University Press, 1995.
Kirkendall, Richard. "Tom C. Clark." In *The Justices of the United States Supreme Court, 1789–1969: Their Lives and Major Opinions,* ed. Leon Friedman and Fred L. Israel, 4:2665–77. New York: Chelsea House Publishers, 1969.
Kizer, George A. "Federal Aid to Education: 1945–1963;" *History and Education Quarterly* 10 (Spring 1970): 84–102.
Klarman, Michael J. "*Brown,* Racial Change, and the Civil Rights Movement." *Virginia Review* 80 (February 1994): 7–150.
———. "How *Brown* Changed Race Relations: The Backlash Thesis." *Journal of American History* 91 (June 1994): 81–118.
———. *From Jim Crow to Civil Rights: The Supreme Court and the Struggle for Racial Equality.* New York: Oxford University Press, 2004.
Klinker, Philip A., and Rogers Smith. *The Unsteady March: The Rise and Decline of Racial Equality in America.* Chicago: University of Chicago Press, 1999.
Kluger, Richard. *Simple Justice: The History of "Brown v. Board of Education" and Black America's Struggle for Equality.* New York: Random House, 1975.
Konvitz, Milton R. *Constitution and Civil Rights.* New York: Columbia University Press, 1946.
Kotlowski, Dean J. "Richard Nixon and the Origins of Affirmative Action." *Historian* 60, no. 3 (Spring 1998): 523–41.
Kryder, Daniel. *Divided Arsenal: Race and the American State during World War II.* New York: Cambridge University Press, 2000.

Kurland, Philip B., and Gerhard Casper, eds. *Landmark Briefs of the Supreme Court of the United States: Constitutional Law*, 80 vols. Arlington, Va.: University Publications of America, 1975.

Kytle, Calvin. "A Long Dark Night for Georgia?" *Harper's*, September 1948, 55–64.

Lash, Joseph P. *Eleanor and Franklin: The Story of Their Relationship Based on Eleanor Roosevelt's Private Papers*. New York: W. W. Norton, 1971.

Lautier, Louis. "Jim Crow in the Nation's Capital." *Crisis* 47 (April 1940): 107, 125.

Lawson, Steven F. *Black Ballots: Voting Rights in the South, 1944–1969*. New York: Columbia University Press, 1976.

Lee, R. Alton. *Truman and Taft-Hartley: A Question of Mandate*. Westport, Conn.: Greenwood Press, 1966.

Lee, Ulysses. *The Employment of Negro Troops: United States Army in World War II*. Washington, D.C.: Government Printing Office, 1966.

Lemmon, Sarah M. "Transportation Segregation in the Federal Courts since 1865." *Journal of Negro History* 38 (April 1953): 174–93.

Lewinson, Paul. *Race, Class, & Party: A History of Negro Suffrage and White Politics in the South*. New York: Russell and Russell, 1963.

Lichtenstein, Nelson. "Walter Reuther in Black and White: A Rejoinder to Herbert Hill." *New Politics* 7, no.2 (Winter 1999): 133–47.

"Lobbyists: Four Negroes Working behind the Scenes to Influence Congress on Civil Rights." *Ebony*, July 1950, 25–28.

Long, Herman H. *Segregation in Interstate Railway Coach Travel*. Nashville, Tennessee: Race Relations Department, American Missionary Association, Board of Home Missions, Congressional Christian Churches, 1952.

———. "Racial Desegregation in Railroad and Bus Transportation." *Journal of Negro Education* 23 (Summer 1954): 214–21.

"Loyalty Check." *New Republic* 115 (December 30, 1946): 898.

Lucas, Scott W. "Is There Any Hope for Civil Rights?" *Negro Digest* 8 (April 1950): 79–82.

MacGregor, Morris J., Jr. *Integration of the Armed Forces, 1940–1965*. Washington, D.C.: Center of Military History, United States Army, 1981.

Marshall, Thurgood. "The Gestapo in Detroit." *Crisis* 50 (August 1943): 232–33, 246–47.

———. "Summary Justice—The Negro GI in Korea." *Crisis* 58 (May 1951): 297–304, 350–55.

Maslow, Will. "FEPC—A Case History in Parliamentary Maneuver." *University of Chicago Law Review* 13 (June 1946): 407–44.

Maslow, Will, and John B. Robinson. "Civil Rights Legislation and the Fight for Equality, 1862–1952." *University of Chicago Law Review* 20 (Spring 1952): 363–413.

Matchette, Robert B., Jan Shelton Davis, United States National Archives and Records Administration, comps. *Guide to Federal Records in the National Archives of the United States*. Washington, D.C.: National Archives and Records Administration, 1995.

Mayer, Kenneth R. *With the Stroke of a Pen: Executive Orders and Presidential Power*. Princeton, N.J.: Princeton University Press, 2001.

McCulloch, Frank W., and Tim Bornstein. *The National Labor Relations Board*. New York: Praeger Publishers, 1974.

McCullough, David. *Truman*. New York: Simon and Schuster, 1992.

McNeil, Genna Rae. *Groundwork: Charles Hamilton Houston and the Struggle for Civil Rights*. Philadelphia: University of Pennsylvania Press, 1983.

McWilliams, Carey. "The Boom Nobody Wanted." *New Republic*, June 30, 1941, 882–84.

Meier, August, and Elliot Rudwick. *Black Detroit and the Rise of the UAW*. New York: Oxford University Press, 1979.

Miller, Loren. "A Right Secured." *Nation*, May 28, 1948, 599–600.
———. "Supreme Court Covenant Decision—An Analysis." *Crisis* 55 (September 1948): 265–66, 285.
Missionary Association, Race Relations Department. "Next Steps in Integration: A Summary of Discussions of the Tenth Race Relations Institute." Fisk University, June 29–July 11, 1953.
Mitchell, Clarence, Jr. "Labor Problems Affecting Negroes." *NAACP Bulletin* 5 (July 1946): 10–11.
———. "Notes on the Taft-Hartley Act." *Crisis* 55 (October 1948): 300–301, 313.
———. "Education UAW Style." *Crisis* 56 (March 1949): 73, 93.
———. "The People v. Winstead of Mississippi." *Crisis* 58 (May 1951): 307–8, 310–11.
———. "Still No FEPC." Editorial. *Crisis* 58 (June–July 1951): 395.
———. "President Truman's 'FEPC.'" *Crisis* 59 (January 1952): 5–8.
———. "These Are the Issues." *Crisis* 59 (October 1952): 483–86.
———. "Negroes Now Eat Upstairs." *Crisis* 60 (December 1953): 585–88, 638.
———. "The Status of Racial Integration in the Armed Services." *Journal of Negro Education* 23, no. 3 (Summer 1954): 208–18.
———. "Foes of Integration in Baltimore and Washington." *Crisis* 61 (November 1954): 533–41, 576–77.
———. "The Warren Court and Congress: A Civil Rights Partnership." *Nebraska Law Review* 48 (1968): 91–128.
Moon, Henry Lee. "Election Post Mortem." *Crisis* 59 (December 1952): 616–17.
———. *Balance of Power: The Negro Vote.* New York: Kraus Reprint, 1969.
Moore, John L., ed. *Congressional Quarterly's Guide to U.S. Elections.* 2nd ed. Washington, D.C.: Congressional Quarterly, 1985.
Moreno, Paul D. *From Direct Action to Affirmative Action: Fair Employment Law and Policy in America, 1933–1972.* Baton Rouge: Louisiana State University Press, 1997.
Morgan, Chester A. *Redneck Liberal: Theodore G. Bilbo and the New Deal.* Baton Rouge: Louisiana State University Press, 1985.
Morrow, E. Frederick. "Virginia Teachers in Revolt." *Crisis* 45 (January 1938): 26.
Motley, Constance. "Wanted: A Compulsory Federal FEPC." *Crisis* 59 (November 1952): 569–71.
Myrdal, Gunnar. *An American Dilemma: The Negro Problem and Modern Democracy.* New York: Harper and Brothers, 1944.
NAACP Legal Defense and Educational Fund, Inc. "School Segregation Cases: Background Material." New York: NAACP Legal Defense and Educational Fund, Inc., December 3, 1953.
———. "Thirty Years of Building American Justice: A Report on Services to the People of the United States by the Legal Defense Fund, 1940–1970." New York: NAACP Legal Defense Fund, 1970.
———. "Toward Equal Justice: The Story of the Work Carried On by the N.A.A.C.P. Legal Defense and Educational Fund." New York: (ca. 1959).
National Association for the Advancement of Colored People (NAACP). "In Court." Editorial. *Crisis* 9 (January 1915): 133–34.
———. Legal Bureau. *Crisis* 9 (January 1915): 137–38.
———. "The Fight in Congress." *Crisis* 9 (March 1915): 246.
———. "Fifth Annual Report, 1914: Report of the Chairman of the Board of Directors." *Crisis* 9 (April 1915): 287–93.
———. "The Jim Crow Car." *Crisis* 11 (November 1915): 33–34.
———. "*Close Ranks.*" Editorial. *Crisis* 16 (July 1918): 111.

———. “The Tenth Anniversary.” *Crisis* 18 (August 1919): 189–93.
———. “Ship Stewards.” *Crisis* 24 (May 1922): 24.
———. “The Status of the Dyer Bill.” *Crisis* 24 (May 1922): 25.
———. “The Dyer Bill.” Editorial. *Crisis* 24 (September 1922): 199.
———. “The Dyer Bill.” *Crisis* 24 (September 1922): 215–16.
———. “The Fight Has Just Begun.” *Crisis* 42 (June 1935): 175, 183.
———. “The Best of the Anti-lynching Fights.” Editorial. *Crisis* 42 (June 1935): 177.
———. “Seven-Point Legislative Program by N.A.A.C.P.” *Crisis* 44 (January 1937): 22.
———. “Unequal Teachers’ Salaries to Be Attacked.” *Crisis* 44 (January 1937): 22.
———. “Seek Equal Salaries for Maryland Teachers.” *Crisis* 44 (February 1937): 53–54.
———. “The New Federal Anti-Lynching Bill.” *Crisis* 44 (March 1937): 72, 94.
———. “For a Federal Anti-Lynching Bill.” *Crisis* 44 (March 1937): 76, 82.
———. “Give Us Our Share.” Editorial. *Crisis* 44 (March 1937): 81.
———. “Sentiment for Anti-Lynching Bill.” *Crisis* 44 (March 1937): 81.
———. “New Anti-lynching Bill Introduced in Congress.” *Crisis* 44 (March 1937): 84.
———. “Anti-lynching Bill Goes to Senate.” *Crisis* 44 (May 1937): 138–40.
———. “Anti-lynch Bill on Senate Calendar Next Session.” *Crisis* 44 (September 1937): 270–80.
———. “Virginia Teachers Will Sue for Equal Pay.” *Crisis* 45 (January 1938): 21
———. “Maryland Governor to Equalize Salaries.” *Crisis* 45 (February 1938): 56.
———. “National Defense and Negroes.” Editorial. *Crisis* 46 (February 1939): 49.
———. “Washington’s Minority Problem.” *Crisis* 46 (June 1939): 170–71.
———. “Air Pilots?” Editorial. *Crisis* 46 (August 1939): 241.
———. “Negro Officers?” Editorial. *Crisis* 46 (November 1939): 337.
———. “Campaign Continued for Jobs in Defense Work.” *Crisis* 47 (October 1940): 324.
———. “Conscription Bill Gets Amendments on Jim Crow.” *Crisis* 47 (October 1940): 324.
———. “White House Blesses Jim Crow.” *Crisis* 47 (November 1940): 350–51.
———. “For Manhood in National Defense.” Editorial. *Crisis* 47 (December 1940): 375.
———. “F.D.R. Regrets That Army Policy Was ‘Misinterpreted.’” *Crisis* 47 (December 1940): 390.
———. “Discrimination in the Draft.” Editorial. *Crisis* 48 (January 1941): 7.
———. “Branches Sent Defense Job Questionnaire.” *Crisis* 48 (January 1941): 21.
———. “The Battle to Save Sharecropper Waller.” *Crisis* 48 (January 1941): 23.
———. “Air Pilots, but Segregated.” Editorials. *Crisis* 48 (February 1941): 39.
———. “Attempt to Smother Senate Resolution 75.” *Crisis* 48 (June 1941): 196.
———. “The Army Must Act.” Editorial. *Crisis* 48 (September 1941): 279.
———. “FEP Committee.” *Crisis* 48 (September 1941): 291.
———. “Jim Crow Wings.” Editorial. *Crisis* 48 (October 1941): 311.
———. “The Defense Job Front.” *Crisis* 48 (October 1941): 327.
———. “Now Is the Time Not to Be Silent.” Editorial. *Crisis* 49 (January 1942): 7.
———. “The Negro in the United States Army.” Editorial. *Crisis* 49 (February 1942): 47.
———. “The American Negro in the United States Army.” *Crisis* 49 (February 1942): 48–49, 67.
———. “Air Corps.” *Crisis* 49 (February 1942): 51.
———. “An Open Letter to President Roosevelt—An Editorial.” *Crisis* 50 (January 1943): 8.
———. “Philadelphia NAACP Seeks 10,000 Members.” *Crisis* 50 (May 1943): 158.
———. “Jim Crow Boomerang.” Editorial. *Crisis* 50 (October 1943): 295.
———. “The Navy Defines ‘Inaptitude.’” *Crisis* 50 (December 1943): 371.
———. “Texas Primary Argument.” *Crisis* 50 (December 1943): 372.
———. “A Declaration by Negro Voters.” *Crisis* 51 (January 1944): 15–16.
———. “FEPC: Its Feckless Friends.” *Crisis* 53 (March 1946): 73–74.

———. "Politics." *Crisis* 53 (March 1946): 86.
———. "The Gillem Report." Editorial. *Crisis* 53 (April 1946): 105.
———. "What Happened at Columbia." *Crisis* 53 (April 1946): 110–11, 125.
———. "New Labor Secretary." *Crisis* 53 (August 1946): 251.
———. "Southern Schrecklichkeit." *Crisis* 53 (September 1946): 276–82.
———. "Negroes! Jews! Catholics!" Editorial. *Crisis* 53 (October 1946): 297.
———. "Today It Is the Senate . . ." *Crisis* 54 (March 1947): 80, 94.
———. "The Negro in the United States Navy." *Crisis* 54 (July 1947): 200–201, 210.
———. "Theodore G. Bilbo." Editorial. *Crisis* 54 (September 1947): 265.
———. "Jim Crow in the Army Camps." *Crisis* 54 (December 1947): 385.
———. "To Secure These Rights." *Crisis* 55 (January 1948): 10–11.
———. "Education." *Crisis* 55 (March 1948): 84–85.
———. "Fighting the Jim Crow Army." Editorial. *Crisis* 55 (May 1948): 136.
———. "Acting Secretary." *Crisis* 56 (July 1949): 213.
———. "FEPC No. 9980." *Crisis* 56 (July 1949): 213–14.
———. "Housing." *Crisis* 56 (July 1949): 213.
———. "First Negro Circuit Judge Sworn In." Picture Caption. *Crisis* 57 (January 1950): 20.
———. "The Civil Rights Mobilization." *Crisis* 57 (February 1950): 100–101.
———. "The FEPC Fight." Editorial. *Crisis* 57 (March 1950): 170.
———. "Push FEPC." Editorial. *Crisis* 57 (April 1950): 238.
———. "FEPC." *Crisis* 57 (April 1950): 240–42.
———. "The NAACP Legislative Scoreboard: 81st Congress, Second Session." *Crisis* 57 (October 1950): 549–52.
———. "Legal." *Crisis* 58 (February 1951): 109–10.
———. "Mr. Marshall Reports." Editorial. *Crisis* 58 (March 1951): 180–81.
———. "Meet Mr. Caldwell." Editorial. *Crisis* 58 (March 1951): 183–84.
———. "Political." *Crisis* 58 (April 1951): 267–75.
———. "Civil Rights Conference." *Crisis* 58 (May 1951): 328, 330.
———. "Still No FEPC." Editorial. *Crisis* 58 (June–July 1951): 395.
———. "Terror in Florida." *Crisis* 59 (January 1952): 35–36.
———. "Resolutions Adopted by the Forty-third Annual Convention of the NAACP at Oklahoma City, Oklahoma, June 28, 1952"—"Political Action." *Crisis* 59 (August–September 1952): 446–47.
———. "These Are the Issues." *Crisis* 59 (October 1952): 480–81.
———. "Somali Youth League." *Crisis* 59 (October 1952): 516.
———. "NAACP Mourns Dr. Louis T. Wright." *Crisis* 59 (November 1952): 548–50.
———. "Africa Awakes." *Crisis* 59 (November 1952): 578–79.
———. "Break the Filibuster." Editorial. *Crisis* 60 (December 1953): 359.
———. "Dr. Lillie M. Jackson: Lifelong Freedom Fighter." *Crisis* 82 (October 1975): 297–99.
———. "The Negro Marches." Editorial. *Opportunity* 19 (July 1941): 194.
———. "The Negroes and the Draft." Editorial reprint from *PM* (April 11, 1948), in *Crisis* 55 (May 1948): 140, 154–55.
New Republic. News in Focus. December 30, 1946.
———. News in Focus. March 31, 1947.
Newsweek. National Affairs. December 9, 1946.
———. National Affairs. March 31, 1947.
———. National Affairs. March 28, 1949.
Nichols, Lee. *Breakthrough on the Color Front.* New York: Random House, 1954.

Norfolk Journal and Guide. "Stand Up and Fight." Editorial of the Month, reprinted in *Crisis* 45 (February 1938): 51.

Norgen, Paul H., and Samuel E. Hill. *Toward Fair Employment.* New York: Columbia University Press, 1964.

Northrup, Herbert R. *Organized Labor and the Negro.* Millwood, N.Y.: Kraus Reprint, 1976.

Northrup, Herbert, and Richard L. Rowan, eds. *The Negro and Employment Opportunities: Problems and Practices.* Ann Arbor: Bureau of Industrial Relations, Graduate School of Business Administration, University of Michigan, 1965.

Ottley, Roi. *New World A-Coming.* Boston: Houghton Mifflin, 1943.

Ovington, Mary White. "How the National Association for the Advancement of Colored People Began." *Crisis* 8 (August 1914): 184–88.

———. *The Walls Came Tumbling Down.* New York: Harcourt, Brace and World, 1947.

Padmore, George. "Fascism Invades West Africa." *Crisis* 46 (October 1939): 297–98.

———. "The Second World War and the Darker Races." *Crisis* 46 (November 1939): 327–28.

Parmet, Herbert S. *Eisenhower and the American Crusades.* New York: Macmillan, 1972.

Patterson, James T. *Mr. Republican: A Biography of Robert A. Taft.* Boston: Houghton Mifflin, 1972.

———. *"Brown v. Board of Education": A Civil Rights Milestone and Its Troubled Legacy.* New York: Oxford University Press, 2001.

"Peace on Earth! Its Magic Light Is Dulled by Riot, Strike, Dissent." *Newsweek,* October 8, 1945, 33–36.

Peck, Gustav. "The Negro Worker and the NRA." *Crisis* 41 (September 1934): 262–63, 279.

Peck, James L. H. "When Do *We* Fly?" *Crisis* 47 (December 1940): 376–78, 388.

Perlman, Mark. *Democracy in the International Association of Machinists.* New York: John Wiley and Sons, 1962.

Pfeffer, Paula F. *A Philip Randolph: Pioneer of the Civil Rights Movement.* Baton Rouge: Louisiana State University Press, 1990.

"The Question of Revising the Taft-Hartley Labor-Management Relations Act." *Congressional Digest* 32 (November 1953): 257–61, 288.

Randolph, A. Philip. "March on Washington Movement Presents Program for the Negro." In *What the Negro Wants,* ed. Rayford Logan. Chapel Hill: University of North Carolina Press, 1944.

Reed, Merl E. *Seedtime for the Modern Civil Rights Movement: The President's Committee on Fair Employment Practice, 1941–1945.* Baton Rouge: Louisiana State University Press, 1991.

"Republicans and FEPC." *Crisis* 52 (July 1945): 193.

Ribble, F. D. G. "The Due Process Clause as a Limitation on Municipal Discretion in Zoning Legislation." *Virginia Law Review* 16 (May 1930): 689–700.

Riddick, Floyd M. *United States Congress, Organization and Procedure.* Washington, D.C.: National Capitol Publishers, Inc., 1949.

Roback, Herbert. "Legal Barriers to Interstate Migration." Pts. 1 and 2. *Cornell Law Quarterly* 28 (March 1943): 286–312; 28 (June 1943): 483–526.

Roberts, Thomas N. "The Negro in World War I and World War II. *Journal of Negro Education* 12 (Summer 1943): 367–75.

Robinson, Spottswood W., III. "The Virginia School Fight—A Clarification." *Crisis* 58 (April 1951): 228–29.

Rorty, James. "The Story of the Chattanooga Choo-Choo." *New Leader* (January 1943).

Ross, Arthur M., and Herbert Hill, eds. *Employment, Race, and Poverty.* New York: Harcourt, Brace and World, 1967.

Ross, B. Joyce. *J. E. Spingarn and the Rise of the NAACP, 1911–1939*. New York: Atheneum, 1972.
Ross, Malcolm. *All Manner of Men*. New York: Reynal and Hitchcock, 1948.
Ruchames, Louis. *Race, Jobs and Politics: The Story of FEPC*. New York: Harcourt, Brace, 1946.
Saunders, Robert W., Sr. *Bridging the Gap: Continuing the Florida NAACP Legacy of Harry T. Moore, 1952–1966*. Tampa, Fla.: University of Tampa Press, 2000.
Saylor, Frances. "The Poll Tax Kills Democracy." *Crisis* 49 (May 1942): 162, 173.
Sherman, Richard B. *The Case of Odell Waller and Virginia Justice, 1940–1942*. Knoxville: University of Tennessee Press, 1992.
"Should District of Columbia Citizens Have the Right to Vote?" *Senior Scholastic* 56, 10–11.
Sinclair, Barbara. *The Transformation of the U.S. Senate*. Baltimore, Md.: Johns Hopkins University Press, 1989.
Sitkoff, Harvard. "Racial Militancy and Interracial Violence in the Second World War." *Journal of American History* 58 (December 1971): 661–81.
———. *A New Deal for Blacks: The Emergence of Civil Rights as a National Issue*. New York: Oxford University Press, 1978.
Sloan, Irving J., comp. and ed. *The Blacks in America, 1492–1976: A Chronology and Fact Book*. 4th rev. ed. Dobbs Ferry, N.Y.: Oceana Publications, 1977.
Smith, Robert. "The Poll Tax—Enemy of Democracy." *Crisis* 46 (April 1939): 106–14.
Stern, Mark. "Presidential Strategies and Civil Rights: Eisenhower—The Early Years, 1953–54." Paper presented at the Annual Meeting of the American Historical Association, Chicago, December 30, 1986.
Stone, I. F. "Robert F. Wagner." *Nation* 159 (October 28, 1944): 507–8.
Summers, Clyde W. "The Right to Join a Union." *Columbia Law Review* 47 (January 1947): 33–74.
Taylor, William L. *The Passion of My Times: My Fifty-Year Journey through the Civil Rights Revolution*. Washington, D.C.: Carroll and Graf Publishers, 2005.
Tiefer, Charles. *Congressional Practice and Procedure: A Reference, Research, and Legislative Guide*. Westport, Conn.: Greenwood Press, 1989.
Time. National Affairs. March 31, 1947.
———. National Affairs. September 18, 1950.
———. National Affairs. September 13, 1954.
———. The Press. January 31, 1955.
"To Have Jobs or to Have Not." *Negro Digest* (January 1946): 73.
Toner, Jerome L. *The Closed Shop*. Washington, D.C.: American Council on Public Affairs, 1942.
To Secure These Rights: The Report of the President's Committee on Civil Rights, with an introduction by Charles E. Wilson, committee chairman. New York: Simon and Schuster, 1947.
"The Trend." *Business Week*, March 29, 1947, 108.
Tucker, William H. *The Funding of Scientific Racism: Wickliffe Draper and the Pioneer Fund*. Urbana: University of Illinois Press, 2002.
Turner, Henry C. "Tolerance on Trial: How New York's Fair Employment Law Is Working after Eight Months in Operation." *American Magazine* 141 (June 1946): 14, 16, 18, 127.
Tushnet, Mark, and Katya Lezin. "What Really Happened in *Brown v. Board of Education*." *Columbia Law Review* 91 (December 1991): 1867–1930.
"Veterans' Benefits, 1945–64." *Congress and the Nation, 1945–1964*. Washington, D.C.: Congressional Quarterly Service, 1965.
Vose, Clement E. *Caucasians Only: The Supreme Court, the NAACP, and the Restrict Covenant Cases*. Berkeley: University of California Press, 1959.

Watson, Denton L. *Lion in the Lobby: Clarence Mitchell, Jr.'s Struggle for the Passage of Civil Rights Laws.* Rev. ed. Lanham, Md.: University Press of America, 2002.

———. "Clarence Mitchell, Jr." *American National Biography.* New York: Oxford University Press, 1999.

Weaver, George C. *Negro Labor: A National Problem.* New York: Harcourt, Brace, 1946.

Weaver, Robert C. "A Wage Differential Based on Race." *Crisis* 41 (August 1934): 236, 237.

———. "Negroes Need Housing." *Crisis* 47 (May 1940): 138–39, 158.

———. "Federal Aid, Local Control, and Negro Participation." *Journal of Negro Education* 11, no. 1 (1942): 47–59.

———. *The Negro Ghetto.* New York: Harcourt, Brace, 1948.

———. "Habitation with Segregation." *Crisis* 59 (June-July 1952): 347–53, 402–3.

Weisbrot, Robert. *Freedom Bound: A History of America's Civil Rights Movement.* New York: W. W. Norton, 1990.

Wesley, Charles H. "Organized Labor's Divided Front." *Crisis* 45 (July 1938): 223–26.

White, Walter. "The Fight Has Just Begun." *Crisis* 42 (June 1935): 75, 183.

———. "Dangerous Federal School Aid." *Crisis* 44 (February 1937): 41–42, 50, 60.

———. "It's Our Country, Too." *Saturday Evening Post,* October–December 1940, 27, 61, 63, 66, 68.

———. *A Man Called White.* Bloomington: Indiana University Press, 1948.

———. "What Negroes Want Now: Interview with Walter White." *U.S. News and World Report* 36, May 28, 1954, 54–62.

"White House Conference." *NAIRO* [National Association of Intergroup Relations Officials] *Reporter* 1 (April 1951): 2.

Wilkins, Roy. "Politicians Win, Education Loses." *Crisis* 50 (November 1943): 333, 348.

———. "The Negro Wants Full Equality." In *What the Negro Wants,* ed. Rayford Logan. Chapel Hill: University of North Carolina Press, 1944, 113–31.

———. "Still a Jim Crow Army." *Crisis* 53 (April 1946): 106–9, 125.

———. "The Negro Vote in 1948." *Crisis* 55 (June 1948): 178, 188.

Williams, Charles. "Harlem at War." *Nation,* January 16, 1943, 88.

Wilson, Walter. "Old Jim Crow in Uniform." *Crisis* 46 (February 1939): 42–44.

———. "Old Jim Crow in Uniform." *Crisis* 46 (March 1939): 71–73, 82.

Zaid, Charles, comp. *Preliminary Inventory of the Records of the Committee on Fair Employment Practice (Record Group 228).* Washington, D.C.: National Archives and Records Service, General Services Administration, 1962.

Zangrando, Robert L. *NAACP Crusade against Lynching, 1909–1950.* Philadelphia: Temple University Press, 1980.

Dissertations and Theses

Chen, Anthony S. "From Fair Employment to Equal Employment Opportunity and Beyond: Affirmative Action and the Politics of Civil Rights during the New Deal Order, 1941–1972." PhD diss., University of California at Berkeley, 2002.

Saucier, Bobby Wade. "The Public Career of Theodore G. Bilbo." PhD diss., Tulane University, 1971.

Smith, Charles Pope. "Theodore G. Bilbo's Senatorial Career: The Final Years, 1941–1947." PhD diss., University of Southern Mississippi, 1983.

Databases and Online Sources

"Advisory Committee on Negro Troop Policies." http://www.trumanlibrary.org/whistleop/study_cp;;ectopms/desegregation/large/documents/.

AFL-CIO. "Working Heroes: Men and Women Who Shaped America's Labor Movement." http://www.aflcio.org/aboutus/history/history/bios.cfm.

African American Biographical Database. http://aabd.chadwyck.com.

African American Registry. "John Artemus, an Ally of Blue Collar Workers!" http://www.aaregistry.com/african_american_history/1787/John_Artemus_an_ally_of_blue_collar_workers.

———. "Lester Granger Worked Hard through the Urban League." http://www.aaregistry.com/african_american_history/1153/Lester_Granger_worked_hard_through_the_Urban_League.

———. "Robert Lee Vann, A Publishing Original." http://www.aaregistry.com/african_american_history/329/Robert_Lee_Vann_a_publishing_original.

"African-Americans-Merchant Marine." http://www.USMM.org.

Air Force Historical Studies Office, Research and Analysis Division. http://www.airforcehistory.hq.af.mil/contact.htm.

Air National Guard History Online. http://www.ang.af.mil/history/.

Alabama Department of Archives and History. "Alabama Moments in American History: Oscar W. Adams, Jr." http://www.alabamamoments.state.al.us/sec65.html.

Alan Mason Chesney Medical Archives of the Johns Hopkins Medical Institutions. "The Jerome Frank Collection." http://www.medicalarchives.jhmi.edu/sgml/frankj.html.

Amateur Athletic Union Sullivan Memorial Award. "Marvin G. Whitfield." http://www.aausullivan.org/winners_1954.html.

American Battle Monuments Commission. http://www.abmc.gov/home.php.

American Jewish Congress. "Will Maslow, General Counsel of A. J. Congress, to Be Honored by Jewish Council for Public Affairs." http://www.ajcongress.org/pages/RELS1998/feb98rel/feb98_01.htm.

American President.org. "Postmaster General: Jesse M. Donaldson (1947–1953)." http://www.americanpresident.org/history/harrytruman/cabinet/postmaster/postmasterCopy2/h_index.shtml.

———. "Presidency in History." http://www.americanpresident.org/history/h_home.shtml.

American University. "About the University: AU Timeline." http://www.american.edu/about/timeline.html.

Ancestor Info. "Genealogy Information for Georgia State Employees and Officials, 1939–1943." http://www.ancestorinfo.com/Georgia%20Officials,%201943.htm.

Ancestry.com. http://www.ancestry.com/.

Arlington National Cemetery Website. http://www.arlingtoncemetery.net/.

Balch Institute for Ethnic Studies of the Historical Society of Pennsylvania. "Register of the Papers of Edwin Lukas, 1937–73." http://www.balchinistitute.org/manuscript_guide/html/lukas.html.

Baltimore Department of Recreation and Parks. http://www.ci.baltimore.md.us/government/recnparks/rec_centers.htm.

Barnett. "What Is 'State' Action under the Fourteenth, Fifteenth, and Nineteenth Amendments of the Constitution," 227.

Baseball Library.com. "Jackie Robinson, 1919–1972." http://www.baseballlibrary.com/baseballlibrary/ballplayers/R/Robinson_Jackie.stm.

Baseball Reference. "Jackie Robinson: Jack Roosevelt Robinson." http://www.baseball-reference.com/r/robinja02.shtml.

Battle of the Bulge. http://ice.mm.com/user/jpk/battle.htm.

Bay Area Paul Robeson Centennial Committee. "Paul Robeson Chronology, 1949 through 1950." http://www.bayarearobeson.org/chronology_6.htm.

Baylor Collections of Political Materials. "Congressional Papers: Ed Lee Gossett." http://www3.baylor.edu/Library/BCPM/Gossett/gossett_scope_content.htm.

Bethune-Cookman College. "Our Founder." http://www.cookman.edu/Welcome/Founder/Default.html.

Biographical Directory of the United States Congress, 1774–Present. http://bioguide.congress.gov/biosearch/biosearch.asp.

Black Facts Online. http://www.blackfacts.com/index.asp.

"Brief History of the NMU." http://ciscohouston.com/essays/nmu.shtml.

Brinson, Claudia Smith. "Unstoppable Courage Drove S.C. NAACP Leaders." http://www.thestate.com/mld/thestate/news/columnists/claudia_smith_brinson/8012304.htm.

Brooklyn College of The City University of New York. "Seventy-sixth Commencement Exercises." Program, Brooklyn, N.Y., June 1, 2001. http://www.brooklyn.cuny.edu/bc/commenc/01/pdf/76th.pdf.

Brown v. Board.com. "An Interactive Civil Rights Chronology." http://www.yale.edu/lawweb/jbalkin/brown/index.html.

Burroughs, Todd Steven. "'Who Is This Man, Louis Lautier?' The NNPA and Louis Lautier, Pt. II." http://www.blackpressusa.com/history/Timeline_Essay.asp?NewsID=106.

Burt, Stephen, and Jessica Bennett. "Millard Cass: A Memorial." http://www.accommodatingly.com/puh.html.

Catholic University of America, American Catholic History Research Center and University Archives. "Finding Aid for the Francis J. Haas Papers." http://libraries.cua.edu/achrcua/haas.html.

———. "Finding Aid for the John A. Ryan Papers." http://libraries.cua.edu/achrcua/ryan .html.

———. "Finding Aid for the John Brophy Papers." http://libraries.cua.edu/achrcua/brophy.html.

———. "Finding Aid for the Joseph D. Keenan Papers." http://libraries.cua.edu/achrcua/keenan.html.

———. "Furfey, Paul Hanly, and Walsh, May Elizabeth. Papers." http://libraries.cua.edu/achrcua/manuA-K.html.

Chattanooga African American Museum. "Today in Black History—July 21, 2003." http://www.caamhistory.com/caam/2dyhsty.htm.

Chicago Public Library. "Harsh Research Collection: Black History Month, 1950s." http://www.chipublib.org/002branches/woodson/afamhistmonth/1950s.html.

Cincinnati Municipal Reference Library. Collections. Finding Aid. http://www.libraries.uc.edu/libraries/arb/archives/collections/MunicipalReferenceLibrary.html.

CityNews Ohio. http://www.citynewsohio.com/.

Clayton Antitrust Act of 10/15/14. http:en.wikipedia.org/wiki/Clayton_Antitust_Act.

Coleman, Kevin J. "The Uniformed and Overseas Citizens Absentee Voting Act: Background and Issues." Order Code RS20764. http://www.thememoryhole.org/crs/more-reports/RS20764.PDC.

Columbia Electronic Encyclopedia. http://www.columbia.edu/cu/cup/cee/cee.html.

Commission on Migratory Workers. http://www.trumanlibrary.org/publicpapers/viewpapers.php?pid=287.

Committee on Equality of Treatment in the Armed Services 1950. http://www.trumanlibrary.org/hstpaper/fahy.htm#series5.

Cornell University Library, Kheel Center for Labor Management Documentation and Archives. "Guide to the International Ladies Garment Workers Union: Charles S. Zimmerman Papers, 1919–1958 [bulk 1920–1945]." http://rmc.library.cornell.edu/EAD/htmldocs/KCL05780–014.html.

Defense Housing and Community Facilities and Services Act of 1951, CIS-NO: 11487 S.rp.189, COC-TYPE: Serial Set Collection, DOC-NO: S.rp189, 82–1, 1951, Congressional Indexes, 1789–1969. http://web.lexis-nexis.com.congcomp/doclist?_m=84ff1dcc025a4c4. . .

Department of the Navy, Naval Historical Center. "Ensign Jesse LeRoy Brown, USN (1926–1950)." http://www.history.navy.mil/photos/pers-us/uspers-b/j-brown.htm.

Department of Veterans Affairs, National Cemetery Administration. "Nationwide Gravesite Locator." http://gravelocator.cem.va.gov/j2ee/servlet/NGL_v1.

Dickinson University. "Encyclopedia Dickinsonia: Honorary Degree Recipients Index." http://chronicles.dickinson.edu/encyclo/h/honorarydegrees/.

Dictionary of Unitarian and Universalist Biography. "A. Powell Davies." http://www.uua.org/uuhs/duub/articles/arthurpowelldavies.

Digges, Brenda V., and Robert R. Fredlund. "From Spoils System to Merit System—60 Years of Progress in Jefferson County, AL." *Public Personnel Management* 26, no.4 (Winter 1997). http://www.findarticles.com/p/articles/mi_qa3779/is_199701/ai_n8757070. Also available in print form.

District of Columbia Public Library. "Frank Smith Horne, 1899–1974." http://www.dclibrary.org/blkren/bios/hornefs.html.

District of Columbia Public Schools. "DCPS Offices: Past DCPS Superintendents, 1869–2000." http://www.k12.dc.us/dcps/offices/dcpastsupers.html.

Dugan, A.K. "Three Decades of Ups and Downs." http://www.mvonline.com/founders/founders-05.html.

Dwight D. Eisenhower Library. "Historical Materials in the Dwight D. Eisenhower Library: List of Holdings." http://www.eisenhower.archives.gov/loh2.htm.

Eisenhower, Dwight David. "Dwight David Eisenhower to James Francis Byrnes, 14 August 1953." The Dwight D. Eisenhower Memorial Commission: The Presidential Papers of Dwight David Eisenhower. http://www.eisenhowermemorial.org/presidential-papers/first-term/documents/382.cfm. Also available in print form.

Encyclopaedia Britannica's Guide to Black History. "Timeline, 1936–59: The Birth of the Civil Rights Movement." http://www.britannica.com/Blackhistory/era.do?nKayValue=5.

Essex County College. "Announcements: ECC Is Saddened to Announce the Passing of Julia Baxter Bates." http://www.essex.edu/news/releases.8release52003.html.

"Explorations in Black Leadership: Oliver W. Hill, Sr." http://www.virginia.edu/blackleadership/bios.html#hill.

FamilyTreeMaker.com. "Descendants of Louis Johnson." http://familytreemaker.genealogy.com/users/j/o/h/Mason-Johnson/ODT11–0001.html.

Federal Judges Biographical Database. http://air.fjc.gov/servlet/uSpage.

Felzenberg, Alvin S., "Alfred Eastlack Driscoll." In *The Governors of New Jersey, 1664–1974: Biographical Essays,* ed. Paul A. Stellhorn and Michael J. Birkner (Trenton, N.J.: The Commission, 1982). http://www.njstatelib.org/NJ_Information/Digital_Collections/Governors_of_New_Jersey/GDRIS.pdf. Also available in print form.

Find A Grave. http://www.findagrave.com.

Fingerhut, Eric. "Civil Rights Proponent Arnold Aronson Dies at 86." *Jewish News Weekly of Northern California,* March 6, 1998. http://www.jewishsf.com/content/2–0-/module/displaystory/story_id/8164/edition_id/155/format/html/displaystory.html.

"Franklin D. (Dewey) Richards, 1900–1987." http://personal.bellsouth.net/w/o/wol3/richafd2.htm.

General Electric. "Past Leaders: Charles E. Wilson." http://www.ge.com/en/company/companyinfo/at_a_glance/bio_wilson.htm.

The Generals of World War II. http://www.generals.dk.

Georgetown University Law Library. http://www.ll.georgetown.edu.

George Washington University, ?Melvin Gelman Library. "Presidents of the University." http://www.gwu.edu/gelman/archives/tours/gwtour/presidents.

Georgia Department of Labor. "About Us." http://www.dol.state.ga.us/about_us.htm.

Georgia Public Service Commission. "Introduction to the Georgia Public Service Commission." http://www.psc.state.ga.us/pscinfo/pscintro.asp.

Georgia State University Library, Special Collections and Archives, Georgia Government Documentation Project. "Stetson Kennedy." http://wwwlib.gsu.edu/spcoll/Collections/GGDP/skennedy.htm.

Georgia State University Library, Special Collections and Archives. "John Gates Ramsay Papers, 1928–1979." http://www.library.gsu.edu/spcoll/Collections/Labor/L1980-05.htm.

Green, Frank. "'Martinsville Seven' Case Drew Worldwide Attention." [Richmond] Times-Dispatch.com. http://www.timesdispatch.com/servlet/Satellite?pagename=RTD/MGArticle/RTD_BasicArticle&c=MGArticle&cid=1031779511373.

Headquarters of the U.S. Army, Europe. "Integration of Negro and White Troops in the U.S. Army, Europe, 1952–1954." http://www.army.mil/cmh-pg/documents/cold-war/EI-FM.htm.

Hernandez-Truyol, Berta Esperanza. "Human Rights through a Gendered Lens: Emergence, Evolution, Revolution." http://www.lic.law.ufl.edu/~hernandez/IntlLaw/lens-b.htm.

Hirsch, Arnold R. "Searching for a 'Sound Negro Policy': A Racial Agenda for the Housing Acts of 1949 and 1954." http://www.fanniemaefoundation.org/programs/hpd/pdf/hpd_1102_hirsch.pdf.

The HistoryMakers. "Dr. Keiffer J. Mitchell, Sr." http://www.thehistorymakers.com/biography/biography.asp?bioindex=578&category=medicalMakers.

———. "Timeline." http://www.thehistorymakers.org/timeline/.

Hoophall.com. "Hall of Famers: Earl Lloyd." http://www.hoophall.com/halloffamers/lloyd_earl.htm.

Howard University School of Law. "Brown @ 50: Fulfilling the Promise." http://www.brownat50.org.

Immigration.com. "Maurice A. Roberts, 1910–2001." http://www.immigration.com/newsletter/maurice.html.

"An Important Figure Who Never Made History." *Laguardia Livewire,* no.21 (December 2002). http://www.lagcc.cuny.edu/livewire/21/article19.asp.

Infoplease. "Benjamin Franklin Fairless." http://www.infoplease.com/ipa/A077893.html.

Interment.net Cemetery Transcription Library. http://www.interment.net/.

Jackson, Emory O. "Letters to Anne Rutledge, 1940–1975." Archival Resources, Birmingham Public Library. http://www.bplonline.org/Archives/collections/arts/jacksonemoryletters.asp.

Jefferson Genealogical Society, Inc. "An Alphabetical Index of Deaths in Metro New Orleans, La., as Published in the Times Picayune." http://us.geocities.com/jeffersongenealogicalsociety/obits/deathnx.htm.

The Jerseyman (April–June 2005). http://www.ussnewjersey.org/thejerseyman/2005%20April.pdf.

Kestenbaum, Lawrence. "The Political Graveyard: A Database of Historic Cemeteries." http://politicalgraveyard.com/index.html.

Lang, Robert E., and Rebecca R. Sohmer. "Legacy of the Housing Act of 1949: The Past, Present, and Future of Federal Housing and Urban Policy." http://www.fanniemaefoundation.org/programs/hpd/pdf/hpd_1102_edintro.pdf.

LexisNexis. http://www.lexisnexis.com.

Library of Congress. "Library of Congress Authorities." http://authorities.loc.gov.

Library of Congress, Manuscript Division. "Labor History Sources in the Manuscript Division of the Library of Congress." http://www.loc.gov/rr/mss/laborlc.html.

"The Life of James E. (Jimmy) Stewart, Sr." http://blackdispatch.smugmug.com/gallery/365257/1/14544915/Large.

Louisiana State University Libraries, Special Collections. "Baton Rouge Bus Boycott: Chronology, 1950–1955." http://www.lib.lsu.edu/special/exhibits/boycott/chronology.html.

Lusignan, Paul R. "Public Housing in the United States, 1933–1949." http://crm.cr.nps.gov/archive/25-0125-01-16.pdf.

Maryland Foundation for Psychiatry, Inc. "Honorary Director Jerome D. Frank M.D., 95, Dies." http://www.mdpsychfoundation.org/archives/2005/05/honorary_direct.html.

Maryland State Archives. "Society of Senates Past, Roster: John B. Funk." http://www.mdarchives.state.md.us/msa/speccol/sc3500/sc3520/002700/002708/html/funk.html.

Matthews, Jessie E. http://wwww.clpgh.org/exhibit/neighborhoods/hill/hill_n103.html.

McKay, Douglas. http://www.nndb.com/people/040/000116689/.

Minnesota Historical Society Library. "History Topics: J. A. A. Burnquist." http://www.mnhs.org/library/tips/history_topics/121burnquist.html.

Moore's Ford Memorial Committee, Inc. http://www.mooresford.org.

Moorland-Spingarn Research Center, Howard University. "Alphabetical List of Processed Manuscript Collections." http://www.howard.edu/library/moorland-spingarn/mssal.htm.

———. "Ralph J. Bunche Oral History Collection." http://www.founders.howard.edu/moorland-spingarn/ohindex.htm.

Myers, Andrew. "Black, White, and Olive Drab: Fort Jackson and the Civil Rights Movement in Columbia." http://www.citadel.edu/civilrights/papers/myers.pdf.

———. "Resonant Ripples in a Global Pond: The Blinding of Isaac Woodard." http://faculty.uscupstate.edu/amyers/.

National Archives. Guide to Federal Records. Records of Temporary Committees, Commissions and Boards. RG 220, 1893–1996: Records of the President's Advisory Commission on Universal Training. http://www.archives.gov/research/guide-fed-records/groups/220.html#220.7.3.

———. Guide to Federal Records. Records of Temporary Committees, Commissions and Boards. RG 220, 1893–1996: Records of the President's Commission on Immigration and Naturalization. http://www.archives.gov/research/guide-fed-records/groups/220.html#220.7.19.

———. Guide to Federal Records. Records of Temporary Committees, Commissions and Boards. RG 220, 1893–1996: Records of the President's Commission on Migratory Labor. http://www.archives.gov/research/guide-fed-records/groups/220.html#220.7.13.

———. Guide to Federal Records. Records of Temporary Committees, Commissions and Boards. RG 220, 1893–1996: Records of the President's Committee on Civil Rights. http://www.archives.gov/research/guide-fed-records/groups/220.html#220.7.2.

———. Guide to Federal Records. Records of Temporary Committees, Commissions and Boards. RG 220, 1893–1996: Records of the President's Committee on Equality of Treatment and Opportunity in the Armed Services. http://www.archives.gov/research/guide-fed-records/groups/220.html#220.7.8.

———. Guide to Federal Records. Records of the Office of the Secretary of the Interior. RG 48, 1826–1985. http://www.archives.gov/research/guide-fed-records/groups/048.html.

———. Guide to the General Records of the Department of Labor. RG 174. http://www.nara.gov/guide/rg174.html.

———. Guide to the Records of the Department of the Navy. RG 80. http://www.nara.gov/guide/rg80.html.

———. Guide to the Records of the War Production Board. RG 179. http://www.nara.gov/guide/rg179.html.

———. World War II Army Enlistment Records, 6/1/2002–9/30/2002: Electronic Army Serial Number Merged File, ca. 1938–1946. RG 64. http://aad.archives.gov/aad/search.jsp?file_id=3475&coll_id=null&data_layout_id=494&table_id=893.

National Farm Labor Union. A History of American Agriculture 1940. http://www.agclassroom.org/gan/timeline/1940.htm.

The Nation Digital Archive: 1865 to the Present. http://www.nationarchive.com/index.asp?.

New Georgia Encyclopedia. "Literature: Lillian Smith (1897–1966)." http://www.georgiaencyclopedia.org/nge/Articl.jsp?path=/Literature/Fiction/Authors&id=h-463.

New York Public Library Digital Library Collections. "Trenton Six Collection, 1949–1956." http://digilib.nypl.org/dynaweb/ead/nypl/sctrentn/@Generic_BookView.

New York Times. "Obituaries." http://www.nytimes.com/pages/obituaries/.

New York University Tamiment Library, Robert F. Wagner Labor Archives. "Guide to the Philip M. Weightman Papers, 1944–1967." http://dlib.nyu.edu:8083/tamwagead/servlet/SaxonServlet?source=weightman.xml&style=saxon01t2002.xsl.

NFL.com. "Bears' Thrower Was NFL's First Black QB." http://www.nfl.com/news/story/5040318.

Norris—La Guardia Act of 1932: http://en.wikipedia.org/wiki/Noris-LaGuardia_Act.

Northwestern University Archives. "James C. Worthy (1910–1998) Papers, 1931–1999." http://www.library.northwestern.edu/archives/findingaids/james_worthy.pdf.

Obits Archive.com. http://oa.newsbank.com/.

Online Archive of California. "Inventory of the U.S. National War Labor Board Records, 1942–1945." http://www.oac.cdlib.org/findaid/ark:/13030/tf4f59n71s.

Orlowski, George, and Erin McDaniel. "The Governor John Charles Vivian Collection at the Colorado State Archives." http://www.colorado.gov/dpa/doit/archives/govs/vivian.html.

Pedersen, Rechs Ann. "Alien Land Laws." http://www.santacruzpl.org/history/ww2/9066/land.shtml.

Pennsylvania Historical and Museum Commission. "Pennsylvania Governors Past to Present: Governor James H. Duff (1883–1969)." http://www.phmc.state.pa.us/bah/dam/governors/duff.asp?secid=31.

Public Broadcasting System. "The Black Press: Soldiers without Swords—Newspapers & Biographies." http://www.pbs.org/blackpress/news_bios.

Quigel, James P. "An Inventory of the Records of the President's Office of the International Union of Electrical, Radio and Machine Workers, ca. 1938–1965." http://www2.scc.rutgers.edu/ead/manuscripts/iueb.html.

Railway Mail Association v. Corsi, Industrial Commissioner of the State of New York et al. 326 U.S. 88. http://web.lexis-nexis.com/universe/document?_m=357b9823fdda8d0d825a959416bea61d. . .

Reber Family Photo Exchange. "Major General Miles Reber." http://home.att.net/~clreber/rebm.02/rebm.02.htm.

Reiff, Janice L. et al., eds. *Encyclopedia of Chicago.* http://www.encyclopedia.chicagohistory.org.

Roark et al. v. Atlantic Coast Line R. Co. et al. 91 F. Supp. 585. http://web.lexis-nexis.com/universe/document?_m=05c434869caf5ad61c741c366849d&. . .

RootsWeb.com. "Social Security Death Index." http://ssdi.genealogy.rootsweb.com/.

70th Infantry Division Association. "Military History Institute Holdings." http://www.trailblazersww2.org/divisionhistory/MHI_listing.htm.

Smith, Dr. J. Clay, Jr. "Frank Daniel Reeves, L'39: Legal and Political Tactician." http://www.law.howard.edu/alumni/legalgiants/huslgiantoct2k1.htm.

Social Security Administration. "Social Security History." http://www.ssa.gov/history/.

Soldiers Vote Bill: Coleman, Kevin J., "The Uniformed and Overseas Citizens Absentee Voting Act: Background and Issues," CRS Report for Congress. http://www.thememoryhole.org/crs/more-reports/RS20764.

Square, Brenda Billips. "Amistad Research Center Remembers 50th Anniversary of the Brown Decision." http://amistadresearchcenter.org/_pdfs/arcnews_summer04.pdf.

Syracuse University Library Archives. "Alexander Albert Liveright Papers, 1934–1969." http://www-distance.syr.edu/aal.html.

Talladega College Historical Collections. "The Reverend John Washington Goodgame Papers." http://www.archives.state.al.us/cornerstone/TalladegaCollegePrivateCollectionsGuide.pdf.

Teaching and Learning Center. "African American Chronology." http://www.k12tlc.net/samplaev.htm.

Texas State Historical Association. *The Handbook of Texas Online.* http://www.tsha.utexas.edu/handbook/online/.

Thevenot, Brian. "Painful Progress." http://nolassf.dev.advance.net/education/painful.html.

Times Picayune 2006 Obituary Index, Orleans Parish, Louisiana. http://ftp.rootsweb.com/pub/usgenweb/la/orleans/obits/times/tpi2006.txt.

Truman, Harry S. Executive Order 10210—Authorizing the Department of Defense and the Department of Commerce to Exercise the Functions and Powers Set Forth in Title II of the First War Powers Act, 1941.

Truman Presidential Museum and Library. "Archival Research: Harry S. Truman Papers." http://www.trumanlibrary.org/hst-pape.htm.

———. "Charles H. McGuire Papers." http://www.trumanlibrary.org/hstpaper/mcguirech.htm.

———. "Earl J. McGrath Papers." http://www.trumanlibrary.org/hstpaper/mcgrath.htm.

———. "Murphy, Charles S." http://www.trumanlibrary.org/profile/viewpro.php?pid=515

———. "Jesse M. Donaldson Papers." http://www.trumanlibrary.org/hstpaper/donaldsonjm.htm.

———. "Oral History Interview with C. Girard Davidson." http://www.trumanlibrary.org/oralhist/davidsn1.htm.

———. "Profile of Julius A. Krug." http://www.trumanlibrary.org/profile/viewpro.php?pid=121.

———. "Raymond M. Foley Papers." http://www.trumanlibrary.org/hstpaper/foleyrm.htm.

———. "Wesley McCune Papers." http://www.trumanlibrary.org/hstpaper/mccune.htm.

United Nations. "The Universal Declaration of Human Rights." http://www.un.org/Overview/rights.html.

United States Conference of Mayors. http://usmayors.org/uscm/home.asp.

"United States Housing Authority." http://en.wikipedia.org/wiki/United_States_Housing_Authority.

United States of America Korean War Commemoration. "Biography: Mark W. Clark (1896–1984)." http://korea50.army.mil/history/biographies/clark.shtml.

United States Tennis Association. "Black Tennis Pioneers." http://www.usta.com/misc_pages/custom.sps?iType=1927&icustompageid=5793.

University of California at Berkeley, Bancroft Library. "Guide to the Harry Lees Kingman Papers, 1921–1975." http://digitalassets.lib.berkeley.edu/findingaids/ucb/ead/m76_173_cubanc.xml.

University of Missouri–St. Louis, Western Historical Manuscript Collection. "Grant, David M. (1903–1985) Papers, 1917–1986." http://www.umsl.edu/~whmc/guides/whm0552.htm.

———. "McNeal, Theodore D. (1906–1982) Scrapbook, 1941–1943. http://www.umsl.edu/~whmc/guides/whm0321.htm.

University of North Carolina University Libraries. "Desegregation of the University of North Carolina at Chapel Hill, 1930–1955." http://www.lib.unc.edu/ncc/ref/unc/uncdesegregation.html.

University of Oregon Scholars' Bank. "C. Girard Davidson Papers, 1934–1980." http://hdl.handle.net/1794/252.

University of South Alabama Archives. "A Guide to the Papers of John L. LeFlore, 1926–1976." http://www.southalabama.edu/archives/html/manuscript/lefloreintro.htm.

University of South Carolina, South Caroliniana Library, Manuscripts Division. "Arthur John Howard Clement, Jr. Papers, 1926–1986." http://www.sc.edu/library/socar/mnscrpts/clement.html.

University of Southern Mississippi Civil Rights Documentation Project. "July 11, 1954." http://www.usm.edu/crdp/html/cd/citizens.htm.

University of Virginia, Arthur J. Morris Law Library: Special Collections. http://www.law.virginia.edu/home2002/html/librarysite/library.htm.

UPA Microform Collection Guides. "Labor Union Periodicals, Part 1: The Metal Trades." http://www.lexisnexis.com/academic/guides/labor_studies/labor_union_per/labor1.asp#pub24.

U.S. Army, Center of Military History. http://www.army.mil/cmh.

U.S. Department of Justice, Office of the Solicitor General. "J. Lee Rankin." http://www.usdoj.gov/osg/aboutosg/rankinbio.html.

U.S. Department of State, Office of the Historian. "Alphabetical List of Chiefs of Mission and Principal Officials, 1778–2004." http://www.state.gov/r/pa/ho/po/c7041.htm.

U.S. Senate. "Oral History Project of the Senate Historical Office." http://www.senate.gov/pagelayout/history/g_three_sections_with_teasers/oralhistory.htm.

U.S. Supreme Court Center. "*District of Columbia v. Thompson Co.*, 346 U.S. 100 (1953)." http://www.justia.us/us/346/100.

Wagner Act of 1935. http://www.stfrancis.edu/ba/ghkickul/stuwebs/btopics/works/watner.htm.

Wagner, Steven. "How Did the Taft-Hartley Act Come About?" http://hnn.us/articles/1036.html.

Waller, Odell. "The Story of a Sharecropper." http://catnyp.nypl.org/search/a?searchtype=X&searcharg=odell+waller&SORT=D&search.

Washington, D.C., Metropolitan Police Department. "Police Chiefs—Past and Present." http://mpdc.dc.gov/mpdc/cwp/view,a,1230,q,540347,mpdcNav_GID,1529,mpdcNav,%7C31458%7C.asp.

Wayne State University, Walter P. Reuther Library of Labor and Urban Affairs. "Roy Reuther Collection: Papers, 1924–1971." http://www.reuther.wayne.edu/collections/hefa_1334.htm.

———. "UAW Fair Practices and Anti-discrimination Department: Records, 1940–1980." http://www.reuther.wayne.edu/collections/hefa_637-uaw.htm.

———. "Wilbur and Mary Alice Baldinger Collection: Papers, 1929–1976." http://www.reuther.wayne.edu/collections/hefa_902.htm.

———. "William Oliver Collection (Part 2): Papers, 1950–1984." http://www.reuther.wayne.edu/collections/hefa_164.htm.

Western Reserve Historical Society, Manuscript Collection. "Charles P. Lucas (1911–1989) Papers, 1880–1973." http://www.wrhs.org/library/template.asp?id=284.

Wexler, Laura. "Fire in a Canebrake: The Last Mass Lynching in America." http://www.fireinacanebrake.com/html/about.html.

William Penn Foundation. "Foundation History." http://www.williampennfoundation.org/info-url_nocat3558/info-url_nocat_show.htm?doc_id=116914.

"With All Deliberate Speed: The Legacy of *Brown v Board*." http://www.brownvboard.info/index.htm.

Wolk, Herman S., "When the Color Line Vanished." *Air Force Magazine* 81, no.7 (July 1998). http://www.afa.org/magazine/july1998/0798integrate.asp. Also available in print form.

World Statesmen: United States Government. http://www.worldstatesmen.org/USA_govt.html.

"Worldwide Guide to Women in Leadership: United States of America." http://www.guide2womenleaders.com/USA_Ministers.htm.

Wynn, Linda T. "William Henry Hastie (1904–1976)." http://www.tnstate.edu/library/digital/hastie.htm.

Encyclopedias, Dictionaries, Indexes, and Biographical Directories

Adams, A. John, and Joan Martin Burke, eds. *Civil Rights: A Current Guide to the People, Organizations, and Events.* New York: R. R. Bowker, 1970.

American Men and Women of Science: The Physical and Biological Sciences, 12th ed. New York: R. R. Bowker, 1971–.

Ancell, R. Manning, and Christine M. Miller, eds. *The Biographical Dictionary of World War II Generals and Flag Officers.* Westport, Conn.: Greenwood Press, 1996.

Bowman, John S., ed. *The Cambridge Dictionary of American Biography.* Cambridge: Cambridge University Press, 1995.

Congressional Information Service. *U.S. Congressional Committee Hearings Index, Part III, 69th Congress–73rd Congress, Dec. 1925–1934: Index by Personal Names, A-Z.* Washington, D.C.: Congressional Information Service, 1984.

———. *U.S. Congressional Committee Hearings Index, Part III, 69th Congress–73rd Congress, Dec. 1925–1934: Index by Subjects and Organizations, N-Z, Supplementary Indexes.* Washington, D.C.: Congressional Information Service, 1984.

———. *U.S. Congressional Committee Hearings Index, Part III, 69th Congress–73rd Congress, Dec. 1925–1934: Reference Bibliography, H395–0–H585–2.* Washington, D.C.: Congressional Information Service, 1984.

———. *U.S. Congressional Committee Hearings Index, Part III, 69th Congress–73rd Congress, Dec. 1925–1934: Reference Bibliography, H586–0–(73) SN–1.* Washington, D.C.: Congressional Information Service, 1984.

———. *U.S. Congressional Committee Hearings Index, Part V, 79th Congress–82nd Congress, 1945–1952: Reference Bibliography, (79) H1040–0–(80) S869–3.* Washington, D.C.: Congressional Information Service, 1983.

———. *U.S. Congressional Committee Hearings Index, Part V, 79th Congress–82nd Congress, 1945–1952: Reference Bibliography, (80) S869–4–(82) SLab-1.* Washington, D.C.: Congressional Information Service, 1983.

———. *U.S. Congressional Committee Hearings Index, Part VI, 83rd Congress–85th Congress, 1953–1958: Index by Personal Names.* Washington, D.C.: Congressional Information Service, 1982.

———. *U.S. Congressional Committee Hearings Index, Part VI, 83rd Congress–85th Congress, 1953–1958: Reference Bibliography, (83) H1389–1–(84) H1789–1.* Washington, D.C.: Congressional Information Service, 1982.

Current Biography Yearbook. New York: H. W. Wilson, 1946–.

Dictionary of American Biography, Allen Johnson, ed. New York: Charles Scribner's Sons, 1946–.

Fink, Gary M., ed. *Biographical Dictionary of American Labor Leaders.* Westport, Conn.: Greenwood Press, 1974.

———. *Biographical Dictionary of American Labor.* Westport, Conn.: Greenwood Press, 1984.

Garraty, John A., and Mark C. Carnes, eds. *American National Biography.* 24 vols. New York: Oxford University Press, 1999.

Harley, Sharon, ed. *The Timetables of African-American History: A Chronology of the Most Important People and Events in African-American History.* New York: Simon and Schuster, 1995.

Hine, Darlene Clark, ed. *Black Women in America: An Historical Encyclopedia.* 2 vols. Brooklyn, N.Y.: Carlson Publishing, 1993.

Hornsby, Alton Jr., ed. *Chronology of African-American History: Significant Events and People from 1619 to the Present.* Detroit, Mich.: Gale Research, 1991.

"In the Second Year." *Business Week,* January 11, 1947, 86, 88.

Joseph, Bea, ed. *Biography Index: A Cumulative Index to Biographical Material in Books and Magazines.* New York: H. W. Wilson, 1949–.

Kinsman, Clare D., ed. *Contemporary Authors: A Bio-bibliographical Guide to Current Authors andTheir Works—Permanent Series.* Detroit, Mich.: Gale Research, 1975–.

Klingamen, William M., ed. *Encyclopedia of the McCarthy Era.* New York: Facts on File, 1996.

Lichtenstein, Nelson, ed. *Political Profiles: The Kennedy Years.* New York: Facts on File, 1977.

Logan, Rayford W., and Michael R. Winston, eds. *Dictionary of American Negro Biography.* New York: W. W. Norton, 1982.

Lowery, Charles D., and John F. Marszalek, eds. *Encyclopedia of African-American Civil Rights: From Emancipation to the Present.* New York: Greenwood Press, 1992.

Murphy, Larry G., J. Gordon Melton, and Gary L. Ward, eds. *Encyclopedia of African American Religions.* New York: Garland Publishing, 1993.

National Cyclopaedia of American Biography. Clifton, N.J.: J. T. White, 1893–.

New York Times Biographical Service. New York: Arno Press, 1974–.

Salzman, Jack, David L. Smith, Cornel West, and David Lionel Smith, eds. *Encyclopedia of African-American Culture and History.* 5 vols. New York: Macmillan Library Reference USA, 1996.

Sandler, Stanley, ed. *The Korean War: An Encyclopedia.* New York: Garland Publishing, 1995.

Schneiderman, Harry, and Itzhak J. Carmin, eds. *Who's Who in World Jewry.* New York: Monde Publishers, 1955–.

Schoenebaum, Eleanora W., ed. *Political Profiles: The Eisenhower Years.* New York: Facts on File, 1977.

———. *Political Profiles: The Truman Years.* New York: Facts on File, 1978.

———. *Political Profiles: The Nixon/Ford Years.* New York: Facts on File, 1979.

Smith, Jesse Carney, ed. *Notable Black American Women.* 2 vols. Detroit, Mich.: Gale Research, 1992–96.

———. *Notable Black American Men.* Detroit, Mich.: Gale Research, 1999.

Sobel, Robert, ed. *Biographical Directory of the United States Executive Branch, 1774–1989.* 2 vols. New York: Greenwood Press, 1990.

Sobel, Robert, and John Raimo, eds. *Biographical Directory of the Governors of the United States, 1789–1978*. 4 vols. Westport, Conn.: Meckler Books, 1978.

Sovern, Michael I. "The National Labor Relations Act and Racial Discrimination." *Columbia Law Review* 62 (1962): 563–622.

Spradling, Mary Mace, ed. *In Black and White: A Guide to Magazine Articles, Newspaper Articles, and Books Concerning More Than 15,000 Individuals and Groups*. 3rd ed., 2 vols. and supplement. Detroit, Mich.: Gale Research, 1980–85.

Standard and Poor's Register of Corporations, Directors, and Executives. New York: Standard and Poor's, 1928–.

Trattner, Walter I., ed. *Biographical Dictionary of Social Welfare in America*. Westport, Conn.: Greenwood Press, 1986.

Waldo, Martin E., and Patricia Sullivan, eds. *Civil Rights in the United States*. New York: Macmillan Reference USA, 2000.

Who's Who among African Americans. Detroit, Mich.: Gale Research, 1976–.

Who's Who among Black Americans. Northbrook, Ill.: Who's Who among Black Americans, 1976–.

Who's Who in America. Wilmette, Ill.: Marquis Who's Who, 1974–81.

Who's Who in American Law. 2nd ed. Chicago: Marquis Who's Who, 1977.

Who's Who in American Politics. New York: R. R. Bowker, 1968–.

Who's Who in Colored America. New York: Who's Who in Colored America, 1927–.

Who's Who in Finance and Industry. Chicago: Marquis Who's Who, 1973–.

Who's Who in Government. Chicago: Marquis Who's Who, 1973–77.

Who's Who in Labor. New York: Arno Press, 1976.

Who's Who in the United Nations and Related Agencies. 1st ed. New York: Arno Press, 1975.

Who Was Who in America. Chicago: Marquis Who's Who, 1943–93.

Government Agencies

Clerk of Council's Office, Cincinnati, Ohio

Cleveland City Archives, Cleveland, Ohio

Internal Revenue Service, Washington, D.C.

National Labor Relations Board Help Center, Washington, D.C.

Selective Service System, Office of Public and Intergovernmental Affairs, Arlington, Va.

Senate Historical Office, Washington, D.C.

U.S. Department of State, Bureau of Public Affairs, Washington, D.C.

Miscellaneous Agencies, Associations, and Organizations

Associate Alumnae of Douglass College, New Brunswick, N.J.

AT&T Archives, Warren, N.J.

Boston University School of Law, Boston, Mass.

Bridgeport Public Library, Historical Collections Department, Bridgeport, Conn.

Brown University Alumni Association, Providence, R.I.

Fisk University, Office of Alumni Affairs, Nashville, Tenn.

Homewood Cemetery, Pittsburgh, Pa.

Kirn Library, Norfolk, Va.

National Alliance of Postal and Federal Employees, Washington, D.C.

National Association for the Advancement of Colored People, Detroit, Mich., Branch
National Labor Relations Board, Washington, D.C.
Second Calvary Baptist Church, Columbia, S.C.
St. John's University, Office of Advancement Services, Queens, N.Y.
Temple University Alumni and Friends, Philadelphia, Pa.
U.S. Steel Corporation, Public Affairs, Pittsburgh, Pa.
University of California at Berkeley Alumni, Parents, and Friends, Berkeley, Calif.
University of Pennsylvania Archives, Philadelphia, Pa.
University of Texas at San Antonio Library, Archives and Special Collections Department, San Antonio, Tex.
Wayne State University Archives of Labor and Urban Affairs, Detroit, Mich.
William Penn Foundation, Philadelphia, Pa.
Wisconsin Alumni Association, Madison, Wis.

ADDITIONAL REFERENCES RELATED TO THE WAR

The following are citations from the *Crisis*, provided chronologically, for which there are no specific textual references:

"Yes, Negroes Know the Issues of War." Editorial, *Crisis* 49 (March 1942): 79.
Mays, Benjamin E. "The Negro and the Present War." *Crisis* 49 (May 1942): 160, 165.
"The Navy: Where Do We Stand?" Editorial reprinted from the *Pittsburgh Courier, Crisis* 49 (May 1942): 161.
"New Navy Policy." *Crisis* 49 (May 1942): 166.
"Prejudice First, Victory Second." Editorial, *Crisis* 49 (July 1942): 215.
"Bright Spot, Black Spot." Editorial, *Crisis* 49 (September 1942): 279.
"Meanest Trick." *Crisis* 50 (April 1943): 105.
Quarles, Benjamin. "Will a Long War Aid the Negro?" *Crisis* 50 (September 1943): 268.
Schuyler, George S. "A Long War Will Aid the Negro." *Crisis* 50 (September 1943): 328–29, 344.
"War and Race Relations: Student Opinion." *Crisis* 50 (September 1943): 269.
"How About Navy Pilots?" Editorial, *Crisis* 50 (October 1943): 295.
"Stimson Scored for Statement on Troops." *Crisis* 51 (April 1944): 115–17.
"White Gives War Department Fourteen Points on Negro Troops Abroad." *Crisis* 51 (June 1944): 198–99.
"Black and White Rape." Editorial, *Crisis* 51 (July 1944): 217.
Reynolds, Grant. "What the Negro Soldier Thinks about This War." *Crisis* 51 (September 1944): 289–91, 299.
———. "What the Negro Soldier Thinks about the War Department." *Crisis* 51 (October 1944): 316–18, 328.
———. "What the Negro Soldier Thinks." *Crisis* 51 (November 1944): 352–53, 357.
"The Negro Soldier Betrayed." *Crisis* 52 (April 1945): 97.

PRINCIPAL CASES CITED

Alston v. Board of Education of City of Norfolk, 112 F.2d 992 (1940), *cert. denied*, 311 U.S. 693 (1940)
Baldwin v. Franks, 120 U.S. 678 (1887)
Benjamin Mays v. Southern Railway Company[1]
Betts v. Easley, 169 P.2d 831 (1946)
Bob-Lo Excursion Company v. Michigan, 333 U.S. 28 (1948)
Breedlove v. Suttles, 302 U.S. 277 (1937)
Briggs v. Elliott, 98 F. 529 (1951)
Brown v. Board of Education, 347 U.S. 483 (1954)
Buchanan v. Warley, 245 U.S. 60 (1917)
California Shipbuilding Corp., 16 Lab. Rel. Rep. 571 (Cal. Sup. 1945)
Chance v. Lambeth, 186 F2d 876 (4th Cir.), *cert. denied*, 341 U.S. 941 (1951)
Chesapeake & Ohio Railway Company v. Commonwealth of Kentucky, 179 U.S. 388 (1900)
Childs v. Chesapeake & Ohio Railway Company, 216 U.S. 71 (1910)
City of Birmingham v. Monk, 185 F.2d 859, *cert. denied*, 341 U.S. 940 (1950)
Civil Rights Cases, 109 U.S. 3 (1883)
District of Columbia v. John R. Thompson Company, Inc., 73 S. Ct. 1007 (1953)
Guinn v. United States, 238 U.S. 347 (1915)
Hall v. DeCuir, 95 U.S. 485 (1877)
Harmon v. Tyler, 273 U.S. 668 (1927)
Henderson v. United States, 339 U.S. 816 (1950)
Hirabayashi v. United States, 320 U.S. 81 (1943)
Hodges v. United States, 203 U.S. 1 (1906)
Housing Authority of the City of San Francisco and County of San Francisco, a Public Corporation, et al. v. Mattie Banks et al., No. 583, 120 Cal. App:2d 1, 260 P.2d 668, *cert. denied*, 377 U.S. 974 (1954)
Hurd v. Hodge, 334 U.S. 24 (1948)
James. v. Bowman, 190 U.S. 127 (1903)
James v. Marinship Corp. 25 C.2d 721 (1944)
Kerr v. Enoch Pratt Library, 149 F.2d 212 (1945)
Korematsu v. United States, 326 U.S. 214 (1944)
Lipke v. Lederer, 259 U.S. 557 (1922)
Louisville v. Mississippi, 133 U.S. 587 (1890)
Marsh v. Alabama, 326 U.S. 501 (1946)
McCabe v. Atchinson, Topeka and Santa Fe Railway Company, 235 U.S. 151 (1914).*McCready v. Byrd*, 195 Md. 131, *cert. denied*, 340 U.S. 827 (1950)
McGhee v. Sipes, 334 U.S. 1 (1948)
McLaurin v. Oklahoma State Regents for Higher Education, 339 U.S. 637 (1950)
Mills v. Anne Arundel County Board of Education, 25 F. Supp. 792 (1939)
Mills v. Anne Arundel County Board of Education, 30 F. Supp. 245 (1939)
Missouri ex rel. Gaines v. Canada et al., 305 U.S. 337 (1938)
Mitchell v. Board of Regents, No. 16–126 (Baltimore City Court, Oct. 3, 1950)

Mitchell v. United States, 313 U.S. 80 (1941)
Morgan v. Commonwealth of Virginia, 328 U.S. 373 (1946)
Murray v. Maryland, 182 A 590 (1936); 169 Md. 478 (1937)
Nebbia v. New York, 291 U.S. 502 (1934)
Nixon v. Condon, 286 U.S. 73 (1932)
Nixon v. Herndon, 273 U.S. 536 (1927)
NLRB v. Jones & Laughlin Steel Corp., 301 U.S. 1 (1937)
Noce v. Edward E. Morgan Co., 106 F2d 746 (1939)
Payne v. Central Pacific RR Co., 255 U.S. 228 (1921)
Plessy v. Ferguson, 163 U.S. 537 (1896)
Railway Mail Association v. Corsi, Industrial Commissioner of the State of New York, et al., No. 691, 326 U.S. 88 (1945)
Richmond v. Deans, 281 U.S. 704 (1930)
Rolax et al. v. Atlantic Coast Line R. Co. et al., 91 F. Supp. 585 (1950)
Santa Fe etc. R.R. Co. v. Lane, 244 U.S. 492 (1917)
Shelley v. Kraemer, 334 U.S. 1 (1948)
Sipuel v. Board of Regents of the University of Oklahoma, 332 U.S. 631 (1948)
Smith v. Allwright, 321 U.S. 649 (1948)
Steele v. Louisville & Nashville Railroad Company, 323 U.S. 192 (1944)
Sweatt v. Painter, 210 S.W.2d 442 (1947), 339 U.S. 629 (1950)
United States v. Lee, 106 U.S. 196 (1882)
United States v. Reese, 92 U.S. 214 (1876)
Urciolo v. Hodge, 334 U.S. 24 (1948)
Whiteside v. Southern Bus Line, 177 F.2d 949 (6th Cir. 1949)
Whittle v. University of Maryland (filed in Baltimore City Court 1950)[2]
Williams v. Carolina Coach Company, 111 F. Supp. 329 (1952), *aff'd* 207 F.2d 408 (4th Cir. 1953)
Williams v. Yellow Cab Company, 200 F.2d 302 (3rd Cir. 1952)

Notes

1. NAACP Legal Files, NAACP II: B-189, DLC.
2. Greenberg, *Crusaders in the Courts*, 535n90.

INDEX

Page numbers in **boldface** refer to the Biographical and Congressional Directories.